INTERFACING
A Laboratory Approach
Using the Microcomputer
for Instrumentation, Data Analysis,
and Control

STEPHEN E. DERENZO

University of California, Berkeley, California

PRENTICE HALL, *ENGLEWOOD CLIFFS, N.J. 07632*

Library of Congress Cataloging-in-Publication Data

DERENZO, STEPHEN E.
  Interfacing : a laboratory approach using the microcomputer for
instrumentation, data analysis, and control / Stephen E. Derenzo.
    p. cm.

  Includes index.
  ISBN 0-13-940685-9
  1. Computer interfaces. 2. Microcomputers. 3. Automatic data
collection systems. 4. Computer interfaces—Laboratory manuals.
5. Microcomputers—Laboratory manuals. 6. Automatic data collection
systems—Laboratory manuals. I. Title.
TK7887.5.D42 1990
004.6—dc19   89-3619
                                                                  CIP

Editorial/production supervision: Joe Scordato
Manufacturing buyer: Mary Noonan
Cover design: Wanda Lubelska

To Stanley, Alice, David,
Carol, Jenny, and Dawn

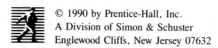

© 1990 by Prentice-Hall, Inc.
A Division of Simon & Schuster
Englewood Cliffs, New Jersey 07632

Printed in the United States of America

10 9 8 7 6 5 4 3 2

ISBN 0-13-940685-9

Prentice-Hall International (UK) Limited, *London*
Prentice-Hall of Australia Pty. Limited, *Sydney*
Prentice-Hall Canada Inc., *Toronto*
Prentice-Hall Hispanoamericana, S.A., *Mexico*
Prentice-Hall of India Private Limited, *New Delhi*
Prentice-Hall of Japan, Inc., *Tokyo*
Simon & Schuster Asia Pte. Ltd., *Singapore*
Editora Prentice-Hall do Brasil, Ltda., *Rio de Janeiro*

Contents

3   ANALOG ↔ DIGITAL CONVERSION AND SAMPLING   102

4   SENSORS AND ACTUATORS   150

Preface

This text describes in practical terms how to use the microcomputer to sense real-world quantities such as temperature, force, sound, light, etc., to rapidly analyze the data, to display the results, or to use the results to perform a control function. It was written for practicing engineers and scientists and as a textbook for laboratory courses in electronic transducers and microcomputer interfacing.

Our approach takes full advantage of the recent availability of relatively low-cost microcomputers that are powerful enough to support high-speed parallel input/output ports and data-acquisition circuit boards, disk operating systems, high-level programming languages, and arithmetic coprocessors. This book shows in practical terms the range of problems in data acquisition, analysis, display, and control that can be tackled in a cost-effective manner without delving into the bus protocol or native language of a particular microprocessor.

The book contains five chapters, covering digital tools, analog tools, conversion between analog and digital signals, sensors and actuators, and data analysis and control. The 24 laboratory exercises can be used either in a college-level laboratory course or as working examples for practicing engineers and scientists who wish to apply sensor, low-level amplification, and microcomputer principles in their work in a practical and immediate way.

This material was developed for 2 one-semester laboratory courses in the Electrical Engineering and Computer Science Department at the University of California in Berkeley, EECS 145L: "Electronic Transducer

Laboratory" and EECS 145M: "Microcomputer Interfacing Laboratory". The purpose of these two courses is to provide upper-level undergraduate students with the tools needed to sense and control "real-world" quantities, such as temperature and force, as well as to display the results of "real-time" analyses, such as least-squares fitting, the Student's t test, fast Fourier transforms, digital filtering, etc. **It is assumed that the students have had some exposure to elementary analog and digital electronics, differential calculus and linear algebra, and the C programming language.**

Over the years, we have used several different microcomputer systems in the laboratory at the same time, and the laboratory exercises were designed to be as machine-independent as possible. Special instructions (such as Appendices E and F) were provided to each student group so they could program the particular counter/timer, parallel I/O port, and data-acquisition board that they were using.

The C programming language was chosen because it is available for almost almost all microcomputers and is well-suited to data acquisition, analysis, and control. It provides word and byte I/O, bit manipulation, powerful conditional and data structures, a wide choice of accuracy and bit length for integer and floating point numbers, and high-speed execution.

Chapter 1, "Digital Tools" briefly describes the overall organization of the microcomputer, binary and 2's complement number systems, and the digital components needed to perform data acquisition and control, such as digital timers, latches, registers, tristate buffers, and parallel input/output ports. It goes on to describe the digital and control aspects of several data-acquisition procedures.

Laboratory Exercise 1 introduces the microcomputer disk operating system, the editor, the C programming language, and the many ways that binary bit patterns can be interpreted as numerical quantities. Exercise 2 provides examples of initializing and reading the AM9513 digital counter/timer to measure human reaction times, and Exercise 3 introduces the parallel I/O ports, debouncing and reading switches, and controlling lights.

Chapter 2, "Analog Tools," covers commonly-used op-amp circuits, the instrumentation amplifier used for low-level differential amplification of sensor signals, noise sources, and the analog signal processing that can be used to enhance the signal-to-noise ratio. It goes on to discuss other useful building blocks: the sample-and-hold amplifier, the comparator, and the power amplifier.

Laboratory Exercises 4 and 5 explore op-amp circuits, instrumentation amplifiers, differential amplification, and noise considerations. Exercise 6 explores analog signal processing using the op amp, including active high-pass, low-pass, and notch filters.

Chapter 3, "Analog $\leftrightarrow$ Digital Conversion," covers the data-conversion components needed to perform data acquisition and control, such as digital-to-analog and analog-to-digital converters. It describes the commonly used methods for data sampling and introduces the notion of frequency aliasing resulting from inadequate sampling. (Considerations of aliasing in the Fourier domain are deferred to Chapter 5.) It lists and describes several commercially available circuit boards

Laboratory Exercise 7 uses a commercial analog I/O board to provide an overview of both digital-to-analog and analog-to-digital conversion for those courses that are not doing Exercises 8 and 9. The conversion between analog and digital is explored in Exercises 8 and 9, using D/A and A/D integrated circuit chips. Exercise 8 involves interfacing a D/A converter to a parallel input port and waveform generation. Exercise 9 involves building a data-acquisition board and interfacing it to a parallel output port, using the "clear-to-send", "strobe", and status-bit handshaking protocol. Exercise 10 uses a commercial data-acquisition board for the periodic sampling of waveforms and demonstrates the concept of frequency aliasing.

Chapter 4, "Sensors and Actuators," covers the sensors (the first element in many data-acquisition systems), the real-world quantities that they sense, the nature of the signals (and the noise) that they produce, and actuators (essential in any control system).

Laboratory Exercises 11–14 explore the basic electronic transducers used to measure position, temperature, strain, force, and light. The thermoelectric heat pump is explored in Laboratory Exercise 15. Exercise 16 investigates the ac and dc electrical properties of bare metal and Ag(AgCl) electrodes. Exercises 17–19 explore physiological signals from the heart, skeletal muscles, and eyes.

Chapter 5, "Data Analysis and Control," covers data analysis, including statistical analysis, Student's t test, least-squares and Chi-squared fitting, fast Fourier transforms, and some algorithms used for the control of real-world quantities.

Laboratory Exercise 20 explores analog-to-digital conversion for the storage of analog signals, digital-to-analog conversion for the analog recovery of those signals, and least-squares fitting for determining the accuracy of signal recovery. Exercise 21 involves the sampling of sine, square, and triangle waves and the computation of their fast Fourier transforms (FFT). These techniques are applied in Exercise 22 to the sampling and FFT of the human voice. Exercise 23 compares analog to real-time digital filtering and Exercise 24 provides experience with temperature sensing and control using several algorithms.

Each chapter is provided with problems derived from recent examination questions. Defined terms appear in the index with boldface page numbers, and appear in the text with boldface in the sentence that defines them.

Appendix A provides some physical and electronic units and constants for the problems at the end of the chapters, and Appendix B discusses the issues of electrical shielding and grounds. Appendix C summarizes some hints useful in C programming. Appendix D provides C code listings and flow charts of some numerical methods, including the fast Fourier transform, nonlinear function minimization (used to fit curves to data), numerical integration using adaptive quadrature, and function inversion using both

Newton's method and quadratic approximation. A program to compute the probability of exceeding Student's t is given as an example.

Appendix E describes the hardware and software needed to use the IBM Data Acquisition and Control Adapter, and Appendix F does the same for the Metra Byte CTM-05 parallel I/O and counter/timer board. Appendix G discusses some potential electrical hazards and methods used to prevent them. Appendices H1 to H10 contain data sheets for the less common integrated circuits used in the Laboratory Exercises.

Guide for the Instructor

Although the entire book would serve for a full-year course, it is also possible to cover portions of the material in separate one-semester courses, as we do at Berkeley.

A one-semester course on **digital interfacing, data analysis, and control** would include Chapters 1, 3, and 5, and Laboratory Exercises 1–3, 8–10, and 20–24.

A one-semester course on **sensors, low-level amplification, and analog signal processing** would include Chapters 2 and 4, and Laboratory Exercises 4–6 and 11–19.

A one-semester course on **bioengineering** would include Chapters 2, 4, and 5, and selections from Laboratory Exercises 2, 4–7, 11–19, and 20–22, depending on course emphasis.

Acknowledgments

I am indebted to Kenneth Krieg, who was the cofounder of EECS 145M "Microcomputer Interfacing Laboratory" and, as teaching associate over a period of several years, made important contributions to most of the laboratory exercises. I also thank the numerous TAs and students who contributed to the improvement of the laboratory exercises.

Special thanks to Professor Ted Lewis for contributions to Chapter 4, derived from his course EECS 145A, "Sensors, Actuators, and Electrodes", and to Dr. Thomas Budinger for contributions to Chapter 5, derived from his course EECS 145B, "Computer Applications in Biology and Medicine". Some of the laboratory exercises were derived from EECS 182, "Biological Signals and Transducers," developed by Professors Ted Lewis and Ed Keller at Berkeley during the 1970s, and to them I am grateful. I also thank John Cahoon for numerous discussions of circuit design.

The camera-ready manuscript for this book was prepared by the author using a Macintosh SE with 20 Mbyte disk drive (Apple Computer, Inc.), Word 4 (Microsoft Corporation), TimesTen Roman and Univers fonts (Adobe Systems Inc.), MacDraw II 1.1 (Claris Corporation), MathType 2.05 (Design Science, Inc), and a Linotronic 100 phototypesetter (Allied Linotype Corporation).

1

Digital Tools

1.1 INTRODUCTION

In the past few years, enormous advances have been made in the cost, power, and ease of use of microcomputers and associated digital circuits. It is now possible, with a relatively small expenditure, to purchase a microcomputer system that will take data, quickly analyze it, and display the results or control a process. Normally, the microcomputer is equipped with a number of standard items: the microprocessor chip and associated circuits, random-access memory, removeable floppy disk drives, high-capacity hard disk drives, keyboards, video display screens, serial interfaces, printers, and x–y entry devices such as the mouse, trackball, joystick, and bitpad. However, data acquisition and control requires additional digital components, such as parallel input and output ports and counter/timers. Also, digital circuits control many of the analog/digital interface components used in data acquisition and control, such as the sample-and-hold (S/H) amplifier, the analog-to-digital (A/D) converter, and the digital-to-analog (D/A) converter.

Even for microprocessor-controlled data-acquisition and control circuits that will ultimately be mounted onto a single board, there are considerable advantages to using the resources of the microcomputer during the development stage. These include program code editors and compilers, a disk operating system for the storage and manipulation of code and data files, and ample random access memory.

In this chapter, we discuss digital tools used for microcomputer-based data-acquisition and control systems (Figure 1.1). Analog tools (amplification and filtering) are treated in Chapter 2, digital-to-analog and analog-to-digital conversion and sampling in Chapter 3, and sensors and actuators in Chapter 4.

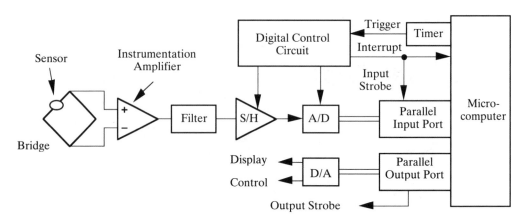

Figure 1.1 A microcomputer system interfaced to sensors and associated analog circuits for data acquisition, analysis, and control.

1.2 THE MICROCOMPUTER

In selecting a system for data acquisition and control, the **microcomputer** itself is a crucial component (Figure 1.2). The microcomputer is sufficiently small to fit on a lab bench (or desktop) and yet contains the following components:

1. The **microprocessor** is an integrated circuit that is connected to memory and peripherals via an address bus, a data bus, and control lines. It reads and executes program instructions from memory, reads data from memory, performs calculations and logic decisions, and transfers data to and from peripherals. Microprocessors vary greatly in their speed and data-handling capability. For example, the eight-bit 8609 has a clock rate of 2 MHz, whereas the 32-bit 80386 has a clock rate of 20 MHz. The latter has a considerable speed advantage when multiplying 64-bit numbers.

2. **Random-access memory (RAM)** usually consists of high-speed semiconductor memory chips that are used to store and retrieve program instructions and data. Commonly used memory chips typically have a storage capacity from 256 kbits to 4 Mbits and an access time less than 200 ns. The highest data-acquisition speeds are achieved when external

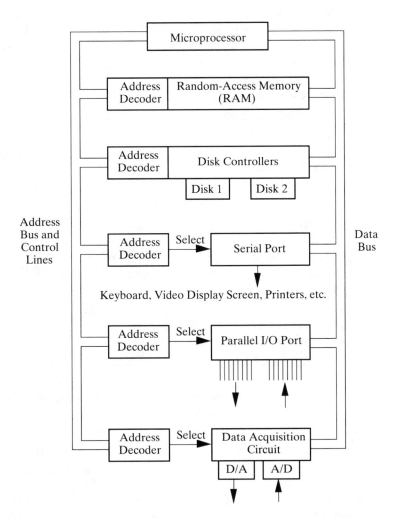

Figure 1.2   The microcomputer consists of a microprocessor that communicates with memory and input/output devices via address and data buses.

data are read directly into RAM, so the size of the RAM places a limit on the number of data values that can be sampled rapidly.

3. Common user interface devices are the keyboard, video display screen, printer, mouse, joystick, and trackball. Some systems provide voice input and synthesized speech output.

4. **Disk memory** is used for the long-term storage of sampled data. Disk memory usually consists of one or more flat circular plates and the storage-and-retrieval mechanism is either magnetic or optical. Magnetic disk capacities range from 500 kbytes to 2 Mbytes for small removable floppy disks and 20 Mbytes to 1000 Mbytes for hard disks. Optical

disks have capacities about ten times larger. Access time consists of a fixed delay of tens of milliseconds (for the read/write head to locate the desired track) and a transfer time of typically 1 μs per 16-bit word.

5. The disk operating system permits the user to manipulate program and data files and supports a high-level compiled programming language (FORTRAN, Pascal, C, compiled BASIC, etc.).

6. A **compiler's** function is to translate a high-level language into micro-processor code. It must be able to

   (i) communicate directly with a data acquisition and control board or parallel I/O port (see below)

   (ii) read and write files to the disk

   Additional useful features include:

   (iii) A full range of scientific functions (sine, cosine, exp, log, etc.), and the ability to compute using floating-point representation, which can handle very small and very large numbers. For example, 80-bit extended precision can handle numbers from $\pm 10^{-4932}$ to $\pm 10^{+4932}$ with a precision of 19 decimal digits.

   (iv) The ability to write functions in assembly code for greater speed during data acquisition. Some compilers permit intermixed assembly code and higher-level code.

   (v) A built-in **editor** that displays lines causing compilation errors and permits immediate correction.

   (vi) A single command that compiles all changed program modules, links all necessary modules, and runs the result.

7. A data-acquisition and control board, with the required speed and the required number of A/D and D/A conversion circuits.

8. A parallel input/output port with sufficient speed, if item 7 is not available. In this case, it becomes necessary to design and build a data-acquisition circuit for connection to the parallel I/O port (see Laboratory Exercise 9).

The microprocessor communicates with the other components of the microcomputer via an address bus, a data bus, and a number of control lines (Figure 1.2). The **address bus** allows the microprocessor to individually select particular components. Each component has a unique assigned **address** whether it is a RAM location, an I/O port register, or other peripheral circuit. An **address decoder** produces a **select** pulse whenever the assigned address appears on the address bus. For example, a 1-Mbyte RAM has an address decoder with 20 input bits and eight million select lines, one for each memory bit that can be selected. (In reality, the address decoder is distributed among many integrated circuit chips and almost all of the eight million select lines are internal to the chips.) The **data bus** is used to transmit data words to and from the microprocessor and its associated circuits.

Note: In some systems, memory locations and external devices are distinguished from each other by a special control bit. In others, a large block of memory address space is reserved for external devices.

Since many devices are attached to the data and address buses and since at any instant only one can be sending data and only one can be receiving data, control lines are used to indicate when the bus is busy, when a device requests use of the bus, when use is granted, etc. These details are beyond the scope of this book and are mentioned only to outline the organization of the microcomputer.

The following sections discuss commercially available devices that automatically handle the details of using the microcomputer bus, such as parallel input and output ports and counter/timers. Digital data-acquisition circuits are described in Chapter 3.

Laboratory Exercise 1 is designed to familiarize the reader with the particular editor and compiler that will be used for the rest of the exercises as well as review 2's complement, hexidecimal, real, and integer interpretations of binary numbers.

1.3 NUMBER SYSTEMS

1.3.1 Representation of Binary Numbers

Many external circuits produce unsigned binary numbers (e.g., A/D converters and counter/timers) or Gray code (e.g., angle and position encoders). Binary numbers are frequently represented in hexadecimal form (base 16) for efficient notation. Note that each eight-bit byte can be represented as two hexadecimal digits. Octal (base 8) is less frequently used.

But, in most microcomputers, internal **2's complement** representation is used to deal efficiently with both negative and positive numbers. In 2's complement representation, the sign of a number is changed by complementing (reversing) all its bits and then adding one. Positive numbers have their most significant bit (**MSB**) equal to zero and negative numbers have their MSB equal to one. By using this operation, the subtraction process $a - b$ can be performed by adding a to the 2's complement of b. For an 8-bit number, 2 is represented as binary 0000 0010 (hexadecimal 02) and –2 is represented as binary 1111 1110 (hexadecimal FE). For example, $5 - 2 = 3$ in 2's complement arithmetic is

$$
\begin{array}{rl}
5 & 0000\ 0101 \\
\underline{-2} & \underline{1111\ 1110} \quad \text{simply add, but ignore the most significant carry bit} \\
3 & 0000\ 0011
\end{array}
$$

Some older computers use signed binary representation, where the leftmost bit represents the sign. While this representation is closer to that of the printed page, arithmetic operations take longer due to the need to process the sign bit.

Table 1.1 shows the typical internal representations available on microcomputers. They are also explored in Laboratory Exercise 1. Each program variable is declared to be one of these. The float, double, and extended have 8-, 11-, and 15- bit exponents and 23, 52, and 63 bits of precision, which correspond to 7, 15, and 19 decimal digits of precision, respectively.

TABLE 1.1   TYPICAL VARIABLE TYPES, STORAGE, AND RANGES OF VALUES

Type	Number of Bits	Range
Char	8	−128 to +127
Unsigned char†	8	0 to 255
Integer	16	−32,768 to +32,767
Unsigned integer	16	0 to 65,535
Long	32	−2,147,483,648 to 2,147,483,647
Unsigned long†	32	0 to 4,294,967,295
Float	32	$\pm1.2 \times 10^{-38}$ to $\pm3.4 \times 10^{+38}$
Double	64	$\pm2.3 \times 10^{-308}$ to $\pm1.7 \times 10^{+308}$
Extended†	80	$\pm1.7 \times 10^{-4932}$ to $\pm1.1 \times 10^{+4932}$

†Not available on all C or Pascal compilers.

Table 1.2 shows the unsigned, **hexadecimal**, Gray, and 2's complement interpretation of binary numbers. The 16-bit and 32-bit numbers are logical extensions.

Warning: Sign Extension

As demonstrated in Laboratory Exercise 1, if the MSB of a number is zero, then conversion from 8-bit to 16-bit or from 16-bit to 32-bit occurs as expected. However, if the MSB is one, then the left half of the longer number will be filled with ones (**sign extension**). In this way, the converted number will have the same numerical value in 2's complement arithmetic. However, if the numbers are read from a counter/timer or A/D converter in blocks of eight bits, some precautions are necessary before they can be packed into 16- or 32- bit numbers. There are two approaches:

1. Mask the left half of the number with zeros.
2. If available on your compiler, declare all relevant variables to be "unsigned." Note that "unsigned long int" is not listed in Kernighan and Ritchie's book (which defines the C programming language), but is included in some compilers (for example, Microsoft C).

TABLE 1.2   VARIOUS INTERPRETATIONS OF BINARY NUMBERS

Binary	Unsigned	Hexadecimal	Gray	2's Complement
0000 0000	0	00	0	0
0000 0001	1	01	1	1
0000 0010	2	02	3	2
0000 0011	3	03	2	3
0000 0100	4	04	7	4
0000 0101	5	05	6	5
0000 0110	6	06	4	6
0000 0111	7	07	5	7
0000 1000	8	08	15	8
0000 1001	9	09	14	9
0000 1010	10	0A	12	10
0000 1011	11	0B	13	11
0000 1100	12	0C	8	12
0000 1101	13	0D	9	13
0000 1110	14	0E	11	14
0000 1111	15	0F	10	15
0001 0000	16	10	31	16
. . .	. . .	. . .	. . .	. . .
0111 1110	126	7E	65	126
0111 1111	127	7F	64	127
1000 0000	128	80	192	−128
1000 0001	129	81	193	−127
. . .	. . .	. . .	. . .	. . .
1111 1110	254	FE	129	−2
1111 1111	255	FF	128	−1

1.3.2 Gray Code

Gray code is used extensively in external devices such as digital position encoders because the transition from any number to the next involves a change of only one bit (Table 1.3). In binary code, many bits can change from one number to the next and since they do not change simultaneously, erroneous codes briefly occur.

The conversion from Gray code to binary code can be done with the exclusive-OR circuit shown in Figure 1.3. See Figure 1.4 for a review of the AND, inclusive-OR, and exclusive-OR logic circuits. It will be noted on the left side of Figure 1.3 that bit 1, for example, cannot be determined until bit 2 is known, and bit 2 cannot be determined until bit 3 is known, etc. Thus the output is valid only after N gate propagation times. A "valid data" signal can be derived by connecting all input bits to an inclusive-OR circuit that is used as the input to a pulse generator. The output is read at the trailing edge of the pulse. Alternatively, a table lookup from computer memory or read-only memory (ROM) can be used to convert between Gray and binary codes.

TABLE 1.3   BINARY AND GRAY CODES AND THEIR DECIMAL EQUIVALENTS

Decimal	Binary	Gray	Decimal	Binary	Gray
0	00000	00000	16	10000	11000
1	00001	00001	17	10001	11001
2	00010	00011	18	10010	11011
3	00011	00010	19	10011	11010
4	00100	00110	20	10100	11110
5	00101	00111	21	10101	11111
6	00110	00101	22	10110	11101
7	00111	00100	23	10111	11100
8	01000	01100	24	11000	10100
9	01001	01101	25	11001	10101
10	01010	01111	26	11010	10111
11	01011	01110	27	11011	10110
12	01100	01010	28	11100	10010
13	01101	01011	29	11101	10011
14	01110	01001	30	11110	10001
15	01111	01000	31	11111	10000

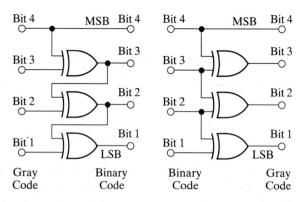

Figure 1.3   Circuits used to convert Gray code to binary and binary code to Gray code. Four bits are shown. The logic elements shown perform the exclusive-OR, which have an output logic state that equals one only if the input logic states differ (see Figure 1.4).

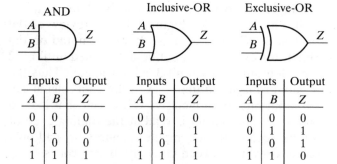

Figure 1.4   AND, **inclusive-OR**, and **exclusive-OR** logic gates. When a circle is shown at the output, the output is complemented and the device is called a NAND or NOR gate.

1.4 DIGITAL COUNTER/TIMERS

Normally, when executing a program, the microcomputer must perform other tasks that make it impossible for the program to keep track of absolute time. A variety of integrated circuit chips have been developed that can constantly keep track of time (and even of the date) while the microcomputer is busy with other tasks (or even turned off). For example, most microcomputers have battery-powered circuits that keep track of the date and time (to the nearest second) and this information is recorded whenever a disk file is created or changed. But for data acquisition involving periodic sampling, a more precise clock is needed that can either be read by the program to the nearest microsecond or can interrupt the program whenever a preset time interval has expired. The use of the digital counter/timer is explored in Laboratory Exercise 2, where human reaction time is measured.

Two of the most popular digital timer chips are now described.

1.4.1 The 8253 Programmable Interval Timer

This integrated-circuit chip (manufactured by Intel and others) has three 16-bit accumulators that can be used to count clock pulses and can be written and read under program control. It has a number of functions that permit it to act as a pulse generator, a digital one-shot, or a digital square-wave generator. These functions are selected by writing to a control register. At 1-MHz clock rates or higher, two problems arise. Firstly, it is not possible to read a rapidly changing accumulator directly and it is first necessary to latch the accumulator into a buffer register. This function is provided by the chip. Secondly, a 16-bit accumulator will overflow in 16 ms or less, and for counting longer periods, it is necessary to hardwire two accumulators in sequence. Since the two accumulators must be latched by different instructions, an ambiguity arises whenever the faster accumulator passes through zero. This problem is not handled by the chip and is most simply resolved by rereading the slower accumulator.

This interval timer is used on the IBM Data Acquisition and Control Adapter and its use is described in Appendix E. The initialization, loading, latching, and reading sequence is shown in Figure 1.5.

1.4.2 The 9513 System Timing Controller

This integrated-circuit chip has many more features than the 8253 and requires more program steps to initialize (Figure 1.6). It has five independent 16-bit counters that can be cascaded or connected to any of five external lines under program control.

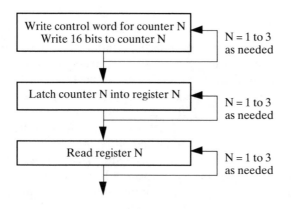

Figure 1.5 Sequence of operations for initializing, loading, latching, and reading the 8253 counter/timer.

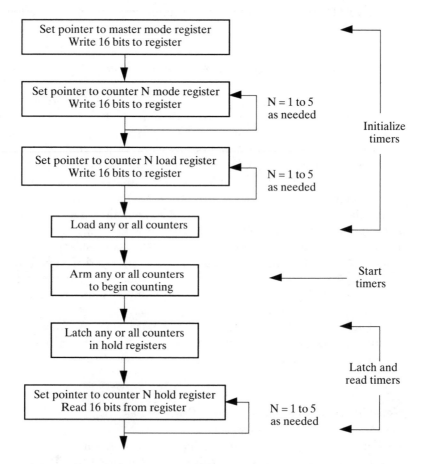

Figure 1.6 Sequence of operations for initializing, loading, latching, and reading the 9513 counter/timer. The counters may be latched and read repeatedly at any time.

On-chip subscalers permit divide-by-N counting for slower rates and longer time ranges. The five counters can be latched in any combination with a single instruction. However, whenever two or more counters are cascaded, the ambiguity mentioned before is still present (although less frequent), and still requires rereading the slower counter. This interval timer is used in the Metra Byte Parallel I/O Board, the National Instruments Analog Data Acquisition Board (among others), and is described in Appendix F.

Warning: Cascading Counter/Timer Chips

When two counter/timer chips are cascaded, the most rapidly moving counter (say, counter 1) receives input pulses from the system clock and increments until it reaches FFFF (for a 16-bit counter). As it transitions to 0000, it sends a carry pulse that increments the least rapidly moving counter (counter 2). Unfortunately, it is not possible to guarantee that these two events happen simultaneously, and erroneous timing information can be read occasionally. For example, suppose that counter 2 reads 01EA and counter 1 has incremented to FFFF. After counter 1 receives its next clock pulse, we would hope that counter 2 and counter 1 would change simultaneously and read 01EB 0000, but if one changes before the other, and we latch the counters during this very brief period, we will get either 01EB FFFF or 01EA 0000. Both are in error by about 64,000 counts! Moreover, it is not possible to latch two different chips simultaneously, even if they could change simultaneously. The solution is shown in the following steps:

1. Latch both counters.
2. Read counter 1 (the most rapidly moving counter).
3. If counter 1 has just passed 0000, relatch counter 2.
4. Read counter 2.

The test condition in step 3 is determined by the maximum number of counter 1 clock pulses that the erroneous condition can last. For the 8253, where the counters decrement and are latched by separate program statements, the conditional in step 3 would be "if counter 1 > 250." For the 9513 in increment mode and "simultaneous" counter latching, the conditional in step 3 would be "if counter 1 < 2."

1.5 PARALLEL AND SERIAL INPUT/OUTPUT PORTS

The parallel input/output (I/O) port allows the microcomputer to communicate directly with the outside digital world and handles most of the problems of control and synchronization with the microprocessor address and data buses. The most convenient is the bidirectional port, which has separate input and output lines, simplifying the connection to external devices. Since all bits are transferred in parallel (at the same time), it is generally faster than the serial port. Laboratory Exercise 3 involves reading switches and writing to lights using a parallel port. Moreover, A/D and D/A converters naturally deal with parallel digital information and can be interfaced directly to a parallel I/O port, as explored in Laboratory Exercises 8 and 9.

The parallel I/O port usually includes the following addressable internal registers:

1. A **Data register** for reading and writing data.

2. A **Control register** that can be written to set the mode of operation and control the logic level of external lines. It permits the program to communicate with external circuits and tell them when the program has new output or is ready to accept new input.

3. A **Status register** that can be read for determining the status of the data register. Its contents can be read by the program to determine (i) when a device connected to the data output port is ready to accept new data, (ii) when it has read the last data output, and (iii) when new data have been latched by the external device on the input port and are ready to be read.

The simpler parallel I/O devices have only data ports, but some of the data bits can be used by the program to communicate with the external circuit. Most have both input and output data lines, whose functions cannot be changed (the bidirectional port), but some permit each data bit to be either input or output, as specified by the contents of a special control register.

The **serial I/O port** also has addresses for setting up the communication protocol and then can transfer data serially in time using only one input and one output line. The advantage over the parallel port is that existing circuits (specifically telephone communication lines) can transmit serial data over long distances, often around the world. Parallel communication lines are usually used to connect circuits within a single building. The disadvantage of serial ports is that they are considerably slower than parallel ports (typically a factor of 10, corresponding to the number of bits per byte sequentially transferred by the serial port).

1.5.1 The Parallel Output Port

The parallel output port reads a number from computer memory and converts the bit pattern to logic voltage levels on wires in the world "outside" the computer. Additional control lines and status registers may also be provided so that (i) the external circuit can notify the computer program that it is ready to receive data, (ii) the output port can notify the external circuit that it has data in its internal registers, and (iii) the external circuit can notify the computer program that the data have been taken.

The basic element in the parallel output port is the edge-triggered **D-type flip-flop**, which differs somewhat from the simple flip-flop that simply toggles from one logic state to the other. The edge-triggered D-type flip-flop has two inputs, a data input (D) and a clock input (C) (Figure 1.7).

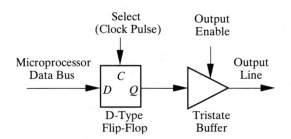

Figure 1.7 Edge-triggered D-type flip-flop as used for microcomputer output. A program write command provides the select pulse and the external circuit provides the output enable.

The output (Q) is set equal to the logic state of the input (D) only when the clock (C) goes from low to high (Figure 1.8). At all other times, the state of Q never changes (even if D changes). Frequently, the outputs have **tristate** drivers so that several outputs can be connected together. The state of Q is only asserted at the output line when the "output-enable" line is asserted. When the output-enable line is not asserted, the output is in a high imped-ance state that neither drives nor loads any other circuit connected to the the output. Whenever two or more outputs are connected to a common line, they must all have tristate outputs.

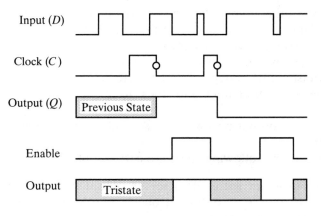

Figure 1.8 Timing diagram for Figure 1.7. Output Q is set equal to the input data D only on a high-to-low edge of clock C. Output Q is asserted on the output lines only when enable is high.

The parallel output port consists of a set of registers that can be addressed and loaded from memory under program control (Figure 1.9). Whenever the output enable line is asserted, the contents of the registers are available on the external output lines.

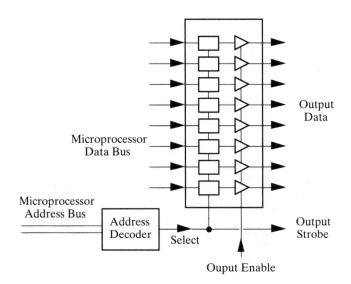

Figure 1.9   Parallel output port using an octal edge-triggered D-type flip-flop, address decoder, and tristate output buffer. When addressed by the microprocessor, data from memory is transferred to the registers and is available at the inputs of the tristate buffers until a new byte is written. The data appears at the output lines whenever the external circuit provides an output enable.

Almost all C compilers written for the IBM PC (and compatible micro-computers) support statements for byte output. For example, the Turbo C compiler (Borland International, Inc.) permits a byte "n" to be written to the parallel output port at address "p" by using the statement "outportb(p,n);". The microcomputer decodes the address "p" and clocks the data "n" onto the D-type flip-flops. The data are then available to the outside world whenever the output-enable line is asserted. By constantly asserting the output-enable line (connecting it high or low, depending on the circuit), the output port can be placed in a "transparent" mode so that a byte written to the port appears immediately on the output lines and does not change until a new byte is written.

A well-designed parallel output port also has several additional features that permit **handshaking**.

In simple handshaking, the following steps are carried out:

1. The microcomputer program writes data to the output port's internal registers, and the port pulses an output strobe line to let the external device know that new data are available.

2. The external device detects the output strobe pulse, asserts the output-enable line, and reads the data.

In full handshaking, two more steps are used:

1. The external circuit pulses a "ready for data" line, which sets a status register that the computer program reads.

2. The computer program writes data to the port's internal registers, and the port pulses an output strobe line to let the external device know that new data are available.

3. The external device detects the output strobe pulse, asserts the output-enable line, and reads the data.

4. The external circuit pulses a "data taken" line, which sets a status register that the computer program can read.

Unfortunately, these features are lacking on many commercial parallel output ports.

1.5.2 The Parallel Input Port

The parallel input port converts a bit pattern of logic voltage levels in the world "outside" the computer to a number in computer memory. Additional control lines and status registers may also be provided so that (i) the computer program can notify the external circuit that it is ready to receive data, (ii) the external circuit can notify the program that it has written data to the port's internal registers, and (iii) the computer program can notify the external circuit that the data have been read.

As in the output port, the basic element in the parallel input port is the **register**, usually an edge-triggered D-type flip-flop followed by a tristate buffer (Figure 1.10). When an external device asserts a high-to-low transition on the **strobe** line, the register output Q is set equal to the input D. Until the next high-to-low transition, the output Q does not change (even if D changes). When an output enable occurs, then the output is set equal to Q. In the absence of an output enable, the output is in a high-impedance state and neither drives nor loads the microprocessor data bus.

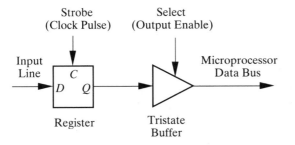

Strobe
(Clock Pulse)

Select
(Output Enable)

Input
Line

Microprocessor
Data Bus

C

D   *Q*

Register

Tristate
Buffer

Figure 1.10   Edge-triggered D-type flip-flop as used for microcomputer input. The external circuit provides the strobe edge, and a program read command provides the select pulse. See Figure 1.8 for the timing diagram.

A variation of this circuit is the **latch**, which makes the output Q equal to the input D only when the gate G is high (transparent mode). When G is low, the output Q does not change (even if D changes). This is shown in Figures 1.11 and 1.12.

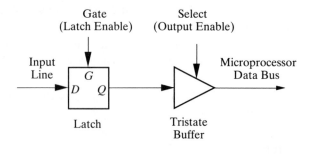

Figure 1.11 Transparent latch followed by a tristate output buffer for parallel input. See Figure 1.12 for the timing diagram.

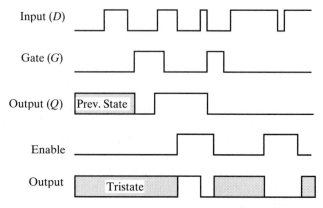

Figure 1.12 Timing diagram for Figure 1.11. Q out is set equal to input data D only when gate G is high. Q out is asserted on output lines only when the enable is high.

The parallel input port (Figure 1.13) consists of a set of registers that stores whatever data are on the external input lines at the instant the input strobe line is pulsed. The microcomputer program can address and read these registers at a later time.

Almost all C compilers written for the IBM PC (and compatible microcomputers) support byte input. For example, the Turbo C compiler (Borland International, Inc.), permits a byte "n" to be read from the parallel port at address "p" by using the statement "n = inportb(p);". Note that the number read by the program corresponds to the data on the input lines when the strobe line was pulsed, not when the program executed the read statement.

For full handshaking, the following steps are typical:

1. The microcomputer program pulses a "clear-to-send" line to notify the external device that it is ready to read new data.

2. When the external device has new data, it asserts the data lines and pulses the strobe line, which latches the data onto the input-port registers.

3. The external circuit or the input port sets a status register that notifies the computer program that new data have been stored on the port's internal registers.

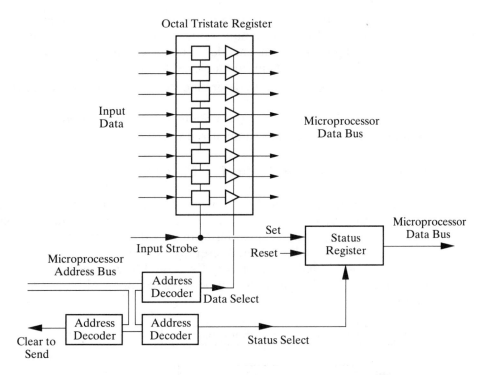

Figure 1.13   Parallel input port using a tristate octal register for data and an RS flip-flop for a status register.

4. The computer program reads the port registers into memory and clears the status register.

Alternatively, if other tasks simultaneously require attention, the external circuit would pulse the "interrupt" line at step 3, causing program execution to be temporarily paused, and a small service program would read the registers and then transfer control back to the main program.

Commercial parallel input ports usually use the 74LS374 octal register, if a high-to-low edge strobe is desired (Figures 1.7 and 1.8), or the 74LS373 octal latch, if a control-level strobe (high = sample, low = hold) is desired (Figures 1.11 and 1.12).

1.6 DIGITAL DATA-ACQUISITION PROCEDURES

Periodic data acquisition from an external device usually requires the following:

1. A digital clock that provides a uniform sampling period, independent of variable software delays.

2. The ability to latch data from the external device onto registers that can also be read by the program. This external device can be an A/D converter, digital-position encoder, or any circuit that senses a physical quantity and converts in into a digital form.

3. A way for the program to determine that new data has been latched.

To perform these tasks, the parallel I/O ports and counter/timers are used in a variety of ways, as summarized in the sections that follow.

1.6.1 Software-Trigger Status-Poll Method

The simplest method uses the "software-trigger status-poll" to initiate sampling and to determine when the data were ready to be read into computer memory. **Polling** is the sequential testing of the status word of all relevant peripherals to determine whenever service is required. This method (shown in Figure 1.14) is used in Laboratory Exercise 9 to demonstrate interfacing an A/D to the parallel input port and periodic sampling. It consists of looping over steps 1 to 5:

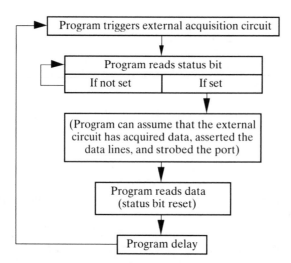

Figure 1.14 Flow chart for software-trigger status-poll method.

1. Produce an external pulse under program control to trigger the external acquisition circuit, usually the clear-to-send pulse from a parallel input port or the output of a counter/timer. Software loop delays are not accurate, and the best way for the program to reliably produce periodic pulses with long periods is by reading the hardware timers in a loop. For short periods, the hardware-trigger method is recommended (see the following section).

2. After the external circuit has new data, it asserts them on the input lines of the parallel port, pulses the strobe line to latch the data, and sets the status bit.

3. Meanwhile, the program has been reading the status bit in a continuous loop, waiting for it to be set.

4. When the status bit is set, the program detects it and reads the data. The program or the input port resets the status bit.

5. After the predetermined delay, go back to step 1.

1.6.2 Hardware-Trigger Status-Poll Method

The hardware-trigger status-poll method (shown in Figure 1.15) provides trigger pulses that are uniformly spaced in time, but still uses software polling of the status bit, which is not a limitation if the program has no other tasks.

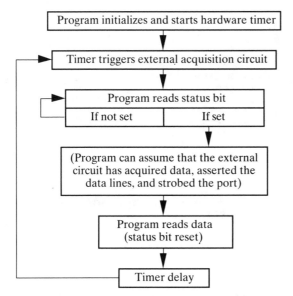

Figure 1.15 Flow chart for hardware-trigger, status-poll method.

1. The program initializes the hardware timer to repetitively load a number and put out a pulse every time the terminal count is reached. The counter is then armed to initiate counting.

2. Each pulse triggers the external circuit.

3. After the external circuit has new data, it asserts them on the input lines of the parallel port, and pulses the strobe line to latch the data and set the status bit.

4. Meanwhile, the program has been reading the status bit in a continuous loop, waiting for it to be set.

5. When the status bit is set, the program detects it and reads the data. The program or the input port resets the status bit.

6. Go to step 2.

1.6.3 Hardware-Trigger Hardware-Interrupt Method:

The hardware-trigger hardware-interrupt method permits data analysis during data acquisition, because the reading of the parallel input port is initiated by an **interrupt**, which causes the program to pause whatever it is doing while a special jump occurs to an interrupt-service routine (Figure 1.16). When the routine has serviced the interrupt, it transfers back to the main program.

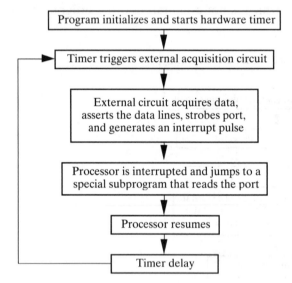

Figure 1.16 Flow chart for hardware-trigger hardware-Interrupt method.

1. The program initializes the hardware timer to repetitively load a number and put out a pulse every time the terminal count is reached. The counter is then armed to initiate the trigger pulses. An interrupt-service routine is initialized.

2. Each pulse triggers the external circuit.

3. After the external circuit has new data, it asserts them on the input lines of the parallel port, pulses the strobe line to latch the data and set the status bit, and generates an interrupt pulse.

4. The interrupt pulse causes a number of registers to be saved in a "stack", and a jump to a special interrupt service routine that reads the parallel input port, restores the registers, and returns to the main program.

5. Go to step 2.

1.6.4 Hardware-Trigger Direct-Memory-Access (DMA) Method:

The hardware-trigger DMA method permits the direct transfer of data to memory without interrupting program execution (Figure 1.17).

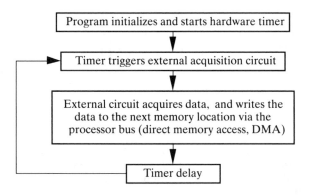

Figure 1.17 Flow chart for hardware-trigger direct-memory-access (DMA) method.

1. The program initializes the hardware timer to repetitively load a number and put out a pulse every time the terminal count is reached. The counter is then armed to initiate the trigger pulses.
2. Each pulse triggers the external circuit.
3. When the external circuit has new data, it accesses the microprocessor bus and stores the data directly into the next location in memory.
4. Go to step 2 until a predetermined number of data values are sampled.

1.7 SWITCH DEBOUNCING

Switches are used to manually change logic levels, such as in keyboards or start buttons. After the switch is thrown, the moveable contact strikes the intended opposing contact and rebounds, so that the output is briefly in an open-circuit condition (Figure 1.18). After many bounces, the switch reaches the intended state. This effect is demonstrated in Laboratory Exercise 3, where a mechanical switch is used to generate a parallel port input strobe. Methods for generating a clean logic pulse are called **debouncing**, and include the use of cross-coupled NAND gates, the one-shot, and software.

1.7.1 Cross-Coupled NAND Gates

This method uses a pair of cross-coupled NAND gates to produce an output that does not change even when the switch is in the open-circuit condition

(Figure 1.19). When the switch momentary touches with the top contact, the output becomes low and remains low until the switch touches the bottom contact. This circuit is available as an integrated circuit (for example, the TTL 74LS279 quad set–reset latch).

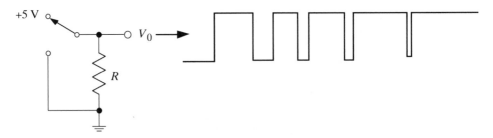

Figure 1.18 Single-pole double-throw switch used to connect load R either to +5 V or to ground. The output waveform shows the effect of contact bounce after the switch has been thrown to the +5-V position. The output V_0 is not stable for a period of tens of milliseconds.

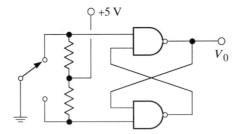

Figure 1.19 Cross-coupled NAND gates used to debounce a single-pole double-throw switch.

1.7.2 One-Shot

This solution uses an edge-triggered one-shot to produce a fixed-duration pulse after the input changes state. The pulse width is chosen to be longer than the maximum settling time of the switch. This method produces a fixed-width pulse even if the switch bounce is so violent that temporary contact is made with the initial contact. In addition, the pulse width is not changed even if the switch or button is held for a long time. Only after the switch is released can a new edge be produced to trigger a new output pulse.

1.7.3 Software Debouncing

In this method, the switch output to the microcomputer is allowed to exhibit contact bounce, but the program detects the first contact, and then uses a delay to ignore subsequent data until the switch has had time to stabilize.

The program can even be written to ask the user to toggle the switch several times, and then observe the maximum contact bounce duration. The program can then use the experimentally determined delay.

1.8 PROBLEMS

1.1 You are given a data-acquisition system consisting of four major components:

- A circuit that senses temperature and digitizes the signal whenever it receives a trigger pulse. At 0°C it produces an output of 0, and at 128°C it produces an output of approximately 2048. When the digitized input is ready, it produces a 12-bit data word (corresponding to the temperature), and a strobe pulse.
- A parallel I/O port with
  - 16 input data lines and corresponding internal registers,
  - a strobe input line for latching the data onto the registers, and
  - a status register that is set every time a strobe pulse is received, and
    is reset when the registers are read by the computer program.
- A digital counter/timer that
  - is set up under program control, and
  - produces output pulses at regular time intervals.
- A microcomputer that, under program control, can
  - set up the digital counter/timer, and
  - read the I/O registers and the status register into computer memory.

Your design goals are
- to measure the temperature at a number of regular time intervals specified by the user, and
- to read the digitized values of temperature into computer memory for later analysis.

a. Sketch a block diagram of all components and essential interconnections, and label each.

b. List the program steps needed to initialize the system for the periodic acquisition of temperature data.

c. Give the sequence of events (hardware and software) that takes place every time this system makes one temperature measurement and stores the result in computer memory.

1.2 Write a program that uses the 9513 counter/timer chip to generate a series of 1-μs-wide pulses that occur at regular time intervals. The value of the time interval (in milliseconds) is to be entered during program execution. Assume that the 9513 is interfaced as described in the Metra Byte board data sheets (see Appendix F). Write the program statements (or a flow chart) you would use to implement this task, including the sequence of binary (or hex) numbers that would be sent to the counter/timer. (*Hint*: Mode D is desired here.)

1.3 Repeat Problem 1.2, but produce a single active low pulse under program control after a delay of at most 1 μs. The desired pulse width (in microseconds) is to be entered during program execution. (*Hint*: Mode G is desired here).

1.4 Show how you would convert Gray code numbers to unsigned binary using software only. Prepare a flow chart or a list of program steps.

1.5 Given an eight-bit binary number where all bits are one, what is the numerical value when it is interpreted as
   a. 2's complement integer
   b. unsigned integer
   c. hexadecimal

1.6 Show explicitly that the 2's complement of the eight-bit number 128 is 128 (i.e., show that $-128 = 128$).

1.9 ADDITIONAL READING

1.1 Michael Andrews, *Programming Microprocessor Interfaces for Control and Instrumentation*, Prentice Hall, Englewood Cliffs, NJ, 1982.

1.2 Bruce A. Artwick, *Microcomputer Interfacing*, Prentice Hall, Englewood Cliffs, NJ, 1980.

1.3 David M. Auslander and Paul Sagues, *Microprocessors for Measurement and Control*, Osborne/McGraw-Hill, Berkeley, CA, 1981.

1.4 George C. Barney, *Intelligent Instrumentation*, Prentice Hall, Englewood Cliffs, NJ, 1988.

1.5 S. J. Cahill, *Designing Microprocessor-Based Digital Circuitry*, Prentice Hall, Englewood Cliffs, NJ, 1985.

1.6 Brian W. Kernighan and Dennis M. Ritchie, *The C Programming Language*, Prentice Hall, Englewood Cliffs, NJ, 1978.

1.7 Harold S. Stone, *Microcomputer Interfacing*, Addison-Wesley, Reading, MA, 1982.

1.8 Willis J. Tompkins and John G. Webster, *Interfacing Sensors to the IBM PC*, Prentice Hall, Englewood Cliffs, N J, 1988.

Laboratory Exercise 1

Introduction to

C Programming

PURPOSE

To use a compiler/editor to write and compile a simple C program. To investigate the 2's complement, unsigned, and hexadecimal representation of 8-bit, 16-bit, and 32-bit numbers, to use the printf function for printed output, and the scanf function for interactive program control and data entry.

EQUIPMENT

- IBM AT microcomputer with disk operating system (DOS) and C compiler
- printer (shared with other lab stations)

ADDITIONAL READING

Appendix C: C Programming Hints

Chapter 1, Section 1.3: Number Systems

B. W. Kernighan and D. M. Ritchie, *The C Programming Language*, Prentice Hall, Englewood Cliffs, NJ, 1978, or Stephen G. Kochan, *Programming in C*, Hayden Book Co., Hasbrouck Heights, NJ, 1983, or any of the many other books on this subject.

PROCEDURE

1 Program

Use the editor to write the following C program, which prompts the user for
a starting integer n1 and a final integer n2, and then prints out various bit-
pattern representations of the numbers from n1 to n2:

```
#include <stdio.h>
main ()
{
char c;
int i,n1,n2,number;
long k;
float f;
while(1)
{
printf("enter first number: ");
scanf("%d",&n1);
printf("%d\n",n1);
printf("enter last number: ");
scanf("%d",&n2);
printf("%d\n",n2);
for (number=n1; number <= n2; number++)
    {
    c=number;
    i=number;
    k=number;
    f=number;
    printf("char:(dec)=\t%12d  (uns dec)=%12u  (hex)=%12x\n",c,c,c);
    printf("int:(dec)=\t%12d  (uns dec)=%12u  (hex)=%12x\n",i,i,i);
    printf("long:(dec)=\t%12ld  (uns dec)=%12lu  (hex)=%12lx\n",k,k,k);
        /* note well- this is %12 followed by the letters ld, not 121 followed by d */
    printf("f: (float)=\t %12.3f\n\n\n", f);
    }
}
}
```

2 Numerical Representation

Run the program and investigate numbers in the ranges from 0 to 5, from 125
to 130, and from –130 to –125. Note that small positive integers such as 0 and
1 have the same representation, whereas a negative number such as –129 has
six different representations, depending on the variable type and the printf
format type.

3 Packing 8 bit bytes into 16 bit integers

Write a function pack(a,b) to pack two 8-bit "char" variables *a* and *b* into a 16-bit "int" variable. (*Hint*: Look at Laboratory Exercise 2 for the use of the left shift operator.) Enter *a* and *b* from the keyboard as hex input and print the packed variable as a decimal number.

Check your pack function for the following cases:

pack(0,80) = 128   pack(0,7F) = 127
pack(1,0) = 256   pack(0,FF) = 255
pack(80,00) = –32,768   pack(7F,FF) = 32,767
pack(FF,01) = –255   pack(FF,00) = –256

LABORATORY REPORT

1 Discussion and Conclusions

1.1 Numerical representation. Discuss how different representations of the same numbers depend on the variable type and the printf format.

1.2 Pack function. Draw a simple flow diagram for your function pack(a,b).

2 Program and Output

Include printouts of your program code and output.

Laboratory Exercise 2

Measuring Event Times

PURPOSE

To write and test a C program that uses a digital counter/timer integrated circuit to measure the time interval between two events and to use that program to measure human response times. To use the Student's t test to determine whether the difference of two means is statistically significant.

EQUIPMENT

- IBM AT with DOS and C compiler
- Metra Byte CTM-05 parallel I/O and timer board
  (with AM9513 counter/timer chip)
- printer (shared with other lab stations)

BACKGROUND

1 Hardware

The Metra Byte CTM-05 board uses the AM9513 System Timing Controller chip, which has five independent 16-bit counters with programmable pulse source selection and clock rates (1.023 MHz maximum). Counters can be connected sequentially under software control. See the AM9513 description in Appendix F. A base address (hexadecimal) of 300 is usually used.

2 Software

You will use the C callable function outportb(p,n) to initialize and latch the timers. The port address is p (16 bits) and the data are n (8 bits). For the AM9513, p=301(hex) is used to initialize the timers, and p=300(hex) is used to read and write the timers. You will use the C callable function inportb(p) to read the two timers as four separate eight-bit bytes. These four bytes are then assembled into a 32-bit number.

3 Student's *t*

Given two sets of values a_i, $i = 1$ to m_a and b_i, $i = 1$ to m_b, measured under different experimental conditions, the averages $\bar{a}$ and $\bar{b}$ are given by

$$\bar{a} = \frac{1}{m_a} \sum_{i=1}^{m_a} a_i \quad \text{and} \quad \bar{b} = \frac{1}{m_b} \sum_{i=1}^{m_b} b_i$$

Use Table 5.2 in Chapter 5 to determine the probability that the difference between $\bar{a}$ and $\bar{b}$ could have arisen by chance. The number of degrees of freedom is given by $n_f = m_a + m_b - 2$, the value of Student's t is given by

$$t = \frac{\bar{a} - \bar{b}}{\sqrt{\sigma_a^2/m_a + \sigma_b^2/m_b}}$$

and the rms deviations σ_a and σ_b are given by

$$\sigma_a^2 = \frac{1}{m_a-1} \sum_{i=1}^{m_a} (a_i - \bar{a})^2 \quad \text{and} \quad \sigma_b^2 = \frac{1}{m_b-1} \sum_{i=1}^{m_b} (b_i - \bar{b})^2$$

If the probability of exceeding t is very low (say, below 0.1%), we may conclude that the different experimental conditions *caused* the averages $\bar{a}$ and $\bar{b}$ to differ.

If the difference between $\bar{a}$ and $\bar{b}$ is real, but small compared to the rms deviations σ_a and σ_b, and the number of measurements m_a and m_b is relatively small, then $|t|$ will be small, and we will not be able to conclude that the difference is statistically significant. Under these circumstances, increasing the number of measurements can increase the value of $|t|$ to the point where the difference can be statistically detected by the Student's t test.

ADDITIONAL READING

Chapter 5, Section 5.2: The Gaussian-Error Distribution and Section 5.3:, Student's *t*.

For more complete treatments, see the following:

George W. Snedicor, *Statistical Methods*, Iowa State University Press, Ames, IA, 1965.

Lyman Ott and William Mendenhall, *Understanding Statistics*, Duxbury Press, Boston, MA, 1985.

PROCEDURE

1 Program

1. Define variables as follows:

```
long i1, i2, i3, i4, i14, j1, j2, j3, j4, j14;
float time;
int k1, k2, k, i;
char dummy;
```

2. Set master mode and counter 1 and 2 mode registers for cascaded 1-MHz counting:

```
outportb(0x301,0x17);      /* set pointer to master mode register
                              (000 10 111) */
outportb(0x300,0xB0);      /* load least significant byte = 1011 0000
                              (1-MHz source F1) */
outportb(0x300,1);         /* load most significant byte = 0000 0001
                              (divide by 1) */
outportb(0x301,1);         /* set pointer to counter 1 mode register
                              (000 00 001) */
outportb(0x300,0x2D);      /* load least significant byte = 00101 101
                              (binary count up, repetitively, active low output) */
outportb(0x300,0x1B);      /* load most significant byte = 000 11011
                              (no gate, 1 MHz source F1, falling edge ) */
outportb(0x301,2);         /* set pointer to counter 2 mode register
                              (000 00 010) */
outportb(0x300,0x2D);      /* load least significant byte = 00101 101
                              (binary count up, active low output) */
outportb(0x300,0);         /* load most significant byte = 000 00000
                              (source from counter 1 out, rising edge) */
```

3. Load counters 1 and 2 with zeros:

```
outportb(0x301,9);              /* set pointer to counter 1 load register
                                (000 01 001) */
outportb(0x300,0);              /* load least significant byte = 0 */
outportb(0x300,0);              /* load most significant byte = 0 */
outportb(0x301,0x0A);           /* set pointer to counter 2 load register
                                (000 01 010) */
outportb(0x300,0);              /* load least significant byte = 0 */
outportb(0x300,0);              /* load most significant byte = 0 */
```

Note: You may wish to combine steps 2 and 3 in a function that you can "include" in programs of future laboratory exercises to initialize the timers with a desired mode and starting count.

4. Start counting:

```
outportb(0x301,0x63);           /* load and arm counters 1 and 2 (011 00011) */
```

5. Loop to delay about five seconds:

```
for(k1 = 0; k1 < 100; ++k1) {
   for (k2 = 0; k2 < 5500; ++k2);
   }
```

6. Latch and read counters 1 and 2:

```
outportb(0x301,0xA3);           /* save counters 1 and 2 in hold registers 1 and 2
                                (101 00011) */
outportb(0x301,0x11);           /* set pointer to counter 1 hold register
                                (000 10 001) */
i1 = inportb(0x300);            /* read least significant byte of hold register 1 */
i2 = inportb(0x300);            /* read most significant byte of hold register 1 */
if(i2 == 0)                     /* if counter 1 has just passed 0, */
   outportb(0x301,0xA2);        /*    then save counter 2 again in hold register */
outportb(0x301,0x12);           /* set pointer to counter 2 hold register
                                (000 10 010) */
i3 = inportb(0x300);            /* read least significant byte  of hold register 2 */
i4 = inportb(0x300);            /* read most significant byte of hold register 2 */
```

7. Generate a prompting character or tone:

```
printf("a");                    /* visible prompt- write character to screen*/
for(k = 0; k < 1; ++k);         /* wait for printf to get off bus */

outportb(0x0061,0x0B);          /* audible prompt- turn tone on */
                                /* (specific to IBM XT and AT) */
for(i = 0; i < 5500; ++i);      /* delay for 50 msec */
outportb(0x061,0);              /* turn tone off */
```

Note: On the IBM XT and AT, the statement printf("\007"); is not suitable because it halts execution while it produces its 300-millisecond tone, and it is impossible for the program to detect the pressing of the return key during this period.

8. Pause until the return key is pressed. This can be done by reading a dummy variable from the keyboard with the following statement:

scanf("%c",&dummy);   /* pause until return key is pressed */

Note that the keyboard interface is a 9600-baud (9600 bits per second) serial port and there are about 10 bits per character (an eight-bit byte plus one or two stop bits). So keyboard I/O takes about 1 ms per character.

9. Repeat step 6 using new variables (e.g., j1, j2, j3, j4).

10. Convert each set of four byte values into a 32-bit number and a decimal time (in seconds) using the following code:

```
i14 = i4<<24 | i3<<16 | i2<<8 | i1;  /* pack four bytes into 32-bit integer */
j14 = j4<<24 | j3<<16 | j2<<8 | j1;  /* pack four bytes into 32-bit integer */
time = (j14 – i14)/1023000.;         /* convert from µs to s */
```

Note 1: It is essential that the number 1023000. have a terminating decimal point so that the variable "time" is computed by floating-point division. Otherwise integer division will occur and the variable "time" will always be an integer number of seconds (in your case, mostly 0 and 1).

Note 2: This procedure assumes that the packed 32-bit values are always positive, which limits them to the value 2.15×10^9 (maximum time interval of about 2000 s).

11. Print the time response on the screen.

12. Loop back to step 5 to try again.

13. After 10 tries, compute and print the average, standard deviation, and standard error of the mean.

Warning: Do not save the counters in their hold registers immediately after a printf statement or they may be read incorrectly. (Apparently an outportb statement can access the microprocessor bus before the printf statement has completed its use of the bus.) If you insert a short delay after the printf, such as "for(k = 0; k < 1; ++k);", the counters will be read correctly.

2 Program Flow Chart

Your program should have the flow chart shown in Laboratory Figure 2.1.

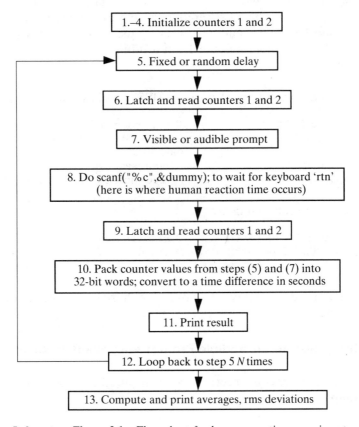

Laboratory Figure 2.1   Flow chart for human reaction experiments.

3 Learning curve

Using a variable prompt and a fixed delay, each lab partner measures several series of 10 response times. Note how the averages change as the task is learned. Any response time less than 50 ms is probably due to pressing the return key *before* the prompt. Such data should be disregarded.

4 Response to a Visible Prompt with Fixed Delay

After the training provided in the previous section, each lab partner measures 10 response times. Here the delay between running the program and the first event (the prompting character) is fixed, so the subject might be able to anticipate it, using an "internal" clock.

5 Response to a Visible Prompt with a Random Delay

Change the program at step 5 to make the delay pseudorandom. Read the least significant byte of the least significant counter as a pseudorandom number. This is the most rapidly varying byte that cycles completely through all values between 0 and 255 every 25 µs. The following program statements will delay a random amount from a minimum of about 5 s to a maximum of about 18 s.

Latch and read counter 1 of the AM9513 with the statements

```
outportb(0x301,0xA1);          /* save counter 1 in hold register 1 (101 0001) */
outportb(0x301,0x11);          /* set pointer to counter 1 hold register
                                  (000 10 001) */
i1=inportb(0x300);             /* read least significant byte of hold register 1 */
i2=inportb(0x300);             /* read most significant byte of hold register 1 */
```

Perform the random delay

```
for (k1=0;k1<(i1+100);++k1) {    /* k1 loops from 100 to 355 */
   for(k2=0;k2<3000;++k2);       /* k2 loops 3000 times (about 50 ms) */
   }
```

With a random delay, it should be harder to anticipate the prompting character.

6 Response to an Audible Prompt with Random Delay

Repeat the previous section using an audible prompt rather than a visible prompt.

7 Computer Response Time

Determine the delay inherent in the measuring process (i.e., your program, transmission to and from the terminal, etc.). (*Hint:* "preload" the scanf by pressing the return key during the delay loop and before the prompt.)

LABORATORY REPORT

1 Data Summary

Tabulate the response times measured for procedure section 3 (learning curve), 4 (visible prompt, fixed delay), section 5 (visible prompt, random delay), section 6 (audible prompt, random delay), and section 7 (computer response time, which represents a systematic error in the above).

2 Analysis

2.1 Average delays and uncertainties. For procedure sections 4 to 7, compute and tabulate average delays, and rms deviations. If you do not have time during the lab, perform the analysis at "home" any way you can (abacus, hand calculator, Cray, etc.).

2.2 Student's *t* test (fixed vs random delay). Compute Student's *t* for the difference between the results of procedure sections 4 and 5 and determine whether the difference is significant.

2.3 Student's *t* test (visible vs audible prompt). Compute Student's *t* for the difference between the results of procedure sections 5 and 6 and determine whether the difference is significant.

2.4 Student's *t* test (different lab partners). Compute Student's *t* for the difference between two lab partners in one of procedure sections 4, 5, or 6 and determine whether the difference is significant.

3 Discussion and Conclusions

3.1 Discuss procedure sections 3 to 7. Include your subjective observations as a subject during the various reaction time tests.

3.2 Discuss what you have learned about the design of experiments for determining whether two different experimental conditions are associated statistically with differences in a measurable quantity.

4 Questions

4.1 Did your results depend on whether the timing of the prompting character could be anticipated by the subject? (*Hint:* Look at the probability of exceeding Student's *t* for these two conditions.)

4.2 Which prompt gives the quicker response: visible or audible? (*Hint:* Look at the probability of exceeding Student's *t* for these two conditions.)

4.3 How did you measure the computer response time, and what assumptions did you make?

4.4 How would you use the AM9513 counter/timer to sound the tone twice a second? (A simple flow chart will be sufficient.) How accurately could you do this?

5 Program and Laboratory Data Sheets

5.1   Include printouts of your program code, data, and output.

5.2   Include your handwritten data sheets (or a copy), which should consist of a log of the procedures you used, any special circumstances, and the measurements you recorded manually.

Laboratory Exercise 3

Digital Interfacing:
Switches and Lights

PURPOSE

To write and test a C program that uses a microcomputer parallel interface to read simple external devices such as switches and to turn on light-emitting diodes, and to gain familiarity with digital interfacing protocols.

EQUIPMENT

- IBM AT with DOS and C compiler
- printer (shared with other lab stations)
- IBM Data Acquisition and Control Adapter (parallel I/O port used)
- Metra Byte CTM-05 card (AM9513 counter/timer used)
- +5-V, ±12-V power supplies
- superstrip circuit board
- parallel port ribbon cable for connecting parallel I/O port to circuit boards
- nine 330-Ω resistors
- one 500-Ω resistor
- one DIP unit of eight switches
- one 74LS244 octal buffer
- eight light-emitting diodes

- one 74LS49 BCD to seven-segment decoder
- one 7-segment LED display

BACKGROUND

1 Parallel I/O Ports

To communicate with the outside world, a microcomputer must have the ability to transfer a byte (eight bits) or a word (16 or 32 bits) to and from another device. Connecting directly to the microprocessor involves many attendant problems, and it is far easier to use a parallel or serial I/O board that connects to the microcomputer bus and handles the details for you.

As described in Chapter 1, section 1.5, the parallel or binary I/O port has addresses for its status register, control register and data register. The **status register** gives the current state of the port and can be read by the program and tested with an 'if' statement to determine whether the device connected to the port is ready to accept output, whether the last byte (or word) has been taken by the device, or whether a byte (or word) is ready for your program to read, etc. The **control register** permits the program to control the logic state of external lines and thereby communicate with external circuits and tell them that the port has new output or is ready to accept new input. The **data registers** are connected to the 16 input and 16 output lines, and are able hold data for as long as necessary until the program or external circuit can read them.

2 Writing to the Parallel Output Port on the IBM DAC Card

The IBM Data Acquisition and Control Adapter has a binary I/O device with a 16-bit parallel input port and a 16-bit output port. Your C program must first select this device by writing 08 to address C2E2. Then you can write two bytes to the port, one at a time. The code is

```
outportb(0xC2E2,8);        /* select binary I/O device */
outportb(0x22E2,data1);    /* output low byte */
outportb(0x22E3,data2);    /* output high byte */
outportb(0x22E2,data1);    /* output low byte */
outportb(0x22E3,data2);    /* output high byte */
```

It is necessary to write twice because the first write is buffered on the data-acquisition board and does not appear on the external lines until the second write.

In this laboratory exercise, we will be using the parallel output port in **transparent output mode** by letting the "BO GATE" line float high. In this mode, you can write two bytes to the port at any time and they will appear on the output lines.

3 Reading from the Parallel Input Port on the IBM DAC Card

To permit the parallel input port to receive data from an external device, that device must first assert the data on the input lines while the external line $\overline{\text{BI HOLD}}$ (pin 33) is high, and then bring $\overline{\text{BI HOLD}}$ to ground to freeze the data on the internal port registers (the ones your program actually reads). Then the device should change the level of the external line BI STROBE (pin 53) to let the program know that new data are ready to be read.

   Note that the purpose of $\overline{\text{BI HOLD}}$ is to control the port input registers (high or no connection for transparent mode, low for hold mode), whereas the purpose of BI STROBE is to allow the external circuit to communicate to the computer program. BI STROBE does not affect the port registers. Bit 0 of the binary status register (which can be read by your program) is one or zero, depending on whether the external BI STROBE line is high or low, respectively. Since BI STROBE floats high when disconnected, it is easiest for you to momentarily disconnect it from ground whenever you want your program to read data. The data will be held in the registers for your C program to read as long as $\overline{\text{BI HOLD}}$ is low. Before your program can read the data from the registers, it must first read the status bit (bit 0 of the binary status register) to see whether any new data are available. This is done by the statement:

```
while((inportb(0x02E2)&1)==0);    /* pause until status bit is set */
```

which causes the program to pause until BI STROBE is disconnected from ground during which time the status bit is set to 1. When the bit is set and the while condition is no longer satisfied, then the while loop falls through to an instruction reads the new data into memory.

   In summary, here are the steps in time sequence:

1. The program initiates some data-acquisition command (via timer pulses, attention pulse, keyboard prompt, etc.);
2. The program loops, waiting for the status bit to be set;
3. The external device makes $\overline{\text{BI HOLD}}$ high while it asserts data on the parallel input port lines;
4. The external device then makes BI STROBE high, which sets status bit to one;
5. The program detects status bit and reads latches (transfers data from latches to memory).

The code is

```
outportb(0xC2E2,8);              /* select Binary I/O device */
```

```
while((inportb(0x02E2)&1)==0);    /* wait for status bit to be set when
                                     BI STROBE goes high */
data1=inportb(0x22E2);            /* read low byte */
data2=inportb(0x22E3);            /* read high byte */
```

ADDITIONAL READING

Appendix E (The IBM Data Acquisition and Control Adapter), Section 1: Pin Assignments, Section 2: Binary output, and Section 3: Binary Input.

PROCEDURE

1 Circuit

1. As shown in Laboratory Figure 3.1, connect the eight DIP switches between ground and input bits 0-7 of the the binary input port (pins 35, 37, ..., 49). Refer to the cable connector diagram in Appendix Figure E.2 and the list of pin assignments in Appendix Table E.1. The input port already has internal "pull up" resistors so that an open line is "high" and a grounded line is "low".

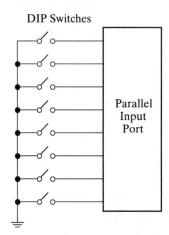

DIP Switches   74LS244 Pinout

Enable 1–4	1	20	+5 V
Input 1	2	19	Enable 5–8
Output 8	3	18	Output 1
Input 2	4	17	Input 8
Output 7	5	16	Output 2
Input 3	6	15	Input 7
Output 6	7	14	Output 3
Input 4	8	13	Input 6
Output 5	9	12	Output 4
Ground	10	11	Input 5

Top View

Laboratory Figure 3.1   Left: Circuit diagram for switches connected to the parallel input port. Right: Pinout for 74LS244 octal buffer used to drive LEDs from the parallel output port.

2. Leave BO GATE (pin 34) unconnected so that it will float high.

3. Ground $\overline{\text{BI HOLD}}$ (pin 33) and BI STROBE (pin 53).

4. As shown in Laboratory Figure 3.2, connect output bits 0-7 of the binary output port (pins 36, 38, ..., 50) to the inputs of the 74LS244 octal buffer. Connect the outputs to the current limiting resistors and LEDs as shown. Ground pin 1 to enable buffers 1-4 and ground pin 19 to enable buffers 5-8.

5. Connect the IBM Data Acquisition and Control Adapter ground (pins 15 and 60) to your external power supply ground.

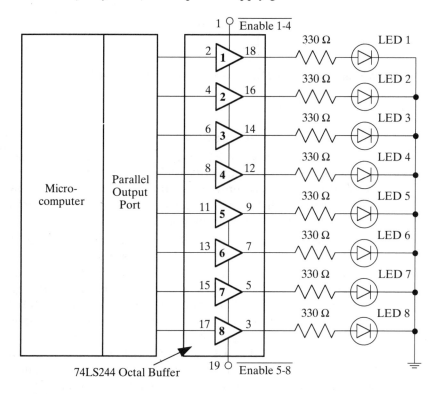

Laboratory Figure 3.2 Schematic for parallel output port, octal buffer, current-limiting resistors, and LEDs.

Note: Use your 5-Volt power supply for the 74LS244 buffer. Never connect anything to the microcomputer power supply lines. One mistake could short the microcomputer power supply, causing expensive damage.

2 Program

Write a C program that does the following:

1. Asks the user to set the eight switches, to momentarily disconnect $\overline{\text{BI HOLD}}$ from ground, and then to momentarily disconnect BI STROBE from ground.

2. Selects the binary I/O device :   outportb(0xC2E2,8);
3. Waits until the status bit is set: while((inportb(0x02E2)&1)==0);
4. Reads the eight switches: n=inportb(0x22E2);
5. Writes the value to the lowest   outportb(0x22E2,n);
   eight bits of the output port: outportb(0x22E3,n);
                                     outportb(0x22E2,n);
                                     outportb(0x22E3,n);

6. Writes the value to the terminal screen.
7. Loops back to step 1.

3 Reading from Switches and Writing to Lights

Run the program of procedure section 2 as follows:

1. Set a bit pattern on the switches.
2. Momentarily disconnect $\overline{\text{BI HOLD}}$ from ground. When the $\overline{\text{BI HOLD}}$ line goes high, the input port registers will take on the value of the external switches. When the $\overline{\text{BI HOLD}}$ line goes back low, the input port registers will retain those values. This is important, since your program may not read them immediately.
3. Momentarily disconnect BI STROBE from ground, which momentarily sets the BI STATUS bit 1 to one and causes the program to fall through the "while" loop and read the data. Note that both external lines may bounce between high to low a few times before reaching their final value (see Figure 1.18). When you unground BI STROBE and then ground it again, it may bounce between high and low many times, but will soon return to its grounded state. Since step 1 takes a while, you may safely assume that BI STROBE is low and that the program will hold at step 3 until it is ungrounded again. In a higher-speed-data acquisition situation, however, this contact bounce can cause trouble, and requires a "debouncing" circuit, which consists of a pulse generator that can be triggered by a leading edge only after the input has been stable for a certain time.
4. The program will detect the BI STATUS bit and read the data.
5. The program will write the data to the lights and the terminal screen.

Repeat the procedure, varying the bit pattern set on the switches. Verify that the pattern of LED lights agrees.

4 Testing the function of $\overline{\text{BI HOLD}}$ and BI STROBE

Do the following:

1. Set a bit pattern in the switches.

2. Momentarily unground $\overline{\text{BI HOLD}}$

3. Change the bit pattern in the switches.

4. Momentarily unground BI STROBE, which causes your program to read the port.

5. Record both the pattern set in the switches and the pattern of lit LEDs. Note whether the value read by your program was the value on the switches during the $\overline{\text{BI HOLD}}$ pulse or during the read statement.

Note: If the input port you are using has a STROBE line that simultaneously latches the data onto the input ports and sets a status register (unlike the IBM DACA port), write your program as follows:

1. Set a bit pattern in the switches.

2. Pulse the STROBE line.

3. Use a dummy "scanf" to pause.

4. Change the switch settings and then press return.

5. Read the input port.

6. Write the data to the lights and terminal screen.

5 From Switches to Timer to Lights

Change the program of procedure section 2 as follows:

1. Cascade counters 1 and 2 as you did in Laboratory Exercise 2. Counter 1 should increment every microsecond and counter 2 should increment every 64 ms. (This program change is easier if you use the counter/timer initialization function developed in Laboratory Exercise 2.)

2. Instead of simply writing the eight switch values to the lights, load the values into the least significant byte of counter 2 and begin counting.

3. Read the least significant byte of counter 2 and write the value to the lights in a tight loop. This will constantly display the state of that counter byte.

4. The program should stop when the byte sent to the lights reaches FF.

This involves combining the procedures you used to initialize, latch and read the counters in Laboratory Exercise 2, with those you used in the preceeding section to read the switches and write to the lights. The result should be a pattern of LEDs that starts with the values that were set into the switches, increments once every 64 ms, and stops with all the lights on.

Run the program with varying switch settings and record the time taken to count from 0 to 255.

6 Seven-Segment Decoder Driver

Connect the three most slowly varying bits of counter 2 to the input of a
seven-segment decoder driver and connect the output to a seven-segment
LED display. This demonstrates the conversion of binary to octal using a
single chip.

LABORATORY REPORT

1 Setup

Draw a simple block diagram of your experimental setup, showing all components on your circuit board as well as the connections to the timer and I/O
ports.

2 Data Summary

Summarize your observations from procedure sections 3, 4, 5, and 6.

3 Discussion and Conclusions

3.1 Discuss procedure sections 3, 4, 5, and 6.

3.2 Describe a computer program to read four switches, put the bits
in a binary number ranging from 0000 to 1001, and light up the various segments of a seven-segment LED array to display the equivalent decimal digit.
(Use only software commands and a parallel I/O port, not the seven-segment
decoder circuit used in procedure section 6).

3.3 Give two examples where a strobe pulse is needed before valid
digital input data can be read by a computer.

4 Questions

4.1 In procedure section 3, did the data read with "inportb" correspond to the switch values during the $\overline{\text{BI HOLD}}$ pulse or during the read?

4.2 In procedure section 7, how long did the count from 0 to FF take?
Was it what you expected?

4.3 When a simple pushbutton is used to strobe data onto a parallel
port, what precaution is necessary so that subsequent data will strobe
properly?

4.4   What are the major functions of the parallel input port in acquiring digital data?

5 Program and Laboratory Data Sheets

5.1   Include a printout of your program code.

5.2   Include your handwritten data sheets (or a copy), which should consist of a log of the procedures you used, any special circumstances, and the measurements you recorded manually.

2

Analog Tools

2.1 INTRODUCTION

This chapter describes the amplification and analog filtering that most sensor signals require before they can be digitized and read by the microcomputer, some of the factors that determine the signal-to-noise ratio, and the simpler circuits that link the analog and digital world, such as the sample-and-hold amplifier and the comparator.

2.2 OPERATIONAL-AMPLIFIER CIRCUITS

One of the most useful building blocks in analog circuit design is the operational amplifier, or op amp, which is available as an integrated circuit at very low cost (Figure 2.1).

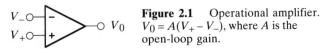

Figure 2.1   Operational amplifier. $V_0 = A(V_+ - V_-)$, where A is the open-loop gain.

The **ideal op amp** has the following characteristics:

1. Differential amplification with infinite gain.
2. Infinite input impedance (no current enters the two inputs V_- and V_+).

3. Zero output impedance.

The **realistic op amp** differs in the following important ways:

1. Inputs V_+ and V_- produce an output $V_0 = A(V_+ - V_-)$, where the open-loop gain A is finite and decreases as 1/frequency. The product of gain and frequency is typically 10^5 to 10^8 Hz.

2. The input impedance is finite, typically 10^6 Ω for bipolar and 10^{12} Ω for FET input.

3. When $V_- = V_+$, V_0 is not zero, but exhibits an offset potential due to unbalanced internal potentials and currents.

4. The input terminals V_- and V_+ have external bias currents that are unequal. These can produce an output offset potential even if the external impedances are equal.

5. The output current is typically limited to 10 mA at ±10 volts.

2.2.1 Inverting Amplifier

One common amplifier circuit uses the op amp with negative feedback (Figure 2.2). As we shall see in Laboratory Exercise 4, the negative feedback establishes a well-defined **voltage gain** $G = V_0/V_1$ (the ratio of the output to the input voltage) over a wide range of frequencies. G is also called the **closed-loop gain**.

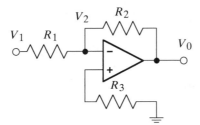

Figure 2.2   Inverting Amplifier. $G = V_0/V_1 \approx -R_2/R_1$.

We compute the closed-loop gain G using the ideal op amp defining relationships given in the last section. The output voltage is given by $V_0 = -AV_2$. Since the op amp has very high input impedance, no current flows into its input, and resistors R_1 and R_2 form a voltage divider with the relationship $(V_0 - V_1)/(R_2 + R_1) = (V_2 - V_1)/R_1$.
Solving for V_0/V_1, we have

$$V_0 R_1 - V_1 R_1 = V_2(R_1 + R_2) - V_1 R_1 - V_1 R_2$$

$$V_0 R_1 + \left(\frac{V_0}{A}\right)(R_1 + R_2) = -V_1 R_2$$

$$G = \frac{V_0}{V_1} = \left(\frac{R_2}{R_1}\right)\left(\frac{R_1 A}{R_1 A + R_1 + R_2}\right) \approx -\frac{R_2}{R_1}$$

Note that $V_2 = -V_0/A$, and is therefore a very small voltage. It is commonly said that point V_2 is at a "virtual ground." Conversely, measurements of V_0 and V_2 for a sine wave input can be used to compute the open-loop gain $A = -V_0/V_2$ as a function of frequency. As measured in Laboratory Exercise 4, V_2 increases in magnitude at high frequency due to the decrease in open-loop gain A. For minimum offset error we want to equalize the dc path resistances to ground and choose $R_3 = R_1 \parallel R_2 = R_1 R_2/(R_1+R_2)$. See Section 2.3.1 (Input Offset Voltage).

2.2.2 Noninverting Amplifier

It is also possible to arrange the feedback to create a noninverting amplifier with very high input impedance (Figure 2.3).

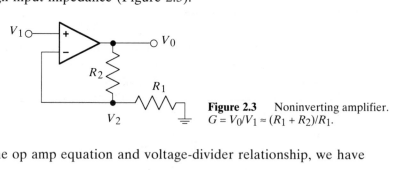

Figure 2.3   Noninverting amplifier.
$G = V_0/V_1 \approx (R_1 + R_2)/R_1$.

From the op amp equation and voltage-divider relationship, we have

$$V_0 = A\left(V_1 - V_2\right) \quad \text{and} \quad \frac{V_2}{V_0} = \frac{R_1}{R_1 + R_2}$$

Eliminating V_2 and solving for V_1 in terms of V_0, we have

$$V_0 = A V_1 - \frac{A V_0 R_1}{R_1 + R_2} \qquad V_1 = V_0\left(\frac{R_1}{R_1 + R_2} + \frac{1}{A}\right) = V_0\left(\frac{R_1 + (R_1 + R_2)/A}{R_1 + R_2}\right)$$

The gain is given by

$$G = \frac{V_0}{V_1} = \frac{R_1 + R_2}{R_1 + (R_1 + R_2)/A} \approx \frac{R_1 + R_2}{R_1}$$

For minimum offset error, $R_1 \parallel R_2 = R$ (source).

2.2.3 Differential Amplifier

By combining these circuits, we have a differential amplifier with a fixed gain over a range of frequencies (Figure 2.4). The input impedance is determined

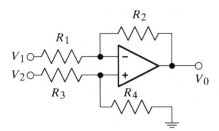

Figure 2.4   Differential amplifier.

by the value of resistors R_1 and R_3, which must be much higher than the source impedance. If this condition is not met, the amplifier circuit will reduce the potential produced by the source and degrade accuracy.

For general values of R_1, R_2, R_3, and R_4 the output is given by

$$V_0 = V_2 \frac{(R_1 + R_2)R_4}{(R_3 + R_4)R_1} - V_1 \frac{R_2}{R_1}$$

For the special case where $R_1 = R_3$, and $R_2 = R_4$, we have

$$\boxed{V_0 = \frac{R_2}{R_1}(V_2 - V_1)}$$

For minimum offset error, $R_1 \| R_2 = R_3 \| R_4$.

2.2.4 Voltage Follower

A special case of the noninverting amplifier is the **voltage follower**, or unity-gain buffer, which is very useful for amplifying small currents from sensors having sufficient voltage but a high output impedance (Figure 2.5).

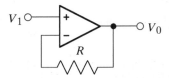

Figure 2.5   Unity-gain buffer. $V_0 = V_1$.

The op-amp equation and voltage-divider equations are

$$V_0 = A(V_1 - V_0) \quad \text{and} \quad V_0 + AV_0 = AV_1$$

Solving, we have
$$\boxed{V_0 = \frac{V_1 A}{1 + A} \approx V_1}$$

For minimum offset error, $R = R$ (source).

2.2.5 Current-to-Voltage Converter

By setting the input resistor R_1 in Figure 2.2 to zero, we have the current-to-voltage converter (Figure 2.6). In this case, the negative feedback through R cancels the input current I and produces an output voltage $V_0 = IR$. It is important that the impedance of the input current source not be too large, or op-amp leakage currents (to be discussed) will cause a large offset voltage or even output saturation.

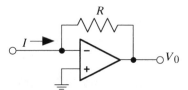

Figure 2.6   Current-to-voltage converter. $V_0 = IR$.

2.2.6 Summing Amplifier

The previous principle can be used to build a voltage summing amplifier, shown in Figure 2.7. The current reaching the virtual ground at the negative op-amp terminal is $I = I_1 + I_2 + I_3 = V_1/R_1 + V_2/R_2 + V_3/R_3$, and the output voltage V_0 is given by

$$V_0 = IR = \left(I_1 + I_2 + I_3\right)R = \left(\frac{V_1}{R_1} + \frac{V_2}{R_2} + \frac{V_3}{R_3}\right)R$$

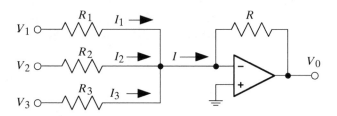

Figure 2.7   Summing amplifier. For equal input resistors R_1, R_2, and R_3, the output voltage is the sum of the input voltages.

This assumes that the negative terminal of the op amp is a good virtual ground, which requires a high open-loop gain over the frequencies of interest. In the case where $R_1 = R_2 = R_3 = R$, we have a voltage-summing amplifier $V_0 = V_1 + V_2 + V_3$. In the case where $V_1 = V_2 = V_3 = V$, we have a current-summing amplifier, and the current through each input leg is determined by the corresponding resistor value. The latter is used in the digital-to-analog converter (Chapter 3).

2.2.7 Full-Wave Rectifier

The **full-wave rectifier** is an op-amp circuit whose output is equal to the absolute value of the input. High open-loop gain permits operation for very small input signals. It is used to rectify a waveform to determine the envelope of a carrier (such as in amplitude demodulation) or the average peak-to-peak amplitude of a noisy signal (such as in processing the electromyogram in Laboratory Exercise 18). The op-amp circuit shown in Figure 2.8 is commonly used for this purpose.

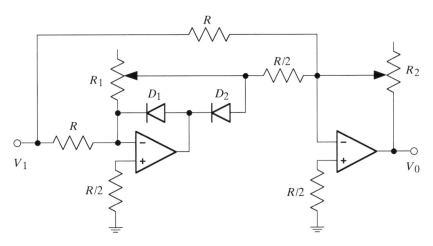

Figure 2.8   Full wave rectifier circuit. Ideally, $R_1 = R_2 = R$, and $V_0 = |V_1|$. See Figures 2.9 and 2.10 for $V_1 < 0$ and $V_1 > 0$ equivalent circuits.

The circuit can be analyzed as two equivalent circuits. For the case $V_1 < 0$ (Figure 2.9), diode D_1 conducts and effectively removes the first op amp from the circuit by making its output a virtual ground. The current into the second op amp is V_1/R and its output is $V_0 = -V_1(R_2/R)$.

For the case $V_1 > 0$ (Figure 2.10), diode D_2 conducts and the first op amp becomes an inverting amplifier with an output $-V_1(R_1/R)$. The current into the second op amp is $+V_1/R - 2V_1R_1/R^2 = (V_1/R)(1 - 2R_1/R)$ and its output is given by

$$V_0 = V_1 \left(\frac{R_2}{R} \right) \left(\frac{2R_1}{R} - 1 \right)$$

To adjust resistors R_1 and R_2, use a sine wave as a test input. If alternate lobes of the rectified waveform have different amplitudes, the gain of the first stage should be adjusted by varying its feedback resistor R_1. If the input and output have different magnitudes, the gain of the second stage should be

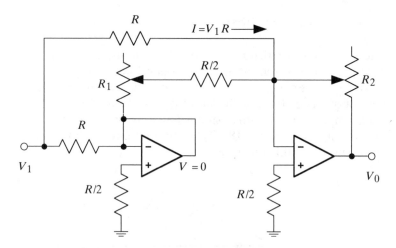

Figure 2.9   Equivalent full-wave rectifier circuit for $V_1 < 0$.

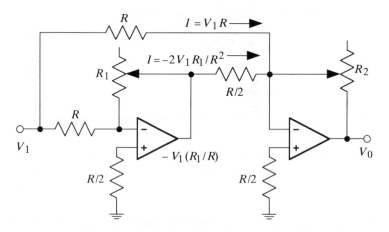

Figure 2.10   Equivalent full-wave rectifier circuit for $V_1 > 0$.

adjusted by varying its feedback resistor R_2.   Ideally, proper operation occurs when R_1 and R_2 are equal to R.

2.3 OP-AMP CHARACTERISTICS

2.3.1 Input and Output Offset Voltages

For an ideal op amp, when the two inputs are both connected to ground (V_- = V_+ = 0 volts), the output V_0 should be zero. However, differences in the input leakage currents of the two inputs to ground can create a nonzero output called the **output offset voltage** (Figure 2.11). The **input offset voltage** is defined as the output offset voltage divided by the closed-loop gain. Note

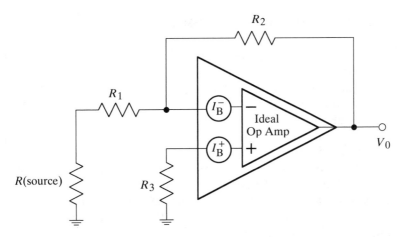

Figure 2.11   Offset voltage produced by unbalanced leakage currents and/or resistance paths to ground.

that the input offset voltage is not directly measurable. For an input offset voltage V_{RTI}, an output offset voltage V_{RTO}, and a closed-loop gain G, the overall offset voltage is approximately $GV_{\text{RTI}} + V_{\text{RTO}}$.

The input and output offset voltages are affected by several factors: power-supply variations, temperature, and unequal resistance paths.

Temperature variations.   The internal offset voltages and bias currents are all generally functions of temperature, so that it is necessary to refer to the data sheets to estimate the variation in input and output offset over the anticipated temperature range.

Unequal resistance paths.   Even if both op-amp input terminals have equal bias currents, an offset voltage can develop due to unequal external resistance paths. This effect can be minimized by choosing external resistors as described in the text for Figures 2.2 to 2.10. On the other hand, the op-amp bias currents can be measured by intentionally making the external resistance paths unequal. Suppose that when both inputs are grounded, the output voltage is V_0. Now if we ground one of the inputs through an external resistor R (say, 1 MΩ), any change in V_0 can be related to the bias current I_B of that input and the closed-loop gain G:

$$I_B = \frac{\Delta V_0}{RG}$$

Caution: The input bias currents of many op amps can cause large output offset voltages or even saturation if the external input resistors are too large. For example, if one input is grounded and the other is connected only by a capacitor so that its dc voltage is allowed to "float," then a leakage current of only 10 pA acting on an input impedance of 10^{12} Ω will try to develop 10 volts at the input!

2.3.2 Op-Amp Dynamic Response

The primary dynamic characteristics of the operational amplifier are as follows:

The **slewing rate** is the maximum rate of output change (V/μs) for a large input step change. It is usually determined by the maximum output current and the capacitive load.

The **unity-gain frequency** is the frequency at which the open-loop gain has fallen to unity.

The **gain at 1 Hz** is the open-loop gain at a frequency of 1 Hz. To provide stability at low frequencies, op-amp manufacturers often provide a small amount of internal negative feedback to limit the gain at very low frequencies (say, below 10 Hz). For this reason, the gain at 1 Hz is usually less than the unity-gain frequency.

The **gain-bandwidth product** is the open-loop gain integrated over frequency. This characteristic depends on the open-loop gain at very low frequencies where the gain is large. For example, the LF356 has a nearly constant open-loop gain for frequencies below 100 Hz and its gain-bandwidth product is considerably larger than its 1-Hz gain. On the other hand, the AD OP-07 is constant below 0.1 Hz and falls as 1/frequency for higher frequencies. Its gain-bandwidth product is considerably less than the 1-Hz gain.

Table 2.1 shows some commercially available monolithic (single integrated-circuit) operational amplifiers. Note the wide range of offset currents and maximum slew rates.

TABLE 2.1 SOME COMMERCIALLY AVAILABLE OPERATIONAL AMPLIFIERS

Model	LF356	AD OP-07A	AD OP-37E	ADLH003
Manufacturer	National Semi.	Analog Dev.	Analog Dev.	Analog Dev.
Gain = 1 frequency	3 MHz	300 kHz	10 MHz	100 MHz
Gain at 1 Hz	2×10^5	3×10^5	10^6	
Input Impedance	$10^{12}\ \Omega$	5 MΩ	5 MΩ	$10^{11}\ \Omega$
Input offset current	< 3 pA	< 2 nA	< 50 nA	
Input bias current	< 50 pA	< 2 nA	< 60 nA	< 150 pA
Input offset voltage	< 1 mV	< 60 μV	< 20 μV	< 10 mV
Common-mode rejection	100 dB	126 dB	126 dB	
Maximum slew rate	12 V/μs	0.17 V/μs	11 V/μs	1000 V/s
Input noise voltage ($nV\ Hz^{-1/2}$)(at 1 kHz)	12	10	4	18

2.3.3 Dynamic Response with Negative Feedback

By using negative feedback, as shown in the previous circuits, it is possible to design an amplifier that has a constant gain over a wide range of frequencies (Figure 2.12).

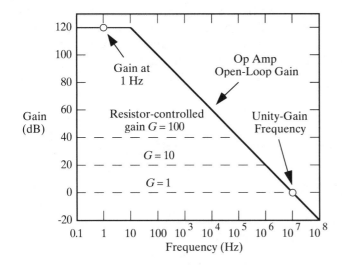

Figure 2.12   Bode plot of gain vs. frequency, where G is the closed-loop gain.

The **gain-bandwidth product** of an amplifier is the product of the closed-loop gain and frequency band over which the gain is approximately constant (usually taken between the 3-dB corner frequencies). Because the gain-bandwidth product of the amplifier is usually determined by the open-loop-gain of the op amp at high frequencies, it is not necessarily equal to the rated gain-bandwidth of the op amp itself (see the example that follows). As the closed-loop gain is increased, the corner frequency formed by the intersection with the open-loop gain decreases and the gain-bandwidth product remains nearly constant.

The **settling time** of an amplifier is the time required for the output to remain within a specified error band of its final value after a step input. The settling time is limited by the closed-loop bandwidth of the op-amp circuit and should be independent of input step size, provided that the output is sufficiently small so that it is not limited by the op-amp slewing rate. The 0.1% settling time for an ideal linear 6.02-dB/octave amplifier is 6.9 exponential time constants, or $6.9/\omega_c = 1.10/f_c$, where ω_c is the 3.01-dB corner frequency in rad/s and f_c is the corner frequency in Hz.

The **rise time** of an amplifier is the time required for the output to rise from 10 to 90% of its final change after a step input. This requires only about two exponential time constants and for quantitative work is not as important a specification as the settling time.

EXAMPLE

The AD OP-37 op amp has a rated gain-bandwidth product of 63 Mhz, a gain of 10^6 from dc to 30 Hz, and a unity-gain frequency of 10 MHz. When used in an amplifier with a closed-loop gain of 100, the 3-dB corner frequency and the bandwidth are both 200 kHz. Thus, the closed-loop gain-bandwidth is

20 MHz, less than the op amp gain-bandwidth product. The reason for the difference is that the open-loop gain-bandwidth product is determined by the low frequency response, whereas the closed-loop gain-bandwidth product is determined by the high-frequency response. Since the corner frequency is 200 kHz, after a step input, the output will reach 0.1% of its final change in approximately 1.1/200 kHz = 5.5 µs.

2.4 INSTRUMENTATION AND ISOLATION AMPLIFIERS

2.4.1 Instrumentation Amplifiers

The **instrumentation amplifier** has all the properties of the op amp: (1) differential amplification, (2) high input impedance, and (3) low output impedance; but it has additional important properties: (4) the gain can be accurately set by choosing resistor values, and (5) the gain is constant over a wide frequency band. Table 2.2 lists the properties of several of the amplifiers discussed in the preceding section and compares them to the instrumentation amplifier.

TABLE 2.2   COMPARISON OF AMPLIFICATION TECHNIQUES

	Op Amp	Inverting Amplifier	Noninverting Amplifier	Differential Amplifier	Instrumentation Amplifier
High Z_{in}	Yes	No	Yes	No	Yes
Differential input	Yes	No	No	Yes	Yes
Defined gain	No	Yes	Yes	Yes	Yes

While many of the previously discussed op-amp circuits have constant gain, one must choose between high input impedance Z_{in} (e.g., the noninverting amplifier in Figure 2.3) and differential amplification (e.g., the differential amplifier in Figure 2.4). The instrumentation amplifier provides both properties.

The instrumentation amplifier is usually constructed using three op amps: the first two provide high input impedance and differential amplification and the third provides a buffered output referenced to ground (Figure 2.13). In this way, the primary deficiency of the single op-amp differential amplifier (Figure 2.4) is overcome (i.e., its low input impedance). It is good practice to get most of the voltage gain from the first stage to reduce the effect of noise from the third op amp. Note that the first stage has good common-mode rejection and can handle large common-mode signals even at high gain (see the example that follows).

Instrumentation amplifiers are available in integrated-circuit chips as well as hybrid and discrete forms.

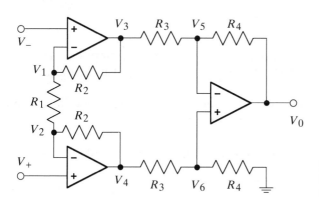

Figure 2.13   Classical instrumentation amplifier design using three op amps. See equation 2.1 for the gain.

An instrumentation amplifier has two inputs, V_+ and V_-, with a common ground. A single output is produced, V_0, also referenced to the common ground. Ideally, the **differential gain** $G_\pm$ is given by:

$$G_\pm = \frac{V_0}{V_+ - V_-}$$

In addition, every instrumentation amplifier is also sensitive to signals that are common to both inputs, and this is described by the **common-mode gain** G_c. Under the conditions of a common-mode signal V_c and no differential signal ($V_c = V_+ = V_-$), $G_c = V_0/V_c$. By combining these, when both common-mode and differential signals are present, output V_0 is given by

$$V_0 = G_\pm(V_+ - V_-) + G_c V_c, \quad \text{where} \quad V_c \approx \tfrac{1}{2}(V_+ + V_-)$$

Normally, $G_\pm$ is the useful signal gain, G_c should be as small as possible, and their ratio is defined as the common-mode rejection ratio (CMRR):

"CMRR" = $G_\pm/G_c$ (typically 10^3 to 10^7)

Converting to dB, we have the common-mode rejection (CMR):

"CMR" = $20 \log_{10}(G_\pm/G_c)$ (typically 60 to 140)

For the circuit in Figure 2.13, we have

$$G_\pm = \frac{V_0}{V_+ - V_-} = \frac{R_4}{R_3}\left(1 + \frac{2R_2}{R_1}\right) \tag{2.1}$$

By varying the resistor values, typically gains from 10 to 1000 can be selected.

The instrumentation amplifier, its gain as a function of frequency, and its common-mode rejection ratio are studied in Laboratory Exercise 5.

EXAMPLE

Derive Equation 2.1, the gain of the instrumentation amplifier, and determine the maximum differential and common-mode input potentials.

Step 1: The first two op amps have infinite open-loop gains so that the negative feedback current sets $V_1 = V_-$ and $V_2 = V_+$

Step 2: The same current flows through the upper R_2, R_1, and the lower R_2, so

$$\frac{V_2 - V_1}{R_1} = \frac{V_4 - V_3}{R_1 + 2R_2}$$

Thus, the differential gain of the first stage is given by

$$\frac{V_4 - V_3}{V_+ - V_-} = \frac{R_1 + 2R_2}{R_1}$$

To compute the common-mode gain, set $V_+ = V_- = V_c$, and we have $V_2 = V_1 = V_c$.

This means that there is no current flowing through R_1. Since the two input op amps have zero current flowing into their negative input terminals, the current through either resistor R_2 is also zero, and $V_3 = V_4 = V_c$, so that the common-mode gain is unity, and the maximum value of V_4 is given by

$$V_{4\max} = V_c + (V_+ + V_-)\left(\frac{R_1 + 2R_2}{2R_1}\right)$$

The maximum common-mode voltage can approach the maximum output voltage of the op amps minus half of whatever output is being produced by the amplification of the differential signal. Typically, when using ±12 volts, the maximum output voltage is 10 volts.

Step 3: No current enters the third op-amp inputs, so

$$\frac{V_0 - V_5}{R_4} = \frac{V_0 - V_3}{R_3 + R_4} \quad \text{and} \quad \frac{V_6}{V_4} = \frac{V_4}{R_3 + R_4}$$

Step 4: Assume that the third op amp has infinite open-loop gain, so that $V_5 = V_6$. The equations in step 3 can be combined to give

$$\frac{V_0}{R_4} - \frac{V_0}{R_3 + R_4} = \frac{V_5}{R_4} - \frac{V_3}{R_3 + R_4} = \frac{V_4 - V_3}{R_3 + R_4}$$

which can be simplified to give

$$\frac{V_0 R_3}{R_4} = V_4 - V_3$$

and the second stage gain is given by

$$\frac{V_0}{V_4 - V_3} = \frac{R_4}{R_3}$$

Step 5: Combining, we have the overall gain

$$G_{\pm} = \frac{V_0}{V_+ - V_-} = \frac{R_4}{R_3}\left(\frac{R_1 + 2R_2}{R_1}\right)$$

2.4.2 Isolation Amplifier

The **isolation amplifier** is similar to the instrumentation amplifier, having a fixed differential gain over a wide range of frequencies, high input impedance, and low output impedance, but it also has an input circuit that is isolated from the output circuit and its power supply. This isolation is designed so that relatively large dc or 60-Hz voltages applied to the output circuit do not appear on the input circuit. Of course, the output depends on the input just as it does for an instrumentation amplifier. Two commonly used methods of isolation are electromagnetic isolation and optical isolation.

Electromagnetic isolation involves modulating the amplified signal with a high-frequency carrier and coupling the signal to the output circuit using a transformer. The transformer provides efficient coupling at the carrier frequency, but is a high-impedance path at frequencies where dangerous currents might occur, such as dc and 60 Hz. A simplified schematic is shown in Figure 2.14.

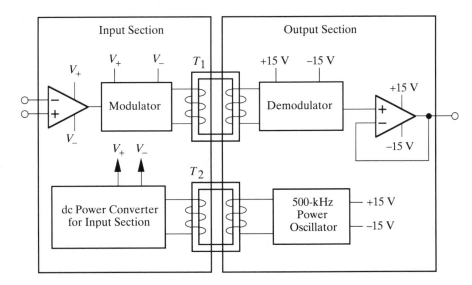

Figure 2.14 Simplified schematic of transformer-coupled isolation amplifier.

The signal is amplified differentially in the input section and then modulated. Transformer T_1 carries the modulated signal from the input amplifier to the output section, where it is demodulated and further amplified. Transformer T_2 carries high-frequency power to the input section where it is converted into direct current for the input amplifier and modulator. By using this design, isolated power is provided to the input section without using batteries.

Optical isolation involves modulating the output of a solid-state photoemitter with the amplified signal and then detecting the light with a photodetector in the output circuit. The advantage of this approach is the complete elimination of electrical paths between the input and output sections, and the disadvantage is the need for battery power for the input section.

2.5 NOISE SOURCES

Noise is any unwanted component in the signal of interest, and can be due to external interference or generated in the circuit itself. It can be repetitive or random. **White noise** has equal power in each frequency interval, and **pink noise** has equal power in each frequency decade. In the following sections, random noise is described in terms of the **rms** (the root mean square, or the square root of the average of the squares of the random fluctuations). See Chapter 5 for a discussion of random processes and the rms deviation.

2.5.1 Johnson Noise

Johnson noise is a white-noise voltage developed across a resistor due to the thermal agitation of the charge carriers (electrons) within the resistor. Although there is a vast number of electrons moving in all directions within the resistor, their motion is random and from instant to instant, there are more electrons moving in one direction than another. Since these random motions never cease, the imbalance varies endlessly and results in a fluctuating noise voltage across the resistor. The average voltage is zero, and the rms voltage is given by

$$V_{rms} = \sqrt{4kTRB}$$

where k (Boltzman's constant) $= 1.380 \times 10^{-23}$ JK $= 1.380 \times 10^{-23}$ V^2 s Ω^{-1} K^{-1}, R is the resistance in ohms; T is the temperature in degrees Kelvin; and $B = F_2 - F_1$ is the bandwidth in Hz.

At 300 K (close to room temperature), the Johnson noise in resistor R at bandwidth B can be expressed as

$$V_{rms} = D_J\sqrt{RB}, \quad \text{where} \quad D_J = 1.287 \times 10^{-10} \text{ V } \Omega^{-1/2} \text{ Hz}^{-1/2}$$

For $B = 10^6$ Hz and $R = 10^6$ Ω, $V_{rms} = 129$ μV. For $B = 10^9$ Hz and $R = 50$ Ω, $V_{rms} = 28.8$ μV.

2.5.2 Shot Noise

Shot noise arises because an electrical current is not a smooth flow of charge but the motion of a finite number of charge carriers (electrons) per unit time. These electrons are moving independently, so that the actual number passing any point per unit time varies randomly. As discussed in Chapter 5, Section 5.5 (The Chi-Squared Statistic), these statistical fluctuations result in an rms (root-mean-square) deviation from the mean that is equal to the square root of their number. For large currents (> 1 mA) the number of electrons per microsecond is very large (6.242×10^9), but in many cases, the signal consists of a much smaller current, in the nA or pA range. Amplifying such a small current also amplifies the shot noise.

For an average current I, the number of electrons passing in time T is $N = IT/q$ and the shot-noise fluctuations are described by

$$I_{rms} = \frac{q\sqrt{N}}{T} = \frac{q}{T}\sqrt{\frac{IT}{q}} = \sqrt{\frac{qI}{T}}$$

Converting to the bandwidth $B = F_2 - F_1$, we have

$$I_{rms} = \sqrt{2qIB}$$

where $q = 1.602 \times 10^{-19}$ Coul (charge of the electron). For $I = 1$ μA and $F_2 - F_1 = 10^6$ Hz, $I_{rms} = 0.56$ nA. For $I = 1$ pA, $I_{rms} = 0.56$ pA, a significant fraction of the average current.

The voltage noise V_{rms} across a resistor R due to the shot noise of a current I through it is given by

$$V_{rms} = R\sqrt{2qIB} = \sqrt{2qV}\sqrt{RB}$$

2.5.3 Amplifier Noise

Noise in an amplifier is a combination of Johnson and shot noises from the various elements of the circuit, both of which are proportional to the square root of the bandwidth. As a result, the noise specifications for the input and output sections of an amplifier are of the form $V_{rms} = D\sqrt{B}$, where D is a constant, and B is the bandwidth. Typical values are $D_1 = 5$ nV Hz$^{-1/2}$ with respect to the input and $D_0 = 50$ nV Hz$^{-1/2}$ with respect to the output (measured when the input is grounded). Since these input and output noise sources are uncorrelated, we combine them as the square root of the sum of the squares. For closed-loop gain G, the overall noise at the output is

$$V_{rms} = \sqrt{B\left[(D_1 G)^2 + (D_0)^2\right]}$$

2.5.4 Electrical Interference

In our modern world, electricity controls and powers nearly everything. As a result, there are wires in the walls of every building, carrying hundreds or thousands of amperes of 60 Hz. A 1-m long unshielded wire can pick up 100 mV of 60 Hz from these sources. Note that the actual amplitude (and phase) of the induced emf depends critically on conductor geometry. By using two wires close together, it is possible to detect very small signals using *differential amplification* because the 60 Hz induced on the two wires has very nearly the same amplitude and phase. The use of a pair of shielded cables reduces the pickup still further.

Electrical interference can also arise from high frequency communication sources (radio and television) and from high-speed switching (digital electronics, computers). This can be greatly reduced by a conductive shield placed around signal lines and circuits. Effectiveness is reduced if the conductive shield is also used to carry current back to the power supply.

2.5.5 Inadequate Grounds

The circuit ground is generally a common reference point through which currents are sent before being returned to the power supply. Digital circuits especially have large current transients that can generate brief potentials due to the resistance and inductance of the "ground" wires. For this reason, it is important to keep the analog and digital grounds separate. Remember that whereas digital circuits have some noise immunity, *analog circuits have none.*

2.6 ANALOG FILTERING

Analog filtering is used to reduce selected frequency components of the signal. It is useful whenever the signal of interest has a frequency content that is different than the frequency content of unwanted signals, electromagnetic pickup, or other noise. Frequency filtering should be used to reduce electromagnetic pickup *only after* proper shielding and differential amplification has reduced it as much as is practical. The following are common applications of filtering:

1. Reducing a fundamental noise such as Johnson or flicker ($1/f$ noise).

2. Rejecting input frequencies that are higher than half the sampling frequency of a data-acquisition system. (This point is discussed further in Chapters 3 and 5.)

3. Extracting a signal from a residual carrier wave after frequency demodulation.

4. Rejecting an unwanted waveform that is an unavoidable product of the transducer or some other component of the measuring system.

The general characteristics of analog filters are as follows:

1. The **passband**, the range of frequencies that are passed unfiltered.
2. The variations in voltage gain in the passband.
3. The **stop band**, the range of frequencies that are rejected.
4. The incomplete rejection of frequencies in the stop band.
5. The **corner frequency**, where the amplitude has dropped by 3.01 dB (a factor of $2^{-1/2} = 0.707$) from the passband.
6. The **phase shift** between the input and the output as a function of frequency.
7. The **settling time**, the time required for the output to rise to within 10% of its final value after a step input.

The **low-pass filter** is designed to pass frequencies below a specified corner frequency and attenuate higher frequencies. It is most commonly used to suppress carrier waves, frequency aliasing, and Johnson noise.

The **high-pass filter** is designed to pass high frequencies and attenuate low frequencies.

The **band-pass filter** has a passband between two stop bands. It is used whenever the signal of interest has a narrow frequency content compared with other unwanted signals. Since all filters have an upper frequency cutoff, all "high-pass" filters are actually band-pass filters.

The expressions for the frequency-dependent gain $G = V_{out}/V_{in}$ can be derived by remembering that the voltage gain of an op amp with a negative feedback network is simply the ratio of the feedback impedance to the input impedance. Note that both of these impedances may be complex numbers, that the impedance of a resistor is R, and that the impedance of a capacitor is $1/(j\omega C)$, where $j = \sqrt{-1}$.

In Laboratory Exercise 6, we explore the low-pass one-pole filter, the high-pass one-pole filter, the Butterworth low-pass two-pole filter, and the notch filter, which are described in the following sections.

2.6.1 Low-Pass, One-Pole Filter

The gain of the low-pass one-pole filter (Figure 2.15) is the ratio of the feedback impedance to the input impedance:

$$G = -\frac{Z_f}{Z_i} = -\frac{R_2 \| C}{R_1} = -\frac{1}{R_1\left(1/R_2 + j\omega C\right)}$$

$$= -\left(\frac{R_2}{R_1}\right)\left(\frac{1}{1 + j\omega R_2 C}\right) = -\frac{R_2}{R_1}\left[\frac{1 - j\omega R_2 C}{1 + \left(\omega R_2 C\right)^2}\right]$$

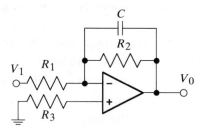

Figure 2.15   Low-pass one-pole filter.

We assume that the open-loop gain of the op amp is very large for all the frequencies in the passband.

It is also possible to analyze filters in the complex frequency plane ($s = j\omega$ plane). The function G is also the amplitude of the complex function

$$\frac{V_0}{V_1} = -\frac{R_2}{R_1}\left[\frac{1/(R_2 C)}{s+1/(R_2 C)}\right]$$

along the real axis. In this form, the circuit has a pole at $s = -1/(R_2 C)$.

The **magnitude** of G is given by

$$|G| = \sqrt{G_r^2 + G_i^2} \tag{2.2}$$

where G_i and G_r are the imaginary and real parts, respectively.

$$\left| |G| = \frac{-R_2/R_1}{\sqrt{1+(\omega R_2 C)^2}} = \frac{-R_2/R_1}{\sqrt{1+(f/f_c)^2}} \right| \tag{2.3}$$

where $f_c = (2\pi R_2 C)^{-1}$ is the corner frequency.

The phase ϕ of G is given by

$$\tan\phi = -\omega R_2 C = -f/f_c$$

For frequencies well below the corner frequency ($f \ll f_c$) the gain is independent of frequency and the phase shift is $-180°$, determined by the amplifier inversion. At the corner frequency ($f = f_c$), the gain has dropped by the square root of 2, or 3.01 dB (decibels) and the phase shift is $-45° -180° = -225°$. Somewhat above the cutoff frequency, the gain drops 6.02 dB per octave or 20 dB per decade. For large frequencies ($f \gg f_c$), the phase shift is $-90° -180° = -270°$. An octave is a factor of 2 in frequency, and a change of $20N$ dB corresponds to a factor of 10^N in voltage, or a factor of 10^{2N} in power.

2.6.2 Low-Pass Two-Pole Filter

For the low-pass two-pole filter (Figure 2.16), there are two independent corner frequencies f_{c1} and f_{c2}:

$$|G| = \frac{-R_3/(R_1 + R_2)}{\sqrt{\left[1 + (f/f_{c1})^2\right]\left[1 + (f/f_{c2})^2\right]}}$$

where $f_{c1} = (R_1 \| R_2)/(2\pi C_1)$ and $f_{c2} = (2\pi R_3 C_2)^{-1}$. At frequencies well above these, the roll-off is 12.04 dB per octave or 40 dB per decade.

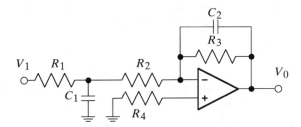

Figure 2.16   Low pass two-pole filter.

For the case of equal corner frequencies, $f = f_{c1} = f_{c2}$, the magnitude of G is:

$$|G| = \frac{-R_3/(R_1 + R_2)}{1 + (f/f_c)^2}$$

The corner frequency $f = f_c$ corresponds to an amplitude drop of a factor of 2, or 6 dB.

2.6.3 High-Pass One-Pole Filter

By placing a capacitor and resistor in series as the input impedance, we have the high-pass one-pole filter (Figure 2.17).

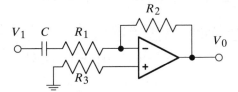

Figure 2.17   High-pass one-pole filter.

We compute the gain as the (complex) ratio of the feedback impedance to the input impedance. The magnitude of the gain is the square root of the sum of the squares of the real and imaginary parts.

$$G = \frac{-R_2}{R_1 + 1/j\omega C} = -\omega R_2 C \left[\frac{j + \omega R_1 C}{1 + (\omega R_1 C)^2} \right]$$

$$\boxed{|G| = \frac{\omega R_2 C}{\sqrt{1 + (\omega R_1 C)^2}}} \qquad (2.4)$$

At frequencies well below the corner frequency, $\omega_c = (R_1 C)^{-1}$, $|G| = \omega R_2 C$. At frequencies well above ω_c, $|G| = R_2/R_1$. However, all op amps have a limited gain-bandwidth product, which results in a decrease in gain at sufficiently high frequencies. Strictly speaking, all active high-pass filters are actually band-pass filters. See the example that follows.

EXAMPLE

Compute the gain of the high-pass, one-pole filter, taking under consideration the finite gain-bandwidth product of the op amp.

Using the open-loop gain equation, we have

$$V_0 = -A V_2$$

The voltage-divider relationship gives

$$\frac{V_0 - V_1}{1/j\omega C + R_1 + R_2} = \frac{V_0 - V_2}{R_2} = \frac{V_0 + V_0/A}{R_2}$$

Simplifying, we have

$$R_2(V_0 - V_1) = (1 + 1/A)(1/j\omega C + R_1 + R_2)$$

$$V_1 R_2 = V_0 R_2 - V_0(1 + 1/A)(1/j\omega C + R_1 + R_2)$$

Solving for the gain,

$$G = \frac{V_0}{V_1} = \frac{R_2}{R_2 - (1 + 1/A)(1/j\omega C + R_1 + R_2)}$$

$$= \frac{-R_2 \omega C \left[R_1 \omega C + (R_1 + R_2)\omega C/A + j(1 + 1/A) \right]}{\left[R_1 \omega C + (R_1 + R_2)\omega C/A \right]^2 + \left[1 + 1/A \right]^2}$$

Computing the magnitude,

$$|G| = \left| \frac{V_0}{V_1} \right| = \frac{A R_2 \omega C}{\sqrt{(\omega C)^2 (A R_1 + R_1 + R_2)^2 + (1 + A)^2}} \qquad (2.5)$$

At lower frequencies, where the open-loop gain $A \gg (R_1+R_2)/R_1$, this reduces to equation (2.4), as expected. At high frequencies, where the open-loop gain A has fallen, so that $A \ll (\omega C)(R_1 + R_2) - 1$ and $A \ll (R_1 + R_2)/R_1$, Equation (2.5) reduces to

$$|G| = \left|\frac{V_0}{V_1}\right| \approx \frac{AR_2}{R_1 + R_2} = \frac{KR_2/\omega}{R_1 + R_2}$$

where $K = A\omega$ is the gain-bandwidth product of the op amp. The op amp introduces a pole at high frequencies, so that $|G|$ decreases linearly with increasing frequency.

2.6.4 Notch Filter

The **notch filter** rejects a narrow band of frequencies and passes all others. It is particular useful in eliminating a specific frequency (such as 60 Hz) while retaining higher and lower frequencies.

The circuit consists of two parallel T filters (Figure 2.18). The R–2C–R section is a low pass filter with corner frequency $f_c = (4\pi RC)^{-1}$. The C–R/2–C section is a high-pass filter with $f_c = (\pi RC)^{-1}$. For ideal components, the phases of these two filters cancel perfectly at the notch frequency, $f_n = (2\pi RC)^{-1}$. In a practical circuit, it is possible to achieve notch depths of 30 dB, using 5% components, and 60 dB, using 1% components. At frequencies above 1 kHz, the capacitors become small, and stray capacitances degrade circuit performance.

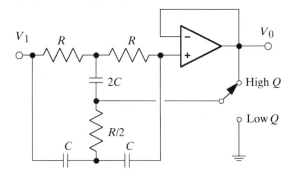

Figure 2.18   Notch filter. Notch frequency $f_n = (2\pi RC)^{-1}$.

In Laboratory Exercise 6, we explore the properties of a notch filter designed to reject 60 Hz.

2.6.5 High-Order Low-Pass Filters

The basic RC filters discussed in Sections 2.6.1 to 2.6.3 are used primarily for noncritical applications where sharp frequency selection is not needed. The Butterworth, Bessel, transitional, and Chebyshev filters described in this section are designed for more critical requirements, such as a constant gain for all frequencies in the passband, a rapid falloff from the passband to the stop band, a low gain for frequencies in the stop band, and the ability to transmit a pulse with little change in shape.

The **Butterworth** filter has a flat frequency response below the characteristic frequency f_0, but responds poorly to transients because the phase–frequency relationship is nonlinear. It is commonly used for antialiasing in circuits that sample analog waveforms (described in Chapters 3 and 5) because it transmits signal amplitudes faithfully. The **Bessel** filter has a linear phase variation for frequencies below f_0, and, hence, has a constant delay in this range. Since each Fourier component is shifted by the same time, the signal is transmitted without a change in shape but a constant delay is introduced. The **transitional**, or **Paynter** filter (also called the "Besselworth") has properties intermediate between those of either the Butterworth or Bessel filter. The **Chebyshev** filter maximizes the sharpness of the frequency roll-off, but introduces ripples in the passband. This filter is actually a family of filters classified by the amplitude of the ripples (in dB). Achieving the intended response requires accurate component values (typically 1 to 5%) and low-leakage capacitors. Inductors are rarely used as they are bulky and not very ideal.

The basic circuit realizations are the unity-gain Sallen–Key filter (Figures 2.19 and 2.20, Table 2.3) and the equal-component-value (or VCVS, voltage-controlled voltage source) Sallen–Key filter (Figures 2.21 and 2.22, Table 2.4). Each of these circuits provides two poles of low-pass or two poles of high-pass filtering. Higher-order filters use cascaded stages. The equal-component design has the advantage of providing gain as the bandwidth is reduced, which reduces the effect of amplifier noise.

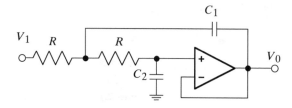

Figure 2.19   Unity-gain Sallen–Key low-pass two-pole filter. $RC_1\omega_0 = k_1$ and $RC_2\omega_0 = k_2$. Higher-order filters use cascaded stages. See Table 2.3 for values of k_1 and k_2.

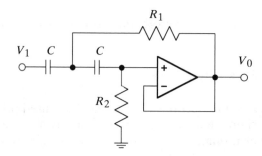

Figure 2.20   Unity-gain Sallen–Key high-pass two-pole filter. $R_1C\omega_0 = 1/k_1$ and $R_2C\omega_0 = 1/k_2$. Higher-order filters use cascaded stages. See Table 2.3 for values of k_1 and k_2.

TABLE 2.3 UNITY-GAIN SALLEN–KEY LOW-PASS AND HIGH-PASS FILTERS. REFER TO FIGURES 2.19 AND 2.20 FOR CIRCUIT DIAGRAMS.

Poles	Butterworth		Transitional		Bessel		Chebyshev (0.5 dB)	
	k_1	k_2	k_1	k_2	k_1	k_2	k_1	k_2
2	1.414	0.707	1.287	0.777	0.907	0.680	1.949	0.653
4	1.082	0.924	1.090	0.960	0.735	0.675	2.582	1.298
	2.613	0.383	2.206	0.472	1.012	0.390	6.233	0.180
6	1.035	0.966	1.060	1.001	0.635	0.610	3.592	1.921
	1.414	0.707	1.338	0.761	0.723	0.484	4.907	0.374
	3.863	0.259	2.721	0.340	1.073	0.256	13.40	0.079
8	1.019	0.981	1.051	1.017	0.567	0.554	4.665	2.547
	1.202	0.832	1.191	0.876	0.609	0.486	5.502	0.530
	1.800	0.556	1.613	0.615	0.726	0.359	8.237	0.171
	5.125	0.195	3.373	0.268	1.116	0.186	23.45	0.044

Source: Brian K. Jones, *Electronics for Experimentation and Research.* By permission of Prentice-Hall International (UK), Ltd., London.

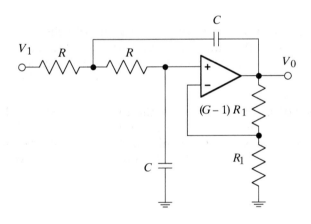

Figure 2.21 Equal-component-value Sallen–Key low-pass two-pole filter. $RC\omega_0 = k_3$ and R_1 is chosen for convenience. See Table 2.4 for values of gain G and k_3.

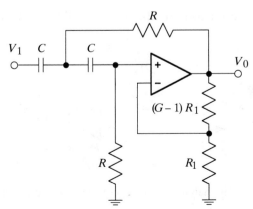

Figure 2.22 Equal-component-value Sallen–Key high-pass two-pole filter. $RC\omega_0 = 1/k_3$ and R_1 is chosen for convenience. See Table 2.4 for values of gain G and k_3.

TABLE 2.4   EQUAL-COMPONENT-VALUE SALLEN–KEY LOW-PASS AND HIGH-PASS FILTERS. REFER TO FIGURES 2.21 AND 2.22 FOR CIRCUIT DIAGRAMS.

Poles	Butterworth		Transitional		Bessel		Chebyshev (0.5 dB)	
	k_3	G	k_3	G	k_3	G	k_3	G
2	1.000	1.586	1.000	1.446	0.785	1.268	1.129	1.842
4	1.000	1.152	1.023	1.123	0.704	1.084	1.831	1.582
	1.000	2.235	0.977	2.035	0.628	1.759	1.060	2.660
6	1.000	1.068	1.030	1.056	0.622	1.040	1.332	2.627
	1.000	1.586	1.009	1.492	0.591	1.364	1.355	2.448
	1.000	2.483	0.962	2.293	0.524	2.023	1.029	2.846
8	1.000	1.038	1.034	1.032	0.561	1.024	3.447	1.522
	1.000	1.337	1.021	1.284	0.544	1.213	1.708	2.379
	1.000	1.889	0.996	1.765	0.510	1.593	1.188	2.711
	1.000	2.610	0.951	2.436	0.455	2.184	1.017	2.913

Source: Brian K. Jones, *Electronics for Experimentation and Research.* By permission of Prentice-Hall International (UK), Ltd., London.

For a given order, the various filters differ in the rate of rolloff near the corner frequency ω_0, but in the stop band far from ω_0, the amplitude response for all filters drops $6N$ dB per octave, or $20N$ dB per decade, where N is the order of the filter.

As an example, consider a Butterworth low-pass four-pole filter with f_0 = 10 kHz (ω_0 = 62.83 krad/s). From Table 2.3, the first stage has k_1 = 1.082 and k_2 = 0.924. Thus, $RC_1 = k_1/\omega_0 = 1.722 \times 10^{-5}$ and $RC_2 = k_2/\omega_0 = 1.471 \times 10^{-5}$. Choosing R = 10 kΩ, we have C_1 = 1722 pF and C_2 = 1471 pF. Similarly, the second stage has k_1 = 2.613 and k_2 = 0.383. Choosing R = 10 kΩ, we have C_1 = 4159 pF and C_2 = 610 pF.

EXAMPLE

Derive the voltage-response function for the low-pass filter in Figure 2.23.

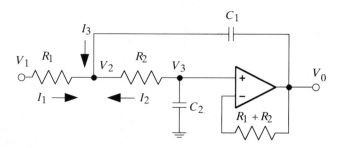

Figure 2.23   Diagram for analysis of unity-gain Sallen-Key, two-pole low-pass Filter.

The op-amp feedback establishes $V_3 = V_0$.

$$I_1 = \frac{V_1 - V_2}{R_1} \qquad I_2 = \frac{V_0 - V_2}{R_2} = -V_0 j\omega C_2 \qquad I_3 = (V_0 - V_2) j\omega C_1$$

Since no current flows into the op amp inputs, we have $I_1 + I_2 + I_3 = 0$.

$$I_1 + I_2 + I_3 = (V_1 - V_2) / R_1 - V_0 j\omega C_2 + (V_0 - V_2) j\omega C_1 = 0$$

Solving for V_1,

$$V_1 / R_1 = V_2 / R_1 + j\omega V_0 C_2 + j\omega V_2 C_1 - j\omega V_0 C_1$$

Using the previous equation involving I_2,

$$V_2 = V_0(1 + j\omega R_2 C_2)$$

$$\frac{V_1}{R_1} = \left(\frac{V_0}{R_1}\right)(1 + j\omega R_2 C_2) + j\omega V_0 C_2 - V_0 j\omega C_1(1 + j\omega R_2 C_2) - j\omega V_0 C_1$$

$$V_1 = V_0 \left[1 - \omega^2 R_1 R_2 C_1 C_2 + j\omega C_2 (R_1 + R_2) \right]$$

Substituting $s = j\omega$, we then have the s-space amplitude:

$$\frac{V_0}{V_1} = \frac{1}{s^2 R_1 R_2 C_1 C_2 + s(R_1 + R_2)C_2 + 1}$$

which has poles defined by the characteristic equation

$$s^2 - 2s\omega_0 \cos\theta + \omega_0^2 = s^2 + \omega_0 s / Q + \omega_0^2 = 0$$

where ω_0 is the corner frequency, θ is the polar angle of the pole on the s plane, and Q is the fractional energy loss per cycle. The overall gain of a series of low-pass filters is the product of the V_0/V_1 terms.

2.6.6 High-Order High-Pass Filters

The Butterworth, Bessel, transitional, and Chebyshev high-pass filters are analogous to the low-pass filters of the previous section. The unity-gain Sallen–Key high-pass filter is shown in Figure 2.22 and the equal-component-value Sallen–Key high-pass filter is shown in Figure 2.23.

As an example, consider a unity-gain Sallen-Key, Butterworth high-pass four-pole filter with $f_0 = 10$ kHz ($\omega_0 = 62.83$ krad/s). From Table 2.3, the first stage has $k_1 = 1.082$ and $k_2 = 0.924$. Thus, $R_1 C = 1/(k_1\omega_0) = 1.471 \times 10^{-5}$ and $R_2 C = 1/(k_2\omega_0) = 1.722 \times 10^{-5}$. Choosing $C = 1000$ pF, we have $R_1 = 14.71$ kΩ and $R_2 = 17.22$ kΩ. Similarly, the second stage has $k_1 = 2.613$ and $k_2 = 0.383$. Choosing $R = 1000$ pF, we have $R_1 = 6.10$ kΩ and $R_2 = 41.55$ kΩ.

2.7 THE SAMPLE-AND-HOLD AMPLIFIER

The **sample-and-hold amplifier** operates as a typical op amp in the sample mode, but in the hold mode, the output is ideally constant, independent of the input (Figure 2.24). This constant value is the output value present when the mode was last switched from sample to hold. The mode is controlled by a digital (logic-level) input. The operation is shown in Figure 2.25. The sample-and-hold amplifier is used to provide a steady input during analog-to-digital conversion (described in Chapter 3).

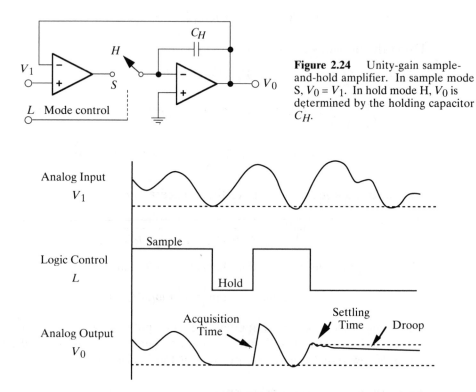

Figure 2.24   Unity-gain sample-and-hold amplifier. In sample mode S, $V_0 = V_1$. In hold mode H, V_0 is determined by the holding capacitor C_H.

Figure 2.25   Output response of the sample-and-hold amplifier to an arbitrary waveform when the logic control is exercised.

The primary characteristics of the sample-and-hold amplifier are as follows:

1. The **acquisition time** is the time required for the output of the sample-and-hold amplifier to reach its final value (within a specified error band) after it has been switched from the hold mode to the sample mode. This includes the switch delay time, the slewing interval, and the amplifier settling time. The acquisition time is reduced by reducing the value of the holding capacitor C_H.

2. The **aperture delay** is the time required for the switch to open fully after the sample-and-hold amplifier has been switched from the sample mode to the hold mode.

3. The **aperture jitter** is the range in random variation in aperture delay. If the aperture delay is compensated, then the aperture jitter establishes the ultimate timing error.

4. The **charge transfer** is the effect of the charge transferred to the holding capacitor C_H via stray capacitance when switching from the sample mode to the hold mode. The associated voltage error can be reduced by using a larger storage capacitor, but this increases the acquisition time.

5. The **settling time** is the time required for the output of the sample-and-hold to reach its final value (within a specified error band) after it has been switched from the sample mode to the hold mode. Ideally, the settling time is zero because the output does not need to change, but in practice, there is a small amount of ringing due to charge transfer.

6. The **droop** is the rate of change in output voltage while in the hold mode due to leakage bias currents discharging the storage capacitor. The associated voltage error can be reduced by using a larger storage capacitor, but this increases the acquisition time.

7. **Feedthrough** is the fraction of the input waveform that appears on the output in the hold mode. It is caused by stray capacitance coupling the input across the open switch to the storage capacitor.

8. The **sample-to-hold offset** is the shift in output level during the transition from the sample mode to the hold mode after the charge transfer has been accounted for. It may depend on the characteristics of the input signal and is also called the offset nonlinearity.

Table 2.5 lists some representative monolithic (single integrated-circuit) sample-and-hold amplifiers.

TABLE 2.5   SOME AVAILABLE MONOLITHIC SAMPLE-AND-HOLD AMPLIFIERS

Model	AD582	AD389	AD683	CXA1008P
Manufacturer	Analog Dev.	Analog Dev.	Analog Dev.	Sony
Linearity	0.01%	0.001%	*	0.1%
Unity gain bandwidth	1.5 MHz	1.5 MHz	10 MHz	N/A
Acquisition time	6 μs (0.1%)	2.5 μs (0.003%)	500 ns (0.01%)	20 ns
Max slew rate	3 V/μs	30 V/μs	130 V/μs	100 V/μs
Settling time	0.5 μs	1 μs	*	*
Aperture delay	200 ns	30 ns	2.5 ns	6 ns
Aperture jitter	15 ns	0.4 ns	20 ps	*
Droop current or rate	< 0.1 nA	< 1 μV/μs	0.01 μV/μs	< 20 mV/μs

* Not provided in data sheets.

Note 1: Usually the combination of aperture delay and settling time is much shorter than the acquisition time, so in analog-to-digital conversion applications, the device is normally kept in the sample mode and only switched to the hold mode during conversion.

Note 2: A small value of C_H reduces the acquisition time, while a large value of C_H reduces charge-transfer error and droop. Fortunately, for most applications and sample-and-hold amplifiers, there is a range of good choices.

2.8 THE COMPARATOR

The **comparator** is a high-gain differential amplifier whose output is limited between two logic levels (Figure 2.26). It is similar to the op amp without negative feedback, but it is not frequency compensated and has a much higher slewing rate. For inputs V_+ and V_-, the logic output L is high whenever $V_+ > V_-$ and L is low whenever $V_+ < V_-$. The output is clamped at logic voltages V_{low} and V_{high} by the diodes, and R_3 is a current-limiting resistor.

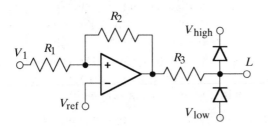

Figure 2.26 Voltage comparator with hysteresis, whose output is a logic V_{high} when $V_1 > V_{ref}$ and V_{low} when $V_1 < V_{ref}$.

The output is poorly defined when V_+ and V_- are nearly equal, and the output may "chatter" between high and low states at the crossing point. A small amount of **positive feedback**, or **hysteresis**, is used to stabilize the comparator. The first output transition feeds back to reinforce the same logic state and can overcome moderate amounts of input noise that would otherwise reverse the state. The amount of this hysteresis applied to the input is $V_f = V_0 R_1/(R_1 + R_2)$, where V_0 is the op amp output (V_{low} or V_{high}). When V_0 is high, an input voltage $V_1 < V_{ref} - V_f$ is required to change the state of V_0 to V_{low}. When V_0 is low, an input voltage $V_1 > V_{ref} + V_f$ is required to change the state of V_0 to V_{high}. For the normal comparator, R_2 is much larger than R_1 and the hysteresis is small. The Schmitt trigger has a large amount of hysteresis, which is accomplished by making R_1 and R_2 approximately equal.

2.9 THE POWER AMPLIFIER

As we shall see in Chapter 3, the microcomputer can generate analog voltages by using a digital-to-analog converter, but the currents available are too small to operate most actuators. The digital-to-analog converter, the op amp, and the instrumentation amplifier can only provide a few tens of mA at most, while many actuators, such as motors and heating elements require many amperes. Basically, what is required is current amplification, using discrete power transistors.

Figure 2.27 shows a dc current amplifier using two NPN power transistors in a cascaded emitter follower (Darlington) configuration. The output voltage V_0 is two diode drops (approximately 1.2 V) lower than the input voltage V_1.

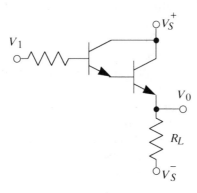

Figure 2.27   Cascaded-emitter follower used for current amplification. $V_0 \approx V_1 - 1.2$ volts.

2.10 PROBLEMS

2.1 For the differential amplifier circuit shown in Figure 2.4, and assuming that the open loop gain A is infinite, do the following:

a. Compute the output V_0 as a function of the four variables R_1, R_2, R_3, and R_4. Your result should be of the form $V_0 = aV_2 - bV_1$.

b. Compute the differential gain $G_\pm$ and the common mode gain G_c using the following:

$$V_0 = aV_2 - bV_1 = (a + b)(V_2 - V_1)/2 + (a - b)(V_2 + V_1)/2$$
$$= G_\pm (V_2 - V_1) + G_c V_c, \text{ where } V_c = (V_1 + V_2)/2$$

c. Compute the CMRR. Comment on the resistor accuracy needed for CMRR > 120 dB.

d. Under what conditions does $G_c = 0$

e. When $G_c = 0$ is satisfied, what does your expression for $G_\pm$ reduce to?

2.2 For the differential amplifier circuit shown in Figure 2.4, and finite open-loop gain A, do the following:

a. Derive the differential gain $G_\pm$ and common-mode gain G_c as a function of R_1, R_2, R_3, R_4, and open-loop gain A (see problem 2.1b).

b. For $R_1 = R_3 = 1$ kΩ, $R_2 = R_4 = 9$ kΩ, and open-loop gain-bandwidth product AB = 10^7 Hz, sketch the Bode amplitude plot (dB gain vs. log frequency).

2.3 You want to evaluate the LM363A instrumentation amplifier for an audio biofeedback project.

   a. For the 16-pin package, show external connections and components for gains of 100 and 250. *Note:* Finding data sheets for this integrated circuit is part of the exercise.

   b. What would you have to add to be able to adjust (i) the input bias current, (ii) the input offset voltage, and (iii) the output offset voltage? (Look at the data sheets and prepare a parts list.)

   c. Devise a set of procedures for adjusting the input and output offset voltages so that when the inputs are connected to ground through equal 1-kΩ resistors, the output voltage is nearly zero, both at a gain of 1 and at a gain of 1000. (Do not worry about adjusting input bias current.)

   d. After performing the procedures in part **c**, at a gain of 1000, how large could the output voltage be if one of the 1-kΩ resistors were replaced with a 10-kΩ resistor? (*Hint:* Look at the data sheets for the maximum input bias current over the full temperature range.)

   e. How would you measure the small signal gain for frequencies from dc to 1 MHz? Prepare a diagram and a list of procedures.

   f. How would you measure the common-mode rejection for the same frequencies? Prepare a diagram and a list of procedures.

   g. Analyze the following data, assuming zero output when both inputs are connected to ground through equal-value resistors. Compute the differential gain, the common-mode gain, and the common-mode rejection ratio at 10 kHz.
   Case I: The differential input is a 10-kHz, 1-mV p-p sine wave. The output is a 10-kHz, 100 mV sine wave.
   Case II: The common-mode input is a 10-kHz, 5 V p-p sine wave connected to both inputs through equal resistors. The output is a 10-kHz, 2.5 mV p-p sine wave.

   h. In the frequency range from 10 Hz to 10 kHz and with a gain of 100, what is the input noise in nV Hz$^{-1/2}$? (*Hint:* Look at the data sheets.) What value resistor has the same Johnson noise in nV Hz$^{-1/2}$?

   i. For a gain of 100 and both inputs connected to ground, estimate the output noise (in μV) in the full bandwidth of the amplifier. What value input resistor would produce an equivalent amount of output noise?

   j. Look at the data sheets for the AD625A and the LM363A and prepare a table that compares the following quantities:
   – Input offset voltage and its temperature dependence
   – Input bias current and its temperature dependence
   – Bandwidth for gains of 10, 100, and 1000
   – Common-mode rejection for gains of 10, 100, and 1000

– Settling time

– Maximum slew rate

2.4 You are given an instrumentation amplifier set for a gain of 100. Both input terminals are connected to ground with 5-MΩ resistors. At a gain of 100, the bandwidth is 10^5 Hz.

    a. If the input leakage currents on the two inputs are 0.5 nA and 1.5 nA, what is resulting offset at output?

    b. What is the output noise in the 10^5-Hz bandwidth due only to the Johnson noise in the 5-MΩ resistors? (*Hint:* If two equal uncorrelated noise sources are added, the resulting noise amplitude is $\sqrt{2}$ larger than the individual noise sources.)

    c. The inputs are grounded, and the output is connected to an rms voltmeter with a dc- to 10^5-Hz bandwidth. At a gain of 100 the output-voltage noise is 1.0 mV rms. At a gain of 1 the output-voltage noise is 0.5 mV rms. What is the amplifier noise due to the input (D_1) and the output (D_0)? (Express the noise in units of nV Hz$^{-1/2}$.)

2.5 Design a system for the filtering of EEG (brain-wave) data, given that

    • the EEG signal amplitude is 50 μV in the 0.5- to 30-Hz frequency band

    • the EMG background amplitude from the head muscles is 100 μV in the 100-Hz to 3-kHz band

    • the EM interference is 10 mV at 60 Hz

    a. What type of filtering would you use to see the EEG signal undistorted while reducing all other backgrounds to 1 μV? (Do not work it out in detail, just give the number of poles, corner frequency, etc.)

    b. Sketch the response of the filter circuit, showing $|V_{out}/V_{in}|$ from 0.1 Hz to 10 kHz, marking the values at 0.5, 30, 60, 100, and 3000 Hz.

2.6 Design an inverting high-pass single-pole filter using the op-amp circuit shown in Figure 2.17. The op amp specifications are

    • infinite input impedance, no input leakage currents

    • above 10 Hz, the open-loop gain varies as 1/frequency and reaches unity gain at 10^7 Hz

The high-pass filter circuit specifications are:

    • low-frequency 3 dB point at 100 Hz

    • gain = 10 in the passband

    a. Sketch the circuit, using C = 1.59 μF, and show values for all resistors.

b. What is the 3-dB high-frequency cutoff? (*Hint:* Don't forget the limited gain-bandwidth product of the op amp.)

c. Give typical values for the input and output impedances of the filter circuit at 10 kHz.

d. Sketch the Bode plot on semilog paper (dB gain vs. log frequency).

2.7 Design a Butterworth high-pass four-pole filter using the circuit shown in Figure 2.22 and the filter parameters in Table 2.4.

a. For a 3-dB corner frequency of 1 kHz and $C = 0.1$ µF, determine the R_1 and R_2 values for each of the two op-amp stages of the filter.

b. Sketch the Bode plot assuming that the op amp has an infinite open-loop gain at all frequencies.

c. What happens when you apply a 100-Hz square wave? Sketch the approximate resulting waveform (amplitude vs. time) and explain. (*Hint:* Think in terms of the time domain, rather than the frequency domain.)

2.8 Design a Butterworth filter that passes frequencies from 0 Hz to 1 kHz with an accuracy of 0.1 dB and rejects frequencies above 10 kHz by a factor of 100 dB.

The nth order Butterworth filter has a gain magnitude $|G|$ and phase shift ϕ given by:

$$|G| = \frac{1}{\sqrt{1 + (f/f_c)^{2n}}} \qquad \tan\left(\frac{\phi}{n}\right) = \frac{f}{f_c}$$

a. What is the minimum order n and the corresponding corner frequency f_c that will satisfy the requirements?

b. What are the phase shifts at 100 Hz and 1 kHz?

c. What are the time delays at 100 Hz and 1 kHz associated with those phase shifts?

d. What can you say about the ability to preserve the shape of a 100 Hz square wave? Consider both the effects of the filter on amplitude and phase. The 100 Hz square wave may be represented by the Fourier series

$$V(t) = \sum_{n=1}^{\infty} \frac{(-1)^{n+1}}{n} \cos(2\pi n f_0 t)$$

e. The Bessel filter has a phase shift that is proportional to frequency. How would this filter preserve the shape of the 100 Hz square wave?

2.9   A power amplifier with a gain $V_0 = G V_1$ can be described by the equivalent circuit shown in Figure 2.28.

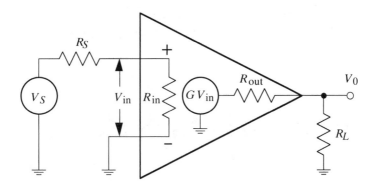

Figure 2.28   Power amplifier equivalent circuit.

a. What is V_0 in terms of V_{in}?
b. What is V_{in} in terms of V_s?
c. What is V_0 in terms of V_s?
d. You want to use this circuit to amplify 1-mV signals from a magnetic tape head (output impedance 1 MΩ) and drive a speaker (input impedance 8 Ω) at 10 volt amplitude. What are the requirements on R_{in} and R_{out} so that V_{in} is within 1% of V_s and V_0 is within 1% of GV_{in}?
e. Comment on the design requirements for R_{in} and R_{out} necessary for specific applications.

2.11   ADDITIONAL READING

2.1   Glenn M. Glasford, *Analog Electronic Circuits,* Prentice Hall, Englewood Cliffs, NJ, 1986.

2.2   John L. Hilburn, *Manual of Active Filter Design,* McGraw-Hill, New York, 1983.

2.3   Paul Horowitz and Winfield Hill, *The Art of Electronics,* Cambridge University Press, New York, 1980.

2.4   Robert G. Irvine, *Operational Amplifier Characteristics and Applications,* Prentice Hall, Englewood Cliffs, NJ, 1987.

2.5   Brian K. Jones, *Electronics for Experimentation and Research,* Prentice Hall, Englewood Cliffs, NJ, 1986.

2.6   Daniel H. Sheingold, *Transducer Interfacing Handbook,* Analog Devices, Norwood, MA, 1981.

2.7   Soclof, *Application of Analog Integrated Circuits,* Prentice Hall, Englewood Cliffs, NJ, 1985.

Laboratory Exercise 4

Operational-Amplifier Circuits

PURPOSE

To gain familiarity with the properties and limitations of the operational amplifier (op amp) such as open-loop gain, offset voltage, noise, and bandwidth. To construct several op-amp circuits used for voltage and current amplification and to measure their Bode plot of gain vs. frequency.

EQUIPMENT

- superstrip circuit board with ground plane and connections for ground, +5 V, ±12 V
- three 10-μF electrolytic capacitors (put between power and ground at circuit board)
- two 0.1-μF CK05 bypass capacitors (put between power and ground on all chips)
- three LF356 op amps
- oscilloscope
- three 25-kΩ trimpots
- seven 1-kΩ resistors
- one 9-kΩ resistor
- four 100-kΩ resistors

- one 10-MΩ resistor
- +5-V, ±12-V power supplies
- wave generator
- heat gun (shared with other lab groups)
- dial thermometer

BACKGROUND

The operational amplifier is one of the most important building blocks in analog-circuit design and is used both for amplification and filtering. Chapter 2 describes the fundamental properties of the op amp and the effect of negative feedback on gain, bandwidth, and input impedance.

The pin assignments for the LF356 op-amp that you will be using is shown in Laboratory Figure 4.1. Pins 1, 4, 5, and 7 are to be connected as shown in Laboratory Figure 4.2.

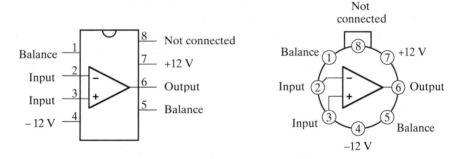

Laboratory Figure 4.1   LF356 pinout for dual inline package (DIP) and T0-5 metal can (top views).

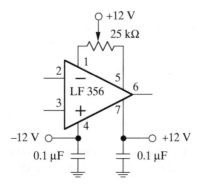

Laboratory Figure 4.2   LF356 external connections. The bypass capacitors at pins 4 and 7 are required for circuit stability and noise reduction. The trimpot between pins 1 and 5 is used to adjust output offset.

Note: For all laboratory exercises, be sure to connect 15-μF electrolytic capacitors between each power supply voltage (+ 5 V, +12 V, –12 V) and ground at the binding posts of your circuit boards. Observe capacitor polarity! Electrolytics can explode when connected backwards! These capacitors help stabilize the supply voltage levels at low frequencies (such as 60 Hz), but are not effective in reducing spikes caused by fast (< 1 μs) circuit-switching transients. To reduce the fast spikes, connect 0.1-μF capacitors between power and ground at all integrated circuits.

ADDITIONAL READING

Chapter 2, Section 2.2: Operational Amplifier Circuits, and Section 2.3: Op-Amp Characteristics.

PROCEDURE

1 Inverting Amplifier with Gain = –100

Construct the amplifier circuit shown in Laboratory Figures 4.1, 4.2, and 4.3 on your superstrip breadboard, but do not connect the 25-kΩ trimpot yet. Laboratory Figure 4.1 shows the pinout diagram of the LF356 op amp, Laboratory Figure 4.2 shows the connection for pins 1, 4, 5, and 7, and Laboratory Figure 4.3 shows the signal connections and op-amp feedback components.

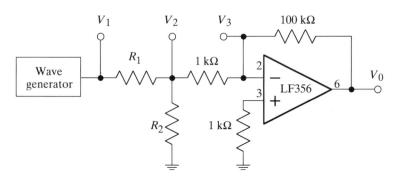

Laboratory Figure 4.3   Inverting amplifier with gain $G = V_0/V_2 = -100$. See Laboratory Figure 4.1 for pinout. Connect pins 1, 4, 5, and 7 as shown in Laboratory Figure 4.2.

1.1 dc offset.   With R_1 open and $R_2 = 0$ Ω, do the following:

1. Unadjusted offset: record the output offset voltage V_0 (25-kΩ offset adjust trimpot not connected).
2. Offset range: connect the 25-kΩ trimpot as shown in Laboratory Figure 4.2 and record V_0 for the two extreme values of the trimpot (full clock-

wise and full counterclockwise). *Note:* 20 turns of the adjusting screw will be required.

3. Temperature effect: adjust the trimpot for $V_0 = 0$. Heat the op amp about 10°C (check with dial thermometer), and record V_0.

4. Reproducibility: wait about 5 min, for the op amp to return to room temperature, and again record V_0.

5. Leakage currents: adjust the trimpot for $V_0 = 0$. Then change R_2 to 10 MΩ and record V_0.

1.2 Noise.   With R_1 open and $R_2 = 0$ Ω, adjust the trimpot for $V_0 = 0$ V.   Record the amplitude of the output noise (extreme oscilloscope gain required).   Distinguish between random "fuzz" and repeating waveforms such as 60-Hz interference.

1.3 Small-signal gain.   Change R_1 to 100 kΩ, change R_2 to 1 kΩ, and adjust the generator output for a 1-kHz sine wave with $V_1 = 1$ volt peak-to-peak (p-p) as seen on your oscilloscope.   Measure the p-p sine-wave amplitudes of V_1, V_2, and V_0 at 1 Hz, 10 Hz, 100 Hz, 1 kHz, 10 kHz, 100 kHz, and 1 MHz. Note that the wave generator amplitude V_1 will vary somewhat as the frequency is changed.

1.4 Open-loop gain.   Increase the generator output V_1 to 10 volts p-p and measure V_0 and V_3 at the same frequencies (extreme oscilloscope gain required for V_3). In the analysis section you will compute the open loop gain A as V_0/V_3.

2 Noninverting Amplifier with Gain = 101

Construct the circuit shown in Laboratory Figures 4.1, 4.2 and 4.4, but do not connect the 25-kΩ trimpot yet.

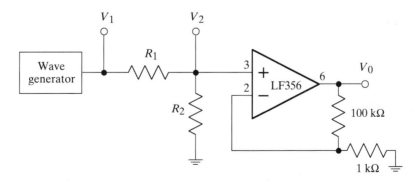

Laboratory Figure 4.4   Noninverting amplifier with gain $G = V_0/V_2 = +101$.

2.1 dc offset.   With R_1 open and $R_2 = 1$ kΩ, do the following:

1. Unadjusted offset: record the output offset voltage V_0 (25-kΩ offset-adjust trimpot not connected).
2. Offset range: connect the 25-kΩ trimpot, as shown in Laboratory Figure 4.2 and record V_0 for the two extreme values of the trimpot (full clockwise and full counterclockwise). *Note:* 20 turns of the adjusting screw will be required.
3. Temperature effect: adjust the trimpot for $V_0 = 0$. Heat the op amp about 10°C (check with dial thermometer), and record V_0.
4. Reproducibility: wait about 5 min for the op amp to return to room temperature, and again record V_0.
5. Leakage currents: adjust the trimpot for $V_0 = 0$. Then change R_2 to 10 MΩ and record V_0.

2.2 Noise.   Record the output noise as you did in procedure section 1.2.

2.3 Small-signal gain.   Change R_1 to 100 kΩ, change R_2 to 1 kΩ, and adjust the generator output for a 1-kHz sine wave with $V_1 = 1$ volt peak-to-peak (p-p) as seen on your oscilloscope.   Measure the p-p sine-wave amplitudes of V_1, V_2, and V_0 at 1 Hz, 10 Hz, 100 Hz, 1 kHz, 10 kHz, 100 kHz, and 1 MHz.

3 Buffer Amplifier

Set up the circuit shown in Laboratory Figures 4.1, 4.2 and 4.5, but do not connect the 25-kΩ trimpot yet.

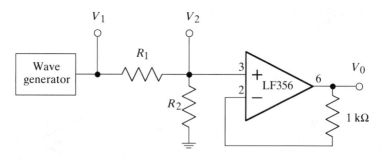

Laboratory Figure 4.5   Buffer amplifier with gain $G = V_0/V_2 = 1$.

3.1 dc offset.   With R_1 open and $R_2 = 1$ kΩ, do the following:

1. Unadjusted offset- record the output offset voltage V_0 (25-kΩ offset-adjust trimpot not connected).

2. Offset range: connect the 25-kΩ trimpot as shown in Laboratory Figure 4.2 and record V_0 for the two extreme values of the trimpot (full clockwise and full counterclockwise). *Note:* 20 turns of the adjusting screw will be required.

3. Temperature effect: adjust the trimpot for $V_0 = 0$. Heat the op amp about 10°C (check with dial thermometer), and record V_0.

4. Reproducibility: wait about 5 min for the op amp to return to room temperature, and again record V_0.

5. Leakage currents: adjust the trimpot for $V_0 = 0$. Then change R_2 to 10 MΩ and record V_0.

3.2 Noise. Record the output noise as you did in procedure section 1.2.

3.3 Small-signal gain. Change R_1 to 9 kΩ, change R_2 to 1 kΩ, and adjust the generator output for a 1-kHz sine wave with $V_1 = 1$ volt peak-to-peak (p-p) as seen on your oscilloscope. Measure the p-p sine-wave amplitudes of V_1, V_2, and V_0 at 1 Hz, 10 Hz, 100 Hz, 1 kHz, 10 kHz, 100 kHz, and 1 MHz.

LABORATORY REPORT

1 Setup

Sketch a simple block diagram of the major components you used and their interconnections.

2 Data Summary

Summarize your observations from procedure sections 1, 2, and 3.

3 Analysis

3.1 Offset voltage. For each of the three amplifier circuits, tabulate the five measured offset output voltages and compute the corresponding input offset voltages as output divided by the closed-loop gain G. (*Note:* Since the actual input voltage V_1 was zero, the input offset voltages you compute are fictitious.) Compute the change of input and output offset voltages with temperature (μV/°C). Compute the leakage current using the change in input offset voltage that occurred when the 10-MΩ was used.

3.2 Noise. From your measurements of closed-loop gain G, rms output noise V_{rms}, and bandwidth B (3-dB frequency) for each of the three circuits, compute the input noise figure

$$D = \frac{V_{rms}}{G\sqrt{B}}$$

which is usually expressed in the units nV $Hz^{-1/2}$.

3.3 Bode amplitude plot. From the small-signal gain data you took for the three op-amp circuits (procedure sections 1.3, 2.3, and 3.3), tabulate gain $G = V_0/V_2$ vs. frequency. Either plot G vs. frequency on semilog paper or plot decibels (dB) = $20\log_{10}(|G|)$ vs. frequency on linear graph paper.

3.4 Open-loop gain. From your measurements of V_0 and V_3 in procedure section 1.4, tabulate and plot the open-loop gain of the LF356 as a function of frequency. For comparison, include open loop-gain data from the LF356 data sheet.

3.5 Summary table. Compare your measurements with the claims in the data sheets: input and output voltage offset, adjustment range, temperature dependence, and input noise (nV $Hz^{-1/2}$). Add entries for data-sheet values of input impedance and slew rate (V/μs). For definitions of these and other parameters, see Chapter 4 of the Course Reader.

4 Discussion and Conclusions

Briefly discuss the principles covered in each of procedure sections 1, 2, and 3.

5 Questions

5.1 Why were V_2 and V_0 less for the inverting amplifier than for the noninverting amplifier?

5.2 How well does your measured open-loop unity gain frequency agree with the data sheet?

5.3 How accurately do you think you were able to measure the open-loop gain at 1 Hz? Are your data consistent with the data sheet?

5.4 Which depends most on the op amp and least on external components- the input or the output offset voltage?

6 Laboratory Data Sheets

Include your handwritten data sheets (or a copy), which should consist of a log of the procedures that you used, any special circumstances, and the measurements you recorded manually.

Laboratory Exercise 5

Instrumentation Amplifiers

PURPOSE

To gain familiarity with the instrumentation amplifier, to demonstrate differential amplification, to measure the common-mode rejection with balanced and unbalanced inputs, and to measure the Bode plot of gain vs. frequency. To measure the ability of differential amplification and coaxial cable to suppress electromagnetic interference.

EQUIPMENT

- superstrip circuit board with ground plane and connections for ground, 5 V, ±12 V
- three 10-μF electrolytic capacitors (put between power and ground at circuit board)
- two 0.1-μF CK05 bypass capacitors (put between power and ground on all chips)
- +5-V, ±12-V power supplies
- wave generator
- AD625 instrumentation amplifier chip
- two 1-m long coax cables
- two 1-m insulated wires

- two BNC-to-alligator clip adapters (POMONA 91836)
- one 25-kΩ trimpot
- one 100-Ω resistor
- one 400-Ω resistor
- one 10-kΩ resistor
- two 20-kΩ resistors
- one 40-kΩ resistor
- four 1-MΩ resistors
- one heat gun (shared with other lab groups)
- one dial thermometer

BACKGROUND

The instrumentation amplifier (shown in Laboratory Figure 5.1) is a very useful circuit element, especially when the signal to be amplified is the difference between two potentials (as from a bridge) and the amplifier input impedance must be very high.

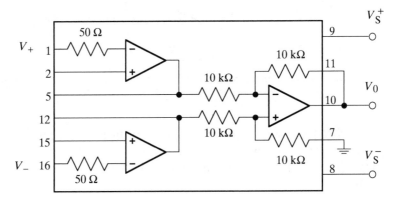

Laboratory Figure 5.1   Simplified circuit of the AD 625 instrumentation amplifier.

ADDITIONAL READING

Chapter 2, Section 2.4: Instrumentation and Isolation Amplifiers and Section 2.5: Noise Sources.

PROCEDURE

1 Circuit Construction

Set up the circuit shown in Laboratory Figure 5.2. Use $R_F = 20$ kΩ and $R_G = 400$ Ω for a differential gain of 101. Set the power supply for $V_S^+ = +12$ volts and $V_S^- = -12$ volts.

2 Offset Voltage

2.1 Unadjusted offset. With the 25-kΩ trimpot removed, and both inputs shorted to ground ($V_- = V_+ = 0$ volts), measure the unadjusted output offset voltage V_0.

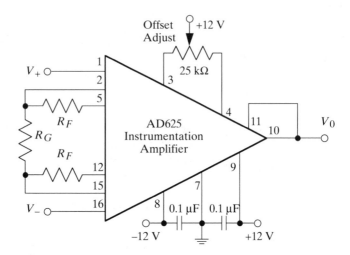

Laboratory Figure 5.2 AD625 instrumentation amplifier circuit. Differential gain is given by $G_\pm = V_0/(V_+ - V_-) = 1 + 2R_F/R_G$.

2.2 Offset adjustment range. With both inputs shorted to ground, install the trimpot and record the output offset voltage for the full trimpot range (full clockwise and full counterclockwise). *Note:* this will require 20 turns.

2.3 Effect of temperature on offset. With both inputs still shorted to ground, first adjust the trimpot for $V_0 = 0$, and then heat the circuit about 10°C with the heat gun (monitor with dial thermometer), and record any change in V_0.

2.4 Effect of power supply voltage on offset. Increase the +12-volt power supply by 5% to 12.6 volts and record any change in V_0. Make sure that you do not change the –12-volt supply. Then readjust the +12-volt supply and adjust the 25-kΩ trimpot for zero output.

3 Noise

With both inputs shorted to ground ($V_- = V_+ = 0$ volts), use the oscilloscope to observe the noise at V_0 (extreme gain required). Record the amplitude and nature of the noise. Distinguish between electromagnetic interference (fixed frequency content, amplitude depends on conductor geometry) and Johnson noise (wideband noise with random fuzzy waveform).   A sketch may be helpful here.

With both inputs connected to ground through 1-MΩ resistors, record the amplitude and nature of the noise.

4 DC Common-Mode Rejection Ratio (CMRR)

4.1 Balanced CMRR.   Connect V_- and V_+ to +5 volts through 1-kΩ resistors and record V_0. Since the differential input is zero, we can determine the common-mode gain G_c as V_0/V_+. The CMRR is $G_\pm/G_c$, where the differential gain $G_\pm$ will be determined in procedure section 5.

4.2 Unbalanced CMRR and heating.   Change one of the 1-kΩ resistors to 1 MΩ and record V_0. This will be used to compute the leakage current. Heat the circuit about 10°C with the heat gun (monitor with the dial thermometer), and record any change in V_0.

5 Small-Signal Differential Gain

Set up the circuit shown in Laboratory Figure 5.3 with an AD625 gain of 100.

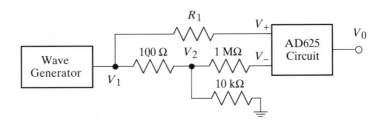

Laboratory Figure 5.3   Circuit for measuring the small-signal differential gain.

Using $R_1 = 1$ MΩ, set the sine-wave generator for 1 kHz, and adjust the amplitude for 1 volt peak-to-peak (p-p) at V_1 as seen on your oscilloscope. Record the amplitude at V_2. Measure V_0 and V_1 at 1 Hz, 10 Hz, 100 Hz, 1 kHz, 10 kHz, 100 kHz, and 1 MHz. Because a large common-mode signal is present at the input, the output will be a differential term $G_\pm(V_1 - V_2)$ and a (hopefully small) common-mode term $G_c V_1$.

6 ac common-mode rejection ratio (CMRR)

Set up the circuit shown in Laboratory Figure 5.4.

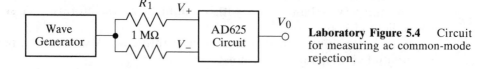

Laboratory Figure 5.4   Circuit for measuring ac common-mode rejection.

6.1 Balanced CMRR.   With $R_1 = 1$ MΩ and V_1 set to the maximum undistorted sine-wave amplitude (not to exceed ±5 volts), measure V_0 at frequencies 1 Hz, 10 Hz, 100 Hz, 1 kHz, 10 kHz, 100 kHz, and 1 MHz. Since the differential input is zero, we can determine the common-mode gain G_c as V_0/V_1. The CMRR can then be computed as $G_\pm/G_c$.

6.2 Unbalanced CMRR.   Change R_1 to 0 Ω and measure the CMRR for sine-wave frequencies as before.

7 Electromagnetic Pickup

7.1 Electromagnetic pickup with insulated wires.   As shown in Laboratory Figure 5.5, attach a 1-m long insulated wire to one of the instrumentation amplifier inputs, connect the same input to ground with a 1-MΩ resistor, and ground the other input. Record the output amplitude and any prominent frequencies.

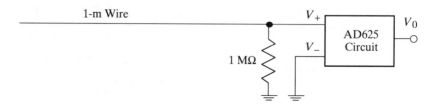

Laboratory Figure 5.5   Circuit for measurement of electromagnetic pick-up with one input grounded.

As shown in Laboratory Figure 5.6, attach 1-m insulated wires to both inputs, and connect both inputs to ground with 1-MΩ resistors. Arrange the wires so that they run parallel to each other but do not touch. Again record the amplitude and prominent frequencies. Now twist the wires around each other without letting the conductors touch. Again record the amplitude and frequency.

7.2 Electromagnetic pickup with coaxial cables.   As before, record for the following: (1) Coaxial cable with alligator adapter on one differential input, the other input grounded. (2) Coaxial cables with alligator adapters on both differential inputs.

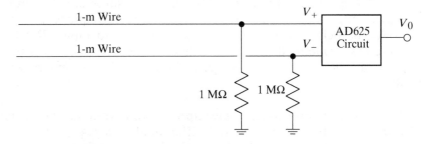

Laboratory Figure 5.6   Circuit for measurement of differential electromagnetic pick-up.

LABORATORY REPORT

1 Setup

Sketch a simple block diagram of the major components used and their
interconnections.

2 Data Summary

Summarize your observations from procedure sections 2 to 7.

3 Analysis

3.1 Offset voltages.   For procedure section 2, tabulate the input and
output offset voltages. Compute the input offset as the observed output offset
divided by the amplifier gain. Note that the actual input voltage was zero
and this input offset is fictitious.

3.2 Power supply rejection.   Compute the power supply rejection
ratio (PSRR) as $G_{\pm}/G_P$, where $G_{\pm}$ is the differential gain and the power-
supply sensitivity G_P is the ratio of the change in output voltage ΔV_0 to a
change in the power-supply voltage ΔV_S:

$$G_P = \frac{\Delta V_0}{G\,\Delta V_S}$$

The data-sheet specification "offset referred to the input vs. supply" is
$G_P/G_{\pm}$.

3.3 Input leakage current.   From your observations in section 4.2,
estimate the input leakage current (pA) and its dependence on temperature
(pA/°C). *Hint:* Calculate the leakage current as (input offset voltage)/
(1 MΩ).

3.4 Noise coefficient. Use your measurements of amplifier noise, closed-loop gain, and bandwidth (3-dB corner frequency) to compute the noise coefficient in nV $Hz^{-1/2}$ with reference to input (R.T.I.). Johnson noise has a random distribution with $V_{rms} = K \sqrt{B}$, where B is the bandwidth in Hz and K is the noise coefficient in nV $Hz^{-1/2}$. Compare with the data-sheet values.

3.5 Common-mode rejection. From your data of common-mode gain G_c (sections 4 and 6) and differential gain $G_\pm$ (part 5) compute the common-mode rejection CMRR = $G_\pm/G_c$ and plot as a function of frequency on semilog paper.

3.6 Bode amplitude plot. From your data of differential gain (procedure section 5), plot gain vs. frequency on semilog paper. Assume that $V_1 - V_2 = V_1/101$.

3.7 Data-sheet comparison. Compare the data-sheet values with your measurements of gain vs. frequency, CMR, noise, offset vs temp, and power supply rejection ratio.

3.8 60 Hz pick-up. Using your data from procedure section 7, pre-pare a table of 60-Hz noise amplitude as follows:

Amplifier Input	60-Hz Amplitude
One 1-m straight wire on one input, other input grounded	
Two 1-m straight wires, one on each input	
Two twisted 1-m wires, one on each input	
One coax with alligator adapter on one input, other input grounded	
Two coax with alligator adapters, one on each input	

4 Discussion and Conclusions

Briefly discuss the significance of your observations for sections 2 to 7.

5 Questions

5.1 Does offset depend on equality of the +12 volt and –12 volt power supplies?

5.2 What are the advantages of the differential amplification?

5.3   In procedure section 3, did the observed Johnson noise agree with the formula given in Chapter 2? (*Hint:* Use the 3-dB corner frequency for the bandwidth.)

5.4   Which type of signal leads permits the observation of the smallest signals, twisted pair or coaxial cable?

6 Laboratory Data Sheets

Include your handwritten data sheets (or a copy), which should consist of a log of the procedures that you used, any special circumstances, and the measurements you recorded manually.

Laboratory Exercise 6

Analog Filtering

PURPOSE

To construct active high-pass, low-pass, and notch filter circuits using the LF356 op-amp integrated-circuit chip. To measure the filtering characteristics of these circuits (Bode amplitude and phase plots.)

EQUIPMENT

- superstrip circuit board with ground plane and connections for ground, 5 V, ±12 V
- three 10-µF electrolytic capacitors (put between power and ground at circuit board)
- two 0.1-µF CK05 bypass capacitors (put between power and ground on all chips)
- one LF356 op amp
- +5-V, ±12-V, power supplies
- wave generator
- oscilloscope
- two 5-kΩ resistors
- four 10-kΩ resistors
- one 100-kΩ resistor

- one 1-MΩ resistor
- one 1-MΩ resistor (5%)
- two 2-MΩ resistors (5%)
- one 0.011-μF capacitor
- one 0.015-μF capacitor
- one 0.022-μF capacitor
- two 1300-pF capacitors (5%)
- one 2600-pF capacitor (5%)

ADDITIONAL READING

Chapter 2, Section 2.6: Analog Filtering.

PROCEDURE

Warning: The inputs to op-amp filter circuits must be provided with a current path to ground, or input leakage currents will cause very large output offsets and possibly saturation. In this Laboratory Exercise the ground path is provided by the wave generator.

1 Low-Pass One-pole Filter

Set up the circuit shown in Laboratory Figure 6.1. The op-amp pinout is shown in Laboratory Figure 4.1. Connect pins 1, 4, 5, and 7 as shown in Laboratory Figure 4.2. Adjust the 25-kΩ trimpot for zero output offset voltage.

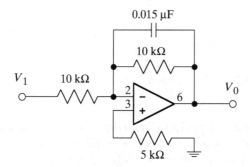

Laboratory Figure 6.1 Low-pass one-pole filter. Input requires a current path to ground.

1.1 Sine-wave response. Connect the output of the wave generator to the input of the filter. With a 1 V peak-to-peak (p-p) sine-wave input, observe the filter input and output on your oscilloscope. Record: (i) input p-p amplitude, (ii) output p-p amplitude, and (iii) the phase shift between the input and output for frequencies of 1 Hz, 10 Hz, 100 Hz, 1 kHz, 10 kHz, 100 kHz, and some intermediate frequencies close to the corner frequency f_c.

Note that the output amplitude of the wave generator may vary with frequency.

Measurement of phase shift. An accurate way to use an oscilloscope to measure the phase shift between two sine-waves is the "zero crossing method," described in the following steps:

1. Display both waves in an alternating mode, always triggering on the positive slope of the reference wave (usually the filter input).
2. Choose a vertical amplification so that both waves span >50% of the screen.
3. Choose the vertical adjustment to center the waves approximately about the center horizontal line (the "zero" line).
4. For the reference wave, as shown in Laboratory Figure 6.2, measure A_1 at its first upward crossing with the zero line, A_2 at the first downward crossing with the line, and A_3 at the second upward crossing with the line.
5. For the phase-shifted wave, measure B_1 as the first upward crossing with the zero line and B_2 as the first downward crossing with the line.

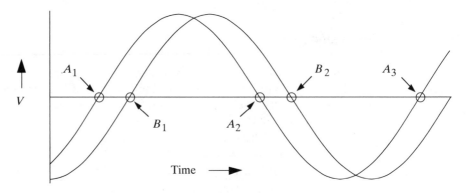

Laboratory Figure 6.2   "Zero crossing" method for using an oscilloscope to determine phase shift.

Since $A_3 - A_1$ is one full period (2π), $(A_1 + A_2)/2$ is the position of the first peak of the reference wave, and $(B_1 + B_2)/2$ is the position of the first peak of the phase-shifted wave, the phase shift P is given by

$$P = \frac{\pi(B_1 + B_2 - A_1 - A_2)}{A_3 - A_1}$$

Note 1: This method uses measurements taken where dV/dt is large, and is more accurate than using the peaks themselves, where dV/dt is zero. Since the uncertainty in time is given by $\Delta T = \Delta V/(dV/dt)$, we want to make measurements where the slope dV/dt is as large as possible.

Note 2:   The computed phase shift is relatively insensitive to the accuracy of the vertical adjustment in step 3.

1.2 Square-wave response.   Observe the output waveform for an input square-wave having a repeat frequency about three times the cutoff frequency. Sketch the output waveforms.

2 Butterworth Low-Pass Two-Pole Filter

Set up the unity-gain Butterworth two-pole filter shown in Laboratory Figure 6.3. Connect pins 1, 4, 5, and 7 as shown in Figure 4-2.

From Chapter 2, Table 2.3, this filter has $k_1 = 1.414$ and $k_2 = 0.707$, where $k_1 = RC_1\omega_0$ and $k_2 = RC_2\omega_0$. Use $R = 10$ kΩ, $C_1 = 0.022$ μF, and $C_2 = 0.011$ μF. Set $V_1 = 1$ V for 1 Hz, 10 Hz, 100 Hz, 1 kHz, 10 kHz, 100 kHz, and some frequencies close to f_c. Record sine-wave and square-wave data as in the previous procedure sections 1.1 and 1.2.

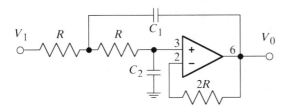

Laboratory Figure 6.3   Butterworth low-pass two-pole filter. Unity-gain Sallen–Key realization. Input requires a current path to ground.

3 High-Pass One-Pole Filter

Set up the circuit shown in Laboratory Figure 6.4. Connect pins 1, 4, 5, and 7 as shown in Laboratory Figure 4.2.

Set $V_1 = 1$ V for 1 Hz, 10 Hz, 100 Hz, 1 kHz, 10 kHz, 100 kHz, and some frequencies close to f_c. Record sine-wave and square-wave data as in procedure sections 1.1 and 1.2, except use a square-wave repeat frequency one-third that of the high-pass cutoff frequency. Sketch the output waveforms.

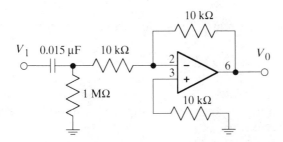

Laboratory Figure 6.4   High-pass one-pole filter. 1-MΩ resistor provides path for input leakage currents.

4 Low-Q Notch Filter

Set up the circuit shown in Laboratory Figure 6.5 in low Q mode, which is a twin-T notch filter followed by a unity-gain follower. Connect pins 1, 4, 5, and 7 as shown in Laboratory Figure 4.2.

Set $V_1 = 1$ V for 1 Hz, 10 Hz, 100 Hz, 1 kHz, 10 kHz, and 100 kHz. Find the notch frequency f_n and take sufficient data to plot the gain and phase shift from $f_n/4$ to $4f_n$. Record sine-wave and square-wave data as in sections 1.1 and 1.2, except use several square-wave frequencies above, at, and below the notch frequency.

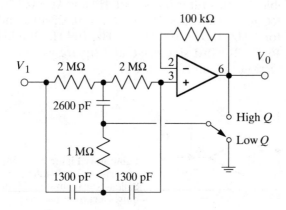

Laboratory Figure 6.5 Notch filter designed to suppress 60 Hz.

5 High-Q Notch Filter

If time permits, switch the notch filter circuit to the high-Q mode and take data near the notch frequency. If the RC components are sufficiently matched, the notch should be much narrower than it was in section 4 above.

LABORATORY REPORT

1 Setup

Sketch a block diagram of the major components used in this exercise.

2 Data Summary

2.1 Gain and phase shift. Tabulate data that you took using the four circuits. Include input p-p amplitude, output p-p amplitude, and phase shift at all frequencies measured.

2.2 Response to a square-wave.   For the high and low pass filters, sketch the output for a square wave input whose fundamental frequency is $3f_c$ (low pass) or $f_c/3$ (high pass). For the notch filter, sketch of the output for a square wave input.

3 Analysis

3.1 Bode amplitude plot.   For each filter, tabulate the voltage gain as output/input for the frequencies used. Plot gain vs. frequency on log–log paper (Bode plot). Note that each factor of 10 in voltage gain corresponds to 20 dB.

3.2 Bode phase plot.   For each filter, plot phase shift vs. frequency on semilog paper (Δ phase vs. log frequency).

3.3 Corner frequencies and slopes.   Tabulate values of corner or notch frequencies, and roll-off slopes (dB of gain per decade of frequency). Compare with expected values.

4 Discussion and Conclusions

4.1   Compare the characteristics of the filtering circuits.

4.2   Comment on any discrepancies between your results and expected values.

4.3   Comment on the shapes of the filter output for square-wave input.

5 Questions

5.1   To double the corner frequency in the low-pass two-pole filter, how would you change the values of the resistors and capacitors?

5.2   How would you change the values of the resistors and capacitors in the notch filter for a notch frequency of 600 Hz?

6 Laboratory Data Sheets

Include your handwritten data sheets (or a copy), which should consist of a log of the procedures that you used, any special circumstances, and the measurements you recorded manually.

3

Analog ↔ Digital Conversion and Sampling

3.1 INTRODUCTION

In this chapter, we discuss the two components that convert data between the digital world of the microcomputer and its I/O ports and the analog world of continuously varying voltages. These are the digital-to-analog (D/A) converter and the analog-to-digital (A/D) converter. We then go on to discuss some of the fundamental limits to sampling time-varying analog signals, including the need for a sample-and-hold amplifier, and the minimum sampling frequency.

Laboratory Exercise 7 is designed as an introduction to the characteristics of the D/A and A/D converters and uses an analog I/O board. Laboratory Exercise 8 interfaces a D/A converter to the binary input port, measures its transfer characteristics, and uses it in waveform generation. Laboratory Exercise 9 interfaces an A/D converter to the binary input port and performs periodic sampling of sine waves. Laboratory Exercise 10 samples and recovers sine waves of various frequencies and explores the aliasing problems that arise when the input frequency is greater than one-half of the sampling frequency.

3.2 DIGITAL-TO-ANALOG CONVERTER CIRCUITS

The digital-to-analog (D/A) converter changes an N-bit binary number to an analog output voltage that can have 2^N distinct values. Usually, the relationship between the input number and the output voltage is **linear**, but other relationships (e.g., logarithmic) are also used.

3.2.1 D/A Converter Characteristics

For an N-bit linear D/A converter, the **ideal** analog output voltage $V(n)$ is a linear function of digital input n between two reference voltages V_{ref}^- and V_{ref}^+.

$$V(n) = V_{ref}^- + n\left(\frac{V_{ref}^+ - V_{ref}^-}{2^N}\right) = V_{ref}^- + n\,\Delta V \qquad (3.1)$$

At the minimum value $n = 0$, the output is V_{ref}^-, but the maximum value of n is $2^N - 1$ so the output can never quite reach V_{ref}^+. Figure 3.1 shows an example where $V_{ref}^- = 0$ V and $V_{ref}^+/2^N = 10$ mV. The average **step size** is ΔV, which is also called the **least significant bit (LSB)** because it corresponds to a change in the least significant bit of the input number.

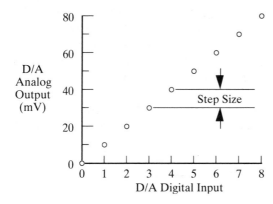

Figure 3.1   Ideal response of D/A converter. The analog output = 0 V for 0 input and increases in discrete 10-mV steps as the input is increased by successively larger integers.

Many D/A converters have fixed reference voltages established by internal circuits. The **multiplying D/A converter** permits V_{ref}^- and V_{ref}^+ to be set by external circuits over a wide range of voltages and even vary with time. As we shall see, the output of this D/A converter is V_{ref}^- plus the product of $(V_{ref}^+ - V_{ref}^-)$ times the fractional equivalent of the digital input number.

As explored in Laboratory Exercises 7 and 8, the main characteristics of the D/A converter are as follows:

1. The **resolution**, or **quantizing error**, of an N-bit D/A converter is the largest difference between any voltage within the full output range and the closest possible output voltage. In the case of the ideal D/A converter, this is one-half the step size, or 0.5 LSB. Because of the close association between resolution and the number of bits, the description "N-bit resolution" is frequently used.

2. The **absolute-accuracy error** is the difference between the actual output and the ideal output, before adjustments for zero offset and gain. It is usually expressed in units of 1 LSB for comparison with the quantizing error.

3. The **relative-accuracy error** is the difference between the actual output and the straight line passing through the measured end points of the full-scale range. Since this error is relative to a straight line, it is also called the **linearity error.** Note that calibration of the end points (by adjusting zero offset and gain) does not affect the relative-accuracy error. It is usually expressed in units of 1 LSB for comparison with the quantizing error.

4. The **zero-offset error** is the D/A output when the digital input is zero.

5. The **differential linearity error** is the difference between the output step sizes and the average step size. It is usually expressed in units of 1 LSB. If the differential linearity error is large enough, a nonmonotonic response can result.

6. A **glitch** is a transient spike in the output of a D/A that occurs when more than one bit changes in the input code and the corresponding internal switches do not change simultaneously. For a short time, the switches contain an erroneous input number. The worst glitch usually occurs at the half-scale transition, when the bits change from 0111...1111 to 1000...0000 (Figure 3.2). The severity of the glitch is given by the product of the duration and magnitude, computed as the area under the time–amplitude curve. Note that a low-pass filter can reduce the magnitude of the glitch, but not the area. A better solution is a **deglitcher**, a sample-and-hold circuit that holds the output constant until the switches settle.

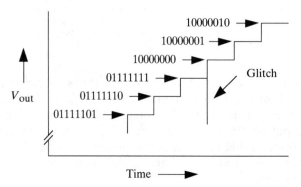

Figure 3.2   D/A output as a function of time for successively larger input values. A voltage spike (glitch) can occur when many bits change state, such as between 01111111 and 10000000.

7. The **power-supply sensitivity** is the percentage change in output voltage per 1% change in supply voltage. It is also expressed as the change in the full-scale output (in LSB) for a standard (usually 3%) change in the power-supply voltage. This is an important specification for battery operation.

8. The **settling time** is the time required for the output to settle to typically 1/4 LSB after a large change in D/A output. It is expressed in units of ns or μs.

9. The **slewing rate** is the maximum rate of change in output voltage, usually imposed by the maximum driving current in the D/A output amplifier and the capacitive load. It is expressed in units of V/μs.

By using the measured end points $V(0) = V_{min}$ and $V(2^N - 1) = V_{max}$, the straight-line response is given by

$$V(n) = V_{min} + n\left(\frac{V_{max} - V_{min}}{2^N - 1}\right) \tag{3.2}$$

The **rms linearity error** is the rms, or "root mean square" of the residuals $R_n = V(n) - V_n$. The measured voltage values are V_n (corresponding to D/A input numbers n), and $V(n)$ is given in equation 3.2.

$$V_{rms} = \sqrt{\frac{1}{2^N}\sum_{n=0}^{2^N-1} R_n^2}, \quad \text{where} \quad R_n = V(n) - V_n$$

3.2.2 Weighted-Adder D/A Converter

One of the simplest D/A designs uses a weighted adder, where current is individually switched through a set of parallel resistors to be summed at the input of an amplifier (Figure 3.3). An input bit logic HIGH turns on an analog switch (usually a field-effect transistor, FET), causing the corresponding current to be summed. (The current-summing circuit using an op amp is shown in Figure 2.7.) The successive resistors have values that differ by a factor of 2, so that the current controlled by the successive switches differs by a factor of 2. When the ith bit has a logic HIGH, it turns on an analog switch that causes a current

$$I_i = \frac{V_{ref}^+ - V_{ref}^-}{2^{N-i}R}$$

to flow through the corresponding $2^{N-i}R$ resistor. When converting the number n, the total current I through the resistors to the summing junction is equal to the current from the op-amp output.

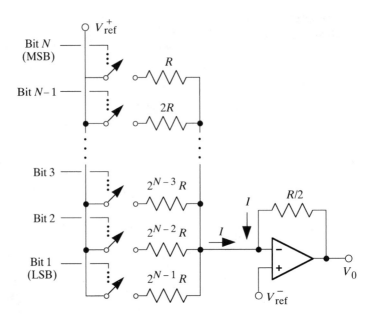

Figure 3.3 D/A converter circuit using a weighted adder. Currents through the binary sequence of resistors are summed at the input of the op amp. See Figure 2.7.

$$I = n\,\Delta I = n\left[\frac{V_{ref}^{+} - V_{ref}^{-}}{2^{N-1}R}\right] = \frac{V_0 - V_{ref}^{-}}{R/2}$$

Solving for V_0, we have the result

$$V_0 = V_{ref}^{-} + n\left(\frac{V_{ref}^{+} - V_{ref}^{-}}{2^{N}}\right)$$

3.2.3 *R-2R* Resistive-Ladder D/A Converter

One requirement of the D/A design shown before is a set of accurate resistors values spanning a large range. While this does not present a problem when using discrete components, it is not possible to fabricate such a wide range of resistor values in the same integrated-circuit chip. For this reason, the most common integrated-circuit D/A design uses the ***R–2R* resistor ladder**, which establishes a binary sequence of currents that can be selectively summed to produce the analog output (see Figure 3.4).

Note that the same currents flow through the resistors to the same potential V_{ref}^{-} no matter how the bit switches are set. At each node along the left-hand side, the current is split into two equal parts so that the bit 1 switch

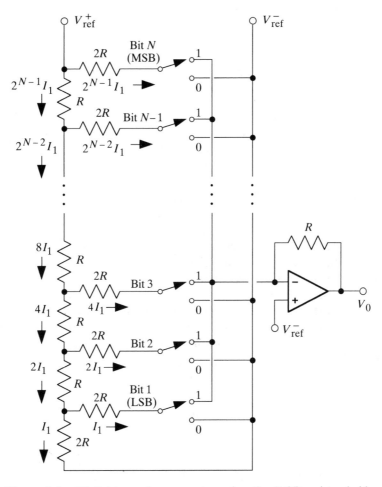

Figure 3.4   Digital-to-analog converter using the R-$2R$ resistor ladder. Note that at each node, the current is split into two equal parts to provide a binary series. The bit switches determine which currents are summed at the virtual ground of the amplifier.

controls the current I_1 and the bit i switch controls the current $2^{N-i} I_1$. Each switch sends its current either to V_{ref}^- or to the negative feedback point that is maintained at V_{ref}^- by the amplifier. As discussed in Chapter 2, the op amp produces whatever output voltage is necessary to drive current through the feedback resistor R and cancel the currents entering through the bit switches. When converting the number n, the current into the op amp is $I = n \, \Delta I$, where

$$\Delta I = \frac{V_{ref}^+ - V_{ref}^-}{2^N R}$$

Current cancellation requires

$$I = n\,\Delta I = n\left(\frac{V_{ref}^+ - V_{ref}^-}{2^N R}\right) = \frac{V_0 - V_{ref}^-}{R}, \quad \text{and} \quad V_0 = V_{ref}^- + n\left(\frac{V_{ref}^+ - V_{ref}^-}{2^N}\right)$$

The output voltage V_0 is therefore proportional to the digital value of the switch pattern.

3.2.4 Subranging D/A Converter

In some applications, such as digital control of an analog process, it is only necessary that the D/A converter have many small steps and that the analog output be a monotonic function of the digital input. This can be achieved by using the **subranging D/A converter,** which uses a pair of D/A converters to provide the reference voltages for a third. An example is shown in Figure 3.5. Two D/A converters are used for the N most significant bits and the third is used for the M least significant bits. Note that while the precision is $N+M$ bits, the absolute accuracy and the differential linearity are no better than the N-bit converters.

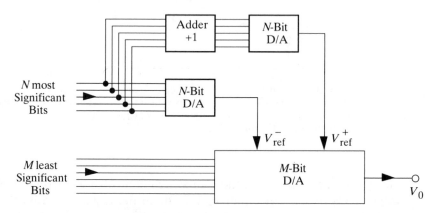

Figure 3.5   Subranging D/A converter with 2^{N+M} monotonic output steps constructed from three D/A converters. Absolute accuracy is only N bits, however.

Table 3.1 describes some commercially available monolithic (single integrated-circuit) D/A converters.

TABLE 3.1   SOME AVAILABLE MONOLITHIC D/A CONVERTERS

Model	AD7545	AD668K	CX20202A-1	CXA1236
Manufacturer	Analog Dev.	Analog Dev.	Sony	Sony
Number of bits	12	12	10	8
Relative accuracy	±0.5 LSB	±0.25 LSB	N/A	±0.5 LSB
Differential linearity	±1 LSB	±0.5 LSB	±0.5 LSB	±0.5 LSB
Maximum update rate	>500 kHz	15 MHz	160 MHz	500 MHz

3.3 ANALOG-TO-DIGITAL CONVERTER CIRCUITS

The analog-to-digital (A/D) converter changes a voltage level (the analog input) into a binary number (the digital output). Usually, the relationship between the input voltage and the output number is **linear** (Figure 3.6). The A/D converter divides the input voltage range into $2^N - 1$ bands, where N is the number of bits in the output word. Some A/D converter circuits require that the input voltage remain steady during the conversion process, which can take many microseconds. To provide a steady level, the sample-and-hold amplifier (described in Chapter 2) is used.

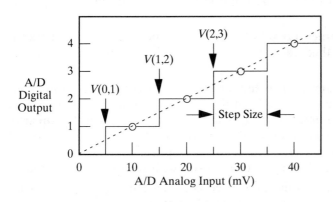

Figure 3.6   Ideal response of an A/D converter to a varying analog input for $V_{ref}^- = 0$ V. At the transition voltage $V(n, n + 1)$ the output toggles between n and $n + 1$.

3.3.1 A/D Converter Characteristics

For an **ideal** linear N-bit A/D converter, the digital output n is a linear function of the analog input voltage V between two reference voltages V_{ref}^- and V_{ref}^+. The range of analog inputs from V_{ref}^- to V_{ref}^+ is divided into $2^N - 1$ equal bands of width ΔV.

$$n = \left\lfloor \frac{V - V_{ref}^-}{\Delta V} + \frac{1}{2} \right\rfloor_{\text{INTEGER}} \quad , \quad \text{where} \quad \Delta V = \frac{V_{ref}^+ - V_{ref}^-}{2^N - 1} \tag{3.3}$$

The ideal response curve passes through the center of the steps (the dashed line in Figure 3.6). Because the same output is produced for a range of analog inputs, the response curve is best measured at the **transition voltages**, where the output changes by one bit. The center of any step can then be computed as the midpoint between the nearest transition voltages. In the ideal case, the first transition voltage $V(0, 1)$ occurs at 0.5 LSB, and the second $V(1, 2)$ occurs at 1.5 LSB. The nth transition voltage is at $V(n - 1, n) = V_{\text{ref}}^- + (n - 0.5) * \Delta V$. While a given value of n corresponds to a range of V that has width ΔV, the transition between $n - 1$ and n corresponds to a definite value of V.

Linearity is measured by how well the transition voltages (or the midpoint of the steps) lie on a straight line. Differential linearity is measured by the equality of the step sizes.

As explored in Laboratory Exercises 7 and 9, the main characteristics of the A/D converter are:

1. The **resolution**, or **quantizing error**, of an N-bit A/D converter is the largest difference between any input voltage within the full range and the voltage corresponding to the output number (the midpoint of the step). In the case of the ideal A/D converter, this is one-half the step size, or 0.5 LSB. Because of the close association between resolution and the number of bits, the description "N bit resolution" is frequently used.

2. The **absolute-accuracy error** is the difference between the input transition voltages and their ideal values, before adjustments for zero offset and gain.

3. The **relative-accuracy error** is the difference between the transition voltages at a straight line passing from the first to the last transition voltage. Since this error is relative to a straight line, it is also called the **linearity error.** Note that calibration of the end points (by adjusting zero offset and gain) does not affect the relative-accuracy error. It is usually expressed in units of 1 LSB for comparison with the quantizing error.

4. The **zero-offset error** is the difference between the first transition voltage and 0.5 LSB (the center of the ideal first step).

5. The **differential-linearity error** is the difference between the spacing of the transition voltages and their average spacing. It is usually expressed in units of 1 LSB. If the differential linearity error is large enough, **missed codes** (output numbers that cannot be produced by any input voltage) can result. Differential linearity error is usually the result of inaccurate resistor values.

6. The **conversion time** is the time required to produce the output number after the "start conversion" command has been given.

7. The **conversion rate (maximum)** is the largest rate that the A/D converter can perform conversions. For simple A/D converters, the maximum conversion rate is the inverse of the conversion time. More

advanced converters can begin the next conversion before the previous one has completed, and their maximum conversion rate can be considerably higher than the inverse of the conversion time.

8. The **power-supply sensitivity** is the percentage change in the transition voltages per 1% change in supply voltage. It is also expressed as the change in the last transition voltage (in LSB) for a standard (usually 3%) change in the power-supply voltage. This is an important specification for battery operation.

3.3.2 Relationship Between A/D and D/A Conversion

As explored in Laboratory Exercises 7, 8, 9, and 20, the ideal A/D converter produces an output n for input voltages in the range from $V(n - 1, n) = V_{min} + (n - 0.5)*\Delta V$ to $V(n, n + 1) = V_{min} + (n + 0.5)*\Delta V$. The midpoint of this range is $V_{mid} = V_{min} + n \Delta V$, which is the output voltage produced by the ideal D/A converter with input n. We see that the conversions in equations 3.1 and 3.3 are defined so that if a set of analog signals are converted and stored digitally, the analog waveform can be recovered without systematic error. The analog output will differ from the corresponding analog input values by $\pm 0.5 \Delta V$, but the average error will be zero.

3.3.3 Integrating A/D Converter

The **integrating, or dual-slope, A/D converter** accumulates the input on a capacitor for a fixed time and then measures the time it takes to discharge the same capacitor at a fixed discharge rate (Figures 3.7 and 3.8). A clock is used to measure the discharge time, and the number of clock pulses is the digital output. It is relatively slow, but has extreme accuracy and linearity. This method is most commonly used in pulse-height analyzers, which accumulate a distribution of pulse heights, such as in nuclear spectroscopy, because its high differential linearity avoids spectral distortion.

The steps are

1. Integrate the analog input on the capacitor for N clock ticks (fixed time T).
2. Restart the clock and discharge the capacitor at a known rate linearly with time.
3. When the capacitor is at zero (use a comparator), store the clock.

The result is quite accurate, and the accuracy does not depend on knowing the exact clock rate or the exact value of the capacitor. In addition, high input frequencies are averaged to zero during the integration period, especially those that are an integral multiple of $1/T$.

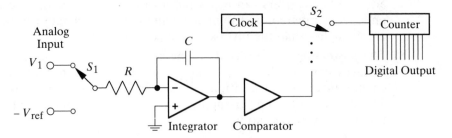

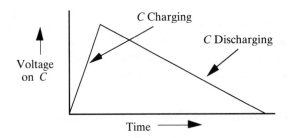

Figure 3.7   Simplified diagram of an integrating dual-slope A/D converter. Switch S_1 connects the input V_1 to the integrator for a set number of clock cycles, charging capacitor C to a voltage proportional to the time average of V_1. Then S_1 connects $-V_{ref}$ to the integrator to discharge C at a constant rate while S_2 closes to accumulate clock pulses in the counter. The number of clock pulses when the comparator input reaches zero is the digitized form of the integral of V_1.

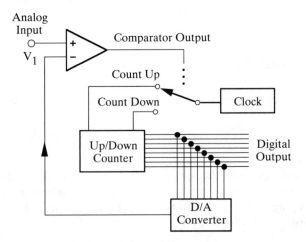

Figure 3.8   Voltage on capacitor C of the integrating dual-slope A/D converter during charging and discharging phases.

3.3.4 Tracking A/D Converter

The **tracking A/D converter** repeatedly compares its input with the output of a D/A converter (Figure 3.9). If the analog input is larger, the D/A input is incremented. If the analog input is smaller, the D/A input is decremented.

Figure 3.9   Tracking A/D converter. The voltage to be converted is compared with the output of a D/A converter that is connected to an up/down counter. If the voltage is larger, the counter is increased by one, otherwise the counter is decreased.

The conversion time is slow relative to the clock frequency. This may be seen by considering the Ferranti ZN433, a low cost 10-bit tracking A/D converter, with a clock rate of 1 Mhz (1 count/µs). A minimum time of 1 ms is thus required to cover the full scale of 1024 counts, which corresponds to the maximum slope of a sine wave with a period of 2π ms. Thus, the maximum frequency that can be reliably tracked is only 180 Hz.

3.3.5 Successive-Approximation A/D Converter

The **successive-approximation A/D converter** uses a binary search to sequentially determine the bits of the output number. The flow chart is shown in Figure 3.10 and the block diagram is shown in Figure 3.11.

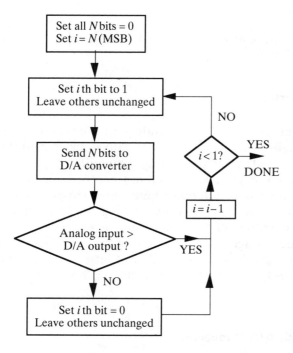

Figure 3.10 Flow chart for the method of successive approximation.

The method is analogous to weighing an object using a balance and a binary sequence of known weights (e.g., 1, 2, 4, 8, and 16 grams). In the first cycle, the analog input is compared with the 16-g weight. If the object is heavier, the weight is left and the 8-g weight is added. If the object is lighter, the 16-g weight is removed and the 8-g weight is added. The process continues, testing each weight in the descending sequence, leaving it in place if the object is heavier than the sum, and removing it if the object is lighter. The balance is analogous to the comparator (discussed in Chapter 2), whose output is a logic 0 or 1, depending on the relative amplitudes of its two analog inputs (Figure 2.26). The binary set of weights is analogous to the

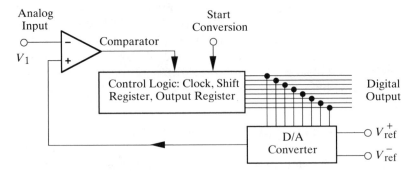

Figure 3.11   Block diagram for the method of successive approximation. The control logic is a hardware implementation of the flow diagram in Figure 3.10.

internal D/A converter, whose analog output is proportional to the weighted sum of the binary input bits.

3.3.6 Flash A/D Converter

The **flash A/D converter** uses $2^N - 1$ comparators to determine simultaneously all N bits of the digital output (Figure 3.12). Since the comparators are constantly sampling the input, a sample-and-hold amplifier is generally not needed. A set of exclusive-OR gates (discussed in Chapter 1) determines the location of the comparator whose reference input most closely matches the analog input. Conversion is accomplished by latching the logic state of the exclusive-OR gates. The address of that comparator is the N-bit binary representation of the input voltage. The number of comparators needed is $2^N - 1$, which grows quite rapidly with the number of bits. Common units are four-bit (15 comparators), six-bit (63 comparators), and eight-bit (255 comparators).

3.3.7 Subranging Flash A/D Converter

The flash converter has the advantage of high speed, but it is costly to use this technique for a large number of bits. A practical solution to this problem is the **subranging flash A/D converter,** which is a hybrid between the successive-approximation and the flash converters. One flash A/D converter determines the most significant bits, which are sent to a D/A converter. A differential amplifier computes the difference, which is used by a second flash converter to determine the least significant bits.

By way of example, let us examine the AD7820 eight-bit "half-flash" converter, which is shown in Figure 3.13.

The sequence of operation follows (RD mode):

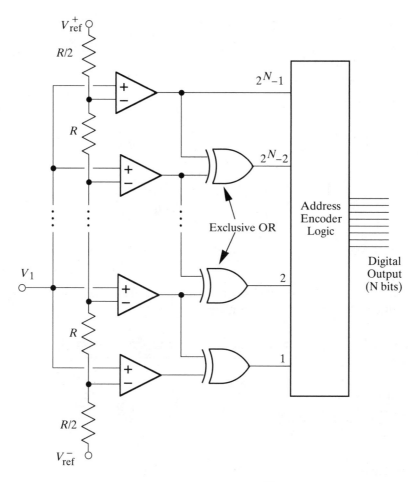

Figure 3.12   The N-bit flash converter uses $2^N - 1$ parallel comparators and exclusive-OR gates for high-speed conversion

1. $\overline{\text{WR}}$/RDY is normally low and the comparators sample the input.
2. Conversion is initiated by taking $\overline{\text{RD}}$ low.
3. After 1.6 to 2.5 µs, $\overline{\text{WR}}$/RDY goes high and the four most significant bits are latched.
4. 20 to 50 ns later, the four least significant bits are latched and all eight output bits are valid.
5. After $\overline{\text{RD}}$ goes high, data are held for an additional 60 to 80 ns.
6. After 500 to 600 ns, conversion may be repeated by taking $\overline{\text{RD}}$ low.

Another example is the 10-bit 20-MHz Sony CX20220A-1 A/D converter. The A/D and D/A for the five most significant bits use the same resistor ladder to reduce error.

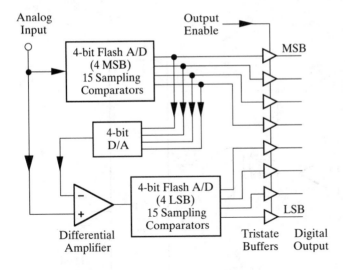

Analog Input

Output Enable

MSB

4-bit Flash A/D (4 MSB) 15 Sampling Comparators

4-bit D/A

4-bit Flash A/D (4 LSB) 15 Sampling Comparators

LSB

Differential Amplifier

Tristate Buffers

Digital Output

Figure 3.13   Subranging eight-bit A/D converter using two four-bit flash A/D converters and a four-bit D/A converter.

Table 3.2 shows some commercially available monolithic (single integrated-circuit) A/D converters.

TABLE 3.2   SOME AVAILABLE MONOLITHIC A/D CONVERTERS

Model	CX20220A-1	AD574	AD367	CXA1176
Manufacturer	Sony	Analog Dev.	Analog Dev.	Sony
Number of bits	10	12	16	8
Integral linearity	±1 LSB	±0.5 LSB	±2 LSB	±0.5 LSB
Differential linearity	±1 LSB	±1 LSB	±4 LSB	±0.5 LSB
Conversion method	Subranging flash	Successive approx.	Successive approx.	Flash
Input voltage range	0 to –2 V	–10 to +10 V	0 to +20 V	0 to –2 V
Conversion time	50 ns	35 µs	17 µs	3.3 ns
Aperture jitter	†	†	†	3.6 ps
Max. conversion rate	20 MHz	29 kHz	59 kHz	300 MHz

†Requires an external sample-and-hold amplifier.

3.4   SAMPLING ANALOG WAVEFORMS

Waveform sampling requires the close coordination of a number of elements, especially when speed and accuracy are required. The process typically has the following steps:

1. The conversion command is initiated under software control or by a digital timer. This switches the sample-and-hold amplifier (if used) from the sample to the hold mode and initiates A/D conversion. As discussed in Chapter 2, the sample-and-hold amplifier has a rapid response when switching from sample to hold, but it may be necessary

to delay conversion while the charge transfer from the digital control pulse to the output settles.

2. When conversion is complete, an I/O status bit is set or an interrupt is produced that notifies the microcomputer that new data are available.

3. The microcomputer reads and stores the A/D output.

For high-speed operation, the data may be transferred directly into memory. This is called "direct memory access," or DMA, and combines steps 2 and 3.

3.4.1 Sampling-Speed Limitations

Suppose we want to sample a sine wave with frequency f (cycles/second) and a peak-peak amplitude of $2V_0$. The waveform is given by

$$V(t) = V_0 \sin (2\pi f t)$$

Note that the 2π is needed to convert from cycles/second to radians/second. The first derivative gives the rate of change

$$dV/dt = 2\pi f V_0 \cos (2\pi f t)$$

which has a maximum value of $2\pi f V_0$. If the A/D converter has N bits of resolution and an input sampling time T, a conversion accuracy of 1/2 LSB requires that the input not change by 1 part in $2^{N+1} = V_0 2^{-N}$ during the time T:

$$2\pi f V_0 < \frac{V_0}{2^N T} \quad \text{or} \quad f_{\max} = \frac{1}{2^{(N+1)}\pi T}$$

If we do not use a sample-and-hold amplifier for the AD670 ($N = 8$, $T = 10$ μs), then $f_{\max} = 62$ Hz, which is very low. On the other hand, using the AD582 sample-and-hold amplifier reduces T to 15 ns (the aperture jitter) and $f_{\max} = 41$ kHz, which is considerably higher. Note that this happens to be nearly equal to the Nyquist frequency limit of 50 kHz, corresponding to the AD670 maximum sampling rate of 100 kHz (see the following section).

The AD7820, on the other hand, uses sampling comparators, and its input sampling time is less than 50 ns (the maximum delay between the latching of the four MSBs and the four LSBs). Even without the sample-and-hold amplifier, $f_{\max} = 12$ kHz.

3.5 FREQUENCY ALIASING

When a sine wave is sampled six times per cycle (Figure 3.14), a smooth curve passed through the data is close to the original sampled curve and the observed frequency f_0 is equal to the true frequency f. When a sinewave is sampled three times per cycle (Figure 3.15), a smooth curve passed through

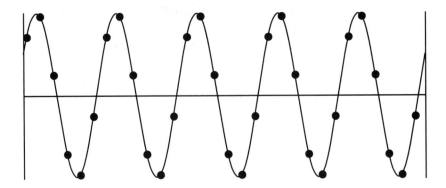

Figure 3.14   When a sine wave is sampled six times per cycle ($f_s = 6f$), the observed frequency is equal to the true frequency.

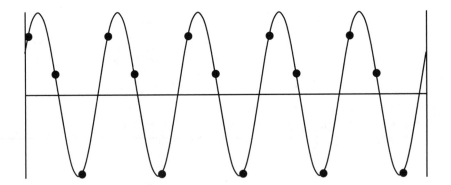

Figure 3.15   When a sine wave is sampled three times per cycle ($f_s = 3f$), the observed frequency is equal to the true frequency.

the data are a less reliable representation of the original sampled waveform, but the observed frequency f_0 is equal to the true frequency f. When the sampling frequency is $(6/5)f$, a smooth curve passed through the data appears to be a sine wave, just like the original sampled data, but severe aliasing has occurred (Figure 3.16). The apparent frequency f_0 is $f/5$, much lower than the true frequency.

The apparent frequency f_0 as a function of true frequency f and the sampling frequency f_s is shown in Figure 3.17. For $f/f_s < 0.5$, $f_0 = f$. When f exceeds $f_s/2$, the apparent frequency f_0 drops linearly and reaches zero at $f = f_s$, when the waveform is sampled exactly once per cycle. In general, if the sampling frequency is any multiple of the true frequency, the waveform is sampled at the same phase and the apparent frequency is zero. This is seen in Laboratory Exercise 10 when the input sine-wave frequency is chosen to be close to the sampling frequency and the recovered wave has a low apparent frequency.

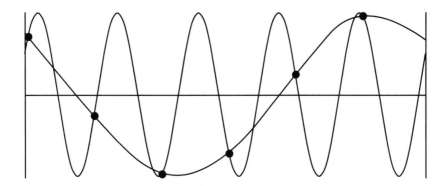

Figure 3.16   When a sine wave is sampled six times in five cycles, the observed sine wave has a much lower frequency than the original sine wave.

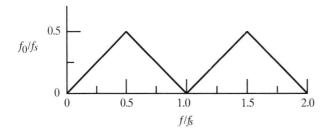

Figure 3.17   Apparent frequency f_0 as a function of true frequency f for a sine wave sampled at frequency f_s. The apparent frequency is equal to the true frequency only when $f/f_s < 0.5$.

It is important to realize that if any frequencies **above** $f_s/2$ exist in the sampled signal, they will appear in the sampled data as waves of **lower** frequency. This frequency aliasing is avoided if the frequencies above $f_s/2$ are removed by analog filtering **before** sampling. The Nyquist sampling requirement that the sampling frequency must be at least twice the highest frequency in the signal is discussed further in Chapter 5.

3.6 AVAILABLE DATA-ACQUISITION CIRCUITS

The following is a brief summary of data-acquisition boards for the IBM PC/XT/AT class and the Apple Macintosh II microcomputers. It is expected that much faster products will soon be available for the Apple Macintosh II and IBM Personal System/2.

3.6.1 Data Acquisition and Control Adapter (IBM, Boca Raton, FL)

Analog input section

1. Analog multiplexer (AD7502) with four differential input channels and a 20-µs settling time (see Figure 3.18).
2. Sample-and-hold amplifier (AD583) with a differential input.
3. A/D converter (AD4574) with 12-bit resolution and 25-µs conversion time. Ranges are ±5 V, ±10 V, or 0 to +10 V, switch selectable.
4. Octal output register is 74LS244, tristate.

Analog outputs: two AD7545 12-bit D/A converters. Ranges are ±5 V, ±10 V, or 0 to +10 V, switch selectable.

32-bit timer: counters 0 and 1 of the 8253-5 Programmable Interval Timer (cascaded), operating at a 1.023-MHz clock rate.

16-bit counter: counter 2 of 8253-5 Programmable Interval Timer.

Parallel input port: 16 bits (2 × 8 bits) latches using 74LS373.

Parallel output port: 16 bits (2 × 8 bits) registers using 74LS374.

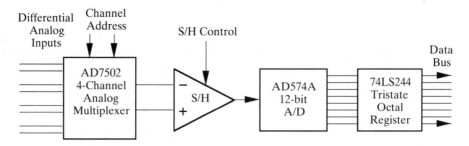

Figure 3.18   IBM Data Acquisition Circuit, featuring an analog multiplexer with four differential inputs, a sample-and-hold amplifier, a 12-bit A/D converter, and tristate output buffers.

3.6.2 PCI-20000 System (Burr-Brown, Tucson, Arizona)

This data-acquisition and control system uses a general "carrier board" that plugs into the IBM PC/XT/AT expansion slot. Modules that perform analog or digital I/O and counter/timer functions plug into the carrier board. One of these is the PCI-20019M-1 High Speed Data Acquisition Module, which has eight single-ended analog input channels, an analog multiplexer, a sample-and-hold amplifier, and a 12-bit A/D converter with a 12-µs conversion time and a maximum conversion rate of 89 kHz. The "LABTECH Notebook" is a general-purpose software package for data acquisition, monitoring, and real-time control using the PCI-20000 circuit board system.

3.6.3 NB-MIO-16 (National Instruments, Austin, TX)

This analog and digital I/O interface plugs into an expansion slot of the Apple Computer Corp., Macintosh SE or Macintosh II. It has 16 single-ended or eight differential analog input channels (A/D conversion time 9 µs), two multiplying D/A converters, eight bits of digital I/O, and three 16-bit counter/timers. The "LabVIEW" software package allows data I/O and counter/timer modules as well as data analysis, recording, and display to be configured in software using the "user friendly" Macintosh graphics interface.

3.6.4 RTI-815 Analog and Digital Board (Analog Devices, Inc., Norwood, MA)

Analog input section:

1. 16 analog input channels with software selectable gains of 1, 10, 100, and 500.
2. Sample-and-hold amplifier.
3. A/D converter with 12-bit resolution and 25-µs conversion time. Input ranges are ±5 V, ±10 V, or 0 to +10 V, switch selectable.

Analog outputs: two 12-bit D/A converters. Ranges are 0 to +10 V, or ±10 V, switch selectable.

16-bit counter/timers: three.

Parallel I/O port: eight lines input, eight lines output.

3.6.5 DT2821-F (Data Translation, Inc., Marlboro, MA)

Analog inputs: 16 single-ended or eight differential 12-bit programmable with gains of 1, 2, 4, or 8. 150-kHz maximum conversion rate.

Analog outputs: two independent 12-bit. 130-kHz maximum rate.

3.6.6 PIO-12 (MetraByte Corp., Taunton, MA)

Binary input/output: two 8-bit ports and two 4-bit ports that can be selected either for input or output.

3.6.7 DAS-4 (MetraByte Corp., Taunton, MA)

Analog inputs: eight-channel multiplexor, sample-and-hold amplifier, and an eight-bit A/D converter, input range ±5 V, maximum sampling rate 5 kHz.

Binary input: 4 bits.

Binary output: 3 bits.

3.6.8 DAS-20 (MetraByte Corp., Taunton, MA)

Input ranges (software selectable): 0 to 100 mV, ± 50 mV, 0 to 1 V, ±0.5 V, 0 to 10 V, ±5 V, and ±10 V.

Analog inputs: 16 single-ended or 8 differential 12-bit.

Analog outputs: two 12-bit. Update time 4 μs.

3.6.9 DAP 1200 (Microstar Laboratories, Redmond, WA)

Analog inputs: 16 single-ended with programmable gain amplifiers.

Analog outputs: two 12-bit.   **Digital I/O:** 32 lines.

3.7 PROBLEMS

3.1 You are given the following components:
- a sample-and-hold amplifier with 50-ns aperture jitter from the sample to hold mode and a 0.5 μs risetime from the hold to sample mode
- a 12-bit analog-to-digital successive-approximation converter with 5-μs conversion time
- a 16-bit parallel input port with 10-μs read time

   a. Using the sample-and-hold amplifier, what is the maximum input frequency such that the aperture jitter corresponds to less than 0.5 LSB during the conversion time?

   b. If you did not use a sample-and-hold amplifier, what is the maximum input frequency such that the change is less than 0.5 LSB during the conversion time?

   c. What is the maximum sampling frequency? What component would you change to improve it?

   d. Limited by the Nyquist sampling requirement, what is the highest frequency in the input waveform that you can reliably sample and store?

   e. For 10 V full scale, what is the resolution of the A/D?

   f. How would your answers to parts **a** and **b** change if the A/D were eight-bit?

3.2 You are using a 16-bit A/D converter with a full scale of 10 V and a conversion time of 100 μs. The sample-and-hold amplifier has a holding capacitor C_H, an acquisition time T_a, and a droop rate R_d related by

$$T_a = 5 \text{ μs} + (10,000 \text{ μs/μF})C_H \quad \text{and} \quad C_H R_d = 10 \text{ μV μF/s}$$

(*Note:* These characteristics describe the AD582 sample-and-hold amplifier used in Laboratory Exercise 9.) For $T_a < 20$ μs and $R_d < 0.5$ LSB per 100 μs, what are the constraints on C_H?

3.3 Design a system to sample and print *eight* slowly varying analog signals. The eight signals are to be sampled as simultaneously as possible, then stored under computer control. The sampling frequency is entered by the user during initial setup. The components provided are

- Eight 12-bit, successive-approximation A/D converters, which initiate conversion whenever they receive a positive edge on a "start-conversion line," take 20 μs to perform the conversion, and then signal a "data-ready line" with a 200 ns wide positive-going output pulse. Data on the eight output lines (HIGH or LOW) are valid slightly before the "data-ready" pulse and do not change until the next conversion.

- Eight tristate 12-bit buffers that clock data onto internal registers whenever a low-to-high edge appears on their "strobe" input. The data remain on the internal registers until new data are strobed. These buffers have output lines that are asserted to the state of the internal registers only when the "select" input is high. At all other times, the outputs are in their high-impedance mode and neither drive nor load any other circuit connected to them.

- You have decided not to use a sample-and-hold amplifier.

- A 16-bit parallel output port. Assume that the write operation takes 3 μs and that you can make a positive going pulse 3 μs wide on a (normally LOW) output line by writing 1 then 0 to that line.

- A 16-bit parallel input port that latches data and sets a status bit whenever a low-to-high strobe edge is received. Assume that the microcomputer read operation takes 3 μs.

- An eight-input OR gate. Has eight inputs and one output. Output is LOW only if all inputs are LOW. Output is HIGH if any input is HIGH.

- A 32-bit digital timing module that increments at 1 MHz. It can be set to zero or read under program control in 10 μs.

a. Draw a block diagram of all components and essential interconnections. Label all components, control lines, and data lines.

b. Draw a timing diagram that shows the data-acquisition sequence for **one** of the eight input signals.

c. How frequently could your system sample all eight inputs in sequence? What is the corresponding Nyquist frequency on each line?

d. Draw a flow chart (or a list of what the steps do) of your microcomputer control program.

e. What is the highest frequency input that you can sample to an accuracy of 1/2 LSB, considering that you do not have a sample-and-hold amplifier?

f. What is the frequency limit in part **e** if you use a sample-and-hold amplifier with an aperture time jitter of 10 ns?

3.4 You are designing a system that uses a sample-and-hold amplifier and a 12-bit successive-approximation A/D converter with an input range that has been accurately trimmed from 0.000 to 10.000 V. The conversion time is 10 μs.

a. Ideally, at what input voltage would you expect the first transition voltage $V(0,1)$ to occur?

b. Ideally, what is the input step size?

c. What is the percent resolution for a 10-mV input?

d. What is the percent resolution for a 5-V input?

e. What is the maximum droop rate (V/s) that the sample-and-hold amplifier can have for 1/2 LSB accuracy?

3.5 You are given a 16-bit D/A converter with an absolute accuracy of 1 LSB and a microcomputer with separate 16-bit parallel input and output ports. Your job is to use these to measure the properties of a new type of eight-bit A/D converter under computer control.

a. Draw a block diagram of the major components. Show and label all important data and control lines.

b. How would you measure the absolute accuracy of the A/D? (Explain in words or with a flow diagram.)

c. How would you measure the linearity (relative to the end points)?

d. How would you measure differential linearity?

3.6 Describe the method of operation of the following A/D converters:

a. integrating (or dual slope)

b. flash

c. tracking

3.7 Consider four types of analog-to-digital converters:

- integrating (or dual-slope)   DS
- successive approximation   SA
- flash   FL
- tracking   TR

Write the best match or matches (N = number of output bits):

	DS	SA	FL	TR
Requires 2^N clock cycles				
Requires N clock cycles				
Requires 1 clock cycle				
Good accuracy and differential linearity				
Low cost (per 2^N steps)				
High speed				
Slow				

3.8 ADDITIONAL READING

3.1 Daniel H. Sheingold, ed., *Analog-Digital Conversion Handbook,* Prentice Hall, Englewood Cliffs, NJ, 1986.

Laboratory Exercise 7

Introduction to A/D
and D/A Conversion

PURPOSE

To use an analog I/O board and to measure the characteristics of analog-to-digital and digital-to-analog converters.

EQUIPMENT

- IBM AT with Data Acquisition and Control Adapter
- oscilloscope
- digital multimeter
- ±12-V power supplies
- superstrip circuit board
- one 10-kΩ resistor
- one 10-kΩ 10-turn helipot (helical potentiometer)
- 10-µF electrolytic capacitor

ADDITIONAL READING

Chapter 3 (Analog↔Digital Conversion and Sampling).

Appendix E (Summary of IBM Data Acquisition and Control Adapter).

PROCEDURE

1 Circuit Construction

Construct a voltage divider as shown in Laboratory Figure 7.1, using a 10-turn 10-kΩ helipot connected between –11 V and +11 V. Connect the wiper to your digital multimeter and the positive input of the data-acquisition circuit (Channel 0+, pin 6). Connect the power supply ground to the negative input (Channel 0–, pin 5) and pins 4, 13, 15, and 60.

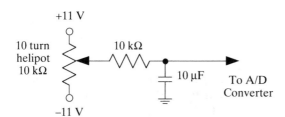

Laboratory Figure 7.1   Voltage source for A/D converter.

2 A/D Conversion

The IBM Data Acquisition and Control Adapter uses the AD574A 12-bit analog-to-digital converter, connected for a ±10 V input range. An input of –10 V produces a digital output of 0. An input of 0 V produces a digital output of about 2047. An input of +10 V produces a digital output of about 4095. One output count corresponds to an input change of about 5 mV.

You will use a computer program that controls the analog to digital conversion and prints the result on the screen in an endless loop. This program is started by typing "ADC" and then pressing the return key. The program takes a number of samples, prints them on the screen, and prints the average.

2.1 End-point voltages.   Adjust the 10-kΩ trimpot to find the largest voltage that gives an A/D digital output of 0. Record the multimeter value. Then find and record the smallest voltage that gives an A/D digital output of 4095. These numbers are the full input range of the A/D. If 60-Hz noise prevents accurate A/D conversions, put a low-pass *RC* filter between the trimpot and the data acquisition circuit. (*Note:* Always observe the polarity of large electrolytic capacitors because reversing the polarity can cause them to explode.)

2.2 Transition voltages.   Adjust the input voltage to produce an output of 2047. Slowly increase the input voltage. Observe and record the *exact* voltage at which the V(2047, 2048) transition occurs. This will be indicated by an average of 2047.5. Repeat for the $V(2048, 2049)$ transition. These values should occur near 0.0 V where the multimeter has an accuracy of about 0.2 mV. Repeat for several pairs of neighboring transition voltages spanning the full range, such as

$V(0, 1)$	$V(1, 2)$
$V(999, 1000)$	$V(1000, 1001)$
$V(1699, 1700)$	$V(1700, 1701)$
$V(2049, 2050)$	$V(2050, 2051)$
$V(2399, 2400)$	$V(2400, 2401)$
$V(2999, 3000)$	$V(3000, 3001)$
$V(3999, 4000)$	$V(4000, 4001)$

3 D/A Conversion

The IBM Data Acquisition and Control Adapter uses the AD7545 12-bit digital-to-analog converter, connected for ±10 V operation. In analogy with the A/D converter, digital inputs of 0, 2047, and 4095 produce corresponding analog outputs of about –10 V, 0 V, and +10 V.

You will use a computer program that reads digital input (decimal) from the keyboard and converts the result to an analog output that appears on "D/A output 1." Start the digital-to-analog program by typing "DAC" and pressing return.

3.1 End point voltages. Record the output voltages corresponding to input numbers of 0 and 4095.

3.2 Output voltages. Record the outputs for several pairs of neighboring input numbers spanning the full range, such as

0	1
999	1000
1699	1700
2047	2048
2049	2050
2399	2400
2999	3000
4000	4001

LABORATORY REPORT

1 Setup

Draw a simple block diagram of your experimental set-up.

2 Data Summary

2.1 A/D transition voltages.   Using your data from procedure section 2, tabulate transition voltages $V(n, n + 1)$ vs. n.

2.2 A/D differential linearity.   Using your data from procedure section 2.3, tabulate the differences $V(n, n - 1) - V(n + 1, n)$ between neighboring transition voltages. The uniformity of the intervals between transition voltages is a measure of differential linearity.

2.3 D/A response.   Using your data from procedure section 3, tabulate output voltage $V(n)$ vs. D/A input number n.

2.4 D/A differential linearity.   Using your data from procedure section 3.2, tabulate the differences between neighboring output voltages $V_n - V_{n-1}$. The uniformity of output step size is a measure of differential linearity.

3 Analysis

3.1 A/D measurements.   Plot transition voltages vs. digital output for the A/D converter and draw a best-fit line through the data (eyeball).

3.2 A/D model.   Using the end-point voltages, compute the slope and intercept of the A/D data and derive a linear formula relating the transition voltage $V(n, n + 1)$ to n.

3.3 A/D comparison between measurements and model.
Tabulate your A/D model values, your measured transition voltages, and compute the differences between them.

3.4 D/A measurements.   Plot output voltages vs. digital input for the D/A converter and draw a best-fit line through the data (eyeball).

3.5 D/A model.   Using the end-point voltages, compute the slope and intercept of the D/A data and derive a linear formula relating the input number n and the output voltage $V(n)$.

3.6 D/A comparison between measurements and model.
Tabulate your D/A model values, your measured values, and compute the differences between them.

4 Discussion and Conclusions

Discuss your measured values and compare with the data sheets.

5 Questions

5.1   How linear were the responses of the A/D and D/A converters?

5.2   Were the differential linearities of the A/D and D/A converters within specifications?

5.3   Were the slopes and zero intercepts what you expected?

5.4   For the A/D and D/A converters, what were the largest deviations between your data and the best-fit lines?

6 Laboratory Data Sheets

Include your handwritten data sheets (or a copy), which should consist of a log of the procedures that you used, any special circumstances, and the measurements you recorded manually.

Laboratory Exercise 8

D/A Conversion
and Waveform Generation

PURPOSE

To interface a microcomputer to a D/A converter, and to write a C program that generates static voltage levels and time-varying waveforms. To determine the deviation between the output and a linear model.

EQUIPMENT

- IBM AT with IBM Data Acquisition and Control Adapter (binary I/O device used)
- printer (shared with other lab stations)
- +5-V, ±12-V power supplies
- digital multimeter
- three 10-µF, 20-V electrolytic capacitors
- parallel port ribbon cable for connecting binary I/O port to student circuit boards
- superstrip circuit board
- one AD558 D/A converter chip

ADDITIONAL READING

Chapter 3, Section 3.2: Digital-to-Analog Converter Circuits.

Appendix E (Summary of IBM Data Acquisition and Control Adapter), Section 1: Cable Pinout and Section 2: Binary Output.

PROCEDURE

1 Circuit Construction

Connect the AD558 D/A converter to the binary output bits 0 to 7 of the IBM Data Acquisition and Control Adapter ribbon cable. Refer to the cable connector diagrams given in Appendix E, Section 1, and the AD558 pinout in Laboratory Figure 8.1.

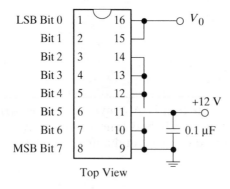

Top View

Laboratory Figure 8.1   Pinout for AD558 D/A converter. Output is 0 to 10 V for an input from 0 to 255.

Connect BO-0 to BO-7 to pins 1–8 of the D/A converter. Connect a 0.1 µF capacitor between +12 volts and ground. Connect the power supply ground to the digital grounds of the IBM Data Acquisition and Control Adapter (pins 15 and 60).

2 End-Point Voltages

Write a simple program that asks the user for a number between 0 and 255, writes that number into the D/A, and loops back for another number. See Appendix E, Section 2, for the code that performs binary output without handshaking.

Load 0 and record the minimum analog output voltage V_{min} (should be near 0.00 volts).

Load 255 and record the maximum analog output voltage V_{max} (should be near 9.96 volts).

3 Power-Supply Sensitivity

3.1 Reduce the +12-volt power supply to +11.6 volts (a 3% decrease). Record the output voltages for D/A inputs 0, 128, and 255.

3.2 Restore the power supply to +12 volts and recheck the output voltages for D/A inputs 0 and 255.

4 Glitches and Settling Time

Write a C program to alternately output 0x7F (127 decimal) and 0x80 (128 decimal) to the D/A. Look at the output on the oscilloscope. Using ac scope coupling, sketch the appearance of the waveform. Observe the voltage steps, and record the height (in mV) and the width (in μs). Look at the step edges and record the settling time. Look at the glitches and record the amplitude, width, and shape. If time permits, repeat for one other major bit transition, such as between 0x3F (63 decimal) and 0x40 (64 decimal).

5 Linearity

Write a C program that does the following:

1. Ask the user for a number n ranging from 0 to 255.
2. Write the number entered by the user to the parallel output port.
3. Ask the user to enter the voltage V_n measured by the digital multimeter and then reads and stores the value as type "float."

Run the program for about 10 neighboring values of n spanning the full range. Example:

0	1
3	4
9	10
19	20
29	30
49	50
99	100
149	150
199	200
254	255

6 Waveform Generation

6.1 Ramp waveform.
Change your program to send the series

$$0, 1, 2, \ldots, 255, 0, 1, \ldots, 255, 0, 1, \ldots$$

to the D/A as rapidly as you can. Look at the output of the D/A with the oscilloscope to determine the time between peaks. Expand the horizontal (time) and vertical (amplitude) scales of the oscilloscope so that you can clearly see the individual "steps" of the ramp. Describe the waveform and record the step height (in mV), step width (in μs).

6.2 Other waveform. Devise some other waveform (sine, decaying sine, decaying exponential, etc.) and write a program to rapidly send it to the D/A converter. If your waveform is noncyclic, you will have to compute each new value before you can send it to the D/A. If your waveform is cyclic, you can precompute the values and store them in an array. Then these values can be sent much more quickly to the D/A in an endless loop. Record the time interval between D/A output steps.

LABORATORY REPORT

1 Setup

Draw a simple block diagram of your experimental setup, showing the components on your circuit board as well as the connections to the parallel output port.

2 Data Summary and Analysis

2.1 Comparison between measurements and model. Compare your data with the linear model $V(n) = V_0 + n \, \Delta V$. The average voltage step $\Delta V = (V_{255} - V_0)/255$ corresponds to 1 LSB. Have your program print your results in a table with the following headings:

- n
- V_n measured D/A output voltages
- Linear model $V(n) = V_0 + n \, \Delta V$
- Difference $V_n - V(n)$ in mV
- Difference $[V_n - V(n)]/\Delta V$ in LSB
- Difference $[V_n - V(n)]/V(n)$ in percent

2.2 rms deviation. Have your program compute the rms deviation V_{rms} between your data and the linear model:

$$V_{\text{rms}} = \sqrt{\frac{1}{N} \sum_{n=1}^{N} \left[V(n) - V_n \right]^2}$$

2.3 Differential linearity.   Tabulate $V_n - V_{n-1}$ from your measured data for several values of n.   Estimate differential nonlinearity in units of LSB.

2.4 Power-supply sensitivity.   For $n = 0$, 128, and 255, compute the power-supply sensitivity G_P as

$$G_P = \frac{\Delta V_n}{\Delta V_S}$$

where ΔV_n is the change in D/A output for a power supply change ΔV_S.

3 Discussion and Conclusions

3.1   Discuss procedure sections 2 to 6.

3.2   Describe how the AD558 D/A you used differs from the specifications promised in the data sheets in terms of accuracy, linearity, differential linearity, glitch amplitude, settling time, and power-supply sensitivity.

4 Questions

4.1   How rapidly (in numbers per second) were you able to send data to the D/A?

4.2   What was the maximum millivolt deviation between your observed D/A output and the straight-line model? What was the maximum percentage deviation?

4.3   How does your answer to Question 4.2 compare with the rated accuracy of your digital multimeter (typically 0.1% plus 1 digit)?

5 Program and Laboratory Data Sheets

5.1   Include printouts of your program code, data, and output.

5.2   Include your handwritten data sheets (or a copy), which should consist of a log of the procedures you used, any special circumstances, and the measurements you recorded manually.

Laboratory Exercise 9

A/D Conversion
and Periodic Sampling

PURPOSE

To interface a microcomputer to an A/D converter, to gain familiarity with the timing relationship between digital control pulses and converted data, to explore the properties of the A/D converter, and to sample a sine wave.

EQUIPMENT

- IBM AT with Data Acquisition and Control Adapter
- printer (shared with other lab stations)
- +5-V, ±12-V power supplies
- additional +5-V supply (for V_{ref}^+ if using the AD7820)
- parallel port ribbon cable
- superstrip circuit board with ground plane and connections for ground, +5 V, ±12 V
- three 10-µF, electrolytic capacitors (put between power and ground at circuit board)
- ten 0.1-µF CK05 bypass capacitors (put between power and ground on all chips)
- digital multimeter

- one AD670 or AD7820 analog-to-digital converter chip
- one AD582 sample-and-hold amplifier chip
- one 74LS123 dual one-shot chip
- one 74LS74 dual D-type flip-flop (if using the AD760)
- one 300-pF capacitor
- two 0.001-µF capacitors
- two 5-kΩ resistors
- one 10-kΩ resistor
- one 1-kΩ trimpot
- one 20-kΩ trimpot
- one 50-kΩ trimpot

ADDITIONAL READING

Chapter 1, Section 1.5.2: The Parallel Input Port and Section 1.6: Digital Data-Acquisition Procedures.

Chapter 2, Section 2.7: The Sample-and-Hold Amplifier.

Chapter 3, Section 3.3: Analog-to-Digital Converter Circuits.

Appendix E (Summary of the IBM Data Acquisition and Control Adapter), Section 1: Introduction and Section 3: Binary Input.

PROCEDURE

1 Circuit Construction

Set up one of the data-acquisition circuits shown in Laboratory Figure 9.1 (if using the AD670 A/D converter) or Laboratory Figure 9.2 (if using the AD7820 A/D converter). See Laboratory Figures 9.3 and 9.4 for chip pinouts. The AD670 A/D converter uses the successive approximation method, has 8 output bits, and converts in 10 µsec. The AD7820 A/D converter uses a subranging flash method, has 8 output bits and converts in 2 µsec. Connect the power-supply ground to the digital grounds of the IBM Data Acquisition and Control Adapter (pins 15 and 60 of the ribbon cable). Let pin 34 (BI HOLD) float, which will make the binary input port transparent. Mark all supply voltage points and the exact location of the ribbon cable with masking tape. This is important since these connections will be taken apart every time the circuit is put away.

Note that a larger holding capacitor on the sample-and-hold amplifier slows acquisition time, whereas a smaller holding capacitor loses its charge more rapidly (see Chapter 3, Problem 3.2). Here we have chosen 300 pF.

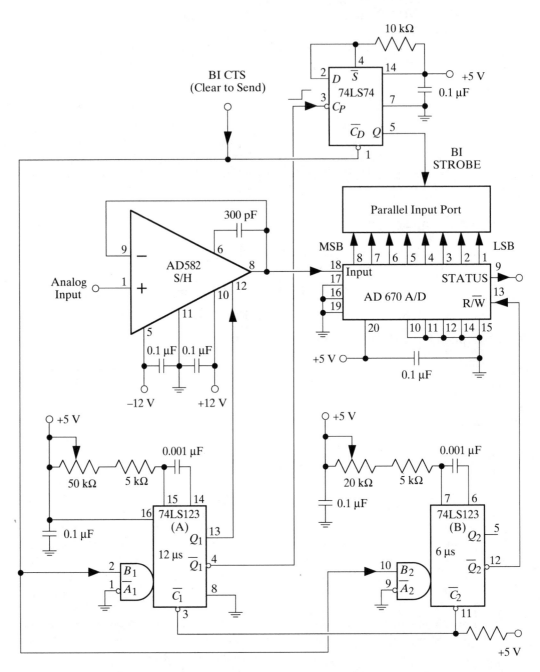

Laboratory Figure 9.1 AD670 data acquisition circuit. See Laboratory Figures 9.3 and 9.4 for chip pinouts.

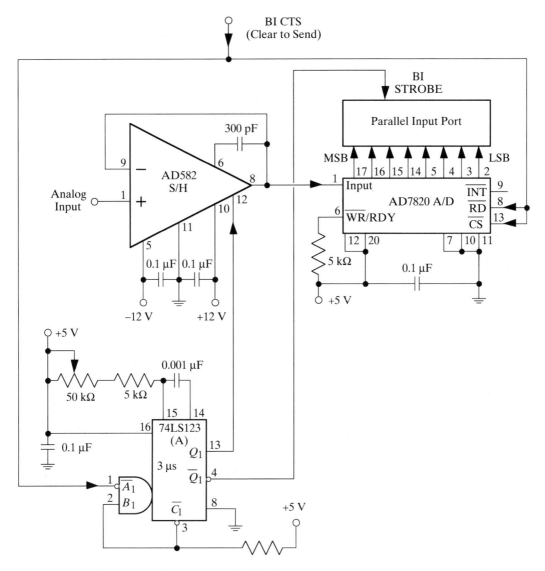

Laboratory Figure 9.2   AD7820 Data acquisition circuit. See Laboratory Figures 9.3 and 9.4 for chip pinouts.

1.1 AD670 Circuit Operation

Set the range of the AD670 A/D converter from 0 to +2.55 volts (10 mV/count) by connecting pins 17 and 19 to ground. Pin 16 is $-V_{in}$ and pin 18 is $+V_{in}$. [For a 0- to +0.255-volt range (1 mV/count), you would tie pins 16 and 17 together ($-V_{in}$) and tie pins 18 and 19 together ($+V_{in}$).] Connect 11 and 12 to ground for unipolar/straight binary.

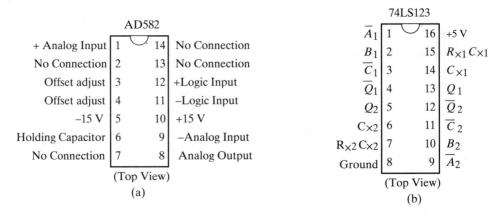

Laboratory Figure 9.3   Pinouts for (a) the AD 670 A/D converter and (b) the AD7820 A/D converter (b).

AD670 (Top View) (a):

Data Bit 0 (LSB)	1	20	+5 V
Data Bit 1	2	19	$+V_{in}$ LOW
Data Bit 2	3	18	$+V_{in}$ HIGH
Data Bit 3	4	17	$-V_{in}$ LOW
Data Bit 4	5	16	$-V_{in}$ HIGH
Data Bit 5	6	15	$\overline{CE}$
Data Bit 6	7	14	$\overline{CS}$
Data Bit 7 (MSB)	8	13	$R/\overline{W}$
STATUS Output	9	12	2's compl./$\overline{binary}$
Power ground	10	11	Bipolar/$\overline{unipolar}$

AD7820 (Top View) (b):

V_{in}	1	20	+5 V
Data Bit 0 (LSB)	2	19	No connection
Data Bit 1	3	18	$\overline{OFL}$
Data Bit 2	4	17	Data Bit 7 (MSB)
Data Bit 3	5	16	Data Bit 6
WR/$\overline{RDY}$	6	15	Data Bit 5
MODE	7	14	Data Bit 4
$\overline{RD}$	8	13	$\overline{CS}$
$\overline{INT}$	9	12	V_{ref}^+
Power ground	10	11	V_{ref}^-

Laboratory Figure 9.4   Pinouts for (a) the AD582 sample-and-hold amplifier and (b) the 74LS123 dual one-shot.

AD582 (Top View) (a):

+ Analog Input	1	14	No Connection
No Connection	2	13	No Connection
Offset adjust	3	12	+Logic Input
Offset adjust	4	11	−Logic Input
−15 V	5	10	+15 V
Holding Capacitor	6	9	−Analog Input
No Connection	7	8	Analog Output

74LS123 (Top View) (b):

$\overline{A}_1$	1	16	+5 V
B_1	2	15	$R_{\times 1}C_{\times 1}$
$\overline{C}_1$	3	14	$C_{\times 1}$
$\overline{Q}_1$	4	13	Q_1
Q_2	5	12	$\overline{Q}_2$
$C_{\times 2}$	6	11	$\overline{C}_2$
$R_{\times 2}C_{\times 2}$	7	10	B_2
Ground	8	9	$\overline{A}_2$

The following steps describe the operation of the data acquisition circuit using the AD670 A/D converter. See Laboratory Figure 9.5 for the timing diagram and Appendix E, Section 3, for the details on binary input.

1. Your program selects the binary I/O device on the IBM Data Acquisition and Control Adapter.
2. The program puts the external line BI CTS (Clear To Send) high, and the low-to-high transition starts the 2 one-shots on your circuit board.

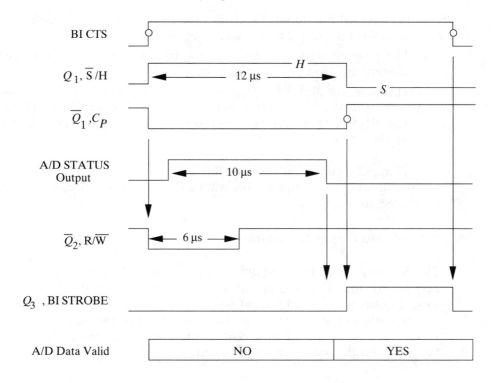

Laboratory Figure 9.5   Timing diagram for AD670 data-acquisition circuit.

3. The first one-shot is adjusted to produce 12-µs wide pulses and performs two functions. Firstly, Q_1 goes high to switch the sample-and-hold amplifier from the sample to the hold mode. Secondly, the high-to-low edge of Q_1 clocks the D-type flip-flop and starts the BI STROBE pulse that the program recognizes as the signal to read new data.

4. The second one-shot is adjusted for a 6-µs wide low pulse. The high-to-low edge of Q_2 starts the AD670 A/D converter chip, and the low-to-high edge enables the AD670 to put the converted data onto its output lines. *Check with an oscilloscope:* The Q_2 low-to-high edge should occur while the AD670 STATUS Output line is still high.

5. When the sample-and-hold amplifier switches to the hold mode, the 5-volt logic transition causes the output to ring for a few hundred nanoseconds. The circuit is designed to switch the S/H to the hold mode as soon as possible, on the low-to-high edge of the first one-shot. Conversion starts 700 ns after this edge, when the S/H output has stabilized.

6. When the AD670 STATUS line goes high to low, **its output lines do not have valid data until 250 ns later.** *Check with an oscilloscope:* Q_1 high-to-low edge occurs at least 500 ns after the high-to-low edge of the STATUS line and the low-to-high edge of Q_1 edge clocks the D-type flip-flop, whose output Q_3 makes the BI STROBE pulse high. This, in turn, sets bit 0 of the binary status register to 1.

7. The program waits for bit 0 of the binary status register to become nonzero and then reads the new data.

8. The program puts BI CTS low, which clears the D-type flip-flop and terminates the BI STROBE pulse. *Check with an oscilloscope:* BI CTS and BI STROBE return to ground simultaneously and have pulse widths < 50 μs.

To rapidly sample analog waveforms, do steps 2 to 8 in a tight loop. Do not perform any printf operations within the data-acquisition loop or it will be slowed considerably.

1.2 AD7820 Circuit Operation

The range of the AD7820 input is from V_{ref}^- (pin 11) to V_{ref}^+ (pin 12). Connect pins 10 and 11 to ground and connect pin 20 to + 5 volts. Connect pin 12 to +2.55 volts using an additional power supply. The following steps describe the operation of the data-acquisition circuit using the AD7820 A/D converter. See Laboratory Figure 9.6 for the timing diagram and Appendix E, Section 3, for the details on binary input.

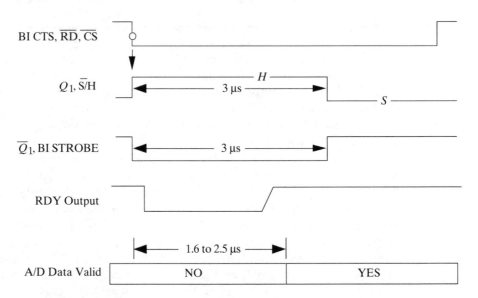

Laboratory Figure 9.6   Timing diagram for AD7820 data acquisition circuit.

1. Your program selects the binary I/O device on the IBM Data Acquisition and Control Adapter, and then puts the external line BI CTS (Binary Input Clear To Send) high.

2. The program puts BI CTS (Binary Input Clear To Send) low, which also makes $\overline{\text{RD}}$ low, initiating A/D conversion. ($\overline{\text{RD}}$ must be kept low until the digital data have been read.)

3. The BI CTS high-to-low transition starts the one-shot on the circuit board.

4. The one-shot is adjusted for a 3 μs wide pulse, and performs the following functions:

(i) The leading low-to-high edge of Q_1 switches the sample-and-hold amplifier to the hold mode.

(ii) The leading high-to-low edge of $\overline{Q}_1$ pulls BI STROBE down, which prevents the program from reading the data until conversion is complete.

(iii) *Check with an oscilloscope:* BI STROBE goes high after RDY goes high by an interval in the range from 1 to 20 μsec.

5. The program waits for bit 0 of the binary status register to become non-zero and then reads the new data.

6. The program puts BI CTS high, which also puts $\overline{\text{RD}}$ high.

To rapidly sample analog waveforms, do steps 2 to 6 in a tight loop. Do not perform any printf operations within the data-acquisition loop or it will be slowed considerably. These steps should be done in a subsequent loop.

2 Measurement of A/D Characteristics

2.1 Program. Write a C program that loops endlessly over the following two steps:

1. Reads the I/O port.

2. Writes the number to the terminal screen.

2.2 Voltage divider. As shown in Laboratory Figure 9.7, construct a voltage divider using a 20-turn 1-kΩ trimpot connected between +5 volts and ground. Connect the wiper to the input of the data-acquisition circuit and your digital multimeter. Bypass the sample-and-hold amplifier in this section and connect the wiper directly to the A/D converter if noise makes it difficult to measure transition voltages accurately.

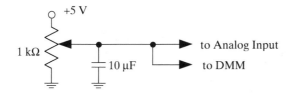

Laboratory Figure 9.7 Voltage source for S/H amplifier.

2.3 Transition voltage measurements. Start with zero input voltage. Slowly increase until reaching the first transition voltage $V(0, 1)$ where the digital output toggles between 0 and 1 and has an average value of 0.5. Record the *exact* input voltage displayed on the digital multimeter. Record a table of neighboring pairs of transition voltages spanning the full range, such as

$V(0,1)$	$V(1,2)$
$V(2,3)$	$V(3,4)$
$V(49, 50)$	$V(50, 51)$
$V(99, 100)$	$V(100, 101)$
$V(149, 150)$	$V(150, 151)$
$V(199, 200)$	$V(200, 201)$
$V(253, 254)$	$V(254, 255)$

2.4 Hysteresis. Slowly reduce the input voltage and record the transition voltages for $V(2, 1)$ and $V(1, 0)$. The reversed indices here mean that the transition voltage was approached from above.

2.5 Power supply sensitivity. Change the +5-volt power supply (pin 20 on both the AD670 and the AD7820) to +4.85 volts (a 3% decrease). Leave the + 15-volt and –15-volt supplies unchanged. Record the $V(0, 1)$ and $V(254, 255)$ transition voltages. Restore the power supply to +5 volts.

3 Sampling a Sine Wave

Set the wave generator for a 100 Hz sine wave oscillating between about 0.5 volts and 2 volts as measured on your oscilloscope. Connect the wave generator to the sample-and-hold amplifier input. Connect the sample-and-hold output to the input of the A/D converter. Change your program to sample 100 values in a tight data-acquisition loop and then store the values in a file for display and printing using the PLOT program. You should have enough data for at least two full cycles.

LABORATORY REPORT

1 Setup

1.1 Draw a simple block diagram of your experimental setup.

1.2 Draw your timing diagram as you saw it on the oscilloscope. Include slightly more than one sampling cycle.

2　Data Summary and Analysis

2.1 Comparison between measurements and model.　Define $V(n, n + 1)$ as the measured transition voltage (where the output toggles between n and $n + 1$).　The linear model is given by

$$V^*(n, n + 1) = V(0, 1) + n\,\Delta V, \text{ where } \Delta V = [V(254, 255) - V(0, 1)]/254.$$

Note that this line passes through the measured end points, since $V^*(0, 1) = V(0, 1)$ and $V^*(254, 255) = V(254, 255)$.　Have your program compare the data with the linear model by printing the results in a table with the following headings:

- n
- $V(n, n + 1)$ measured transition voltages
- Linear model $V^*(n, n + 1) = V_0 + n\,\Delta V$
- Difference $V(n, n + 1) - V^*(n, n + 1)$ in mV
- Difference $[V(n, n + 1) - V^*(n, n + 1)]/\Delta V$ in LSB
- Difference $[V(n, n + 1) - V^*(n, n + 1)]/V^*(n, n + 1)$ in percent

2.2 Differential linearity.　Tabulate $V(n, n + 1) - V(n - 1, n)$ from your data to determine differential linearity error.

2.3 rms deviation.　Compute the rms deviation between $V(n, n + 1)$ and $V^*(n, n + 1)$.

2.4 Sampling frequency.　From the 100-Hz sine wave in procedure section 3, compute your sampling frequency in samples per second. (Frequency aliasing will not occur if you sample more than twice per sine wave.)

2.5 Power supply sensitivity.　For the V(0, 1) and V(254, 255) transition voltages, compute the power-supply sensitivity G$_P$ as

$$G_P = \frac{\Delta V(n, n + 1)}{\Delta V_S}$$

where $\Delta V(n, n + 1)$ is the change in transition voltage for a change in power supply voltage V_S.

3　Discussion and Conclusions

3.1　Discuss procedure sections 2 and 3.

3.2　Describe how your A/D differed from the specifications promised in the data sheets in terms of resolution, absolute (unadjusted) accuracy, linearity, differential linearity, conversion speed, and power-supply rejection.

4 Questions

4.1   Was the $V(0, 1)$ transition voltage what you expected? The $V(254, 255)$ transition?

4.2   What was the largest millivolt deviation between your transition data and the best straight line fit?   What was the largest percentage deviation?

4.3   What was your sampling frequency in procedure section 3? What is the maximum frequency sine wave that your system can sample without aliasing?

5 Program and Laboratory Data Sheets

5.1   Include printouts of your program code, data, and output.

5.2   Include your handwritten data sheets (or a copy), which should consist of a log of the procedures you used, any special circumstances, and the measurements you recorded manually.

Laboratory Exercise 10

Frequency Aliasing

PURPOSE

To use the analog I/O device on the IBM Data Acquisition and Control Adapter to sample sine waves of various frequencies, to output the sampled data in analog form, and to observe frequency aliasing.

EQUIPMENT

- IBM AT with IBM Data Acquisition and Control Adapter
- printer (shared with other IBM AT lab stations)
- wave generator
- oscilloscope

ADDITIONAL READING

Chapter 3, Section 3.4: Sampling Analog Waveforms and Section 3.5: Frequency Aliasing.

Appendix E (Summary of the IBM Data Acquisition and Control Adapter), Section 5: Analog Input and Section 6: Analog Output.

PROCEDURE

1 Program

As described in Appendix E, Section 5 (Analog Input), write a program to perform A/D conversion of 512 samples of an analog waveform in a tight loop, and then (as described in Section 6, Analog Output) to convert the stored values back into analog form. Since the A/D input loop is slower than the D/A output loop, you have to delay the D/A loop to get the same play-back rate.

2 Sampling a 100-Hz Sine Wave

Set the sine wave generator at 100 Hz and 5 V p-p as measured on your oscil-loscope. Connect the output to the input of the analog input device (pin 6). Connect the wave generator ground to pins 4, 5, 13, 15, and 60. Run your program to convert the sine wave into digital form, and write the numbers to a file for printing and plotting. These data will be used to compute the sampling frequency R_S of your program and the IBM analog input device.

3 Analog Recovery of Sampled Data

Change your program so that it is able to store the digital values, convert the values back into analog form, and display the recovered waveform on the oscilloscope.

4 Frequency Aliasing

4.1   Increase the sine-wave frequency to 0.5 R_S. Sample 512 values of the waveform in a tight acquisition loop, and display the recovered waveform on the oscilloscope in another loop. Use the "plot" program to display and print these values. Note that since the frequency is not exactly 0.5 R_S, the phase will drift and the amplitude of the observed oscillations will itself slowly oscillate. The rapid oscillations have the frequency of the sine-wave while the slow oscillations have a "beat" frequency equal to the difference between the sine wave and 0.5 R_S.

4.2   Increase the sine wave frequency to R_S, 1.5 R_S, and 2 R_S. For each, print enough of the recovered wave to estimate its apparent frequency. In each case compare the frequency of the original sine wave with the appar-ent frequency of the recovered wave.

4.3   Repeat procedure steps 4.1 and 4.2 with a triangle wave. Print enough of the recovered wave to see its frequency and shape.

LABORATORY REPORT

1 Setup

Draw a simple block diagram of your experimental setup.

2 Data Summary and Analysis

2.1   From the 100-Hz sine wave in procedure section 2, compute your sampling frequency in samples per second.   Frequency aliasing will not occur with a slow sine wave.

2.2   For all the sine-wave and triangle-wave frequencies you sampled, compare the actual frequency with the apparent frequency of the recovered waveform.

3 Discussion and Conclusions

Discuss procedure sections 2 to 4.   Explain how you measured the sampling frequency in procedure section 2, and discuss the waveforms you observed.

4 Questions

4.1   What was your sampling frequency in procedure section 2?

4.2   What is the maximum frequency sine wave that your system can sample without aliasing?

4.3   Did aliasing change the shape of the triangle wave?   Why?

5 Program and Laboratory Data Sheets

5.1   Include printouts of your program code, data, and output.

5.2   Include your handwritten data sheets (or a copy), which should consist of a log of the procedures you used, any special circumstances, and the measurements you recorded manually.

4

Sensors and Actuators

4.1 INTRODUCTION

The **transducer** is a device that converts one form of energy to another. For interfacing to a microcomputer, we are primarily interested in the **electronic transducer,** which has an input or an output that is electrical in nature, such as a voltage, current, or resistance. The **sensor** is an electronic transducer that converts a physical quantity into an electrical signal. An **actuator** is an electronic transducer that converts electrical energy into a physical quantity, and is an essential element in control systems.

Sensors are used to detect displacement, temperature, strain, force, light, etc. Almost all sensors require additional circuits to produce the voltage and current needed for analog-to-digital conversion. As we shall see in this chapter, the thermistor changes its electrical resistance as a function of temperature, and a bridge is needed to produce a corresponding voltage, whereas the silicon photodiode produces a current, and a stage of amplification is needed to produce a voltage. Often, the term "sensor" includes both the transducer and the circuits needed to produce an output voltage.

Laboratory Exercise 11 uses a circular resistor and a computer to record angle and the oscillations of a damped pendulum. Laboratory Exercise 12 explores the measurement of temperature using the dial thermometer, a platinum resistance thermometer, the thermocouple, and the thermistor. Laboratory Exercise 13 measures force, using four metal foil strain gauges bonded to a plastic rod and wired in opposing pairs to form a bridge circuit. Laboratory Exercise 14 uses a silicon photodiode to measure light and the absorption of light by colored solutions. Laboratory Exercise 15 explores the thermoelectric heat pump and its ability to heat and cool a small system. Laboratory Exercise 16 measures the offset potential and frequency-dependent complex impedance for bare metal and Ag(AgCl) electrodes. Laboratory Exercise 17 measures the human electrocardiogram (ECG), phonocardiogram, and blood pressure. Laboratory Exercise 18 amplifies and processes the electromyogram (EMG) from the skin surface and relates it to the mechanical tension produced by the underlying muscles. Laboratory Exercise 19 measures the position of the eyes using the electrooculogram (EOG) to determine the maximum angular velocity of voluntary and involuntary eye motion.

Several important characteristics that are common to most sensors are now described.

1. The **response** of a sensor is its output as a function of the quantity being sensed. It is usually expressed in terms of a curve or a formula.

2. The **sensitivity** of an sensor is defined as the change in output for a unit change in the quantity being sensed. This is the first derivative of the response curve and generally depends on the value of the quantity being measured. For example, the Iron-Constantan thermocouple has a sensitivity of 50 μV/°C at 0°C.

3. The **linearity error** of a sensor is the difference between the sensor response and either a best-fit straight line or a straight line passing through the end points. In either case, the value of the linearity will depend on the range of measurements used. Generally, sensors become more linear as the measurement range is restricted. For example, the thermocouple output depends almost linearly on temperature over a wide range. On the other hand, the thermistor resistance depends exponentially on temperature and the linear approximation is poor even over a small temperature range.

4. The **accuracy error** of a sensor is the difference between the measured quantity and the "true" value, as defined by accepted standards. The measured quantity is determined from the sensor output and the "ideal" relationship between output and input.

5. The **precision** of a sensor is the ability to detect reliably small changes in the measured quantity, and the ability to measure the same value under repeated identical conditions.

6. The **stability** of a sensor is the ability to maintain the same response and noise level, despite the effects of time and usage.

7. The **noise** of a sensor is any component of the output that would be interpreted as a signal but does not depend on the quantity being

sensed. This includes thermal noise in resistors, shot noise in amplifier elements, external electrical interference, etc.

8. The **response time** of a sensor is the characteristic time required to respond to an abrupt change in the quantity being sensed. Under these conditions, the sensor output typically changes quickly at first, and then levels off asymptotically to a new steady value. For a simple system, this behavior is often described by

$$V(t) = V_2 + (V_1 - V_2)\, e^{-t/\tau}$$

where V_1 is the initial output value, V_2 is the final (asymptotic) value, and τ is the exponential response time. To estimate τ, plot $V(t)$ and draw a horizontal line 63.2% of the way from V_1 to V_2. The curve will pass through this line at $t = \tau$. Several time constants may be required before the output agrees with its final value within the desired accuracy. For example, if an accuracy of 0.5% of $V_2 - V_1$ is desired (and the previous formula is appropriate), then it is necessary to wait 5.3τ.

9. The **temperature coefficient** of a sensor is the change in a quantity per unit temperature change. This is an important characteristic of sensors used to measure quantities other than temperature but are nonetheless sensitive to temperature. For example, the temperature coefficient applies to the leakage current and offset voltage of an amplifier, the dark current of a silicon photodiode, the change in resistance of a strain gauge, etc.

10. The **hysteresis** of a sensor is the dependence of its output on previous history. It is very common in magnetic and mechanical systems (backlash).

Table 4.1 lists a some examples of physical quantities and the associated sensors and actuators.

TABLE 4.1   EXAMPLES OF SENSORS AND ACTUATORS

Real-World Quantity	Sensor	Actuator
Motion	Digital encoder	Stepping motor
Temperature	Thermocouple	Resistor
Strain	Resistive wire	Piezoelectric
Force	Load cell	Motor
Light	Photocell	Light bulb
Image	CCD camera	Laser printer
Pressure	Strain gauge membrane	Pump
Radiation (p, α, β, γ, etc.)	Geiger counter	Cyclotron
Radio Waves	Radio receiver	Radio transmitter

4.2 POSITION SENSORS

4.2.1 The Potentiometer

The potentiometer consists of a resistive element distributed around an arc or along a line and a sliding contact connected to a shaft. Electrical connections are provided to each end of the resistor and the sliding contact (Figure 4.1). By providing a fixed voltage across the entire resistor, the potential of the sliding contact depends on the position or angle of the connected shaft. This sensor is used in Laboratory Exercise 11 to measure angle and the damped pendulum.

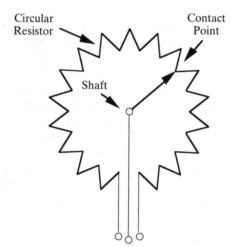

Figure 4.1   Rotary potentiometer, which relates a shaft angle to a contact point along a circular resistor.

The common 3/4-turn potentiometer has limited range and accuracy when used as an angle transducer, but 5- to 20-turn rotary potentiometers are made with accuracies and linearities of 0.1% In many cases, this is sufficient for the application and much simpler and less costly than the digital encoders discussed in the next section.

For sensing linear motion, tensioned steel cables and pulleys are used with accurate multiturn rotary potentiometers. Another approach is to use a linear potentiometer, as shown in Figure 4.2.

4.2.2 Digital Rotary Encoders

The digital rotary encoder provides a very precise conversion from a shaft angle to a digital number. There are two basic types. The **relative-position encoder** consists of a disk with a pattern of uniformly spaced marks and a

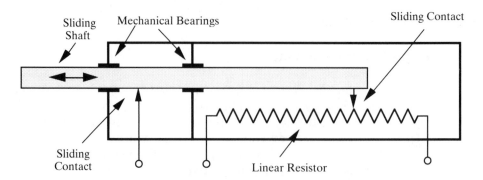

Figure 4.2 Linear potentiometer, which relates a position to a contact point along a linear resistor.

sensor that detects the marks and produces pulses as the disk is rotated. The pulses are counted to give a number whose value is proportional to relative position.

The **absolute-position encoder** has several concentric circular patterns of marks that can be uniquely related to the absolute angle or position. Unlike the absolute-position encoder, the relative-position encoder loses track of position after a power shutdown and accuracy is lost if any bit error occurs. Early designs of absolute-position encoders used patterns of insulating and conducting regions. The conducting regions were detected by electrical contacts made by "brushes" (similar to those in small electric motors), and these encoders are called "brush encoders." The primary problem with the brush encoder is bit errors due to dust, oil, oxide layers, and the occasional loss of electrical contact with the rotating surface. Modern "optical encoders" use patterns of opaque and transparent regions, where the transparent regions are detected optically (using light-emitting diodes and silicon photodiodes).

If the pattern is arranged in a binary code, as shown in the left side of Figure 4.3, and an array of light-emitting diodes and photodiodes are placed on opposite sides of the pattern, the angular position is transformed to a series of "zeros" and "ones", depending on whether light can pass through the segments of the pattern. However, many bits can switch at a single transition (e.g., between 01111 and 10000), and since there is no way of ensuring that all bits will switch at exactly the same instant, it is possible to read an incorrect code at the transition. Adding an additional timing bit to the pattern will provide a pulse that can be used to latch the data into a buffer only when all bits are stable, but it is more common to overcome this problem by arranging the pattern in the Gray code, where only one bit switches at a time (Figure 4.3, Table 1.3). With Gray code, all bits are always valid and may be read at any time. However, the circuit that converts from Gray to binary code (Figure 1.9) does not have reliable data during the conversion and should be read only after conversion is complete.

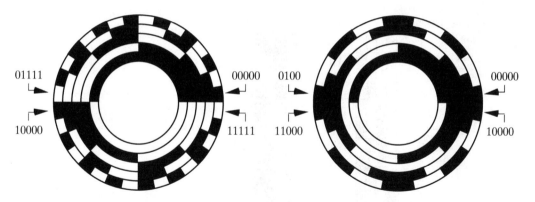

01111   00000   0100   00000

10000   11111   11000   10000

Figure 4.3 Optical-encoder patterns. The dark portion of the pattern represents a "zero" (blocks light) and the white portion of the pattern represents a "one" (lets light through). On the left is the binary code, where the outermost ring is the LSB and the innermost ring is the MSB. On the right is the Gray code, where only one bit switches at a time.

In both cases, 00000 is to the right and the code advances counterclockwise. Whereas five bits are shown here as an example, optical encoders range from 10 to 20 or more bits. They are more expensive than the simple potentiometer described in the previous section, but are used extensively whenever high accuracy is required. Applications include numerically controlled milling machines and optical and radio telescopes.

One technical problem that arises is the difficulty of making the photoemitters and photodetectors small enough to fit in a line across the optical mask. Usually, these elements are arranged in a spiral, and the encoder disk circles are rotated to correspond.

4.2.3 Digital Linear Encoders

The linear version of the digital encoder is shown in Figure 4.4 It is used in handheld precision digital calipers, which include batteries, Gray code to BCD conversion circuits, and digital display in English or metric units. The light emitters and sensors are shown in Figure 4.5.

4.3 TEMPERATURE TRANSDUCERS

One of the most common temperature sensors that you have seen is the mercury or alcohol thermometer, which consists of a bulb connected to a sealed capillary tube. As the temperature of the bulb changes, the liquid expands or contracts and the change in volume is transduced to a change in length in the capillary tube.

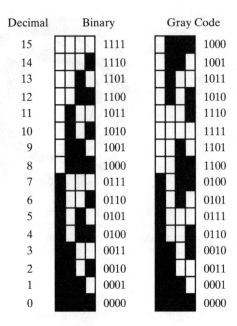

Decimal	Binary	Gray Code
15	1111	1000
14	1110	1001
13	1101	1011
12	1100	1010
11	1011	1110
10	1010	1111
9	1001	1101
8	1000	1100
7	0111	0100
6	0110	0101
5	0101	0111
4	0100	0110
3	0011	0010
2	0010	0011
1	0001	0001
0	0000	0000

Figure 4.4   Digital encoder pattern for linear position.

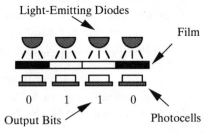

Figure 4.5   Arrangement of light-emitting diodes and photocells for reading the digital encoder pattern of Figure 4.4.

Note that there are two transduction processes: the change in temperature to a change in volume (which assumes that the temperature coefficient of the liquid is non-zero and does not change its sign over the temperature of interest) and a change in volume to a change in length (which assumes that the volume of the thermometer changes less than the volume of the liquid). Another non-electric temperature transducer is the liquid crystal thermometer, which can be purchased in drugstores and placed on the forehead to indicate fever. The most important electric temperature transducers (the platinum resistance thermometer, the thermocouple, and the thermistor) are explored in Laboratory Exercise 12.

4.3.1 Temperature Standards

The primary temperature standards are fixed temperatures produced by physical phenomena. Examples are the triple point of hydrogen at 13.81K, the triple point of water at 273.16K, and the freezing point of gold at 1337.58K.

The triple point is a specific point in the temperature vs. pressure plane where all three phases (solid, liquid, and gas) coexist in equilibrium. These are expressed in the **Kelvin** absolute thermodynamic temperature scale, where 0K corresponds to the minimum possible thermal energy. It was developed in the early 1800s by Lord Kelvin and based on the coefficient of expansion of an ideal gas.

In science and engineering, the **Celsius** temperature scale is also used and is defined with 0°C at the freezing point and 100°C at the boiling point of water at standard pressure. The triple point of water occurs at a lower pressure (6.11 mbar or 4.58 mm Hg) and is slightly warmer (0.01°C). The freezing point of water is at 273.15K, and to convert from Celsius to Kelvin scales, add 273.15. This scale was developed around 1742 by Anders Celsius.

The **Fahrenheit** temperature scale is defined by 32°F at the ice point and 212°F at the boiling point of water at standard pressure. Its use is discouraged for scientific writing. To convert from Fahrenheit to Celsius, subtract 32 and multiply by 5/9. This scale was developed in the early 1700s by Gabriel Fahrenheit, a Dutch instrument maker, who based it on a mixture of ice, water, and ammonium chloride (the lowest temperature that he could reliably produce) at 0°F and the temperature of the human body at 96°F.

The **Rankine** temperature scale is the Fahrenheit equivalent of the Kelvin temperature scale. To convert from Rankine to Fahrenheit, add 459.67.

Absolute zero is the temperature corresponding to the minimum possible thermal energy and is defined as 0K, –273.15°C, –459.67°F, and 0°R.

The **calorie** is the quantity of thermal energy required to raise 1 g of water 1°C at 15°C. It is equal to 4.1868 watt seconds. The Calorie used in nutrition (note the capital C) is 1000 times larger.

Between these fixed temperature standards, interpolation standards are used. The most practical of these is the platinum resistance thermometer.

4.3.2 Platinum Resistance Thermometer

Platinum is a noble metal that can withstand high temperatures and harsh chemical environments with good stability. The standard **platinum resistance temperature detector** (PRTD), or **platinum resistance thermometer**, is a fine platinum wire carefully trimmed to a resistance of 100.0 Ω at 0°C. The fractional change in resistance with temperature $dR/(R\,dT)$ is called "alpha" or the temperature coefficient. There are two common values for alpha, 0.00392 per °C (American alloy) and 0.00385 per °C (European alloy). Alpha drops with increasing temperature, and a more accurate expression is given for the American alloy by

$$R = 100 + 0.391T - 0.00006T^2$$

where R is the resistance in Ω, and T is the temperature in degrees Celsius. See Table 4.2 for R vs. T over a large temperature range. Usually, the platinum is used in a resistance bridge, but a digital multimeter may be used as well. For faster response and improved ruggedness, the platinum resistance thermometer is also available in the form of a thick film of platinum metal on an alumina (Al_2O_3) substrate.

TABLE 4.2   PLATINUM RESISTANCE R VS TEMPERATURE T

T (°C)	R (Ω)	T (°C)	R (Ω)	T (°C)	R (Ω)
−200	18.49	−100	60.25	0	100.00
−190	22.80	−90	64.30	10	103.90
−180	27.08	−80	68.33	20	107.79
−170	31.32	−70	72.33	30	111.67
−160	35.53	−60	76.33	40	115.54
−150	39.71	−50	80.31	50	119.40
−140	43.87	−40	84.27	60	123.24
−130	48.00	−30	88.22	70	127.07
−120	52.11	−20	92.16	80	130.89
−110	56.19	−10	96.09	90	134.70
−100	60.25	0	100.00	100	138.50

4.3.3 The Bimetallic Switch and the Dial Thermometer

One of the most common temperature sensors is the bimetallic switch, which opens and closes an electrical contact, depending on whether the temperature is above or below a set value (Figure 4.6). It consists of two layers of materials (usually metal alloys) with different thermal-expansion coefficients (Table 4.3), so that mechanical bending occurs as the temperature changes.

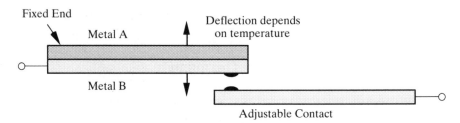

Figure 4.6   Bimetal switch, whose deflection depends on the temperature. Contact is made or broken at a temperature value set by the adjustable contact.

If the bimetallic strip is wound into a helix, with one end fastened and the other end connected to a needle indicator, the angle of the needle will depend on the temperature. Equipped with a temperature scale, this device is the "dial thermometer" and is commonly found in kitchens for measuring the temperature of meat or candy. It is used to determine approximate temperature values in Laboratory Exercises 4, 5, 12, 13, 15, and 24. If the rotating end is connected to an angle sensor (described in the previous section), the

TABLE 4.3   LINEAR THERMAL EXPANSION COEFFICIENTS α OF MATERIALS AT 20°C. $\alpha = dL/(LdT)$ (10^{-6} per C°)

Al_2O_3 (∥ c axis)	5.6	Platinum	8.9
Al_2O_3 (⊥ c axis)	5.0	Silicon	2.5
Aluminum	23.0	SiO_2 (∥ to axis)	7.4
Carbon	7.8	SiO_2 (⊥ to axis)	13.1
Copper	16.7	SiO_2 (vitreous)	0.35
Gold	14.2	Silver	19.0
Iron	11.8	Stainless Steel 304	15.9
Invar	1.2	Tungsten	4.5
Lead	28.7	Yellow brass	19.0
Nickel	12.8		

result is a rugged temperature sensor with good sensitivity and linear response. The main disadvantages are the length and thermal mass of the sensing element.

4.3.4   The Thermocouple

Thompson EMF.   When a bar of metal or semiconductor is heated at one end, some of the conduction electrons diffuse from the warmer end to the colder end. Although the electrons are free to move throughout the bar, they spend more time at the cooler end where their agitation velocity is lower. The positive ions, on the other hand, are immobile. The **Thompson emf** is the electrostatic potential difference that results after this thermal rearrangement. At equilibrium, the diffusion force (caused by the difference in temperature) and the electrostatic force (caused by the charge separation) are balanced (Figure 4.7). Note that the actual number of electrons separated is very small compared to the number of conduction electrons in the metal.

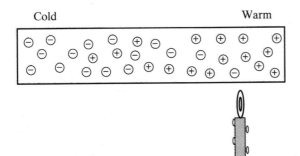

Figure 4.7   Distribution of charge in a conductor that is warmer at one end.

If you connect the ends of the bar to a voltmeter, the voltage will read zero (electric fields are zero in conductors), but if you connect the metal bar to a battery, the resistance will be lower in the direction of electron flow that is facilitated by the thermal diffusion. This current will transport warm electrons to the cooler end of the bar and *convert heat to electrical energy.* On the other hand, if the current opposes the thermal diffusion, the resistance will be higher and *electrical energy will be converted into heat.*

Peltier EMF.   When two unlike conductors are brought into electrical contact, there will be a diffusion of electrons from the high-mobility metal to the low-mobility metal (Figure 4.8). The **Peltier emf** is the resulting diffusion potential. Again, zero voltage will be measured across the opposite end of the two conductors, but the electrical resistivity will be different in the two directions of current flow.

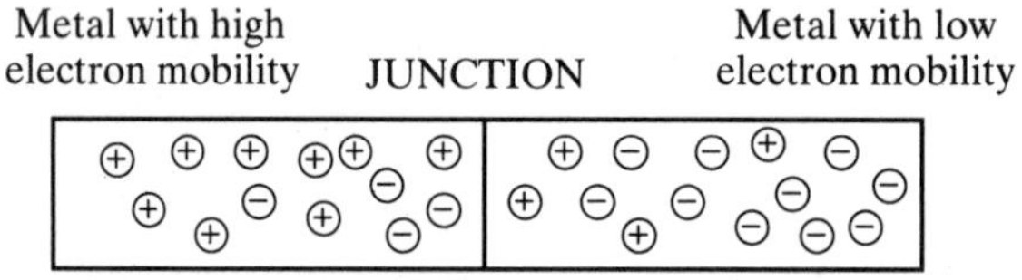

Metal with high
electron mobility   JUNCTION

Metal with low
electron mobility

Figure 4.8   Distribution of charge when two metals of dissimilar electron mobility are brought into contact.

If electrons move from the low-mobility conductor to the high-mobility conductor, the effect is like an expanding gas, and the junction will be cooled. If the electrons move from the high-mobility conductor to the low-mobility conductor, the effect is like compressing a gas, and the junction will be heated. Note that this emf depends on temperature.

Seebeck EMF.   If a closed circuit is formed by two different metals (Figure 4.9) and if the junctions are at different temperatures, the net result is the Seebeck emf (the sum of two Thompson emfs and two Peltier emfs), and a current will flow around the circuit.

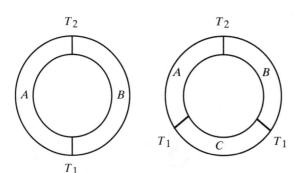

Figure 4.9   Circuits formed when dissimilar conductors *A* and *B* are joined and the junctions are at different temperatures T_1 and T_2. In the thermocouple temperature sensor, the conductor is broken at *C* and the voltage developed is approximately proportional to the temperature difference, $T_1 - T_2$.

The thermocouple as a temperature sensor. If the circuit in Figure 4.9 is broken, a potential difference will develop (the thermocouple potential) that depends on the temperature difference between the two junctions. In practice, the two dissimilar thermocouple wires are welded together at one end to form the sensing junction and welded at the other two ends to copper wires for connection to a voltmeter (Figure 4.10). Use of a high-impedance meter keeps the current very low and resistive heating (Joule) and heat transfer between the junctions (Peltier effect) is then negligible. During use, the connections to the copper wire (which constitutes a single junction) are kept at a known reference temperature. To justify the inclusion of the copper wire, note that the Thompson emf in conductor C is zero (both ends at same temperature) and the Peltier emf across junction AB in the diagram on the left is the same as the sum of the Peltier emfs across junctions AC and CB (both at the same temperature).

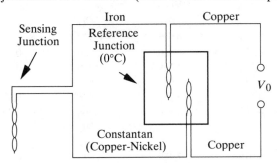

Figure 4.10 Iron–Constantan thermocouple for sensing the temperature difference between the reference junction and the sensing junction.

Table 4.4 lists the commonly available thermocouples, which cover a wide variety of temperature ranges. Table 4.5 lists the Seebeck emf as a function of temperature of the more commonly used thermocouples. Alumel is an aluminum–nickel alloy, chromel is a chromium–nickel alloy, and constantan is a copper–nickel alloy.

TABLE 4.4 PHYSICAL PROPERTIES OF THERMOCOUPLES

+ Element	− Element	Type	Temp. Range (°C)	Sensitivity (μV/°C)	Environment
Copper	Constantan	T	−200 to 370	40.5	Reducing, inert, or vacuum
Chromel	Constantan	E	−200 to 900	67.9	Oxidizing or inert
Iron	Constantan	J	0 to 760	52.6	Reducing, inert, or vacuum
Chromel	Alumel	K	−200 to 1250	38.8	Oxidizing or inert
Pt(13% Rh)	Platinum	R	0 to 1450	12.0	Oxidizing or inert
Pt(10% Rh)	Platinum	S	0 to 1450	10.6	Oxidizing or inert
Pt(30% Rh)	Pt(6% Rh)	B	0 to 1700	7.6	Oxidizing or inert
W(5% Rh)	W(26% Rh)		0 to 2320	16.6	Vacuum, inert, or hydrogen
W	W(26% Rh)		0 to 2320	16.0	Vacuum, inert, or hydrogen
W(3% Rh)	W(25% Rh)		0 to 2320	17.0	Vacuum, inert, or hydrogen

Source: Omega Temperature Measurement Handbook and Encyclopedia. Reproduced with the permission of Omega Engineering, Inc., Stamford, CT.

TABLE 4.5 THERMOELECTRIC OUTPUT (mV) OF COMMON THERMOCOUPLES

T (°C)	Copper– Constantan	Chromel– Constantan	Iron– Constantan	Chromel– Alumel	Platinum– Pt (10%Rh)
–260	–6.232	–9.797			
–240	–6.105	–9.604			
–220	–5.889	–9.274			
–200	–5.603	–8.824	–7.890	–5.891	
–180	–5.261	–8.273	–7.402	–5.550	
–160	–4.865	–7.631	–6.821	–5.141	
–140	–4.419	–6.907	–6.159	–4.669	
–120	–3.923	–6.107	–5.426	–4.138	
–100	–3.378	–5.237	–4.632	–3.553	
–80	–2.788	–4.301	–3.785	–2.920	
–60	–2.152	–3.306	–2.892	–2.243	
–40	–1.475	–2.254	–1.960	–1.527	
–20	–0.757	–1.151	–0.995	–0.777	
0	0.000	0.000	0.000	0.000	0.000
20	0.789	1.192	1.019	0.798	0.111
40	1.611	2.419	2.058	1.611	0.232
60	2.467	3.683	3.115	2.436	0.363
80	3.357	4.983	4.186	3.266	0.501
100	4.277	6.317	5.268	4.095	0.647
120	5.227	7.683	6.359	4.919	0.800
140	6.204	9.078	7.457	5.733	0.959
160	7.207	10.501	8.560	6.539	1.124
180	8.235	11.949	9.667	7.338	1.294
200	9.286	13.419	10.777	8.137	1.468
250	12.011	17.178	13.553	10.151	1.923
300	14.860	21.033	16.325	12.207	2.400
350	17.816	24.961	19.089	14.292	2.896
400	20.869	28.943	21.846	16.395	3.407
450		32.960	24.607	18.513	3.933
500		36.999	27.388	20.640	4.471
600		45.085	33.096	24.902	5.582
700		53.110	39.130	28.128	6.741
800		61.022		33.277	7.949
900				37.325	9.203
1000				41.269	10.503
1100				45.108	11.846
1200				48.282	13.224
1300				52.398	14.624
1400					16.035
1500					17.445
1600					18.842
1700					20.215

Source: Omega Temperature Measurement Handbook and Encyclopedia. Reproduced with the permission of Omega Engineering, Inc., Stamford, CT.

If the data-acquisition system is capable of accurately recording the thermocouple voltage V, the National Bureau of Standards (NBS) polynomials (Table 4.6) can be used to estimate the temperature T (°C):

$$T = a_0 + a_1 V + a_2 V^2 + \ldots + a_n V^n \tag{4.1}$$

TABLE 4.6 POLYNOMIAL COEFFICIENTS FOR ESTIMATING TEMPERATURE (°C) AS A FUNCTION OF THERMOCOUPLE OUTPUT (mV). [SEE EQUATION (4.1)]

	Copper–Constantan	Chromel–Constantan	Iron–Constantan	Chromel–Alumel	Platinum–Pt (10%Rh)
Range (°C)	–160 to 400	–100 to 1000	0 to 760	0 to 1370	0 to 1750
Accuracy (°C)	±0.5	±0.5	±0.7	±0.7	±1
a_0	0.100860910	0.104967248	-0.048868252	0.226584602	0.927763167
a_1	25727.94369	17189.45282	19873.14503	24152.10900	169526.5150
a_2	–767345.8295	–282639.0850	–218614.5353	67233.42488	–31568363.94
a_3	78025595.81	12695339.5	11569199.78	2210340.682	8990730663
a_4	–9247486589	–448703084.6	–264917531.4	–860963914.9	-1.63565×10^{12}
a_5	6.97688×10^{11}	1.10866×10^{10}	2018441314	4.83506×10^{10}	1.88027×10^{14}
a_6	-2.66192×10^{13}	-1.76807×10^{11}		-1.18452×10^{12}	-1.37241×10^{16}
a_7	3.94078×10^{14}	1.71842×10^{12}		1.38690×10^{13}	6.17501×10^{17}
a_8		-9.19278×10^{13}		-6.33708×10^{13}	-1.56105×10^{19}
a_9		2.06132×10^{13}			1.69535×10^{20}

Source: Omega Temperature Measurement Handbook and Encyclopedia. Reproduced with the permission of Omega Engineering, Inc., Stamford, CT.

For iron–constantan, T is given to an accuracy of 0.1°C over the 0°C to 760°C range by the coefficients in Table 4.6. As seen from Table 4.7, the fit is excellent within the 0°C to 670°C range and rather poor below 0°C, where the polynomial was not fit to the data.

Peltier thermoelectric device.   By running a thermocouple backwards, it is possible to convert electrical energy into a temperature difference. The electrical energy is basically used to compress an electron gas at the "hot" junction, which then expands to cool the "cold" junction (Figure 4.11). If one side is kept at ambient temperature by means of a heat reservoir or flowing water or air, the other side can be used for heating or cooling, depending on the direction of the electric current. The maximum cooling that can be achieved is limited by the rate at which the hot junction can be cooled, the heat load from the current passing through the device, and the heat from the surrounding medium.

The rate of heat removal from the cold surface of the heat pump is given by

$$Q = \pi I - I^2 R / 2 - K \Delta T$$

TABLE 4.7   THERMOELECTRIC VOLTAGE V OF IRON CONSTANTAN AS A FUNC-
TION OF TEMPERATURE T AND THE NBS POLYNOMIAL [TABLE 4.6, EQN (4.1)]

Temp. (°C)	Output (mV)	Polynomial Temp. (°C)	Temp. (°C)	Output (mV)	Polynomial Temp. (°C)
−200	−7.890	−177.23	160	8.560	159.97
−180	−7.402	−164.66	180	9.667	179.94
−160	−6.821	−150.05	200	10.777	199.93
−140	−6.159	−133.84	220	11.887	219.91
−120	−5.426	−116.40	240	12.998	239.92
−100	−4.632	−98.07	260	14.108	259.93
−80	−3.785	−79.08	280	15.217	279.95
−60	−2.892	−59.65	300	16.325	299.98
−40	−1.960	−39.93	350	19.089	350.06
−20	−0.995	−20.05	400	21.846	400.09
0	0.000	−0.05	450	24.607	450.06
20	1.019	19.99	500	27.388	499.98
40	2.058	40.02	550	30.210	549.91
60	3.115	60.06	600	33.096	599.92
80	4.186	80.08	650	36.066	650.02
100	5.268	100.07	700	39.130	700.10
120	6.359	120.05	750	42.283	749.99
140	7.457	140.01	760	42.922	759.93

Electron Expansion (Cooling)

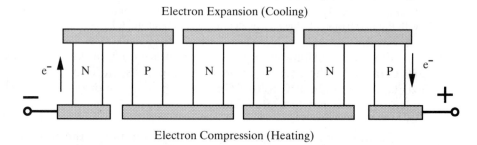

Electron Compression (Heating)

Figure 4.11   Peltier thermoelectric heat pump. Usually, the materials are
P- and N-doped alloys of semiconductors such as Bi_2Te_3 and Sb_2Te_3.
Reversing the flow of electrical current reverses the flow of heat.

The first term is due to the Peltier effect, where π is the Peltier coefficient. The second term is Joule heating, where R is the ratio between the
voltage V across the device and the current I through the device. The third
term is due to thermal conductivity K through the device.

Note that at low currents, the first term can be larger than the second,
resulting in a net cooling. However, as the current is increased, the I^2 term
can dominate, resulting in net heating.

4.3.5 The Thermistor

Practical thermistors for temperature measurement consist of a piece of sintered metal oxide that exhibits a large decrease in electrical resistance with increasing temperature. In semiconductors, electrical conductivity is due to the electrons in the conduction band. If the temperature is increased, some electrons are promoted from the valence band into the conduction band (Figure 4.12), and the conductivity also increases. The electrical conductivity is described by the Boltzmann relation, which states that the number of electrons in the conduction band depends on temperature as exp $(-E/kT)$, where E is the band gap, typically 0.3 eV; and k is Boltzman's constant, equal to 8.61709×10^{-5} eV/K. Since the resistance is the inverse of the conductivity, resistance is proportional to exp $(+E/kT)$ = exp $(3500/T)$.

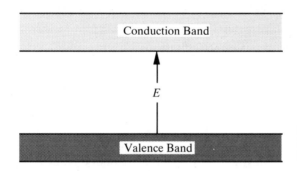

Figure 4.12   Diagram of energy levels of the valence and conduction bands and the bandgap E.

To the first order in $1/T$, the relationship between resistance R and temperature T is given by

$$R(T) = R(T_0) \exp\left[\beta\left(1/T - 1/T_0\right)\right]$$

where T is in degrees Kelvin, T_0 is the reference temperature, and β is the temperature coefficient of the material (Figure 4.13, Table 4.8). The rapid exponential drop in resistance with increasing temperature is due to the increase in the concentration of electrons in the conduction band with temperature. A more accurate description is given by

$$1/T = A + B(\ln R) + C(\ln R)^3 \tag{4.2}$$

where A, B, and C are empirical constants determined by a best fit to measured data. Since the equation is linear in A, B, and C the least-squares fitting techniques of Chapter 5 can be used. As an initial approximation, $A \approx \ln R_0 - \beta/T_0$ and $B \approx \beta$.

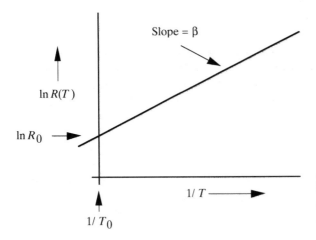

Figure 4.13 Relationship between $1/T$ and $\ln R$ for the thermistor, where the $(\ln R)^3$ term in Equation (4.2) has been neglected.

TABLE 4.8 TYPICAL THERMISTOR RESISTANCE R VS. TEMPERATURE T.
(β = 3000K, R = 10 kΩ at 0°C)

$T(°C)$	$R(k\Omega)$	$T(°C)$	$R(k\Omega)$	$T(°C)$	$R(k\Omega)$
−50	117.2	−10	15.2	30	3.4
−40	65.8	0	10.0	40	2.5
−30	38.8	10	6.8	50	1.8
−20	23.8	20	4.7	60	1.4

The typical **time constant** for a thermistor in an insulating liquid (such as oil) is several seconds, but for use in aqueous media (such as in water or in the mouth), a teflon tube is used for electrical insulation and to maintain sterility, which increases the response time by about a factor of 10. The **dissipation constant** is the power required to raise the temperature 1°C above the surrounding media. For a thermistor suspended by its leads in a "well stirred" oil bath, the dissipation constant is about 10 mW/°C and a factor of 10 less in still air. It is therefore important that the current through the thermistor be kept sufficiently small so that Joule heating does not affect the temperature measurement.

To sense temperature, thermistors are used in a bridge circuit such as that shown in Figure 4.14.

The bridge equation is

$$V_0 = V_+ - V_- = V_b \left(\frac{R_3}{R_T + R_3} - \frac{R_2}{R_1 + R_2} \right)$$

Solving for R_T:

$$R_T = R_3 \left[\frac{V_b R_1 - V_0(R_1 + R_2)}{V_b R_2 + V_0(R_1 + R_2)} \right]$$

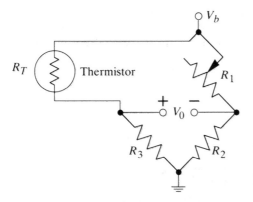

Figure 4.14   Thermistor in bridge circuit. Variable resistor R_1 may be adjusted to produce a zero output voltage at a selected temperature.

Optimization of thermistor-bridge sensitivity.   The sensitivity Q in this case is the change in bridge output per unit change in temperature, and we now ask what choice of bridge resistors maximizes Q:

$$Q = \frac{dV_0}{dT} = R_T \frac{dV_0}{dR_T} \frac{1}{R_T} \frac{dR_T}{dT}$$

From the thermistor relationship, we have

$$\frac{1}{R_T} \frac{dR_T}{dT} = \frac{\beta}{T^2}$$

From the bridge relationship, we have

$$R_T \frac{dV_0}{dR_T} = - \frac{R_3 R_T}{(R_T + R_3)^2} = \frac{\alpha}{(1 + \alpha^2)}$$

where $\alpha = R_3/R_T$ and $R_2 = R_3$.
    Combining, we have

$$Q = \frac{\alpha\beta}{(1 + \alpha^2)T^2}$$

To maximize Q, we set $dQ/d\alpha = 0$ and find a maximum at $\alpha = 1$:

$$\frac{dQ}{d\alpha} = \frac{\beta(1 - \alpha^2)}{T^2(1 + \alpha^2)^2} = 0$$

The conclusion is that to maximize the sensitivity of the thermistor bridge in Figure 4.14 at temperature T (which maximizes the change in bridge output voltage for a given temperature change around the value T), we want to select $R_2 = R_3 = R_T$. This is a surprisingly simple result, considering the nature of the equations for $R(T)$ and V_0 just given.

Thermal dynamics. When a thermal mass that is in thermal equilibrium with a medium at temperature T_1 is suddenly moved to a medium at temperature T_2, its temperature changes with time t according to:

$$T = T_2 + (T_1 - T_2) e^{-t/\tau}$$

where τ is the exponential time constant.

4.3.6 The Solid-State Temperature Sensor

The junction potential of silicon transistors and diodes changes linearly about 2.2 mV/C° over a wide range of temperature (–55°C to + 150°C). This effect can be used to measure differences in temperature.

It is also possible to measure the temperature in degrees Kelvin without the need for linearization circuits or cold-junction compensation. This uses the effect that for a matched pair of transistors with different currents, the difference in base–emitter voltages is only a function of the absolute temperature and the logarithm of the ratios of the currents:

$$V_T = V_{\text{BE2}} - V_{\text{BE1}} = \frac{kT}{q} \ln\left(\frac{I_1}{I_2}\right)$$

where I_1 and I_2 are the collector currents, T is the absolute temperature, and $k/q = 86.1709\ \mu\text{V/K}$. By accurately dividing a current so that the ratio I_1/I_2 is known, the voltage V_T becomes proportional to the absolute temperature.

The Analog Devices AD590 solid-state temperature sensor consists of a pair of transistors that divides a current I_T into two equal parts (Figure 4.15). One-half I_T passes through a transistor and the other half of I_T passes through eight transistors connected in parallel. All nine transistors are identical. The difference in base-emitter voltages $V_T = (86.1\ \mu\text{V/K}) (\ln 8)\ T = (179\ \mu\text{V/K})\ T$. This voltage appears across a 358 Ω resistor through which one-half of I_T flows. The total device current is $I_T = (1\ \mu\text{A/K})\ T$, and is proportional to the absolute temperature. This sensor is operated by applying a bias in the range from 3 to 40 volts and measuring the current. It can be used with an external 1-kΩ resistor to give a sensitivity of 1 mV/K, which is about 20 times larger than the thermocouple. For measurements of temperature relative to 0°C, a difference amplifier is used to subtract 273 mV.

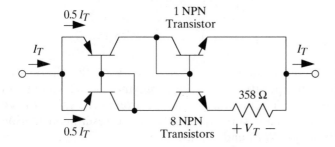

Figure 4.15 Analog Devices AD590 solid-state temperature sensor. The device is biased at 4 to 30 volts and the resulting current is proportional to the absolute temperature. Typical sensitivity is 1 μA/K.

4.4 STRAIN-SENSING ELEMENTS

When a mechanical structure is subject to a force, it undergoes deformation. **Stress** describes the intensity of the force on the structure as the force per unit area (F/A) and **strain** describes the deformation as the fractional change in length ($\Delta L/L$). **Young's modulus** describes the stiffness of the structure as the ratio of stress to strain. If the structure is very stiff, a large stress is required to produce a given strain and the Young's modulus is large.

One of the simplest resistive strain gauges is a rubber tube filled with mercury. As the rubber tube is stretched, its length L increases and its cross-sectional area A decreases. The electrical resistance R is given by $R = \rho L/A$, where ρ is the resistivity in ohm cm, and for constant volume $V = AL$, $R = \rho L^2/V$. For small changes in length ΔL, and a constant electrical resistivity ρ, $\Delta R = 2\rho L\, \Delta L/V$ and $\Delta R/R = 2\, \Delta L/L$ is the measure of the strain. The mercury tube strain gauge has been used for respiration monitoring.

4.4.1 The Bonded Resistance Strain Gauge

The metal-foil strain gauge consists of a pattern of metal on a mylar backing (Figure 4.16) that changes its resistance as it is placed under tension or compression (Figure 4.17).

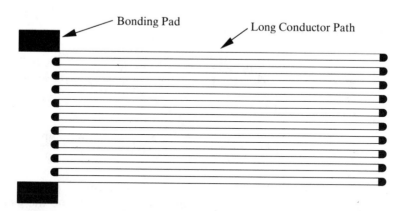

Figure 4.16 Metal-foil strain gauge. For most metals, the fractional change in electrical resistance ($\Delta R/R$) is equal to twice the fractional change in length ($\Delta L/L$).

When metals are placed under tension, their length L will increase but the girth D will not necessarily decrease to keep the volume a constant, as it was for the mercury tube strain gauge. Defining the longitudinal strain $\varepsilon_l = \Delta L/L$ and the transverse strain $\varepsilon_t = \Delta D/D$, **Poisson's Ratio** υ is defined as

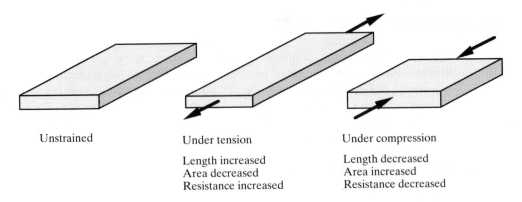

Unstrained   Under tension   Under compression

Length increased   Length decreased
Area decreased   Area increased
Resistance increased   Resistance decreased

Figure 4.17   The metal-foil element in the strain gauge changes its shape during tension and expansion, resulting in a change in electrical resistance.

$-\varepsilon_t/\varepsilon_l$. Because the cross-sectional area A varies as the square of the girth D, $\Delta A/A = 2\,\Delta D/D = -2\upsilon(\Delta L/L)$.

The electrical resistance of a rectangular bar of metal of volume resistivity ρ is given by

$$R = \frac{L\rho}{A}$$

Taking partial derivatives,

$$dR = \frac{\rho}{A}\partial L - \frac{\rho L}{A^2}\partial A + \frac{L}{A}\partial\rho = R\frac{\partial L}{L} - R\frac{\partial A}{A} + R\frac{\partial\rho}{\rho}$$

In differential form,

$$\frac{\Delta R}{R} = \frac{\Delta L}{L} - \frac{\Delta A}{A} + \frac{\Delta\rho}{\rho} = (1 + 2\upsilon)\frac{\Delta L}{L} + \frac{\Delta\rho}{\rho}$$

The term $\Delta L/L$ is dimensional and the term $\Delta\rho/\rho$ is piezoresistive. For the constant-volume mercury strain gauge, $\sigma = 0.50$ and the **gauge factor** G in the expression $\Delta R/R = G\,\Delta L/L$ has the value $G = 2$. For most metals, $\upsilon = 0.30$ (increase in volume with strain), but the piezoresistive term increases G so that it is also about 2. The gauge factor ranges from 2 to 4.5 for metals and can be as high as 150 for semiconductors. The high gauge factor for semiconductive strain elements is because the resistivity ρ is a strong function of the strain.

Strain gauges are used extensively on buildings, bridges, and ships to constantly monitor the strain on structural members. Excessive strain indicates the buildup of forces that could cause a failure.

4.5 FORCE AND PRESSURE TRANSDUCERS

4.5.1 Force Transducers

A common method of measuring the force of gravity F on a mass m uses a spring and position sensor. $F = mg = kx$, where g is the gravitational acceleration, k is the spring constant, and x is the difference between the loaded and unloaded lengths of the spring. Since the gravitational force does not depend on displacement, we can use a spring that permits a significant displacement, which helps the accuracy of the measurement. In many cases, however, a displacement in the direction of the force (i.e. "yielding" to the force) significantly reduces the magnitude of the force, so it is important to measure the force with very little displacement. One of the best methods for accomplishing this uses the piezoelectric crystal, which produces a voltage that is proportional to the force. Another method uses one or more strain gauges cemented to a flexible rod (Figure 4.18). One end of the rod is fixed and the other is attached to the force. The stiffness of the rod is chosen to provide an accurate measurement over the loads of interest without excessive displacement.

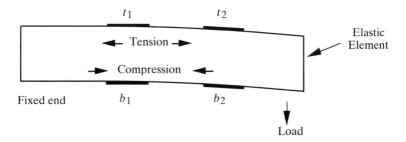

Figure 4.18   Force transducer consisting of four strain gauges mounted in opposing pairs to an elastic element.

The resistance of the strain gauge is measured by placing it in one arm of an initially balanced Wheatstone bridge. If a single strain element is used (left-hand side of Figure 4.19), the output will be sensitive to thermal expansion of the elastic element. A better design uses four strain elements in opposing pairs (right-hand side of Figure 4.19). This results in a fourfold improvement in sensitivity and a relative insensitivity to temperature changes.

For the single-element bridge (left-hand side of Figure 4.19) with an excitation voltage V_b, the output is given by

$$V_0 = V_b\left(\frac{R}{2R} - \frac{R}{2R + \Delta R}\right) = V_b\left(\frac{\Delta R}{4R + 2\Delta R}\right) \approx V_b\left(\frac{\Delta R}{4R}\right) = V_b\left(\frac{G}{4}\frac{\Delta L}{L}\right)$$

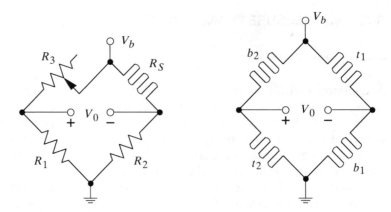

Figure 4.19   Force-transducer bridge circuits using a single strain element R_S, or four strain elements, t_1, t_2, b_1, and b_2, in opposing pairs. The four-element bridge has four times the sensitivity of the single-element bridge.

For the four-element bridge (right-hand side of Figure 4.19), assuming that all four strain elements have the same unstrained resistance R, we have

$$V_0 = V_b \left(\frac{R + \Delta R}{R + \Delta R + R - \Delta R} - \frac{R - \Delta R}{R + \Delta R + R - \Delta R} \right) = V_b \left(\frac{2 \Delta R}{2R} \right) = V_b \left(G \frac{\Delta L}{L} \right)$$

Note that the relationship for the four-element bridge is naturally linear, whereas that of the single-strain-element bridge is not. In addition, the four element force transducer has four times the sensitivity. A typical maximum strain $\Delta L/L$ would be 0.5%, so that for a gauge factor $G = 2$, $\Delta R/R$ would be only 1% and V_0 would be 1% of V_b.

It should also be noted that a uniform change in temperature will cause a change in the length of the bar and put an equal strain on all the gauges. Therefore, the single-element force transducer is sensitive to temperature changes, while the four-element force transducer is not.

4.5.2 Pressure Transducers

The pressure of a gas or a fluid is the force per unit area exerted perpendicularly on the surface of the surrounding container. One of the most sensitive pressure transducers is the piezoresistive diaphragm, which consists of four nearly identical semiconductor piezoresistors buried in the surface of a thin circular silicon diaphragm. Pressure causes the diaphragm to bend, inducing a stress on the diaphragm and the buried piezoresistors. Two of the resistors increase in value and two decrease, depending on their orientation with respect to the crystalline direction of the silicon material. Gold pads attached to the silicon diaphragm provide connection from the piezoresistors to a full bridge similar to the force transducer described in the previous section. Silicon is elastic throughout its operating range and fails by rupturing. Units are available for measuring pressures up to 15,000 psi. For measuring absolute pressure, one side of the diaphragm is evacuated and sealed. For measuring differential pressure, both sides are used.

4.6 MEASURING LIGHT

4.6.1 The Silicon Photodiode

The best commercially available photodiode for the measurement of low light levels is the PIN photodiode, which is manufactured by diffusing donor (*n*-type) impurities (usually boron) and acceptor (*p*-type) impurities (usually phosphorous or arsenic) into opposite sides of a high-purity silicon crystal (Figure 4.20).

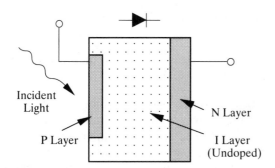

Figure 4.20   Electronic structure of the PIN photodiode. Photons pass through the P layer and produce electron-hole pairs in the I layer.

Photovoltaic mode.   The doping of the PIN diode produces free negative carriers (and fixed positive ions) in the N layer and free positive carriers (and fixed negative ions) in the P layer. These free carriers (in the absence of any other forces) will diffuse to fill the space available. This driving force is the **diffusion emf**. However, since these carriers leave their oppositely charged fixed ions behind, the diffusion emf is opposed by a **coulomb emf**. At equilibrium, the two emfs are balanced and do not produce an external voltage or current, but the charge separation produces an electric field in the I layer. In this field, excess free negative carriers will drift toward the N layer and excess free positive carriers will drift toward the P layer.

Photons shining into the intrinsic layer (through the thin transparent P layer) produce electron–hole pairs that are separated by the internal electric field to produce an external emf (called the **photovoltaic potential**). In an open circuit, the potential developed is in the range of 200 to 600 mV over a wide range of light intensities (shown as the intercept with the +*V* axis in Figure 4.21). On the other hand, the short-circuit current is linearly proportional to the light intensity over many decades (shown as the intercept with

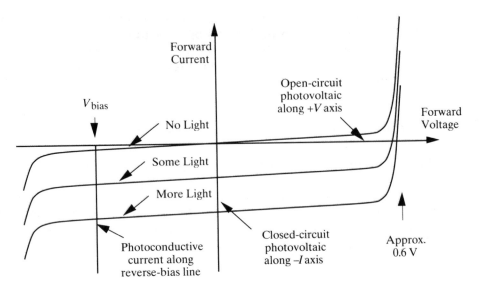

Figure 4.21   *V–I* characteristics of the PIN photodiode for various incident-light levels.

the *–I* axis in Figure 4.21). If a load resistor is used, then the voltage–current relationship is the intercept with the usual load line.

Photoconductive mode.   When a reverse bias is applied, and if the material is sufficiently pure, the I layer is almost totally depleted and devoid of charge carriers. This results in a lowering of capacitance (by typically a factor of 3) and an increase in speed, which is especially important in communication applications. In darkness, the *V–I* curve for the photodiode is similar to a conventional diode, except that the reverse-bias current is much lower, typically a few nanoamperes for the S1723. Illumination mainly shifts the curve *downward* in the direction of reverse current. As seen in Figure 4.21, and explored in Laboratory Exercise 14, this current is the best indicator of light intensity.

Amplification.   To convert current to voltage, a noninverting amplifier is used (Figure 4.22). The voltage-to-current converter shown in Figure 2.5 is not recommended because op-amp leakage currents can develop a large voltage drop across the photodiode (typical reverse-bias impedance is 10^{12} Ω) and saturate the amplifier.

4.6.2 Lambert–Beer Law

The photodiode is often used to measure transmission through a colored solution of unknown concentration. The optical transmission is defined as the intensity $I(L)$ measured through path length L divided by the intensity $I(0)$ at zero path length:

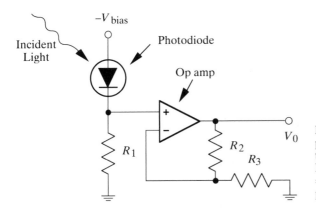

Figure 4.22   Circuit for biasing a photodiode and converting the photoconduction current into a voltage. For $R_1 = 1$ MΩ, $R_2 = 900$ kΩ, and $R_3 = 100$ kΩ, the op-amp output is 10 V per nA of photodiode current.

$$I(L) = I(0)e^{-kCL} \tag{4.3}$$

where C is the concentration of the solution, and L is the path length through the solution (Figure 4.23). The constant of proportionality k is usually determined by using known standards.

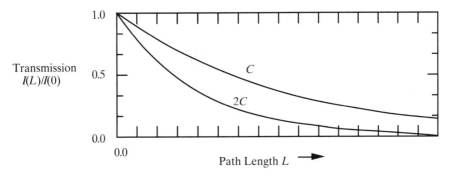

Figure 4.23   Transmitted intensity as a function of path length for colored solutions of concentration C and $2C$.

4.6.3 The Vacuum Photomultiplier Tube

The vacuum photomultiplier is one of the most sensitive photodetectors and combines a special photosensitive layer called the photocathode with a high-gain electron multiplier. The photocathode converts incident photons into photoelectrons released into the vacuum with typically 25% efficiency. The electron multiplier consists of a series of 8 to 14 plates (called dynodes) coated with high secondary emission material so that the electrons multiply as they cascade from plate to plate (Figure 4.24). The overall electron gain in this process is typically 10^5 to 10^7.

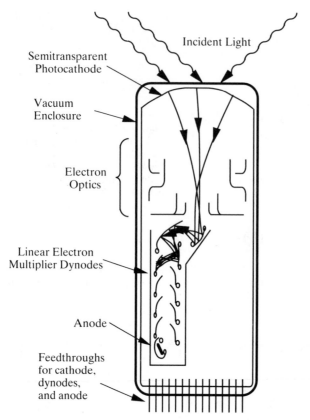

Incident Light

Semitransparent
Photocathode

Vacuum
Enclosure

Electron
Optics

Linear Electron
Multiplier Dynodes

Anode

Feedthroughs
for cathode,
dynodes,
and anode

Figure 4.24   Photomultiplier tube.
For clarity, only the electron amplification at the first three dynodes is
shown.

4.7 IONIC POTENTIALS

4.7.1 Origin of the Ionic Potential

Two important examples of ionic potentials are those that appear on the surface of the skin as a result of the electrochemical activity of neurons and
muscles, and those that are measured in test tubes to determine ionic
concentration.

   In the first case, ionic potentials are measured at the surface of the skin
to study the electrical activity of the heart (the electrocardiogram, or ECG),
the brain (the electroencephalogram, or EEG), the skeletal muscles (the
electromyogram, or EMG), and the position of the eyes (the electrooculogram, or EOG).

   It is important to note that these ionic potentials are not the result of a
concentration of electrons, but a concentration of ions that are not free to
travel down wires to our amplifiers. As a result, it is necessary to transduce a
current of ions in solution to a current of electrons in a conductor.

4.7.2 Bare-Metal Electrodes

Bare-metal electrodes are poor for the detection of ionic potentials because:

1. The skin provides a barrier to charge transport

2. The ionic potentials are small (1 mV for the ECG and much less for the EEG) and can only transform a small amount of ion charge into electrons in the metal before the electrode polarizes.

3. Reactions such as

   Cu (anode) $\rightarrow$ e⁻ (in anode) + Cu⁺ (in solution)   and

   Cu⁺ (in solution)+ e⁻ (in cathode) $\rightarrow$ Cu (solid)

   are limited at low voltages (mV) by the potential barriers associated with removing a metal atom from the crystal lattice and ionizing it. At higher voltages (0.1 volts) the current is limited by the rate of diffusion. Even when no current flows, there is a Cu⁺ space charge around the wire which can produce a transient potential on the electrode whenever the solution is disturbed (microphonic effect).

4. Reactions such as the following require potentials of several volts

   $2H_2O \rightarrow O_2 + 4H^+ + 4e^-$ (into anode)

   $2H^+ + 2e^-$ (from cathode) $\rightarrow H_2$

   $2Cl^-$ (in solution) $\rightarrow 2e^-$ (into anode) + Cl_2 (gas)

4.7.3 Ag(AgCl) Electrodes

The Ag(AgCl) gel electrode has a silver core surrounded by a sintered AgCl layer. The reaction

$$Ag \text{ (solid)} + Cl^- \text{ (aqueous)} \leftrightarrow AgCl \text{ (solid)} + e^- \text{ (in AgCl)}$$

allows an efficient transfer of e⁻ charge in the Ag wire to and from the Cl⁻ ion charge in solution for the following reasons:

1. AgCl is insoluble and stays with the Ag core.

2. AgCl is porous, so that the Cl⁻ ions in solution can reach the Ag in the core.

3. AgCl is slightly conductive, and can receive e⁻ from the Ag core.

4. The NaCl in the gel reduces the skin resistance to the passage of ions.

Note that while Ag and AgCl are both present in the electrode, it can act either as a positive terminal (Ag and Cl⁻ are converted to AgCl and e⁻) or as a negative terminal (AgCl and e⁻ are converted to Ag and Cl⁻).

Due to the cost of the Ag(AgCl) electrode, copper electrodes smeared with a special ECG paste are also used, but this is much more subject to off-set potentials (i.e., battery potentials) and polarization.

The dc electrical resistance of the skin varies greatly from person to person and depends on how "dry" the skin is. A pair of bare dry metal electrodes applied to the skin about 15 cm apart will generally show a resistance in the 1-to-10-MΩ range. By using water, the resistance will drop to the 100-to-1-MΩ range. Ag(AgCl) floating electrodes typically show a resistance in the 20-to-50-kΩ range.

A commonly used model for electrodes is shown in Figure 4.25. It has several components as follows:

1. a resistance due to charge transfer from electrode into solution.
2. a resistance due to diffusion velocity of ions away from electrode.
3. an equilibrium voltage emf.
4. a Helmholtz capacitance due to charge layer.

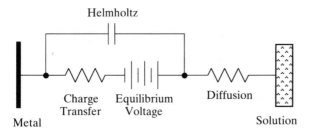

Figure 4.25   Equivalent circuit for a metal electrode in an ionic solution.

4.8 PROBLEMS

4.1 You have just joined a team to design incubators (temperature-controlled enclosures) for hatching chicken eggs and raising baby chickens. Your part of the project is to develop a temperature sensor that can be read by a data-acquisition board connected to a microcomputer.

The data-acquisition board has a 10-bit A/D converter with a full-scale input range from 0 to 5 volts and an input impedance of 1 kΩ. The temperature range of interest is 20 to 60°C, with maximum sensitivity at 40°C, near the optimum temperature of the incubators. The thermistor has a calibration scale shown in part in the following table:

T	R	T	R	$\Delta R/\Delta T$
20 °C	10,000 Ω	21 °C	9,700 Ω	300 Ω/°C
40 °C	5,000 Ω	41 °C	4,800 Ω	200 Ω/°C
60 °C	2,500 Ω	61 °C	2,425 Ω	75 Ω/°C

You also use the standard bridge circuit shown in Figure 4.14, with $V_b = 1$ volt.

a. For maximum bridge output sensitivity V_0 at 40 °C, and zero output at 20 °C, what should be the values of resistors R_1 and R_2?

b. What is the sensitivity of your bridge circuit (in mV/°C) at 20, 40, and 60°C?

$$Hint: \text{If } F = \frac{A}{A+x} + B, \quad \text{then } dF = \frac{-A}{(A+x)^2} dx$$

c. What is the bridge output voltage V_0 at the maximum temperature of 60°C?

d. What type of amplifier would you use to provide the input signal to the A/D converter? What gain would you choose? What would be reasonable values for the specifications on input impedance, output impedance, and common-mode rejection?

e. What limit does the resolution of the A/D place on the precision of the temperature measurements near 40 °C? (Give your answer in °C.)

4.2 You are given the following components and asked to design the hardware for a temperature-measurement system:

1. A solid-state temperature sensor and amplifier whose output is proportional to the absolute temperature from 200K to 400K (–73 to +127°C). The output voltage is 2.000 volts at 200K, 4.000 volts at 400K, and perfectly linear in between.

2. A successive-approximation 12-bit A/D converter with an input range from 0.000 to 4.095 volts. Conversion time is 10 μs. Conversion is initiated 100 ns after a low-to-high edge on the "conversion start" input line. The "conversion status" output line is high only when a conversion is in progress and the digital output data are valid 100 ns before the "conversion status" goes from high to low.

3. A sample-and-hold amplifier that is in the hold mode when its input control line is high and is in the sample mode when its control line is low. Assume that the output is stable 100 ns after the transition from sample to hold.

4. A 12-bit parallel input port that simultaneously (i) latches data onto its input registers and (ii) sets bit 0 of a status register to 1, whenever a high-to-low edge appears on its "input strobe" line. Your computer program can read the eight-bit status register with the statement "inp(3);", the low eight bits on its data registers with the statement "inp(1);" and the high four bits with the statement "inp(2);". If all 12 bits are ones, then the "inp(1);" will read FF and the "inp(2);"

will read 0F. The read process causes the port to reset the status register.

5. A one-bit output port that produces a 1 μs positive pulse using the statement "outp(1,1);".

6. A microcomputer with keyboard, CRT screen, with components 4 and 5 as plug-in boards.

a. Draw a block diagram of all essential components and interconnections, and label same.

b. What voltage transformation is needed to match the range of the temperature sensor to the A/D converter?

c. Draw timing diagrams for the following lines and registers:
A/D conversion start input (show logic level)
A/D conversion status output (show logic level)
Sample-and-hold control input (show logic level)
Parallel port input strobe (show logic level)
Parallel port data registers (show new vs. old data)
Bit 0 of the parallel port status word (show zero or one)

4.3 Design a computer code for the hardware system of Problem 4.2 to display the temperature (in °C) on the screen whenever the user asks for it.

a. Show the computer code (or a list of what the program steps do) for the following:
• receive a prompt from the user,
• initiate data conversion,
• read the temperature data,
• convert to degrees Celsius,
• display the answer on the user's screen. *(do not omit any essential steps)*.

b. If the A/D has an absolute accuracy of 1 LSB, how accurate is the temperature value that is displayed?

c. What is the smallest temperature change that the system can reliably detect?

4.4 You are given a force transducer consisting of a single-element strain gauge cemented to the top of an aluminum bar (Figure 4.26). The gauge factor of the strain gauge is $G = 2$. The flexibility of the rod is such that the strain at the top of the bar (where the strain gauge is located) is 1 microstrain per gram of mass. Aluminum has a thermal-expansion coefficient of 23 ppm/°C.

a. Draw the bridge circuit you would use (excitation = 1 volt). *(Hint:* the equations are easier if all resistors have the same value as the

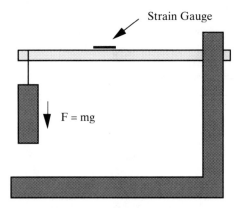

Strain Gauge

F = mg

Figure 4.26   Force transducer using a flexible bar and a single strain gauge.

unloaded strain gauge and one end of the strain gauge is connected to ground.)

b. derive the bridge equation for this transducer (i.e., relate output voltage to strain $\Delta L/L$).

c. Give the sensitivity in μV per gram for a very small mass on the bar.

d. What is the bridge output for a 10-kg mass on the bar? What would you have expected from your answer to part c, assuming perfect linearity?

e. With a fixed mass on the bar, how will the bridge output change if the temperature changes by 10°C?   To what load does this correspond?

f. How could you use a second identical strain gauge to compensate for such temperature-caused errors?

4.5 You are given four identical resistive strain gauges with the following resistance/strain relation: $\Delta R/R = G(\Delta L/L)$, where $G = 2$. These are cemented to opposite sides of a flexible bar: two on one side and two on the other as shown in Figure 4.27. Using the assembly as a force trans- ducer, we have $\Delta L/L = KF = Kmg$, where K is a constant, m is the mass, g is the acceleration of gravity, and $\Delta L/L$ is the strain experienced at the top of the bar.

a. Draw the bridge circuit you would use.

b. Derive the bridge equation for 1 volt excitation and solve for the output voltage V_0 as a function of m.

c. If $V_0 = 1$ mV for 1 kg, what is the value of K?

d. Is this force transducer linear?

e. What limits the maximum m that can be measured?

f. How sensitive is this force transducer to temperature?

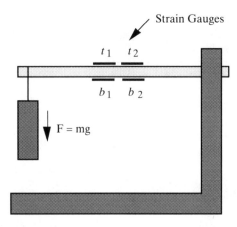

Strain Gauges

t_1 t_2

b_1 b_2

$F = mg$

Figure 4.27   Force transducer consisting of a flexible bar and two opposing pairs of strain gauges.

g. What would be the effect of a second power term? $\Delta R/R = G(\Delta L/L) + \alpha(\Delta L/L)^2$. (*Hint:* this new term does not depend on the sign of ΔL.)

4.6 A railroad track support column has four solid-state strain gauges cemented to it, as shown in Figure 4.28. The force on the column is straight down (no bending, only compression). Your goal is to be able to measure the strain on the column as trains pass over it. Two of the strain gauges are P type, with the strain relationship: $\Delta R/R = 100\,\Delta L/L + 10{,}000\,(\Delta L/L)^2$, and the other two are N type, with the strain relationship: $\Delta R/R = -100\,\Delta L/L + 10{,}000\,(\Delta L/L)^2$. Assume that all gauges have the same unstrained resistance R.

a. Draw a bridge circuit to measure the compressive strain on the beam. Indicate the positions of the P-type and N-type strain gauges.
b. Derive an expression relating the bridge output to the compressive strain on the column.
c. What is the sensitivity of the bridge in terms of millivolts per microstrain at very small strain? (Assume a 1 volt bridge excitation.)
d. For a strain of $\Delta L/L = 0.1\%$ (1000 microstrains), how far does the actual output deviate from a straight line passing through zero with the slope given in part c? (Assume that the gauge factor remains constant.)

4.7 Design a thermocouple-based system for measuring the Space Shuttle main engine exhaust temperature with the following requirements:
1. The response time is 1 s or less.
2. The temperature range is 20 to 2300°C.
3. The electronics must be located in a forward compartment, 20 m from the sensing junction.

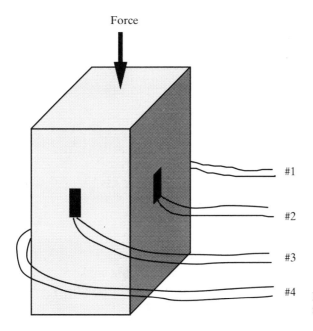

Force

#1

#2

#3

#4   **Figure 4.28**   Four strain gauges
mounted on a column.

4. There is considerable electromagnetic radiation in the 1-kHz to 100-MHz range from other circuits in the spacecraft.

5. The electrical output of your circuit will be sampled at 10 Hz with a data-acquisition circuit similar to the one you built in the lab.

a. Draw a block diagram, labeling all essential components and wires. *Hint 1:* Your circuit must reject interference that appears on both thermocouple wires.   *Hint 2:* You will need a low-pass filter so that the data-acquisition circuit does not see unwanted frequencies.

b. Label the drawing with the typical voltages that would be present at various points in your circuit when the sensing junction is at a temperature of 2000°C.

c. What sensor would you use to measure the temperature inside an astronaut's space suit?

d. Estimate the accuracy and precision of the systems in parts **a** and **c**.

4.8   You are developing a spectrophotometer system that uses a PIN photodiode to measure the concentration of a colored solution in a test tube. The op amp you are using has an input impedance of 10^{14} Ω. With a reverse bias of 10 volts, the photodiode dark current is 10 nA and the maximum light level you need to detect produces a photodiode current of 1 μA.

You first try the circuit shown in Figure 4.29, with $R_1 = 9$ kΩ and $R_2 = 1$ kΩ:

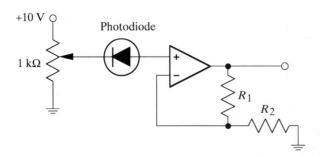

Figure 4.29   Faulty photodiode amplifier circuit.

a. With this circuit, the output saturates. What is the problem with the circuit?

b. Draw a modification of the circuit that would make it work so that the output voltage is a linear function of the intensity of the light falling on the photodiode (i.e., $V_0 = a + b\,I$).

c. Describe briefly how would you bias the circuit for the photovoltaic mode and for the photoconductive mode.

d. Draw the block diagram for a complete microcomputer-based system for measuring the concentration of a colored solution. Label all essential components.

e. How would the output voltage depend on the concentration of the solution? (Give a formula with an unknown constant multiplier.)

4.9 You are developing a spectrophotometer system that uses a PIN photodiode, and want to design a circuit that produces an output that is linearly proportional to the *concentration* of a colored solution.

a. First, derive the closed-loop gain V_0/V_1 for the op-amp circuit shown in Figure 4.30 that uses a standard diode (not a photodiode) as a feedback element.

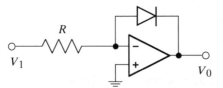

Figure 4.30   Op-amp circuit with a diode as a feedback element.

Assume an ideal op amp, $V_1 > 0$, and a diode current $I_D = I_S$ exp (V_D/V_T), where I_S and V_T are constants, and V_D is the voltage across the diode ($V_D > 0$ for forward bias) (Figure 4.31.)

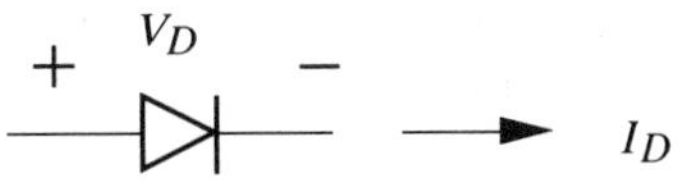

Figure 4.31   Forward-biased diode.

   b. Draw a modification of the circuit of Figure 4.30 that could be used for measuring the concentration of solutions such as you did in Laboratory Exercise 14. (*Hint:* The photodiode acts as a current source, not a voltage source.)

   c. Assuming that the photodiode current is directly proportional to incident light, and neglecting dark current, how would this circuit aid data processing for the measurement of concentration? (*Hint:* Derive an expression for V_0 as a function of concentration.)

4.10   Give two significant sources of error for the following sensors or transducers. (*Hint:* Call upon your experiences in the laboratory.)

   a. Thermistor in a bridge circuit.

   b. Thermocouple and differential amplifier.

   c. A force transducer consisting of four strain gauges mounted in opposing pairs and used in a bridge circuit.

   d. A potentiometer used to measure angle.

   e. PIN photodiode with current-to-voltage amplifier.

4.11   Recently, a test kit has become available for testing the levels of lead in eating utensils (cups, bowls, plates, etc.). The utensil is first soaked in hot acetic acid (vinegar) and the acid is mixed with a reagent. If no lead is present, the mixture is clear. If a small amount of lead is present, the mixture is yellow. If a dangerous amount of lead is present, the mixture is dark orange. The light intensity passing through the solution is given by $I = I_0 e^{-kLC}$, where C is the lead concentration in ppm, L is the thickness of the solution in cm, and the extinction coefficient for green light is $k = 1$ ppm^{-1} cm^{-1}. Design a system for determining the concentration of lead in ppm, using a green LED, a photodiode, and a microcomputer with A/D converter.

   a. Sketch a block diagram including and labeling all essential components. (You can show the A/D and microcomputer as a single block).

   b. Derive an expression for the A/D input voltage as a function of lead concentration, thickness of solution, dark current (if any), amplifier offset (if any) and any calibration factors.

   c. Describe how a user would calibrate the system.

d. How accurately do you estimate that the concentration of lead could be measured? List sources of error and the estimated amount of error.

e. What is the highest lead concentration that you think you could measure? Give reason.

4.12 When designing circuits for transducers, non-ideal characteristics must frequently be taken under consideration. Consider the three cases below:

a. Explain how the circuit in Figure 4.32 converts the photodiode current I_D into the output voltage V_0.

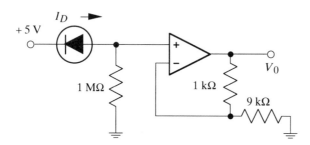

Figure 4.32   Photodiode circuit.

b. What happens if the 1 MΩ resistor is taken out of the circuit in Figure 4.32? Justify your answer.

c. Given the following specifications of the op-amp and photodiode in Figure 4.32, what is the amplifier output when no light reaches the photodiode? Show work.

Assume that the op amp has the following characteristics:

Leakage current	0.1 nA
Input offset voltage	3 mV
Noise	18 nV/Hz$^{-1/2}$
R_{in}	10^{10} Ω
Unity gain bandwidth	10^7 Hz

Assume that the photodiode has a dark current of 1 nA at 5 volt reverse bias.

d. There is a problem with the thermocouple circuit shown in Figure 4.33. How does this relate to the problem discussed above?

e. A thermistor is set up to measure the temperature in still air using the bridge circuit shown in Figure 4.14. Under these conditions, self heating causes the temperature of the thermocouple to rise 1 °C for every 10 mW of power. The thermistor resistance is 10 kΩ at 0°C,

5 kΩ at 20°C and 1 kΩ at 60°C. The resistor values are R_1 = 10 kΩ, and R_2 = R_3 = 5 kΩ.

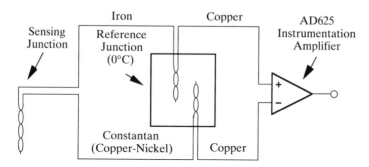

Figure 4.33   Thermocouple connected directly to an instrumentation amplifier.

At 20 °C, and 1 volt bridge bias V_b, how much power is dissipated by the thermistor? What is the temperature rise?

At 60 °C and 1 volt bridge bias V_b, how much power is dissipated by the thermistor? What is the temperature rise?

At 20 °C, when the bridge bias is increased to 10 volts, how much power is dissipated by the thermistor? What is the temperature rise?

4.13 There are almost always tradeoffs associated with any given design consideration. Before deciding which tradeoffs to make, the specific application must be considered.

    a. For a photodiode, when would you use a 5 volts reverse bias and when would you use zero volt bias?

    b. For a force transducer using an elastic rod, when would you use four strain elements and when would you use one strain element?

    c. For a bandpass filter to extract a signal in a noisy environment, when would you use a high Q (narrow) filter and when would you use a low Q (wide) filter?

    d. For sensing temperature, when would you use a thermistor and when would you use a thermocouple?

4.9 ADDITIONAL READING

4.1 George C. Barney, *Intelligent Instrumentation*, Prentice Hall, Englewood Cliffs, NJ, 1985.

4.2 Richard S. C. Cobbold, *Transducers for Biomedical Measurements*, Wiley, New York, 1974.

4.3 Leslie Cromwell, Fred J. Weibell, and Erich A. Pfeiffer, *Biomedical Instrumentation and Measurements,* Prentice Hall, Englewood Cliffs, NJ, 1980.

4.4 Robert L. Powell, William J. Hall, Clyde H. Hyink, et al., *Termcouple Reference Tables Based on the IPTS-68,* National Bureau of Standards Monograph 125, National Institute of Standards and Technology, Gaithersburg, MD.

4.5 Daniel H. Sheingold, ed., *Transducer Interfacing Handbook,* Analog Devices, Norwood, MA, 1981.

4.6 Peter Strong, *Biophysical Measurements,* Tektronix, Beaverton, OR, 1970.

4.7 Willis J. Thompkins and John G. Webster, *Interfacing Sensors to the IBM PC,* Prentice Hall, Englewood Cliffs, NJ, 1988.

4.8 Omega Engineering, *Omega Temperature Measurement Handbook and Encyclopedia,* Stamford, CT, 1987.

Laboratory Exercise 11

Measuring Angular Position

PURPOSE

To use a potentiometer to measure angle and to determine the linearity, accuracy, and backlash. To use the microcomputer to measure the angle of the decaying pendulum as a function of time.

EQUIPMENT

- IBM AT with Data Acquisition Adapter
- printer (shared with other lab groups)
- pendulum and 250-Ω potentiometer mounted on a wooden frame
- ±5-V power supplies
- oscilloscope
- digital multimeter

BACKGROUND

Damped-Harmonic Oscillator

The damped-harmonic oscillator consists of a mass that is subject to two forces, (1) the force of gravity, which is proportional to the displacement x and oppositely directed, and (2) friction, which exerts a force proportional to the velocity v and oppositely directed. The force equation is

$$F = ma = -kx - cv$$

which results in the equation of motion

$$m\,(d^2x/dt^2) + c\,(dx/dt) + kx = 0$$

where k is the restoring-force constant, and c is the friction-force constant.

This differential equation has the characteristic equation:

$$mr^2 + cr + k = 0 \quad \text{with the solution} \quad r = \frac{-c - \sqrt{c^2 - 4km}}{2m}$$

There are three cases:

Case 1: The underdamped oscillator. When $c^2 < 4km$, the solution is:

$$x = e^{-\alpha t}\left[A\cos(\omega t) + B\sin(\omega t)\right] = R\,e^{-\alpha t}\cos(\omega t + \delta)$$

where $R = \sqrt{A^2 + B^2}$, $\tan(\delta) = B/A$, $\alpha = c/2m$, and $\omega = \dfrac{\sqrt{4km - c^2}}{2m}$

The undamped natural frequency is given by $\omega_0 = \sqrt{k/m}$ and the damping factor α reduces the frequency of oscillation.

$$\omega^2 = \omega_0^2 - \alpha^2$$

The constants A and B are determined from the initial position x_0 and velocity v_0.

$$x_0 = A \quad v_0 = \omega B$$

Case 2: The critically-damped oscillator. When $c^2 = 4km$, the solution is:

$$x = (A + Bt)\,e^{-\alpha t} \quad \text{where} \quad \alpha = \frac{c}{2m} = \frac{2k}{c} = \sqrt{k/m}$$

The constants A and B are determined from the initial position x_0 and velocity v_0.

$$x_0 = A \quad v_0 = B - \alpha A$$

Note: Case 2 is of particular importance in electrical and mechanical engineering because when a harmonic oscillator (such as a circuit or building) is critically damped, it recovers from an impulse disturbance more quickly than with any other damping.

Case 3: The overdamped oscillator. When $c^2 > 4km$, the solution is:

$$x = A e^{-\alpha t} + B e^{-\beta t}$$

$$\text{where} \quad \alpha = \frac{c + \sqrt{c^2 - 4km}}{2m} \quad \text{and} \quad \beta = \frac{c - \sqrt{c^2 - 4km}}{2m}$$

The constants A and B are determined from the initial position x_0 and velocity v_0.

$$x_0 = A + B \quad v_0 = -\alpha A - \beta B$$

Note: When the damping term c is large, α_2 is small, and after a disturbance the system returns slowly to $x = 0$.

ADDITIONAL READING

Chapter 4, Section 4.2: Position Sensors.

Appendix E (Summary of the IBM Data Acquisition and Control Adapter), Section 4: Analog Output and Section 5: Analog Input.

PROCEDURE

1 Setup

Attach +5 volts and –5 volts to opposite contacts of the potentiometer mounted on the pendulum board (Laboratory Figure 11.1). Connect the wiper (center contact) to your digital multimeter and to analog input 0^+ (pin 6) of the IBM Data Acquisition and Control Adapter. Connect the power supply ground to analog input 0^- (pin 5) and pins 4, 13, 15, and 60. See Appendix E, Table E.1, for pin assignments.

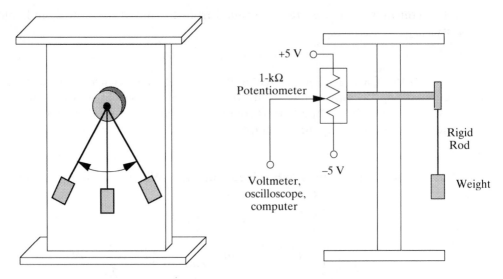

Laboratory Figure 11.1   Pendulum with a potentiometer for the measurement of angle.

2 Static Measurement of Angle

Place the wooden frame flat and measure the output for five different angles using the polar graph paper attached. Check reproducibility and see if the result depends on whether you approach the angle from the right or from the left (backlash). Run the computer program and record the digitized output for each angle measured.

3 Dynamic Measurement of Angle

3.1 Oscilloscope Output.   Set the wooden frame upright and observe the output on the oscilloscope after the pendulum has been allowed to swing (use a slow sweep, about 1 s per division). Draw the waveform and make a rough estimate of the period (time per cycle) and decay time (time for the sine-wave envelope to decay to $e^{-1} = 0.368$ of its original amplitude).

3.2 Computer Output.   Run the microcomputer program "sample" to digitize and print the amplitude of the decaying pendulum as a function of time.

LABORATORY REPORT

1 Setup

Draw a simple block diagram of your experimental setup.

2 Data Summary and Analysis

2.1 Tabulate output voltage and computer output as a function of angle (data from procedure section 2). Do you see any deviations from linearity?

2.2 Plot the computer output vs. time (data from procedure section 3) and describe in simple analytic form.

3 Discussion and Conclusions

Discuss the principles covered in procedure sections 2 and 3.

4 Questions

4.1 If the pendulum were frictionless (did not decay), had a period of 0.5 s, and you took three samples per sec, what would your data look like?

4.2 How accurate is this potentiometer when used to measure angle? What is the sensitivity in degrees per A/D count? Did you observe any backlash?

4.3 If the potentiometer had a resistance of 10 kΩ and the data-acquisition circuit had an input impedance of 10 kΩ, would you expect the digitized values to be a linear function of angle?

5 Computer Output and Laboratory Data Sheets

5.1 Include your computer output.

5.2 Include your handwritten data sheets (or a copy), which should consist of a log of the procedures you used, any special circumstances, and the measurements you recorded manually.

Laboratory Exercise 12

Measuring Temperature

PURPOSE

To use three important temperature transducers: the thermocouple, the thermistor, and the platinum resistance thermometer (or dial thermometer). To compare their response time, sensitivity, linearity, precision, and accuracy.

EQUIPMENT

- IBM AT with Data Acquisition and Control Adapter
- platinum resistance thermometer (or dial thermometer)
- +5-V, ±12-V power supplies
- AD625 instrumentation amplifier
- iron–constantan thermocouple
- digital multimeter with 0.1-mV sensitivity and 0.1-Ω accuracy on 200-Ω full scale
- precision thermistor (Omega type YSI 44004 (1207), 2252 Ω at 25°C) coated with insulator for water immersion
- one 25-kΩ trimpot
- two 1-MΩ resistors
- two 2.5-kΩ resistors

- one 2-kΩ resistor
- two 20-kΩ resistors
- one 400-Ω resistor
- one 40-Ω resistor
- electronics breadboard
- three 15-μF, 20-V electrolytic capacitors (put between power and ground on the superstrip breadboard)
- three 0.1-μF CK05 capacitors (put between power and ground on all chips)
- crushed ice
- hot plate
- two 500-ml pyrex beakers and stirring rod (wood or glass)

ADDITIONAL READING

Chapter 2, Section 2.4.1: Instrumentation Amplifiers.

Chapter 4, Section 4.3: Temperature Transducers.

PROCEDURE

1 Setup

1.1 Circuit construction. Set up your instrumentation amplifier with a gain of about 100 by using $R_F = 20$ kΩ and $R_G = 400$ Ω. You will use it to amplify the thermocouple signal, which is quite small. Set up the thermistor bridge, as shown in Laboratory Figure 12.1 with $V_S = 1$ volt, $R_1 = 25$ kΩ, and $R_2 = R_3 = 2.5$ kΩ. Measure the amplifier voltage gain, which will be needed for your thermocouple data analysis. The bridge output may be accurately read with the digital multimeter without amplification.

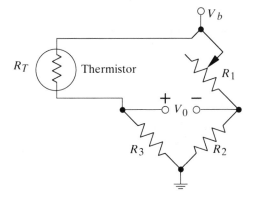

Laboratory Figure 12.1   Thermistor bridge circuit. The thermistor resistance is 2.5 kΩ at 25°C, the trimpot R_1 is 25 kΩ and the two resistors R_2 and R_3 are 2.5 kΩ.

1.2 Reference bath. Place crushed ice in a beaker of tap water and stir. This will serve as your 0°C reference. You will also use the platinum resistance thermometer (or dial thermometer) to provide a standard temperature measurement. See Chapter 4, Table 4.1, for platinum resistance vs. temperature.

2 Thermocouple

2.1 Connections and reference junction. Connect the copper leads of the thermocouple to the differential inputs of the AD625 instrumentation amplifier. The external connections for the AD625 are shown in Laboratory Figure 5.2. Connect the amplifier output to the digital multimeter and immerse the copper reference junctions in the 0°C ice bath, as shown in Laboratory Figure 12.2.

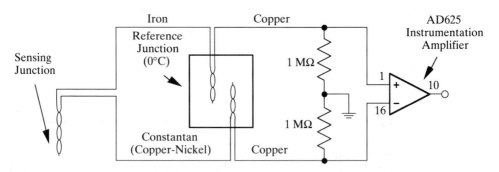

Laboratory Figure 12.2   Thermocouple junctions and instrumentation amplifier.

2.2 Calibration of sensing junction. Place the sensing junction and a small amount of crushed ice in a second beaker and stir. When the standard thermometer reads 0°C, record the thermocouple DVM reading. Now place the second beaker on the hot plate and warm slowly while stirring. At 5 or 10°C intervals, record the standard thermometer reading and the thermocouple DVM reading. Continue until 100°C is reached.

3 Thermistor

3.1 Thermistor bridge. You will be using a thermistor with a resistance of 2252 Ω at 25°C (Laboratory Figure 12.1). We select $R_2 = R_3 = 2.5$ kΩ, since the bridge output is in its most linear range when R_2 and R_3 are both equal to the thermistor resistance. R_1 is a 25-kΩ variable resistor, sufficiently high to balance the thermistor at 0°C.

The bridge equation is

$$V_0 = V_+ - V_- = V_b \left(\frac{R_3}{R_T + R_3} - \frac{R_2}{R_1 + R_2} \right)$$

Solving for R_T we have:

$$R_T = R_3 \frac{V_b R_1 - V_0 (R_1 + R_2)}{V_b R_2 + V_0 (R_1 + R_2)}$$

3.2 Thermistor calibration. Place the thermistor in the 0°C bath and adjust R_1 so that V_0 (measured by your DVM) is zero volts on the most sensitive scale. As before, record the temperature and the DVM reading as you heat a beaker of water from 0 to 100°C. Leave the water boiling gently for the next step. *Note:* You will need to measure accurately the values of R_1, R_2, and R_3 for your analysis.

Suggestion: To save time, you may want to calibrate the thermocouple and the thermistor simultaneously.

3.3 Self-heating. With the thermistor in still air, let the bridge output come to equilibrium and record the output voltage. Increase the bridge excitation to 3 volts, let the bridge output come to equilibrium and again record the output voltage. Restore the bridge to 1 volt and again record the output voltage.

4 Dynamic Measurement of Temperature

4.1 Thermistor. Prepare two beakers of water, one at room temperature, the other at about 40°C. (*Caution:* If the temperature difference is too great, the thermistor may crack when it is rapidly transferred between the two beakers.) Set up the thermistor bridge and the AD625 instrumentation amplifier circuit with a gain of about 20 ($R_G = 2$ kΩ). This should provide an output of about –5 volts for the cooler beaker and +5 volts in the warmer beaker. Connect the AD625 output to analog input 0+ (pin 6). Connect the power supply ground to analog input 0– (pin 5) and pins 4, 13, 15, and 60. Use the microcomputer to record the transient that occurs when the thermistor is rapidly transferred from one beaker to the other. After equilibrium is established, rapidly transfer to the first beaker. Print the results.

4.2 Thermocouple. Repeat procedure section 4.1 for the thermocouple. To provide a 2-volt output change for the data acquisition board, you will need an AD625 voltage gain of 1000 ($R_G = 40$ Ω).

5 Reproducibility

To check reproducibility, remeasure the 40°C bath with the standard thermometer, thermistor, and thermocouple.

LABORATORY REPORT

1 Setup

Draw a simple block diagram of your experimental setup.

2 Data Summary and Analysis

2.1 Thermocouple data.   From the data of procedure section 2 (thermocouple), tabulate and plot the amplifier output and thermocouple output (computed by using the measured gain) as a function of temperature. Compute and tabulate the thermocouple sensitivity before and after amplification in mV/°C.

2.2 Thermistor data.   From the data of procedure section 3 (thermistor), tabulate the bridge output as a function of temperature. Compute and tabulate the thermistor bridge sensitivity in mV/°C as a function of temperature.

2.3 Thermistor resistance and beta.   Use the bridge equation to compute the thermistor resistance as a function of temperature. Tabulate your data and results. Plot ln (log base e) resistance vs. inverse temperature (in degrees Kelvin!) and estimate (by eyeball) the best-fit value and uncertainty in β for your thermistor.

2.4 Thermistor self-heating.   From the self-heating data of procedure section 3.3, compute the thermistor resistance, power dissipation, and temperature in still air for 1-volt and 3-volt bridge excitations. Estimate the dissipation constant as the power required to raise the thermistor temperature 1 °C.

2.5 Dynamic response.   Plot temperature as a function of time for the dynamic temperature data of procedure section 4. Estimate the thermal time constant of the thermistor.

2.6 Reproducibility.   Tabulate the thermistor and thermocouple outputs measured at the same temperature but at different times (procedure section 5).

3 Discussion and Conclusions

Discuss the principles covered in each of procedure sections 2 to 5.

4 Questions

4.1   What accuracy and precision (in °C) would you estimate for the thermocouple and the thermistor? (*Note:* accuracy means adherence to a standard, whereas precision means reproducibility and the ability to reliably detect small changes.)

4.2   What was the range of power dissipated by your thermistor during your measurements? Considering the dissipation constant estimated in analysis section 2.4, do you think that self-heating affected your measurements? By what factor would the dissipation increase if the bridge supply voltage were increased from 1 to 10 volts?

4.3   What value of $R_2 = R_3$ gives the largest bridge sensitivity to temperature? *Hint:* Define $\alpha = R_3/R_T$, and find the value of α that maximizes the quantity $R_T(dV_0/dR_T)$.

4.4   What are the two most important factors that determine the response time of a temperature transducer?

5 Computer Output and Laboratory Data Sheets

5.1   Include your computer output.

5.2   Include your handwritten data sheets (or a copy), which should consist of a log of the procedures you used, any special circumstances, and the measurements you recorded manually.

Laboratory Exercise 13

Measuring Strain and Force

PURPOSE

To investigate the sensitivity, linearity, hysteresis, and temperature dependence of two force transducers. The first uses a single strain element cemented to a lucite rod. The second uses four strain elements mounted in opposing pairs.

EQUIPMENT

- one AD625 Instrumentation Amplifier
- one 400-Ω resistor
- two 20-kΩ resistors
- two 120-Ω 1% resistors
- one 200-Ω trimpot
- +1-V, ±12 V power supplies
- superstrip circuit board
- three 15-μF, 20-V electrolytic capacitors (put between power terminals and ground on superstrip circuit board)
- two 0.1-μF CK05 bypass capacitors (put between power and ground on AD625)
- digital multimeter

- strain gauge unit (lucite rod with four strain elements)
- set calibration weights (50 g to 1 kg, shared with other lab groups)
- heat gun (shared with other lab groups)
- dial thermometer
- four strain gauges: BLH Electronics, 42 Forth Ave, Waltham MA 02254. Type FAE-25-35-SO (SR-4) resistance 120.0 Ω, gauge factor 2.04.
- Aluminum plate, vertical support rod, and clamps to hold the strain gauge unit as shown in Laboratory Figure 13.1.

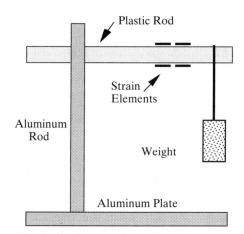

Laboratory Figure 13.1   Setup for force measurement.

ADDITIONAL READING

Chapter 2, Section 2.4.1: Instrumentation Amplifiers.

Chapter 4, Section 4.4: Strain-Sensing Elements and Section 4.5.1: Force Transducers.

PROCEDURE

1 Single-Strain-Element Force Transducer

Set up the single-strain-element bridge circuit shown in Laboratory Figure 13.2. Set up the instrumentation amplifier for a gain of 100. See Laboratory Figure 5.2 for connections. With no load on the rod, adjust the 200-Ω trimpot for $V_0 = 0$.

1.1 Force calibration.   Hang 0, 50, 100, 200, 300, 500, 700 and 1000 g weights and for each; record V_0. With the 1000-g weight, measure the gain of the instrumentation amplifier as $V_0/(V_+ - V_-)$.

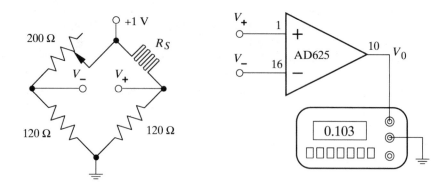

Laboratory Figure 13.2   Single-strain-element bridge and AD625 instrumentation amplifier.

1.2 Drift.   Remove the 1000 g weight, and immediately record V_0. Record every minute for 5 min.

1.3 Reproducibility.   Replace the 1000 g weight, and record V_0. Remove the weight, and again record V_0.

1.4 Effect of heating.   Gently heat the *top* of the rod (no load). Record any changes in V_0 while heating. Estimate the temperature rise using a dial thermometer. Do not heat more than 10°C. Repeat, heating the *bottom* of the rod. Repeat, heating the top and bottom at the same time.

2 Four-Strain-Element Force Transducer

Set up the four element bridge circuit shown in Laboratory Figure 13.3. With no load, adjust the instrumentation amplifier offset (25-kΩ trimpot in Laboratory Figure 5.2) for $V_0 = 0$. Repeat procedure section 1 for this force transducer.

LABORATORY REPORT

1 Setup

Draw a simple block diagram of your experimental setup.

2 Data Summary and Analysis

2.1 Bridge equations.   Derive the bridge equations for V_0 as a function of strain $\Delta L/L$ for both force transducers. Assume that the elongation

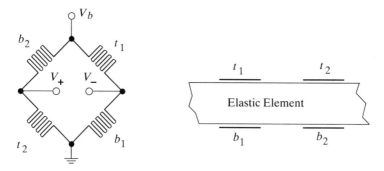

Laboratory Figure 13.3   Force transducer bridge using four strain
elements.

$\Delta L/L$ is proportional to the load, $\Delta R/R = G(\Delta L/L)$, and all strain gauges
have the same resistance when $\Delta L/L = 0$.

2.2 Output vs. load plots.   Plot amplifier output V_0 as a function of
load for both force transducers. Compute the sensitivity in mV/g.

2.3 Comparison between measurements and a linear model.
Derive a linear expression for output voltage vs. load for the two force transducers. For the loads that you used, tabulate your measured data, the value
of the expression, and the difference between them. *Note:* You will want to
examine your data and adjust the slope and intercept of the line to minimize
the deviations from the data.

3 Discussion and Conclusions

Based on your analysis, discuss the relative merits of the single- and four-
element force transducer from the standpoint of sensitivity, linearity, and the
effect of uniform heating.

4 Questions

4.1   What is the effect of uniform and nonuniform heating that you
observed on the two force transducers? Express in terms of amplifier output
V_0 and load in g.

4.2   Why was it important to limit the temperature rise in procedure
sections 1.4 and 2.4?

4.3   For both transducers, what strain $\Delta L/L$ occurred for a 1000 g
load?

4.4   What was the largest deviation between your data and your straight-line fit? What does this mean in terms of load in g?

4.5   Does the relative sensitivity (mV/g) of the four-element bridge and the one-element bridge agree with what was expected?

5 Laboratory Data Sheets

Include your handwritten data sheets (or a copy), which should consist of a log of the procedures you used, any special circumstances, and the measurements you recorded manually.

Laboratory Exercise 14

Measuring Light with a Photodiode

PURPOSE

To measure the I-V characteristics, dark current, noise, and linearity of a high-sensitivity PIN silicon photodiode and to use it in a simple photometer to measure the concentration of solutions.

EQUIPMENT

- +5-V, ±12-V power supplies
- three 15-µF, 20-V electrolytic capacitors (put between power terminals and ground on superstrip circuit board)
- DMM (digital multimeter)
- wooden block for PIN photodiode, LED source, and test tube
- hollow black cylinder, taped on one end, to cover top of test tube
- solid black cylinder to block light when no test tube is present
- red light-emitting diode (LED) (≥20 mA maximum current)
- PIN silicon photodiode
- two 10-kΩ trimpots
- one 25-kΩ trimpot
- one 330-Ω resistor
- three 10-kΩ resistors

- two 1-MΩ resistors
- two LF 356 op-amps
- four 0.1-μF, CK05 bypass capacitors (put between power and ground on all chips)
- one vial of 0.01-molar potassium permanganate ($KMnO_4$, deep purple color)
- one vial of 0.005-molar potassium permanganate
- one vial of 0.002-molar potassium permanganate
- one vial of 0.001-molar potassium permanganate
- one vial of potassium permanganate of unknown concentration
- one vial of water

ADDITIONAL READING

Chapter 2, Section 2.2: Operational Amplifier Circuits.

Chapter 4, Section 4.6: Measuring Light.

PROCEDURE

1 Setup

The silicon PIN photodiode and the LED are mounted in a wooden block as shown in Laboratory Figure 14.1.

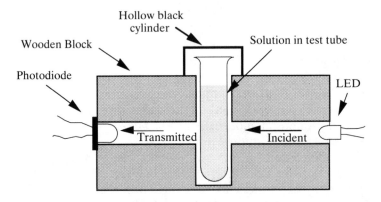

Laboratory Figure 14.1   Setup for measuring light transmission through a solution.

1.1 Photodiode biasing and amplifier circuits.   Construct the photodiode biasing and current amplifier circuit shown in Laboratory Figure 14.2. Note that positive bias voltages cause the photodiode to be reverse biased. A photodiode current of 1 mA should produce an op-amp output

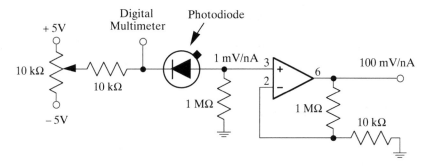

Laboratory Figure 14.2 Circuit for biasing a photodiode and converting the photoconduction current into a voltage. Metal tab on the case is toward the anode lead.

voltage of 100 mV. The LF 356 op-amp pinout and connections to the external components are shown in Laboratory Figures 4.1 and 4.2. Adjust the 25-kΩ trimpot for zero output offset voltage.

1.2 LED biasing circuit. Construct the controlled-current LED circuit shown in Laboratory Figure 14.3.

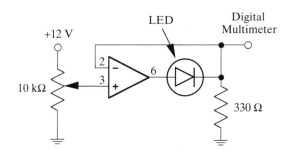

Laboratory Figure 14.3 Op-amp circuit for providing a controlled current through a light-emitting diode. Output is 3 mA/V.

2 Photodiode *I-V* Characteristics and Noise with Dark Conditions

To exclude room light, tape the test tube hole with black tape.

2.1 Reverse bias. Measure the dc current as a function of bias on the photodiode. Suggested bias-voltages are 0.0, 0.1, 0.3, 1, 2, and 5 volts. At each bias voltage, record the dc output voltage level as seen on your oscilloscope and estimate the rms noise (use aluminum foil for shielding if necessary).

2.1 Forward bias. Determine the bias voltages required to produce forward currents of 1, 2, 5, 10, 20, and 50 nA.

3 Photodiode Light Response

3.1 Photovoltaic mode.   With a photodiode bias of 0 volts, measure photodiode current vs. LED current for six values of LED current: 1, 2, 5, 10, 15, and 20 mA (the maximum output of the op-amp).

3.2 Photoconductive mode.   Repeat procedure section 3.1 with a 5-volt reverse bias .

4 Photodiode *I-V* Characteristics and Noise with Illumination

Repeat procedure section 2 with an LED current of 20 mA.

5 Measuring the Concentration of a Solution

Set the LED current to 20 mA and set the photodiode reverse bias to 0 volts (photovoltaic mode).   Record the photodiode output for the four known solutions and for the unknown.

The photodiode current is given by $I = I_0\, e^{-kLC} + I_B$, where L is the path length, C is the concentration, and k is the extinction coefficient.   Use the water-filled test tube ($C = 0$) to measure $I_0 + I_B$, and turn off the LED to measure I_B (due to amplifier offset).   To use Beer's law, plot $(I - I_B)/I_0$ vs. concentration C on semi-log graph paper.

$$\boxed{\begin{array}{c} \text{Beer's Law:} \\[4pt] \dfrac{\text{transmitted light}}{\text{incident light}} = e^{-kLC} \end{array}}$$

LABORATORY REPORT

1 Setup

Draw a simple block diagram of your experimental setup.

2 Data Summary and Analysis

2.1 Photodiode I-V curves.   Plot photodiode current as a function of voltage for LED currents of 0 mA (procedure section 2) and 20 mA (procedure section 4).   Be sure to include both forward- and reverse-biased data, and to consider any voltage drop across the 1 MΩ input resistor (between op-amp pin 3 and ground).

2.2 Noise vs. dark current.   Plot rms noise as a function of photodiode current (procedure sections 2 and 4).

2.3 Noise model.   Devise an empirical expression that describes the noise and incorporates Johnson and shot noise as separate terms. (Remember that shot noise varies as $\sqrt{I}$, whereas Johnson noise is independent of I.)

2.4 Photodiode vs. LED currents.   Tabulate and plot photodiode current vs. LED current (procedure section 3).

2.5 Beer's law plot.   Using your photovoltaic measurements from procedure section 5, plot the natural logarithm of photodiode current vs. solution concentration. Use Beer's law to estimate the concentration of your unknown solution. Estimate your uncertainty.

3 Discussion and Conclusions

Briefly discuss the principles covered in this laboratory exercise.

4 Questions

4.1   Was the photodiode current linearly proportional to the LED current? If not, what could be the reasons?

4.2   If the maximum photodiode power dissipation is 0.1 W, what is the maximum safe current in forward-biased mode? In reverse-biased mode?

4.3   Does the plot from analysis section 2.1 agree with the graph in Chapter 4, Figure 4.21?

5 Laboratory Data Sheets

Include your handwritten data sheets (or a copy), which should consist of a log of the procedures you used, any special circumstances, and the measurements you recorded manually.

Laboratory Exercise 15

The Thermoelectric Heat Pump

PURPOSE

To investigate the application of a thermoelectric device as a heat pump to heat and cool a small object.

EQUIPMENT

- digital multimeter
- Cambion # 801-3959-01 thermoelectric device (maximum current 10 A at 5 V)
- high current power supply: 5 V at 10 A
- thick aluminum plate (heat sink)
- small beaker, approx 10 ml
- heat sink compound: zinc oxide in silicone paste
- small 5 mil mylar sheet
- dial thermometer

BACKGROUND

1 Peltier and Seebeck Effects

While the Peltier and Seebeck effects have been known for over 100 years, practical applications for the production of electrical power and as a heat pump have been exploited only recently. Examples include power generators in space vehicles, cooling devices for low-temperature instrumentation, precision temperature references, temperature stabilization of precision instrumentation, etc.

You will be using a Bi_2Te_3 semiconductor Peltier heat pump with P and N doping as shown in Figure 4.11. The rate of heat removal Q from the cold surface of the heat pump is given by

$$Q = \pi I - I^2 R / 2 - K \Delta T$$

The first term on the right-hand side is due to the Peltier effect, where π is the Peltier coefficient. The second term is Joule heating, where R is the ratio between the voltage V across the device and the current I through the device. The third term is due to thermal conductivity K through the device.

At low currents, the first term can be larger than the second, resulting in net cooling. However, as the current is increased, the I^2 term will eventually dominate, resulting in net heating. There is, therefore, a value of I that maximizes Q. This can also been seen from the quadratic form for $Q(I)$.

If the system is at equilibrium, $Q = 0$ because the cooling factor πI is equal to the sum of the Joule heating $I^2 R$ and the thermal conduction losses $K \Delta T$. If the current I is abruptly changed, then the heat transfer Q will be such as to drive the system to a new equilibrium.

2 Estimation of T_{equ} from T vs. Time Measurements

For a simple (one compartment) thermal system, the time rate of change in temperature dT/dt is proportional to the difference between the current temperature T and some equilibrium temperature T_{equ}.

$$\frac{dT}{dt} = k (T_{equ} - T)$$

The solution is:

$$T_n = T_{equ} - (T_{equ} - T_0) e^{-t_n/\tau}$$

where $\tau = 1/k$, the initial temperature is T_0 at $t_0 = 0$, and the temperature asymptotically approaches T_{equ} as t_n becomes very large.

In a realistic thermal system, after a change in the heat input or the system being heated, the initial change in temperature does not necessarily obey the above equation, but after a few time constants τ, the equation is usually accurate enough to predict the equilibrium value T_{equ} without having to wait forever!

We have two objectives here: (i) determining when the above equation describes the measured asymptotic behavior of the thermal system, and (ii) estimating T_{equ} from the data.

If the equation is valid, we expect that the ratio of successive differences will be constant:

$$Q = \frac{T_{n+2} - T_{n+1}}{T_{n+1} - T_n} = \frac{\left(T_{equ} - T_0\right)\left(e^{-t_{n+2}/\tau} - e^{-t_{n+1}/\tau}\right)}{\left(T_{equ} - T_0\right)\left(e^{-t_{n+1}/\tau} - e^{-t_n/\tau}\right)} = e^{-\Delta t/\tau}$$

where the t_n are equally spaced in time and $\Delta T = t_{n+1} - t_n$.

So the procedure is to compute Q for successive time intervals and when it is reasonably constant, use the following analysis to estimate T_{equ}:

$$T_{equ} = T_{n+1} + (T_{n+2} - T_{n+1}) + (T_{n+3} - T_{n+2}) + (T_{n+4} - T_{n+3}) + \ldots$$

$$= T_{n+1} + (T_{n+2} - T_{n+1}) + (T_{n+2} - T_{n+1}) \frac{(T_{n+3} - T_{n+2})}{(T_{n+2} - T_{n+1})}$$

$$+ (T_{n+2} - T_{n+1}) \frac{(T_{n+3} - T_{n+2})}{(T_{n+2} - T_{n+1})} \frac{(T_{n+4} - T_{n+3})}{(T_{n+3} - T_{n+2})} + \ldots$$

$$= T_{n+1} + (T_{n+2} - T_{n+1})(1 + Q + Q^2 + \ldots)$$

the working result is:

$$\boxed{T_{equ} = T_{n+1} + \frac{T_{n+2} - T_{n+1}}{1 - Q}}$$

ADDITIONAL READING

Chapter 4, Section 4.3.4: The Thermocouple.

PROCEDURE

1 Setup

As shown in Laboratory Figure 15.1, paste a sheet of mylar or paper to the aluminum heat sink plate with ZnO cream, paste the thermoelectric device (TED) to the top of the mylar or paper, and then paste a 10 ml beaker of

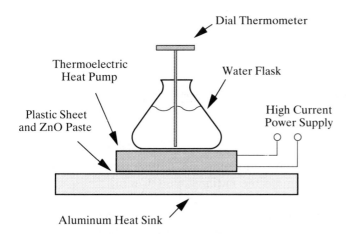

Laboratory Figure 15.1   Setup for using a thermoelectric heat pump to heat and cool a beaker of water.

water on top of the TED. Fill the beaker about half full of water and place a dial thermometer into the beaker. Record the amount of water in the beaker for later calculations.

2 Thermoelectric Efficiency

Abruptly apply 5 A of current to the TED and record the voltage and temperature every 30 s for 5 min. Observe whether the water temperature is increasing or decreasing. The initial slope of the temperature-vs.-time curve will be used to compare the power consumed by the TED with the caloric power received (or extracted from) the water in the beaker. (*Note:* Initially, the temperature of the beaker is close to room temperature and the thermal energy pumped by the TED acts only to change the temperature of the beaker.)

Wait 10 min for the system to approach thermal equilibrium with the room, reverse the polarity of the power leads, and apply 5 A, recording the voltage and temperature every 30 s for 5 min.

3 Thermoelectric Capacity

Reduce the current to 1 A and wait for the temperature to stabilize. Record the voltage and temperature. Slowly increase the current from the power supply in 1-A steps, wait for the temperature to stabilize, and record the voltage and temperature. (*Note:* At equilibrium, the temperature does not change and the thermal energy pumped by the TED is equal to that lost to the surroundings.)

Reverse the polarity of the power into the TED and repeat the series of measurements.

LABORATORY REPORT

1 Setup

Draw a simple block diagram of your experimental setup.

2 Data Summary and Analysis

2.1 Initial slope.   Tabulate and plot the temperature-vs.-time data from procedure section 2. Estimate the initial slope (°C/min).

2.2 Thermoelectric efficiency.   From your initial slope data of procedure section 2 and the known weight of the water, compute the caloric thermal power received by (or extracted from) the beaker and the electrical power consumed by the thermoelectric device. The thermal power needed to change the temperature of 1 g of water at the rate of 1°C/s is 4.19 W. Use these to compute the thermal power that must have been transferred to the heat sink. (Assume that the beaker temperature was sufficiently close to room temperature, so that you can ignore the heat transfer with the surroundings.) Compute the thermoelectric efficiency as ratio of the power received by (or extracted from) the beaker to the electrical power consumed by the thermoelectric device.

2.3 Thermoelectric capacity.   Tabulate and plot the equilibrium temperature vs. current (procedure section 3). Include a column for power input. Do an "eyeball" fit of the model

$$T_{equ} = T_{room} - AI + BI^2$$

to your data.

3 Discussion and Conclusions

Discuss procedure sections 1 to 3.

4 Questions

4.1   What power supply wattage was required to achieve a beaker equilibrium temperature 10°C above ambient? 10°C below ambient?

4.2   When you cooled the beaker you noticed a point for which further increases in current (and power to the TED) did not result in further cooling. Why did this occur? What are the major factors (in the real world) that determine the lowest temperature that you can achieve?

4.3   How would thermal insulation around the beaker affect the temperature-vs.-current curve and the thermal time constant of the system.

4.4   Was the thermoelectric efficiency the same for cooling as for heating? Why?

5 Laboratory Data Sheets

Include your handwritten data sheets (or a copy), which should consist of a log of the procedures you used, any special circumstances, and the measurements you recorded manually.

Laboratory Exercise 16

Electrodes
and Ionic Media

PURPOSE

To measure and compare several important properties of Ag(AgCl) electrodes and bare-metal electrodes: offset potential, stability, and complex impedance as a function of frequency.

EQUIPMENT

- +5-V, ±12-V power supplies
- superstrip circuit breadboard
- digital multimeter
- sine-wave signal generator
- oscilloscope
- two Ag(AgCl) skin electrodes with the gel and adhesive removed
- two stainless steel or copper plates
- 1% NaCl solution
- tap water

BACKGROUND

1 Electrodes Used as Sensors and Actuators

Electrodes are used as sensors to record potentials from the heart (electro-cardiogram, or ECG), from the muscles (electromyogram, or EMG), from the eyes (electrooculogram or EOG), from the brain (electroencephalogram, or EEG), and even from individual cells. Electrodes are essential compo-nents in electromagnetic flowmeters, pH meters, and ion meters. They are also used as actuators to stimulate nerve conduction and muscle contraction. The skin electrodes studied in this laboratory exercise will also be used for the ECG in Laboratory Exercise 17, the EMG in Laboratory Exercise 18, and the EOG in Laboratory Exercise 19.

An understanding of the electrical nature of the recording or stimulat-ing electrodes and the properties of the ionic media (the tissue fluids or salt solution) is necessary for a better understanding of the resultant effects or measurements.

2 Complex Impedance Analysis

To better understand the nature of your electrode measurements, we review some basic material relating phase shifts with reactive components. The gen-eralized complex impedance and the graphical relationship between resistive and reactive impedance are shown in Laboratory Figure 16.1.

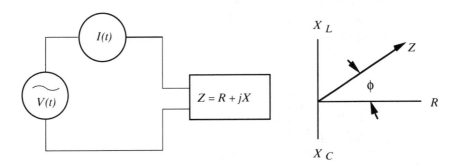

Laboratory Figure 16.1   Left: circuit for complex impedance measure-ment. Right: Graphical relationship between phase angle and amplitudes of resistive and reactive impedance.

Exciting potential: $V(t) = V_0 \sin(\omega t)$ Resulting current: $I(t) = I_0 \sin(\omega t + \phi)$

$$\tan(\phi) = \frac{X}{R} \qquad I_0 = \frac{V_0}{\sqrt{R^2 + X^2}}$$

Resistor: $Z = R$ Inductor: $Z = j\omega L = jX_L$ Capacitor: $Z = -j/\omega C = -jX_C$

Pure R: $\phi = 0°$, $V(t)$ and $I(t)$ in phase

Pure L: $\phi = 90°$, $I(t)$ lags $V(t)$ by $90°$

Pure C : $\phi = -90°$, $I(t)$ leads $V(t)$ by $90°$

R, L, and C in series: $Z = R + jX$, $X = \omega L - 1/\omega C$

add Z's in series $Z_{12} = Z_1 + Z_2$ add Z's in parallel $\dfrac{1}{Z_{12}} = \dfrac{1}{Z_1} + \dfrac{1}{Z_2}$

ADDITIONAL READING

Chapter 4, Section 4.7: Ionic Potentials.

Peter Strong, *Biophysical Measurements,* Tektronix, Beaverton, OR, 1970, Chapter 16.

Getzel and Webster, "Minimizing Silver-Silver Chloride Electrode Impedance," IEEE Trans. Biomed. Eng. BME-23, No. 1, (1976): pp 87–88.

PROCEDURE

1 Preparation of Electrodes and Ionic Medium

1. Remove the adhesive from two Ag(AgCl) skin electrodes. Leave the foam and electrolyte gel in place.
2. Fill a 500-ml beaker with 1% NaCl solution.
3. Suspend the Ag(AgCl) electrodes so that the gel touches the top of the solution (Laboratory Figure 16.2).

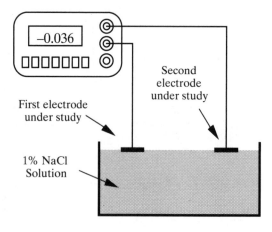

Laboratory Figure 16.2   Setup for measurement of offset potential.

2 Electrode Offset Potential, Stability, and Microphonics

Metals in contact with ionic media often undergo chemical reactions that produce a potential difference in the absence of a current, very much like a weak battery. This potential may depend on layers of charge near the surface that can change with time and can be displaced by a mechanical disturbance.

2.1 Two Ag(AgCl) electrodes. With the two Ag(AgCl) electrodes, use your digital multimeter to record the offset potential every 30 s for 5 min. Then determine how microphonic the electrodes are by observing the oscilloscope deflection (slow sweep) when the table is given a "standard" tap.

2.2 Ag(AgCl) vs. bare metal electrodes. Repeat procedure section 2.1 using one Ag(AgCl) electrode and a bare-metal electrode (a copper alligator clip).

2.3 Two bare metal electrodes. Repeat the measurement using two bare-metal electrodes.

3 AC Electrode Impedance

In tissue stimulation, knowledge of the electrical impedance of the stimulation electrode is important, because it will determine the actual level of current passed into the tissue for a given voltage. In another type of study, measurement of the actual impedance across or through some types of tissue or organ is desired. In this case, the impedance of the electrode–tissue interface may be significantly greater than the impedance of the tissue itself. For both of these reasons, we need to measure electrode impedance. In addition, under normal conditions, we want to minimize this impedance.

Set up the electrode-impedance measuring apparatus as shown in Laboratory Figure 16.3. Test the circuit by measuring the impedance of a 100-Ω resistor and of a 100-Ω resistor in series with a 1-μF capacitor.

Choose one of your Ag(AgCl) electrodes as a reference, and at $V(t) =$ 0.1 V measure $I(t)$ and the $V(t)$–$I(t)$ phase difference for the other Ag(AgCl) and bare-metal electrodes at 1 Hz, 10 Hz, 100 Hz, 1 kHz, 10 kHz, and 100 kHz. For each electrode and at each frequency, you will need to adjust the oscillator output for $V(t) = 0.1$ V amplitude. This is necessary because different electrode impedances load the oscillator differently.

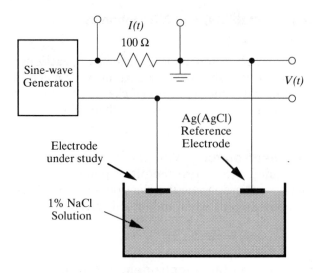

Laboratory Figure 16.3   Setup for measuring the complex impedance of electrodes as a function of frequency.

LABORATORY REPORT

1 Setup

Draw a simple block diagram of your experimental setup.

2 Data Summary and Analysis

2.1 Offset potential vs. time.   Plot the offset potential as a function of time for the three electrode pairs.

2.2 Microphonics.   Tabulate the effect of a standard tap for the three electrode pairs.

2.3 Complex impedance vs. frequency.   For the three electrode pairs, tabulate the amplitude of $V(t)$ and $I(t)$ and the phase difference between them as a function of frequency. Compute the real (resistive) and imaginary (reactive) parts of the impedance and enter them into the table.

2.4 Equivalent circuits.   From the results of analysis part 2.3, deduce the equivalent circuits that describe the individual electrodes. (*Hint:* See Figure 4.25. Use your 1 Hz data to determine the sum of the charge transfer and diffusion resistance, and use your 100 kHz data to estimate the diffusion resistance).

3 Discussion and Conclusions

Discuss procedure sections 1 to 3, and draw conclusions about the nature of the individual electrodes.

4 Questions

4.1 From your measurements of the complex impedance of the Ag(AgCl) and bare-metal electrodes, what can you conclude about the relative capacitive, inductive, and resistive components as a function of frequency?

4.2 Were any of your electrodes microphonic? Were any not microphonic? Explain your answers in terms of ionic events.

4.3 Which of your electrodes had the best properties (low resistive impedance, low offset potential, low noise, good stability)? Which was worst?

5 Laboratory Data Sheets

Include your handwritten data sheets (or a copy), which should consist of a log of the procedures you used, any special circumstances, and the measurements you recorded manually.

Laboratory Exercise 17

The Human Heart

PURPOSE

To gain familiarity with basic cardiovascular physiology and the origin of the most commonly used noninvasive indicators of heart activity. To measure the electrocardiogram (ECG), the phonocardiogram, and blood pressure; and to observe the effect of light exercise on these indicators.

EQUIPMENT

- IBM microcomputer with Data Acquisition Adapter
- Cambridge ECG unit with strip chart recorder
- Ag(AgCl) ECG skin electrodes
- digital oscilloscope
- headphone to record heart sounds
- stethoscope
- pressure cuff and sphygmomanometer

BACKGROUND

1 Ag(AgCl) Electrodes

We will be using "floating" skin electrodes, consisting of a sintered plug of Ag and AgCl in contact with a piece of foam containing electrolyte gel. An adhesive pad keeps the foam pad in contact with the skin and allows for small amounts of movement without breaking electrical contact.

2 The Circulatory System

Laboratory Figure 17.1 shows a simplified schematic of the human circulatory system, including the heart, lungs, and organs. Note that oxygenated blood is so important that the lungs are in "series" with all the other organs, and have their own pumping chambers.

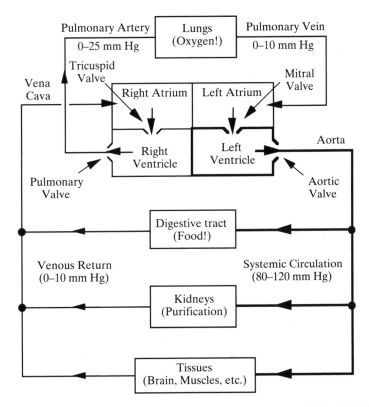

Laboratory Figure 17.1 The human circulatory system (simplified). Heavy lines show the high-pressure portion of the system.

3 The Cardiac Cycle

Laboratory Table 17.1 gives the times, signals, and arterial pressures associated with the major events in the cardiac cycle at 75 beats/min (see Rudd, 9-6, Figure 78).

LABORATORY TABLE 17.1   EVENTS IN THE CARDIAC CYCLE AT 75 BEATS/MIN

Time (ms)	Event	Signal	Arterial Pressure (mm Hg)	Ventricular Pressure (mm Hg)
0	Depolarization SA node		90	0
0–50	Depolarization atria	P wave	85	0
50–120	AV node delay; atrial contraction	P–R segment; 4th heart sound	80	3
130–200	Depolarization ventricles; repolarization atria	QRS complex	80	2–80
170–200	AV valves close; isovolumetric ventricular contraction; end ventricular diastole; begin ventricular systole	Start 1st heart sound	80	2–80
200	Semilunar valves open		80	80
200–300	Ventricular contraction; rapid ejection	S–T segment	80–120	80–120
320–480	Ventricular repolarization	T wave	120–100	120-100
440	Semilunar valves close; end ventricular systole; begin ventricular diastole	Dichrotic notch; start 2nd heart sound	100	100
480	AV valves open		100	5
480–800	Ventricular diastole; ventricular filling	3rd heart sound at end of rapid filling	100–90	0

4 Sequence of Cardiac Depolarization

1. SA node fires.
2. Depolarization proceeds right to left over both atria.
3. Delay at AV node during atrial contraction.
4. Bundle of His (prounounced "hiss") at top of ventricular septum.
5. Bundle branches along inner surfaces of ventricles down the septum, around the apex, and back up toward the base.
6. Purkinje network from inner to outer surfaces of ventricle *Note:* The sequence of ventricular contraction is controlled by the bundle branches.

5 Glossary

apex: Bottom of the heart.

Atrial systole: Period of active atrial contraction between the P wave and the closing of the AV valves.

AV (atrioventricular) node: A cluster of cells leading from the lower portion of the right atrium to the ventricular septum that conducts the depolarization wave very slowly (70 ms) to allow the atrial systole to reach completion before the ventricular systole begins.

AV (atrioventricular) valves: The tricuspid valve between the right atrium and the right ventricle; and the mitral valve between the left atrium and the left ventricle.

base: Top of heart, where valves and great vessels are located.

bundle branches: Conduct the depolarization wave from the bundle of His around the inner (endocardial) surface of the ventricles.

diastole: When used alone, means ventricular diastole, the period of ventricular relaxation between the closing of the semilunar valves and the closing of the AV valves.

dichrotic notch: Brief drop in arterial pressure due to backflow associated with the closing of the semilunar valves.

Purkinje network: Conducts the depolarization wave through the ventricular wall from the inner (endocardial) to the outer (epicardial) surfaces.

SA (sinoatrial) node: Cluster of highly conductive cells in the back wall of the right atrium where the cardiac depolarization wave is initiated.

semilunar valves: The aortic valve between the left ventricle and the aorta; and the pulmonary valve between the right ventricle and the pulmonary artery.

septum: Muscular wall between the left and right ventricles. Contains the bundle of His where ventricular depolarization originates.

systole: When used alone, means ventricular systole, the period of active ventricular contraction between the closing of the AV valves and the closing of the semi-lunar valves. See also atrial systole.

ADDITIONAL READING

Leslie Cromwell, Fred J. Weibell, and Erich A. Pfeiffer, *Biomedical Instrumentation and Measurements*, Prentice Hall, Englewood Cliffs, NJ, Chapter 5, Chapter 6: Sections 6.1 and 6.2.

Rudd, *Basic Concepts of Cardiovascular Physiology,* Hewlett-Packard, Waltham, MA, 1973, Chapters 8 and 9.

R. F. Rushmer, *Cardiovascular Dynamics,* W.B. Saunders Co., Philadelphia, 1970.

Peter Strong, *Biophysical Measurements,* Tektronix, Beaverton, OR, 1970, Chapters 2, 5, and section 8.2.

PROCEDURE

1 Electrocardiogram (ECG) (Demonstrated by a Physician)

Attach four electrodes to both wrists and ankles, as shown in Laboratory Figure 17.2. Record the ECG, leads I, II, and III, with the subject at rest and during *light* exercise (*walking* up and down two flights of stairs).

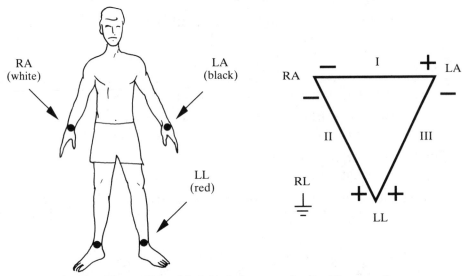

Laboratory Figure 17.2   Limb lead placement for the Electrocardiogram and the Einthoven triangle.

2 Phonocardiogram

Clean the ear pieces of the stethoscope with cotton and alcohol and listen to your heart sounds (pick a quiet place). Describe what you hear in terms of pitch, quality, duration, and repetition of sounds. Note that the heart sounds are loudest after an exhalation, when the heart is pressed against the chest wall.

Connect the microphone (one side of the headphones) to the digital oscilloscope, as shown in Laboratory Figure 17.3. Since the microphone output is about 5 mV, you will need to use an instrumentation amplifier to increase the signal level. Hold the microphone over your chest and observe the phonocardiogram on the oscilloscope. For best results, sit or stand perfectly still while a lab partner triggers the digital oscilloscope. The first and second heart sounds should be visible. Use the microcomputer to store and plot the phonocardiogram on the printer. Do at rest and after light exercise.

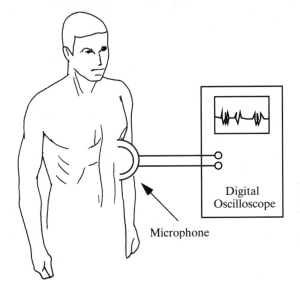

Digital
Oscilloscope

Microphone

Laboratory Figure 17.3
Procedure for recording a phonocardiogram, using a large foam-covered dynamic headphone as a microphone.

3 Blood Pressure

Have the subject sit down next to a table so that the left arm can rest level with the heart. Make sure that the garment sleeve is not too light. Circle the arm with the pressure cuff midway between the shoulder and elbow and fasten it by touching the Velcro surfaces together. The cuff should be snug but not uncomfortable.

Locate the brachial artery. It is above and slightly to the right of the bend in the elbow. Feel for its pulse with the first two fingers of the right hand. Measure and record the pulse rate. Note that the normal pulse variations in this artery produce audio frequencies that are in the 1-Hz range and very little in the 60- to 10-kHz range that can be heard by the human ear.

Tighten the screw valve and inflate the cuff to 150 mm Hg. Place the stethoscope head firmly over the brachial artery and listen with the stethoscope. You should hear nothing. Open the screw valve a bit and deflate the cuff at a rate of 2 to 3 mm/s. Laboratory Figure 17.4 shows the pulsing arterial pressure and the decreasing cuff pressure.

As the pressure falls, sounds (called Korotkoff sounds) become audible and pass through the following five phases:

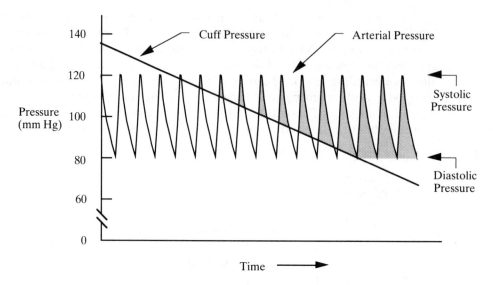

Laboratory Figure 17.4   Pulsatile flow occurs when the cuff pressure is close to either the systolic or diastolic pressure.

Phase I.   Faint, clear tapping sounds that gradually increase in intensity, caused by the abrupt distention of the arterial wall as a jet of blood surges under the cuff.   These short duration pulses have higher harmonics that can be heard by the human ear.

Phase II.   A swishing quality is heard, due to turbulence of the jet of blood in the artery.

Phase III.   The sounds become crisper and increase in intensity, as the volume of blood in the jet increases.

Phase IV.   A distinct, abrupt muffling of sound so that a soft blowing quality is heard.   At this point, the blood flow in the artery is not interrupted, but is restricted enough to produce an audible turbulent flow.

Phase V.   The point at which sound disappears completely because the cuff pressure is too low to restrict the flow of arterial blood.

Systolic blood pressure.   The point in phase I where the initial tapping sound is heard for two consecutive beats.

Diastolic blood pressure.   The point in phase IV where there is a distinct muffling of sound.

Potential sources of error. If the limb is thick in relation to the width of the cuff or if the cuff is loosely applied so that the rubber bag must be partially inflated before it exerts pressure on the tissues, which reduces the area of contact, the pressure in the cuff will significantly exceed the pressure in the tissues surrounding the artery. The result is an overestimate of the systolic and diastolic pressures.

In the general population, the systolic pressure can be as high as 180 mm Hg, a starting pressure of 200 mm Hg is generally used.

In some individuals, the sounds emitted by the artery disappear over a fairly large range of pressure between the systolic and diastolic pressures. This is called an "auscultatory gap" and the cause is not known. If the cuff pressure is initially set to a pressure within this gap, the pressure at the lower end of this silent range may be mistaken for a normal systolic pressure when, in fact, the actual systolic pressure is considerably higher.

Measurement of blood pressure. Measure the systolic and diastolic blood pressure for the following conditions:

1. subject is seated and has the arm at heart level
2. subject is seated and has the arm above the head
3. repeat condition 1 after light exercise

CAUTION

When fully inflated, the cuff stops blood flow completely.
Do not leave in this condition for more than 30 seconds.

LABORATORY REPORT

1 Setup

Draw a simple block diagram of your experimental setup.

2 Data Summary and Analysis

2.1 Electrocardiogram. The ECG record is traditionally calibrated at 0.1 mV per vertical mm and 40 ms per horizontal mm. On your ECG recordings, label the P wave, QRS complex, and T wave. For both resting and exercise conditions measure and tabulate the amplitude of the P, R, and T waves and the R–R, P–R, R–T, and T–P intervals for lead II. Compute the percentage change in these four intervals due to light exercise.

2.2 Phonocardiogram. From your phonocardiogram, measure and tabulate the duration of the first and second heart sounds and the interval between them. Compare the resting with the exercise values.

2.3 Blood pressure. Tabulate all systolic and diastolic blood pressures that you measured as well as the pulse pressure (systolic minus diastolic pressure). Estimate the pressure difference due to arm elevation and compare with the observed difference. (*Hint:* 1 atmosphere pressure = 760 mm Hg = 10.3 meters water.)

3 Discussion and Conclusions

Discuss the three major parts of the exercise (ECG, phonocardiogram, and blood pressure) and how you would use sensors, amplifiers, and the microcomputer to take the measurements and display useful results.

4 Questions

4.1 Will a heart murmur show up on an ECG? Explain.

4.2 What events produce the P, R, and T waves?

4.3 When are the highest and lowest pressures reached in the arteries?

4.4 What events produce the first and second heart sounds?

4.5 When you measured the blood pressure using the cuff, why was it best to have the arm at the same level as the heart?

4.6 How would you automate the non-invasive measurement of human blood pressure using the method of this laboratory exercise?

4.7 Which interval was affected most by light exercise: P–R, R–T, or T–P?

4.8 How much work (in joules) is done by the heart per beat? What is the power level (watts)?

Hints:
- work = mean ventricular pulse pressure × ejection volume + 1/2 × mass × velocity^2
- 1 joule (work) = 1 newton meter = 1 kg m^2 s^{-2} = 10^7 gm cm^2 s^{-2}
- 1 newton (force) = 1 kg × 9.8 m s^{-2}

- 760 mm Hg (pressure) = 76 cm $\times$ 13 g cm^{-3} $\times$ 980 cm s^{-2}
  = 96,800 kg/(m s^2) = 968,000 g/(cm s^2)
- mean ventricular pulse pressure = 1/2 (systolic + diastolic)
- ejection volume = 80 cm^3 aortic velocity = 10 cm/s

5 Laboratory Data Sheets

Include your handwritten data sheets (or a copy), which should consist of a log of the procedures you used, any special circumstances, and the measurements you recorded manually.

Laboratory Exercise 18

The Electromyogram (EMG)

PURPOSE

To investigate the electrical potentials produced by skeletal muscles; to build a circuit that amplifies, rectifies, and filters these signals; to relate the processed signal to the force of muscular contraction, and to determine the possibilities and limitations of using the EMG for control purposes.

EQUIPMENT

- IBM AT microcomputer with data-acquisition circuit
- set of weights with finger loop
- three floating Ag(AgCl) skin electrodes
- +5-V, ±12-V power supplies
- superstrip circuit board
- oscilloscope
- two coaxial cables
- headphone
- two 1N914 diodes
- four LF356 op-amps
- eight 0.1-μF bypass capacitors (put between power and ground on all chips)
- two 1-kΩ resistors

- four 10-kΩ resistors
- one 25-kΩ resistor
- two 50-kΩ resistors
- one 100-kΩ resistor
- capacitors (one each): 1, 3.3, and 10 μF

BACKGROUND

Individual muscle cells conduct action potentials similar to those conducted by axons. In an actively contracting muscle, the many parallel fibers (cells) making up the muscle will be conducting such action potentials at various repetition rates. With suitable electrodes, this barrage of electrical activity can be detected and recorded as the electromyogram (EMG). In some cases, needle electrodes are inserted through the skin directly into the muscle under study. If the needles are fine enough, little damage results. For most practical purposes, however, the activity is detected by electrodes placed on the skin surface over the muscle. After pickup by the electrodes, the signal can be processed and used for control purposes. EMG activity has commonly been used in the control of orthotic–prosthetic devices such as artificial hands and arms but it need not be limited to control aids for the physically handicapped.

In almost all practical control uses to date, the EMG activity has been detected by electrodes placed on the skin surface over the contracting muscle and then differentially amplified to reject the much stronger power-line interference present in normal environments. Because of the electrode placement and the relatively large recording areas, the EMG waveform is a spatial–temporal summation of the many muscle-fiber potentials reaching the electrodes. As a result, the waveform observed at the amplifier output is primarily marked by a peak-to-peak amplitude that increases with increasing contraction. In addition, the number of peaks per second similarly increases. For even a constant contraction level, the peak-to-peak amplitude can only be defined in a statistical sense.

Because of the nature of the raw EMG waveform, some initial analog-signal processing is done to extract a feature that is monotonically related to contraction intensity. In this laboratory exercise, you will differentially record this signal, amplify it, rectify it, and then smooth it with a low-pass filter. You should consider how this processed signal depends on contraction force and what problems you would encounter in using this signal to control a powered prosthetic device.

ADDITIONAL READING

Leslie Cromwell, Fred J. Weibell, and Erich A. Pfeiffer, *Biomedical Instrumentation and Measurements*, Prentice Hall, Englewood Cliffs, NJ, Chapter 16.

John Kreifeldt, IEEE Trans Bio-Medical Engineering BME-18, No 1, (1971): pp16-19.

Peter Strong, *Biophysical Measurements*, Tektronix, Beaverton, OR, 1970, Chapter 3 and Chapter 12, Sections 12.5 and 12.6.

PROCEDURE

1 EMG Signal-Processing Circuit

The overall circuit you will use is shown in Laboratory Figure 18.1. The isolation amplifier has differential inputs (V_+ and V_-) and an input ground that is not connected to the output of the circuit. It consists of an AD625 instrumentation amplifier and a Burr-Brown 3656 isolation amplifier. To reject electrode drift, select ac coupled output. Build the full-wave rectifier (Laboratory Figure 18.2) and a single pole low-pass filter (Laboratory Figure 18.3) on your circuit breadboard. See Laboratory Figure 4.2 for the LF356 op-amp external connections.

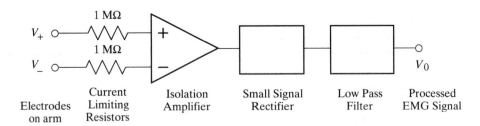

Laboratory Figure 18.1   Block diagram of EMG amplification and processing circuit.

Test the rectifier circuit with a 1-V p-p sine wave at test point 1. If alternate lobes of the output waveform (test point 2) are not equal, adjust the first 20-kΩ trimpot. If the lobes do not have 0.5 V amplitude, adjust the second 20-kΩ trimpot.

To test the entire circuit, use a 1-MΩ/10-kΩ voltage divider to provide a 2-mV sine wave into the isolation amplifier. The output of the low-pass filter should be a slowly varying waveform with a level that depends on input wave amplitude and offset level, but does not depend on frequency.

2 Skin Electrodes

Use the bare-metal probes of your digital multimeter to record the dry and wet electrical resistances between two points about 10 cm apart on the forearm of one of your lab partners. Obtain three Ag(AgCl) skin electrodes and

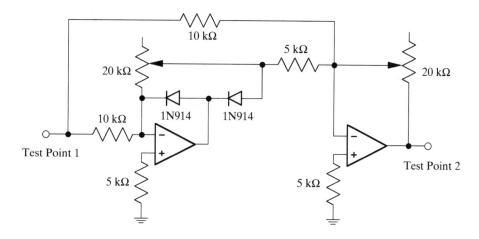

Laboratory Figure 18.2 Full-wave rectifier circuit used after the isolation amplifier. The 20-kΩ trimpots are nominally set at 10 kΩ.

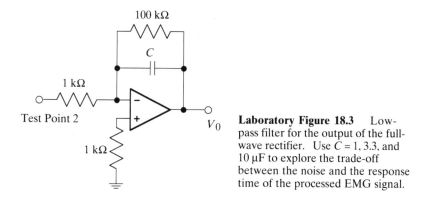

Laboratory Figure 18.3 Low-pass filter for the output of the full-wave rectifier. Use $C = 1, 3.3$, and 10 μF to explore the trade-off between the noise and the response time of the processed EMG signal.

apply them as demonstrated on the forearm. They should be placed to record the EMG signal from the group of muscles that control the flexion of the long finger. Record the electrical resistance between the two electrodes.

3 Experimental Setup

Position the forearm with the palm up and the long finger in the lifting hole of one of the weights provided, as shown in Laboratory Figure 18.4. Practice raising the finger to pick up one of the weights provided.

4 The Unprocessed EMG

Attach the three skin electrodes to the differential inputs V_-, V_+, and the input ground of the isolation amplifier using the coaxial cables provided. Observe the amplifier output at test point 1 with the digital oscilloscope and

Skin Electrodes

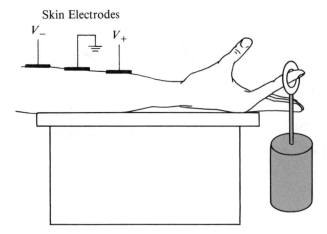

Laboratory Figure 18.4   Experimental setup relating force and the EMG signal.

describe the amplitude, average value, and quality of the "raw" EMG signal as a function of finger tension. For a maximum signal, remove the finger from the ring and clench the fist as tight as possible.

Listen to the amplified raw EMG signal with the headphones during high and low muscle tension. Describe what you hear.

Check that the rectified signal is present at test point 2.

5 EMG vs. Mechanical Load

Measure the average EMG signal (output of the low-pass filter) for zero load and when lifting each weight with the finger. Use either the oscilloscope or the digital multimeter. Some EMG signal may occur at zero load due to muscle tone. Pick up the weight abruptly as your lab partner triggers the computer data-acquisition circuit. Print the waveform, which will be used in your analysis of response time. Estimate the average peak-to-peak noise amplitude. Repeat for the other two filter capacitors.

6 Response Time

For three low-pass filter time constants, record the response time of the processed EMG signal after an abrupt application of force by the finger. Estimate response time and noise amplitude.

7 Voluntary Control of EMG

Under no-load conditions, flex your forearm muscles without moving your fingers and see how well you can produce EMG-processing circuit outputs that correspond to actually lifting weights. Record the largest processed EMG signal you can produce this way.

LABORATORY REPORT

1 Setup

Draw a simple block diagram of your experimental setup.

2 Data Summary and Analysis

2.1 Summarize your data from procedure sections 2, and 4 to 7.

2.2 Plot the processed EMG signal as a function of load.

2.3 Plot the response time as a function of the filter time constant for the three capacitors.

3 Discussion and Conclusions

3.1 Discuss the principles apparent from this laboratory exercise.

3.2 Discuss how an artificial hand would be controlled using skin electrodes on the forearm.

4 Questions

4.1 Why is the amplified EMG signal rectified before filtering? (*Hint:* How would the output change if the rectification were omitted?)

4.2 What are the high- and low-frequency cutoffs at test point 1? Using the 10-μF capacitor, what are the high- and low-frequency cutoffs for the low-pass filter circuit?

4.3 Signals from nerves going to muscles have been rejected by prosthetics designers as a possible source of control signals. Discuss any possible reasons for this.

5 Laboratory Data Sheets

Include your handwritten data sheets (or a copy), which should consist of a log of the procedures you used, any special circumstances, and the measurements you recorded manually.

Laboratory Exercise 19

The Electrooculogram (EOG)

PURPOSE

To record the human EOG during various sequences of horizontal eye movements; to identify smooth pursuit and saccadic eye movements.

EQUIPMENT

- +5-V, ±12-V power supplies
- isolation amplifier circuit
- digital multimeter
- gear motor with controller for the range 10 to 300 rpm. Mount with vertical axis and attach lucite rod with battery above center of rotation and small light at outer edge
- cardboard with 1-in wide black strips on 6-in centers
- board with three LEDs on 2-ft centers

BACKGROUND

1 Origin of the EOG

There exists between the cornea and retina of the eye a potential difference thought to be due to the difference in potential between the interior ends of the photoreceptors (rods and cones) and the pigment epithelium in which they are imbedded. This potential is relatively steady, although changes do occur in response to different light levels. Under constant background illumination, this potential may be considered an electrical dipole that rotates about the center of orbit as the eye rotates. The potential at any point on the head may be estimated by volume conductor theory. In practice, the best placement of the sensing electrodes are on the skin just over the bony ridge just lateral to the eye. An indifferent center electrode can be used as the ground for the coaxial cables that carry the differential signal to an instrumentation amplifier. A horizontal plane through the eye and recording electrodes is shown in Laboratory Figure 19.1, where O is the center of rotation, OA is the direction of the dipole, OB is the direction of the eyeball, OC defines the straight-ahead position, and angle AOB is about $14°$ in a human. By using electrodes on both temples, the observed differential potential is given by

$$V_{EOG} = K \cos 14° \sin \theta$$

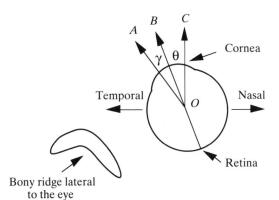

Laboratory Figure 19.1 The direction AO of the occular dipole and the line of vision BO relative to the direction CO of the head. The angle BOC is θ, the direction of vision. The angle $AOB = \gamma$ is about $14°$ in a human.

ADDITIONAL READING

Theodore C. Ruch and Harry D. Patton, *Physiology and Biophysics,* Saunders, Philadelphia, PA, 1982, Chapter 3, pp 85-91.

PROCEDURE

1 EOG Signal vs. Eye Position

Place the subject 4 ft away from the bar pattern shown in Laboratory Figure 19.2. Measure the distance between bars and calculate the angular separation as seen by the subject.

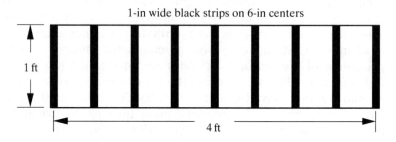

1-in wide black strips on 6-in centers

1 ft

4 ft

Laboratory Figure 19.2   Bar pattern for determining the relationship between EOG amplitude and eye angle.

Place two skin electrodes on either side of the forehead and connect to the signal leads of two coaxial cables. Place a third skin electrode between the two and connect to the ground shield of both coaxial cables. Connect both coaxial cables to the isolation amplifier.

Fixate on the center bar and record the EOG signal for a few minutes to estimate drift. Fixate on each bar in turn and measure the EOG signal vs. angle. Periodically return to the center bar to recheck the zero angle.

Shift from one bar to another bar at the edge of the pattern *as rapidly as possible.* Using the oscilloscope, measure the maximum voluntary velocity of the eyes. Repeat for a smaller angular shift.

2 Response Time

Place the subject 4 ft away from the LED board (Laboratory Figure 19.3). Perform as many of the following experiments as time permits:

  1. The subject fixates on the center LED (on) with earphones on to prevent hearing switch noise. A partner switches to the right or left LED. Trigger the scope on the switch pulse and record the EOG. Measure the latency time.

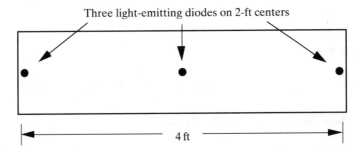

Laboratory Figure 19.3   LED board for measuring maximum voluntary angular speed.

2. The subject knows which way the light will "move" but not when and cannot hear switch noise.

3. As step 1 but the subject can hear the switch closure by electrical connection to the earphones.

4. Change the lit diode back and forth at random. Measure the latency as the subject tries to fixate on the lit LED. See if there is a minimum interval between fixation shifts. See if you can devise a pattern that produces an exceptionally long latency (see Robinson).

3 Smooth Pursuit and Saccadic Motion

Place the subject 4 ft away from the center of the revolving light (Laboratory Figure 19.4). At slow speed, the EOG signal will be a familiar curve. Slowly increase the speed and determine the maximum angular velocity (as seen by the subject) for smooth pursuit. Increase the speed still further and note what happens to the EOG signal. Record the angular velocity of any rapid shift.

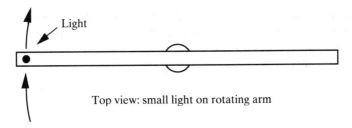

Laboratory Figure 19.4   Rotating light for determining maximum smooth-pursuit and involuntary saccade velocities.

LABORATORY REPORT

1 Setup

Draw a simple block diagram of your experimental setup.

2 Data Summary and Analysis

2.1   Plot EOG vs. angle from your data of procedure section 1.

2.2   Plot the relationship between the angular velocity and the angular displacement involved in the voluntary and involuntary saccades. Can saccades be the step-function response of a linear mechanical system?

3 Discussion and Conclusions

Discuss procedure sections 1 to 3.

4 Questions

4.1   Since it is known from other better methods of measuring eye position that humans can maintain fixation for long periods within 15 min of arc, the EOG signal drift must come from your recording setup. What source do you hypothesize? Is the drift random?

4.2   What is the maximum smooth-pursuit angular velocity observed (procedure section 3)?

4.3   What are the maximum angular velocities of the involuntary (procedure section 3) and voluntary (procedure section 2) saccades?

5 Laboratory Data Sheets

Include your handwritten data sheets (or a copy), which should consist of a log of the procedures you used, any special circumstances, and the measurements you recorded manually.

5

Data Analysis and Control

5.1 INTRODUCTION

One of the major advantages of the microcomputer is its use to quickly analyze data even while it is being taken. The result of the analysis can be a meaningful display or control of the system being measured. This chapter discusses data analysis, including statistical analysis, least-squares fitting, fast Fourier transforms, and control.

5.2 THE GAUSSIAN-ERROR DISTRIBUTION

5.2.1 Repeated Measurements of the Same Quantity

Ideally, if repeated measurements are made of the same quantity under identical conditions, the results should be the same. In the real world, however, all measurements are influenced to some extent by random factors, and repeated measurements exhibit unavoidable and unpredictable fluctuations. The measured values will cluster about some special value – most of them will be close to the average value, but some will lie farther away. An example of such a distribution is shown in Figure 5.1. An alternative method for showing such data is to divide the horizontal axis into "bins," and use the vertical axis to show the number of events in each bin, as shown in Figure 5.2.

Figure 5.1 Distribution of 25 measurements. Each vertical line represents a single measurement placed along the horizontal axis according to the measured value. The average of all the measurements is very close to 10.

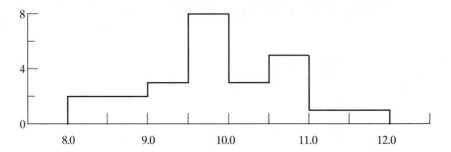

Figure 5.2 Data of Figure 5.1 plotted in bins 0.5 units wide. The vertical axis is the number of measured values in each bin.

If a very large number of measurements are made, and if the bins are made very narrow, the famous "bell-shaped" curve results, also called the gaussian curve of error (Figure 5.3). This distribution is given analytically by the following formula:

$$G(a) = \frac{\exp\left[-\frac{1}{2}\left(\frac{a-\mu}{\sigma}\right)^2\right]}{\sqrt{2\pi\sigma^2}}$$

where $G(a)$ is dN/da, dN is the number of measurements in the interval (or very small bin) between a and $a + da$, and σ is a constant called the "root mean square" or "rms" (the average of the squares of the deviations from the mean μ). $G(a)$ is the relative probability of obtaining a particular measured value a, given that the average is μ and the rms is σ.

While there is no upper bound to the magnitude of random error, it is comforting to know that very large errors are extremely unlikely (Table 5.1). While the probability of exceeding one standard deviation is 32%, a random process that occurs 10^{16} times per second would be expected to exceed 12 standard deviations only once in the entire history of the universe (10^{10} years, or 3.2×10^{17} seconds).

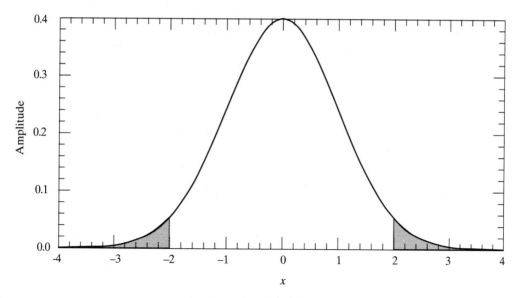

Figure 5.3   The gaussian curve of error, shown with a mean of 0, a standard deviation of 1, and unit area. The shaded region |x| > 2 is the 4.55% probability of exceeding two standard deviations.

TABLE 5.1   PROBABILITY OF EXCEEDING ±x STANDARD DEVIATIONS

x	Probability	x	Probability	x	Probability
0	1.00	5	5.73×10^{-7}	15	7.34×10^{-51}
1	3.17×10^{-1}	6	1.97×10^{-9}	20	5.51×10^{-89}
2	4.55×10^{-2}	8	1.24×10^{-15}	30	9.81×10^{-198}
3	2.70×10^{-3}	10	1.52×10^{-23}	50	2.16×10^{-545}
4	6.33×10^{-5}	12	3.55×10^{-33}	100	2.69×10^{-2174}

5.2.2 Estimating the Sample Mean and Standard Deviation

Suppose we make repeated experimental measurements a_i $(i = 1 \rightarrow m)$ of some quantity whose "true" value is μ. As mentioned before, these repeated measurements will not all be exactly equal, but will have some average value that is presumably close to the true value μ. Two important questions we can ask are: "How can we best estimate the quantity μ from our measurements?" and "How reliable is that estimation?" The estimator of μ is simply the average of the a_i (called the **sample mean**):

$$\mu \approx \bar{a} = \frac{1}{m} \sum_{i=1}^{m} a_i$$

To answer the question about the reliability of the average, we must first examine an important index of how much variability exists in our measurements a_i. To do this, we define a quantity called the **residual** R_i, which is the difference between the measurements a_i and their average:

$$R_i = a_i - \bar{a}$$

Whereas the sum of the R_i is zero, the average of the sum of the squares of R_i (the square of the **standard deviation** σ) is an important statistical quantity called the **variance**:

$$\sigma^2 = \text{Var}(a) = \frac{1}{m-1}\sum_{i=1}^{m} R_i^2 = \frac{1}{m-1}\sum_{i=1}^{m}(a_i - \bar{a})^2$$

$$\text{Var}(a) = \sum_{i=1}^{m}\frac{(a_i - \bar{a})^2}{m-1} = \frac{\sum a_i^2 - 2\bar{a}\sum a_i + m\bar{a}^2}{m-1} = \frac{\sum a_i^2 - m\bar{a}^2}{m-1} \qquad (5.1)$$

The latter form is preferred for programming because it can be formed by summing the data and the square of the data in a single loop.

Note: It is tempting to use m for the denominator in the Equation (5.1), like a simple average, but this assumes that the average value of a is a constant, not a random variable. Because we have estimated Var (a) from the same data that was used to compute the average value of a, the residuals are "biased" toward lower values. To correct for this, the denominator $(m-1)$ is used.

Another important question is how variances combine when the quantity of interest is a function of random quantities. Consider $f(a_1, a_2, \ldots, a_n)$, which is a well-defined, linear function of the independent random variables $a_1, a_2, \ldots, a_n$. The variance in f is given by

$$\text{Var}(f) = \left(\frac{\partial f}{\partial a_1}\right)^2 \text{Var}(a_1) + \left(\frac{\partial f}{\partial a_2}\right)^2 \text{Var}(a_2) + \cdots + \left(\frac{\partial f}{\partial a_n}\right)^2 \text{Var}(a_n)$$

Since f is a linear function of the a_i, each first partial derivative $\partial f/\partial a_i$ is a constant.

5.2.3 Estimating the Standard Error of the Mean

Let us apply this to the computation of the variance in the average of the measurements a_i, noting that each $\partial f/\partial a_i$ is equal to $1/m$, and that Var (a) represents the variance in each of the measurements a_i:

$$\text{Var}(\bar{a}) = \frac{1}{m^2}\sum_{i=1}^{m}\text{Var}(a_i) = \frac{\text{Var}(a)}{m} = \frac{\sum a_i^2 - m\bar{a}^2}{m(m-1)}$$

The root-mean-square (rms) deviation from the mean (σ) is given by

$$\boxed{\sigma = \sqrt{\text{Var}(a)}}$$

The **standard error of the mean** (sem) is given by

$$\boxed{\sigma_\mu = \sqrt{\text{Var}(\bar{a})}}$$

For binned data, where f_i is the number of measurements falling into the *i*th bin centered at a_i, the weighted average is given by

$$\bar{a} = \frac{1}{M} \sum_{i=1}^{m} a_i f_i$$

The weighted total M is given by

$$M = \sum_{i=1}^{m} f_i$$

The variance of the weighted data is given by

$$\boxed{\text{Var}(a) = \frac{1}{M-1} \sum_{i=1}^{m} f_i \left(a_i - \bar{a} \right)^2 = \frac{1}{M-1} \left(\sum_{i=1}^{m} f_i a_i^2 - M\bar{a}^2 \right)} \qquad (5.2)$$

5.3 STUDENT'S *t* TEST

5.3.1 Unpaired Data

Suppose we make m_a repeated measurements a_i under some experimental condition *A* and m_b repeated measurements b_i under condition *B*. In the unpaired case, there is no particular correspondence between a_i and b_i. (In the next section, we discuss the paired-data case, where a_i and b_i are measurements of the same *m* individuals under conditions *A* and *B*.) The means (averages) are given by

$$\bar{a} = \frac{1}{m_a} \sum_{i=1}^{m_a} a_i \quad \text{and} \quad \bar{b} = \frac{1}{m_b} \sum_{i=1}^{m_b} b_i$$

Clearly, if the distributions of the a_i and the b_i are so far apart that there is very little overlap, then we may safely conclude that there is a clear difference between condition *A* and condition *B*, as far as the measurements are concerned. However, we must frequently deal with the case where the a_i and b_i distributions have a significant overlap, as shown in Figure 5.4.

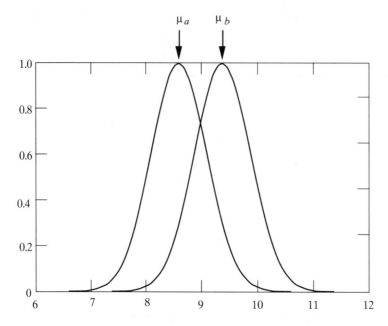

Figure 5.4   Case where two distributions have different means μ_a and μ_b but overlap considerably. The Student's t test is used to determine if the difference in the means of measurements made during two different experimental conditions could have occurred purely by chance.

The question we ask in this case is whether the difference $\Delta = \bar{a} - \bar{b}$ is statistically significant. In other words, what is the probability that the difference arose by chance? To answer this question, we must know the variance in the difference Δ itself. From the equation for combining variances:

$$\mathrm{Var}(\Delta) = \mathrm{Var}(\bar{a}) + \mathrm{Var}(\bar{b})$$

Student's t is defined as the difference in the averages divided by the standard error of that difference, and is the number of standard deviations that Δ differs from zero:

$$t = \frac{\Delta}{\sqrt{\mathrm{Var}(\Delta)}} = \frac{\bar{a} - \bar{b}}{\sqrt{\mathrm{Var}(\bar{a}) + \mathrm{Var}(\bar{b})}} = \frac{\bar{a} - \bar{b}}{\sqrt{\mathrm{Var}(a)/m_a + \mathrm{Var}(b)/m_b}}$$

where Var (a) and Var (b) can be computed from Equations (5.1) or (5.2), depending on whether the data are individual measurements or binned.

If we can assume that the variances of the a and b distributions are the same, we estimate the variance in Δ by combining both data sets:

$$\mathrm{Var}(a) = \mathrm{Var}(b) = \frac{1}{m_a + m_b - 2}\left(\sum_{i=1}^{m_a} a_i^2 + \sum_{i=1}^{m_b} b_i^2 - m_a \bar{a}^2 - m_b \bar{b}^2\right)$$

Combining, we have

$$t = \frac{\bar{a} - \bar{b}}{\sqrt{\left(\dfrac{1}{m_a + m_b - 2}\right)\left(\dfrac{1}{m_a} + \dfrac{1}{m_b}\right)\left(\displaystyle\sum_{i=1}^{m_a} a_i^2 + \sum_{i=1}^{m_b} b_i^2 - m_a \bar{a}^2 - m_b \bar{b}^2\right)}} \qquad (5.3)$$

Since the two sample means were determined from the data, the number of degrees of freedom is the number of independent data values minus 2, $n_f = m_a + m_b - 2$.

5.3.2 Paired Data

In the case where different conditions are applied to an assortment of individuals, Student's *t* is computed using the differences between the individual pairs of measurements, rather than the sample means. For $i = 1$ to m, measurements a_i and b_i are made under conditions A and B, respectively. There may be relatively large differences between the set a_i and the set b_i due to differences among the individuals; however, the paired differences $d_i = a_i - b_i$ may have much less variation because the individuals are being used as their own controls. For paired data, the number of degrees of freedom $n_f = m - 1$, and Student's *t* is given by

$$t = \frac{\bar{d}}{\sqrt{\mathrm{Var}(\bar{d})}} = \frac{\bar{d}}{\sqrt{\left(\dfrac{1}{m}\right)\left(\dfrac{1}{m-1}\right)\left(\sum d_i^2 - m \bar{d}^2\right)}}$$

5.3.3 Using the Student's *t* Test

Now *t* is a random variable that will be different every time the experiment is performed, and can take any value even if the experimental conditions A and B did not cause a difference between the data sets a_i and b_i (Figure 5.4). Initially, we must assume that differences in the measured values are due to chance alone (the "**null hypothesis**"). Only if |*t*| is so large that its probability is sufficiently small (say, less than 0.1%), can we reject the null hypothesis and conclude that something about the experimental conditions A and B *caused* the measured values to differ. Probabilities above 1% are not considered statistically significant.

Figure 5.5 shows the distribution of Student's t, and the tails of the distribution are shaded to show the values of t that correspond to a probability below 5%. Table 5.2 lists the values of t corresponding to the probability factors in the first column. The number of degrees of freedom $n_f = m_a + m_b - 2$ for unpaired and $n_f = m - 1$ for paired data) determines the column to be used.

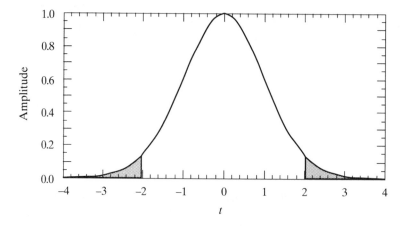

Figure 5.5   Distribution of Student's t for 30 degrees of freedom. Shaded areas show the probability that the absolute value of t will exceed 5% purely by chance.

5.3.4 Computing the Probability of Exceeding |t|

After acquiring data, it is natural to not only compute the value of student's t, but also the probability that that value (or larger) could have arisen by chance. The probability of exceeding $|t|$ is given by

$$P(>|t|) = \frac{2\Gamma\left(\frac{n+1}{2}\right)}{\sqrt{n\pi}\ \Gamma(n/2)} \int_t^\infty \left(1 + \frac{x^2}{n}\right)^{-(n+1)/2} dx$$

For a very large number of degrees of freedom, it is difficult to compute the gamma functions, and the approximation

$$\Gamma(x) \approx x^x e^{-x} \sqrt{2\pi/x}$$

yields the more convienient form

$$P(>|t|) \approx \sqrt{\frac{2}{e\pi}} \left(\frac{n+1}{n}\right)^{n/2} \int_t^\infty \left(1 + \frac{x^2}{n}\right)^{-(n+1)/2} dx$$

which has an error $\leq 1.5 \times 10^{-8}$ for $n \geq 3000$.

TABLE 5.2   STUDENT'S *t* TEST OF SIGNIFICANCE

$P(> |t|)$	$n_f = 1$	2	3	5	7	10	15	20
1.00000	0.0000	0.0000	0.0000	0.0000	0.0000	0.0000	0.0000	0.0000
0.90000	0.1584	0.1421	0.1366	0.1322	0.1303	0.1289	0.1278	0.1273
0.80000	0.3249	0.2887	0.2767	0.2672	0.2632	0.2602	0.2579	0.2567
0.70000	0.5095	0.4447	0.4242	0.4082	0.4015	0.3966	0.3928	0.3909
0.60000	0.7265	0.6172	0.5844	0.5594	0.5491	0.5415	0.5357	0.5329
0.50000	1.0000	0.8165	0.7649	0.7267	0.7111	0.6998	0.6912	0.6870
0.40000	1.3764	1.0607	0.9785	0.9195	0.8960	0.8791	0.8662	0.8600
0.30000	1.9626	1.3862	1.2498	1.1558	1.1192	1.0931	1.0735	1.0640
0.20000	3.0777	1.8856	1.6377	1.4759	1.4149	1.3722	1.3406	1.3253
0.10000	6.3138	2.9200	2.3534	2.0150	1.8946	1.8125	1.7531	1.7247
0.05000	12.7062	4.3027	3.1824	2.5706	2.3646	2.2281	2.1314	2.0860
0.02000	31.8205	6.9646	4.5407	3.3649	2.9980	2.7638	2.6025	2.5280
0.01000	63.6567	9.9248	5.8409	4.0321	3.4995	3.1693	2.9467	2.8453
0.00500	127.3213	14.0890	7.4533	4.7733	4.0293	3.5814	3.2860	3.1534
0.00200	318.3088	22.3271	10.2145	5.8934	4.7853	4.1437	3.7328	3.5518
0.00100	636.6193	31.5991	12.9240	6.8688	5.4079	4.5869	4.0728	3.8495
0.00050	1273.2393	44.7046	16.3263	7.9757	6.0818	5.0490	4.4166	4.1460
0.00020	3183.0988	70.7001	22.2037	9.6776	7.0634	5.6938	4.8800	4.5385
0.00010	6366.1977	99.9925	28.0001	11.1777	7.8846	6.2111	5.2391	4.8373
0.00005	12732.3955	141.4161	35.2979	12.8928	8.7825	6.7568	5.6070	5.1388
0.00002	31830.9889	223.6034	47.9277	15.5469	10.1027	7.5270	6.1089	5.5428
0.00001	63661.9778	316.2254	60.3968	17.8969	11.2148	8.1503	6.5017	5.8537

$P(> |t|)$	$n_f = 30$	50	70	100	150	200	500	∞
1.00000	0.0000	0.0000	0.0000	0.0000	0.0000	0.0000	0.0000	0.0000
0.90000	0.1267	0.1263	0.1261	0.1260	0.1259	0.1258	0.1257	0.1257
0.80000	0.2556	0.2547	0.2543	0.2540	0.2538	0.2537	0.2535	0.2533
0.70000	0.3890	0.3875	0.3869	0.3864	0.3861	0.3859	0.3855	0.3853
0.60000	0.5300	0.5278	0.5268	0.5261	0.5255	0.5252	0.5247	0.5244
0.50000	0.6828	0.6794	0.6780	0.6770	0.6761	0.6757	0.6750	0.6745
0.40000	0.8538	0.8489	0.8468	0.8452	0.8440	0.8434	0.8423	0.8416
0.30000	1.0547	1.0473	1.0442	1.0418	1.0400	1.0391	1.0375	1.0364
0.20000	1.3104	1.2987	1.2938	1.2901	1.2872	1.2858	1.2832	1.2816
0.10000	1.6973	1.6759	1.6669	1.6602	1.6551	1.6525	1.6479	1.6449
0.05000	2.0423	2.0086	1.9944	1.9840	1.9759	1.9719	1.9647	1.9600
0.02000	2.4573	2.4033	2.3808	2.3642	2.3515	2.3451	2.3338	2.3263
0.01000	2.7500	2.6778	2.6479	2.6259	2.6090	2.6006	2.5857	2.5758
0.00500	3.0298	2.9370	2.8987	2.8707	2.8492	2.8385	2.8195	2.8070
0.00200	3.3852	3.2614	3.2108	3.1737	3.1455	3.1315	3.1066	3.0902
0.00100	3.6460	3.4960	3.4350	3.3905	3.3566	3.3398	3.3101	3.2905
0.00050	3.9016	3.7231	3.6509	3.5983	3.5584	3.5387	3.5037	3.4808
0.00020	4.2340	4.0140	3.9257	3.8616	3.8130	3.7891	3.7468	3.7190
0.00010	4.4824	4.2283	4.1268	4.0533	3.9978	3.9705	3.9222	3.8906
0.00005	4.7292	4.4385	4.3229	4.2396	4.1767	4.1458	4.0913	4.0556
0.00002	5.0540	4.7110	4.5757	4.4784	4.4052	4.3694	4.3062	4.2649
0.00001	5.2995	4.9139	4.7626	4.6542	4.5728	4.5330	4.4629	4.4172

In the limit $n \to \infty$, $P(> |t|)$ simplifies to

$$P(>|t|) = \sqrt{\frac{2}{\pi}} \int_t^\infty e^{-t^2/2}\, dt$$

See Appendix D for the numerical methods (adaptive quadrature integration and Newton's method) used in computing Table 5.2.

5.4 LEAST-SQUARES FITTING

Least-squares fitting is a method for finding the coefficients of an analytical curve so that the sum of the squares of the differences between the function and a data set is minimized.

5.4.1 Fitting a Straight Line to Measured Data

Let us say we have measured a quantity $f(x)$ at different values x_i, where i varies from 1 to m, and the measured values are f_i. The straight line we wish to fit to the data has the form $f(x) = a_0 + a_1 x$ (Figure 5.6).

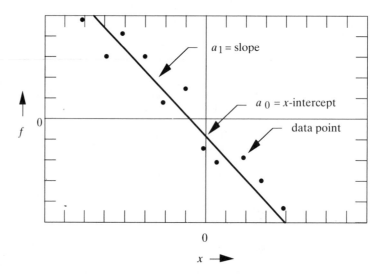

Figure 5.6   Straight-line fit to measured data (circles).

The data provide a set of simultaneous equations:

$$f_1 = a_0 + a_1 x_1$$
$$f_2 = a_0 + a_1 x_2$$
$$\vdots$$
$$f_m = a_0 + a_1 x_m$$

Since there are many more equations than the two unknowns a_0 and a_1, it is in general impossible for all the equations to be satisfied simultaneously. Instead, we define the difference between f_i and the quantity $a_0 + a_1 x_i$ as the **residual** R_i:

$$R_i = f_i - a_0 - a_1 x_i$$

Then our task is to find the values of a_0 and a_1 that minimize the sum of squares of the residuals:

$$\sum_{i=1}^{m} R_i^2 = \text{minimum}$$

To do this, we set the first partial derivatives equal to zero:

$$\frac{\partial}{\partial a_0} \sum_{i=1}^{m} R_i^2 = 2 \sum_{i=1}^{m} R_i \frac{\partial R_i}{\partial a_0} = 0 \quad \text{and} \quad \frac{\partial}{\partial a_1} \sum_{i=1}^{m} R_i^2 = 2 \sum_{i=1}^{m} R_i \frac{\partial R_i}{\partial a_1} = 0$$

which is equivalent to:

$$\sum_{i=1}^{m} \left(f_i - a_0 - a_1 x_i \right)(-1) = 0 \quad \text{and} \quad \sum_{i=1}^{m} \left(f_i - a_0 - a_1 x_i \right)(-x_i) = 0$$

Rearranging, we have two equations in two unknowns:

$$\sum f_i = n a_0 + a_1 \sum x_i \quad \text{and} \quad \sum f_i x_i = a_0 \sum x_i + a_1 \sum x_i^2$$

which has the solutions:

$$a_0 = \frac{\sum f_i \sum x_i^2 - \sum f_i x_i \sum x_i}{m \sum x_i^2 - \left(\sum x_i \right)^2} \qquad a_1 = \frac{m \sum f_i x_i - \sum f_i \sum x_i}{m \sum x_i^2 - \left(\sum x_i \right)^2}$$

The rms deviation σ from the best-fit straight line (a measure of linearity) is given by

$$\sigma = \sqrt{\frac{1}{m-2} \sum R_i^2}$$

5.4.2 Fitting a Curve to Measured Data

We now generalize this treatment to handle any function with linear coefficients:

$$f(x) = \sum_{j=1}^{n} a_j g_j(x)$$

Again, let the data set be x_i, f_i, where i varies from 1 to m. The residuals are given by

$$R_i = f_i - f(x_i) = f_i - \sum_{j=1}^{n} a_j g_j(x_i)$$

Minimizing the sum of the squares of the residuals produces the set of equations:

$$\frac{\partial}{\partial a_j}\left(\sum_{i=1}^{m} R_i^2\right) = 2\sum_{i=1}^{m} R_i \frac{\partial R_i}{\partial a_j} = 2\sum_{i=1}^{m} R_i g_j(x_i) = 0$$

which is equivalent to

$$\sum_{i=1}^{m}\left[f_i - \sum_{k=1}^{n} a_k g_k(x_i)\right] g_j(x_i) = 0$$

By rearranging the order of the summation, we have

$$\sum_{k=1}^{n} a_k \sum_{i=1}^{m} g_k(x_i) g_j(x_i) = \sum_{i=1}^{m} f_i g_j(x_i)$$

Writing this equation in matrix form:

$$\begin{bmatrix} g_1(x_1) & g_1(x_2) & \cdots & g_1(x_m) \\ g_2(x_1) & g_2(x_2) & \cdots & g_2(x_m) \\ \vdots & \vdots & \ddots & \vdots \\ g_n(x_1) & g_n(x_2) & \cdots & g_n(x_m) \end{bmatrix}\begin{bmatrix} g_1(x_1) & g_2(x_1) & \cdots & g_n(x_1) \\ g_1(x_2) & g_2(x_2) & \cdots & g_n(x_2) \\ \vdots & \vdots & \ddots & \vdots \\ g_1(x_m) & g_2(x_m) & \cdots & g_n(x_m) \end{bmatrix}\begin{bmatrix} a_1 \\ a_2 \\ \vdots \\ a_n \end{bmatrix}$$

$$= \begin{bmatrix} g_1(x_1) & g_1(x_2) & \cdots & g_1(x_m) \\ g_2(x_1) & g_2(x_2) & \cdots & g_2(x_m) \\ \vdots & \vdots & \ddots & \vdots \\ g_n(x_1) & g_n(x_2) & \cdots & g_n(x_m) \end{bmatrix}\begin{bmatrix} f_1 \\ f_2 \\ \vdots \\ f_m \end{bmatrix}$$

which can be written in the more compact notation:

$$(\mathbf{g}^T\mathbf{g})\mathbf{a} = \mathbf{g}^T\mathbf{f}$$

where $\mathbf{g}$ is an n × m matrix, $\mathbf{g}^T$ is its transpose, $\mathbf{a}$ is a column vector of dimension n, and $\mathbf{f}$ is a column vector of dimension m. These operations sum over the m data points and result in a set of n linear equations in n unknowns, which is usually solved by matrix inversion. In the case of least-squares fitting of a straight line (where $n = 2$), the resulting equations are readily solved by hand.

5.5 THE CHI-SQUARED STATISTIC

5.5.1 Use of Chi-Squared in Fitting a Model to Data

The Student's t statistic discussed before is most frequently used to compare two measured distributions and determine the probability that the difference between them could have arisen by chance. If this probability is very small, then some factor (presumably part of the experiment) has caused the difference.

Chi-squared (χ^2) is the sum of the squares of the differences between the data and the model to be fitted to the data, weighted by the inverse of the uncertainty. It is used to compare a measured distribution with a function and determine the probability that the difference between them could have arisen by chance. If this probability is very small, then we may conclude that the function does not describe the system being measured. However, the task of science is generally to determine the equations that describe the measurable universe, and we would seek another function that does describe the measured distribution. Quite often, this is done with a family of functions, with one or more parameters that are varied to minimize the χ^2 value.

$$\chi^2 = \sum_{i=1}^{n} \frac{\left[d_i - f(a, x_i) \right]^2}{\sigma_i^2} \tag{5.4}$$

Equation (5.4) describes the difference between the function $f(a,x)$ and measurements d_i made at coordinates x_i in terms of the experimental uncertainties σ_i. The parameter a describes the members of the family of functions. The assumption is that the data d_i are normally distributed with an rms uncertainty σ_i. If the data d_i are counts N_i within intervals of x, then we have

$$\chi^2 = \sum_{i=1}^{n} \frac{\left[N_i - f(a, x_i) \right]^2}{N_i} \tag{5.5}$$

The N_i can be regarded as being normally distributed with an rms uncertainty of $\sqrt{N_i}$, provided that the $N_i \geq 30$. For smaller statistics, it is better to use maximum-likelihood techniques that consider the Poisson nature of the data. Equation (5.5) suffers from the problem that downward fluctuations in the N_i cause the difference $N_i - f(x_i)$ to be weighted more than equal upward fluctuations. For this reason, Equation (5.5) is considered "biased" in favor of the smaller values of N_i but is widely used because of the relative ease in taking derivatives with respect to the parameter a for least-squares minimization. The unbiased equation is as follows:

$$\chi^2 = \sum_{i=1}^{n} \left[\frac{N_i - f(a,x_i)}{f(a,x_i)} \right]^2$$

The number of degrees of freedom n_f is equal to the number of independent data points minus the number of parameters that are varied to minimize χ^2.

A general note: The least-squares and chi-squared statistics described before have the general form

$$\sum_{i=1}^{n} W_i R_i^2$$

where $R_i^2 = N_i - f(a,x_i)$ is the residual, and W_i is a weighting factor.

For simple least squares, $W_i = 1$.
For chi-squared, $W_i = f(a, x_i)^{-1}$.
For relative least squares, $W_i = f(a, x_i)^{-2}$.

5.5.2 Computing the Probability of Exceeding χ^2

The probability of exceeding χ^2 by chance is given by

$$P(>\chi^2) = \int_{\chi^2}^{\infty} \frac{x^{(n-2)/2} e^{-x/2}}{2^{n/2}\,\Gamma(n/2)}\,dx \qquad (5.6)$$

Table 5.3 was computed by numerical integration of Equation (5.6), using adaptive quadrature and inverted using Newton's method (Appendix D). Table 5.3 lists the values of χ^2 corresponding to the probability factors in the first column. As a general rule, $\chi^2 \le n_f$ indicates an acceptable fit.

For $n_f > 30$, $P(>\chi^2)$ can be approximated as the gaussian integral:

$$P(>\chi^2) = \sqrt{\frac{2}{\pi}} \int_y^{\infty} e^{-x^2/2}\,dx, \quad \text{where} \quad y = \sqrt{2\chi^2} - \sqrt{2n-1}$$

An example of a poor fit would be $P < 0.1\%$ ($y > 3.09$ standard deviations). This corresponds to

$$\sqrt{2\chi^2} - \sqrt{2n-1} > 3.09 \qquad \text{and} \qquad \chi^2 > 0.5\left(3.09 + \sqrt{2n-1}\right)^2$$

5.6 SOLVING NONLINEAR EQUATIONS

5.6.1 Newton's Method

In his development of the calculus, Newton devised a method for solving $f(x) = 0$ using the first derivative $df/dx = f'(x)$ and a little geometry (Figure 5.7).

TABLE 5.3 $P(> \chi^2)$ PROBABILITY OF EXCEEDING χ^2 FOR n_f DEGREES OF FREEDOM

$P(> \chi^2)$	$n_f = 1$	2	3	5	7	10	15	20
1.00000	0.0000	0.0000	0.0000	0.0000	0.0000	0.0000	0.0000	0.0000
0.90000	0.0158	0.2107	0.5844	1.6103	2.8331	4.8652	8.5468	12.4426
0.80000	0.0642	0.4463	1.0052	2.3425	3.8223	6.1791	10.3070	14.5784
0.70000	0.1485	0.7133	1.4237	2.9999	4.6713	7.2672	11.7212	16.2659
0.60000	0.2750	1.0217	1.8692	3.6555	5.4932	8.2955	13.0297	17.8088
0.50000	0.4549	1.3863	2.3660	4.3515	6.3458	9.3418	14.3389	19.3374
0.40000	0.7083	1.8326	2.9462	5.1319	7.2832	10.4732	15.7332	20.9514
0.30000	1.0742	2.4079	3.6649	6.0644	8.3834	11.7807	17.3217	22.7745
0.20000	1.6424	3.2189	4.6416	7.2893	9.8032	13.4420	19.3107	25.0375
0.10000	2.7055	4.6052	6.2514	9.2364	12.0170	15.9872	22.3071	28.4120
0.05000	3.8415	5.9915	7.8147	11.0705	14.0671	18.3070	24.9958	31.4104
0.02000	5.4119	7.8240	9.8374	13.3882	16.6224	21.1608	28.2595	35.0196
0.01000	6.6349	9.2103	11.3449	15.0863	18.4753	23.2093	30.5779	37.5662
0.00500	7.8794	10.5966	12.8382	16.7496	20.2777	25.1882	32.8013	39.9968
0.00200	9.5495	12.4292	14.7955	18.9074	22.6007	27.7216	35.6276	43.0720
0.00100	10.8276	13.8155	16.2662	20.5150	24.3219	29.5883	37.6973	45.3147
0.00050	12.1157	15.2018	17.7300	22.1053	26.0178	31.4198	39.7188	47.4985
0.00020	13.8311	17.0344	19.6561	24.1855	28.2271	33.7958	42.3288	50.3090
0.00010	15.1367	18.4207	21.1075	25.7448	29.8775	35.5640	44.2632	52.3860
0.00005	16.4481	19.8070	22.5547	27.2937	31.5124	37.3107	46.1678	54.4263
0.00002	18.1893	21.6396	24.4624	29.3272	33.6530	39.5907	48.6455	57.0743
0.00001	19.5114	23.0259	25.9017	30.8562	35.2585	41.2962	50.4930	59.0446

$P(> \chi^2)$	$n_f = 30$	50	70	100	150	200	300	500
1.00000	0.0000	0.0000	0.0000	0.0000	0.0000	0.0000	0.0000	0.0000
0.90000	20.5992	37.6886	55.3289	82.3581	128.2751	174.8353	269.0679	459.9261
0.80000	23.3641	41.4492	59.8978	87.9453	135.2625	183.0028	279.2143	473.2099
0.70000	25.5078	44.3133	63.3460	92.1289	140.4569	189.0486	286.6878	482.9462
0.60000	27.4416	46.8638	66.3961	95.8078	144.9998	194.3193	293.1786	491.3709
0.50000	29.3360	49.3349	69.3345	99.3341	149.3339	199.3337	299.3336	499.3335
0.40000	31.3159	51.8916	72.3583	102.9459	153.7535	204.4337	305.5741	507.3816
0.30000	33.5302	54.7228	75.6893	106.9058	158.5774	209.9854	312.3460	516.0874
0.20000	36.2502	58.1638	79.7146	111.6667	164.3492	216.6088	320.3971	526.4014
0.10000	40.2560	63.1671	85.5270	118.4980	172.5812	226.0210	331.7885	540.9303
0.05000	43.7730	67.5048	90.5312	124.3421	179.5806	233.9943	341.3951	553.1268
0.02000	47.9618	72.6133	96.3875	131.1417	187.6785	243.1869	352.4247	567.0698
0.01000	50.8922	76.1539	100.4252	135.8067	193.2077	249.4451	359.9064	576.4928
0.00500	53.6720	79.4900	104.2149	140.1695	198.3602	255.2642	366.8444	585.2066
0.00200	57.1674	83.6566	108.9295	145.5769	204.7231	262.4338	375.3690	595.8820
0.00100	59.7031	86.6608	112.3169	149.4493	209.2646	267.5405	381.4252	603.4460
0.00050	62.1619	89.5605	115.5776	153.1670	213.6134	272.4226	387.2035	610.6476
0.00020	65.3130	93.2586	119.7240	157.8816	219.1131	278.5859	394.4824	619.6990
0.00010	67.6326	95.9687	122.7547	161.3187	223.1121	283.0603	399.7559	626.2427
0.00005	69.9045	98.6136	125.7061	164.6591	226.9906	287.3941	404.8555	632.5596
0.00002	72.8433	102.0221	129.5009	168.9445	231.9552	292.9335	411.3621	640.6042
0.00001	75.0234	104.5417	132.3000	172.0989	235.6018	296.9968	416.1267	646.4844

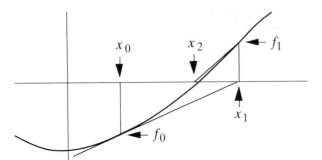

Figure 5.7 Newton's method for finding the roots of an equation.

If the ith approximation is x_i, the next approximation x_{i+1} is given by

$$x_{i+1} = x_i - \frac{f(x_i)}{f'(x_i)}$$

EXAMPLE

To extract the cube root of a number a, we wish to solve the equation: $f(x) = x^3 - a = 0$. Since $f'(x) = 3x^2$, we have the iterative algorithm:

$$x_{i+1} = x_i - \frac{x_i^3 - a}{3x_i^2} = \frac{2x_i^3 + a}{3x_i^2}$$

Table 5.4 shows how this algorithm converges for $a = 10$, using the very poor initial guess $x_0 = 1$. As expected, the linear approximation is very poor far from the correct answer, and, in the first iteration, the algorithm actually jumps over the answer from 1 to 4. However, Newton's linear approximation improves rapidly as the correct answer is approached, and the last three iterations demonstrate impressively rapid convergence to 18 decimal-digit accuracy.

TABLE 5.4 USE OF NEWTON'S METHOD TO SOLVE $\sqrt[3]{10}$

i	x_i	x_i^3
0	1.00000 00000 00000 00	1.00000 00000 00000 00
1	4.00000 00000 00000 00	64.00000 00000 00000 00
2	2.87500 00000 00000 00	23.76367 18750 00000 00
3	2.31994 32892 24952 74	12.48625 23021 57114 08
4	2.16596 15551 77792 79	10.16136 92074 95129 95
5	2.15449 59251 53374 74	10.00085 27090 04352 98
6	2.15443 46917 72292 94	10.00000 00242 34792 06
7	2.15443 46900 31883 72	10.00000 00000 00000 02

5.7 FAST FOURIER TRANSFORMS

5.7.1 The Discrete Fourier Transform

The **discrete Fourier transform** (DFT) determines the sine and cosine components of a periodic waveform. In many cases, these components are more useful than the shape of the waveform itself. The waveform $f(t)$ is sampled at N time intervals $t_0 = 0$, $t_1 = T$, $t_k = kT, \ldots, t_{N-1} = (N-1)T$. The full sampling interval is $S = NT$ (Figure 5.8).

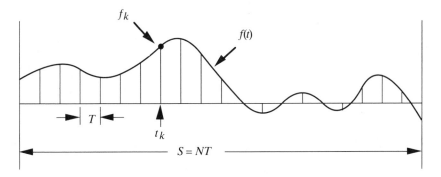

f_k

$f(t)$

T

t_k

$S = NT$

Figure 5.8   Waveform sampled at uniform time intervals T.

By using the notation $f_k = f(t_k)$, the DFT of f_k is defined as

$$F_n = \sum_{k=0}^{N-1} f_k \, e^{-i2\pi nk/N} \tag{5.7}$$

Note: $e^{i\phi} = \cos\phi + i\sin\phi$, $e^{-i\phi} = \cos\phi - i\sin\phi$, $e^0 = e^{i2\pi} = 1$, and $e^{-i\pi} = -1$.

The significance of the DFT coefficients is that F_0 is the Fourier coefficient at frequency 0 (dc component), F_1 is the Fourier coefficient at frequency 1 (1 cycle per S), and F_n is the Fourier coefficient at frequency n (n cycles per S).

To see that this is so, let us calculate a few Fourier coefficients:

$$F_0 = \sum_{k=0}^{N-1} f_k, \quad \text{(the sum of all amplitudes)}$$

Consider the case where $f_k = C$ (a constant). Then $F_0 = NC$ and all other Fourier coefficients are zero.

Let us next consider the example of a sine wave with M complete cycles per sampling interval S:

$$f_k = \sin(2\pi kM/N)$$

$$F_n = \sum_{k=0}^{N-1} \sin(2\pi kM/N)\left[\cos(2\pi kn/N) - i\sin(2\pi kn/N)\right]$$

Due to the orthogonal nature of the sine and cosine series (see the example that follows), for this f_k,

$$F_M = \sum_{k=0}^{N-1} -i\sin^2(2\pi kM/N) = \frac{-iN}{2}$$

$$F_{N-M} = \sum_{k=0}^{N-1} i\sin^2(2\pi kM/N) = \frac{iN}{2}$$

and all the other Fourier coefficients are zero. Thus, we see that the nth Fourier coefficient describes the amplitude of any sine wave component having n complete cycles per sampling interval.

EXAMPLE

Relate the coefficients a_j and b_j in the expansion

$$f_k = \sum_{j=0}^{N-1} a_j\cos(2\pi jk/N) + b_j\sin(2\pi jk/N)$$

to the complex Fourier coefficients F_n.

First, we perform the discrete Fourier transform of f_k :

$$F_n = \sum_{k=0}^{N-1}\left[\sum_{j=0}^{N-1} a_j\cos(2\pi jk/N) + b_j\sin(2\pi jk/N)\right]$$

$$\times\left[\cos(2\pi nk/N) - i\sin(2\pi nk/N)\right]$$

Since

$$\sum_{k=0}^{N-1}\left[\cos(2\pi jk/N)\sin(2\pi nk/N)\right] = 0 \quad \text{for all } j \text{ and } n$$

$$\sum_{k=0}^{N-1}\left[\cos(2\pi jk/N)\cos(2\pi nk/N)\right] = 0 \quad \text{for all } j \neq n$$

$$\sum_{k=0}^{N-1}\left[\sin(2\pi jk/N)\sin(2\pi nk/N)\right] = 0 \quad \text{for all } j \neq n$$

and

$$\sum_{k=0}^{N-1}\left[\cos^2(2\pi nk/N)\right] = \sum_{k=0}^{N-1}\left[\sin^2(2\pi nk/N)\right] = N/2$$

we have for $n = 0$

$$F_0 = \sum_{k=0}^{N-1} a_0 = N\, a_0$$

and for $0 < n < N$

$$F_n = \sum_{k=0}^{N-1}\left[a_n\cos^2(2\pi nk/N) - i\, b_n\sin^2(2\pi nk/N)\right] = (N/2)(a_n - ib_n)$$

$$a_n = (2/N)\,\mathrm{Re}\,(F_n) \quad \text{and} \quad b_n = -(2/N)\,\mathrm{Im}\,(F_n)$$

We see that the real part of F_n is associated with the cosine terms and the imaginary part of F_n is associated with the sine terms of the expansion.

To what do the Fourier coefficients outside the interval from 0 to $N/2$ correspond? From the definition of the DFT, the Fourier amplitude for N cycles per sampling interval S is the same as 0 cycles per S:

$$F_N = \sum_{k=0}^{N-1} f_k\, e^{-i2\pi k} = \sum_{k=0}^{N-1} f_k = F_0$$

Above N samples per S, all the Fourier amplitudes are equal to their lower counterparts:

$$F_{N+n} = \sum_{k=0}^{N-1} f_k\, e^{-i2\pi k}\, e^{-i2\pi kn/N} = \sum_{k=0}^{N-1} f_k\, e^{-i2\pi kn/N} = F_n$$

Between $N/2$ and N samples per S, we have the following result:

$$F_{N-n} = \sum_{k=0}^{N-1} f_k\, e^{-i2\pi k}\, e^{+i2\pi kn/N} = \sum_{k=0}^{N-1} f_k\, e^{+i2\pi kn/N}$$

If f_k is real, then $F_{N-n} = F_n^*$ and $F_{N/2}$ is real (* denotes the complex conjugate). $F_{N/2}$ is the Fourier coefficient at frequency $N/2$ (1 cycle per $2T$). This is the highest frequency that the DFT can determine. All Fourier coefficients for higher frequencies are either equal to or are complex conjugates of coefficients for lower frequencies. Thus, there are only $N/2$ *independent* Fourier coefficients.

If the sampling frequency is inadequate, higher-frequency components of the true waveform $f(t)$ will appear as lower frequency components in the DFT. This is called **frequency aliasing**. There is no way to correct the data after the sampling has been performed. The usual solution to this problem is to use a low-pass analog filter (**anti-aliasing filter**) that eliminates all frequencies above $f_s/2$ before sampling.

One statement of this result is the **sampling theorem**:

> **Sampling Theorem:** To be able to recover completely the continuous signal from its sampled counterpart, the sampling frequency f_s must be at least twice the highest frequency in the signal.

Each Fourier coefficient F_n is in general complex, the real part describing the cosine-like amplitude and the imaginary part describing the sine-like amplitude. The modulus, or magnitude G_n is defined as

$$G_n = \sqrt{\operatorname{Re}(F_n)^2 + \operatorname{Im}(F_n)^2}$$

and the phase angle θ_n is given by $\tan \theta_n = \operatorname{Im}(F_n)/\operatorname{Re}(F_n)$.

The inverse DFT is given by

$$f_k = \sum_{n=0}^{N-1} \frac{F_n}{N} e^{+i2\pi nk/N}$$

Note that the same function is obtained by first performing the forward and then the inverse transformations given before.

What happens if we evaluate f_k outside the sampling interval S?

$$f_{N+k} = \sum_{n=0}^{N-1} \frac{F_n}{N} e^{+i2\pi n} e^{+i2\pi nk/N} = f_k$$

We see that, given a set of N Fourier coefficients, the constructed function repeats endlessly with a periodicity $S = NT$. This is analogous to the previous result that, given a set of N samples, the Fourier coefficients repeat endlessly with a periodicity $N = S/T$.

5.7.2 The Fast Fourier Transform

The **fast Fourier transform**, or **FFT**, is a computationally efficient method for computing the discrete Fourier transform (DFT). As a result, interpreting the results of the FFT only requires an understanding of the DFT. The computational efficiency of the FFT arises from a clever reorganization of the terms in the DFT so that similar terms are computed only once. Direct computation of the DFT equation given before requires N^2 multiplications and $N(N-1)$ additions. The FFT, on the other hand, requires only $N \log_2 N$ multiplications and $2N \log_2 N$ additions. For $N = 1024$, the number of multiplications is reduced by a factor of 100.

$$F_n = \sum_{n=0}^{N-1} f_k \, e^{-i2\pi kn/N} = \sum_{n=0}^{N-1} f_k \, W^{nk}$$

where we define $W = e^{-i2\pi/N}$ and $W^0 = W^N = 1$. Writing this in matrix form and using the relationship $W^{N+nk} = W^{nk}$, we have

$$
\begin{bmatrix} F_0 \\ F_1 \\ F_2 \\ F_3 \end{bmatrix}
=
\begin{bmatrix}
W^0 & W^0 & W^0 & W^0 \\
W^0 & W^1 & W^2 & W^3 \\
W^0 & W^2 & W^4 & W^6 \\
W^0 & W^3 & W^6 & W^9
\end{bmatrix}
\begin{bmatrix} f_0 \\ f_1 \\ f_2 \\ f_3 \end{bmatrix}
=
\begin{bmatrix}
1 & 1 & 1 & 1 \\
1 & W^1 & W^2 & W^3 \\
1 & W^2 & 1 & W^2 \\
1 & W^3 & W^2 & W^1
\end{bmatrix}
\begin{bmatrix} f_0 \\ f_1 \\ f_2 \\ f_3 \end{bmatrix}
$$

The key to the efficiency of the fast Fourier transform is the factorization of the matrix, which is made possible by the interchange of certain rows:

$$
\begin{bmatrix} F_0 \\ F_2 \\ F_1 \\ F_3 \end{bmatrix}
=
\begin{bmatrix}
1 & 1 & 1 & 1 \\
1 & W^2 & 1 & W^2 \\
1 & W^1 & W^2 & W^3 \\
1 & W^3 & W^2 & W^1
\end{bmatrix}
\begin{bmatrix} f_0 \\ f_1 \\ f_2 \\ f_3 \end{bmatrix}
$$

$$
=
\begin{bmatrix}
1 & 1 & 0 & 0 \\
1 & W^2 & 0 & 0 \\
0 & 0 & 1 & W^1 \\
0 & 0 & 1 & W^3
\end{bmatrix}
\begin{bmatrix}
1 & 0 & 1 & 0 \\
0 & 1 & 0 & 1 \\
1 & 0 & W^2 & 0 \\
0 & 1 & 0 & W^2
\end{bmatrix}
\begin{bmatrix} f_0 \\ f_1 \\ f_2 \\ f_3 \end{bmatrix}
$$

In general, there will be $\log_2 N$ matrices with $N/2$ complex multiplications and N complex additions per matrix. Every occurrence of $W^0 = 1$ means a simple addition. Other powers of W involve multiplication by precomputed constants. As N becomes large, we have $\log_2 N$ sparse matrices. The direct method, Equation (5.7), requires N^2 complex multiplications and $N(N-1)$ complex additions. In terms of the number of multiplication operations, the FFT gains a factor of $2N/\log_2 N$ over the direct method, which is greater than 200 for $N = 1024 = 2^{10}$.

5.7.3 Use of the Fast Fourier Transform Function

The fast Fourier transform function and its use is listed in Appendix D. It is used in Laboratory Exercises 21–23.

Figure 5.9 shows the function $f_k = 1 + \sin(3 \times 2\pi k/16)$, which has three complete cycles in the interval from $k = 0$ to $k = 15$. Table 5.5 shows the 16-point discrete Fourier transform of this function. Since the constant term is 1, the F_0 Fourier amplitude is 16 (the sum over 16 terms). Because there are three cycles per full sampling interval, the $n = 3$ and $n = N - 3 = 13$ Fourier amplitudes are non-zero. The $n = 8$ coefficient corresponds to the Nyquist frequency limit.

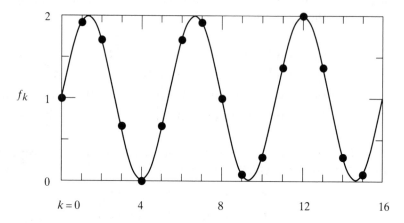

Figure 5.9   Sinewave $f_k = 1 + \sin(3 \times 2\pi k/16)$ sampled 16 times in three complete cycles. See Table 5.5 for the Fourier transform coefficients.

TABLE 5.5   FOURIER TRANSFORM OF $f_k = 1 + \sin(3 \times 2\pi k/16)$

k or n	$\text{Re}(f_k)$	$\text{Im}(f_k)$	$\text{Re}(F_n)$	$\text{Im}(F_n)$
0	1.0000	0	+16	0
1	1.9239	0	0	0
2	1.7071	0	0	0
3	0.6173	0	0	−8
4	0.0000	0	0	0
5	0.6173	0	0	0
6	1.7071	0	0	0
7	1.9239	0	0	0
8	1.0000	0	0	0
9	0.0761	0	0	0
10	0.2929	0	0	0
11	1.3827	0	0	0
12	2.0000	0	0	0
13	1.3827	0	0	+8
14	0.2929	0	0	0
15	0.0761	0	0	0

5.8 THE CONTROL SYSTEM

The true potential of the microcomputer is realized when it is used not merely to sense quantities in the real world and to perform data analysis and display, but to reach out and control those quantities. In this section, we discuss some of the digital control algorithms that are used to perform that control.

To control a system variable, it is first necessary to sense that variable, amplify the resulting signal, and sample with the microcomputer (Figure 5.10). The control algorithm uses these measurements and the desired value, called the set point, to determine the value of the control variable that is converted into analog form, amplified, and used to drive an actuator that is capable of changing the system variable.

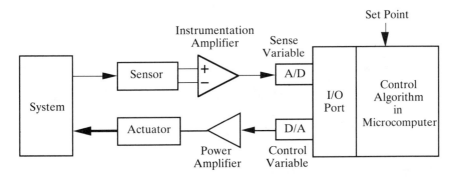

Figure 5.10   Typical microcomputer control system. The control algorithm periodically reads the sense variable and produces a control value that acts on the system to make the sense variable as close as possible to a previously entered set point.

In Laboratory Exercise 24, a temperature-control system is built using a thermistor to sense temperature, a cylindrical resistor to act as an oven, and the microcomputer to perform the control function. This system is used to explore the open- and closed-loop response, described in the sections that follow.

5.8.1 Open-Loop System Response

Before attempting to control a system variable, it is important to understand how the **sense variable** responds in the open-loop mode to changes in the **control variable**. The measured behavior of the sense variable after an abrupt change in the control variable is called the **open-loop step response**. From this, the lag and response times of the system can be measured, which are both important time constants that play a role in the design and behavior of any control system. The **response time** is the time after an abrupt change in the control value for the sense value to make 63% of the change to the final equilibrium value. After a period equal to five times the response time, the sensed variable should approach its asymptotic limit to within 0.7%.

Each value of the control variable will result in a different asymptotic equilibrium value of the sense variable (the open-loop response table). From this, the nonlinearities of the system response can be learned. In Figure 5.11, we show typical open-loop step responses of the sensed variable after an abrupt change in the control variable from zero to three different values. Note that the system responds after a time lag, and that the asymptotic equilibrium sense variable is not a linear function of the control variable.

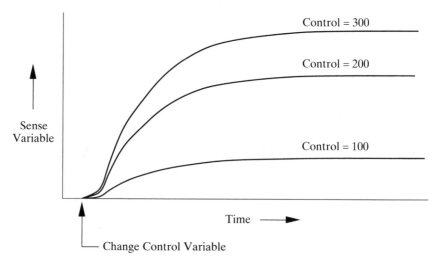

Figure 5.11   Open-loop step response as shown by a plot of the **sense** variable after an abrupt change in the **control** variable from zero to three different values.

5.8.2 Performance Criteria for Control Algorithms

The **control algorithm** compares the sampled sense data to the desired sense value called the **set point**, and periodically derives the value of a **control variable** that is sent to an actuator to control the system and influence the sense data. In the control of motion, the sensor might be a digital position encoder and the actuator might be a motor. In the control of temperature, the sensor might be a thermistor or thermocouple and the actuator might be a resistor or heat pump.

Figure 5.12 shows the typical behavior of a control system after an abrupt change in set point. The **lag time** is the time from the change in set point to the time when the sensed variable first reaches a point 10% away from its initial value and 90% of the way from its final equilibrium value. The **rise time** is the time required for the sensed variable to change from the 10% point to the 90% point. Quite frequently, the sensed variable passes through the set-point value and overshoots before approaching from the other side.

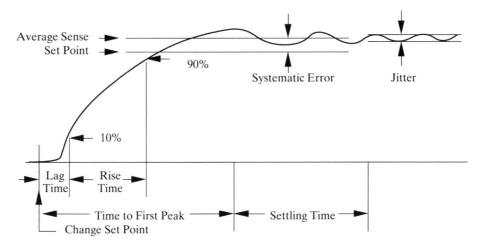

Figure 5.12   Behavior of a typical control system, where the sensed variable is shown as a function of time after an abrupt change in set point. After a lag time, the variable rapidly approaches the new set point, possibly overshoots, and possibly oscillates before settling to the sense point value. In some cases, due to inadequacies in the control algorithm, the oscillations continue indefinitely or there is a systematic error between the sensed variable and the set point that does not diminish with time.

The **time to first peak** is the time between the change in set point and the peak of the first overshoot. Possibly the sensed variable will oscillate about its average equilibrium value, and those oscillations will decay with a **settling time** that is the time required for the amplitude of the oscillations to decay by a factor of $e = 2.71828$. It is also possible that these oscillations do not decay, but continue indefinitely.

Even long after the system has responded to the change in set point, it may exhibit jitter and systematic error. **Jitter** is the rms deviations from the mean value of the sense variable and is frequently due to noise in the control system or oscillations or "hunting" behavior of the control algorithm. **Error** in a control system is the difference between the sensed variable and the set point. The **average error**, or **accuracy**, is the difference between the set point and the time-averaged sensed variable.

5.9 TEMPERATURE CONTROL

One of the most commonly controlled quantities is temperature, for heating
and cooling buildings or for controlling the reaction rates of chemical or
biological processes. When fuel combustion or electrical resistance heating
is used, the control engineer can actively control heating but must rely on
heat losses for cooling. On the other hand, heat pumps or Peltier thermoelectric devices can both heat and actively cool. Figure 5.13 shows the
schematic for the microcomputer-based temperature-control system explored
in Laboratory Exercise 24. A thermistor is used for temperature sensing and
a cylindrical ceramic resistor is used for heating. Note that almost every element in this control system has a nonlinear response:

1. the thermistor, whose resistance depends exponentially on $1/T$,
2. the bridge circuit, whose response is nonlinear when unbalanced, and
3. the ceramic resistor, whose power output is given by $P = RV^2$.

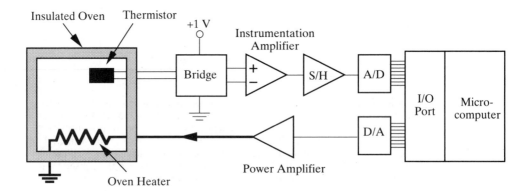

Figure 5.13   Schematic of a typical microcomputer-based temperature-control
system. The thermistor and bridge provide a voltage that is converted with an A/D
and read by the computer program. A control program writes a number to the D/A
converter, whose output is amplified to drive an oven resistor.

5.9.1 ON–OFF Control

ON–OFF temperature control is used most often in the temperature control
of building heating systems and ovens. It works by turning the heater ON
when the **sense** variable is less than the **set point** variable and turning the
heater OFF when the **sense** variable is greater than the **set point** variable.
The **duty factor** is the fraction of time that the heater is ON. When the heater

is turned ON, the temperature will usually rise rapidly until the **set point** is reached, the heater will be turned OFF, but the temperature may still continue to rise while the heating element comes into thermal equilibrium with the rest of the system. When the heater is turned OFF, cooling is accomplished by heat losses to the surroundings through any thermal insulation.

Representing the periodically measured sense variable as S, the set point as S', and the control variable as C, ON–OFF control can be described as the repeated application of the following algorithm:

> ### ON-OFF Control
> If $S \le S'$, then C = maximum.
> If $S \ge S'$, then C = minimum.

For effective control over a range of temperatures, the heater is chosen with sufficient capacity to overcome cooling losses at even the highest temperature. As a result, the rate of temperature rise when the heater is ON is generally much greater than the rate of temperature fall when the heater is OFF. Depending on how closely coupled the heater is to the rest of the system, there will be a lag time between switching the heater ON or OFF and any change in temperature. As seen in Figure 5.14, this results in a systematic error, where the temperature spends more time above the **set point** than below the **set point**, and the average value of the temperature can be considerably above the set point. This systematic error can be reduced by reducing the heater power in the ON state to increase the duty factor, but this reduces the maximum temperature capability of the system.

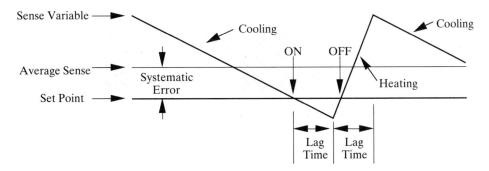

Figure 5.14   The **sense** variable as a function of time for ON–OFF control. The system passively cools until it reaches the set point when the heater is turned ON. After a time lag, the temperature rises. When the temperature exceeds the **set point**, the heater is turned OFF. The rate of heating is usually much greater then the rate of cooling, and the average temperature is above the **set point**.

5.9.2 Hysteresis

Occasionally, hysteresis is used in ON–OFF control to introduce a deadband and reduce that rate at which the heater is turned on and off (Figure 5.15). A **dead band** is a region of the sensed variable where no control action takes place. While this reduces the accuracy of control, it prolongs the life of the switching hardware and heater.

Representing the periodically sampled sense variable as S, the set point as S', the hysteresis dead-band width as H, zone as Z, and the control variable as C, ON–OFF control with hysteresis dead band can be represented as the periodic application of the following algorithm:

**ON-OFF Control with
Hysteresis Dead Band**

If $S \leq S' - H/2$, then $C = Z =$ maximum.
If $S \geq S' + H/2$, then $C = Z =$ minimum.
If $S' - H/2 < S < S' + H/2$, then $C = Z$.

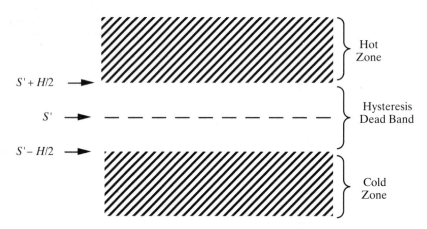

$S' + H/2$ →   Hot
                                                                                Zone

                                                                                Hysteresis
S' →   — — — — — — — — — — — —   Dead Band

$S' - H/2$ →   Cold
                                                                                Zone

Figure 5.15   Temperature zones for ON–OFF control with a hysteresis dead band.

5.9.3 Proportional Control

In **proportional control**, the heater output is controlled in a fairly continuous manner, either by adjusting the voltage or by adjusting the width of a pulsed input. The sensed variable is sampled at time interval T and the open-loop system response time is T_r. The algorithm computes an **error** value as the difference between the **sense** value and the **set point**. The **control** value is changed by the quantity **error** $\times$ **gain** $\times$ T/T_r and then checked to see whether it exceeds the maximum heater input. It is necessary to keep track of small changes in the **control** variable by making it a floating-point number. It is converted to an integer only for writing to the D/A converter. Large values of **gain** result in **ringing**, or oscillations, about the set point that slowly decay, analogous to the underdamped oscillator. Large values of gain cause the **control** variable to jump between its minimum and maximum values so that the behavior is similar to the ON–OFF control.

Representing the sense variable as S (measured periodically with time interval T), the set point as S', the thermal response time as T_r, the gain as G, and the change in the control variable as ΔC, proportional control can be described as the periodic application of the following algorithm:

Proportional Control

$$C = C + \Delta C$$
$$\Delta C = (S - S')GT/T_r$$

If $C >$ maximum, then $C =$ maximum.
If $C <$ minimum, then $C =$ minimum.

5.9.4   PID (Proportional–Integral–Differential) Control

The behavior of the proportional control algorithm is improved substantially by the addition of terms that describe the integral of the **error** and the differential of the **error**. Note that unlike the proportional and integral terms, the difference between successive **error** terms does not depend on the set point and cannot be used by itself for control.

Representing the periodically measured sense variable as S, the set point as S', the most recent change in S as ΔS, the integral of S as $\sum S$, the proportional, integral, and differential control coefficients as D_p, D_i, and D_d, respectively, and the change in the control variable as ΔC, PID control can be described as the periodic application of the following algorithm:

PID Control

$$C = C + \Delta C$$
$$\Delta C = D_p (S - S') + D_i \sum S + D_d \, \Delta S$$

If $C >$ maximum, then $C =$ maximum.
If $C <$ minimum, then $C =$ minimum.

5.10 PROBLEMS

5.1 A new drug has been developed for the treatment of high blood pressure (hypertension). You select a population of 18 patients suffering from hypertension. Half of the population is chosen at random to be the "control" group and these receive an inert substance (called a placebo). The other half is actually treated with the drug. The subjects do not know what group they are in. The table lists the measured systolic blood pressures before and after treatment:

	Before Treatment	After Treatment
Treated group:		
Patient 1	160	140
Patient 2	196	180
Patient 3	158	152
Patient 4	160	135
Patient 5	194	165
Patient 6	159	123
Patient 7	181	159
Patient 8	192	185
Patient 9	216	185
Placebo group:		
Patient 10	169	163
Patient 11	190	174
Patient 12	201	179
Patient 13	194	176
Patient 14	203	204
Patient 15	163	151
Patient 16	171	167
Patient 17	157	137
Patient 18	196	204

a. Calculate the mean, the standard deviation, and the standard error of the mean for the two groups, before and after treatment (12 numbers in all).

b. Calculate the unpaired Student's t for the change in blood pressure for each group (2 numbers). Here we are only comparing the averages of the two groups, and disregarding the fact that the same patients are being used for the "before" and "after" measurements.

c. For the unpaired Student's t, estimate the probability that the observed change in blood pressure could have arisen by chance. What number of degrees of freedom (n_f) did you use?

d. Calculate the paired Student's t for the change in blood pressure for each group (2 numbers). Here we are using the patients as their own controls, which cancels out the variation between patients and should give a more sensitive test for the effect of the drug.

   e. For the paired Student's t, estimate the probability that the observed change in blood pressure could have arisen by chance.

   f. Was the drug effective? Was the placebo effective?

5.2 Ten thousand kernels of corn have been randomly strewn over a tile floor consisting of 100 tiles.

   a. What is the average number of kernels per tile?

   b. How many tiles do you expect would have less than 80 kernels?

   c. How many would have more than 150?

5.3 Calculate chi-squared for the following data:

x_i	Model $f(x_i)$	Data Value f_i	Standard Deviation
0	80.0	90.0	5.0
10	50.0	55.0	2.5
20	30.0	18.5	1.5
30	20.0	18.5	1.5

   a. Estimate the probability of getting a higher chi-squared by chance.

   b. How many degrees of freedom are there?

   c. How well does the above model fit the data?

5.4 If m and n are positive integers, show that

$$\int_{-\pi}^{\pi} \sin(mx)\sin(nx)\,dx = \int_{-\pi}^{\pi} \cos(mx)\cos(nx)\,dx \begin{cases} = 0 \text{ for } n \neq m \\ = \pi \text{ for } n = m \end{cases}$$

$$\int_{-\pi}^{\pi} \sin(mx)\cos(nx)\,dx = 0 \text{ for all } n,m$$

$$\textit{Hint}: \sin A \sin B = \tfrac{1}{2}\left[\cos(A-B) - \cos(A+B)\right]$$

$$\cos A \cos B = \tfrac{1}{2}\left[\cos(A-B) + \cos(A+B)\right]$$

$$\sin A \cos B = \tfrac{1}{2}\left[\sin(A-B) + \sin(A+B)\right]$$

5.5 You have a data-acquisition system that can sample an analog waveform, digitize it, and transfer the resulting digital number into computer memory every 10 μs. (*Note*: This system has no analog filtering before digitizing.)

   a. What is the sampling frequency?

b. You sample a sine wave with frequency $f = 25$ kHz, look at the resulting data, and observe that there are four samples per sinewave. How many samples per apparent sinewave would you expect to observe if the input frequency were 10, 50, 75, and 100 kHz?

c. You acquire 1024 samples of a 9766-Hz sine wave oscillating between 0 and 2 V, and take the fast Fourier transform of the resulting data. List the location (frequency indices) of all non-zero Fourier amplitudes. (*Hint*: $1.024 \times 0.9766 = 1.0000$.)

5.6 You have been using the system described in Problem 5.5 for input frequencies below 20 kHz for some time and with great success until a colleague in the next room turns on a pure 1.000-MHz (± 1 Hz) sine-wave oscillator and some of the unwanted signal gets into the analog input of your system.

a. What would be the effect of the 1-MHz signal on your digitized data?

b. If you took several 1024 point data sets, where the start time was determined at random (such as by the push of a button), would the effect of the 1-MHz signal be the same for each data set? Give a reason for your answer.

c. How could you most easily eliminate the effect of the unwanted 1-MHz signal on your digitized data?

5.7 You sample exactly 10 cycles of a 1-kHz square wave at a sampling frequency at 100 kHz, and take the fast Fourier transform. (For this problem, you may assume the approximation $1000 \approx 1024$.)

a. Over what period of time have you sampled?

b. How many samples did you take?

c. To what frequency does the Fourier coefficient F_1 correspond? (*Hint*: F_0 is the zero frequency or dc coefficient)

d. At what Fourier coefficient do you expect the fundamental frequency to occur?

e. At which Fourier coefficient do you expect the next nonzero harmonic to occur?

f. At what Fourier coefficient is the highest frequency harmonic that can appear in your FFT?

5.8 You wish to develop a microcomputer-based system for monitoring the depth of liquid in a large tank by measuring the resonant frequency of the volume of air above the liquid (Figure 5.16). The tank is 50 ft high and you want to determine the depth of the liquid to an accuracy of 0.5 ft.

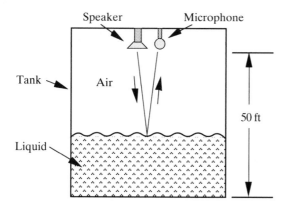

Figure 5.16 Measurement of liquid level in a tank using acoustic reflection.

- You have a speaker and microphone mounted inside the tank, at its top.
- The speed of sound in the air of the tank is 1000 ft per second.
- The fundamental resonance frequency (first harmonic) is inversely proportional to the height of the air column above the liquid, (i.e., the distance from the speaker to the liquid surface and back to the microphone equals one wavelength). When the tank is empty, the round trip path is 100 ft and the resonant frequency is 10 Hz. The tank is considered full when the level is 0.5 ft below the speaker and microphone.
- The speaker is driven by a white-noise generator, which excites all frequencies equally. Assume that the speaker and microphone have good response from 5 Hz to 10 kHz. (You have decided not to use acoustic reflection (sonar) or a sine-wave generator whose frequency can be computer controlled.)
- You decide to sample the microphone output, perform an FFT, and determine the fundamental resonant frequency by examining the Fourier amplitudes (similar to the first formant in the Laboratory Exercise 22, fast Fourier transforms of the human voice, but the mouth is very large!).

a. For a sampling interval $S = NT$ (where T is the time interval between samples and N is the number of samples), what is the frequency (in Hz) of the first Fourier coefficient F_1?

b. What is the frequency corresponding to the Fourier index F_n?

c. What is the resonant frequency when the liquid is 0.5 ft from the top?

d. To satisfy the 0.5-ft accuracy requirement for both nearly full and empty conditions, what are the requirements on N and T?

5.9 You are designing a system to sample analog data at a sampling frequency of 20 kHz in the presence of noise. An important consideration is the maximization of the signal-to-noise power ratio R, defined as

$$R = \frac{\int_0^\infty S^2 df}{\int_0^\infty N^2 df}$$

where S is the signal amplitude and N is the noise amplitude .

Your signal S has amplitude A from 0 Hz to 10 kHz and is zero above 10 kHz.
The noise $N = 0.1$ A from 0 Hz to 100 kHz and is zero above 100 kHz.

a. What is R before sampling or filtering?
b. What is R before sampling using an ideal low-pass filter with a sharp cut-off $f_c = 10$ kHz? (Here most of the noise is excluded.)
c. What is R after sampling but before using the filter in part b? (Remember how high frequencies can appear in the sampled data as lower frequencies.)
d. What is R after sampling and after using the filter in part b?

5.10 Since an ideal low-pass filter is not commercially available, you are to design and build your own Butterworth four-pole low-pass filter for the system in problem 5.8 above with corner frequency $f_c = 10$ kHz. The amplitude response $G(f)$ of the filter is given by:

$$G(f) = \frac{1}{\sqrt{1 + (f/f_c)^8}}$$

a. What is R before sampling using the four-pole filter? *Hint:* Use the following table for the filter response integral F:

$$F = \int_0^{f_{max}} \left[G(f) \right]^2 df$$

f_{max} =	0	$0.5 f_c$	$1.0 f_c$	$1.5 f_c$	$2.0 f_c$	$5.0 f_c$	∞
F =	0	$0.500 f_c$	$0.924 f_c$	$1.017 f_c$	$1.024 f_c$	$1.025 f_c$	$1.025 f_c$

b. You note that the filter of part **a** has an amplitude of only 0.707 at f_c = 10 kHz. What should f_c be so that the filter has an amplitude accuracy of 1/2 LSB at 10 kHz for an eight-bit A/D converter?
Hint: for small ε,

$$\frac{1}{\sqrt{1+\varepsilon}} \approx \frac{1}{1+\varepsilon/2} \approx 1 - \frac{\varepsilon}{2}$$

c. What is the signal-to-noise power ratio R before sampling using this more accurate filter?

d. What is the signal-to-noise power ratio R after sampling using this more accurate filter?

e. What is the signal-to-noise power ratio R after doubling the sampling frequency and using this more accurate filter?

5.11   Given the digital filter: $y_i = x_{i-1} - x_{i-2}$.

a. What is the impulse response? (*Hint*: An impulse has $x_0 = 1$ and $x_i = 0$ for $i \neq 0$)

b. What is the response to the pulse $x_0 = x_1 = x_2 = 1$?

c. To what does this digital filter most closely correspond: (i) low-pass filter, (ii) smoothing filter, (iii) integration, or (iv) differentiation?

5.12   Given the following digital filter $y_i = x_{i-1} - 2\, x_{i-2} + x_{i-3}$.

a. What is the impulse response? (*Hint*: An impulse has $x_0 = 1$ and $x_i = 0$ for $i \neq 0$)

b. What is the response to the pulse $x_0 = x_1 = x_2 = x_3 = x_4 = x_5 = 1$? (All other $x_i = 0$.)

c. To what does this digital filter most closely correspond: (i) low-pass filter, (ii) integration, (iii) first derivative, or (iv) second derivative?

5.13 You want to design a temperature-control system for an electrically heated incubator for hatching chicken eggs. You are provided with a thermistor, an A/D converter, a microcomputer with parallel interface, a power relay (a device that can switch a large current ON or OFF and is controlled by a small current), and assorted electronic components.

a. Draw a block diagram of your design for simple ON–OFF control and label all essential components.

b. Describe the steps involved in simple ON–OFF control (or draw a flow diagram).

c. How would part **b** be modified to implement ON–OFF control with hysteresis?

d. Do either of the techniques in part **b** or part **c** (theoretically) stabilize *at* the set point?

e. How would the *hardware* be changed to implement proportional control?

5.14 Design a temperature control system using a thermoelectric heat pump, a thermistor, and a microcomputer with –10 volt to +10 volt A/D and D/A converters. The heat pump and thermistor are in a steel box insulated with glass fibers.

a. Draw a block diagram for the sensor side of the system, from the thermistor to the A/D converter. Include and label all essential components and show typical signal voltage levels at all important points.

b. Draw a block diagram for the actuator side of the system, from the D/A converter to the thermoelectric heat pump. Include and label all essential components and show typical voltage and current levels at all important points.

c. What minimum and maximum temperatures do you think that this control system could achieve? Give reasons for your limits.

5.15 Show explicitly that if f_k is defined by:

$$f_k = \sum_{j=0}^{N-1} a_j \cos(2\pi jk/N) + b_j \sin(2\pi jk/N)$$

then the Fourier transform coefficient F_{N-n} is given by

$$F_{N-n} = (N/2)(a_n + i b_n)$$

5.11 ADDITIONAL READING

5.1 Michael Andrews, *Programming Microprocessor Interfaces for Control and Instrumentation,* Prentice Hall, Englewood Cliffs, NJ, 1982.

5.2 Karl J. Åström and Björn Wittenmark, *Computer Controlled Systems*, Prentice-Hall, Englewood Cliffs, NJ, 1984.

5.3 E. Oran Brigham, *The Fast Fourier Transform and its Applications,* Prentice Hall, Englewood Cliffs, NJ, 1988.

5.4 Robert W. Hornbeck, *Numerical Methods,* Prentice Hall, Englewood Cliffs, NJ, 1975.

5.5 Benjamin C. Kuo, *Digital Control Systems,* Holt, Rinehart, and Winston, New York, 1980.

5.6 Benjamin C. Kuo, *Automatic Control Systems,* Prentice Hall, Englewood Cliffs, NJ, 1987.

5.7 Lyman Ott and William Mendenhall, *Understanding Statistics,* Duxbury Press, Boston, MA, 1985.

5.8 Charles L. Phillips and Royce D. Harbor, *Feedback Control Systems,* Prentice Hall, Englewood Cliffs, NJ, 1988.

5.9 Charles L. Phillips and H. Troy Nagle, Jr., *Digital Control System and Design,* Prentice Hall, Englewood Cliffs, NJ, 1984.

5.10 George W. Snedecor, *Statistical Methods*, Iowa State University Press, Ames, IA, 1965.

5.11 Samuel D. Stearns and Ruth A. David, *Signal Processing Algorithms*, Prentice Hall, Englewood Cliffs, NJ, 1988.

Laboratory Exercise 20

Analog ↔ Digital Conversion and Least-Squares Fitting

PURPOSE

To digitize a set of analog voltages with an A/D converter, to use a D/A converter to recover the voltages, and to use the least-squares technique to determine the accuracy and linearity of the procedure.

EQUIPMENT

- IBM AT with Data Acquisition and Control Adapter
- printer (shared with other lab stations)
- +5-, and ±12-V power supplies
- one 10 kΩ trimpot
- digital multimeter
- superstrip circuit board

BACKGROUND

1 Analog-to-Digital (A/D) Converter Characteristics

The purpose of the A/D converter is to transform an analog voltage into a binary number. For an ideal linear A/D, the digital representation n corresponding to the analog voltage V is given by

$$n = \left[\frac{V - V_{\min}}{\Delta V} + \frac{1}{2} \right]_{\text{INTEGER}}$$

$V_{\min} + \Delta V/2$ is the transition voltage $V(0,1)$ at which n switches between 0 and 1. ΔV is the average difference between neighboring transition voltages:

$$\Delta V = \frac{V(2^N - 2, 2^N - 1) - V(0,1)}{2^N - 2}$$

For an N-bit A/D, the maximum transition voltage is $V(2^N - 2, 2^N - 1)$.

2 Digital-to-Analog (D/A) Converter Characteristics

The purpose of the D/A converter is to convert a binary number to an analog output voltage. For an ideal linear D/A, the output voltage $V(n)$ corresponding to the digital input n is given by

$$V(n) = V_{\min} + n\,\Delta V, \quad \text{where} \quad \Delta V = \frac{V_{\max} - V_{\min}}{2^N - 1}$$

where $V_{\min} = V(0)$ is the lowest output voltage and $V_{\max} = V(2^N - 1)$ is the highest output voltage. This may be verified by evaluating the equation for $V(n)$ at $n = 0$ and $n = 2^N - 1$.

3 Relationship between A/D and D/A Conversion

If the A/D and D/A converters have linear responses and the same values of $V_{\min}$ and ΔV, then the two conversion processes do not introduce systematic errors. The A/D output n is produced only by input voltages in the range between the transition voltages:

$$V(n-1, n) = V_{\min} + (n - 0.5)\,\Delta V \quad \text{and} \quad V(n, n+1) = V_{\min} + (n + 0.5)\,\Delta V$$

The average input value in this range is $V_{\min} + n\,\Delta V$, which is the same value given by the D/A equation for $V(n)$. As a result, when an arbitrary input voltage is digitized by an A/D and when the digital value is converted back by a D/A, the analog values may differ by as much as $\Delta V/2$, but the average value of the difference will be zero.

4 Two-Parameter Least-Squares Fit

The model is $y = a + bx_i$, where x_i are measured values, $i = 1$ to m, and a and b are unknown. As shown in Chapter 5, the least-squares best-fit coefficients are given by

$$a = \frac{st - rq}{ms - r^2} \quad \text{and} \quad b = \frac{mq - rt}{ms - r^2}$$

where

$$r = \sum x_i, \quad s = \sum x_i^2, \quad q = \sum x_i y_i, \quad \text{and} \quad t = \sum y_i$$

The residuals are $R_i = a + bx_i - y_i$, where y_i is the measured analog output value corresponding to the analog input x_i. The rms deviation between the data the best fit straight line (a measure of linearity) is given by:

$$\text{rms} = \sqrt{\frac{1}{m} \sum_i R_i^2}$$

ADDITIONAL READING

Chapter 3, Section 3.2: Digital-to-Analog Converter Circuits and Section 3.3: Analog-to-Digital Converter Circuits.

Chapter 5, Section 5.4: Least-Squares Fitting.

Appendix E (Summary of IBM Data Acquisition and Control Adapter), Section 1: Pin Assignments, Section 4: Analog Output, and Section 5: Analog Input.

PROCEDURE

1 Circuit

Construct a voltage divider using a 20-turn 10-kΩ trimpot connected between –11 volts and +11 volts. Connect the wiper to the digital multimeter and the positive input of the data-acquisition circuit (channel 0+, pin 6). Connect the power-supply ground to the negative input (channel 0–, pin 5) and to pins 4, 13, 15, and 60.

2 Program

Write a program that does the following:

1. Asks the user to (i) connect the multimeter to the trimpot, (ii) set an analog input voltage with the trimpot, (iii) enter the multimeter value into the keyboard, and (iv) press return.

2. Digitizes the voltage with the A/D converter.

3. Stores the digital number and sends it to the D/A.

4. Asks the user to (i) connect the multimeter to the analog output, (ii) enter the multimeter value into the keyboard, and (iii) press return.

5. For each step, stores three numbers: the analog input, the converted digital equivalent, and the analog output.

3 Data

Run the program for about 40 analog voltage levels spaced over the full range from –10 volts to +10 volts. Uniform spacing is not necessary; it is better if the input voltage values are randomly chosen.

LABORATORY REPORT

1 Setup

Draw a simple block diagram of your experimental setup.

2 Data Summary and Analysis

2.1 Do a two-parameter least squares fit of a and b of the model $y = a + bx$ to your data, where x is the analog input to the A/D and y is the analog output from the D/A. Print your results in a table with the following headings:

Index i	Input x_i	Measured Output y_i	Best linear fit $a + bx_i$	residual $R_i = a + bx_i - y_i$ (mV)	$100R_i/x_i$ (%)

2.2 Do a two-parameter least-squares fit to the A/D converter using the model

$$n = a + bV_i.$$

2.3 Do a two-parameter least squares fit to the D/A converter using the model

$$V = a + bn_i.$$

3 Discussion and Conclusions

3.1   Discuss how the principles of this laboratory exercise relate to the recording and playback used in compact digital disks and digital audio tapes.

3.2   Discuss how a 12-bit D/A converter can be used to test an 8-bit A/D converter entirely under program control.

3.3   From your analysis, determine whether the A/D or the D/A converter contributed more to the departures from linearity of the entire system. Did some of their non-linearities cancel?

4 Questions

4.1   How did the A/D and D/A V_{min} values compare?

4.2   How does the least-squares parameter a of the entire system relate to the A/D and D/A V_{min} values?

4.3   How well did the best least-squares fit values of a and b agree with your expectations?

4.4   Why is it best to choose random voltages in testing A/D converters?

5 Program and Laboratory Data Sheets

5.1   Include printouts of your program code, data, and output.

5.2   Include your handwritten data sheets (or a copy), which should consist of a log of the procedures you used, any special circumstances, and the measurements you recorded manually.

Laboratory Exercise 21

Fast Fourier Transforms
of Sampled Data

PURPOSE

To sample sine, square, and triangle waves, and to compute and display their fast Fourier transforms. To observe the effect of windowing on the purity of the Fourier components and to compare the observed harmonic amplitudes of the square and triangle waves with expected values.

EQUIPMENT

- IBM AT with IBM Data Acquisition and Control Adapter
- printer (shared with other IBM AT lab stations)
- wave generator

BACKGROUND

1 Use of the fft.c Function

Your program should have the following form:

```
#include <DOS.h>
#include "fft.c"
main()
{
float xr[512],xi[512];
int nu,ie;
. . .
fft(xr,xi,nu,ie);
. . .
}
```

If ie = −1, fft.c performs the forward Fourier transform $f_k \rightarrow F_n$.
If ie = +1, fft.c performs the reverse Fourier transform $F_n \rightarrow f_k$.
The number of points N is given by $N = 2^{nu}$. For $N = 512$, nu = 9.

To perform the discrete Fourier transform of a real time series, set xr[k] = f_k, and xi[k] = 0. The fft.c function will return with the complex Fourier amplitudes in the same xr and xi arrays. Note that the xr frequency amplitudes correspond to the cosine-like terms and the xi frequency amplitudes correspond to the sine-like terms.

The ratio of the real and imaginary parts of the Fourier coefficients depend on the point (phase) of the waveform at which you start sampling. Since the wave generator and the computer program are not synchronized, the phase angle ϕ will vary randomly from run to run and is not too important. However, the modulus $|F_n|$ of the Fourier coefficient F_n does not depend on ϕ.

$$\tan \phi = \text{Im}(F_n) / \text{Re}(F_n) \qquad |F_n| = \sqrt{\text{Re}(F_n)^2 + \text{Im}(F_n)^2}$$

ADDITIONAL READING

Chapter 5, Section 5.7: Fast Fourier Transforms.

E. Orhan Brigham, *The Fast Fourier Transform and its Applications*, Prentice Hall, Englewood Cliffs, NJ, 1988.

PROCEDURE

1 Circuit

Connect your wave generator to one of the analog inputs of the IBM Data Acquisition and Control Adapter. Ground pins 4, 13, 15, and 60.

2 Program

Write a C program that does the following:

1. Samples 1024 amplitude values at about 15 kHz and stores them in an array.

2. Writes the 1024 values to a disk file for plotting.

2. Performs the FFT and computes the modulus array.

3. Writes the modulus values to a disk file for plotting.

The data acquisition loop should look like the one you used in Laboratory Exercise 10 to demonstrate aliasing.

3 FFT of Periodic Waveforms

Set your wave generator for 100 Hz and sample 1024 values of the sine waveform at your maximum rate (approximately 15 kHz). The full sampling interval should contain about 7 sine waves. You will need to adjust the amplitude and offset knobs to produce a sine wave that swings between about –5 and +5 volts. Use the FFT function to get 1024 real and imaginary components of the frequency amplitudes. This should take about one minute, so be patient. Set up your program to compute the modulus of the 1024 values, and write them to a file on disk. Display and print the values using the plot program.

Set up your program to print the first 512 modulus values, 64 lines, 8 per line. Thus, the four data sets that follow should take at most three pages each for a total of 12 pages. DO NOT print one modulus value per line; it uses too much paper.

3.1 FFT of a nonintegral number of sine waves. As described above, print the data and plot the modulus values for a nonintegral number of cycles per full sampling interval (data set 1). Adjust the frequency slightly if a nearly integral number of cycles is sampled.

3.2 FFT of windowed sine waves. Change your program to multiply the data by a cosine window before taking the Fourier transform. Your modulus vector should now have only two large values (other than $|F_0|$). Print the data and plot the modulus values (data set 2).

3.3 FFT of windowed square waves. Without changing the frequency or amplitude, switch the wave generator from sine-wave to square-wave mode. Print the data, and plot the modulus values (data set 3).

3.4 FFT of windowed triangle waves. Without changing the frequency or amplitude, switch the wave generator from square-wave to triangle-wave mode. Print the data and plot the modulus values (data set 4).

LABORATORY REPORT

1 Setup

Draw a simple block diagram of your experimental setup.

2 Data Summary and Analysis

For the non-integral sine wave (data set 2), combine the two or three largest modulus values, and compare with the modulus value for the integral sine wave. Note that modulus values from neighboring Fourier coefficient should be combined in quadrature (the square root of the sum of the squares).

For the square and triangle waves (data sets 3 and 4), note the peaks in the modulus values, and identify the corresponding harmonic numbers. The nth harmonic has a frequency n times the primary frequency of the square or triangle wave. For each peak, combine the two or three largest modulus values in quadrature. For each peak, tabulate the frequency, the harmonic number, the combined modulus, and the ratio of the combined modulus to that of the first harmonic. Compare this last column with the expected values for the square and triangle wave. Note that the modulus values for the square wave should decrease with increasing frequency as f^{-1} and the modulus values for the triangle wave should decrease as f^{-2}.

3 Discussion and Conclusions

3.1 Discuss procedure sections 1 to 3.

3.2 Explain why the Fourier amplitudes occur where they do.

3.3 Discuss the differences in the purity of the Fourier coefficients between nonwindowed and windowed data when there are a nonintegral number of cycles per full sampling interval.

3.4 Discuss the limitations of the spectrum-analysis technique used in this laboratory exercise.

4 Questions

4.1 How would you expect the last 511 values of the modulus (i.e. $|F_{513}| \rightarrow |F_{1023}|$) to compare with the first 511 values after the dc term (i.e. $|F_1| \rightarrow |F_{511}|$)? Give an explicit relationship.

4.2 Could the difference in combined modulus between the windowed and nonwindowed non-integral sine wave data be explained by "leakage" into other Fourier coefficients?

4.3 How would you change the exercise to control the phase angle between the real and imaginary Fourier coefficients in procedure section 3?

5 Program and Laboratory Data Sheets

5.1 Include printouts of your program code, data, and output transforms of nonintegral sine-wave sampling, and integral sine wave, square wave, and triangle wave.

5.2 Include your handwritten data sheets (or a copy), which should consist of a log of the procedures you used, any special circumstances, and the measurements you recorded manually.

Laboratory Exercise 22

Fast Fourier Transforms
of the Human Voice

PURPOSE

To periodically sample the audio waveform produced by the human voice
when uttering various vowel sounds and to perform a fast Fourier transform
(FFT). To investigate which features in the FFT depend on the identity of
the speaker and which features depend on the vowel that is spoken.

EQUIPMENT

- IBM AT with IBM Data Acquisition and Control Adapter
- printer (shared with other IBM AT lab stations)
- +5- and ±12-V power supplies
- superstrip circuit breadboard
- three 10-µF electrolytic capacitors (put between power and ground at
  circuit board)
- six 0.1-µF CK05 bypass capacitors (put between power and ground at all
  chips)
- AD625 instrumentation amplifier for microphone
- two LF356 op amps for antialiasing filter
- N3568 NPN power transistor
- MJE3055 NPN power transistor
- microphone

- small loudspeaker
- one 50-Ω resistor (10 W)
- one 100-Ω resistor
- one 400-Ω resistor
- four 5-kΩ resistors
- two 20-kΩ resistors
- two 100-kΩ resistors
- one 20-kΩ trimpot
- one 2400-pF capacitor
- one 5600-pF capacitor
- one 6800-pF capacitor
- one 18000-pF capacitor
- two 1-μF capacitors
- one 10-μF capacitor

BACKGROUND

Voiced sounds are produced by forcing air through the glottis (the opening between the vocal chords) with the tension of the vocal chords adjusted so that they vibrate to produce quasi-periodic pulses of air that excite the vocal tract. The vocal tract consists of the pharynx (connection between the esophagus and the mouth) and the mouth. The jaw, lips and tongue can be moved to change the acoustical properties of the vocal tract. In addition, by lowering the velum, the nasal tract can be used to produce nasal sounds.

Vowels are voiced sounds produced with a fixed vocal tract. English examples are *a* as in father, *e* as in see, *o* as in go, *u* as in up.

Diphthongs are gliding voiced sounds that begin with one vowel and end with another. English examples are "bay", "boy", "you".

Nasals are voiced sounds produced by total constriction of the vocal tract and the lowering of the velum so that the air passes through the nasal cavity and the sound is radiated at the nostrils. The mouth still plays an important role as a resonant cavity. English examples are *m* (vocal tract constricted at the lips) and *n* (vocal tract constricted just back of the teeth). Nasals have a concentration of low frequency energy and the mid-range shows no prominent peaks.

Unvoiced Fricatives are produced by exciting the vocal tract by a steady flow of air that becomes turbulent in the region of a constriction in the vocal tract. The vocal chords do not vibrate. Examples are *f* (constriction near lips), *s* (constriction near middle of vocal tract), and *sh* (constriction near back of vocal tract). In these cases, the waveform is nonperiodic and similar to white noise. There are also many other identified speech components, such as semivowels (such as *w*, *l*, and *r*), voiced fricatives (such as *v* and *z*), voiced stops (such as *b*,*d*, and *g*), unvoiced stops (such as *p*, *t*, and *k*), and affricatives (such as *j* and *h*).

In this Laboratory Exercise, we will concentrate on the vowels, because they have characteristic frequency spectra. The resonant frequencies associated with each vowel are called "formants". For example, for the average male speaker, the o in hot should have its first formant F_1 at 730 Hz, the second F_2 at 1090 Hz, and the third F_3 at 2440 Hz. See Laboratory Table 22.1 for additional examples.

LABORATORY TABLE 22.1   AVERAGE FORMANT FREQUENCIES FOR THE VOWELS

IPA Symbol	Typical Word	F_1 (Hz)	F_2 (Hz)	F_3 (Hz)	F_2/F_1	F_3/F_1
i	beet	270	2290	3010	8.5	11.1
I	bit	390	1990	2550	5.1	6.5
E	bet	530	1990	2480	3.8	4.7
æ	bat	660	1720	2410	2.6	3.7
Λ	but	520	1190	2390	2.3	4.6
a	hot	730	1090	2440	1.5	3.3
O W	bought	570	840	2410	1.5	4.2
U	foot	440	1020	2240	2.3	5.1
u	boot	300	870	2240	2.9	7.5
ER	bird	490	1350	1690	2.8	3.4

Source: Gordon E. Peterson and Harold L. Barney, "Control Methods used in a Study of the Vowels", *J. Accoust. Soc. Am.*, Vol. 24 (1952): 175-184. Reprinted with permission of AT&T Corp., NJ.

A simple model for human speech vowels is an impulse generator (vocal chords) followed by a time-varying filter (mouth and tongue). The regular impulses are characteristic of the speaker and produce a FFT where only certain frequency amplitudes have nonzero magnitudes, similar to the primary frequency and higher harmonics that you observed in Laboratory Exercise 21 for the square wave and triangle wave. The mouth and tongue transmit these harmonics to the outside world with an intensity pattern that is characteristic of the vowel being spoken. By doing an FFT of a steady vowel sound, you should be able to identify two or three primary resonances (called formants) that are characteristic of that particular vowel. Note that the actual frequencies of the formants depend on the pitch of the speaker's voice and the ratios of the formant frequencies are more indicative of the vowel spoken.

ADDITIONAL READING

R. W. Broderson, P. J. Hurst, and D. J. Allstot, "Switched-Capacitor Applications in Speech Processing," *IEEE Symp. Circ. Sys.*, Vol. 3 (1980): 732-737.

Gordon E. Peterson and Harold L. Barney, "Control Methods used in a Study of the Vowels", *J. Accoust. Soc. Am.*, Vol. 24 (1952): 175-184.

L. R. Rabiner and R. W. Schafer, *Digital Processing of Speech Signals,* Prentice Hall, Englewood Cliffs, NJ, 1978.

PROCEDURE

1 Microphone Preamplifier

Build the AD625 instrumentation amplifier shown in Laboratory Figure 5.2. Use R_F = 20 kΩ and adjust R_G to get the necessary output. R_G should be 400 Ω for a gain of 100. Build the microphone circuit as shown in Laboratory Figure 22.1 and connect it to the instrumentation amplifier inputs. The amplifier output should be in the –5-volt to +5-volt range for the antialiasing filter, which has unity gain.

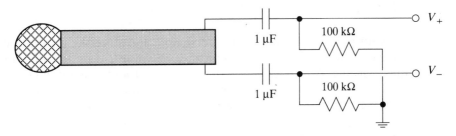

Laboratory Figure 22.1   Dynamic microphone and circuit for connection to instrumentation amplifier.

2 Antialiasing Filter

Build the Butterworth four-pole filter shown in Laboratory Figure 22.2 with a 3db corner frequency at 5 kHz. See Laboratory Figures 4.2 and 4.3 for op-amp pin assignments and external connections. See Chapter 2, Section 2.6 and Table 2.3 for filter component values.

Test the filter using your sine-wave generator. The filter should attenuate frequencies at and above 8 kHz (the Nyquist limit of the data acquisition circuit), reduce the amplitude to 0.707 at 5 kHz (the corner frequency of the filter), and preserve the amplitude at frequencies below 5 kHz.

Connect the filter circuit input to the output of the instrumentation amplifier and check that the filter output does not exceed the –5- to +5-volt range when speaking into the microphone in a moderate voice.

For f_c = 5 kHz and $R_1 = R_2 = R_3 = R_4$ = 5 kΩ, we want

C_1 = 6800 pF, marked "682" C_2 = 5600 pF, marked "562"
C_3 = 18,000 pF, marked "183" C_4 = 2400 pF, marked "242"

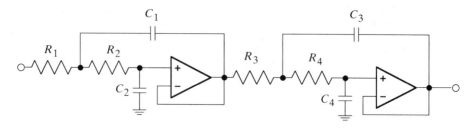

Laboratory Figure 22.2   Butterworth 4-pole antialiasing filter.

3 Data-Acquisition and Playback Circuit

Connect the output of the filter to analog input channel 0^+. Connect the power-supply grounds, input 0^- (pin 5), and pins 4, 13, 15, and 60 together. Connect the analog output to the current amplifier and speaker for playback.

4 Program

Use your previous program code to sample and store the data in a tight data-acquisition loop. Store and window 1024 values. Use the FFT function to transform the 1024 data values into 1024 real and imaginary components of the frequency coefficients. Compute the 512 modulus values, print them out, and write them to a file for plotting, as in Laboratory Exercise 21.

5 FFT of Vowel Sounds

Using the microphone, antialiasing filters, and computer, sample 1024 values for two different vowel sounds chosen from Laboratory Table 22.1, as spoken by both lab partners.

As you did in Laboratory Exercise 21, perform an FFT, compute the modulus array (513 values), print them on the printer, 8 per line, and write them to a file for plotting. You should have at least four data sets: two speakers and two vowel sounds. As there are individual differences between speakers, do not be too concerned if your data do not agree closely with Laboratory Table 22.1.

6 Sampling and Playback of Human Speech

6.1 Program.   Modify your program to write the stored data to the IBM analog output device to recover the human speech waveform. Since the power amplifier can only amplify positive signals, you must bias your values for > 0 volt output. If the input is in the range from -5 volts to $+5$ volts (digital 1024 to 3072), add 1024 to shift the output to the range from 0 volts to $+10$ volts (digital 2048 to 4096).

6.2 Power amplifier. Connect the analog output to an emitter-follower power transistor circuit shown in Laboratory Figure 22.3. Connect the output of the emitter follower to the small speaker. The 10 μF capacitor is necessary to block the dc current that would overheat the speaker coil.

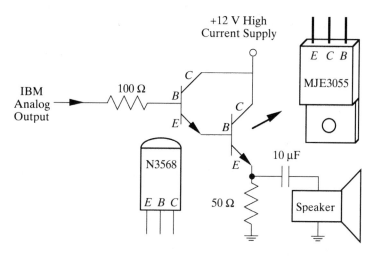

Laboratory Figure 22.3   Output circuit for playback of human speech.

6.3 Sampling and playback. Sample 2 seconds or more of speech (use an array of 30 kbytes or larger) and play it back on a speaker or headphone. Put a short delay in your playback loop so that the data are played back at the same rate they were recorded.

LABORATORY REPORT

1 Setup

Draw a simple block diagram of your experimental setup.

2 Data Summary and Analysis

2.1   Plot the magnitudes of the major periodic harmonics as a function of frequency for the four data sets (two vowels spoken by two speakers). If two or three adjacent Fourier coefficients have significant magnitudes, combine them by adding the squares of the magnitudes and then take the square root.

$$|M| = \sqrt{\sum M_i^2}$$

Label the first harmonic with the integer 1, mark the second harmonic (at double the frequency) with 2, mark the third harmonic with 3, etc.

2.2   You should see that the magnitude of the harmonics varies with frequency with the formants corresponding to broad peaks. Identify the pattern for each vowel and compute the ratio of the formant frequencies. Compare your ratios with those in Laboratory Table 22.1.

2.3   Estimate the fundamental vibration frequency of the vocal chords for each of the two speakers.

3 Discussion and Conclusions

3.1   Discuss procedure sections 5 and 6.

3.2   Examine the four data sets to compare different vowels spoken by the same speaker and the same vowels spoken by different speakers. Discuss which features of the FFT magnitude vector are characteristic of the vowel sound and which are characteristic of the speaker.

3.3   Prepare a flowchart for a computer program designed to determine which vowel was spoken, independent of speaker. Comment on any major problems.

3.4   Comment on the fidelity of digitized speech using your system.

4 Questions

4.1   To what frequency (in Hz) did your highest Fourier coefficient (N/2) correspond?

4.2   What was the frequency difference (in Hz) between neighboring Fourier coefficients?

5 Program and Laboratory Data Sheets

5.1   Include printouts of your program code and output of FFT magnitude values.

5.2   Include your handwritten data sheets (or a copy), which should consist of a log of the procedures you used, any special circumstances, and the measurements you recorded manually.

Laboratory Exercise 23

Digital Filtering

PURPOSE

To filter sine waves with analog and digital low-pass filters and to compare their properties as a function of frequency.

EQUIPMENT

- IBM AT with Data Acquisition and Control Adapter
- printer (shared with other IBM AT lab stations)
- +5-V and ±15-V power supplies
- sine-wave generator

BACKGROUND

1 Analog Low-Pass Single-Pole Filter

As described in Chapter 2, Section 2.6.1, the analog low-pass single-pole filter shown in Laboratory Figure 23.1 has a closed-loop gain G given as follows:

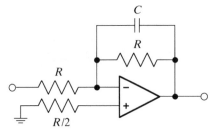

Laboratory Figure 23.1 Single-pole Low-pass Analog filter. See Laboratory Figure 4.3 for external components.

$$|G| = \frac{1}{\sqrt{1+(f/f_c)^2}}$$

where f is the frequency and $f_c = (2\pi R\underline{C})^{-1}$ is the corner frequency. For low frequencies, $|G| = 1$. At $f = f_c$, $|G| = 1/\sqrt{2}$. At very high frequencies, $|G| = f_c/f$.

This analog filter has an impulse response $e^{-t/RC}$, as shown in Laboratory Figure 23.2. The impulse basically puts a charge on the output of capacitor C, which decays with time constant RC.

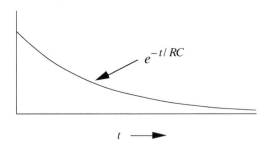

Laboratory Figure 23.2 Impulse response of a low-pass single-pole analog filter.

2 Digital Filters

A real-time digital filter has the general form:

$$y_i = A_1 x_{i-1} + A_2 x_{i-2} + \ldots + A_M x_{i-M} + B_1 y_{i-1} + \ldots + B_N y_{i-N}$$

If all the B's are zero, the filter will have a finite impulse response (FIR). If some or all of the B's are nonzero and sufficiently small, the filter will have an infinite impulse response (IIR) with decreasing amplitude for increasingly longer times. If some of the B's are not sufficiently small, the filter may be unstable.

The primary advantages of the digital filter is that it is easy to change (software rather than circuit components) and permits the use of certain classes of filters that are very difficult to implement with analog components.

2.1 Examples of Finite Impulse Response (FIR) Filters

Example I. $y_i = x_{i-1}$ The identity filter. The output is equal to the input, shifted in time by one cycle of the acquire/filter/output procedure.

Example II. $y_i = x_{i-1} - x_{i-2}$ The linear approximation to the first derivative filter. The output is equal to the differential of the input shifted in time by 1.5 cycles.

Example III. $y_i = x_{i-1} - 2x_{i-2} + x_{i-3}$ The quadratic approximation to the second derivative filter. The output is equal to the second differential of the input shifted by 2 cycles.

Example IV. $y_i = 0.25x_{i-1} + 0.50x_{i-2} + 0.25x_{i-3}$ A smoothing filter. The output is smoothed and shifted by 2 cycles.

Example V. $y_i = (x_{i-1} + x_{i-2} + ... + x_{i-n+1} + x_{i-n})/n$ An averaging filter. The output is the average of the input over n samples shifted by $1 + n/2$ cycles.

2.2 Example of an Infinite Impulse Response (IIR) Filter

Example I. $y_i = x_{i-1} + 0.9\,y_{i-1}$ A low-pass digital filter. The impulse response is computed by setting $y_0 = 0$, $x_0 = 1$ and $x_i = 0$ for $i > 0$. We then have $y_1 = 1$, $y_2 = 0.9$, $y_3 = 0.81$, $y_4 = 0.729$, and $y_i = (0.9)^{i-1}$.

ADDITIONAL READING

Samuel D. Stearns and Ruth A. David, *Signal Processing Algorithms,* Prentice Hall, Englewood Cliffs, NJ, 1988.

PROCEDURE

1 Analog Filtering

Build the low-pass single-pole analog filter shown in Laboratory Figure 23.1 with $R = 10$ kΩ and $C = 0.05$ μF. The corner frequency is at $f_c = (2\pi RC)^{-1} =$ 318 Hz. Using the setup shown in Laboratory Figure 23.3, measure the response of the analog filter at 10, 30, 100, 300, 1000, and 3000 Hz. Record both V_{out}/V_{in} and the phase shift.

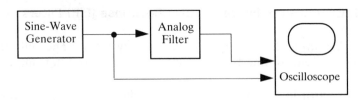

Laboratory Figure 23.3   Setup for analog filtering of sinewaves.

2 Digital Filtering

Using the setup shown in Laboratory Figure 23.4, sample the sine-wave generator with the IBM data-acquisition circuit at the frequencies listed above.
Connect the power-supply ground to pins 4, 13, 15, and 60. You will not need
the antialiasing filter used in Laboratory Exercise 22. Adjust the sine wave
for a peak-to-peak amplitude of about 10 V and an average amplitude of zero.

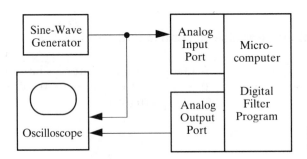

Laboratory Figure 23.4   Setup for
digital filtering of sine waves.

Write a program to sample the sine wave, perform the digital filtering

$$y_i = (1-\alpha)x_{i-1} + \alpha y_{i-1} \tag{23.1}$$

and write the result to the D/A converter as rapidly as possible   See Laboratory Figure 23.5 for the flow chart. In Equation (23.1), x_{i-1} is the most recent
value read by the A/D, y_{i-1} is the previous output value, and $0 < \alpha < 1$ is a
filter-design parameter. The impulse response of this low-pass, single-pole
digital filter is $y_i = \alpha^{i-1}$, which we wish to equate to the impulse response of
the analog filter:

$$y_i = \alpha^{i-1} = e^{-(i-1)T/RC} \qquad \alpha = e^{-T/RC}$$

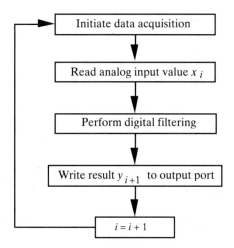

Laboratory Figure 23.5   Flow chart for digital filtering program.

Before you can calculate α, you will need to measure accurately the sampling interval T of your system. You will need to implement the multiplications by $(1 - \alpha)$ and α in Equation (23.1) by using multiplication and division by integers. A floating point multiplication will greatly decrease the speed of the digital filter.

When you begin filtering, the values of y_{i-1} will be inaccurate, particularly if you choose $y_0 = 0$. As the filter is implemented many times, the successive values of y_i "forget" the initial erroneous value used for y_0, with a time constant of RC. It is thus necessary to discard the first $5\,RC/T = -5/\ln\alpha$ samples.

LABORATORY REPORT

1 Setup

Draw a simple block diagram of your experimental setup.

2 Data Summary and Analysis

2.1   Tabulate and plot V_{out}/V_{in} for both filters as a function of frequency.

2.2   Tabulate and plot phase for both filters as a function of frequency.

2.3   Compare the measured properties of both filters.

3 Discussion and Conclusions

Discuss your results from procedure sections 1 and 2, and the analysis section.

4 Questions

4.1   What value of α did you use for your low-pass digital filter?

4.2   What value of α would you use in this exercise if your sampling and digital filtering frequency were $100\ \text{kHz}$?

4.3   Compute the impulse responses for the following filters:

$$y_i = x_{i-1} + 0.5y_{i-1} + 2y_{i-2}$$

$$y_i = x_{i-1} + 0.9y_{i-4}$$

$$y_i = x_{i-1} - y_{i-1}$$

5 Program and Laboratory Data Sheets

5.1   Include printouts of your program code and output.

5.2   Include your handwritten data sheets (or a copy), which should consist of a log of the procedures you used, any special circumstances, and the measurements you recorded manually.

Laboratory Exercise 24

Temperature Control

PURPOSE

To sense the temperature of a small oven with a thermistor bridge circuit and instrumentation amplifier, to digitize the analog signal, and to write a C program to implement and compare several algorithms for the digital control of temperature.

EQUIPMENT

- IBM AT with Data Acquisition and Control Adapter
- printer (shared with other IBM AT lab stations)
- parallel port ribbon cable
- superstrip circuit breadboard
- Analog Devices AD625 instrumentation amplifier
- 5-V and ±12-V power supplies
- 2-A +12-V power supply
- one precision thermistor (Omega type YSI 44004 [1207]- 2252 Ω at 25°C)
- one dial thermometer (temperature range –10°C to +110°C, with 0.15-in diameter metal stem, 5 in long)
- three ceramic 5-Ω, 12-W resistors (to be connected in series, mechanically and electrically)
- one N3568 NPN power transistor

- one MJE3055 NPN power transistor on heatsink
- one 100-Ω resistor
- one 20-kΩ trimpot
- two 2.5-kΩ resistors
- five 20-kΩ resistors

BACKGROUND

1 Control Modes

Three 12-W, 5-Ω ceramic resistors connected in series will act as a small cylindrical oven. The temperature inside the oven will be sensed by a thermistor and a dial thermometer. The thermistor will be one element of a bridge circuit with one variable resistor. This resistor is adjusted so the bridge has a small positive output voltage at room temperature and about 50 mV at 40°C. An instrumentation amplifier will be used to amplify this signal by about 100 to provide 0 to 5 volts for the IBM analog input device. You will write a program that digitizes this **sense signal**, compares it with a previously entered **set point**, and generates the difference as an **error signal**. You will program one of several control algorithms to generate a number that is sent out via the digital-to-analog converter. The resulting analog signal is amplified by a Darlington power amplifier and used to drive the ceramic resistors. Note that almost every element in this control system has a nonlinear response: (i) the thermistor, whose resistance depends exponentially on $1/T$, (ii) the bridge circuit, (iii) the Darlington amplifier, which has an offset, and (iv) the ceramic resistor, whose power output is given by $P = RV^2$.

Write a program (or use a program provided by the instructor) that provides one manual and two automatic control modes. The program first asks for a sampling interval T (sec), then every time that interval passes, read and display (i) the A/D value, (ii) the error signal, and (iii) the D/A control signal.

Mode 0 (Manual). The program asks for a control signal (0-4095) and sends this value to the D/A. At each multiple of the sampling time T you will be able to see the effect on the A/D sense signal. Use this mode when measuring the open loop step response and the relationship between the control signal and the sense signal.

Mode 1 (On–Off). The program asks for a set point (0-4095). Every time T the sense signal is sampled and an error signal is computed as sense signal minus set point. The control variable is then determined as follows:

If error signal < 0, control D/A is set to 4095.
If error signal > 0, control D/A is set to 0.

Mode 2 (Proportional).   The program asks for a set point (0-4095) and a gain value. Every time interval T the sense signal is sampled, an error signal computed, and control D/A is changed by the quantity (–gain × error). A typical value for gain is $0.5(T/T_r)$, where T_r is the thermal response time. Large values of gain cause the algorithm to oscillate and small values of gain result in very slow response. This is very analogous to the underdamped and overdamped harmonic oscillator except that thermal systems generally have large phase lags. If you write the program, calculate control D/A as a floating variable (so that it can keep track of small changes) and convert it to an integer for output to the D/A.

Mode 3 (Proportional-Derivative).   As above, but the change in the control variable has an additional term proportional to the change in sense.

2 Performance Criteria

In this laboratory exercise we will begin with the oven at some thermal equilibrium temperature T_0, abruptly change the set point S, and observe the change in temperature T with time t. The oven temperature will first change toward the desired temperature, possibly overshoot, and possibly oscillate. There are several criteria used to evaluate the performance of control algorithms, as described in chapter 5. These are: lag time, risetime, time to first peak, settling time, jitter, and accuracy.

ADDITIONAL READING

Chapter 5, Section 5.8: The Control System and Section 5.9: Temperature Control.

PROCEDURE

1 Circuit

The overall schematic of the control system is shown in Laboratory Figure 24.1. Set up the thermistor bridge as shown in Chapter Figure 4.14 with V_b = 1 volt, R_T = 2.5 kΩ (room temperature), $R_3 = R_4$ = 2.5 kΩ, and R_1 = 15 kΩ (variable). Amplify V_0 with with your instrumentation-amplifier circuit shown in Laboratory Figure 5.2. Adjust the gain as needed to provide a suitable voltage swing for the A/D converter. Connect the instrumentation-amplifier output to the data acquisition circuit. Power all the above circuits with the low-current power supplies. Connect the output of the D/A to the input of the power Darlington amplifier (Laboratory Figure 24.2). The three 12 W ceramic load resistors are to be connected in series to act an oven. *You must use the +12-V, 2-A supply for the Darlington.* Note that a 1.2 volt drop

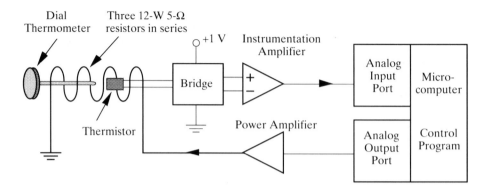

Laboratory Figure 24.1 Block diagram of the temperature control system. See Laboratory Figure 12.1 for the thermistor bridge circuit and Laboratory Figure 5.2 for the instrumentation amplifier circuit.

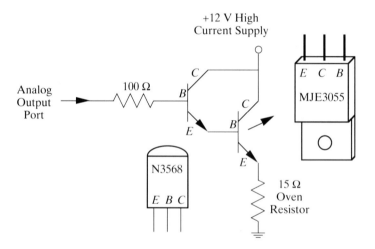

Laboratory Figure 24.2 Darlington power amplifier circuit.

will occur between the D/A output and the Darlington output. As a result, the output of the Darlington will be zero unless the D/A output exceeds 1.2 volts. Connect the power-supply grounds to pins 4, 13, 15, and 60.

2 Program

Write a program to implement Mode 0 (Manual), Mode 1 (On-off), and Mode 2 (Proportional) *or* Mode 3 (Proportional-Derivative). At the start of your program, ask the user for a value T for the sampling interval. Read the timer (as you did in Laboratory Exercises 2 and 3) and sample the A/D value every T seconds. Mode 0 requires entering a D/A control value, Modes 1 to

3 require entering a set point, and Mode 3 requires entering a proportional gain value.

3 Open-Loop Response Table

1. In manual mode 0, set the control variable to produce a D/A output of 2 volts. Wait for the temperature to stabilize, and measure and record the temperature in the oven with your dial thermometer. Also record the A/D input voltage, the A/D output number, the resistor voltage, and compute the resistor power.

2. Repeat for D/A outputs of 3, 4, 5, and 6 volts. The result is a table that relates the D/A input (and resistor power) to the dial thermometer temperature and A/D output. Ideally, the gain of the thermistor bridge amplifier should be chosen so that (at temperature equilibrium) a low value of D/A input corresponds to a low value of A/D output, and an D/A input of about 3500 corresponds to an A/D output of about 3500. Do not approach 0 or 4095 too closely to avoid the danger of saturation.

3. In Mode 0, set the D/A output to 2 volts and record the time required to cool down from 90% to 10% of the temperature difference. (This is the same temperature excursion measured as the rise time.)

4 Open-Loop Step Response

In manual mode 0, abruptly change the D/A output from 2 to 5 volts, and record the open loop step response in 5-s time intervals. For each sample, print out the time and the A/D output number.

5 On-Off Closed-Loop Response

In Mode 0 with a D/A output voltage value that corresponds to an A/D value of about 500, wait for the temperature to stabilize. Enter Mode 1 and abruptly change the A/D set point to some value between 1000 and 2000. Record the closed loop step response in 5-s intervals. For each sample, print the time, the A/D output number, the error value, and the D/A input number.

6 Proportional Closed-Loop Step Response

In Mode 0 with a D/A value that corresponds to an A/D value of about 500, wait for the temperature to stabilize. Enter Mode 2 and abruptly change the A/D set point to some value between 1000 and 2000. A typical value for the gain is $0.5(T/T_r)$, where T is the sampling time interval and T_r is the open loop response time. For each sample, print the time, the A/D output number, the error value, and the D/A output number.

7 Proportional–Derivative Closed Loop Step Response

As Mode 2, with the addition of a derivative coefficient.

LABORATORY REPORT

1 Setup

Include a simple block diagram of your experimental setup.

2 Data Summary and Analysis

2.1   Plot open loop sense and dial thermometer temperature vs control D/A at equilibrium (data of section 3)

2.2   Plot the open loop step response, and tabulate lag time, rise time, and jitter.

2.3   For the closed loop step responses of the two control algorithms used (section 5 and 6 or 7), tabulate lag time, rise time, time to first peak, settling time, jitter, and systematic error.

3 Discussion and Conclusions

Discuss procedure sections 3 to 5 and 6 or 7

4 Questions

4.1   Which of the two control algorithms you used had the least jitter? The least systematic error? To what temperature errors in °C do these correspond?

4.2   After an abrupt change in set point, which control algorithm reached 90% first (sum of lag time and rise time)?

5 Program and Laboratory Data Sheets

5.1   Include printouts of your program code and output.

5.2   Include your handwritten data sheets (or a copy), which should consist of a log of the procedures you used, any special circumstances, and the measurements you recorded manually.

A

Units and Constants

Angle

1 radian (rad)= $180°/\pi$ = 57.2958°

1 mrad = 0.0572958° = 3.43775 arc min = 206.265 arc s

Avogadro's Number

6.0228×10^{26} molecules mole^{-1}

Boltzmann's Constant

$k = 8.61709 \times 10^{-5}$ eV/K

Charge

1 coulomb (C) = 6.241×10^{18} electron charges

1 electron charge = 1.6022×10^{-19} C

1 faraday = 1 mole of electron charge = 96,487 C

Colors (Visible)

Pure color =	Violet	Blue	Green	Yellow	Orange	Red
λ (nm) =	420	450	550	580	600	700

Current

1 ampere (A) = 1 C/s = 6.241×10^{18} electrons/s

Density

Water (4°C) = 1.000 g cm^{-3}
Mercury (Hg) = 13.6 g cm^{-3}

Energy

1 electron volt (eV) = 1.6021×10^{-12} erg = 1.6021×10^{-19} J
1 electron Volt/molecule = 1.6021×10^{-12} ergs/molecule = 23.060 kcal/mole
1 erg = 1 dyn cm = 1 g cm^2 s^{-2} = 6.241×10^{11} eV
1 joule (J) = 1 newton meter = 1 kg m^2 s^{-2} = 1 V C = 10^7 erg = 6.241×10^{18} eV
1 kWh = 3.600×10^6 J = 3409.54 Btu = 8.5918×10^5 cal
1 calorie (g) (cal) = 4.1900 joules (J) = 3.974×10^3 Btu = 1.1639×10^{-6} kWh
$\quad$ = 6.9468×10^{-17} erg = 4.3361×10^{-5} eV
1 calorie (kg) = 1 kcal
1 ton TNT = 4.2×10^{16} erg

Force

1 dyne (dyn) = 1 g cm s^{-2}
1 newton (N) = 1 kg m s^{-2} = 10^5 dyn = 0.2247 lb (at surface of earth)

Gravitational Force

$F = GM_1M_2/R^2$, where $G = 6.67 \times 10^{-11}$ N m^2 kg^{-2} = 6.67×10^{-8} dyn cm^2 g^{-2}

Inductance

1 henry (H) = 1 V s A^{-1} turn^{-1}

Length

1 angstrom (Å) = 10^{-8} cm = 10^{-10} m = 0.1 nm
1 astronomical unit (AU) = 1.496×10^{13} cm = 9.296×10^7 mi
1 cm = 0.032808 ft = 0.39370 in = 0.10936 yd
Earth radius (equatorial) = 6.3782×10^8 cm
1 ft = 30.48 cm (exactly)
1 in = 2.54 cm (exactly) = 25,400 μm
1 km = 10^5 cm = 0.6214 mi = 3280.8 ft
1 light year (LY) = 9.4606×10^{17} cm = 0.3066 pc = 63,280 AU
1 m = 1.094 yd = 39.37 in = 3.2808 ft
1 mi = 1.60934 km = 5280 ft (exactly) = 1760 yd = 8 furlongs
1 light ns = 29.979 cm = 0.9836 ft
1 parsec (pc) = 3.262 LY = 206,265 AU = 3.086×10^{18} cm
Solar radius = 6.960×10^{10} cm

Magnetic Fields

1 Tesla = 10^4 Gauss (g) = 1 Weber m^{-2}

• Ampere-Biot law: $d\mathbf{B} = \dfrac{k'I \, d\mathbf{L} \times \mathbf{R}}{R^3}$

where the magnetic field $d\mathbf{B}$ at $\mathbf{R}$ is due to line element $d\mathbf{L}$ carrying current I; and $k' = 10^{-7}$ Wb A^{-1} m^{-1} = 10^{-3} G m A^{-1} = $\mu_0/4\pi$.

• Biot-Savart law: $B_T = 2\,k'\,I/R$, where B_T is the tangential magnetic field at distance R from an infinitely long straight wire carrying current I.

• $B_A = \mu_0 IN$, where B_A is the magnetic field along the axis of an air solenoid of N turns per cm carrying current I, and μ_0 (the permeability of empty space) = $0.4\,\pi$ G A^{-1} (turn cm^{-1})$^{-1}$.

Mass

1 g = 1 cm^3 water (4°C) = 0.35274 oz (avdp) = 15.432 grains (gr)
   = 980.665 dyn at surface of earth
1 karat = 100 points = 0.2 g
1 kg = 1 liter water (4°C) = 2.2046 lb (avdp) = 35.274 oz (avdp) = 10^{-3} ton (metric)
1 lb (avdp) = 453.592 g = 16 oz (avdp) = 256 drams (avdp) = 7000 gr
l lb (apoth or Troy) = 373.42 g = 12 oz (apoth or Troy) = 5760 gr
1 ton (metric) = 1 m^3 water (4°C) = 10^6 g = 1000 kg = 2204.6 lb (avdp)
1 ton (short) = 2000 lb (avdp) = 0.90718 ton (metric)

Avoirdupois (pronounced av'ur du poyz') is the most commonly used system of weights in the United States and Great Britain. Apothecary is used for drugs and Troy is used for precious metals and gems.

Earth mass = 5.977×10^{27} g
Electron mass = 9.1066×10^{-34} g
Proton mass = 1.67248×10^{-30} g
Solar mass = 1.991×10^{33} g = 3.32×10^5 earth mass

Maxwell's Equations

$\nabla \bullet \mathbf{B} = 0$ Absence of free magnetic poles

$\nabla \bullet \mathbf{D} = 4\pi\rho$ Coulomb's law

$\nabla \times \mathbf{H} = \dfrac{4\pi}{c}\mathbf{J} + \dfrac{1}{c}\dfrac{\partial \mathbf{D}}{\partial t}$ Ampere-Biot law

$\nabla \times \mathbf{E} = \dfrac{\partial \mathbf{B}}{\partial t}$ Faraday's law of induction

Photon Energy

$E = h\upsilon$, where $h = 6.6254 \times 10^{-27}$ erg s
$E = hc/\lambda$, where $hc = 1240$ eV nm, and λ = wavelength

Planck's Constant h

$h = 6.6254 \times 10^{-27}$ erg s

Power

1 horsepower (hp) = 746 watts (W) = 178.298 cal s^{-1} = 2547.2 Btu h^{-1}
    = 550.22 ft lb s^{-1}
1 W = 1 V A = 0.238 cal s^{-1} = 10^7 erg s^{-1}

Astronomical examples:
solar flux at 1 AU (earth) = 1.37×10^6 erg cm^{-2} s^{-1} (–26.5 stellar magnitude)
solar flux at 10 pc = 3.2×10^{-7} erg cm^{-2} s^{-1} (4.6 magnitude)
solar luminosity = 3.86×10^{33} erg s^{-1}
spiral galaxy luminosity = 10^8 to 10^{10} solar luminosity
quasar (3C273) optical luminosity = 10^{46} erg s^{-1} if at a distance of 10^9 LY

Pressure

1 atmosphere (atm) = 760 mm Hg = 29.9213 in Hg = 1.01325×10^6 dyn cm^{-2}
    = 14.6960 lb in^{-2}
1 bar = 10^6 dyn cm^{-2}
1 dyn cm^{-2} = 9.86923×10^{-7} atm = 7.5006×10^{-4} mm Hg = 1.45038×10^{-5} lb in^{-2}

Quadratic Equation

$$ax^2 + bx + c = 0 \quad x = \frac{-b \pm \sqrt{b^2 - 4ac}}{2a}$$

Velocity

Velocity of light in vacuum = c = 2.99792458×10^8 m s^{-1}
1 mi h^{-1} = 1.6093 km h^{-1} = 1.4667 ft s^{-1} = 88 ft min^{-1} = 0.44704 m s^{-1}
1 ft s^{-1} = 1.0973 km h^{-1} = 0.3048 m s^{-1} = 0.68182 mi h^{-1}
1 m s^{-1} = 3.2808 ft s^{-1} = 2.2369 mi h^{-1}

Volume

1 liter (L) = 1000 cm^3

B

Shielding and Grounds

INTRODUCTION

Noise in electronic circuits includes three basic categories:

1. transmitted noise, received with the original signal and indistinguishable from it,
2. intrinsic noise in the circuit (Johnson, shot, etc.), and
3. interference noise generated by components in the circuit or picked up from outside the circuit.

This appendix considers only the last category, which is the only form of noise that can be influenced by choices of wiring and shielding. The addition of capacitors can also reduce voltage spikes appearing on power-supply wires.

GENERAL RULES TO FOLLOW

- Think where the currents flow: all the current that enters your circuit from the power supplies must somehow return to those same power supplies. Since every conductor has a finite dc resistance and ac impedance, the conductors that carry that current may be called "ground" but may have dc shifts and voltage spikes.

- Keep digital and analog ground returns separate: conductors that serve as the "digital ground" can carry large voltage spikes as the digital circuits change logic state, and these grounds serve as very poor analog circuit grounds. Remember that analog circuits have no "noise immunity."

- Printed circuit boards and well-designed breadboards have a "ground plane" that is best used as electromagnetic shielding from outside electrical interference. Do not use this plane as a conductor to return current to the power supply.

- Both the power-supply and the ground-return leads should be sufficiently heavy wire to reduce both dc and ac voltage drops to acceptable levels.

- Put electrolytic capacitors (in the 1- to 100-μF range) between the power-supply conductors and their ground-return conductors at the point where they connect to the circuit board. Their purpose is to stabilize the supply voltages from external electrical interference (60 Hz to 1 MHz), and brief (μs to ms) drops in supply voltage due to momentary current demands by both external circuits and internal circuit components. These capacitors are not useful in protecting against the 1- to- 10-nsec voltage spikes caused by switching in digital circuits.

- Put mylar capacitors (in the 0.1-μF range) across the voltage supplies of all digital integrated-circuit chips that demand very brief surges of current and across all analog chips that have to be protected from such surges.

- Never blindly trust your power supply and ground connections; look at them with an oscilloscope while the circuit is running.

- An op amp is usually shown with only three signal terminals, the two differential inputs and an output that is referenced to "ground". In reality, however, one or both of the power-supply terminals acts as a fourth output conductor, which is expected to be a low impedance at all frequencies within the amplifier bandwidth. For example, some amplifiers such as the 741 have excellent low-frequency power-supply rejection, but are limited in their ability to compensate for variations in the negative supply that are faster than the closed-loop bandwidth. Thus, other high-speed switching circuits that draw current pulses from the negative supply can cause fluctuations in the output of such op amps.

C

C Programming Hints

1 DECLARE ALL VARIABLES

char	8-bit integer: −128 to 127
uns char	8-bit unsigned integer: 0 to 255
int	16-bit integer: −32,768 to 32,767
uns int	16-bit unsigned integer: 0 to 65,535
long or long int	32 bit integer: −2,147,483,648 to 2,147,483,647
uns long†	32 bit unsigned integer: 0 to 4,294,967,295
float	32 bits: 7 significant digits from $\pm 1.2 \times 10^{-38}$ to $\pm 3.4 \times 10^{+38}$
double or long float	64 bits: double precision float from $\pm 2.3 \times 10^{-308}$ to $\pm 1.7 \times 10^{+308}$

† not defined by some compilers

For example, to declare an integer array a of dimension 10, put the following statement at the top of your program:

int a[10];

In C, subscripts start from 0, so that valid elements are a[0], a[1], . . . ,a[9]. Writing into a[10] may do serious damage to other data!

• Note the square brackets and the ";" after every statement.

• Note that the following will overflow if b*b has more than 16 bits:

```
long a;
int b;
a=b*b;
```

The solution is to make both a and b long.

2 ARITHMETIC STATEMENTS

Arithmetic statements always end in ";" :

```
a=b+c;        /* addition */
a=b-c;        /* subtraction */
a=b*c;        /* multiplication */
a=b/c;        /* division */
a=b%c;        /* b modulo c   (b and c both "int") */
```

• Note that there is no low-level exponentiation operator such as a**b or a^b.

```
a=1459;       /* a = decimal 1459 */
b=0127;       /* b = octal 127 (note leading zero) */
c=0xA3FC;     /* c = hexadecimal A3FC (note leading 'zero ex') */
```

3 CONDITIONAL TESTS

```
if (expression)
    statement 1
else
    statement 2
```

• "expression" uses conditional operators, such as a < b or a != b or a == b or a <= b (see Section 4).

• "statement" can be a single statement line ending with ";" or many statement lines, each ending in ";", enclosed between "{" and "}".

4 CONDITIONAL OPERATORS

These operators are used with conditional tests; see Section 3.

```
==      equal to
!=      not equal to
<       less than
<=      less than or equal to
>       greater than
>=      greater than or equal to
&&      logical AND
| |     logical OR
```

5 INDEXED LOOPING

```
for (expression 1; expression 2;  expression 3)
    statement;
```

is equivalent to:

```
expression 1;
while(expression 2) {
    statement;
    expression 3;
    }
```

Usually, expressions 1 and 3 are assignments and expression 2 is relational, e.g.,

```
for (i=0; i<100 ; ++i)
    expression;
```

will loop 100 times with i taking on the values 0, 1, 2, 3, . . . , 99.

6 BITWISE LOGICAL OPERATORS

```
&      AND
|      inclusive-OR
^      exclusive-OR
<<     left  shift
>>     right shift
~      complement
```


7 INCREMENT AND DECREMENT OPERATORS

```
++i    increments i by 1 and then uses its value as the value in the expression
i++    uses i as the value in the expression, then increments i by 1
--i    decrements i by 1 and then uses its value as the value in the expression
i--    uses i as the value in the expression, then decrements i by 1
```


8 THE printf STATEMENT

The first part of the argument is in quotes (") and may contain text to be printed and special format commands, always beginning with % or /. The second part of the argument is a list of quantities (numbers or text data) to be printed according to the % commands. Each such quantity in the list is associated with the corresponding % command.

Example of printf use: printf("index=%d   data=%10.3f",a,b);

Examples of % format commands:

Format	Variable Type	Output Printed As
%5d	"int"	decimal, field width = 5
%10ld	"long"	decimal, field = 10
%10.3f	"float"	decimal, field = 10, 3 places after "."
%15.8lf	"double"	decimal, field = 15, 8 places after "."
%4x	"int"	hexadecimal (4 bits, 0 to F), field = 4
%10lx	"long"	hexadecimal, field =10
%c	"char"	single ASCII character

Summary of "\" commands (Stephen G. Kochan, *Programming in C*, Hayden Publishing Co., Hasbrouck Heights, NJ, 1983, p. 323):

\n	new line
\r	carriage return (no linefeed)
\b	backspace (to make ϕ, θ, etc.)
\t	horizontal tab (note use in Section 10)
\nnn	ASCII character corresponding to nnn (octal)

9 DEFINING YOUR OWN FUNCTIONS

```
main()
{
float fun();      /* declare function variable type */
float x,y,z;      /* define other variables */
 . . .            /* your main program goes here */
z=fun(x,y);       /* call to function */
 . . .            /* more of your program */
}                 /* end of main program */


float fun(x,y)    /* note: no final semicolon */
float x,y;        /* declare external variables */
{
float u,v;        /* declare local variables */
 . . .            /* body of code to compute fun(x,y) */
return(u);        /* return local variable value */
}
```

Note 1: The function name "fun" can be any name of your choosing.
Note 2: If the function code appears before main(), then the initial type declaration of the function is not required.

10 "INCLUDING" YOUR OWN FUNCTIONS

It is very common practice to maintain a "library" of functions that can be used by many different programs. In this way, only one copy of each function need be maintained. The code for each function is in a file by itself and that file is "included" in the main program code to be compiled as though it were all in one file. For example, the file "fun.c" might look like

```
float fun(x,y)   /* note: no final semicolon */
float x,y;       /* declare external variables */
{
float u,v;       /* declare local variables */
. . .            /* body of code to compute fun(x,y) */
return(u);       /* return local variable value */
}
```

And the main program would look like

```
#include "fun.c"
main()
{
float fun();     /* declare function variable type */
float x,y,z;     /* define other variables */
. . .            /* your main program goes here */
z=fun(x,y);      /* call to function */
. . .            /* more of your program */
}                /* end of main program */
```

Note: Since the included file precedes its first call, a separate type declaration in the main program code is not necessary.

11 OPENING AND WRITING TO FILES OF ARBITRARY NAME

This very important feature is to be used for most of the data recording in systems where several microcomputers share a printer. It allows you to save your data on disk and then print it later, whenever the printer is free.

At the top of your program, put the statements

```
char    out_file_name[16];
FILE    *out_file;
```

Later in your program, ask the user for a filename, read it, and open the file:

```
printf("Output file name:\t");
scanf("%s", out_file_name);
out_file = fopen(out_file_name,"w");
```

To write to the newly created file:

```
fprintf(out_file, "This file is %s", out_file_name);
```

(or anything else you want to write).

12 USING LIBRARY FUNCTIONS

To use the standard I/O library, put "#include <stdio.h>" before "main()". This is necessary for all programs that use printf, scanf, fprintf, fscanf, etc.

To use the math function library, put "#include <math.h>" before "main()". All the math functions listed below have type "double" arguments and return type "double".

cos(x)	cosine of x, x in radians
sin(x)	sine of x, x in radians
tan(x)	tan of x, x in radians
atan(x)	arc tangent of x in radians
atan2(y,x)	arc tangent of y/x (range spans 2π)
exp(x)	exponential, base e
log(x)	base e (natural) logarithm
log10(x)	base 10 logarithm
pow(x,y)	power function x^y
sqrt(x)	square root
fabs(x)	absolute value (use abs(i) for type "int")

13 GENERAL FORMAT RULES FOR C PROGRAMS

- Every single-line statement must end in ";".
- Multiline statements must be inclosed between "{" and "}".
- Every variable must be declared (char, int, long, float, double).
- Comments must be inclosed between /* and */.

D

Numerical Methods
and C Functions

1 INTRODUCTION

This appendix describes some numerical methods useful in microcomputer-based data analysis. The fast Fourier transform function performs a discrete Fourier transform of a waveform sampled at periodic time intervals. The STREAM function permits nonlinear fitting by varying parameters to minimize a goodness-of-fit quantity (such as chi-squared). The ADSINT function performs numerical integration using adaptive quadrature and dynamically divides the integration interval into smaller steps to evaluate the integral with the desired accuracy and the minimum number of integrand evaluations. An example is given for computing the probability of exceeding a particular value of Student's t. Several methods for function inversion are given using both Newton's method and quadratic approximation. The ADSINT function and Newton's method were used to compute the chi-squared and Student's t probability tables in Chapter 5.

2 FAST FOURIER TRANSFORM

The fast Fourier transform is discussed in Chapter 5 (Data Analysis and Control), Section 5.7. This algorithm is basically a way to compute the discrete Fourier transform rapidly.

The C code listing (Section 2.1) was adapted by the author from the FORTRAN code in E. Orhan Brigham, *The Fast Fourier Transform*, © 1974, P. 164, by permission of Prentice-Hall, Inc., Englewood Cliffs, N. J. This C function is used with the statement fft(xr,xi,nu,ie);, where xr and xi are the real and imaginary parts, respectively, of a coefficient array having 2^{nu} elements. If ie < 0, the forward transform is performed (time samples into frequency coefficients), and if ie $\geq$ 0, the reverse transform is performed (frequency coefficients into time samples). The function returns the result of the transformation in the arrays xr and xi. Note that raising 2 to an integer power and bit reversal are performed using shifts rather than multiplication and division by 2.

2.1 C Code

```
#include "stdio.h"
#include "math.h"
fft(xr,xi,nu,ie)
float xr[ ],xi[ ];                        /* define global variables */
int nu,ie;
{
float stab[1025],ctab[1025];              /* define local variables */
int n,n1,n2,nu1,p,k1n2,i,k,l;
float arg,c,s,tr,ti;
#define TWOPI 6.283185307      /* 2 PI */
#define PITWO 1.570796327      /* PI/2 */
n=1<<nu;
n2=n/2;
nu1=nu-1;
for (i=0; i<n; ++i)
    {
    arg=TWOPI*i/n;
    stab[i]=sin(arg);
    ctab[i]=sin(arg+PITWO);
    }
k=0;
for (l=0; l<nu; ++l)
    {
    while (k<n)
    {
    for(i=0; i<n2; ++i)
        {
        n1=1<<nu1;
        p=ibitr(k/n1,nu);
        s=stab[p];
        c=ctab[p];
        if(ie>0) s=-s;
        k1n2=k+n2;
        tr = xr[k1n2]*c + xi[k1n2]*s;
```

```
                ti = xi[k1n2]*c - xr[k1n2]*s;
                xr[k1n2] = xr[k] - tr;
                xi[k1n2] = xi[k] - ti;
                xr[k] = xr[k] + tr;
                xi[k] = xi[k] + ti;
                k=k+1;
                }              .            /* end i loop */
            k=k+n2;
            }                               /* end while */
            k=0;
            nu1=nu1-1;
            n2=n2/2;
            }                               /* end l loop */
    for (k=0; k<n; ++k)
        {
        i=ibitr(k,nu);
        if(i>k)
            {
            tr=xr[k];
            ti=xi[k];
            xr[k]=xr[i];
            xi[k]=xi[i];
            xr[i]=tr;
            xi[i]=ti;
            }
        }
    if (ie>0)
        {
        for(i=0; i<n; ++i)
            {
            xr[i]=xr[i]/n;
            xi[i]=xi[i]/n;
            }
        }
    return;
    }
int ibitr(j,nu)
int j,nu;
{
int rm,lm,i,bitr;
rm=1;
lm=1<<(nu-1);
bitr=0;
for (i=0; i<nu; ++i)
    {
    if ((j&rm)!=0) bitr=bitr|lm;
    rm=rm<<1;
    lm=lm>>1;
    }
return (bitr);
}
```

3 MINIMIZATION FUNCTION STREAM

The STREAM function was developed by the author to perform nonlinear fitting of functions to data on a small computer. A user-defined function, called fun(m,n,x), computes a goodness-of-fit for any set of parameters x. STREAM calls fun repeatedly and seeks the first minimum downhill from the starting point. The primary advantages are its robustness, small size, and its ability to handle non-stationary correlations (i.e., be able to turn corners in its pursuit of the minimum).

The function is called using the statement

stream(m,n,x,e,conv,maxit,nprint);,

where the initial arguments of the function are in the array x of dimension n. The initial step size is in the array e. If any e[i] is < 0, then the corresponding parameter x[i] is never varied. The parameter maxit is the maximum number of iterations. The parameter nprint controls printing to the standard output device. If nprint > 0, then stream prints output for every iteration that is an integral multiple of nprint. If nprint is ≤ 0, output is suppressed. The message "MINIMUM NOT FOUND" should not be suppressed. The function returns when the change in the x vector is less than the vector e*conv or when the iteration counter exceeds maxit.

3.1 Flow Chart

1. From the first, guess, vary each function parameter in turn, and minimize the function using quadratic approximations.

2. Compute the direction that the function parameters moved in Step 1 and minimize the function along this direction.

3. If the convergence criteria is not met and if the maximum iteration number is not exceeded, go back to Step 1.

3.2 C Code

```
#include<stdio.h>
#include<math.h>

stream(m,n,x,e,conv,maxit,nprint)
double x[ ],e[ ],conv;
int m,n,maxit,nprint;
{
static double c[20],abse[20],d[20],xp[20],y[20],fstep[20],fx1[20],fx2[20];
static int i, ifconv=0, iit, nfcls, ifprint, nfc;
static double dmin, sconv, fx, sd, sdmax;

/*   description of local variables used:
```

```
    c[i]        change in x between last two iterations
    d[i]        step size for this iteration
    xp[i]       value of x at the end of the last iteration
    y[i]        intermediate values of x (output from min1)
    fstep[i]    temp storage    (step size for flow)
    fx1[i]      values of x from previous iteration before step 1
    fx2[i]      values of x from previous iteration after step 1
*/

iit=0; nfcls=1; dmin=conv; sconv=sqrt(conv);
for (i=0; i<n; ++i)
    {
    abse[i]=fabs(e[i]);
    d[i]=abse[i];
    }
fun(m,n,x);
fx=x[n];
while ( (ifconv==0) && (iit<maxit) )  /* main iteration loop */
    {
    ifprint=0;
    if ( (nprint!=0) && (iit%nprint==0) ) ifprint=1;
    for (i=0; i<n; ++i)
        {
        xp[i]=x[i];  /* save values of x from previous iteration  */
        if (e[i]!=0)
            { /* insure that d[i] does not exceed user step size */
            if (d[i]>abse[i]) d[i]=abse[i];
                /*  insure that d[i] does not get too small */
            if (d[i]<(dmin*abse[i])) d[i]=dmin*abse[i];
            }
        }
    if (ifprint!=0)
        {
        printf(" Iteration %5d   %7d function calls    fun=%15.5f\n",
        iit,nfcls,fx);
        for (i=0; i<n; ++i) printf("%12.4f ",x[i]);
        printf("\n");
        }
/*  Step 1- vary each x[i] in turn to find minima */
    for (i=0; i<n; ++i) fstep[i]=0;
    for (i=0; i<n; ++i)
        {
        if (e[i]!=0)
            {
            fstep[i]=d[i];
            nfc=3;  /* call fun 3 or 4 times  */
            x[n]=fx;
            flow(m,n,x,fstep,conv,nfc);
            fx=x[n];
            nfcls=nfcls+nfc;
            fstep[i]=0;
            }
        }
```

```
/* Step 2 - minimize function along direction of improvement indicated by last
iteration */
/* if this is the first iteration , skip averaging  */
if (iit==0)  for (i=0; i<n; ++i) fstep[i]=x[i]-xp[i];
if (iit>0)
    {
    for (i=0; i<n; ++i)
        {
        fstep[i]=0;
/* average to estimate trough bottom direction  */
        if (e[i]!=0)
        fstep[i]=(xp[i]-fx1[i])*(i)+(x[i]-fx2[i])*(n-i);
        }
    }
/* insure that no s[i] is greater than its d[i]*/
/* save values of x before (xp[i]) and after (x[i])  step 1  */
for (i=0; i<n; ++i)
    {
    fx1[i]=xp[i]; fx2[i]=x[i];
    }
sdmax=0;
for (i=0; i<n; ++i)
    {
    if (d[i]>=0)
        {
        sd=fabs(fstep[i])/d[i];
        if (sdmax<sd) sdmax=sd;
        }
    }
if (sdmax>0)
    {
    for (i=0; i<n; ++i) fstep[i]=fstep[i]/sdmax;
    }
nfc=5;   /* call fun 5 or 6 times  */
x[n]=fx;
flow(m,n,x,fstep,conv,nfc);
fx=x[n];
nfcls=nfcls+nfc;
for (i=0; i<n; ++i)  c[i]=fabs(x[i]-xp[i])+sconv*d[i];
/* add change in x to sqrt(conv) times the current step size  */
/* test for convergence  - quit when each delta x is less than e[i]*conv */
    ifconv=1;
    for (i=0; i<n; ++i)
        {
        if ( (e[i]!=0) && (c[i]>fabs(e[i]*conv)) ) ifconv=0;
        }
    if ( ifconv!=0 )
        {
        printf(" Iteration %5d    %7d function calls    fun=%15.5f\n",
        iit,nfcls,fx);
        for (i=0; i<n; ++i) printf("%12.4f  ",x[i]);
        printf("\n");
        }
```

```
/*  adjust size of d hyperbox  */
/*  if x did not change during the last iteration (not sufficiently quadratic)  */
/*  then reduce current step size by a factor of ten  */
    for (i=0; i<n; ++i) d[i]=c[i];
    iit=iit+1;
    }  /* end iteration loop  */
if (ifconv==0) printf("minimum not found\n");
if (ifconv!=0) printf("minimum found\n");
}


/*  function flow - performs a one parameter minimization along
    any direction */
flow(m,n,x,fstep,conv,nfmax)
double x[],fstep[],conv;
int m,n,nfmax;
{
static double y[20], f1[20],f2[20],f3[20];
static double fx,fn,fm,fp,xden,xnum,xs;
static int i,il;
/*
     y[i]     intermediate values of x[i]
     fstep[i]    step size used by flow
*/
fn=x[n]; il=1;
for (i=0; i<n; ++i)
    {
    f1[i]=x[i]; /* store x in temp buffer f1[i]  */
    /*      set x to x-     f2[i] to x0        f3[i] to x+  */
    x[i]=x[i]-fstep[i];
    f2[i]=f1[i];
    f3[i]=f1[i]+fstep[i];
    }
fun(m,n,x);
fm=x[n];
    if ( fm<fn )
    {
/* if first step goes lower, flip xm and fn and continue in same direction */
    fp=fn; fn=fm; fm=fp;
    for (i=0; i<n; ++i)
        {
        f2[i]=x[i];
        f3[i]=f2[i]-fstep[i];
        }
    }
while (il<nfmax)
    {
    for (i=0; i<n; ++i) x[i]=f3[i];
    fun(m,n,x);
    fp=x[n];
    il=il+1;
    xden=2*(fm-2*fn+fp);
    xnum=fm-fp;
    if( (fabs(xden)<fabs(xnum)) || (xden<=0) )
```

```
/*  case where extremum lies outside interval or is not concave up -
    pick lowest edge  */
        {
        if(xnum==0)
/*  case where xnum=0, which means that fm, fn, and fp are
    equal to machine accuracy - stay put and decrease step size by 2x */
            {
            for (i=0; i<n; ++i)
                {
                y[i]=f2[i];
                f3[i]=0.5*(f2[i]+f3[i]);
                }
            fx=fn;
            }
        if(xnum<0)
            {
/*  case where quadratic minimum lies below xm  */
/*  double step size in xm direction */
            for (i=0; i<n; ++i)
                {
                y[i]=2.*f2[i]-f3[i];
                f2[i]=y[i];
                f3[i]=2.*y[i]-f3[i];
                }
            fx=fm;  fn=fm;  fm=fp;
            }
        if(xnum>0)
            {
/*  case where quadratic minimum lies above xp  */
/*  double step size in xp direction */
            for(i=0; i<n; ++i)
                {
                y[i]=f3[i];
                f3[i]=3.*y[i]-2.*f2[i];
                f2[i]=y[i];
                }
            fn=fp;  fx=fp;
            }
        }
    if ( (xden>0) && (fabs(xden)>fabs(xnum)) )
        { /* concave up and minimum bracketed - compute and test new minimum */
        xs=xnum/xden;
        for(i=0; i<n; ++i)
            {
            y[i]=f2[i]+(f3[i]-f2[i])*xs;
            x[i]=y[i];
            }
        il=il+1;
        fun(m,n,x);
        fx=x[n];
        if(fn<=fx)
            { /*  if fx is larger - nonquadratic region  */
            for (i=0; i<n; ++i)
```

```
            {
            f3[i]=2.*f2[i]-y[i];
            y[i]=f2[i];
            }
            fm=fx;  fx=fn;
        }
    if(fn>fx)
        { /*  usual case - fx is smaller  */
        for (i=0; i<n; ++i)
            {
            f3[i]=2.*y[i]-f2[i];
            f2[i]=y[i];
            }
            fm=fn;  fn=fx;
        }
    }
} /* end of iteration loop */
for (i=0; i<n; ++i)
    {
    if (fstep[i]==0) y[i]=f1[i];
    x[i]=y[i];
    }
for (i=0; i<n; ++i)
if (fstep[i]!=0) fstep[i]=f3[i]-f2[i];
/* printf(" flow: x= %12.4f %12.4f %12.4f %12.4f fx= %12.4f\n",
x[0],x[1],x[2],x[3],fx); */
x[n]=fx;
}
```

4 NUMERICAL EVALUATION OF FUNCTIONS DEFINED BY INTEGRALS

A number of methods have been devised for the numerical evaluation of integrals, including the trapezoidal rule and Simpson's rule, that integrate the function tabulated on a uniform spacing, and more sophisticated methods, such as gaussian quadrature, that use a carefully chosen spacing (corresponding to zeros of a particular polynomial) and special weighting.

The disadvantage of the former is that a large number of function calls are necessary to cover the whole range of integration with sufficient density, even if significant contributions come from only a small part of the range. This is a particular problem for integrals that have an infinite integration limit and do not permit a change of variable that simultaneously avoids infinities in both the limits of integration and the integrand. The disadvantage of the latter methods is that the points of function evaluation must be chosen before the integral (and its accuracy) can be evaluated.

The method that follows uses adaptive quadrature, where the points of function tabulation and the accuracy are determined as the method proceeds. Without using any pre-determined set of function points, the method develops a fine spacing, where the quadratic approximation results in the greatest error, and a relatively coarse spacing, where the contributions to the error are small. The method can even be used for functions with infinite limits of integration without having to find a suitable change of variable.

4.1 Flow Chart

The algorithm to numerically evaluate the integral of a function $F(x)$ to an accuracy e by using adaptive quadrature, given the limits of integration a and b:

1. Initialize the first segment by dividing the interval from a to b into four equal parts and by evaluating the integrand at the five boundary points. Compute the error for this segment and declare this segment as having the largest error.

2. Move all data beyond the segment with the maximum error four places to create space for a new segment.

3. Divide the segment with the largest error into two equal segments, using the old integrand values and evaluating only the new values needed.

4. Compute and store the errors for the two new segments.

5. Add the errors for all segments thus far created and determine the segment with the largest error. If the sum is greater than the desired error and if the number of segments is less than the limit, loop back to Step 2.

6. Exit the function, returning the value of the integral, the estimated upper limit on the error, and the number of segments created.

4.2 C Code

```
/* adaptive quadrature integration function */
double adsint(a,b,m,errmax,errptr,nsegptr)

/*
*    nmax is the maximum number of segments calculated
*    integral taken over a,b interval
*    if positive, errmax is maximum error of the integral
*    if negative, - errmax is the maximum fractional error of the integral
*    user must define a function igrand(x,n) that evaluates the
*        integrand of type n
*/

double a,b,errmax;
int m;
double *errptr;
int *nsegptr;
{
int n,i,iseg,nseg,isegm;
```

```
#define NMAX 201        /* absolute max number of segments*/
#define NMAX4 801
#define NSEGMAX 199
double x[NMAX4], f[NMAX4],s[NMAX],e[NMAX];
double h,dx,xtemp,emax,s1,s2,sum,err;

if(a==b)
    {
    *errptr=0;
    *nsegptr=0;
    return(0);
    }

/* initialize first segment */
nseg=1;
iseg=0;
h=b-a;
dx=h/4.;
for(i=0;i<5;++i)
    {
    x[i]=a+i*dx;
    xtemp=x[i];
    f[i]=igrand(xtemp,m);
    }
s1=(f[0]+4.*f[2]+f[4])*h/6.;
s2=(f[0]+4.*f[1]+2.*f[2]+4.*f[3]+f[4])*h/12.;
err=fabs(s1-s2)/15.;
e[iseg]=err;
s[iseg]=s2;
isegm=0;

/* loop until error summed over all segments is less than errmax
    or until maximum number of segments is reached */

while(1)
    {
    /* move down all segments above isegm */
    n=nseg*4+4;
    x[n]=x[n-4];
    f[n]=f[n-4];
    for (iseg=nseg;iseg>(isegm+1);--iseg)
        {
        s[iseg]=s[iseg-1];
        e[iseg]=e[iseg-1];
        for (i=0;i<4;++i)
            {
            n=iseg*4+i;
            x[n]=x[n-4];
            f[n]=f[n-4];
            }
        }
    nseg=nseg+1;
```

```
/* expand segment isegm */

n=isegm*4;
x[n+6]=x[n+3];
x[n+4]=x[n+2];
x[n+2]=x[n+1];
f[n+6]=f[n+3];
f[n+4]=f[n+2];
f[n+2]=f[n+1];

x[n+1]=(x[n]+x[n+2])/2.;
x[n+3]=(x[n+2]+x[n+4])/2.;
x[n+5]=(x[n+4]+x[n+6])/2.;
x[n+7]=(x[n+6]+x[n+8])/2.;
xtemp=x[n+1];
f[n+1]=igrand(xtemp,m);
xtemp=x[n+3];
f[n+3]=igrand(xtemp,m);
xtemp=x[n+5];
f[n+5]=igrand(xtemp,m);
xtemp=x[n+7];
f[n+7]=igrand(xtemp,m);

/*

f[n+1]=(*fun)(x[n+1]);
f[n+3]=(*fun)(x[n+3]);
f[n+5]=(*fun)(x[n+5]);
f[n+7]=(*fun)(x[n+7]);

*/

/* determine integrals and errors for the two new segments */

for(iseg=isegm;iseg<isegm+2;++iseg)
    {
    n=iseg*4;
    h=x[n+4]-x[n];
    s1=(f[n]+4.*f[n+2]+f[n+4])*h/6.;
    s2=(f[n]+4.*f[n+1]+2.*f[n+2]+4.*f[n+3]+f[n+4])*h/12.;
    e[iseg]=fabs(s1-s2)/15.;
    s[iseg]=s2;
    }

/* loop to find total error and the index isegm corresponding to max error*/

emax=-999.;
err=0.;
sum=0.;
for(iseg=0;iseg<nseg;++iseg)
    {
    err=err+e[iseg];
    sum=sum+s[iseg];
    n=iseg*4;
    if(e[iseg]>emax)
```

```
            {
            emax=e[iseg];
            isegm=iseg;
            }
        }
    if(nseg>=NSEGMAX) break;
    if(errmax>=0 && err<errmax) break;
    if(errmax<0 && (err/sum)<-errmax) break;

    }    /* end main while loop */

/* final statistics */

sum=0;
err=0;
for(iseg=0;iseg<nseg;++iseg)
    {
    sum=sum+s[iseg];
    err=err+e[iseg];
    }
*errptr=err;
*nsegptr=nseg;
return(sum);
}
```

4.3 Example of a Program to Compute the Probability of Exceeding a Particular Value of Student's *t* (of Either Sign)

```
#include<stdio.h>
#include<math.h>

double igrand(x,m)
double x;
int m;
{
double a;
if (m==0)
    {
    a=exp(-x*x/2);
    }
else
    {
    a=1.+x*x/m;
    a=exp(-log(a)*(m+1.)/2.);
    }
return(a);
}

#include "gamman2.c"
#include "adsint.c"

main()   /* program for computing P(>|Student's t|)*/
```

```
{
double a,b,an,q,gamma1,gamma2,err,errmax,ng,st,ans;
int nseg,ndeg,np,n,n1,i;
double q1,q2,q3;
while(1)
{
printf(" Prob of exceeding Itl\n");
printf(" enter Student's t (<0 quits):");
scanf(" %lf",&st);
if (st<0) break;
printf(" enter ndeg (0 means inf., <0 quits):");
scanf(" %d",&ndeg);
if (ndeg<0) break;

if(st<2.)
    {
    a=0;
    b=st;
    }
    else
    {
    a=st;
    b=1.e15;
    }

printf(" a = %12.4lf  b = %15.6le  ndeg= %5d\n",a,b,ndeg);

/* maximum ndeg is between 3500 and 4000*/

if(ndeg==0) q = sqrt(2./PI);
if(ndeg>0 && ndeg<3000)
    {
    gamma1=gamman2(ndeg);
    gamma2=gamman2(ndeg+1);
    q=2.*gamma2/(gamma1*sqrt(PI*ndeg));
    }
if(ndeg>=3000)
    {
    q1=ndeg;
    q2=(q1+1.)/q1;
    q3=pow(q2,q1/2.);
    q=2.*q3/sqrt(2.*E*PI);
    }

printf("ndeg =%5d   q=%15.9lf\n",ndeg,q);
errmax=-1.e-8;  /* specify fractional error */
ans=q*adsint(a,b,ndeg,errmax,&err,&nseg);
if (st<2.) ans=1.-ans;
printf("probability of exceeding = %20.10le\n",ans);
printf("error=%20.10le    %d segments\n\n",q*err,nseg);
}
}
```

4.4 Function to Compute the Gamma Function of Integral or Half-Integral Arguments

```
double gamman2(n)
int n;

{
double ng,n1,n2,gamma;
int np;
ng=n/2;
np=n%2;
if (np==1)
    {
    gamma = sqrt(PI);
    n1=0.5;
    }
    else
    {
    gamma=1;
    n1=1;
    }
for (n2=n1;n2<ng;++n2) gamma=gamma*n2;
return(gamma);
}
```

5 FUNCTION INVERSION USING NEWTON'S METHOD

Frequently, it is necessary to invert a function $F(x)$ that does not have a sufficiently simple form for analytic inversion, but can be differentiated. In this case, we approximate the value x_n that yields a function value $F(x_n)$ that is very close to a given F_n by iterating over the algorithm that follows. This method is particularly applicable to functions that are defined by integrals (e.g., gaussian error function, probability of exceeding Student's t or χ^2, gamma function), because the magnitude of $F'(x)$ is simply the integrand. See the previous section for the adaptive quadrature method of numerical evaluation of such functions.

5.1 Flow Chart

The algorithm to find the value x_n such that $|F(x_n) - F_n| < e$, given a function $F(x)$, its derivative function $F'(x)$, the desired value F_n, an initial guess x_0, and the maximum error e:

Loop over steps 1 to 5:

1. Evaluate $F_0 = F(x_0)$.

2. If $|F_0 - F_n| < e$, then quit loop.

3. Evaluate $F_1 = F'(x_0)$.

4. Use linear extrapolation to find a better value for x_0:

$$x_0 = x_0 + \frac{F_n - F_0}{F_1}$$

5. If x_0 is out of legal range, set x_0 to the edge of the range.

6 FUNCTION INVERSION USING QUADRATIC APPROXIMATION

Frequently, it is necessary to invert a function $F(x)$ that does not have a sufficiently simple form for analytic inversion. Furthermore, it may be difficult or impossible to take the first derivative and use Newton's method. In these cases, it is more convenient to use numerical methods that evaluate $F(x)$ at suitably chosen points to find the value $x = x_n$ such that $F(x_n)$ is nearly equal to a given value F_n. The method shown uses a first guess and a step size to evaluate the function about the first guess, do a quadratic approximation to find a better value of x_n, and iterate until $F(x_n)$ is sufficiently close to F_n.

6.1 Flow Chart

The algorithm to find the value x_n such that $|F(x_n) - F_n| < e$, given a function $F(x)$, the desired value F_n, an initial guess x_0, an initial step size Δx, and the maximum error e:

Loop over Steps 1 to 6:

1. Evaluate $F_0 = F(x_0)$.

2. If $|F_0 - F_n| < e$, then quit loop.

3. Compute $x_- = x_0 - \Delta x$ and $x_+ = x_0 + \Delta x$.

   If x_- and/or x_+ are outside the legal range, adjust their values to the edge of the range.

4. Evaluate $F_- = F(x_-)$, and $F_+ = F(x_+)$.

5. Compute the point $x = c$, where the quadratic curve defined by x_-, x_0, x_+, F_-, F_0, and F_+ passes through F_n.

   $a = x_0 + (x_- - x_0) (F_0 - F_n)/(F_0 - F_-)$
   $b = x_0 + (x_+ - x_0) (F_0 - F_n)/(F_0 - F_+)$
   $c = a + (b - a) (F_- - F_n)/(F_- - F_+)$

6. Compute the distance between x_0 and the new estimate c, which is to be used as the next step size.

   If $x_- \geq c \geq x_+$, then $\Delta x = c - x_0$ and $x_0 = c$.
   If $c < x_-$, then $x_0 = x_-$ and $\Delta x = 2 \Delta x$.
   If $c > x_+$, then $x_0 = x_+$ and $\Delta x = 2 \Delta x$.

E

*Summary of IBM® Data Acquisition and Control Adapter**

1 INTRODUCTION

The IBM Personal Computer Data Acquisition and Control Adapter is directly accessible via C programming statements. It includes the following I/O devices:

- A 16-bit parallel output port with full handshaking capability and tristate output latches (two 74LS374).
- A 16-bit parallel input port with full handshaking capability and tristate input latches (two 74LS373).
- Four differential analog input channels, using a four-input multiplexer (MUX), a single sample-and-hold amplifier (AD583), a single 12-bit A/D converter (AD4574) with 25-µs conversion time, and tristate output registers (74LS244). The input ranges are –5 to +5 volts, –10 to +10 volts, or 0 to +10 volts, switch selectable.
- Two independent analog output channels, using two D/A converters (AD7545). The output ranges are –5 to +5 volts, –10 to +10 volts, or 0 to +10 volts, switch selectable.
- A 16-bit counter (counter 2 of the 8253 counter/timer chip)

*Reprinted by permission from the IBM Personal Computer Data Acquisition and Control Adapter Technical Reference © 1984 by International Business Machines Corporation.

- A 32-bit timer, operating at a clock rate of 1.023 MHz (cascaded counters 0 and 1 of the 8253 counter/timer chip)

The external 60-pin connector shown in Figure E.1 can be connected by a ribbon cable to plugs shown in Figure E.2 for use with a superstrip circuit board. The pin assignments are given in Table E.1. Connect pins 4, 15, and 60 to the power-supply ground of the external circuits.

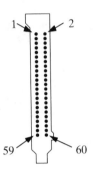

Figure E.1 Distribution panel connector J-4 of the IBM Data Acquisition and Control Adapter Expansion Card as viewed from the rear of the chassis.

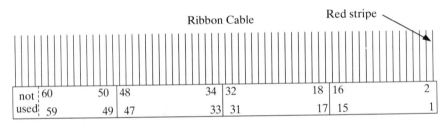

Figure E.2 Pin numbering for ribbon cable and plugs used to connect IBM Data Acquisition and Control Adapter Expansion Card (Figure E.1) to a circuit board. Top view.

2 PARALLEL OUTPUT

Parallel output is accomplished by first selecting the binary I/O device, and then writing two bytes to the binary output register. The code for simple output to card position 0 with no handshaking is

```
outportb(0xC2E2,8);        /* select binary I/O device */
outportb(0x22E2,data1);    /* output low byte */
outportb(0x22E3,data2);    /* output high byte */
outportb(0x22E2,data1);    /* output low byte */
outportb(0x22E3,data2);    /* output high byte */
```

TABLE E.1 PIN ASSIGNMENTS FOR THE IBM DATA ACQUISITION ADAPTER

Pin	Signal Name	Pin	Signal Name
1	D/A output 1	2	D/A Output 0
3	+10 Volt Ref. (do not use)	4	Analog Ground
5	Analog Input 0⁻	6	Analog Input 0⁺
7	Analog Input 1⁻	8	Analog Input 1⁺
9	Analog Input 2⁻	10	Analog Input 2⁺
11	Analog Input 3⁻	12	Analog Input 3⁺
13	Analog Ground	14	A/D Convert Enable input (low inhibits)
15	Digital Ground	16	A/D Converter Output (high = busy)
17	Binary Input Bit 8	18	Binary Out Bit 8
19	Binary Input Bit 9	20	Binary Out Bit 9
21	Binary Input Bit 10	22	Binary Out Bit 10
23	Binary Input Bit 11	24	Binary Out Bit 11
25	Binary Input Bit 12	26	Binary Out Bit 12
27	Binary Input Bit 13	28	Binary Out Bit 13
29	Binary Input Bit 14	30	Binary Out Bit 14
31	Binary Input Bit 15 (MSB)	32	Binary Out Bit 15 (MSB)
33	Binary Input Latch Control ($\overline{\text{BI HOLD}}$)	34	Binary Out Gate (BO Gate)
35	Binary Input Bit 0 (LSB)	36	Binary Out Bit 0 (LSB)
37	Binary Input Bit 1	38	Binary Out Bit 1
39	Binary Input Bit 2	40	Binary Out Bit 2
41	Binary Input Bit 3	42	Binary Out Bit 3
43	Binary Input Bit 4	44	Binary Out Bit 4
45	Binary Input Bit 5	46	Binary Out Bit 5
47	Binary Input Bit 6	48	Binary Out Bit 6
49	Binary Input Bit 7	50	Binary Out Bit 7
51	Rate Out	52	Delay Out
53	BI STROBE	54	BO STROBE
55	$\overline{\text{BO CTS}}$ (Clear To Send)	56	BI CTS (Clear To Send)
57	$\overline{\text{IRQ}}$ (Interrupt Request)	58	Count Out
59	Count In	60	Digital Ground

For a card in expansion slot position 1, 2, or 3, the second hexadecimal digit of the address is 6, A, and E, respectively. (See Section 7 for a synopsis of the address structure.) Data are written to a 16-bit register – the low byte is the 8 least significant bits and the high byte is the 8 most significant bits. It is necessary to write each byte twice because the first write is buffered on the data-acquisition board and does not appear on the external lines until the second write.

If the external circuit requires a pulse to tell it that new data are available, the C program can put a short pulse on the external line "BO STROBE" with the following code:

```
outportb(0x02E2,1);      /* set BO STROBE */
outportb(0x02E2,0);      /* reset BO STROBE */
outportb(0x02E2,0);
```

When the external device is ready to read the data (which in principle could be some time later), it should take the "BO GATE" line high (or unground it and let it "float" high). This causes the parallel output port to assert the data on the output lines. When two or more parallel output ports are connected to a common bus, the BO GATE lines are normally grounded so that the unasserted output lines are placed in a high-impedance state and neither drive or load the bus.

The parallel output port can be put in **transparent mode** by bringing the BO GATE line high. In this mode, two bytes can be written to the port at any time and they will immediately appear on the output lines. This mode can only be used when the external device is connected to a single parallel output port.

For full handshaking, the procedure is as follows:

1. The program selects the binary I/O device by loading 8 into the device number register using the statement

   ```
   outportb(0xC2E2,8);
   ```

2. When the external circuit is ready for new data, it pulls the external line "BO CTS" (Binary Out Clear To Send) high. This sets bit 2 of the binary status register to 1.

3. When the program has new data, it checks that bit 2 of the binary status register is nonzero and writes to the binary output register using the statements

   ```
   while((inportb(0x02E2)&4)==0);
   outportb(0x22E3,data2);
   outportb(0x22E2,data1);
   outportb(0x22E3,data2);
   outportb(0x22E2,data1);
   ```

4. The program puts a pulse on the external BO STROBE line using the statements

   ```
   outportb(0x02E2,1);
   outportb(0x02E2,0);
   outportb(0x02E2,0);
   ```

5. The external circuit reads the data and sets BO CTS low.

3 PARALLEL INPUT

Parallel input can be accomplished by first selecting the binary I/O device, and then reading the binary input register.

```
outportb(0xC2E2,8);              /* select binary I/O device */
data1=inportb(0x22E2);           /* input low byte */
data2=inportb(0x22E3);           /* input high byte */
```

This method has a serious flaw, however, in that the program has no way of knowing for sure whether the data that are read are new data or old data that are accidently the same. It is very common to read FFFF because lines tend to float high when they are not asserted. Even worse, it is possible for one or more bits to be in transition during the read, which would make the data in error.

Except in the simplest cases, some handshaking is always required for parallel input. The steps for full handshaking follow:

1. The program selects the Binary I/O Device by loading 8 into the device number register using the statement

```
outportb(0xC2E2,8);
```

2. The program puts "BI CTS" (Binary Input Clear To Send) high by writing a 1 to bit 2 of the binary control register using the statements

```
outportb(0x02E2,4);
outportb(0x02E2,4);
```

3. The external circuit detects that the BI CTS line is high, asserts new data on the input lines, and then puts the external line BI STROBE high. This causes bit 0 of the binary status register to be set to 1. If necessary, the external circuit can latch the data onto the binary input register by putting BI HOLD high.

4. The program waits for bit 0 of the binary status register to be set to 1 and then reads the data using the statements

```
while((inportb(0x02E2)&1)==0);
data1=inportb(0x22E2);
data2=inportb(0x22E3);
```

5. The program puts BI CTS low by writing a 0 to bit 2 of the binary control register using the statements

```
outportb(0x02E2,0);
outportb(0x02E2,0);
```

Note 1: In many cases, the input port is always available, and it is not necessary to use the BI CTS line at all.

Note 2: The above procedure does not allow the computer to be used for other purposes during the wait for the binary status register to be set (such as analyzing previously acquired data).

4 ANALOG OUTPUT

The analog output device is used as follows:

1. The program selects the analog I/O device by loading 9 into the lower byte of the device number register using the statement

```
outportb(0xC2E2,9);
```

2. The program sets the analog output channel N (0 or 1) by loading N into the upper byte of the AO control register using the statements

```
outportb(0x12E3,N);
outportb(0x12E3,N);
```

3. The program converts the integer data into two bytes using the statements

```
data1=data%256;
data2=data/256;
```

4. The program writes the data to the AO data register using the statements

```
outportb(0x32E2,data1);    /* write low byte */
outportb(0x32E3,data2);    /* write high byte */
```

For writing a sequence of data to a single channel, the following code would be typical:

```
#define IMAX 1024
char data1[IMAX],data2[IMAX];
int i,data[IMAX];
outportb(0xC2E2,9);                /* select the analog I/O device */
outportb(0x12E3,0);                /* select analog channel 0 */
outportb(0x12E3,0);
for (i=0;i<IMAX;++i) {             /* data output loop */
    data1[i]=data[i]&255;         /* mask low byte */
    data2[i]=data[i]>>8;          /* extract high byte */
    outportb(0x32E2,data1[i]);    /* write low byte */
    outportb(0x32E3,data2[i]);    /* write high byte */
    }
```

5 ANALOG INPUT

The analog input device has the following components:

1. An analog multiplexer (AD7502) with four differential input channels and a settling time of 20 µs.

2. A sample-and-hold amplifier (AD583) with differential inputs.

3. An A/D converter (AD4574) with 12-bit resolution and 25-μs conversion time. The input ranges are –5 to +5 volts, –10 to +10 volts, or 0 to +10 volts, switch selectable.

4. A 16-bit tristate output register using two octal buffers (74LS244). The highest four bits are always 0.

The analog input device (Chapter 3, Figure 3.18) is used as follows:

1. The program selects the analog I/O device by loading 9 into the lower byte of the device number register using the statement

```
outportb(0xC2E2,9);
```

2. The program writes 16 bits to the AI control register to clear the A/D conversion start bit (bit 0) and set the analog multiplexer to input channel N (0, 1, 2, or 3) using the statements

```
outportb(0x02E2,0)        /* disable conversion, clear conversion
                             start bit */
outportb(0x02E3,N);       /* set analog multiplexer channel */
```

3. The program waits at least 20 μs for the multiplexer to settle.

4. The program starts an A/D conversion by setting the conversion start bit (bit 0 of the AI control register) to 1 and resetting the analog multiplexer input channel using the statements

```
outportb(0x02E2,1);       /* set conversion start bit */
outportb(0x02E3,N);       /* set analog multiplexer channel */
```

Note: all 16 bits must be transmitted or conversion will not start.

5. At the end of conversion (which takes about 25 μsec), bit 1 of the AI status register is set to 1. The program waits for this using the statement

```
while((inportb(0x02E2)&2)==0);   /* wait for end of conversion */
```

6. The program disables the A/D converter and enables reading of converter data by setting the convert start bit to 0 using the statements

```
outportb(0x02E2,0);       /* clear conversion start bit */
outportb(0x02E3,0);       /* set analog multiplexer channel */
```

7. The program reads the data using the statements

```
data1=inportb(0x22E2);    /* read low byte */
data2=inportb(0x22E3);    /* read high byte */
```

8. Loop back to Step 4.

For reading a sequence of data from a single channel, the following code would be typical:

```
#define IMAX 1024
char data1[IMAX],data2[IMAX];
int i,data[IMAX];
outportb(0xC2E2,9);                    /* select the analog I/O device */
outportb(0x02E2,0);                    /* clear conversion start bit */
outportb(0x02E3,0);                    /* set MUX to channel 0 */
for (i=0;i<IMAX;++i) {                 /* data acquisition loop */
    outportb(0x02E2,1);                /* start conversion */
    outportb(0x02E3,0);                /* set MUX to channel 0 */
    while((inportb(0x02E2)&2)==0);     /* wait for conversion complete */
    outportb(0x02E2,0);                /* clear start bit to enable read */
    outportb(0x02E3,0);                /* set MUX to channel 0 */
    data1[i]=inportb(0x22E2);          /* read low byte */
    data2[i]=inportb(0x22E3);          /* read high byte */
    }
for (i=0;i<IMAX;++i)  data[i] = data1[i] | (data2[i]<<8);
```

The speed of the above code can be doubled by using in-line assembly instructions in place of the byte I/O function calls:

```
#pragma inline
#define IMAX 1024
char data1[IMAX],data2[IMAX];
int i,data[IMAX];
asm push ax;                           /* save ax register */
asm push dx;                           /* save dx register */
asm mov ax,9;                          /* put 9 in ax register */
asm mov dx,c2E2h;                      /* put hex c2E2 in dx register */
asm out dx,ax;                         /* select the Analog I/O Device */
asm mov ax,0;                          /* put 0 in ax register */
asm mov dx,02E2h;                      /* put hex 02E2 in dx register */
asm out dx,ax;                         /* clear conversion start bit */
asm mov ax,0;                          /* put 0 in ax register */
asm mov dx,02E3h;                      /* put hex 02E3 in dx register */
asm out dx,ax;                         /* set MUX to channel 0 */
for (i=0;i<IMAX;++i) {                 /* data acquisition loop */
    asm mov ax,1;                      /* put 1 in ax register */
    asm mov dx,02E2h;                  /* put hex 02E2 in dx register */
    asm out dx,ax;                     /* start conversion */
    asm mov ax,0;
    asm mov dx,02E3h;
    asm out dx,ax;                     /* set MUX to channel 0 */
    asm mov dx,02E2h;
    asm in al,dx;
    status = _AX;
    while((status&2)==0);              /* wait for conversion complete */
    asm mov ax,0;                      /* put 0 in ax register */
    asm mov dx,02E2h;                  /* put hex 02E2 in dx register */
    asm out dx,ax;                     /*clear conversion start bit to enable read*/
    asm mov ax,0;
    asm mov dx,02E3h;
    asm out dx,ax;                     /* set MUX to channel 0 */
```

```
    asm mov dx,22E2h;
    asm in al,dx;
    data1[i]=_AX;                          /* read low byte */
    asm mov dx,22E3h;
    asm in al,dx;
    data2[i]=_AX;                          /* read low byte */
    }
asm pop dx;                                /* restore dx register */
asm pop ax;                                /* restore ax register */
for (i=0;i<IMAX;++i)  data[i] = data1[i] | (data2[i]<<8);
```

In some compilers (such as Turbo C) the doubling in speed can be achieved simply by putting "include <DOS.h>" at the top of the program. This cause the compiler to replace the inportb and outportb function calls with assembly code.

Some older data acquisition boards may not respond quickly enough, and the assembly code will read before the data are ready. It is then necessary to put "dummy" instructions in the program to slow its execution.

6 Intel 8253 COUNTER/TIMER DEVICE

The IBM Data Acquisition and Control Adapter uses the Intel 8253-5 timer chip, which contains three 16-bit programmable digital counters (0, 1, and 2). Counters 0 and 1 have been cascaded to form a 32-bit timer, where counter 0 is clocked at 1.023 MHz and counter 1 is clocked with the overflow of counter 0 (15.61 Hz). Counter 2 is available as an independent 16-bit counter.

The following code initializes counters 0 and 1 for cascaded 1-MHz counting:

```
outportb(0xB2E2,0x30);        /* load control word 0011 0000
                              (counter 0, 2 bytes, mode 0, binary) */
outportb(0x82E2,0xFF);        /* prepare to load FF (all 8 bits on) as least
                              significant byte */
outportb(0x82E2,0xFF);        /* prepare to load FF as most significant byte */
outportb(0xB2E2,0x58);        /* load control word 0101 1000
                              (counter 1, 1 byte, mode 4, binary) */
outportb(0x92E2,0x01);        /* increment counter 1 with an overflow pulse
                              from counter 0, since timer 1 has been
                              disconnected from the system clock */
outportb(0xB2E2,0x34);        /* load control word 0011 0100
                              (counter 0, mode 2) */
outportb(0x82E2,0xFF);        /* load FF into least significant byte */
outportb(0x82E2,0xFF);        /* load FF into most significant byte */
```

Note 1: Because we have set both counters to mode 2, we must always read and write two bytes in sequence. Omitting one of the byte reads will cause unpredictable behavior.

Note 2: You must load FF (all bits on) into timer 1 because in mode 2 that is the value that will be automatically loaded every time the timer decrements through 0.

To latch and read counters 0 and 1:

```
outportb(0xB2E2,0x40);        /* latch counter 1 into register 1 */
outportb(0xB2E2,0x0);         /* latch counter 0 into register 0 */
i1= inportb(0x82E2);          /* read least significant byte register 0 */
i2= inportb(0x82E2);          /* read most significant byte register 0 */
if (i2> 253)                  /* if i2>253 */
   outportb(0xB2E2,0x40);     /*    then latch counter 1 again */
i3= inportb(0x92E2);          /* read LSB register 1 */
i4= inportb(0x92E2);          /* read MSB register 1 */
```

The counters constantly decrement without regard to what the program is doing; if the program tried to read them at some random time, bits could be changing during the read, resulting in erroneous information. It is thus necessary to "latch" the counters and "freeze" their values in other registers. The registers may then be read by the program at a later time (although they reflect the numbers that were in the counters at the instant of latching).

Unfortunately, the 8253 does not permit us to latch two counters simultaneously — there is the possibility that counter 0 passed through zero and decremented counter 1 during the short interval between the two latching instructions. In this case, the counter values do not correspond and will result in an erroneous time value. We test for this possibility by checking the value of i2. If it is large (254 or 255), then we know that counter 0 passed through zero recently and we have to relatch counter 1, which will then be valid.

Each set of four byte values can be converted into a 32-bit number and a decimal time (in seconds) using the following code:

```
i14 = i4 <<24 | i3<<16 | i2<<8 | i1;
j14 = j4 <<24 | j3<<16 | j2<<8 | j1;
time =(i14-j14)/1023000.;
```

Note 1: i14 and j14 have very large values that are decrementing. If the variable "time" is to be a positive number, we take the difference between i14 and j14, because i14 is always larger.

Note 2: It is essential that the number 1023000. have a terminating decimal point so that "time" is computed by floating-point division. Otherwise, integer division will occur and the "time" will always be an integer number of seconds.

Note 3: This procedure assumes that the packed 32-bit values are always positive, which limits them to the value 2.15×10^9, which corresponds to a maximum time interval of about 1000 seconds.

7 SYNOPSIS OF ADDRESS AND DATA STRUCTURE

The IBM Data Acquisition and Control Adapter is used by writing to or reading from various 16-bit registers. The writing is done with a statement of the form "outportb(address,data);" and reading is done with a statement of the form "data=inportb(address);."

"Address" is a 16-bit number of binary form RRRR CC10 1110 001B, and "data" is an 8-bit byte. RRRR is a 4-bit register address, CC is a 2-bit card address, and B is a 1-bit byte select. Up to four Data Acquisition and Control Adapters may be installed, and the switches on each can be set to CC = 00, 01, 10, or 11. B = 1 selects the most significant (high) byte of the register, and B = 0 selects the least significant (low) byte of the register.

RRRR = 1100 (decimal 12 or hexadecimal C) is used to select the binary I/O device (Data = 8) or the analog I/O device (Data = 9), by writing "Data" into the lower byte of the Device Register. Other registers are listed in Tables E.2 and E.3.

The Address and Data codes for the Timer/Counter device are shown in Table E.4.

TABLE E.2   BINARY I/O DEVICE ADDRESS/DATA CODES

Register Address		Register Name	Data Bits
0000	Write	Binary Control	0 controls BO STROBE
			2 controls BI CTS (clear to send)
	Read	Binary Status	0 shows BI STROBE
			2 shows BO CTS (clear to send)
0010	Write	Binary Output	0–15 are data
	Read	Binary Input	0–15 are data

TABLE E.3   ANALOG I/O DEVICE ADDRESS/DATA CODES

Register Address		Register Name	Data Bits
0000	Write	AI Control	0 controls conversion start (set 1 starts)
			2 controls end of conversion interrupt enable
			8–15 controls channel number
	Read	AI Status	0 shows busy status (1 = busy)
			1 shows end of conversion interrupt state
			(1 = end of conversion interrupt)
			3 shows end of conversion interrupt enable
0001	Write	AO Control	8–15 controls channel number
0010	Read	AI Data	0–11 are data
0011	Write	AO Data	0–11 are data

TABLE E.4   TIMER/COUNTER DEVICE ADDRESS/DATA CODES

Register Address		Register Name	Data Bits
1000	Write	Counter 0	0-15 are data
	Read	Counter 0	0-15 are data
1001	Write	Counter 1	0-15 are data
	Read	Counter 1	0-15 are data
1010	Write	Counter 2	0-15 are data
	Read	Counter 2	0-15 are data
1011	Write	Control	SSRR MMMB (see below)

SS = 00, 01, 10 to select counters 0, 1, or 2, respectively.
RR = 00 to latch counter (MMM and B bits are ignored).
RR = 10 read/load most significant byte (MSB) only.
RR = 01 read/load least significant byte (LSB) only.
RR = 11 read/load LSB first, then MSB.

MMM = 000	Mode 0 (edge on terminal count):
	Output is low after mode set and load, goes high on terminal count, and remains high, while counter continues to decrease
MMM = 001	Mode 1 (not used on IBM Data Acquisition and Control Adapter)
MMM = X10	Mode 2 (divide by N clock):
	Output high after mode set and load, goes low for one clock pulse on terminal count, goes high for N – 1 clock pulses, then repeats (X= don't care)
MMM = X11	Mode 3 (square-wave generator):
	Output high for N/2 clock pulses, low for N/2 clock pulses, then repeats
MMM = 100	Mode 4 (pulse on terminal count):
	Output is high after mode set and load, goes low for one clock period on terminal count,
MMM = 101	Mode 5 (not used on IBM Data Acquisition and Control Adapter)

B = 0 Binary counter (16 bits)
B = 1 BDC (binary coded decimal)counter (4 decades)

Note 1: Reading valid counter data first requires latching (counter control bits RR = 00).
Note 2: It is not possible to latch more than one counter at a time.
Note 3: All counters are down counters.
Note 4: The control register can only be written to, not read.
Note 5: The program must load the control register before loading or reading the corresponding counter.
Note 6: A count register is not loaded until the count value is written and the register receives a rising and falling edge of the clock.

Note 7: Loading of control or counter registers can be in any sequence, and counter loading does not have to immediately follow the loading of the control register, but the counter byte or bytes must be loaded and read as specified in bits RR of the counter's control register.

F

Summary of Metra Byte CTM-05 I/O Card with AM9513 Timer*

1 INTRODUCTION

The Metra Byte CTM-05 I/O is an expansion board for the IBM PC, XT, and AT. It includes the following features:

1. Five independent 16-bit up/down counters with programmable input and output polarity selection, count source selection, and prescaling (AM9513 chip)
2. 8 bits TTL digital input (no handshaking) with latch (74LS373)
3. 8 bits TTL digital output (no handshaking) with latch

The CTM-05 uses four consecutive addresses in the IBM PC I/O address space, starting from a base address that can range from 100 to 3FC (hex). The eight most significant bits of the 10-bit base address are set by eight switches. The ON position means zero (grounded) and the OFF position means one (floating high). The following description assumes a base address of 300 (hex), which is the "Prototype Card" reserved I/O address.

*Based on the CTM-05 Counter-Timer and Digital I/O Expansion Board Manual (with permission of MetraByte Corp., Taunton, MA 02780) and the AM9513 System Timing Controller Manual (with permission of Advanced Micro Devices, Inc., Sunnyvale, CA 94086).

The external 37-pin D connector shown in Figure F.1 has pin assignments given in Table F.1. The ribbon cable and plugs for connection to an external circuit board are shown in Figure F.2.

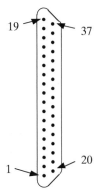

Figure F.1   D connector for the Metra Byte CTM-05 board as viewed from the rear of the chassis.

TABLE F.1   PIN ASSIGNMENTS FOR THE METRA BYTE CTM-05 CARD

Pin	Signal Name	Pin	Signal Name
1	INTERRUPT INPUT	20	+5 V (do not use)
2	INTERRUPT ENABLE	21	STROBE input
3	Data Output Bit 7 (MSB)	22	Data Input Bit 7 (MSB)
4	Data Output Bit 6	23	Data Input Bit 6
5	Data Output Bit 5	24	Data Input Bit 5
6	Data Output Bit 4	25	Data Input Bit 4
7	Data Output Bit 3	26	Data Input Bit 3
8	Data Output Bit 2	27	Data Input Bit 2
9	Data Output Bit 1	28	Data Input Bit 1
10	Data Output Bit 0 (LSB)	29	Data Input Bit 0 (LSB)
11	Digital Ground	30	FOUT
12	Counter 5 Gate	31	Counter 5 Output
13	Source 5	32	Counter 4 Output
14	Counter 4 Gate	33	Counter 3 Output
15	Source 4	34	Counter 2 Output
16	Counter 3 Gate	35	Counter 1 Output
17	Source 3	36	Source 1
18	Counter 2 Gate	37	Counter 1 Gate
19	Source 2		

2 PARALLEL OUTPUT PORT

The Metra Byte CTM-05 has an eight-bit parallel output port at address 303 (hex) that is independent of its eight-bit parallel input port. You can write a byte to the port at any time with the statement outp(0x303,n); and the byte n

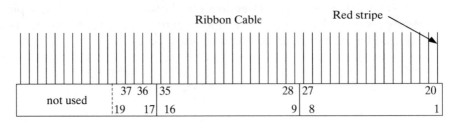

Figure F.2   Pin numbering for ribbon cable and plugs used to connect Metra Byte CTM-05 Counter/Timer and digital I/O board to circuit board. Top view.

will appear on the output lines. This port uses 74LS373 latches (output = input when STROBE is high, output fixed when STROBE is low).

3 PARALLEL INPUT PORT

Unfortunately, the CTM-05 board lacks even the simplest input handshaking, so it is necessary to improvise:

(1) The 74LS373 registers are "transparent" (output = input) whenever the STROBE line is high, and the output is "frozen" whenever the STROBE line is low. Thus, the data must remain asserted as long as the STROBE line is high.

(2) The CTM-05 input port does not have a STATUS BIT, which is normally used to determine whenever new data have been latched onto the parallel input port registers. Instead, send the STROBE pulse to one of the counters on the AM9513 chip (which can be read by the program) to indicate whenever new data have been received.

(3) The CTM-05 output port does not have an ATTENTION line, but the AM9513 chip can be used to generate a data-acquisition command pulse.

In summary, here are the data-acquisition steps in time sequence:

1. The program initializes counter 3.

```
outp(0x301,0x03);      /* set pointer to counter 3 mode register (000 00 011) */
outp(0x300,0x2D);      /* load least significant byte = 00101 101
                          (binary count up repetitively, active low output) */
outp(0x300,0x13);      /* load most significant byte = 000 10011
                          (no gating, count on falling edge, source 3) */
outp(0x301,0x0B);      /* set pointer to counter 3 load register (000 01 011) */
outp(0x300,0);         /* load least significant byte = 0 */
outp(0x300,0);         /* load most significant byte = 0 */
outp(0x301,0x64);      /* load and arm counter 3 (011 00100) */
c3=0;                  /* initialize counter 3 variable */
d3=0;
```

2. The program or a timer initiates some data-acquisition command.

3. The program reads counter 3 in an endless loop until it changes:

```
outp(0x301,0xA4);          /* save counter 3 in hold register 3 (101 00100) */
outp(0x301,0x13);          /* set pointer to counter 3 hold register (000 10 011) */
i1=inp(0x300);             /* read least significant byte of hold register 3 */
i2=inp(0x300);             /* read most significant byte of hold register 3 */
d3=i2<<8|i;                /* assemble 16-bit number */
c3=d3;                     /* save current value */
while(d3==c3){
    outp(0x301,0xA4);      /* save counter 3 in hold register 3 (101 00100) */
    outp(0x301,0x13);      /* set pointer to counter 3 hold register (000 10 011) */
    i1=inp(0x300);         /* read least significant byte of hold register 3 */
    i2=inp(0x300);         /* read most significant byte of hold register 3 */
    d3=i2<<8|i1;           /* assemble 16-bit number */
}                          /* exit while loop when counter changes */
```

4. Meanwhile, the external device asserts data on the parallel input port lines and sends a STROBE pulse to the parallel port and counter 3.

5. The parallel input port that latches the data onto the input registers and counter 3 is incremented.

6. The program detects the change in counter 3 and reads the parallel input registers (transfers data from registers to memory) using the statement n=inp(0x302);.

7. Loop back to step 2.

4 AM9513 COUNTER/TIMER DEVICE

Chapter 1, Figure 1.6 shows a flow chart for initializing, starting, latching, and reading the AM9513 counter/timer. Laboratory Exercise 2 explores the code needed to perform these functions. In the sections that follow, we describe this device in general.

4.1 Initialization

The AM9513 and its five counter/timers are initialized with the following steps:

1. Write a **command code** to the command register at input port 301 (hex) that causes an internal **pointer register** to be loaded with a code that selects the **master mode register**. This may seem complicated, but using a pointer register to select other registers avoids "using up" an input port address for each of the 20 registers in the AM9513. See Table F.2 for the command codes.

TABLE F.2 COMMAND REGISTER CODES

C_7	C_6	C_5	C_4	C_3	C_2	C_1	C_0	Function
0	0	0	F_2	F_1	1	1	1	Load control register group
0	0	0	E_2	E_1	0	0	1	Load counter 1 register group
0	0	0	E_2	E_1	0	1	0	Load counter 2 register group
0	0	0	E_2	E_1	0	1	1	Load counter 3 register group
0	0	0	E_2	E_1	1	0	0	Load counter 4 register group
0	0	0	E_2	E_1	1	0	1	Load counter 5 register group
0	0	1	S_5	S_4	S_3	S_2	S_1	Arm (start) specified counters
0	1	0	S_5	S_4	S_3	S_2	S_1	Load specified counters
0	1	1	S_5	S_4	S_3	S_2	S_1	Load and arm specified counters
1	0	0	S_5	S_4	S_3	S_2	S_1	Disarm and hold specified counters
1	0	1	S_5	S_4	S_3	S_2	S_1	Hold specified counters
1	1	0	S_5	S_4	S_3	S_2	S_1	Disarm (stop) specified counters
1	1	1	0	0	N_4	N_2	N_1	Clear output bit N ($N = 001, \ldots, 101$)
1	1	1	0	1	N_4	N_2	N_1	Set output bit N ($N = 001, \ldots, 101$)
1	1	1	1	0	N_4	N_2	N_1	Step counter N ($N = 001, \ldots, 101$)
1	1	1	0	0	0	0	0	Enable data-pointer sequencing (clear bit 14 of master mode register)
1	1	1	0	0	1	1	0	Gate FOUT on (clear bit 12 of master mode register)
1	1	1	0	1	0	0	0	Disable data-pointer sequencing (set bit 14 of master mode register)
1	1	1	0	1	1	1	0	Gate FOUT off (set bit 12 of master mode register)
1	1	1	1	1	1	1	1	Master reset

$F_2, F_1 = 00$ for alarm register 1, $= 01$ for alarm register 2, $= 10$ for master mode register.
$E_2, E_1 = 00$ for mode register, $= 01$ for load register, $= 10$ for hold register.
$E_2, E_1 = 11$ for hold register cycle.
$S_1, \ldots, S_5$ specify counters $1, \ldots, 5$.
"load" means transfer data from load register to counter.
"hold" means transfer data from counter to hold register.

2. Write a 16-bit code to the **master mode register**. This code controls the overall operation of the AM9513 and should be the first register initialized. See Table F.3 for the function of each bit.

3. Write a command code to the command register that causes the pointer register to be loaded with a code that selects one of five **counter mode registers**.

4. Write a 16-bit code to the **counter mode register** just selected. See Table F.4 for the function of each bit.

5. Write a command code to the command register that causes the pointer register to be loaded with a code that selects one of five **counter load registers**.

TABLE F.3   MASTER MODE REGISTER CODES

Bits	Function	Values
15	Scalar control	0: $F_1 = 1$ MHz, $F_2 = F_1/16$, $F_3 = F_1/256$, $F_4 = F_1/4096$, $F_5 = F_1/65{,}536$ 1: $F_1 = 1$ MHz, $F_2 = 100$ kHz, $F_3 = 10$ kHz, $F_4 = 1$ kHz, $F_5 = 100$ Hz
14	Data-pointer control	0: enable automatic incrementing of data-pointer register 1: disable automatic incrementing
13	Data bus width	0: 8-bit data bus (only legal value for IBM PC)
12	FOUT gate	0: FOUT on 1: FOUT off (low to ground)
11-8	FOUT divider	0000: divide by 16, 0001: divide by 1 $\vdots$ 0101: divide by 5 $\vdots$ 1111: divide by 15
7-4	FOUT source	0000: F_1 0001: Source 1 0101: Source 5 0110: Gate 1 0111: Gate 2 1000: Gate 3 1001: Gate 4 1010: Gate 5 1011: F_1 1100: F_2 1101: F_3 1110: F_4 1111: F_5
3	Compare 2 enable	0: disabled 1: enabled Counter 2 out = high if counter 2 = alarm 2
2	Compare 1 enable	0: disabled 1: enabled Counter 1 out = high if counter 1 = alarm 2
1-0	Time of day mode	00: disabled 01: time of day enabled for 50-Hz input 10: time of day enabled for 60-Hz input 11: time of day enabled for 100-Hz input (counter 2: most sig byte = hours, least sig byte = minutes) (counter 1: most sig byte = sec, least sig byte = ticks)

Bit 15 = most significant bit, bit 0 = least significant bit.

6. Write 16 bits to the **counter load register** just selected. These 16 bits are the initial value of the counter when counting starts.

7. Write a command code to the command register to (i) transfer the contents of any combination of the five load registers to their corresponding counters, (ii) arm (start) any combination of the five counters, or both (i) and (ii).

TABLE F.4 COUNTER MODE REGISTER CODES

Bits	Function	Values
15-13	Gating control	000: no gating
		001: active high-level TCN − 1
		010: active high-level gate N + 1
		011: active high-level gate N − 1
		100: active high-level gate N
		101: active low-level gate N
		110: active high-edge gate N
		111: active low-edge gate N
12-8	Count source selection	0XXXX: count on rising edge
		X0000: output of counter N − 1
		X0001: Source 1
		X0010: Source 2
		X0011: Source 3
		X0100: Source 4
		X0101: Source 5
		X0110: Gate 1
		X0111: Gate 2
		X1000: Gate 3
		X1001: Gate 4
		X1010: Gate 5
		X1011: F_1
		X1100: F_2
		X1101: F_3
		X1110: F_4
		X1111: F_5
7	Count control	0XXXX: disable special gate
6	Count control	0: reload from load
		1: reload from load or hold
5	Count control	0: count once
		1: count repetitively
4	Count control	0: binary count
		1: BCD count
3	Count control	0: count down
		1: count up
2-0	Output control	000: inactive, output low
		001: active high during terminal count clock pulse
		010: toggles between high and low on terminal count
		100: inactive high impedance
		101: active low during terminal count clock pulse

Bit 15 = most significant bit, bit 0 = least significant bit.

By setting bit 14 of the master mode register to zero, the data pointer is automatically incremented. To use this mode, set the pointer register to select the first register and subsequent write statements will cycle through the registers, as shown in Figure F.3. The mode/load/hold register cycle occurs when E_2,E_1 are set to 0,0 or 0,1 or 1,0 (that is, when either one of the

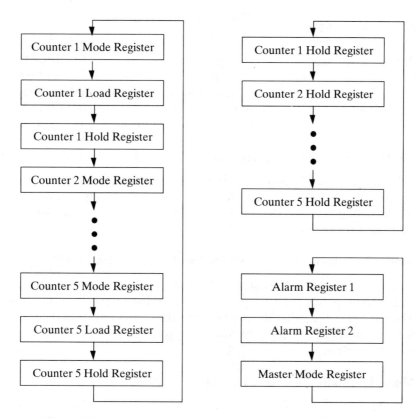

Figure F.3   Pointer cycling that occurs when master mode register bit 14 is zero.

mode, load, or hold registers is selected). The hold register cycle occurs when E_2, E_1 are set to 1,1. The control register cycle occurs when one of the alarm registers or master register is selected.

4.2 Latching and Reading

The five counter/timers are latched and read with the following steps:

1. Write a command code to the command register to transfer any combination of the five counters to their corresponding hold registers. This is necessary because the counters themselves are changing too rapidly for direct reading.

2. Write a command code to the command register that causes the pointer register to be loaded with a code that selects one of five **counter hold registers**.

3. Read the 16 bits of the **counter hold register**.

4.3 Counter Modes

A number of standard operating modes have been defined for the AM9513 counter/timer. A few of the more common modes are described below and others may be inferred by examining the counter mode register codes in Table F.4. In the descriptions below, "CM 5–7" are counter mode bits 5, 6, and 7 and "CM 13–15" are gate control counter mode bits 13, 14, and 15.

Mode A. Software-Triggered Strobe. CM 5–7 = 000. CM 13–15 = 000.

The counter begins counting when it receives an arm command. On terminal count (TC), the counter will produce an output pulse, reload from the load register, and disarm itself. Counting will resume when a new arm command is received.

Mode D. Rate Generator. CM 5–7 = 100. CM 13–15 = 000.

Once armed, the counter will count to TC repetitively. On each TC, the counter will produce an output pulse and reload itself from the load register. The load register value determines the time between output pulses. Square-wave counter output is specified by setting counter mode bit 1 to one (toggled output).

Mode F. Nonretriggerable One-Shot. CM 5–7 = 100. CM 13–15 = edge.

The counter must be armed before it will function. Application of a gate edge to the armed counter will begin counting. When the counter reaches TC, it will produce an output pulse, reload itself from the load register, and stop counting. A new gate edge will resume counting and new arm command is not needed. A gate edge during counting is ignored.

Mode G. Software-triggered Delayed-Pulse One-Shot. CM 0–2 = 010, CM 5–7 = 010. CM 13–15 = 000.

Once armed, the counter will count to TC twice and then automatically disarm itself. The counter will be loaded initially from the load register. Upon coming to the first TC, the counter will toggle the output and reload itself from the hold register. Counting will continue until the second TC, when the counter will toggle the output, reload itself from the load register and automatically disarm itself. The cycle will repeat when a new ARM command is received. Operation is not affected by the GATE.

Mode R. Retriggerable One-Shot. CM 5–7 = 101. CM 13–15 = edge.

As mode F, but a new gate edge during counting will immediately reload the counter from the load register and counting will continue.

G

Electrical Hazards and Prevention

1 INTRODUCTION

An intact dry 1 cm^2 patch of skin has a typical electrical resistance of about 100 kΩ, which is primarily provided by epithelium, the horny outermost layer of skin. Under normal circumstances, the skin provides considerable protection against brief contact with electrical potentials even as high as 120 volts. However, if the skin is wet or perspiring, the electrical resistance is greatly reduced and dangerous currents can be conducted. If the skin has a cut, or if Ag(AgCl) electrodes with electrode paste are used, the resistance can decrease to below 1 kΩ. Under these conditions, dangerously high currents can be produced by potentials as low as 12 volts. See Table G.1 for the physiological effects of various current levels. With a skin resistance of 100 kΩ, 500 volts would be required to produce a current of 5 mA, but with a skin resistance of 1 kΩ, only 5 volts will produce the same current.

Note that ventricular fibrillation can occur with currents as low as 20 μA passing directly through the heart. This is of particular concern to designers of equipment that uses electrodes placed near or on the surface of the heart, such as coronary catheters, or during surgery.

TABLE G.1 PHYSIOLOGICAL EFFECTS OF 60-Hz CURRENTS FROM A 1-SECOND CONTACT WITH THE BODY EXTREMITIES

Current	Effect
500 µA	Threshold of perception.
5 mA	Unpleasant, but accepted safe level.
>20 mA	Pain, fatigue, possible physical injury, inability to "let go" due to involuntary muscular contraction.
>75 mA	Possible respiratory paralysis and loss of normal rhythm of heart muscle contraction (ventricular fibrillation) resulting in death.
>1 A	Sustained contraction of the heart (which may revert to normal rhythm if the duration is sufficiently short).
>10 A	Severe burns and physical injury.

2 TYPICAL ACCIDENT SCENARIOS

1. Due to a fault in electrical insulation, the metal case of a piece of equipment is energized. The victim touches the faulty equipment with one hand and a properly grounded piece of equipment with the other hand.

2. The victim touches live conductors in equipment whose case has been removed for repair. Note that one of these conductors may be at "ground" potential, but should be considered "live" if it can return current to its source.

3. Although the equipment is disconnected from power, the victim touches a charged high voltage capacitor after the case is opened for repair.

3 METHODS OF ACCIDENT PREVENTION

1. Connect all external metal parts to a common ground that does not normally carry current. This is the familiar green "U ground" or "house ground" in electrical receptacles.

2. Double insulate all dangerous voltages. This is used for power tools, but is not effective in the presence of water and is not used for medical equipment due to the danger of a saline solution spill.

3. When designing high-voltage (> 1 kV) systems, especially those that require large capacitors, provide two bleeder resistors in parallel that automatically eliminate dangerous potentials short time after the equipment is turned off. (This is more reliable than a single bleeder resistor which may burn out after several years without being noticed.) When servicing such equipment, firmly attach a grounding strap to all dangerous potentials.

4. Use a ground fault interrupter (GFI) circuit, which uses a differential transformer and amplifier to detect any difference in current between the 120-V "hot" (black) conductor and the "neutral" (white) conductor. If this difference exceeds 5 mA, power is interrupted by a circuit breaker.

5. Isolation of patient-connected parts by a low-capacitance transformer or opto-isolator (LED and photodiode) or by radio telemetry.

6. Use current-limiting circuits in all conductive paths connected to the patient.

H

Data Sheets

1 INTRODUCTION

This appendix contains the data sheets for the less common integrated circuits used in the Laboratory Exercises. The AD OP-07* (Appendix H1) is provided as an alternative to the LF356 op amp explored in Laboratory Exercise 4 and used in Laboratory Exercises 6, 14, 18, 22, and 23. The AD625* instrumentation amplifier (Appendix H2) is explored in Laboratory Exercise 5 and is used in Laboratory Exercises 12, 13, and 24. The Burr-Brown 3656† isolation amplifier (Appendix H3) is used in Laboratory Exercises 18 and 19. The AD590* temperature transducer (Appendix H4) is provided for Laboratory exercises 12, 15, and 24. The AD582* Sample-and-hold amplifier (Appendix H5) is used in Laboratory Exercise 9. The AD558* 8-bit D/A converter (Appendix H6) is used in Laboratory Exercise 8. The AD7545* 12-bit D/A converter (Appendix H7) is in the IBM Data Acquisition and Control Adapter and is used in Laboratory Exercises 7, 10, 20, 21, 23, and 24. The AD574A* 12-bit 25-μs A/D converter (Appendix H8) is also in the IBM Data Acquisition and Control Adapter and is used in Laboratory Exercises 7, 10, 11, 12, 20, 21, 22, 23, and 24. Either the AD670* 8-bit 10-μs A/D converter (Appendix H9) or the AD7820* 8-bit 1.4 μs A/D converter (Appendix H10) can be used in Laboratory Exercise 9.

*Reprinted with the permission of Analog Devices, Inc.
†Reprinted with the permission of Burr-Brown Corp.

Ultra-Low Offset Voltage Op Amp
AD OP-07

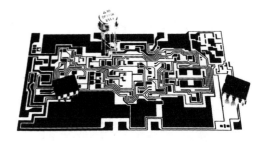

FEATURES
**Ten Times More Gain Than Other OP-07 Devices
(3.0M min)**
Ultra-Low Offset Voltage: 10μV
Ultra-Low Offset Voltage Drift: 0.2μV/$^\circ$C
Ultra-Stable vs. Time: 0.2μV/month
Ultra-Low Noise: 0.35μV p-p
No External Components Required
Monolithic Construction
High Common Mode Input Range: ±14.0V
Wide Power Supply Voltage Range: ±3V to ±18V
Fits 725, 108A/308A Sockets
Military Parts and Plus Parts Available
**8-Pin Plastic Mini-DIP, CERDIP or TO-99 Hermetic
Metal Can**
Available in Wafer-Trimmed Chip Form

PRODUCT DESCRIPTION
The AD OP-07 is an improved version of the industry-standard OP-07 precision operational amplifier. A guaranteed minimum open-loop voltage gain of 3,000,000 (AD OP-07A) represents an order of magnitude improvement over older designs; this affords increased accuracy in high closed loop gain applications. Typical input offset voltages as low as 10μV, typical bias currents of 0.7nA, internal compensation and device protection eliminate the need for external components and adjustments. An input offset voltage temperature coefficient of 0.2μV/$^\circ$C (typ) and long-term stability of 0.2μV/month (typ) eliminate recalibration or loss of initial accuracy.

A true differential operational amplifier, the AD OP-07 has a high common-mode input voltage range (±13V, min) common-mode rejection ratio (typically up to 126dB) and high differential input impedance (50MΩ typ); these features combine to assure high accuracy in noninverting configurations. Such applications include instrumentation amplifiers, where the increased open-loop gain maintains high linearity at high closed-loop gains.

The AD OP-07 is available in five performance grades. The AD OP-07E, AD OP-07C and AD OP-07D are specified for operation over the 0 to +70°C temperature range, while the AD OP-07A and AD OP-07 are specified for -55°C to +125°C operation. All devices are available in either the TO-99 hermetically sealed metal cans or the hermetically sealed CERDIP packages, while the industrial grades are also available in plastic 8-pin mini-DIPs.

PRODUCT HIGHLIGHTS
1. Increased open-loop voltage gain (3.0 million, min) results in better accuracy and linearity in high closed-loop gain applications.

2. Ultra-low offset voltage and offset voltage drift, combined with low input bias currents, allow the AD OP-07 to maintain high accuracy over the entire operating temperature range.

3. Internal frequency compensation, ultra-low input offset voltage and full device protection eliminate the need for additional components. This reduces circuit size and complexity and increases reliability.

4. High input impedances, large common mode input voltage range and high common mode rejection ratio make the AD OP-07 ideal for noninverting and differential instrumentation applications.

5. Monolithic construction along with advanced circuit design and processing techniques result in low cost.

6. The input offset voltage is trimmed at the wafer stage. Unmounted chips are available for hybrid circuit applications.

One Technology Way; P. O. Box 9106; Norwood, MA 02062-9106 U.S.A.
Tel: 617/329-4700   Twx: 710/394-6577
Telex: 174059   Cables: ANALOG NORWOODMASS

SPECIFICATIONS ($T_A = +25°C$, $V_S = \pm 15V$, unless otherwise specified)

MODEL		AD OP-07E			AD OP-07C			AD OP-07D		
PARAMETER	SYMBOL	MIN	TYP	MAX	MIN	TYP	MAX	MIN	TYP	MAX
OPEN LOOP GAIN	A_{VO}	2,000	5,000		1,200	4,000		1,200	4,000	
		1,800	4,500		1,000	4,000		1,000	4,000	
		300	1,000		300	1,000		300	1,000	
OUTPUT CHARACTERISTICS										
Maximum Output Swing	V_{OM}	±12.5	±13.0		±12.0	±13.0		±12.0	±13.0	
		±12.0	±12.8		±11.5	±12.8		±11.5	±12.8	
		±10.5	±12.0			±12.0			±12.0	
		±12.0	±12.6		±11.0	±12.6		±11.0	±12.6	
Open-Loop Output Resistance	R_O		60			60			60	
FREQUENCY RESPONSE										
Closed Loop Bandwidth	BW		0.6			0.6			0.6	
Slew Rate	SR		0.17			0.17			0.17	
INPUT OFFSET VOLTAGE										
Initial	V_{OS}		30	75		60	150		60	150
			45	130		85	250		85	250
Adjustment Range			±4			±4			±4	
Average Drift										
No External Trim	TCV_{OS}		0.3	1.3		0.5	1.8		0.7	2.5
With External Trim	TCV_{OSN}		0.3	1.3		0.4	1.6		0.7	2.5
Long Term Stability	V_{OS}/Time		0.3	1.5		0.4	2.0		0.5	3.0
INPUT OFFSET CURRENT										
Initial	I_{OS}		0.5	3.8		0.8	6.0		0.8	6.0
			0.9	5.3		1.6	8.0		1.6	8.0
Average Drift	TCI_{OS}		8	35		12	50		12	50
INPUT BIAS CURRENT										
Initial	I_B		±1.2	±4.0		±1.8	±7.0		±2.0	±12
			±1.5	±5.5		±2.2	±9.0		±3.0	±14
Average Drift	TCI_B		13	35		18	50		18	50
INPUT RESISTANCE										
Differential	R_{IN}	15	50		8	33		7	31	
Common Mode	R_{INCM}		160			120			120	
INPUT NOISE										
Voltage	e_n p-p		0.35	0.6		0.38	0.65		0.38	0.65
Voltage Density	e_n		10.3	18.0		10.5	20.0		10.5	20.0
			10.0	13.0		10.2	13.5		10.2	13.5
			9.6	11.0		9.8	11.5		9.8	11.5
Current	i_n p-p		14	30		15	35		15	35
Current Density	i_n		0.32	0.80		0.35	0.90		0.35	0.90
			0.14	0.23		0.15	0.27		0.15	0.27
			0.12	0.17		0.13	0.18		0.13	0.18
INPUT VOLTAGE RANGE										
Common Mode	CMVR	±13.0	±14.0		±13.0	±14.0		±13.0	±14.0	
		±13.0	±13.5		±13.0	±13.5		±13.0	±13.5	
Common-Mode Rejection										
Ratio	CMRR	106	123		100	120		94	110	
		103	123		97	120		94	106	
POWER SUPPLY										
Current, Quiescent	I_Q		3.0	4.0		3.5	5.0		3.5	5.0
Power Consumption	P_D		90	120		105	150		105	150
			6.0	9.0		6.0	9.0		6.0	9.0
Rejection Ratio	PSRR	94	107		90	104		90	104	
		90	104		86	100		86	100	
OPERATING TEMPERATURE										
RANGE	T_{min}, T_{max}	0		+70	0		+70	0		+70
PACKAGE OPTIONS										
Plastic Mini-DIP (N8A)			AD OP-07EN			AD OP-07CN			AD OP-07DN	
CERDIP (Q8A)			AD OP-07EQ			AD OP-07CQ			AD OP-07DQ	
TO-99 (H08A)			AD OP-07EH			AD OP-07CH			AD OP-07DH	

NOTES

[1]Input Offset Voltage measurements are performed by automated test equipment approximately 0.5 seconds after application of power. Additionally, the AD OP-07A offset voltage is guaranteed fully warmed up.

[2]Long-Term Input Offset Voltage Stability refers to the averaged trend line of V_{OS} vs. Time over extended periods of time and is extrapolated from high temperature test data. Excluding the initial hour of operation, changes in V_{OS} during the first 30 operating days are typically $2.5\mu V$ – Parameter is not 100% tested; 90% of units meet this specification.

Specifications subject to change without notice.

AD OP-07A			AD OP-07			TEST CONDITIONS	UNITS
MIN	TYP	MAX	MIN	TYP	MAX		
3,000	5,000		**2,000**	5,000		$R_L \geq 2k\Omega$, $V_O = \pm 10V$	V/mV
2,000	4,000		**1,500**	4,000		$R_L \geq 2k\Omega$, $V_O = \pm 10V$, T_{min} to T_{max}	V/mV
300	1,000		300	1,000		$R_L \geq 500\Omega$, $V_O = \pm 0.5V$, $V_S = \pm 3V$	V/mV
±12.5	±13.0		**±12.5**	±13.0		$R_L \geq 10k\Omega$	V
±12.0	±12.8		**±12.0**	±12.8		$R_L \geq 2k\Omega$	V
±10.5	±12.0		**±10.5**	±12.0		$R_L \geq 1k\Omega$	V
±12.0	±12.6		**±12.0**	±12.6		$R_L \geq 2k\Omega$, T_{min} to T_{max}	V
	60			60		$V_O = 0$, $I_O = 0$	Ω
	0.6			0.6		$A_{VCL} = +1.0$	MHz
	0.17			0.17		$R_L \geq 2k$	V/μs
	10	**25**		30	**75**	Note 1	μV
	25	**60[1]**		60	**200[1]**	T_{min} to T_{max}	μV
	±4			±4		$R_P = 20k\Omega$	mV
	0.2	**0.6**		0.3	**1.3**	T_{min} to T_{max}	μV/°C
	0.2	0.6		0.3	1.3	$R_P = 20k\Omega$, T_{min} to T_{max}	μV/°C
	0.2	1.0		0.2	1.0	Note 2	μV/Month
	0.3	**2.0**		0.4	**2.8**		nA
	0.8	**4.0**		1.2	**5.6**	T_{min} to T_{max}	nA
	5	25		8	50	T_{min} to T_{max}	pA/°C
	±0.7	**±2.0**		±1.0	**±3.0**		nA
	±1.0	**±4.0**		±2.0	**±6.0**	T_{min} to T_{max}	nA
	8	25		13	50	T_{min} to T_{max}	pA/°C
30	80		20	60			$M\Omega$
	200			200			$G\Omega$
	0.35	0.6		0.35	0.6	0.1Hz to 10Hz	μV p-p
	10.3	18.0		10.3	18.0	$f_O = 10Hz$	nV/$\sqrt{Hz}$
	10.0	13.0		10.0	13.0	$f_O = 100Hz$	nV/$\sqrt{Hz}$
	9.6	11.0		9.6	11.0	$f_O = 1kHz$	nV/$\sqrt{Hz}$
	14	30		14	30	0.1Hz to 10Hz	pA p-p
	0.32	0.80		0.32	0.80	$f_O = 10Hz$	pA/$\sqrt{Hz}$
	0.14	0.23		0.14	0.23	$f_O = 100Hz$	pA/$\sqrt{Hz}$
	0.12	0.17		0.12	0.17	$f_O = 1kHz$	pA/$\sqrt{Hz}$
±13.0	±14.0		**±13.0**	±14.0			V
±13.0	±13.5		**±13.0**	±13.5		T_{min} to T_{max}	V
110	126		**110**	126		$V_{CM} = \pm CMVR$	dB
106	123		**106**	123		$V_{CM} = \pm CMVR$, T_{min} to T_{max}	dB
	3.0	**4.0**		30	**4.0**	$V_S = \pm 15V$	mA
	90	**120**		90	**120**	$V_S = \pm 15V$	mW
	6.0	**8.4**		6.0	**8.4**	$V_S = \pm 3V$	mW
100	110		**100**	110		$V_S = \pm 3V$ to $\pm 18V$	dB
94	106		**94**	106		$V_S = \pm 3V$ to $\pm 18V$, T_{min} to T_{max}	dB
−55		+125	−55		+125		°C
	AD OP-07AQ			AD OP-07Q			
	AD OP-07AH			AD OP-07H			

Specifications shown in boldface are tested on all production units at final electrical test. Results from those tests are used to calculate outgoing quality levels. All min and max specifications are guaranteed, although only those shown in boldface are tested on all production units.

ABSOLUTE MAXIMUM RATINGS

Supply Voltage. . . . . ±22V
Internal Power Dissipation (Note 1) 500mW
Differential Input Voltage. ±30V
Input Voltage (Note 2). . . . . ±22V
Output Short Circuit Duration. . . . . Indefinite

Storage Temperature Range. . . . . –65°C to +150°C
Operating Temperature Range
    OP-07A, OP-07. . . . . –55°C to +125°C
    OP-07E, OP-07C, OP-07D. . . . . 0 to +70°C
Lead Temperature Range (Soldering, 60sec). . . . . 300°C

NOTES:
Note 1: Maximum package power dissipation vs. ambient temperature.

Package Type	Maximum Ambient Temperature for Rating	Derate Above Maximum Ambient Temperature
TO-99 (H)	80°C	7.1mW/°C
Mini-DIP (N)	36°C	5.6mW/°C
CERDIP (Q)	75°C	6.7mW/°C

Note 2: For supply voltages less than ±22V, the absolute maximum input voltage is equal to the supply voltage.

OUTLINE DIMENSIONS
Dimensions shown in inches and (mm).

CONNECTION DIAGRAMS
(Top View)

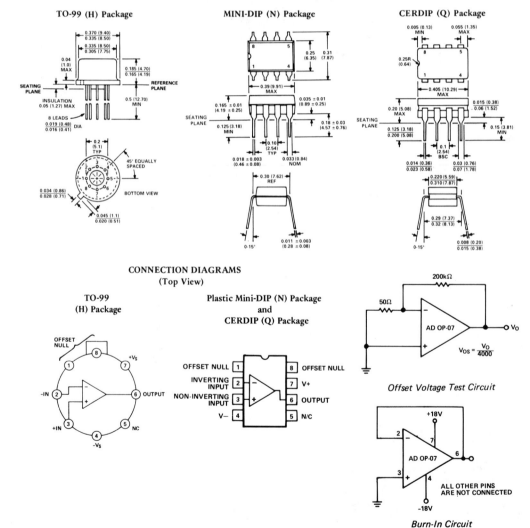

Offset Voltage Test Circuit

$$V_{OS} = \frac{V_O}{4000}$$

Burn-In Circuit

Applying the AD OP-07

The AD OP-07 may be directly substituted for other OP-07's as well as 725, 108/208/308, 108A/208A/308A, 714, OP-05 or LM11 devices, with or without removal of external frequency compensation or offset nulling components. If used to replace 741 devices, offset nulling components must be re-

moved (or referenced to +V$_S$). Input offset voltage of the AD OP-07 is very low, but if additional nulling is required, the circuit shown in Figure 1 is recommended.

The AD OP-07 provides stable operation with load capacitances up to 500pF and ±10V swings; larger capacitances should be decoupled with 50Ω resistor.

Stray thermoelectric voltages generated by dissimilar metals (thermocouples) at the contacts to the input terminals can prevent realization of the drift performance indicated. Best operation will be obtained when both input contacts are maintained at the same temperature, preferably close to the temperature of the device's package.

Although the AD OP-07 features high power supply rejection, the effects of noise on the power supplies may be minimized by bypassing the power supplies as close to pins 4 and 7 of the AD OP-07 as possible, to load ground with a good-quality 0.01μF ceramic capacitor as shown in Figure 1.

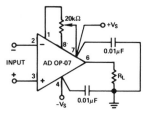

Figure 1. Optional Offset Nulling Circuit and Power Supply Bypassing

Performance Curves (typical @ T$_A$ = +25°C, V$_S$ = ±15V, AD OP-07 Grade Device unless otherwise noted)

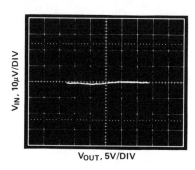

AD OP-07 Open Loop Gain Curve

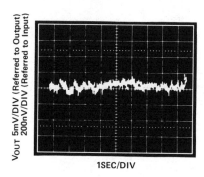

AD OP-07 Low Frequency Noise (See Test Circuit, on the Previous Page)

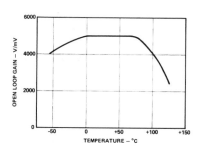

Open Loop Gain vs. Temperature

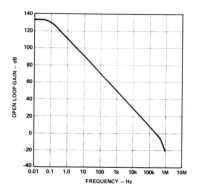

Open Loop Frequency Response

Typical Performance Curves

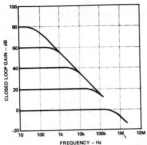

Closed Loop Response for Various Gain Configurations

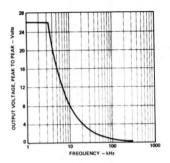

Maximum Undistorted Output vs. Frequency

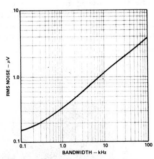

Input Wideband Noise vs. Bandwidth (0.1kHz to Frequency Indicated)

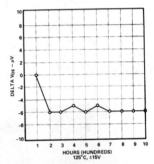

Offset Voltage vs. Time

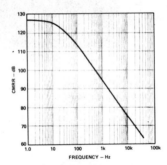

CMRR vs. Frequency

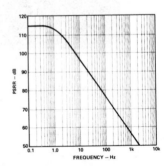

PSRR vs. Frequency

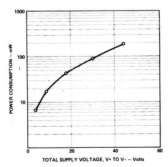

Power Consumption vs. Power Supply

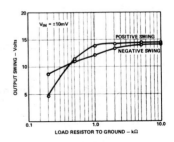

Output Voltage vs. Load Resistance

**ANALOG
DEVICES**

Programmable Gain
Instrumentation Amplifier
AD625

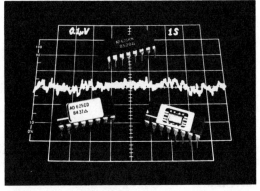

FEATURES
User Programmed Gains of 1 to 10,000
Low Gain Error: 0.02% max
Low Gain TC: 5ppm/°C max
Low Nonlinearity: 0.001% max
Low Offset Voltage: 25µV
Low Noise 4nV/$\sqrt{\text{Hz}}$ (at 1kHz) RTI
Gain Bandwidth Product: 25MHz
16-Pin Ceramic or Plastic DIP Package
MIL-Standard Parts Available
Low Cost

PRODUCT DESCRIPTION
The AD625 is a precision instrumentation amplifier specifically designed to fulfill two major areas of application:
1) Circuits requiring nonstandard gains (i.e., gains not easily achievable with devices such as the AD524 and AD624).
2) Circuits requiring a low cost, precision software programmable gain amplifier.

For low noise, high CMRR, and low drift the AD625JN is the most cost effective instrumentation amplifier solution available. An additional three resistors allow the user to set any gain from 1 to 10,000. The error contribution of the AD625JN is less than 0.05% gain error and under 5ppm/°C gain TC; performance limitations are primarily determined by the external resistors. Common-mode rejection is independent of the feedback resistor matching.

A software programmable gain amplifier (SPGA) can be configured with the addition of a CMOS multiplexer (or other switch network), and a suitable resistor network. Because the ON resistance of the switches is removed from the signal path, an AD625 based SPGA will deliver 12-bit precision, and can be programmed for any set of gains between 1 and 10,000, with completely user selected gain steps.

For the highest precision the AD625C offers an input offset voltage drift of less than 0.25µV/°C, output offset drift below 15µV/°C, and a maximum nonlinearity of 0.001% at G = 1. All grades exhibit excellent ac performance; a 25MHz gain bandwidth product, 5V/µs slew rate and 15µs settling time.

The AD625 is available in three accuracy grades (A, B, C) for industrial (−25°C to +85°C) temperature range, two grades (J, K) for commercial (0 to +70°C) temperature range, and one (S) grade rated over the extended (−55°C to +125°C) temperature range.

PRODUCT HIGHLIGHTS
1. The AD625 affords up to 16-bit precision for user selected fixed gains from 1 to 10,000. Any gain in this range can be programmed by 3 external resistors.
2. A 12-bit software programmable gain amplifier can be configured using the AD625, a CMOS multiplexer and a resistor network. Unlike previous instrumentation amplifier designs, the ON resistance of a CMOS switch does not affect the gain accuracy.
3. The gain accuracy and gain temperature coefficient of the amplifier circuit are primarily dependent on the user selected external resistors.
4. The AD625 provides totally independent input and output offset nulling terminals for high precision applications. This minimizes the effects of offset voltage in gain-ranging applications.
5. The proprietary design of the AD625 provides input voltage noise of 4nV/$\sqrt{\text{Hz}}$ at 1kHz.
6. External resistor matching is not required to maintain high common-mode rejection.

Two Technology Way; Norwood, Massachusetts 02062-9106
Tel: 617/329-4700   **TWX: 710/394-6577**
| **West Coast** | **Mid-West** | **Texas** |
| 714/641-9391 | 312/350-9399 | 214/231-5094 |

SPECIFICATIONS (typical @ V_S = ±15V, R_L = 2kΩ and T_A = +25°C unless otherwise specified)

Model	AD625A/J/S Min	Typ	Max	AD625B/K Min	Typ	Max	AD625C Min	Typ	Max	Units
GAIN										
Gain Equation		$\frac{2\,R_F}{R_G}+1$			$\frac{2\,R_F}{R_G}+1$			$\frac{2\,R_F}{R_G}+1$		
Gain Range	1		10,000	1		10,000	1		10,000	
Gain Error[1]		±.035	±.05		±0.02	±0.03		±0.01	±0.02	%
Nonlinearity, Gain = 1-256			±0.005			±0.002			±0.001	%
Gain>256			±0.01			±0.008			±0.005	%
Gain vs. Temp. Gain<1000[1]		5			5			5		ppm/°C
GAIN SENSE INPUT										
Gain Sense Current		300	**500**		150	**250**		50	**100**	nA
vs. Temperature		5	20		2	15		2	10	nA/°C
Gain Sense Offset Current		150	**500**		75	**250**		50	**100**	nA
vs. Temperature		2	15		1	10		1	5	nA/°C
VOLTAGE OFFSET (May be Nulled)										
Input Offset Voltage		50	200		25	50		10	25	μV
vs. Temperature		1	2/2		0.25	0.50/1		0.1	0.25	μV/°C
Output Offset Voltage		4	5		2	3		1	2	mV
vs. Temperature		20	50/50		10	25/40		10	15	μV/°C
Offset Referred to the Input vs. Supply										
G = 1	70	75		75	85		80	90		dB
G = 10	85	95		90	100		95	105		dB
G = 100	95	100		105	110		110	120		dB
G = 1000	**100**	110		**110**	120		**115**	140		dB
INPUT CURRENT										
Input Bias Current		±30	±50		±20	±25		±10	±15	nA
vs. Temperature		±50			±50			±50		pA/°C
Input Offset Current		±2	±35		±1	±15		±1	±5	nA
vs. Temperature		±20			±20			±20		pA/°C
INPUT										
Input Impedance										
Differential Resistance		1			1			1		GΩ
Differential Capacitance		4			4			4		pF
Common-Mode Resistance		1			1			1		GΩ
Common-Mode Capacitance		4			4			4		pF
Input Voltage Range										
Differ. Input Linear (V_D)			±10			±10			±10	V
Common Mode Linear (V_{CM})		$12V-\left(\frac{G}{2}\times V_D\right)$			$12V-\left(\frac{G}{2}\times V_D\right)$			$12V-\left(\frac{G}{2}\times V_D\right)$		
Common-Mode Rejection Ratio dc to 60Hz with 1kΩ Source Imbalance										
G = 1	70	75		75	85		80	90		dB
G = 10	90	95		95	105		100	115		dB
G = 100	100	105		105	115		110	125		dB
G = 1000	**110**	115		**115**	125		**120**	140		dB
OUTPUT RATING		±10V			±10V			±10V		
		@ 5mA			@ 5mA			@ 5mA		
DYNAMIC RESPONSE										
Small Signal −3dB										
G = 1 (R_F = 20kΩ)		650			650			650		kHz
G = 10		400			400			400		kHz
G = 100		150			150			150		kHz
G = 1000		25			25			25		kHz
Slew Rate		5.0			5.0			5.0		V/μs
Settling Time to 0.01%, 20V Step										
G = 1 to 200		15			15			15		μs
G = 500		35			35			35		μs
G = 1000		75			75			75		μs
NOISE										
Voltage Noise, 1kHz										
R.T.I.		4			4			4		nV/√Hz
R.T.O.		75			75			75		nV/√Hz
R.T.I., 0.1 to 10Hz										
G = 1		10			10			10		μV p-p
G = 10		1.0			1.0			1.0		μV p-p
G = 100		0.3			0.3			0.3		μV p-p
G = 1000		0.2			0.2			0.2		μV p-p
Current Noise										
0.1Hz to 10Hz		60			60			60		pA p-p
SENSE INPUT										
R_{IN}		10			10			10		kΩ
I_{IN}		30			30			30		μA
Voltage Range	±10			±10			±10			V
Gain to Output		1 ± 0.01			1 ± 0.01			1 ± 0.01		%

Model	AD625A/J/S			AD625B/K			AD625C			Units
	Min	Typ	Max	Min	Typ	Max	Min	Typ	Max	
REFERENCE INPUT										
R_{IN}		20			20			20		kΩ
I_{IN}		30			30			30		μA
Voltage Range	± 10			± 10			± 10			V
Gain to Output		1 ± 0.01			1 ± 0.01			1 ± 0.01		%
TEMPERATURE RANGE										
Specified Performance										
J/K Grades	0		+ 70	0		+ 70				°C
A/B/C Grades	− 25		+ 85	− 25		+ 85	− 25		+ 85	°C
S Grade	− 55		+ 125							°C
Storage	− 65		+ 150	− 65		+ 150	− 65		+ 150	°C
POWER SUPPLY										
Power Supply Range		± 5 to ± 18			± 5 to ± 18			± 5 to ± 18		V
Quiescent Current		3.5	5		3.5	5		3.5	5	mA
PRICE (100's)										
J/K Grades		6.95			9.85					$
A/B/C Grades		9.50			13.50			22.50		$
S Grade		27.00								$

NOTES

[1]Gain Error and Gain TC are for the AD625 only. Resistor Network errors will add to the specified errors.

Specifications subject to change without notice.

Specifications shown in boldface are tested on all production units at final
electrical test. Results from those tests are used to calculate outgoing quality
levels. All mim and max specifications are guaranteed, although only those
shown in boldface are tested on all production units.

FUNCTIONAL BLOCK DIAGRAM

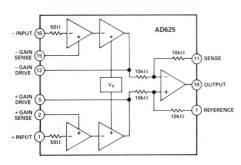

PIN CONFIGURATION

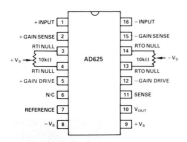

OUTLINE DIMENSIONS

Dimensions shown in inches and (mm).

16-PIN CERAMIC PACKAGE

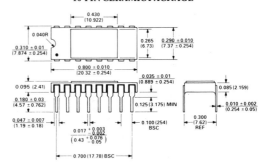

N16B
16-PIN PLASTIC DIP PACKAGE

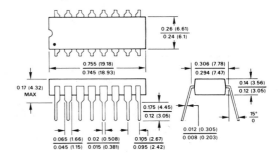

Typical Characteristics

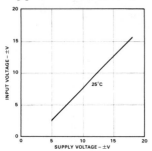

Figure 1. Input Voltage Range vs. Supply Voltage, G = 1

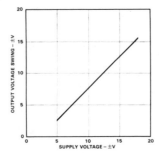

Figure 2. Output Voltage Swing vs. Supply Voltage

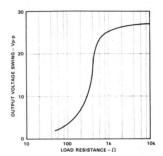

Figure 3. Output Voltage Swing vs. Resistive Load

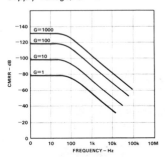

Figure 4. CMRR vs. Frequency RTI, Zero to 1kΩ Source Imbalance

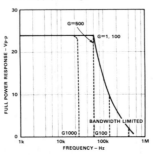

Figure 5. Large Signal Frequency Response

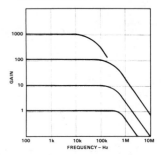

Figure 6. Gain vs. Frequency

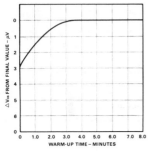

Figure 7. Offset Voltage, RTI, Turn On Drift

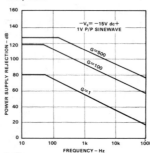

Figure 8. Negative PSRR vs. Frequency

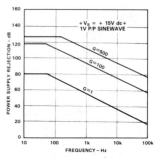

Figure 9. Positive PSRR vs. Frequency

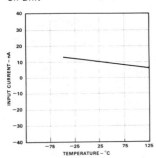

Figure 10. Input Bias Current vs. Temperature

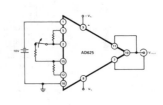

Figure 11. Overange and Gain Switching Test Circuit (G=8, G=1)

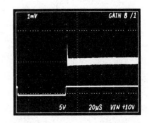

Figure 12. Gain Overange Recovery

Typical Characteristics

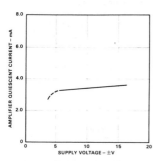

Figure 13. Quiescent Current vs.
Supply Voltage

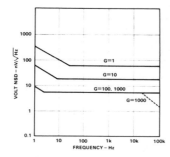

Figure 14. RTI Noise Spectral
Density vs. Gain

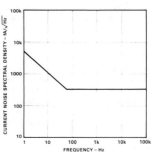

Figure 15. Input Current Noise

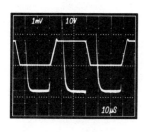

Figure 16. Low Frequency Voltage
Noise, G=1 (System Gain=1000)

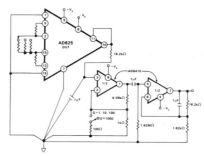

Figure 17. Noise Test Circuit

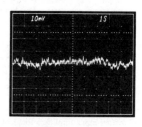

Figure 18. Low Frequency Voltage
Noise, G=1000 (System
Gain=100,000)

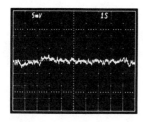

Figure 19. Large Signal Pulse
Response and Settling Time, G=1

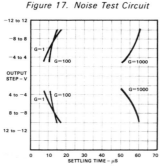

Figure 20. Settling Time to 0.01%

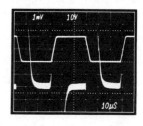

Figure 21. Large Signal Pulse
Response and Settling Time, G = 100

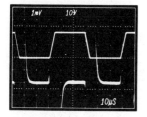

Figure 22. Large Signal Pulse
Response and Settling Time, G = 10

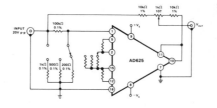

Figure 23. Settling Time Test
Circuit

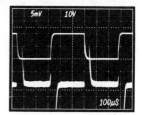

Figure 24. Large Signal Pulse
Response and Settling Time,
G=1000

Theory of Operation

The AD625 is a monolithic instrumentation amplifier based on a modification of the classic three-op-amp approach. Monolithic construction and laser-wafer-trimming allow the tight matching and tracking of circuit components. This insures the high level of performance inherent in this circuit architecture.

A preamp section (Q1-Q4) provides additional gain to A1 and A2. Feedback from the outputs of A1 and A2 forces the collector currents of Q1-Q4 to be constant, thereby, impressing the input voltage across R_G. This creates a differential voltage at the outputs of A1 and A2 which is given by the gain $(2R_F/R_G + 1)$ times the differential portion of the input voltage. The unity gain subtractor, A3, removes any common-mode signal from the output voltage yielding a single ended output, V_{OUT}, referred to the potential at the reference pin.

The value of R_G is the determining factor of the transconductance of the input preamp stage. As R_G is reduced for larger gains the transconductance increases. This has three important advantages. First, this approach allows the circuit to achieve a very high open-loop gain of $(3 \times 10^8$ at programmed gains $\geq 500)$ thus reducing gain related errors. Second, the gain-bandwidth product, which is determined by C3, C4, and the input transconductance, increases with gain, thereby, optimizing frequency response. Third, the input voltage noise is reduced to a value determined by the collector current of the input transistors $(4nV/\sqrt{Hz})$.

INPUT PROTECTION

Differential input amplifiers frequently encounter input voltages outside of their linear range of operation. There are two considerations when applying input protection for the AD625; 1) that continuous input current must be limited to less than 10mA and 2) that input voltages must not exceed either supply by more than one diode drop (approximately 0.6V @ 25°C).

Under differential overload conditions there is $(R_G + 100)\Omega$ in series with two diode drops (approximately 1.2V) between the plus and minus inputs, in either direction. With no external protection and R_G very small (i.e., 40Ω), the maximum overload voltage the AD625 can withstand, continuously, is approximately ±2.5V. Figure 26A shows the external components necessary to protect the AD625 under all overload conditions at any gain.

The diodes to the supplies are only necessary if input voltages outside of the range of the supplies are encountered. In higher gain applications where differential voltages are small, back-to-back zener diodes and smaller resistors, as shown in Figure 26b, provides adequate protection. Figure 26c shows low cost FETs with a maximum ON resistance of 300Ω configured to offer input protection with minimal degradation to noise, $(5.2nV/\sqrt{Hz}$ compared to normal noise performance of $4nV/\sqrt{Hz})$.

During differential overload conditions, excess current will flow through the gain sense lines (pins 2 and 15). This will have no effect in fixed gain applications. However, if the AD625 is being used in an SPGA application with a CMOS multiplexer, this current should be taken into consideration. The current capabilities of the multiplexer may be the limiting factor in allowable overflow current. The ON resistance of the switch should be included as part of R_G when calculating the necessary input protection resistance.

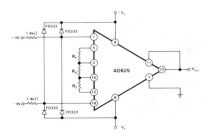

Figure 26a. Input Protection Circuit

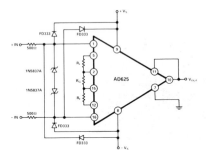

Figure 26b. Input Protection Circuit for G>5

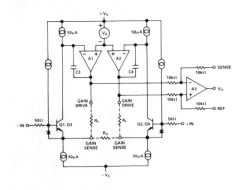

Figure 25. Simplified Circuit of the AD625

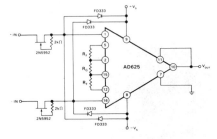

Figure 26c. Input Protection Circuit

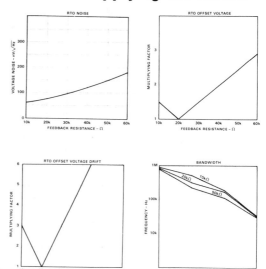

Applying the AD625

Any resistors in series with the inputs of the AD625 will degrade the noise performance. For this reason the circuit in Figure 26b should be used if the gains are all greater than 5. For gains less than 5, either the circuit in Figure 26a or in Figure 26c can be used. The two 1.4kΩ resistors in Figure 26a will degrade the noise performance to:

$$\sqrt{4kTR_{ext} + (4nV/\sqrt{Hz})^2} = 7.9nV/\sqrt{Hz}$$

RESISTOR PROGRAMMABLE GAIN AMPLIFIER
In the resistor-programmed mode (Figure 27), only three external resistors are needed to select any gain from 1 to 10,000. Depending on the application, discrete components or a pretrimmed network can be used. The gain accuracy and gain TC are primarily determined by the external resistors since the AD625C contributes less than 0.02% to gain error and under 5ppm/°C gain TC. The gain sense current is insensitive to common-mode voltage, making the CMRR of the resistor programmed AD625 independent of the match of the two feedback resistors, R_F.

Selecting Resistor Values
As previously stated each R_F provides feedback to the input stage and sets the unity gain transconductance. These feedback resistors are provided by the user. The AD625 is tested and specified with a value of 20kΩ for R_F. Since the magnitude of RTO errors increases with increasing feedback resistance, values much above 20kΩ are not recommended (values below 10kΩ for R_F may lead to instability). Refer to the graph of RTO noise, offset, drift, and bandwidth (Figure 28) when selecting the feedback resistors. The gain resistor (R_G) is determined by the formula $R_G = 2R_F/(G-1)$.

Figure 28. RTO Noise, Offset, Drift, and Bandwidth vs. Feedback Resistance Normalized to 20kΩ

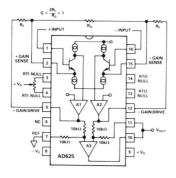

Figure 27. AD625 in Fixed Gain Configuration

A list of standard resistors which can be used to set some common gains is shown in Table I.

For single gain applications, only one offset null adjust is necessary; in these cases the RTI null should be used.

GAIN	R_F	R_G
1	20kΩ	∞
2	19.6kΩ	39.2kΩ
5	20kΩ	10kΩ
10	20kΩ	4.42kΩ
20	20kΩ	2.1kΩ
50	19.6kΩ	806Ω
100	20kΩ	402Ω
200	20.5kΩ	205Ω
500	19.6kΩ	78.7Ω
1000	19.6kΩ	39.2Ω
4	20kΩ	13.3kΩ
8	19.6kΩ	5.62kΩ
16	20kΩ	2.67kΩ
32	19.6kΩ	1.27kΩ
64	20kΩ	634Ω
128	20kΩ	316Ω
256	19.6kΩ	154Ω
512	19.6kΩ	76.8Ω
1024	19.6kΩ	38.3Ω

Table I. Common Gains Nominally within ±0.5% Error Using Standard 1% Resistors

SENSE TERMINAL

The sense terminal is the feedback point for the AD625 output amplifier. Normally it is connected directly to the output. If heavy load currents are to be drawn through long leads, voltage drops through lead resistance can cause errors. In these instances the sense terminal can be wired to the load thus putting the $I \times R$ drops "inside the loop" and virtually eliminating this error source.

Typically, IC instrumentation amplifiers are rated for a full ± 10 volt output swing into $2k\Omega$. In some applications, however, the need exists to drive more current into heavier loads. Figure 29 shows how a high-current booster may be connected "inside the loop" of an instrumentation amplifier. By using an external power boosting circuit, the power dissipated by the AD625 will remain low, thereby, minimizing the errors induced by self-heating. The effects of nonlinearities, offset and gain inaccuracies of the buffer are reduced by the loop gain of the AD625's output amplifier.

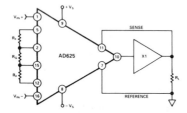

Figure 29. AD625 Instrumentation Amplifier with Output Current Booster

REFERENCE TERMINAL

The reference terminal may be used to offset the output by up to $\pm 10V$. This is useful when the load is "floating" or does not share a ground with the rest of the system. It also provides a direct means of injecting a precise offset. However, it must be remembered that the total output swing is ± 10 volts, from ground, to be shared between signal and reference offset.

The AD625 reference terminal must be presented with nearly zero impedance. Any significant resistance, including those caused by PC layouts or other connection techniques, will increase the gain of the noninverting signal path, thereby, upsetting the common-mode rejection of the In-Amp. Inadvertent thermocouple connections created in the sense and reference lines should also be avoided as they will directly affect the output offset voltage and output offset voltage drift.

In the AD625 a reference source resistance will unbalance the CMR trim by the ratio of $10k\Omega/R_{REF}$. For example, if the reference source impedance is 1Ω, CMR will be reduced to 80dB ($10k\Omega/1\Omega$ = 80dB). An operational amplifier may be used to provide the low impedance reference point as shown in Figure 30. The input offset voltage characteristics of that amplifier will add directly to the output offset voltage performance of the instrumentation amplifier.

The circuit of Figure 30 also shows a CMOS DAC operating in the bipolar mode and connnected to the reference terminal to provide software controllable offset adjustments. The total offset range is equal to $\pm (V_{REF}/2 \times R_5/R_4)$, however, to be symmetrical about 0V $R_3 = 2 \times R_4$.

The offset per bit is equal to the total offset range divided by 2^N, where N = number of bits of the DAC. The range of offset for Figure 30 is $\pm 120mV$, and the offset is incremented in steps of 0.9375mV/LSB.

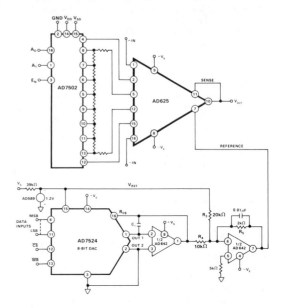

Figure 30. Software Controllable Offset

An instrumentation amplifier can be turned into a voltage-to-current converter by taking advantage of the sense and reference terminals as shown in Figure 31.

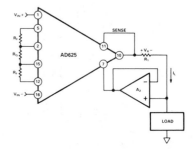

Figure 31. Voltage-to-Current Converter

By establishing a reference at the "low" side of a current setting resistor, an output current may be defined as a function of input voltage, gain and the value of that resistor. Since only a small current is demanded at the input of the buffer amplifier A1, the forced current I_L will largely flow through the load. Offset and drift specifications of A2 must be added to the output offset and drift specifications of the In-Amp.

INPUT AND OUTPUT OFFSET VOLTAGE

Offset voltage specifications are often considered a figure of merit for instrumentation amplifiers. While initial offset may be adjusted to zero, shifts in offset voltage due to temperature variations will cause errors. Intelligent systems can often correct for this factor with an auto-zero cycle, but this requires extra circuitry.

Offset voltage and offset voltage drift each have two components: input and output. Input offset is that component of offset that is generated at the input stage. Measured at the output it is directly proportional to gain, i.e., input offset as measured at the output at G = 100 is 100 times greater than that measured at G = 1. Output offset is generated at the output and is constant for all gains.

The input offset and drift are multiplied by the gain, while the output terms are independent of gain, therefore, input errors dominate at high gains and output errors dominate at low gains. The output offset voltage (and drift) is normally specified at G = 1 (where input effects are insignificant), while input offset (and drift) is given at a high gain (where output effects are negligible). All input-related parameters are specified referred to the input (RTI) which is to say that the effect on the output is "G" times larger. Offset voltage vs. power supply is also specified as an RTI error.

By separating these errors, one can evaluate the total error independent of the gain. For a given gain, both errors can be combined to give a total error referred to the input (RTI) or output (RTO) by the following formula:

Total Error RTI = input error + (output error/gain)

Total Error RTO = (Gain × input error) + output error

The AD625 provides for both input and output offset voltage adjustment. This simplifies nulling in very high perecision applications and minimizes offset voltage effects in switched gain applications. In such applications the input offset is adjusted first at the highest programmed gain, then the output offset is adjusted at G = 1. If only a single null is desired, the input offset null should be used. The most additional drift when using only the input offset null is 0.9μV/°C, RTO.

COMMON-MODE REJECTION

Common-mode rejection is a measure of the change in output voltage when both inputs are changed by equal amounts. These specifications are usually given for a full-range input voltage change and a specified source imbalance.

In an instrumentation amplifier, degradation of common-mode rejection is caused by a differential phase shift due to differences in distributed stray capacitances. In many applications shielded cables are used to minimize noise. This technique can create

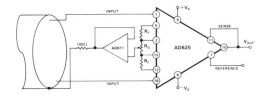

Figure 32. Common-Mode Shield Driver

common-mode rejection errors unless the shield is properly driven. Figures 32 and 33 show active data guards which are configured to improve ac common-mode rejection by "bootstrapping" the capacitances of the input cabling, thus minimizing differential phase shift.

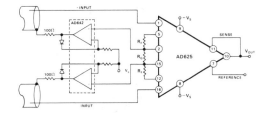

Figure 33. Differential Shield Driver

GROUNDING

In order to isolate low level analog signals from a noisy digital environment, many data-acquisition components have two or more ground pins. These grounds must eventually be tied together at one point. It would be convenient to use a single ground line, however, current through ground wires and pc runs of the circuit card can cause hundreds of millivolts of error. Therefore, separate ground returns should be provided to minimize the current flow from the sensitive points to the system ground (see Figure 34). Since the AD625 output voltage is developed with respect to the potential on the reference terminal, it can solve many grounding problems.

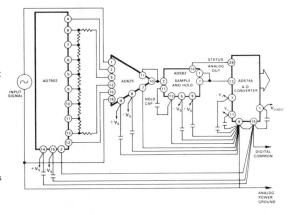

Figure 34. Basic Grounding Practice for a Data Acquisition System

GROUND RETURNS FOR BIAS CURRENTS

Input bias currents are those currents necessary to bias the input transistors of a dc amplifier. There must be a direct return path for these currents, otherwise they will charge external capacitances, causing the output to drift uncontrollably or saturate. Therefore, when amplifying "floating" input sources such as transformers, or ac-coupled sources, there must be a dc path from each input to ground as shown in Figure 35.

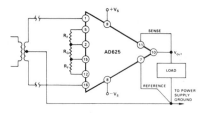

Figure 35a. Ground Returns for Bias Currents with Transformer Coupled Inputs

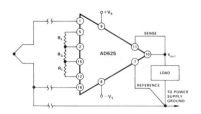

Figure 35b. Ground Returns for Bias Currents with Thermocouple Input

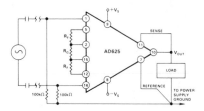

Figure 35c. Ground Returns for Bias Currents with AC Coupled Inputs

AUTO-ZERO CIRCUITS
In many applications it is necessary to maintain high accuracy. At room temperature, offset effects can be nulled by the use of offset trimpots. Over the operating temperature range, however, offset nulling becomes a problem. For these applications the auto-zero circuit of Figure 36 provides a hardware solution.

OTHER CONSIDERATIONS
One of the more overlooked problems in designing ultra-low-drift dc amplifiers is thermocouple induced offset. In a circuit comprised of two dissimilar conductors (i.e., copper, kovar), a current flows when the two junctions are at different temperatures. When this circuit is broken, a voltage known as the "Seebeck" or thermocouple emf can be measured. Standard IC lead material (kovar) and copper form a thermocouple with a high thermoelectric potential (about $35\mu V/°C$). This means that care must be taken to insure that all connections (especially those in the input circuit of the AD625) remain isothermal. This includes the input leads (1, 16) and the gain sense lines (2, 15). These pins were chosen for symmetry, helping to desensitize the input circuit to thermal gradients. In addition, the user should also avoid air currents

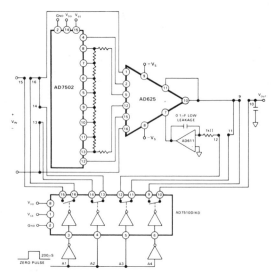

Figure 36. Auto-Zero Circuit

over the circuitry since slowly fluctuating thermocouple voltages will appear as "flicker" noise. In SPGA applications relay contacts and CMOS mux leads are both potential sources of additional thermocouple errors.

The base emitter junction of an input transistor can rectify out of band signals (i.e., RF interference). When amplifying small signals, these rectified voltages act as small dc offset errors. The AD625 allows direct access to the input transistors' bases and emitters enabling the user to apply some first order filtering to these unwanted signals. In Figure 37, the RC time constant should be chosen for desired attenuation of the interfering signals. In the case of a resistive transducer, the capacitance alone working against the internal resistance of the transducer may suffice.

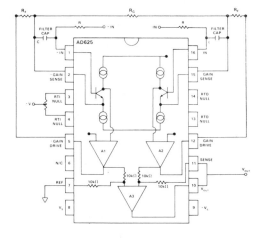

Figure 37. Circuit to Attenuate RF Interference

These capacitances may also be incorporated as part of the external input protection circuit (see section on input protection). As a general practice every effort should be made to match the extraneous capacitance at pins 15 and 2, and pins 1 and 16, to preserve high ac CMR.

SOFTWARE PROGRAMMABLE GAIN AMPLIFIER

An SPGA provides the ability to externally program precision gains from digital inputs. Historically, the problem in systems requiring electronic switching of gains has been the ON resistance (R_{ON}) of the multiplexer, which appears in series with the gain setting resistor R_G. This can result in substantial gain errors and gain drifts. The AD625 eliminates this problem by making the gain drive and gain sense pins available (pins 2, 15, 5, 12; see Figure 39). Consequently the multiplexer's ON resistance is removed from the signal current path. This transforms the ON resistance error into a small nullable offset error. To clarify this point, an error budget analysis has been performed in Table II based on the SPGA configuration shown in Figure 39.

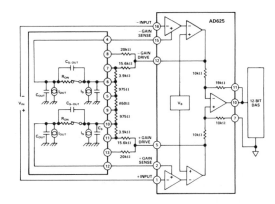

Figure 39. SPGA with Multiplexer Error Sources

Figure 39 shows a complete SPGA feeding a 12-bit DAS with a 0–10V input range. This configuration was used in the error budget analysis shown in Table II. The gain used for the RTI calculations is set at 16. As the gain is changed, the ON resistance of the multiplexer and the feedback resistance will change, which will slightly alter the values in the table.

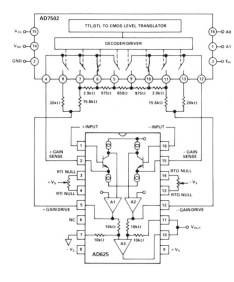

Figure 38. SPGA in a Gain of 16

Figure 38 shows an AD625 based SPGA with possible gains of 1, 4, 16, 64. R_G equals the resistance between the gain sense lines (pins 2 and 15) of the AD625. In Figure 38, R_G equals the sum of the two 975Ω resistors and the 650Ω resistor, or 2600Ω. R_F equals the resistance between the gain sense and the gain drive pins (pins 12 and 15, or pins 2 and 5), that is R_F equals the 15.6kΩ resistor plus the 3.9kΩ resistor, or 19.5kΩ. The gain, therefore equals:

$$\frac{2R_F}{R_G} + 1 = \frac{2(19.5\text{k}\Omega)}{(2.6\text{k}\Omega)} + 1 = 16$$

As the switches of the differential multiplexer proceed synchronously, R_G and R_F change, resulting in the various programmed gain settings.

Induced Error	Specification AD625C	AD7502KN	Calculation	Voltage Offset Induced RTI
RTI Offset Voltage	Gain Sense Offset Current 40nA	Switch Resistance 170Ω	40nA × 170Ω = 6.8μV	6.8μV
RTI Offset Voltage	Gain Sense Current 60nA	Differential Switch Resistance 6.8Ω	60nA × 6.8Ω = 0.41μV	0.41μV
RTO Offset Voltage	Feedback Resistance 20kΩ[1]	Differential Leakage Current (I_S)[2] + 0.2nA − 0.2nA	2(0.2nA × 20kΩ) = 8μV/16	0.5μV
RTO Offset Voltage	Feedback Resistance 20kΩ[1]	Differential Leakage Current (I_{OUT})[2] + 1nA − 1nA	2(1nA × 20kΩ) = 40μV/16	2.5μV

Total error induced by a typical CMOS multiplexer to an SPGA at 25°C   **10.21μV**

NOTES

[1]The resistor for this calculation is the user provided feedback resistance (R_F). 20kΩ is recommended value (see resistor programmable gain amplifier section).

[2]The leakage currents (I_S and I_{OUT}) will induce an offset voltage, however, the offset will be determined by the difference between the leakages of each "half" of the differential multiplexer. The differential leakage current is multiplied by the feedback resistance (see Note 1), to determine offset voltage. Because differential leakage current is not a parameter specified on multiplexer data sheets, the most extreme difference (one most positive and one most negative) was used for the calculations in Table II. Typical performance will be much better.

*The frequency response and settling will be affected by the ON resistance and internal capacitance of the multiplexer. Figure 40 shows the settling time vs. ON resistance at different gain settings for an AD625 based SPGA.

**Switch resistance and leakage current errors can be reduced by using relays.

Table II. Errors Induced by Multiplexer to an SPGA

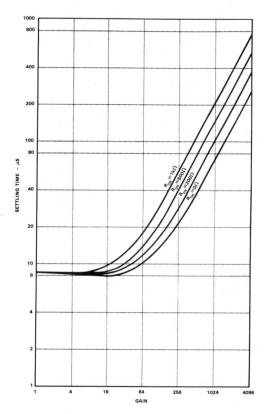

Figure 40. Settling Time to 0.01% of a 20V Step Input for
SPGA with AD625

DETERMINING SPGA RESISTOR NETWORK VALUES

The individual resistors in the gain network can be calculated
sequentially using the formula given below. The equation determines the resistors as labeled in Figure 41. The feedback resistors
and the gain setting resistors are interactive, therefore; the formula
must be a series where the present term is dependent on the
preceding term(s). The formula

$$R_{F_{i+1}} = \left(20k\Omega - \sum_{j=0}^{i} R_{F_j}\right)\left(1 - \frac{G_i}{G_{i+1}}\right) \qquad \begin{matrix} G_0 = 1 \\ R_{F_0} = 0 \end{matrix}$$

can be used to calculate the necessary feedback resistors for any
set of gains. This formula yields a network with a total resistance
of 40kΩ. A dummy variable (j) serves as a counter to keep a

running total of the preceding feedback resistors. To illustrate
how the formula can be applied, an example similar to the calculation used for the resistor network in Figure 38 is examined
below.

1) Unity gain is treated as a separate case. It is implemented
with separate 20kΩ feedback resistors as shown in Figure 41. It
is then ignored in further calculations.

2) Before making any calculations it is advised to draw a resistor
network similar to the network in Figure 41. The network will
have $(2 \times M) + 1$ resistors, where M = number of gains. For
Figure 38 M = 3 (4, 16, 64), therefore, the resistor string will
have 7 resistors (plus the two 20kΩ "side" resistors for unity
gain).

3) Begin all calculations with $G_0 = 1$ and $R_{F_0} = 0$.

$R_{F_1} = (20k\Omega - R_{F_0})(1 - 1/4): R_{F_0} = 0 \therefore R_{F_1} = 15k\Omega$

$R_{F_2} = [20k\Omega - (R_{F_0} + R_{F_1})](1 - 4/16):$

$\qquad R_{F_0} + R_{F_1} = 15k\Omega \therefore R_{F_2} = 3.75k\Omega$

$R_{F_3} = [20k\Omega - (R_{F_0} + R_{F_1} + R_{F_2})](1 - 16/64):$

$\qquad R_{F_0} + R_{F_1} + R_{F_2} = 18.75k\Omega \therefore R_{F_3} = 937.5\Omega$

4) The center resistor (R_G of the highest gain setting), is determined
last. Its value is the remaining resistance of the 40kΩ string,
and can be calculated with the equation:

$$R_G = \left(40k\Omega - 2\sum_{j=0}^{M} R_{F_j}\right)$$

$$R_G = 40k\Omega - 2(R_{F_0} + R_{F_1} + R_{F_2} + R_{F_3})$$

$$40k\Omega - 39.375k\Omega = 625\Omega$$

5) If different resistor values are desired, all the resistors in the
network can be scaled by some convenient factor. However,
raising the impedance will increase the RTO errors, lowering
the total network resistance below 20kΩ can result in amplifier
instability. More information on this phenomenon is given in
the RPGA section of the data sheet. The scale factor will not
affect the unity gain feedback resistors. The resistor network in
Figure 38 has a scaling factor of 650/625 = 1.04, if this factor is
used on R_{F_1}, R_{F_2}, R_{F_3}, and R_G, then the resistor values will
match exactly.

6) Round off errors can be cumulative, therefore, it is advised
to carry as many significant digits as possible until all the values
have been calculated.

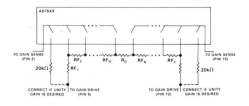

Figure 41. Resistors for a Gain Setting Network

BURR-BROWN®

3656

Integrated Circuit - Transformer Coupled
ISOLATION AMPLIFIER

FEATURES

- INTERNAL ISOLATED POWER
- 8000V ISOLATION TEST VOLTAGE
- $0.5\mu A$ MAX LEAKAGE AT 120V, 60Hz
- 3-PORT ISOLATION
- 125dB REJECTION AT 60Hz
- 1" x 1" x 0.25" CERAMIC PACKAGE

APPLICATIONS

- MEDICAL
  Patient monitoring and diagnostic instrumentation
- INDUSTRIAL
  Ground loop elimination and off-ground signal measurement
- NUCLEAR
  Input/output/power isolation

DESCRIPTION

The 3656 is the first amplifier to provide a total isolation function ... both signal and power isolation ... in integrated circuit form. This remarkable advancement in analog signal processing capability is accomplished by use of a patented modulation technique and minature hybrid transformer.

Versatility and performance are outstanding features of the 3656. It is capable of operating with three completely independent grounds (three-port isolation). In addition, the isolated power generated is available to power external circuitry at either the input or output. The uncommitted op amps at the input and the output allow a wide variety of closed-loop configurations to match the requirements of many different types of isolation applications.

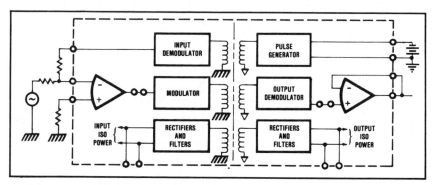

International Airport Industrial Park - P.O. Box 11400 - Tucson, Arizona 85734 - Tel. (602) 746-1111 - Twx: 910-952-1111 - Cable: BBRCORP - Telex: 66-6491

©1979 Burr-Brown Corporation   PDS-403C   Printed in U.S.A. February, 1985

THEORY OF OPERATION

Details of the 3656 are shown in Figure 1. The external connections shown, place it in its simplest gain configuration - unity gain, noninverting. Several other amplifier gain configurations and power isolation configurations are possible. See Installation and Operating Instructions and Applications sections for details.

Isolation of both signal and power is accomplished with a single miniature toroid transformer with multiple windings. A pulse generator operating at approximately 750kHz provides a two-part voltage waveform to transformer T_1. One part of the waveform is rectified by diodes D_1 through D_4 to provide the isolated power to the input and output stages (+V, -V and V+, V-). The other part of the waveform is modulated with input signal information by the modulator operating into the V_2 winding of the transformer.

The modulated signal is coupled by windings W_6 and W_7 to two matched demodulators - one in the input stage and one in the output stage - which generate identical voltages at their outputs, pins 10 and 11 (voltages identical with respect to their respective commons, pins 3 and 17). In the input stage the input amplifier A_1, the modulator and the input demodulator are connected in a negative feedback loop. This forces the voltage at pin 6 (connect as shown

in Figure 1) to equal the input signal voltage applied at pin 7. Since the input and the output demodulators are matched and produce identical output voltages, the voltage at pin 11 (referenced to pin 17, the output common) is equal to the voltage at pin 10 (referenced to pin 3, the input common). In the output stage, output amplifier A_2 is connected as a unity gain buffer, thus the output voltage at pin 15 equals the output demodulator voltage at pin 11. The end result is an isolated output voltage at pin 15 equal to the input voltage at pin 7 with no galvanic connection between them.

Several amplifier and power connection variations are possible:

1. The input stage may be connected in various operational amplifier gain configurations.

2. The output stage may be operated at gains above unity.

3. The internally generated isolated voltages which provide power to A_1 and A_2 may be overridden and external supply voltages used instead.

Versatility and its three independent isolated grounds allow simple solutions to demanding analog signal conditioning problems. See the Installation and Operating Instructions and Applications sections for details.

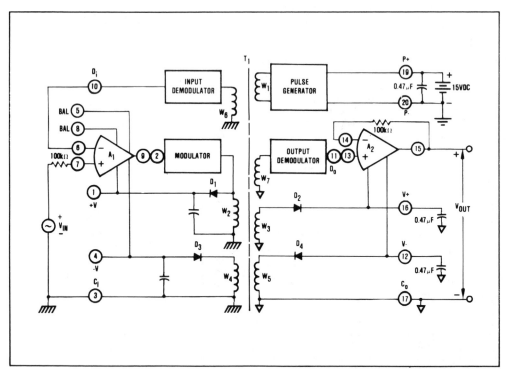

FIGURE 1. Block Diagram.

SPECIFICATIONS
ELECTRICAL

At +25°C, V± = 15VDC and 15VDC between P+ and P-, unless otherwise noted.

PARAMETER	CONDITIONS	3656AG, BG, HG, JG, KG			UNITS
		MIN	TYP	MAX	
ISOLATION					
Voltage					
Rated Continuous[1], DC		3500 (1000)			VDC
Rate Continuous[2], AC		2000 (700)			V, rms
Test, 10sec[1]	G_1 = 10V/V	8000 (3000)			VDC
Rejection					
DC			160		dB
60Hz, < 100Ω in I/P Com[2]			125		dB
60Hz, 5kΩ in I/P Com[2]					
3656HG		108			dB
3656AG, BG, JG, KG		112			dB
Capacitance[1]			6.0 (6.3)		pF
Resistance[1]			10^{12} (10^{12})		Ω
Leakage Current	120V, 60Hz		0.28	0.5	μA
GAIN					
Equations	See Text				
Accuracy of Equations					
Initial[3] 3656HG	G < 100V/V			1.5	%
3656AG, JG, KG				1.0	%
3656BG				0.3	%
vs. Temperature 3656HG				480	ppm/°C
3656AG, JG				120	ppm/°C
3656BG, KG				60	ppm/°C
vs. Time			0.02 (1 + log khrs.)		%
Nonlinearity	$R_A + R_F = R_B \geq 2M\Omega$				
External Supplies used at					
pins 12 and 16, 3656HG	Unipolar or Bipolar Output			±0.15	%
3656AG, JG, KG				±0.1	%
3656BG				±0.05	%
Internal Supplies used for	Bipolar Output Voltage				
Output Stage	Swing, Full Load[4]		±0.15		%
OFFSET VOLTAGE[5]	RTI				
Initial[3], 3656HG	15VP between P+ and P-			±|4 + 40/G_1|	mV
3656AG, JG				±|2 + (20/G_1)|	mV
3656BG, KG				±|1 + (10/G_1)|	mV
vs. Temperature, 3656HG				±|200 + (1000/G_1)|	μV/°C
3656JG				±|50 + (750/G_1)|	μV/°C
3656AG				±|25 + (500/G_1)|	μV/°C
3656KG				±|10 + (350/G_1)|	μV/°C
3656BG				±|5 + (350/G_1)|	μV/°C
vs. Supply Voltage	Supply between P+ and P-				
3656HG				±|0.6 + (3.5/G_1)|	mV/V
3656AG, BG, JG, KG				±|0.3 + (2.1/G_1)|	mV/V
vs. Current[6]		±|0.1 + (10/G_1)|		±|0.2 + (20/G_1)|	mV/mA
vs. Time		±|10 + (100/G_1)| x (1 + log khrs.)			μV
AMPLIFIER PARAMETERS	Apply to A1 and A2				
Bias Current[7]					
Initial				100	nA
vs. Temperature			0.5		nA/°C
vs. Supply			0.2		nA/V
Offset Current[7]			5	20	nA
Impedance	Common-mode	100 || 5			MΩ || pF
Input Noise Voltage	f_B = 0.05Hz to 100Hz		5		μV, p-p
	f_B = 10Hz to 10kHz		5		μV, rms
Input Voltage Range[8]					
Linear Operation	Internal Supply			±5	V
	External Supply			Supply -5V	V
Without Damage	Internal Supply			±8	V
	External Supply			Supply	V
Output Current	V_{OUT} = ±5V				
	±15V External Supply	±5			mA
	Internal Supply	±2.5			mA
	V_{OUT} = ±10V				
	±15V External Supply	±2.5			mA
	V_{OUT} = ±2V, $V_{P-, P-}$ = 8.5V				
	Internal Supply		±1		mA
Quiescent Current			150	450	μA

ELECTRICAL (CONT)

At +25°C, V± = 15VDC and 15VDC between P+ and P-, unless otherwise noted.

PARAMETER	CONDITIONS	3656AG, BG, HG, JG, KG			UNITS
		MIN	TYP	MAX	
FREQUENCY RESPONSE					
±3dB Response	Small Signal		30		kHz
Full Power			1.3		kHz
Slew Rate	Direction measured at output	+0.1, -0.04			V/µsec
Settling Time	to 0.05%		500		µsec
OUTPUT					
Noise Voltage (RTI)	f_B = 0.05Hz to 100Hz		$\sqrt{(5)^2 + (22/G_1)^2}$		µV, p-p
	f_B = 10Hz to 10kHz		$\sqrt{(5)^2 + (11/G_1)^2}$		µV, rms
Residual Ripple[9]			5		mV, p-p
POWER SUPPLY IN	at P+, P-				
Rated Performance			15		VDC
Voltage Range[10]	Derated Performance	8.5		16	VDC
Ripple Current[9]			10	25	mA, p-p
Quiescent Current[11]	Average		14	18	mA, DC
Current vs. Load Current[12]	vs. Currents from +V, -V, V+, V-		0.7		mA/mA
ISOLATED POWER OUT	at +V, -V, V+, V- pins[13]				
Voltage, no load	15V between P+ and P-	8.5	9.0	9.5	V
Voltage, full load	±5mA (10mA sum) load[12]	7.0	8.0	9.0	V
Voltage vs. Power Supply	vs. Supply between P+ and P-		0.66		V/V
Ripple Voltage[9]					
No load			40		mV, p-p
Full load	±5mA load		80	200	mV, p-p
TEMPERATURE RANGE					
Specification 3656AG, BG		-25		+85	°C
3656HG, JG, KG		0		+70	°C
Operation[10]		-55		+100	°C
Storage[14]		-65		+125	°C

NOTES:

1. Ratings in parenthesis and between P- (pin 20) and O/P Com (pin 17). Other isolation ratings are between I/P Com and O/P Com or I/P Com and P-.

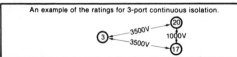

An example of the ratings for 3-port continuous isolation.

MECHANICAL

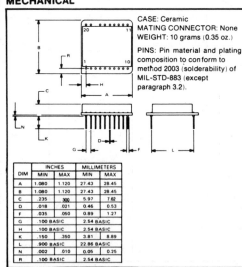

CASE: Ceramic
MATING CONNECTOR: None
WEIGHT: 10 grams (0.35 oz.)

PINS: Pin material and plating composition to conform to method 2003 (solderability) of MIL-STD-883 (except paragraph 3.2).

DIM	INCHES		MILLIMETERS	
	MIN	MAX	MIN	MAX
A	1.080	1.120	27.43	28.45
B	1.080	1.120	27.43	28.45
C	.235	.300	5.97	7.62
D	.018	.021	0.46	0.53
F	.035	.050	0.89	1.27
G	.100 BASIC		2.54 BASIC	
H	.100 BASIC		2.54 BASIC	
K	.150	.350	3.81	8.89
L	.900 BASIC		22.86 BASIC	
N	.002	.010	0.05	0.25
R	.100 BASIC		2.54 BASIC	

2. May be improved with proper shielding. See Performance Curves.

3. May be trimmed to zero.

4. If output swing is unipolar, or if the output is not loaded, specification same as if external supply were used.

5. Includes effects of A_1 and A_2 offset voltages and bias currents if recommended resistors used.

6. Versus the sum of all external currents drawn from V+, V-, +V, -V (= ISO).

7. Effects of A_1 and A_2 bias currents and offset currents are included in Offset Voltage specifications.

8. With respect to I/P Com (pin 3) for A_1 and with respect to O/P Com (pin 17) for A_2. CMR for A_1 and A_2 is 100dB, typical.

9. In configuration of Figure 3. Ripple frequency approximately 750kHz. Measurement bandwidth is 30kHz.

10. Decreases linearly from 16VDC at 85°C to 12VDC at 100°C.

11. Instantaneous peak current required from pins 19 and 20 at turn-on is 100mA for slow rising voltages (50msec) and 300mA for fast rises (50µsec).

12. Load current is sum drawn from +V, -V, V+, V- (= I_{ISO}).

13. Maximum voltage rating at pins 1 and 4 is ±18VDC; maximum voltage rating at pins 12 and 16 is ±18VDC.

14. Isolation ratings may degrade if exposed to 125°C for more than 1000 hours or 90°C for more than 50,000 hours.

PIN DESIGNATIONS

1.	+V	11.	OUTPUT DEMOD
2.	MOD INPUT	12.	V-
3.	INPUT DEMOD COM	13.	A_2 NONINVERTING INPUT
4.	-V	14.	A_2 INVERTING INPUT
5.	BALANCE	15.	A_2 OUTPUT
6.	A_1 INVERTING INPUT	16.	V+
7.	A_1 NONINVERTING INPUT	17.	OUTPUT DEMOD COM
8.	BALANCE	18.	NO PIN
9.	A_1 OUTPUT	19.	P+
10.	INPUT DEMOD	20.	P-

TYPICAL PERFORMANCE CURVES

All specifications typical at +25°C unless otherwise noted.

SMALL SIGNAL FREQUENCY RESPONSE

$G_1 = 10$
$G_1 = 1$
$G_1 = 100$
$G_1 = 1000$
$V_P = 15V$
$V+, V- = +15V$
$-15V$
$V_{OUT} = 300mV, rms$
$G_2 = 2$

Relative Gain (dB) vs Frequency (Hz)

PHASE RESPONSE

$G_1 = 10$
$G_1 = 1$
$G_1 = 100$
$G_1 = 1000$
$V_P = 15V$
$V+, V- = \pm15V$
$V_{OUT} = 300mV, rms$

Phase Shift (°C) vs Frequency (Hz)

OUTPUT SWING VS SUPPLY VOLTAGE

$G_2 = 2$ $(\pm V) = \pm5mA$
$R_L = 3k\Omega$, ext. $V\pm = \pm15V$
$R_L = 2k\Omega$, int. $V\pm$ or $\pm15V$
$R_L = 1k\Omega$, ext. $V\pm = 0$
$1(\pm V) = 0$
$1(\pm V) = 5mA$

Output Voltage $(\pm V)$ vs Power Supply Voltage P± (V)

OUTPUT SWING AND DISTORTION VS FREQUENCY

Output Swing
Distortion
$G = 1000$
$G = 100$
$G = 10$
$G = 1$

Output Voltage $(\pm V)$ / Harmonic Distortion (%) vs Frequency (Hz)

OUTPUT VOLTAGE SWING VS TEMPERATURE AND ISOLATED SUPPLY LOAD

$R_B = 2M\Omega$
$I_{ISO} = 0, +V_{OUT}$
$I_{ISO} = 0, -V_{OUT}$
$I_{ISO} = max, -V_{OUT}$
$I_{ISO} = max, +V_{OUT}$
I_{ISO} (see note 12 of electrical specs)
Derate $V_{P\pm}$

Output Voltage $(\pm V)$ vs Temperature (°C)

NOISE VOLTAGE VS FREQUENCY

Output Stage
Input Stage

Noise Voltage $(nV/\sqrt{Hz})$ vs Frequency (Hz)

QUIESCENT CURRENT VS TEMPERATURE

Derate $V_{P\pm}$

Normalized Quiescent Current (at V_{P-P-}) vs Temperature (°C)

ISOLATED OUTPUT VOLTAGE AND CURRENT VS TEMPERATURE

$\pm V$ at $I_{ISO} = 0$
$\pm V$ at $I_{ISO} = max$
Voltage
Current
Derate $V_{P\pm}$

Maximum Recommended I_{ISO} Current $(\pm mA)$ / Isolated Voltage Out $(\pm V)$ vs Temperature (°C)

QUIESCENT CURRENT AND ISOLATED VOLTAGE OUTPUT VS SUPPLY VOLTAGE

Voltage at $I_{ISO} = 0$
Voltage at $I_{ISO} = +5mA$
Voltage at $I_{ISO} = 0$
Current

Quiescent Current at V_{P-P-} (mA) / Isolated Voltage Output $(\pm V)$ vs Supply Voltage at $V_{P\pm}$ (V)

ISOLATION-MODE REJECTION VS GAIN

$f = 60Hz$
R_C is resistance is series with input common, pin 3
$R_C = 0$
$R_C = 5k\Omega$
Shielded
Unshielded

Isolation-Mode Rejection (dB) vs Gain (V/V)

ISOLATION-MODE REJECTION VS FREQUENCY

Normalized Isolation-Mode Rejection (dB) vs Frequency (Hz)

AC AND DC LEAKAGE CURRENT VS ISOLATION VOLTAGE

DC
AC, 60Hz

AC Leakage Current (μA) / DC Leakage Current (nA) vs Isolation Voltage (V_P)

INSTALLATION AND OPERATING INSTRUCTIONS

The 3656 is a very versatile device capable of being used in a variety of isolation and amplification configurations. There are several fundamental considerations that determine configuration and component value constraints:

1. Consideration must be given to the load placed on the resistance (pin 10 and pin 11) by external circuitry. Their output resistance is $100k\Omega$ and a load resistor of $2M\Omega$ or greater is recommended to prevent a voltage divider loading effect in excess of 5%.

2. Demodulator loadings should be closely matched so their output voltages will be equal. (Unequal demodulator output voltages will produce a gain error.) At the $2M\Omega$ level, a matching error of 5% will cause an additional gain error of 0.25%.

3. Voltage swings at demodulator outputs should be limited to 5V. The output may be distorted if this limit is exceeded. This constrains the maximum allowed gains of the input and output stages. Note that the voltage swings at demodulator outputs are tested with $2M\Omega$ load for a minimum of 5V.

4. Total current drawn from the internal isolated supplies must be limited to less than $\pm5mA$ per supply and limited to t total of 10mA. In other words, the combination of external and internal current drawn from the internal circuitry which feeds the +V, -V, V+ and V- pins should be limited to 5mA per supply (total current to +V, -V, V+ and V- limited to 10mA). The internal filter capacitors for $\pm V$ are $0.01\mu F$. If more than $0.1mA$ is drawn to provide isolated power for external circuitry (see Figure 12), additional capacitors are required to provide adequate filtering. A minimum of $0.1\mu F/mA$ is recommended.

5. The input voltage at pin 7 (noninverting input to A_1) must not exceed the voltage at pin 4 (negative supply voltage for A_1) in order to prevent a possible lockup condition. A low leakage diode connected between pins 7 and 4, as shown in Figure 2, can be used to limit this input voltage swing.

6. Impedances seen by each amplifier's + and - input terminals should be matched to minimize offset voltages caused by amplifier input bias currents. Since the demodulators have a $100k\Omega$ output resistance, the amplifier input not connected to the demodulator should also see $100k\Omega$.

7. All external filter capacitors should be mounted as close to the respective supply pins as is possible in order to prevent excessive ripple voltages on the supplies or at the output. (Optimum spacing is less than 0.5". Ceramic capacitors recommended.)

POWER AND SIGNAL CONFIGURATIONS

NOTE: Figures 2, 3 and 4 are used to illustrate both signal and power connection configurations. In the circuits shown, the power and signal configurations are independent so that any power configuration could be used with any signal configuration.

ISOLATED POWER CONFIGURATIONS

The 3656 is designed with isolation between the input, the output, and the power connections. The internally generated isolated voltages supplied to A_1 and A_2 may be overridden with external voltages greater than the internal supply voltages. These two features of 3656 provide a great deal of versatility in possible isolation and power supply hook-ups. When external supplies are applied, the rectifying diodes (D_1 through D_4) are reverse biased and the internal voltage sources are decoupled from the amplifiers (see Figure 1). Note that when external supplies are used, they must never be lower than the internal supply voltage.

Three-Port

The power supply connections in Figure 2 show the full three-port isolation configuration. The system has three separate grounds with no galvanic connections between them. The two external $0.47\mu F$ capacitors at pins 12 and 16 filter the rectified isolated voltage at the output stage. Filtering on the input stage is provided by internal capacitors. In this configuration continuous isolation voltage ratings are: 3500V between pins 3 and 17; 3500V between pins 3 and 19; 1000V between pins 17 and 19.

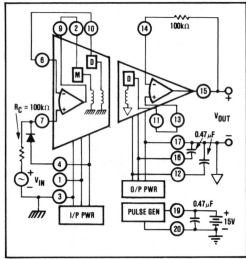

FIGURE 2. Power: Three-port Isolation;
Signal: Unity-gain Noninverting.

Two-Port - Bipolar Supply

Figure 3 shows two-port isolation which uses an external bipolar supply with its common connected to the output stage ground (pin 17). One of the supplies (either + or - could be used) provides power to the pulse generator (pins 19 and 20). The same sort of configuration is possible with the external supplies connected to the input stage. With the connection shown, filtering at pins 12 and 16 is not required. In this configuration continuous isolation voltage rating is: 3500VDC between pins 3 and 17; not applicable between pins 17 and 19; 3500VDC between pins 3 and 19.

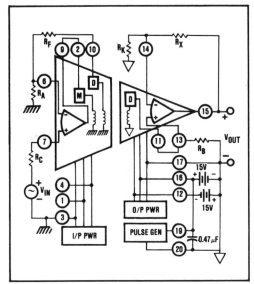

FIGURE 3. Power: Two-port, Dual Supply;
Signal: Noninverting Gain.

Two-Port Single Supply

Figure 4 demonstrates two-port isolation using a single polarity supply connected to the output common (pin 17). The other polarity of supply for A_2 is internally generated (thus the filtering at pin 12). This isolated power configuration could be used at the input stage as well and either polarity of supply could be employed. In this configuration continuous isolation voltage rating is: 3500V between pins 3 and 17; 3500V between pins 3 and 19; not applicable between pins 17 and 19.

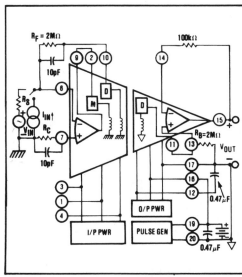

FIGURE 4. Power: Two-port, Single Supply;
Signal: Inverting Gains.

SIGNAL CONFIGURATIONS
Unity Gain Noninverting

The signal path portion of Figure 2 shows the 3656 in its simplest gain configuration: unity gain noninverting. The two 100kΩ resistors provide balanced resistances to the inverting and noninverting inputs of the amplifiers. The diode prevents latch up in case the input voltage goes more negative than the voltage at pin 4.

Noninverting With Gain

The signal path portion of Figure 3 demonstrates two additional gain configurations: gain in the otuput stage and noninverting gain in the input stage. The following equations apply:

Total amplifier gain:

$$G = G_1 \bullet G_2 = V_{OUT} / V_{IN} \tag{1}$$

Input Stage:

$G_1 = 1 + (R_F / R_A)$ (Select G_1 to be less than 5V/full scale V_{In} to limit demodulator output to 5V) $\tag{2}$

$R_A + R_F \geqslant 2M\Omega$ (Select to load input demodulator with at least 2MΩ) $\tag{3}$

$R_C = R_A \parallel (R_F + 100k\Omega) =$

$$\frac{R_A (R_F + 100k\Omega)}{R_A + R_F + 100k\Omega}$$

(Balance impedances seen by the + and - inputs of A_1 to reduce input offset caused by bias current) $\tag{4}$

Output Stage:

$G_2 = 1 + (R_X / R_K)$ (Select ratio to obtain V_{OUT} between 5V and 10V full scale with V_{IN} at its maximum) $\tag{5}$

$R_X \parallel R_K = 100k\Omega$ (Balance impedances seen by the + and - inputs of A_2 to reduce effect of bias current on the output offset) $\tag{6}$

$R_B = R_A + R_F$ (Load output demodulator equal to input demodulator) $\tag{7}$

Inverting Gain, Voltage or Current Input

The signal portion of Figure 4 shows two possible inverting input stage configurations: current and input and voltage input.

Input Stage:
For the voltage input case:

$G_1 = -R_F / R_S$ (Select G_1 to be less than 5V/full scale V_{IN} to limit the demodulator output voltage to 5V) $\tag{8}$

$R_F = 2M\Omega$ (Select to load the demodulator with at least 2MΩ $\tag{9}$

$$R_C = R_S \parallel (R_F + 100k\Omega) = \frac{R_S (R_F + 100k\Omega)}{R_S + R_F + 100k\Omega}$$

(Balance the impedances seen by the + and - inputs of A_1). $\tag{10}$

For the current input case:

$$V_{OUT} = -I_{IN} R_F \bullet G_2 \qquad (11)$$
$$R_C = R_F \qquad (12)$$

R_F may be made larger than 2MΩ if desired. The 10pF capacitors are used to compensate for the input capacitance of A_1 and to insure frequency stability.

Output Stage:

The output stage is the same as shown in equations (5), (6), and (7).

Illustrative Calculations:

The maximum input voltage is 100mV. It is desired to amplify the input signal for maximum accuracy. Non-inverting output is desired.

Input Stage:

Step 1

G_1 max = 5V/Max Input Signal = 5V/0.1V = 50V/V

With the above gain of 50V/V, if the input ever exceeds 100mV, it would drive the output to saturation. Therefore, it is good practice to allow reasonable input overrange.

So, to allow for 25% input overrange without saturation at the output, select;

$$G_1 = 40V/V$$
$$G_1 = 1 + (R_F + R_A) = 40$$
$$\therefore R_F/R_A = 39 \qquad (13)$$

Step 2

$R_A + R_F$ forms a voltage divider with the 100kΩ output resistance of the demodulator. To limit the voltage divider loading effect to no more than 5%, $R_A + R_F$ should be chosen to be at least 2MΩ. For most applications, the 2MΩ should be sufficiently large for $R_A + R_F$. Resistances greater than 2MΩ may help decrease the loading effect, but would increase the offset voltage drift.

The voltage divider with $R_A + R_F = 2MΩ$ is 2MΩ/(2MΩ + 100kΩ) = 2/(2 + 0.1) = 95.2%, i.e., the percent loading is 4.8%.

Choose $R_A + R_F = 2MΩ$ \qquad (14)

Step 3

Solving equations (13) and (14)
$R_A = 50kΩ$ and $R_F = 1.95MΩ$

Step 4

The resistances seen by the + and - input terminals of the input amplifier A_1 should be closely matched in order to minimize offset voltage due to bias currents.

$$\therefore R_C = R_A \parallel (R_F + 100kΩ)$$
$$= 50kΩ \parallel (1.95MΩ + 100kΩ)$$
$$\approx 49kΩ$$

Output Stage:

Step 5

$$V_{OUT} = V_{IN\ MAX} \bullet G_1 \bullet G_2$$

As discussed in Step 1, it is good practice to provide 25% input overrange.

So we will calculate G_2 for 10V output and 125% of the maximum input voltage.

$$\therefore V_{OUT} = (1.25 \times 0.1)(G_1)(G_2)$$
i.e., $10V = 0.125 \times 40 \times G_2$
$$\therefore G_2 = 10V/5V = 2V/V$$

Step 6

$$G_2 = 1 + (R_X/R_K) = 2.0$$
$$\therefore R_X/R_K = 1.0$$
$$\therefore R_X = R_K \qquad (15)$$

Step 7

The resistance seen by the + input terminal of the output stage amplifier A_2 (pin 13) is the output resistance 100kΩ of the output demodulator. The resistance seen by the (-) input terminal of A_2(pin14) should be matched to the resistance seen by the + input terminal.

The resistance seen by pin 14 is the parallel combination of R_X and R_K.

$$\therefore R_X \parallel R_K = 100kΩ$$
i.e., $(R_X \bullet R_K/(R_X + R_K) = 100kΩ$
i.e., $R_K/[1 + (R_K/R_X)] = 100kΩ \qquad (16)$

Step 8

Solving equations (15) and (16) $R_K = 20kΩ$ and $R_X = 200kΩ$.

Step 9

The otuput demodulator must be loaded equal to the input demodulator.

$$\therefore R_B = R_A + R_F = 2MΩ$$
(See equation (14) above in Step 2)

Use the resistor values obtained in Steps 3, 4, 8 and 9, and connect the 3656 as shown in Figure 3.

OFFSET TRIMMING

Figure 5 shows an optional offset voltage trim circuit. It is important that $R_A + R_F = R_B$.

CASE 1: Input and output stages in low gain, use output potentiometer (R_2) only. Input potentiometer (R_1) may be disconnected. For example, unity gain could be obtained by setting $R_A = R_B = 20MΩ$, $R_C = 100kΩ$, $R_F = 0$, $R_X = 100kΩ$, and $R_K = \infty$.

CASE 2: Input stage in high gain and output stage in low gain, use input potentiometer (R_1) only. Output potentiometer (R_2) may be disconnected. For example, $G_T = 100$ could be obtained by setting $R_F = 2MΩ$, $R_B = 2MΩ$ returned to pin 17, $R_A = 20kΩ$, $R_X = 100kΩ$, and $R_K = \infty$.

CASE 3: When it is necessary to perform a two-stage precision trim (to maintain a very small offset change under conditions of changing temperature and changing gain in A_1 and A_2), use step 1 to adjust the input stage and step 2 for the output stage. Carbon composition resistors are acceptable but potentiometers should be stable.

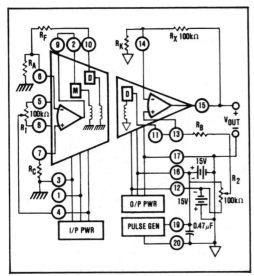

FIGURE 5. Optional Offset Voltage Trim.

Step 1:   Input stage trim ($R_A = R_C = 20k\Omega$, $R_F = R_B = 20M\Omega$, $R_X = 100k\Omega$, $R_K = \infty$, R_2 disconnected); A_1 high, A_2 low gain. Adjust R_1 for 0V ±5mV or desired setting at V_{OUT}, pin 15.

Step 2:   Output stage trim ($R_A = R_B = 20M\Omega$, $R_C = 100k\Omega$, $R_F = 0$, $R_X = 100k\Omega$, $R_K = \infty$, R_1 and R_2 connected); A_1 low, A_2 low gain. Adjust R_2 for 0V ±1mV or desired setting at V_{OUT}, pin 15 (±110mV approximate total range).

Note: Other circuit component values can be used with valid results.

APPLICATIONS

ECG AMPLIFIER

Although the features of the circuit shown in Figure 6 are important in patient monitoring applications, they may also be useful in other applications. The input circuitry uses an external, low quiescent current op amp (OPA21 type) powered by the isolated power of the input stage to form a high impedance instrumentation amplifier input (true three-wire input). R_3 and R_4 give the input stage amplifier of the 3656 a noninverting gain of 10 and an inverting gain of -9. R_1 and R_2 give the external amplifier a noninverting gain of $1 + 1/9$. The inputs are applied to the noninverting inputs of the two amplifiers and the composite input stage amplifier has a gain of 10.

The 330kΩ, 1W, carbon resistors and diodes D_1 - D_4 provide protection for the input amplifiers from defibrillation pulses.

The output stage in Figure 6 is configured to provide a bandpass filter with a gain of 22.7 (68MΩ/3MΩ). The high-pass section (0.05Hz cutoff) is formed by the 1μF capacitor and 2MΩ resistor which are connected in series between the output demodulator and the inverting input of the output stage amplifier. The low-pass section (100Hz cutoff) is formed by the 68MΩ resistor and 22pF capacitor located in the feedback loop of the output stage. The diodes provide for quick recovery of the high-pass filter to overvoltages at the input. The 100kΩ pot and the 100MΩ resistor allow the output voltage to be trimmed to compensate for increased offset voltage caused by unbalanced impedances seen by the inputs of the output stage amplifier.

In many modern electrocardiographic systems, the

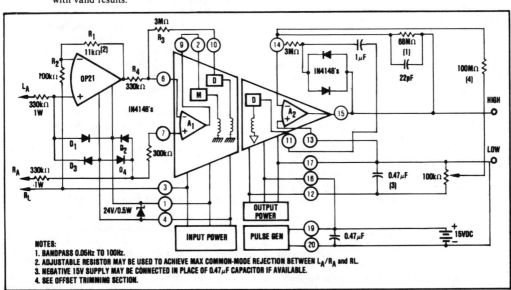

FIGURE 6. ECG Amplifier.

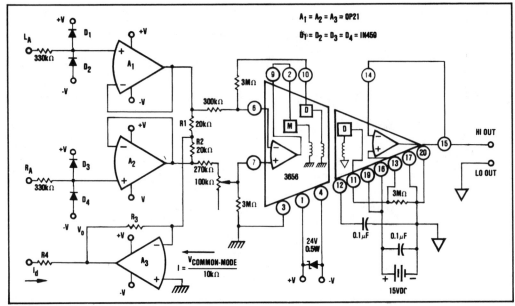

FIGURE 7. Driven Right-Leg ECG Amplifier.

patient is not grounded. Instead, the right-leg electrode is connected to the output of an auxiliary operational amplifier as shown in Figure 7. In this circuit, the common-mode voltage on the body is sensed by the two averaging resistors R_1 and R_2, inverted, amplified, and fed back to the right-leg through resistor R_4. This negative feedback drives the common-mode voltage to a low value. The body's displacement current i_d does not flow to ground, but rather to the output circuit of A_3. This reduces the pickup as far as the ECG amplifier is concerned and effectively grounds the patient.

The value of R_4 should be as large as practical to isolate the patient from ground. The resistors R_3 and R_4 may be selected by these equations:

$$R_3 = (R_1/2)(V_o/V_{CM}) \text{ and } R_4 = (V_{CM} - V_o)/i_d$$

$$(-10V \leqslant V_o \leqslant +10V \text{ and } -10V \leqslant V_{CM} \leqslant +10V)$$

where V_o is the output voltage of A_3 and V_{CM} is the common-mode voltage between the inputs L_A and R_A and the input common at pin 3 of the 3656.

This circuit has the added benefit of having higher common-mode rejection than the circuit in Figure 6 (approximately 10dB improvement).

BIPOLAR CURRENT OUTPUT

The three-port capability of the 3656 can be used to implement a current output isolation amplifier function, usually difficult to implement when grounded loads are involved. The circuit is shown in Figure 8 and the following equations apply:

$$G = I_{OUT}/V_{IN} = 1 + \frac{R_F}{R_A} \times \frac{R_2}{(R_1 + R_2) \cdot R_S}$$

$$I_{OUT} \leqslant \pm 2.5mA$$
$$V_L \leqslant \pm 4V \text{ (compliance)}$$
$$R_L \leqslant 1.6k\Omega$$
$$R_F + R_A = R_1 + R_2 \leqslant 2M\Omega$$

CURRENT OUTPUT - LARGER UNIPOLAR CURRENTS

A more practical version of the current output function is shown in Figure 9. If the circuit is powered from a source greater than 15V as shown, a three-terminal regulator should be used to provide 15V for the pulse generator (pins 19 and 20). The input stage is configured as a unity gain buffer, although other configurations such as current input could be used. The circuit uses the isolation feature between the output stage and the primary power supply to generate the output current configuration that can work into a grounded load. Note that the output transistors can only drive positive current into the load. Bipolar current output would require a second transistor and dual supply.

ISOLATED 4mA TO 20mA OUTPUT

Figure 10 shows the circuit of an expanded version of the isolated current output function. It allows any input voltage range to generate the 4mA to 20mA output excursion and is also capable of zero suppression. The "span" (gain) is adjusted by R_2 and the "zero" (4mA output for minimum input) is set by the 200kΩ pot in the output stage. A three-terminal 5V reference is used to provide a stable 4mA operating point. The reference is

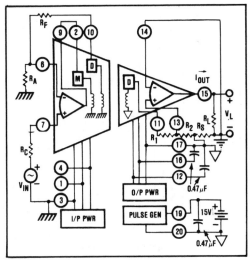

FIGURE 8. Bipolar Current Output.

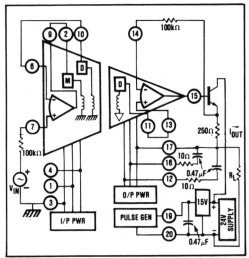

FIGURE 9. Isolated 1 to $5V_{IN}/4$ to 20mA I_{OUT}.

connected to insert an adjustable bias between the demodulator output and the noninverting input of the output stage.

DIFFERENTIAL INPUT

Figure 11 shows the proper connections for differential input configuration. The 3656 is capable of operating in this input configuration only for floating loads (i.e., the source V_{IN} has no connection to the ground reference established at pin 3). For this configuration the usual $2M\Omega$ resistor used in the input stage is split into two halves, R_F and R_{F-}. The demodulator load (seen by pin 10 with respect to pin 3) is still $2M\Omega$ for the floating load as shown. Notice pin 19 is common in Figure 11 whereas pin 20 is common in previous figures.

SERIES STRING SOURCE

Figure 12 shows a situation where a small voltage, which is part of a series string of other voltages, must be

measured. The basic problem is that the small voltage to be measured is 500V above the system ground (i.e., a system common-mode voltage of 500V exists). The circuit converts this system CMV to an amplifier isolation mode voltage. Thus, the isolation voltage ratings and isolation-mode rejection specifications apply.

IMPROVED INPUT CHARACTERISTICS

In situations where it is desired to have better DC input amplifier characteristics than the 3656 normally provides it is possible to add a precision operational amplifier as shown in Figure 13. Here the instrumentation grade Burr-Brown 3510 is supplied from the isolated power of the input stage. The 3656 is configured as a unity-gain buffer. The gain of the 3510 stage must be chosen to limit its full scale output voltage to 5V and avoid overdriving the 3656's demodulators. Since the 3656 draws a

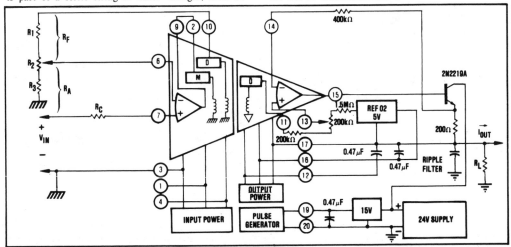

FIGURE 10. Isolated 4mA to 20mA I_{OUT}.

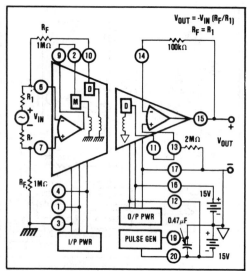

FIGURE 11. Differential Input, Floating Source.

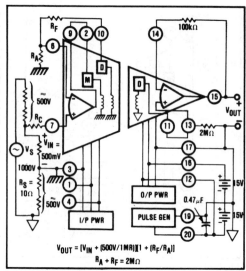

FIGURE 12. Series Source.

significant amount of supply current, extra filtering for the input supply is required as shown (2 x 0.47μF).

ELECTROMAGNETIC RADIATION

The transformer coupling used in the 3656 for isolation makes the 3656 a source of electromagnetic radiation unless it is properly shielded. Physical separation

between the 3656 and sensitive components may not give sufficient attenuation by itself. In these applications the use of an electromagnetic shield is a must. A shield, Burr-Brown 100MS, is specially designed for use with the 3656 package. Note that the offset voltage appearing at pin 15 may change by 4mV to 12mV with use of the shield; however, this can be trimmed (see Offset Trimming section).

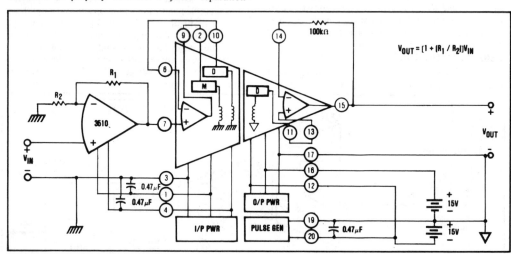

FIGURE 13. Isolator for Low-Level Signals.

Two-Terminal IC
Temperature Transducer
AD590*

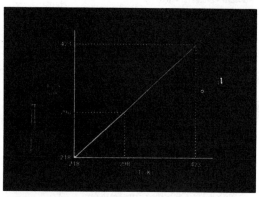

FEATURES
Linear Current Output: 1μA/K
Wide Range: –55°C to +150°C
Probe Compatible Ceramic Sensor Package
Two-Terminal Device: Voltage In/Current Out
Laser Trimmed to ±0.5°C Calibration Accuracy (AD590M)
Excellent Linearity: ±0.3°C Over Full Range (AD590M)
Wide Power Supply Range: +4V to +30V
Sensor Isolation from Case
Low Cost

PRODUCT DESCRIPTION

The AD590 is a two-terminal integrated circuit temperature transducer which produces an output current proportional to absolute temperature. For supply voltages between +4V and +30V the device acts as a high impedance, constant current regulator passing 1μA/K. Laser trimming of the chip's thin film resistors is used to calibrate the device to 298.2μA output at 298.2K (+25°C).

The AD590 should be used in any temperature sensing application below +150°C in which conventional electrical temperature sensors are currently employed. The inherent low cost of a monolithic integrated circuit combined with the elimination of support circuitry makes the AD590 an attractive alternative for many temperature measurement situations. Linearization circuitry, precision voltage amplifiers, resistance measuring circuitry and cold junction compensation are not needed in applying the AD590.

In addition to temperature measurement, applications include temperature compensation or correction of discrete components, biasing proportional to absolute temperature, flow rate measurement, level detection of fluids and anemometry. The AD590 is available in chip form making it suitable for hybrid circuits and fast temperature measurements in protected environments.

The AD590 is particularly useful in remote sensing applications. The device is insensitive to voltage drops over long lines due to its high impedance current output. Any well-insulated twisted pair is sufficient for operation hundreds of feet from the receiving circuitry. The output characteristics also make the AD590 easy to multiplex: the current can be switched by a CMOS multiplexer or the supply voltage can be switched by a logic gate output.

*Covered by Patent No. 4,123,698

PRODUCT HIGHLIGHTS

1. The AD590 is a calibrated two terminal temperature sensor requiring only a dc voltage supply (+4V to +30V). Costly transmitters, filters, lead wire compensation and linearization circuits are all unnecessary in applying the device.

2. State-of-the-art laser trimming at the wafer level in conjunction with extensive final testing insures that AD590 units are easily interchangeable.

3. Superior interference rejection results from the output being a current rather than a voltage. In addition, power requirements are low (1.5mW's @ 5V @ +25°C). These features make the AD590 easy to apply as a remote sensor.

4. The high output impedance (>10MΩ) provides excellent rejection of supply voltage drift and ripple. For instance, changing the power supply from 5V to 10V results in only a 1μA maximum current change, or 1°C equivalent error.

5. The AD590 is electrically durable: it will withstand a forward voltage up to 44V and a reverse voltage of 20V. Hence, supply irregularities or pin reversal will not damage the device.

One Technology Way; P. O. Box 9106; Norwood, MA 02062-9106 U.S.A.
Tel: 617/329-4700   Twx: 710/394-6577
Telex: 924491   Cables: ANALOG NORWOODMASS

SPECIFICATIONS (@ +25°C and V$_S$=5V unless otherwise noted)

Model	AD590J Min	AD590J Typ	AD590J Max	AD590K Min	AD590K Typ	AD590K Max	Units
ABSOLUTE MAXIMUM RATINGS							
Forward Voltage (E+ to E−)			+44			+44	Volts
Reverse Voltage (E+ to E−)			−20			−20	Volts
Breakdown Voltage (Case to E+ or E−)			±200			±200	Volts
Rated Performance Temperature Range	−55		+150	−55		+150	°C
Storage Temperature Range	−65		+155	−65		+155	°C
Lead Temperature (Soldering, 10 sec)			+300			+300	°C
POWER SUPPLY							
Operating Voltage Range	+4		+30	+4		+30	Volts
OUTPUT							
Nominal Current Output @ +25°C (298.2K)		298.2			298.2		μA
Nominal Temperature Coefficient		1			1		μA/K
Calibration Error @ +25°C			±5.0			±2.5	°C
Absolute Error (over rated performance temperature range)							
Without External Calibration Adjustment			±10			±5.5	°C
With +25°C Calibration Error Set to Zero			±3.0			±2.0	°C
Nonlinearity			±1.5			±0.8	°C
Repeatability[1]			±0.1			±0.1	°C
Long Term Drift[2]			±0.1			±0.1	°C
Current Noise		40			40		pA/√Hz
Power Supply Rejection							
+4V≤V$_S$≤+5V		0.5			0.5		μA/V
+5V≤V$_S$≤+15V		0.2			0.2		μA/V
+15V≤V$_S$≤+30V		0.1			0.1		μA/V
Case Isolation to Either Lead		10^{10}			10^{10}		Ω
Effective Shunt Capacitance		100			100		pF
Electrical Turn-On Time		20			20		μs
Reverse Bias Leakage Current[3] (Reverse Voltage = 10V)		10			10		pA

NOTES
[1]Maximum deviation between +25°C readings after temperature cycling between −55°C and +150°C; guaranteed not tested.
[2]Conditions: constant +5V, constant +125°C; guaranteed, not tested.
[3]Leakage current doubles every 10°C.
Specifications subject to change without notice.

Specifications shown in boldface are tested on all production units at final electrical test. Results from those tests are used to calculate outgoing quality levels. All min and max specifications are guaranteed, although only those shown in boldface are tested on all production units.

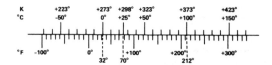

TEMPERATURE SCALE CONVERSION EQUATIONS

$$°C = \frac{5}{9}(°F - 32) \qquad K = °C + 273.15$$

$$°F = \frac{9}{5}°C + 32 \qquad °R = °F + 459.7$$

Model	AD590L			AD590M			
	Min	Typ	Max	Min	Typ	Max	Units
ABSOLUTE MAXIMUM RATINGS							
Forward Voltage (E + to E −)			+44			+44	Volts
Reverse Voltage (E + to E −)			−20			−20	Volts
Breakdown Voltage (Case to E + or E −)			±200			±200	Volts
Rated Performance Temperature Range	−55		+150	−55		+150	°C
Storage Temperature Range	−65		+155	−65		+155	°C
Lead Temperature (Soldering, 10 sec)			+300			+300	°C
POWER SUPPLY							
Operating Voltage Range	+4		+30	+4		+30	Volts
OUTPUT							
Nominal Current Output @ +25°C (298.2K)		298.2			298.2		μA
Nominal Temperature Coefficient		1			1		μA/K
Calibration Error @ +25°C			±1.0			±0.5	°C
Absolute Error (over rated performance temperature range)							
Without External Calibration Adjustment			±3.0			±1.7	°C
With +25°C Calibration Error Set to Zero			±1.6			±1.0	°C
Nonlinearity			±0.4			±0.3	°C
Repeatability[1]			±0.1			±0.1	°C
Long Term Drift[2]			±0.1			±0.1	°C
Current Noise		40			40		pA$\sqrt{Hz}$
Power Supply Rejection							
+4V≤V_S≤ +5V		0.5			0.5		μA/V
+5V≤V_S≤ +15V		0.2			0.2		μA/V
+15V≤V_S≤ +30V		0.1			0.1		μA/V
Case Isolation to Either Lead		10^{10}			10^{10}		Ω
Effective Shunt Capacitance		100			100		pF
Electrical Turn-On Time		20			20		μs
Reverse Bias Leakage Current[3] (Reverse Voltage = 10V)		10			10		pA

OUTLINE DIMENSIONS
AND PIN DESIGNATIONS
Dimensions shown in inches and (mm).
TO-52 PACKAGE: DESIGNATION "H"

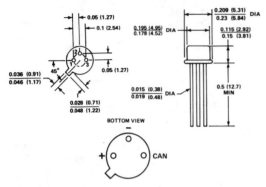

BOTTOM VIEW

+ ○   ○ ○ CAN

The 590H has 60μ inches of gold plating on its Kovar leads and Kovar header. A resistance welder is used to seal the nickel cap to the header. The AD590 chip is eutectically mounted to the header and ultrasonically bonded to with 1 MIL aluminum wire. Kovar composition: 53% iron nominal; 29% ±1% nickel; 17% ±1% cobalt; 0.65% manganese max; 0.20% silicon max; 0.10% aluminum max; 0.10% magnesium max; 0.10% zirconium max; 0.10% titanium max; 0.06% carbon max.

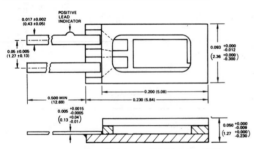

FLAT-PACK PACKAGE: DESIGNATION "F"

The 590F is a ceramic package with gold plating on its Kovar leads, Kovar lid, and chip cavity. Solder of 80/20 Au/Sn composition is used for the 1.5 mil thick solder ring under the lid. The chip cavity has a nickel underlay between the metalization and the gold plating. The AD590 chip is eutectically mounted in the chip cavity at 410°C and ultrasonically bonded to with 1 mil aluminum wire. Note that the chip is in direct contact with the ceramic base, not the metal lid.

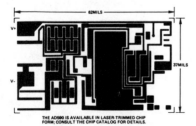

THE AD590 IS AVAILABLE IN LASER-TRIMMED CHIP FORM; CONSULT THE CHIP CATALOG FOR DETAILS.

Metalization Diagram

CIRCUIT DESCRIPTION[1]
The AD590 uses a fundamental property of the silicon transistors from which it is made to realize its temperature proportional characteristic: if two identical transistors are operated at a constant ratio of collector current densities, r, then the difference in their base-emitter voltages will be $(kT/q)(\ln r)$. Since both k, Boltzman's constant and q, the charge of an electron, are constant, the resulting voltage is directly proportional to absolute temperature (PTAT).

In the AD590, this PTAT voltage is converted to a PTAT current by low temperature coefficient thin film resistors. The total current of the device is then forced to be a multiple of this PTAT current. Referring to Figure 1, the schematic diagram of the AD590, Q8 and Q11 are the transistors that produce the PTAT voltage. R5 and R6 convert the voltage to current. Q10, whose collector current tracks the collector currents in Q9 and Q11, supplies all the bias and substrate leakage current for the rest of the circuit, forcing the total current to be PTAT. R5 and R6 are laser trimmed on the wafer to calibrate the device at +25°C.

Figure 2 shows the typical V–I characteristic of the circuit at +25°C and the temperature extremes.

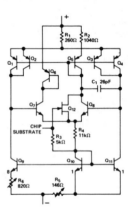

Figure 1. Schematic Diagram

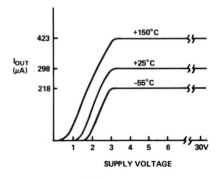

SUPPLY VOLTAGE

Figure 2. V–I Plot

[1] For a more detailed circuit description see M.P. Timko, "A Two-Terminal IC Temperature Transducer," IEEE J. Solid State Circuits, Vol. SC-11, p. 784-788, Dec. 1976.

Understanding the AD590 Specifications

EXPLANATION OF TEMPERATURE SENSOR SPECIFICATIONS

The way in which the AD590 is specified makes it easy to apply in a wide variety of different applications. It is important to understand the meaning of the various specifications and the effects of supply voltage and thermal environment on accuracy.

The AD590 is basically a PTAT (proportional to absolute temperature)[1] current regulator. That is, the output current is equal to a scale factor times the temperature of the sensor in degrees Kelvin. This scale factor is trimmed to $1\mu A/K$ at the factory, by adjusting the indicated temperature (i.e. the output current) to agree with the actual temperature. This is done with 5V across the device at a temperature within a few degrees of $25°C$ (298.2K). The device is then packaged and tested for accuracy over temperature.

CALIBRATION ERROR

At final factory test the difference between the indicated temperature and the actual temperature is called the calibration error. Since this is a scale factor error, its contribution to the total error of the device is PTAT. For example, the effect of the $1°C$ specified maximum error of the AD590L varies from $0.73°C$ at $-55°C$ to $1.42°C$ at $150°C$. Figure 3 shows how an exaggerated calibration error would vary from the ideal over temperature.

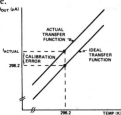

Figure 3. Calibration Error vs. Temperature

The calibration error is a primary contributor to maximum total error in all AD590 grades. However, since it is a scale factor error, it is particularly easy to trim. Figure 4 shows the most elementary way of accomplishing this. To trim this circuit the temperature of the AD590 is measured by a reference temperature sensor and R is trimmed so that $V_T = 1mV/K$ at that temperature. Note that when this error is trimmed out at one temperature, its effect is zero over the entire temperature range. In most applications there is a current to voltage conversion resistor (or, as with a current input ADC, a reference) that can be trimmed for scale factor adjustment.

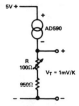

Figure 4. One Temperature Trim

[1] $T(°C) = T(K) -273.2$; Zero on the Kelvin scale is "absolute zero"; there is no lower temperature.

ERROR VERSUS TEMPERATURE: WITH CALIBRATION ERROR TRIMMED OUT

Each AD590 is also tested for error over the temperature range with the calibration error trimmed out. This specification could also be called the "variance from PTAT" since it is the maximum difference between the actual current over temperature and a PTAT multiplication of the actual current at $25°C$. This error consists of a slope error and some curvature, mostly at the temperature extremes. Figure 5 shows a typical AD590K temperature curve before and after calibration error trimming.

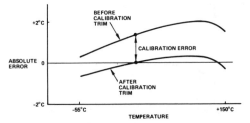

Figure 5. Effect of Scale Factor Trim on Accuracy

ERROR VERSUS TEMPERATURE: NO USER TRIMS

Using the AD590 by simply measuring the current, the total error is the "variance from PTAT" described above plus the effect of the calibration error over temperature. For example the AD590L maximum total error varies from $2.33°C$ at $-55°C$ to $3.02°C$ at $150°C$. For simplicity, only the larger figure is shown on the specification page.

NONLINEARITY

Nonlinearity as it applies to the AD590 is the maximum deviation of current over temperature from a best-fit straight line. The nonlinearity of the AD590 over the $-55°C$ to $+150°C$ range is superior to all conventional electrical temperature sensors such as thermocouples, RTD's and thermistors. Figure 6 shows the nonlinearity of the typical AD590K from Figure 5.

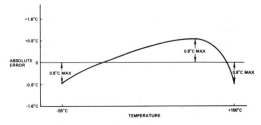

Figure 6. Nonlinearity

Figure 7A shows a circuit in which the nonlinearity is the major contributor to error over temperature. The circuit is trimmed by adjusting R_1 for a 0V output with the AD590 at $0°C$. R_2 is then adjusted for 10V out with the sensor at $100°C$. Other pairs of temperatures may be used with this procedure as long as they are measured accurately by a reference sensor. Note that for +15V output ($150°C$) the V+ of the op amp must be greater than 17V. Also note that V− should be at least −4V: if V− is ground there is no voltage applied across the device.

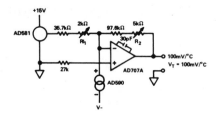

Figure 7A. Two Temperature Trim

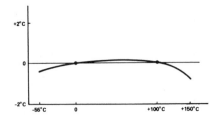

Figure 7B. Typical Two-Trim Accuracy

VOLTAGE AND THERMAL ENVIRONMENT EFFECTS

The power supply rejection specifications show the maximum expected change in output current versus input voltage changes. The insensitivity of the output to input voltage allows the use of unregulated supplies. It also means that hundreds of ohms of resistance (such as a CMOS multiplexer) can be tolerated in series with the device.

It is important to note that using a supply voltage other than 5V does not change the PTAT nature of the AD590. In other words, this change is equivalent to a calibration error and can be removed by the scale factor trim (see previous page).

The AD590 specifications are guaranteed for use in a low thermal resistance environment with 5V across the sensor. Large changes in the thermal resistance of the sensor's environment will change the amount of self-heating and result in changes in the output which are predictable but not necessarily desirable.

The thermal environment in which the AD590 is used determines two important characteristics: the effect of self heating and the response of the sensor with time.

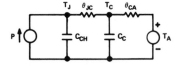

Figure 8. Thermal Circuit Model

Figure 8 is a model of the AD590 which demonstrates these characteristics. As an example, for the TO-52 package, θ_{JC} is the thermal resistance between the chip and the case, about

26°C/watt. θ_{CA} is the thermal resistance between the case and its surroundings and is determined by the characteristics of the thermal connection. Power source P represents the power dissipated on the chip. The rise of the junction temperature, T_J, above the ambient temperature T_A is:

$$T_J - T_A = P\,(\theta_{JC} + \theta_{CA}).\qquad\text{Eq. 1}$$

Table I gives the sum of θ_{JC} and θ_{CA} for several common thermal media for both the "H" and "F" packages. The heatsink used was a common clip-on. Using Equation 1, the temperature rise of an AD590 "H" package in a stirred bath at +25°C, when driven with a 5V supply, will be 0.06°C. However, for the same conditions in still air the temperature rise is 0.72°C. For a given supply voltage, the temperature rise varies with the current and is PTAT. Therefore, if an application circuit is trimmed with the sensor in the same thermal environment in which it will be used, the scale factor trim compensates for this effect over the entire temperature range.

MEDIUM	$\theta_{JC} + \theta_{CA}(^\circ$C/watt$)$		τ (sec)(Note 3)	
	H	F	H	F
Aluminum Block	30	10	0.6	0.1
Stirred Oil[1]	42	60	1.4	0.6
Moving Air[2]				
With Heat Sink	45	–	5.0	–
Without Heat Sink	115	190	13.5	10.0
Still Air				
With Heat Sink	191	–	108	–
Without Heat Sink	480	650	60	30

[1] Note: τ is dependent upon velocity of oil; average of several velocities listed above.
[2] Air velocity $\cong$ 9ft/sec.
[3] The time constant is defined as the time required to reach 63.2% of an instantaneous temperature change.

Table I. Thermal Resistances

The time response of the AD590 to a step change in temperature is determined by the thermal resistances and the thermal capacities of the chip, C_{CH}, and the case, C_C. C_{CH} is about 0.04 watt-sec/$^\circ$C for the AD590. C_C varies with the measured medium since it includes anything that is in direct thermal contact with the case. In most cases, the single time constant exponential curve of Figure 9 is sufficient to describe the time response, T(t). Table I shows the effective time constant, τ, for several media.

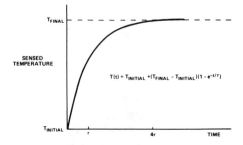

Figure 9. Time Response Curve

Applying the AD590

GENERAL APPLICATIONS

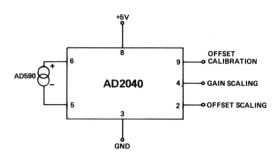

Figure 10. Variable Scale Display

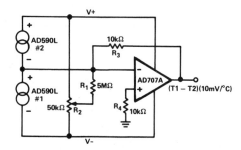

Figure 12. Differential Measurements

Figure 10 demonstrates the use of a low-cost Digital Panel Meter for the display of temperature on either the Kelvin, Celsius or Fahrenheit scales. For Kelvin temperature Pins 9, 4 and 2 are grounded; and for Fahrenheit temperature Pins 4 and 2 are left open.

The above configuration yields a 3 digit display with $1°C$ or $1°F$ resolution, in addition to an absolute accuracy of $±2.0°C$ over the $-55°C$ to $+125°C$ temperature range if a one-temperature calibration is performed on an AD590K, L, or M.

a desired temperature difference. For example, the inherent offset between the two devices can be trimmed in. If V+ and V– are radically different, then the difference in internal dissipation will cause a differential internal temperature rise. This effect can be used to measure the ambient thermal resistance seen by the sensors in applications such as fluid level detectors or anemometry.

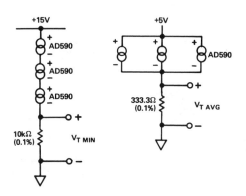

Figure 11. Series & Parallel Connection

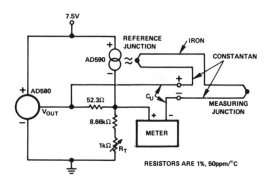

Figure 13. Cold Junction Compensation Circuit for Type J Thermocouple

Connecting several AD590 units in series as shown in Figure 11 allows the minimum of all the sensed temperatures to be indicated. In contrast, using the sensors in parallel yields the average of the sensed temperatures.

The circuit of Figure 12 demonstrates one method by which differential temperature measurements can be made. R_1 and R_2 can be used to trim the output of the op amp to indicate

Figure 13 is an example of a cold junction compensation circuit for a Type J Thermocouple using the AD590 to monitor the reference junction temperature. This circuit replaces an ice-bath as the thermocouple reference for ambient temperatures between $+15°C$ and $+35°C$. The circuit is calibrated by adjusting R_T for a proper meter reading with the measuring junction at a known reference temperature and the circuit near $+25°C$. Using components with the T.C.'s as specified in Figure 13, compensation accuracy will be within $±0.5°C$ for circuit temperatures between $+15°C$ and $+35°C$. Other thermocouple types can be accommodated with different resistor values. Note that the T.C.'s of the voltage reference and the resistors are the primary contributors to error.

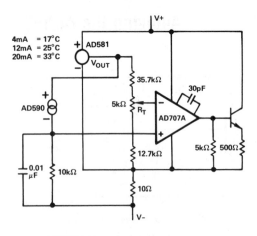

Figure 14. 4 to 20mA Current Transmitter

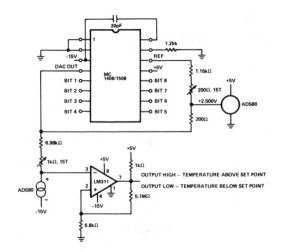

Figure 16. DAC Set Point

Figure 14 is an example of a current transmitter designed to be used with 40V, 1kΩ systems; it uses its full current range of 4mA to 20mA for a narrow span of measured temperatures. In this example the 1μA/K output of the AD590 is amplified to 1mA/°C and offset so that 4mA is equivalent to 17°C and 20mA is equivalent to 33°C. R_T is trimmed for proper reading at an intermediate reference temperature. With a suitable choice of resistors, any temperature range within the operating limits of the AD590 may be chosen.

particular circuit operates from 0 (all inputs high) to +51°C (all inputs low) in 0.2°C steps. The comparator is shown with 1°C hysteresis which is usually necessary to guard-band for extraneous noise; omitting the 5.1MΩ resistor results in no hysteresis.

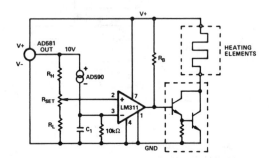

Figure 15. Simple Temperature Control Circuit

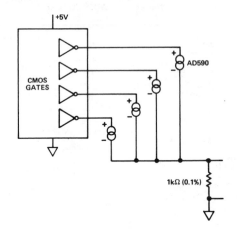

Figure 17. AD590 Driven from CMOS Logic

Figure 15 is an example of a variable temperature control circuit (thermostat) using the AD590. R_H and R_L are selected to set the high and low limits for R_{SET}. R_{SET} could be a simple pot, a calibrated multi-turn pot or a switched resistive divider. Powering the AD590 from the 10V reference isolates the AD590 from supply variations while maintaining a reasonable voltage (~7V) across it. Capacitor C_1 is often needed to filter extraneous noise from remote sensors. R_B is determined by the β of the power transistor and the current requirements of the load.

Figure 16 shows how the AD590 can be configured with an 8-bit DAC to produce a digitally controlled set point. This

The voltage compliance and the reverse blocking characteristic of the AD590 allows it to be powered directly from +5V CMOS logic. This permits easy multiplexing, switching or pulsing for minimum internal heat dissipation. In Figure 17 any AD590 connected to a logic high will pass a signal current through the current measuring circuitry while those connected to a logic zero will pass insignificant current. The outputs used to drive the AD590's may be employed for other purposes, but the additional capacitance due to the AD590 should be taken into account.

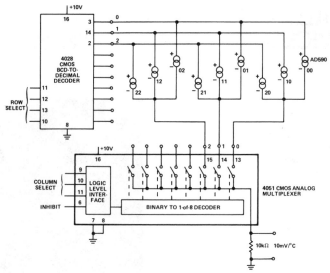

Figure 18. Matrix Multiplexer

CMOS Analog Multiplexers can also be used to switch AD590
current. Due to the AD590's current mode, the resistance of
such switches is unimportant as long as 4V is maintained
across the transducer. Figure 18 shows a circuit which combines
the principal demonstrated in Figure 17 with an 8 channel
CMOS Multiplexer. The resulting circuit can select one of
eighty sensors over only 18 wires with a 7 bit binary word. The
inhibit input on the multiplexer turns all sensors off for minimum dissipation while idling.

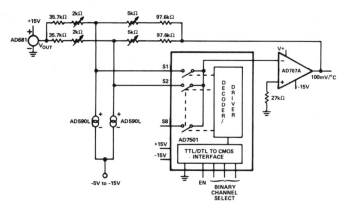

Figure 19. 8-Channel Multiplexer

Figure 19 demonstrates a method of multiplexing the AD590
in the two-trim mode (Figure 7). Additional AD590's and their
associated resistors can be added to multiplex up to 8 channels
of ±0.5°C absolute accuracy over the temperature range of
-55°C to +125°C. The high temperature restriction of +125°C
is due to the output range of the op amps; output to +150°C
can be achieved by using a +20V supply for the op amp.

ANALOG
DEVICES

Low Cost
Sample/Hold Amplifier
AD582

FEATURES
Suitable for 12-Bit Applications
High Sample/Hold Current Ratio: 10^7
Low Acquisition Time: $6\mu s$ to 0.1%
Low Charge Transfer: $<2pC$
High Input Impedance in Sample and Hold Modes
Connect in Any Op Amp Configuration
Differential Logic Inputs

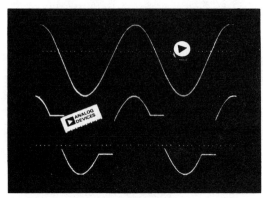

PRODUCT DESCRIPTION

The AD582 is a low cost integrated circuit sample and hold amplifier consisting of a high performance operational amplifier, a low leakage analog switch and a JFET integrating amplifier – all fabricated on a single monolithic chip. An external holding capacitor, connected to the device, completes the sample and hold function.

With the analog switch closed, the AD582 functions like a standard op amp; any feedback network may be connected around the device to control gain and frequency response. With the switch open, the capacitor holds the output at its last level, regardless of input voltage.

Typical applications for the AD582 include sampled data systems, D/A deglitchers, analog de-multiplexers, auto null systems, strobed measurement systems and A/D speed enhancement.

The device is available in two versions: the "K" specified for operation over the 0 to +70°C commercial temperature range and the "S" specified over the extended temperature range, –55°C to +125°C. All versions may be obtained in either the hermetic sealed, TO-100 can or the TO-116 DIP.

PRODUCT HIGHLIGHTS

1. The specially designed input stage presents a high impedance to the signal source in both sample and hold modes (up to ±12V). Even with signal levels up to ±V_S, no undesirable signal inversion, peaking or loss of hold voltage occurs.

2. The AD582 may be connected in any standard op amp configuration to control gain or frequency response and provide signal inversion, etc.

3. The AD582 offers a high, sample-to-hold current ratio: 10^7 The ratio of the available charging current to the holding leakage current is often used as a figure of merit for a sample and hold circuit.

4. The AD582 has a typical charge transfer less than 2pC. A low charge transfer produces less offset error and permits the use of smaller hold capacitors for faster signal acquisition.

5. The AD582 provides separate analog and digital grounds, thus improving the device's immunity to ground and switching transients.

One Technology Way; Norwood, MA 02062-9106 U.S.A.
Tel: 617/329-4700   **Twx: 710/394-6577**
Telex: 174059   **Cables: ANALOG NORWOODMASS**

SPECIFICATIONS (typical @ +25°C, V$_S$ = ±15V and C$_H$ = 1000pF, A = +1 unless otherwise specified)

MODEL	AD582K	AD582S
SAMPLE/HOLD CHARACTERISTICS		
Acquisition Time, 10V Step to 0.1%, C$_H$ = 100pF	6µs	•
Acquisition Time, 10V Step to 0.01%, C$_H$ = 1000pF	25µs	•
Aperture Time, 20V p-p Input, Hold 0V	200ns	•
Aperture Jitter, 20V p-p Input, Hold 0V	15ns	•
Settling Time, 20V p-p Input, Hold 0V, to 0.01%	0.5µs	•
Droop Current, Steady State, ±10V$_{OUT}$	100pA max	•
Droop Current, T$_{min}$ to T$_{max}$	1nA	150nA max
Charge Transfer	5pC max (1.5pC typ)	•
Sample to Hold Offset	0.5mV	•
Feedthrough Capacitance 20V p-p, 10kHz Input	0.05pF	
TRANSFER CHARACTERISTICS		
Open Loop Gain V$_{OUT}$ = 20V p-p, R$_L$ = 2k	25k min (50k typ)	•
Common Mode Rejection V$_{CM}$ = 20V p-p	60dB min (70dB typ)	•
Small Signal Gain Bandwidth V$_{OUT}$ = 100mV p-p, C$_H$ = 100pF	1.5MHz	•
Full Power Bandwidth V$_{OUT}$ = 20V p-p, C$_H$ = 100pF	70kHz	•
Slew Rate V$_{OUT}$ = 20V p-p, C$_H$ = 100pF	3V/µs	•
Output Resistance Hold Mode, I$_{OUT}$ = ±5mA	12Ω	•
Linearity V$_{OUT}$ = 20V p-p, R$_L$ = 2k	±0.01%	•
Output Short Circuit Current	±25mA	•
ANALOG INPUT CHARACTERISTICS		
Offset Voltage	6mV max (2mV typ)	•
Offset Voltage, T$_{min}$ to T$_{max}$	4mV	8mV max (5mV typ)
Bias Current	3µA max (1.5µA typ)	•
Offset Current	300nA max (75nA typ)	•
Offset Current, T$_{min}$ to T$_{max}$	100nA	400nA max (100nA typ)
Input Capacitance, f = 1MHz	2pF	•
Input Resistance, Sample or Hold 20V p-p Input, A = +1	30MΩ	•
Absolute Max Diff Input Voltage	30V	•
Absolute Max Input Voltage, Either Input	±V$_S$	•
DIGITAL INPUT CHARACTERISTICS		
+Logic Input Voltage Hold Mode, T$_{min}$ to T$_{max}$, -Logic @ 0V	+2V min	•
Sample Mode, T$_{min}$ to T$_{max}$, -Logic @ 0V	+0.8V max	•
+Logic Input Current Hold Mode, +Logic @ +5V, -Logic @ 0V	1.5µA	•
Sample Mode, +Logic @ 0V, -Logic @ 0V	1nA	•
-Logic Input Current Hold Mode, +Logic @ +5V, -Logic @ 0V	24µA	•
Sample Mode, +Logic @ 0V, -Logic @ 0V	4µA	•
Absolute Max Diff Input Voltage, +L to -L	+15V/-6V	•
Absolute Max Input Voltage, Either Input	±V$_S$	•
POWER SUPPLY CHARACTERISTICS		
Operating Voltage Range	±9V to ±18V	±9V to ±22V
Supply Current, R$_L$ = ∞	4.5mA max (3mA typ)	•
Power Supply Rejection, ΔV$_S$ = 5V, Sample Mode (see next page)	60dB min (75dB typ)	•
TEMPERATURE RANGE		
Specified Performance	0 to +70°C	−55°C to +125°C
Operating	−25°C to +85°C	−55°C to +125°C
Storage	−65°C to +150°C	•
Lead Temperature (Soldering, 15 sec)	+300°C	

NOTES
*Specifications same as AD582K.
Specifications subject to change without notice.

OUTLINE DIMENSIONS
Dimensions shown in inches and (mm).

TO-100 "H"

TO-116 "D"

PIN CONFIGURATIONS
TOP VIEW

10 PIN TO-100

14 PIN DIP
TO-116

Applying the AD582

APPLYING THE AD582

Both the inverting and non-inverting inputs are brought out to allow op amp type versatility in connecting and using the AD582. Figure 1 shows the basic non-inverting unity gain connection requiring only an external hold capacitor and the usual power supply bypass capacitors. An offset null pot can be added for more critical applications.

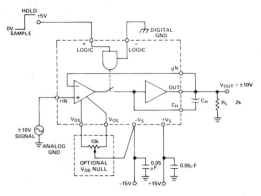

Figure 1. Sample and Hold with A = +1

Figure 2 shows a non-inverting configuration where voltage gain, A_V, is set by a pair of external resistors. Frequency shaping or non-linear networks can also be used for special applications.

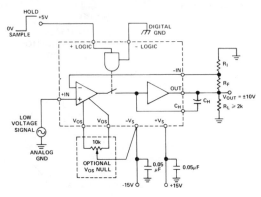

Figure 2. Sample and Hold with A = (1 + R_F/R_I)

The hold capacitor, C_H, should be a high quality polystyrene (for temperatures below +85°C) or Teflon type with low dielectric absorption. For high speed, limited accuracy applications, capacitors as small as 100pF may be used. Larger values are required for accuracies of 12 bits and above in order to minimize feedthrough, sample to hold offset and droop errors (see Figure 6). Care should be taken in the circuit layout to minimize coupling between the hold capacitor and the digital or signal inputs.

In the hold mode, the output voltage will follow any change in the $-V_S$ supply. Consequently, this supply should be well regulated and filtered.

Biasing the +Logic Input anywhere between -6V to +0.8V with respect to the -Logic will set the sample mode. The hold mode will result from any bias between +2.0V and (+V_S - 3V). The sample and hold modes will be controlled differentially with the absolute voltage at either logic input ranging from -V_S to within 3V of +V_S (V_S - 3V). Figure 3 illustrates some examples of the flexibility of this feature.

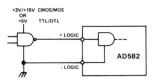

Figure 3A. Standard Logic Connection

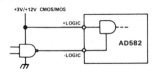

Figure 3B. Inverted Logic Sense Connection

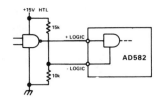

Figure 3C. High Threshold Logic Connection

DEFINITION OF TERMS

Figure 4 illustrates various dynamic characteristics of the AD582.

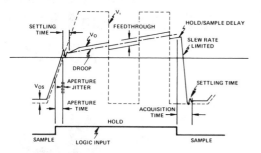

Figure 4. Pictorial Showing Various S/H Characteristics

Aperture Time is the time required after the "hold" command until the switch is fully open and produces a delay in the effective sample timing. Figure 5 is a plot giving the maximum frequency at which the AD582 can sample an input with a given accuracy (lower curve).

Aperture Jitter is the uncertainty in Aperture Time. If the Aperture Time is "tuned out" by advancing the sample-to-hold command 200ns with respect to the input signal, the Aperture Jitter now determines the maximum sampling frequency (upper curve of Figure 5).

Acquisition Time is the time required by the device to reach its final value within a given error band after the sample command has been given. This includes switch delay time, slewing time and settling time for a given output voltage change.

Droop is the change in the output voltage from the "held" value as a result of device leakage. In the AD582, droop can be in either the positive or negative direction. Droop rate may be calculated from droop current using the following formula:

$$\frac{\Delta V}{\Delta T} \text{(Volts/sec)} = \frac{I(pA)}{C_H(pF)}$$

(See also Figure 6.)

Feedthrough is that component of the output which follows the input signal *after* the switch is open. As a percentage of the input, feedthrough is determined as the ratio of the feedthrough capacitance to the hold capacitance (C_F/C_H).

Charge Transfer is the charge transferred to the holding capacitor from the interelectrode capacitance of the switch when the unit is switched to the hold mode. The charge transfer generates a sample-to-hold offset where:

$$\text{S/H Offset (V)} = \frac{\text{Charge (pC)}}{C_H(pF)}$$

(See also Figure 6.)

Sample-to-Hold Offset is that component of D.C. offset independent of C_H (see Figure 6). This offset may be nulled using a null pot, however, the offset will then appear during the sampling mode.

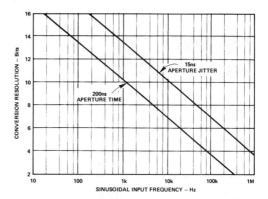

Figure 5. Maximum Frequency of Input Signal for ½LSB Sampling Accuracy

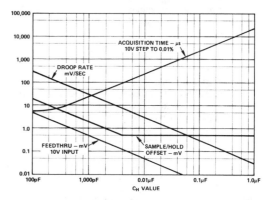

Figure 6. Sample-and-Hold Performance as a Function of Hold Capacitance

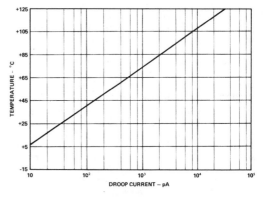

Figure 7. Droop Current vs. Temperature

DACPORT
Low-Cost Complete
μP-Compatible 8-Bit DAC
AD558*

FEATURES
Complete 8-Bit DAC
Voltage Output — 2 Calibrated Ranges
Internal Precision Band-Gap Reference
Single-Supply Operation: +5V to +15V
Full Microprocessor Interface
Fast: 1μs Voltage Settling to ±1/2LSB
Low Power: 75mW
No User Trims
Guaranteed Monotonic Over Temperature
All Errors Specified T_{min} to T_{max}
Small 16-Pin DIP or PLCC Package
Single Laser-Wafer-Trimmed Chip for Hybrids
Low Cost

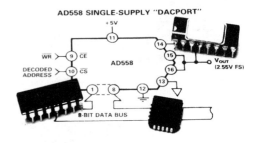

PRODUCT DESCRIPTION
The AD558 DACPORT™ is a complete voltage-output 8-bit digital-to-analog converter, including output amplifier, full microprocessor interface and precision voltage reference on a single monolithic chip. No external components or trims are required to interface, with full accuracy, an 8-bit data bus to an analog system.

The performance and versatility of the DACPORT is a result of several recently-developed monolithic bipolar technologies. The complete microprocessor interface and control logic is implemented with integrated injection logic (I^2L), an extremely dense and low-power logic structure that is process-compatible with linear bipolar fabrication. The internal precision voltage reference is the patented low-voltage band-gap circuit which permits full-accuracy performance on a single +5V to +15V power supply. Thin-film silicon-chromium resistors provide the stability required for guaranteed monotonic operation over the entire operating temperature range (all grades), while recent advances in laser-wafer-trimming of these thin-film resistors permit absolute calibration at the factory to within ±1LSB; thus no user-trims for gain or offset are required. A new circuit design provides voltage settling to ±1/2LSB for a full-scale step in 800ns.

The AD558 is available in four performance grades. The AD558J and K are specified for use over the 0 to +70°C temperature range, while the AD558S and T grades are specified for −55°C to +125°C operation. The "J" and "K" grades are available either in 16-pin plastic (N) or hermetic ceramic (D) DIPS. They are also available in 20-pin JEDEC standard PLCC packages. The "S" and "T" grades are available in 16-pin hermetic ceramic DIP packages.

*Covered by U.S. Patent Nos. 3,887,863; 3,685,045; 4,323,795;
Patents Pending.
DACPORT is a trademark of Analog Devices, Inc.

PRODUCT HIGHLIGHTS
1. The 8-bit I^2L input register and fully microprocessor-compatible control logic allow the AD558 to be directly connected to 8- or 16-bit data buses and operated with standard control signals. The latch may be disabled for direct DAC interfacing.

2. The laser-trimmed on-chip SiCr thin-film resistors are calibrated for absolute accuracy and linearity at the factory. Therefore, no user trims are necessary for full rated accuracy over the operating temperature range.

3. The inclusion of a precision low-voltage band-gap reference eliminates the need to specify and apply a separate reference source.

4. The voltage-switching structure of the AD558 DAC section along with a high-speed output amplifier and laser-trimmed resistors give the user a choice of 0V to +2.56V or 0V to +10V output ranges, selectable by pin-strapping. Circuitry is internally compensated for minimum settling time on both ranges; typically settling to ±1/2LSB for a full-scale 2.55 volt step in 800ns.

5. The AD558 is designed and specified to operate from a single +4.5V to +16.5V power supply.

6. Low digital input currents, 100μA max, minimize bus loading. Input thresholds are TTL/low voltage CMOS compatible over the entire operating V_{CC} range.

One Technology Way; P. O. Box 9106; Norwood, MA 02062-9106 U.S.A.
Tel: 617/329-4700   Twx: 710/394-6577
Telex: 174059   Cables: ANALOG NORWOODMASS

SPECIFICATIONS (@ T_A = +25°C, V_{CC} = +5V to +15V unless otherwise specified)

Model	AD558J Min	Typ	Max	AD558K Min	Typ	Max	AD558S[1] Min	Typ	Max	AD558T[1] Min	Typ	Max	Units
RESOLUTION			8			8			8			8	Bits
RELATIVE ACCURACY[2]													
0 to +70°C		±1/2			±1/4			±1/2			±1/4		LSB
−55°C to +125°C								±3/4			±3/8		LSB
OUTPUT													
Ranges[3]		0 to +2.56			0 to +2.56			0 to +2.56			0 to +2.56		V
		0 to +10			0 to +10			0 to +10			0 to +10		V
Current Source	+5			+5			+5			+5			mA
Sink		Internal Passive Pull-Down to Ground[4]			Internal Passive Pull-Down to Ground			Internal Passive Pull-Down to Ground			Internal Passive Pull-Down to Ground		
OUTPUT SETTLING TIME[5]													
0 to 2.56 Volt Range		0.8	1.5		0.8	1.5		0.8	1.5		0.8	1.5	μs
0 to 10 Volt Range[4]		2.0	3.0		2.0	3.0		2.0	3.0		2.0	3.0	μs
FULL SCALE ACCURACY[6]													
@25°C			±1.5			±0.5			±1.5			±0.5	LSB
T_{min} to T_{max}			±2.5			±1			±2.5			±1	LSB
ZERO ERROR													
@25°C			±1			±1/2			±1			±1/2	LSB
T_{min} to T_{max}			±2			±1			±2			±1	LSB
MONOTONICITY[7]													
T_{min} to T_{max}		Guaranteed			Guaranteed			Guaranteed			Guaranteed		
DIGITAL INPUTS													
T_{min} to T_{max}													
Input Current		±100			±100			±100			100		μA
Data Inputs, Voltage													
Bit On – Logic "1"	2.0			2.0			2.0			2.0			V
Bit On – Logic "0"	0		0.8	0			0			0			V
Control Inputs, Voltage													
On – Logic "1"	2.0			2.0			2.0			2.0			V
On – Logic "0"	0		0.8	0		0.8	0		0.8	0		0.8	V
Input Capacitance		4			4			4			4		pF
TIMING[8]													
t_W Strobe Pulse Width	200			200			200			200			ns
T_{min} to T_{max}	270			270			270			270			ns
t_{DH} Data Hold Time	10			10			10			10			ns
T_{min} to T_{max}	10			10			10			10			ns
t_{DS} Data Set-Up Time	200			200			200			200			ns
T_{min} to T_{max}	270			270			270			270			ns
POWER SUPPLY													
Operating Voltage Range (V_{CC})													
2.56 Volt Range	+4.5		+16.5	+4.5		+16.5	+4.5		+16.5	+4.5		+16.5	V
10 Volt Range	+11.4		+16.5	+11.4		+16.5	+11.4		+16.5	+11.4		+16.5	V
Current (I_{CC})		15	25		15	25		15	25		15	25	mA
Rejection Ratio			0.03			0.03			0.03			0.03	%/%
POWER DISSIPATION, V_{CC} = 5V		75	125		75	125		75	125		75	125	mW
V_{CC} = 15V		225	375		225	375		225	375		225	375	mW
OPERATING TEMPERATURE RANGE	0		+70	0		+70	−55		+125	−55		+125	°C

NOTES
[1] The AD558 S & T grades are available processed and screened to MIL-STD-883 Class B. Consult Analog Devices' Military Databook for details.
[2] Relative Accuracy is defined as the deviation of the code transition points from the ideal transfer point on a straight line from the zero to the full scale of the device.
[3] Operation of the 0 to 10 volt output range requires a minimum supply voltage of +11.4 volts.
[4] Passive pull-down resistance is 2kΩ for 2.56 volt range, 10kΩ for 10 volt range.
[5] Settling time is specified for a positive-going full-scale step to ±1/2LSB. Negative-going steps to zero are slower, but can be improved with an external pull-down.
[6] The full range output voltage for the 2.56 range is 2.55V and is guaranteed with a +5V supply, for the 10V range, it is 9.960V guaranteed with a +15V supply.
[7] A monotonic converter has a maximum differential linearity error of ±1LSB.
[8] See Figure 7.

Specifications subject to change without notice.

AD558 METALIZATION PHOTOGRAPH
Dimensions shown in inches and (mm).

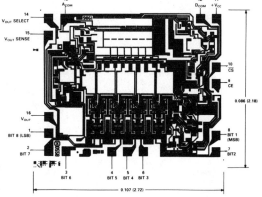

ABSOLUTE MAXIMUM RATINGS

V$_{CC}$ to Ground. . . . . .0V to +18V

Digital Inputs (Pins 1-10) . . . . 0 to +7.0V

V$_{OUT}$ . . . . Indefinite Short to Ground

. . . . Momentary Short to V$_{CC}$

Power Dissipation 450mW

Storage Temperature Range

    N/P (Plastic) Packages . . . . –25°C to +100°C

    D (Ceramic) Package . . . . –55°C to +150°C

Lead Temperature (soldering, 10 second). . . . . 300°C

Thermal Resistance

    Junction to Ambient/Junction to Case

        D (Ceramic) Package . . . . 100/30°C/W

        N/P (Plastic) Packages . . . . 140/55°C/W

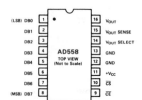

Figure 1a. AD558 Pin Configuration (DIP)

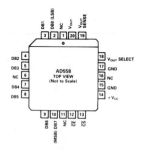

Figure 1b. AD558 Pin Configuration (PLCC)

N (PLASTIC) PACKAGE

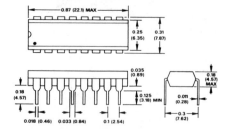

P (PLCC) PACKAGE

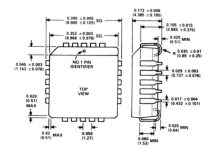

D (CERAMIC) PACKAGE

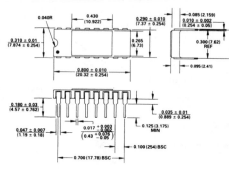

AD558 ORDERING GUIDE

Model	Package	Temperature	Relative Accuracy Error Max T$_{min}$ to T$_{max}$	Full-Scale Error, Max T$_{min}$ to T$_{max}$
AD558JN	Plastic DIP	0 to + 70°C	± 1/2LSB	± 2.5LSB
AD558JP	PLCC	0 to + 70°C	± 1/2LSB	± 2.5LSB
AD558JD	Ceramic DIP	0 to + 70°C	± 1/2LSB	± 2.5LSB
AD558KN	Plastic DIP	0 to + 70°C	± 1/4LSB	± 1LSB
AD558KP	PLCC	0 to + 70°C	± 1/4LSB	± 1LSB
AD558KD	Ceramic DIP	0 to + 70°C	± 1/4LSB	± 1LSB
AD558SD	Ceramic DIP	− 55°C to + 125°C	± 3/4LSB	± 2.5LSB
AD558TD	Ceramic DIP	− 55°C to + 125°C	± 3/8LSB	± 1LSB

(continued from page 1)

7. The single-chip, low power I^{2}L design of the AD558 is inherently more reliable than hybrid multi-chip or conventional single-chip bipolar designs. The AD558S and T grades which are specified over the -55°C to +125°C temperature range, are available processed to MIL-STD-883, Class B.

8. All AD558 grades are available in chip form with guaranteed specifications from +25°C to T_{max}. MIL-STD-883, Class B visual inspection is standard on Analog Devices bipolar chips. Contact the factory for additional chip information.

CIRCUIT DESCRIPTION

The AD558 consists of four major functional blocks, fabricated on a single monolithic chip (see Figure 2). The main D to A converter section uses eight equally-weighted laser-trimmed current sources switched into a silicon-chromium thin-film R/2R resistor ladder network to give a direct but unbuffered 0mV to 400mV output range. The transistors that form the DAC switches are PNPs; this allows direct positive-voltage logic interface and a zero-based output range.

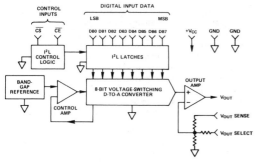

Figure 2. AD558 Functional Block Diagram

The high-speed output buffer amplifier is operated in the non-inverting mode with gain determined by the user-connections at the output range select pin. The gain-setting application resistors are thin-film laser-trimmed to match and track the DAC resistors and to assure precise initial calibration of the two output ranges, 0V to 2.56V and 0V to 10V. The amplifier output stage is an NPN transistor with passive pull-down for zero-based output capability with a single power supply.

The internal precision voltage reference is of the patented band-gap type. This design produces a reference voltage of 1.2 volts and thus, unlike 6.3 volt temperature-compensated zeners, may be operated from a single, low-voltage logic power supply. The microprocessor interface logic consists of an 8-bit data latch and control circuitry. Low-power, small geometry and high-speed are advantages of the I^{2}L design as applied to this section. I^{2}L is bipolar process compatible so that the performance of the analog sections need not be compromised to provide on-chip logic capabilities. The control logic allows the latches to be operated from a decoded microprocessor address and write signal. If the application does not involve a μP or data bus, wiring $\overline{CS}$ and $\overline{CE}$ to ground renders the latches "transparent" for direct DAC access.

MIL-STD-883

The rigors of the military/aerospace environment, temperature extremes, humidity, mechanical stress, etc., demand the utmost in electronic circuits. The AD558, with the inherent reliability of integrated circuit construction, was designed with these applications in mind. The hermetically-sealed, low profile DIP package takes up a fraction of the space required by equivalent modular designs and protects the chip from hazardous environments. To further ensure reliability, military-temperature range AD558 grades S and T are available screened to MIL-STD-883. For more complete data sheet information consult the Analog Devices' Military Databook.

CHIP AVAILABILITY

The AD558 is available in laser-trimmed, passivated chip form. AD558J and AD558T chips are available. Consult the factory for details.

Digital Input Code			Output Voltage	
Binary	Hexadecimal	Decimal	2.56V Range	10.00V Range
0000 0000	00	0	0	0
0000 0001	01	1	0.010V	0.039V
0000 0010	02	2	0.020V	0.078V
0000 1111	0F	15	0.150V	0.586V
0001 0000	10	16	0.160V	0.625V
0111 1111	7F	127	1.270V	4.961V
1000 0000	80	128	1.280V	5.000V
1100 0000	C0	192	1.920V	7.500V
1111 1111	FF	255	2.55V	9.961V

Input Logic Coding

AD558 Applications

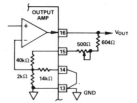

Figure 4. 10.24V Full-Scale Connection

CONNECTING THE AD558

The AD558 has been configured for ease of application. All reference, output amplifier and logic connections are made internally. In addition, all calibration trims are performed at the factory assuring specified accuracy without user trims. The only connection decision that must be made by the user is a single jumper to select output voltage range. Clean circuit-board layout is facilitated by isolating all digital bit inputs on one side of the package; analog outputs are on the opposite side.

Figure 3 shows the two alternative output range connections. The 0V to 2.56V range may be selected for use with any power supply between +4.5V and +16.5V. The 0V to 10V range requires a power supply of +11.4V to +16.5V.

Because of its precise factory calibration, the AD558 is intended to be operated without user trims for gain and offset; therefore no provisions have been made for such user-trims. If a small increase in scale is required, however, it may be accomplished by slightly altering the effective gain of the output buffer. A resistor in series with V_{OUT} SENSE will increase the output range.

For example if a 0V to 10.24V output range is desired (40mV = 1LSB), a nominal resistance of 850Ω is required. It must be remembered that, although the internal resistors all ratio-match and track, the *absolute* tolerance of these resistors is typically ±20% and the *absolute* TC is typically –50ppm/°C (0 to –100ppm/°C). That must be considered when re-scaling is performed. Figure 4 shows the recommended circuitry for a full-scale output range of 10.24 volts. Internal resistance values shown are nominal.

NOTE: Decreasing the scale by putting a resistor in series with GND will not work properly due to the code-dependent currents in GND. Adjusting offset by injecting dc at GND is not recommended for the same reason.

GROUNDING AND BYPASSING*

All precision converter products require careful application of good grounding practices to maintain full rated performance. Because the AD558 is intended for application in microcomputer systems where digital noise is prevalent, special care must be taken to assure that its inherent precision is realized.

The AD558 has two ground (common) pins; this minimizes ground drops and noise in the analog signal path. Figure 5 shows how the ground connections should be made.

It is often advisable to maintain separate analog and digital grounds throughout a complete system, tying them common in one place only. If the common tie-point is remote and accidental disconnection of that one common tie-point occurs due to card removal with power on, a large differential voltage between the two commons could develop. To protect devices that interface to both digital and analog parts of the system, such as the AD558, it is recommended that common ground tie-points should be provided at *each* such device. If only one system ground can be connected directly to the AD558, it is recommended that analog common be selected.

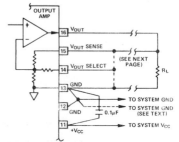

Figure 5. Recommended Grounding and Bypassing

POWER SUPPLY CONSIDERATIONS

The AD558 is designed to operate from a single positive power supply voltage. Specified performance is achieved for any supply voltage between +4.5V and +16.5V. This makes the AD558 ideal for battery-operated, portable, automotive or digital main-frame applications.

The only consideration in selecting a supply voltage is that, in order to be able to use the 0V to 10V output range, the power supply voltage must be between +11.4V and +16.5V. If, however, the 0V to 2.56V range is to be used, power consumption will be minimized by utilizing the lowest available supply voltage (above +4.5V).

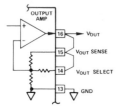

a. 0V to 2.56V Output Range

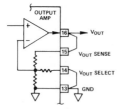

b. 0V to 10V Output Range

Figure 3. Connection Diagrams

*For additional insight, "An IC Amplifier Users' Guide to Decoupling, Grounding and Making Things Go Right For A Change", is available at no charge from any Analog Devices Sales Office.

TIMING AND CONTROL

The AD558 has data input latches that simplify interface to 8- and 16-bit data buses. These latches are controlled by Chip Enable ($\overline{CE}$) and Chip Select ($\overline{CS}$) inputs. $\overline{CE}$ and $\overline{CS}$ are internally "NORed" so that the latches transmit input data to the DAC section when both $\overline{CE}$ and $\overline{CS}$ are at Logic "0". If the application does not involve a data bus, a "00" condition allows for direct operation of the DAC. When either $\overline{CE}$ or $\overline{CS}$ go to Logic "1", the input data is latched into the registers and held until both $\overline{CE}$ and $\overline{CS}$ return to "0". (Unused $\overline{CE}$ or $\overline{CS}$ inputs should be tied to ground.) The truth table is given in Table I. The logic function is also shown in Figure 6.

Input Data	$\overline{CE}$	$\overline{CS}$	DAC Data	Latch Condition
0	0	0	0	"transparent"
1	0	0	1	"transparent"
0	∫	0	0	latching
1	∫	0	1	latching
0	0	∫	0	latching
1	0	∫	1	latching
X	1	X	previous data	latched
X	X	1	previous data	latched

Notes: X = Does not matter
            ∫ = Logic Threshold at Positive-Going Transition

Table I. AD558 Control Logic Truth Table

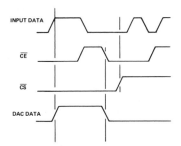

Figure 6. AD558 Control Logic Function

In a level-triggered latch such as that in the AD558 there is an interaction between data setup and hold times and the width of the enable pulse. In an effort to reduce the time required to test all possible combinations in production, the AD558 is tested with $t_{DS} = t_W = 200ns$ at 25°C and 270ns at T_{min} and T_{max}, with $t_{DH} = 10ns$ at all temperatures. Failure to comply with these specifications may result in data not being latched properly.

and 270ns at T_{min} and T_{max}, with $t_{DH}=10ns$ at all temperatures. Failure to comply with these specifications may result in data not being latched properly.

Figure 7 shows the timing for the data and control signals; $\overline{CE}$ and $\overline{CS}$ are identical in timing as well as in function.

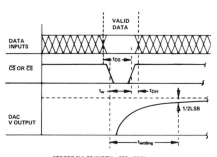

t_W = STROBE PULSE WIDTH = 200ns MIN
t_{DH} = DATA HOLD TIME = 10ns MIN
t_{DS} = DATA SETUP TIME = 200ns MIN
$t_{settling}$ = DAC OUTPUT SETTLING TIME TO ±1/2LSB

Figure 7. AD558 Timing

USE OF V_{OUT} SENSE

Separate access to the feedback resistor of the output amplifier allows additional application versatility. Figure 8a shows how $I \times R$ drops in long lines to remote loads may be cancelled by putting the drops "inside the loop." Figure 8b shows how the separate sense may be used to provide a higher output current by feeding back around a simple current booster.

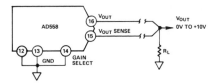

a. Compensation for I x R Drops in Output Lines

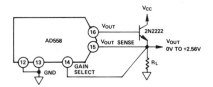

b. Output Current Booster

Figure 8. Use of V_{OUT} Sense

Applying the AD558

OPTIMIZING SETTLING TIME

In order to provide single-supply operation and zero-based output voltage ranges, the AD558 output stage has a passive "pull-down" to ground. As a result, settling time for negative-going output steps may be longer than for positive-going output steps. The relative difference depends on load resistance and capacitance. If a negative power supply is available, the negative-going settling time may be improved by adding a pull-down resistor from the output to the negative supply as shown in Figure 9. The value of the resistor should be such that, at zero voltage out, current through that resistor is 0.5mA max.

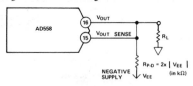

Figure 9. Improved Settling Time

BIPOLAR OUTPUT RANGES

The AD558 was designed for operation from a single power supply and is thus capable of providing only unipolar (0V to +2.56 and 0V to 10V) output ranges. If a negative supply is available, bipolar output ranges may be achieved by suitable output offsetting and scaling. Figure 10 shows how a ±1.28 volt output range may be achieved when a –5 volt power supply is available. The offset is provided by the AD589 precision 1.2 volt reference which will operate from a +5 volt supply. The AD544 output amplifier can provide the necessary ±1.28 volt output swing from ±5 volt supplies. Coding is complementary offset binary.

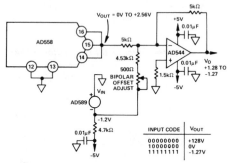

Figure 10. Bipolar Operation of AD558 from ±5V Supplies

INTERFACING THE AD558 TO MICROPROCESSOR DATA BUSES*

The AD558 is configured to act like a "write only" location in memory that may be made to coincide with a read only memory location or with a RAM location. The latter case allows data previously written into the DAC to be read back later via the RAM. Address decoding is partially complete for either ROM or RAM. Figure 11 shows interfaces for three popular microprocessor systems.

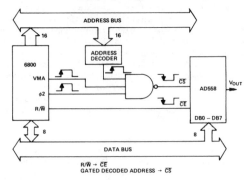

a. 6800/AD558 Interface

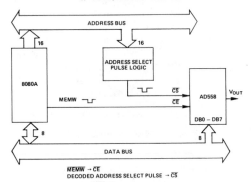

b. 8080A/AD558 Interface

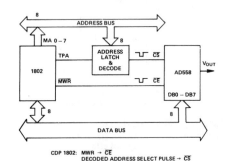

c. 1802/AD558 Interface

Figure 11. Interfacing the AD558 to Microprocessors

*The microprocessor-interface capabilities of the AD558 are extensive. A comprehensive application note, "Interfacing the AD558 DACPORT™ to Microprocessors" is available from any Analog Devices Sales Office upon request, free of charge.

AD558 Performance (typical @ +25°C, V_CC = +5V to +15V unless otherwise noted)

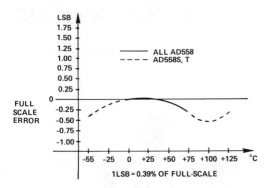

Figure 12. Full-Scale Accuracy vs. Temperature Performance of AD558

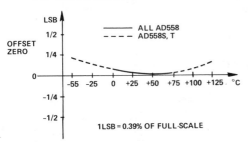

Figure 13. Zero Drift vs. Temperature Performance of AD558

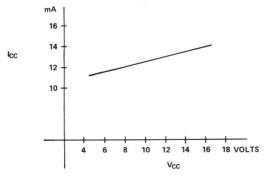

Figure 14. Quiescent Current vs. Power Supply Voltage for AD558

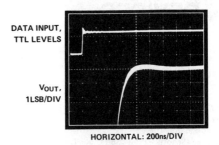

Figure 15. AD558 Settling Characteristic Detail 0V to 2.56V Output Range Full-Scale Step

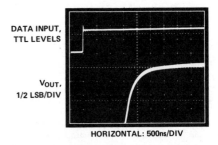

Figure 16. AD558 Settling Characteristic Detail 0V to 10V Output Range Full-Scale Step

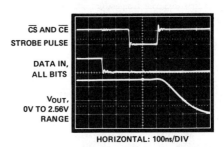

Figure 17. AD558 Logic Timing

**ANALOG
DEVICES**

CMOS 12-Bit
Buffered Multiplying DAC
AD7545

FEATURES
12-Bit Resolution
Low Gain T.C.: 2ppm/°C typ
Fast TTL Compatible Data Latches
Single +5V to +15V Supply
Small 20-Pin 0.3″ DIP
Latch Free (Schottky Protection Diode Not Required)
Low Cost
Ideal for Battery Operated Equipment

GENERAL DESCRIPTION

The AD7545 is a monolithic 12-bit CMOS multiplying DAC with on-board data latches. It is loaded by a single 12-bit wide word and interfaces directly to most 12- and 16-bit bus systems. Data is loaded into the input latches under the control of the $\overline{CS}$ and $\overline{WR}$ inputs; tying these control inputs low makes the input latches transparent allowing direct unbuffered operation of the DAC.

The AD7545 is particularly suitable for single supply operation and applications with wide temperature variations.

The AD7545 can be used with any supply voltage from +5V to +15V. With CMOS logic levels at the inputs the device dissipates less than 0.5mW for V_{DD} = +5V.

AD7545 FUNCTIONAL DIAGRAM

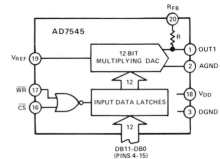

ORDERING INFORMATION

Relative Accuracy	Maximum Gain Error T_A = +25°C V_{DD} = +5V	Temperature Range and Package		
		Plastic 0 to +70°C	Cerdip[1,2] -25°C to +85°C	Ceramic[1] -55°C to +125°C
±2LSB	±20LSB	AD7545JN	AD7545AQ	AD7545SD
±1LSB	±10LSB	AD7545KN	AD7545BQ	AD7545TD
±1/2LSB	±5LSB	AD7545LN	AD7545CQ	AD7545UD
±1/2LSB	±1LSB	AD7545GLN	AD7545GCQ	AD7545GUD

NOTES:
[1]883B version is available. To order add "/883B" to part number shown.
[2]Analog Devices reserves the right to ship ceramic packages in lieu of Cerdip packages.

PIN CONFIGURATION

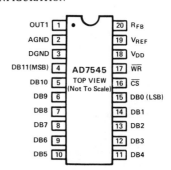

P.O. Box 280; Norwood, Massachusetts 02062 U.S.A.
Tel: 617/329-4700   Twx: 710/394-6577
Telex: 924491   Cables: ANALOG NORWOODMASS

SPECIFICATIONS (V_{REF} = +10V, V_{OUT1} = 0V, AGND = DGND unless otherwise specified)

Parameter	Version	V_{DD} = +5V Limits T_A = +25°C	T_{min}, T_{max}[1]	V_{DD} = +15V Limits T_A = +25°C	T_{min}, T_{max}[1]	Units	Test Conditions/Comments
STATIC PERFORMANCE							
Resolution	All	12	12	12	12	Bits	
Relative Accuracy	J, A, S	±2	±2	±2	±2	LSB max	
	K, B, T	±1	±1	±1	±1	LSB max	
	L, C, U	±1/2	±1/2	±1/2	±1/2	LSB max	
	GL, GC, GU	±1/2	±1/2	±1/2	±1/2	LSB max	
Differential Nonlinearity	J, A, S	±4	±4	±4	±4	LSB max	10-Bit Monotonic T_{min} to T_{max}
	K, B, T	±1	±1	±1	±1	LSB max	12-Bit Monotonic T_{min} to T_{max}
	L, C, U	±1	±1	±1	±1	LSB max	12-Bit Monotonic T_{min} to T_{max}
	GL, GC, GU	±1	±1	±1	±1	LSB max	12-Bit Monotonic T_{min} to T_{max}
Gain Error (Using Internal RFB)[2]	J, A, S	±20	±20	±25	±25	LSB max	DAC Register Loaded with
	K, B, T	±10	±10	±15	±15	LSB max	1111 1111 1111
	L, C, U	±5	±5	±10	±10	LSB max	Gain Error is Adjustable Using
	GL, GC, GU	±1	±2	±6	±7	LSB max	the Circuits of Figures 4, 5 and 6
Gain Temperature Coefficient[3]							
ΔGain/ΔTemperature	All	±5	±5	±10	±10	ppm/°C max	Typical Value is 2ppm/°C for V_{DD} = +5V
DC Supply Rejection[3]							
ΔGain/ΔV_{DD}	All	0.015	0.03	0.01	0.02	% per % max	ΔV_{DD} = ±5%
Output Leakage Current at OUT1	J, K, L, GL	10	50	10	50	nA max	DB0-DB11 = 0V; $\overline{WR}$, $\overline{CS}$ = 0V
	A, B, C, GC	10	50	10	50	nA max	
	S, T, U, GU	10	200	10	200	nA max	
DYNAMIC PERFORMANCE							
Current Settling Time[3]	All	2	2	2	2	µs max	To 1/2LSB. OUT 1 load = 100Ω. DAC output measured from falling edge of $\overline{WR}$. $\overline{CS}$ = 0V.
Propagation Delay[3] (from Digital Input Change to 90% of final Analog Output)	All	300	–	250	–	ns max	OUT1 LOAD = 100Ω C_{EXT} = 13pF[4]
Digital to Analog Glitch Impulse	All	400	–	250	–	nV sec typ	V_{REF} = AGND
AC Feedthrough[5]							
At OUT1	All	5	5	5	5	mV p-p typ	V_{REF} = ±10V, 10kHz Sinewave
REFERENCE INPUT							
Input Resistance	All	7	7	7	7	kΩ min	Input Resistance TC = -300ppm/°C typ
(Pin 19 to GND)		25	25	25	25	kΩ max	Typical Input Resistance = 11kΩ
ANALOG OUTPUTS							
Output Capacitance[3]							
C_{OUT1}	All	70	70	70	70	pF max	DB0-DB11 = 0V, $\overline{WR}$, $\overline{CS}$ = 0V
C_{OUT1}	All	200	200	200	200	pF max	DB0-DB11 = V_{DD}, $\overline{WR}$, $\overline{CS}$ = 0V
DIGITAL INPUTS							
Input High Voltage							
V_{IH}	All	2.4	2.4	13.5	13.5	V min	
Input Low Voltage							
V_{IL}	All	0.8	0.8	1.5	1.5	V max	
Input Current[6]							
I_{IN}	All	±1	±10	±1	±10	µA max	V_{IN} = 0 or V_{DD}
Input Capacitance[3]							
DB0-DB11	All	5	5	5	5	pF max	V_{IN} = 0
$\overline{WR}$, $\overline{CS}$	All	20	20	20	20	pF max	V_{IN} = 0
SWITCHING CHARACTERISTICS							
Chip Select to Write Setup Time	All	280	380	180	200	ns min	See Timing Diagram on next page
t_{CS}		200	270	120	150	ns typ	
Chip Select to Write Hold Time							
t_{CH}	All	0	0	0	0	ns min	
Write Pulse Width							
t_{WR}	All	250	400	160	240	ns min	$t_{CS} \geqslant t_{WR}, t_{CH} \geqslant 0$
		175	280	100	170	ns typ	
Data Setup Time	All	140	210	90	120	ns min	
t_{DS}		100	150	60	80	ns typ	
Data Hold Time							
t_{DH}	All	10	10	10	10	ns min	
POWER SUPPLY							
I_{DD}	All	2	2	2	2	mA max	All Digital Inputs V_{IL} or V_{IH}
		100	500	100	500	µA max	All Digital Inputs 0V or V_{DD}
		10	10	10	10	µA typ	All Digital Inputs 0V or V_{DD}

NOTES
[1] Temperature Ranges as follows: JN, KN, LN, GLN: 0 to +70°C
                              AQ, BQ, CQ, GCQ: -25°C to +85°C
                              ST, TD, UD, GUD: -55°C to +125°C
[2] This includes the effect of 5ppm max gain TC.
[3] Guaranteed but not tested.
[4] DB0-DB11 = 0V to V_{DD} or V_{DD} to 0V.
[5] Feedthrough can be further reduced by connecting the metal lid on the ceramic package (suffix D) to DGND.
[6] Logic inputs are MOS gates. Typical input current (+25°C) is less than 1nA.
[7] Sample tested at +25°C to ensure compliance.
Specifications subject to change without notice.

WRITE CYCLE TIMING DIAGRAM

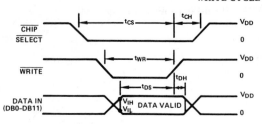

MODE SELECTION

WRITE MODE:
$\overline{CS}$ and $\overline{WR}$ low, DAC responds to data bus (DB0–DB11) inputs.

HOLD MODE:
Either $\overline{CS}$ or $\overline{WR}$ high, data bus (DB0–DB11) is locked out; DAC holds last data present when $\overline{WR}$ or $\overline{CS}$ assumed high state.

NOTES:
V_{DD} = +5V; t_r = t_f = 20ns
V_{DD} = +15V; t_r = t_f = 40ns
All input signal rise and fall times measured from 10% to 90% of V_{DD}.
Timing measurement reference level is V_{IH} + V_{IL}/2.

ABSOLUTE MAXIMUM RATINGS*
(T_A = +25°C unless otherwise noted)

V_{DD} to DGND . . . .–0.3V, +17V
Digital Input Voltage to DGND . . . .–0.3V, V_{DD}
V_{RFB}, V_{REF} to DGND. . . . .±25V
V_{PIN1} to DGND . . . .–0.3V, V_{DD}
AGND to DGND. . . . .–0.3V, V_{DD}
Power Dissipation (Any Package) to 75°C 450mW

Derates above 75°C by . . . . .6mW/°C
Operating Temperature
  Commercial (JN, KN, LN, GLN) Grades . . . . . 0 to +70°C
  Industrial (AQ, BQ, CQ, GCQ) Grades. . . . –25°C to +85°C
  Extended (SD, TD, UD, GUD) Grades. . . . –55°C to +125°C
Storage Temperature . . . . –65°C to +150°C
Lead Temperature (Soldering, 10 Seconds). . . . . +300°C

*Stresses above those listed under "Absolute Maximum Ratings" may cause permanent damage to the device. This is a stress rating only and functional operation at or above this specification is not implied. Exposure to above maximum rating conditions for extended periods may affect device reliability.

CAUTION:
ESD (Electro-Static-Discharge) sensitive device. The digital control inputs are diode protected; however, permanent damage may occur on unconnected devices subject to high energy electrostatic fields. Unused devices must be stored in conductive foam or shunts. The protective foam should be discharged to the destination socket before devices are removed.

TERMINOLOGY

RELATIVE ACCURACY: The amount by which the D/A converter transfer function differs from the ideal transfer function after the zero and full scale points have been adjusted. This is an end point linearity measurement.

DIFFERENTIAL NONLINEARITY: The difference between the measured change and the ideal change between any two adjacent codes. If a device has a differential nonlinearity of less than 1LSB then it will be monotonic, i.e., the output will always increase for an increase in digital code applied to the D/A converter.

PROPAGATION DELAY: This is a measure of the internal delay of the circuit and is measured from the time a digital input changes to the point at which the analog output at OUT1 reached 90% of its final value.

DIGITAL TO ANALOG GLITCH IMPULSE: This is a measure of the amount of charge injected from the digital inputs to the analog outputs when the inputs change state. It is usually specified as the area of the glitch in nVsecs and is measured with V_{REF} = AGND and an ADLH0032CG as the output op amp, C1 (phase compensation) = 33pF.

CIRCUIT INFORMATION – D/A CONVERTER SECTION

Figure 1 shows a simplified circuit of the D/A converter section of the AD7545 and Figure 2 gives an approximate equivalent circuit. Note that the ladder termination resistor is connected to AGND. R is typically $11k\Omega$.

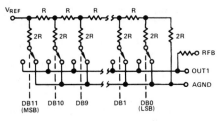

Figure 1. Simplified D/A Circuit of AD7545

The binary weighted currents are switched between the OUT1 bus line and AGND by N-channel switches, thus maintaining a constant current in each ladder leg independent of the switch state.

The capacitance at the OUT1 bus line, C_{OUT1}, is code dependent and varies from 70pF (all switches to AGND) to 200pF (all switches to OUT1).

One of the current switches is shown in Figure 2. The input resistance at V_{REF} (Figure 1) is always equal to R_{LDR} (R_{LDR} is the R/2R ladder characteristic resistance and is equal to value "R"). Since R_{IN} at the V_{REF} pin is constant, the reference terminal can be driven by a reference voltage or a reference current, ac or dc, of positive or negative polarity. (If a current source is used, a low temperature coefficient external R_{FB} is recommended to define scale factor.)

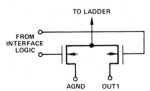

Figure 2. N-Channel Current Steering Switch

CIRCUIT INFORMATION–DIGITAL SECTION

Figure 3 shows the digital structure for one bit.

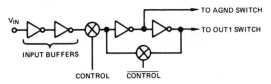

Figure 3. Digital Input Structure

The digital signals CONTROL and $\overline{CONTROL}$ are generated from $\overline{CS}$ and $\overline{WR}$.

The input buffers are simple CMOS inverters designed such that when the AD7545 is operated with $V_{DD} = 5V$, the buffers convert TTL input levels (2.4V and 0.8V) into CMOS logic

levels. When V_{IN} is in the region of 2.0 volts to 3.5 volts the input buffers operate in their linear region and draw current from the power supply. To minimize power supply currents it is recommended that the digital input voltages be as close to the supply rails (V_{DD} and DGND) as is practically possible.

The AD7545 may be operated with any supply voltage in the range $5 \leqslant V_{DD} \leqslant 15$ volts. With $V_{DD} = +15V$ the input logic levels are CMOS compatible only, i.e., 1.5V and 13.5V.

BASIC APPLICATIONS

Figures 4 and 5 show simple unipolar and bipolar circuits using the AD7545. Resistor R1 is used to trim for full scale. The "G" versions (AD7545GLN, AD7545GCQ, AD7545GUD) have a guaranteed maximum gain error of ±1LSB at $+25°C$ ($V_{DD} = +5V$) and in many applications it should be possible to dispense with gain trim resistors altogether. Capacitor C1 provides phase compensation and helps prevent overshoot and ringing when using high speed op amps. Note that all the circuits of Figures 4, 5 and 6 have constant input impedance at the V_{REF} terminal.

The circuit of Figure 4 can either be used as a fixed reference D/A converter so that it provides an analog output voltage in the range 0 to $-V_{IN}$ (note the inversion introduced by the op amp) or V_{IN} can be an ac signal in which case the circuit behaves as an attenuator (2-Quadrant Multiplier). V_{IN} can be any voltage in the range $-20 \leqslant V_{IN} \leqslant +20$ volts (provided the op amp can handle such voltages) since V_{REF} is permitted to exceed V_{DD}. Table II shows the code relationship for the circuit of Figure 4.

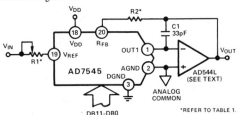

Figure 4. Unipolar Binary Operation

TRIM RESISTOR	JN/AQ/SD	KN/BQ/TD	LN/CQ/UD	GLN/GCQ/GUD
R1	500Ω	200Ω	100Ω	20Ω
R2	150Ω	68Ω	33Ω	6.8Ω

Table I. Recommended Trim Resistor Values vs. Grades for $V_{DD} = +5V$

Binary Number in DAC Register			Analog Output
1111	1111	1111	$-V_{IN} \left\{ \dfrac{4095}{4096} \right\}$
1000	0000	0000	$-V_{IN} \left\{ \dfrac{2048}{4096} \right\} = -1/2\ V_{IN}$
0000	0000	0001	$-V_{IN} \left\{ \dfrac{1}{4096} \right\}$
0000	0000	0000	0 Volts

Table II. Unipolar Binary Code Table for Circuit of Figure 4

Figure 5 and Table III illustrate the recommended circuit and code relationship for bipolar operation. The D/A function itself uses offset binary code and inverter U_1 on the MSB line converts 2's complement input code to offset binary code. If appropriate, inversion of the MSB may be done in software

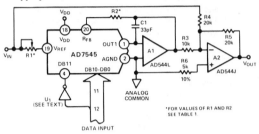

Figure 5. Bipolar Operation (2's Complement Code)

Data Input	Analog Output
0111 1111 1111	$+V_{IN} \cdot \left\{\frac{2047}{2048}\right\}$
0000 0000 0001	$+V_{IN} \cdot \left\{\frac{1}{2048}\right\}$
0000 0000 0000	0 Volts
1111 1111 1111	$-V_{IN} \cdot \left\{\frac{1}{2048}\right\}$
1000 0000 0000	$-V_{IN} \cdot \left\{\frac{2048}{2048}\right\}$

Table III. 2's Complement Code Table for Circuit of Figure 5

using an exclusive –OR instruction and the inverter omitted. R3, R4 and R5 must be selected to match within 0.01% and they should be the same type of resistor (preferably wire-wound or metal foil), so that their temperature coefficients match. Mismatch of R3 value to R4 causes both offset and full scale error. Mismatch of R5 to R4 and R3 causes full scale error.

Figure 6 shows an alternative method of achieving bipolar output. The circuit operates with sign plus magnitude code and has the advantage that it gives 12-bit resolution in each quadrant compared with 11-bit resolution per quadrant for

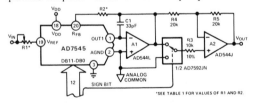

Figure 6. 12-Bit Plus Sign Magnitude D/A Converter

the circuit of Figure 5. The AD7592 is a fully protected CMOS change-over switch with data latches. R4 and R5 should match each other to 0.01% to maintain the accuracy of the D/A converter. Mismatch between R4 and R5 introduces a gain error.

Sign Bit	Binary Numbers in DAC Register			Analog Output
0	1111	1111	1111	$+V_{IN} \cdot \left\{\frac{4095}{4096}\right\}$
0	0000	0000	0000	0 Volts
1	0000	0000	0000	0 Volts
1	1111	1111	1111	$-V_{IN} \cdot \left\{\frac{4095}{4096}\right\}$

Note: Sign bit of "0" connects R3 to GND.

Table IV. 12-Bit Plus Sign Magnitude Code Table for Circuit of Figure 6

APPLICATION HINTS

Output Offset: CMOS D/A converters exhibit a code dependent output resistance which in turn causes a code dependent amplifier noise gain. The effect is a code dependent differential nonlinearity term at the amplifier output which depends on V_{OS} where V_{OS} is the amplifier input offset voltage. To maintain monotonic operation it is recommended that V_{OS} be no greater than (25×10^{-6}) (V_{REF}) over the temperature range of operation. Suitable op amps are AD517L and AD544L. The AD517L is best suited for fixed reference applications with low bandwidth requirements: it has extremely low offset $(50\mu V)$ and in most applications will not require an offset trim. The AD544L has a much wider bandwidth and higher slew rate and is recommended for multiplying and other applications requiring fast settling. An offset trim on the AD544L may be necessary in some circuits.

General Ground Management: AC or transient voltages between AGND and DGND can cause noise injection into the analog output. The simplest method of ensuring that voltages at AGND and DGND are equal is to tie AGND and DGND together at the AD7545. In more complex systems where the AGND and DGND intertie is on the backplane, it is recommended that two diodes be connected in inverse parallel between the AD7545 AGND and DGND pins (1N914 or equivalent).

Digital Glitches: When $\overline{WR}$ and $\overline{CS}$ are both low the latches are transparent and the D/A converter inputs follow the data inputs. In some bus systems, data on the data bus is not always valid for the whole period during which $\overline{WR}$ is low and as a result invalid data can briefly occur at the D/A converter inputs during a write cycle. Such invalid data can cause unwanted glitches at the output of the D/A converter. The solution to this problem, if it occurs, is to retime the write pulse $\overline{WR}$ so that it only occurs when data is valid.

Another cause of digital glitches is capacitive coupling from the digital lines to the OUT1 and AGND terminals. This should be minimized by screening the analog pins of the AD7545 (Pins 1, 2, 19, 20) from the digital pins by a ground track run between pins 2 and 3 and between pins 18 and 19 of the AD7545. Note how the analog pins are at one end of the package and separated from the digital pins by V_{DD} and DGND to aid screening at the board level. On-chip capacitive coupling can also give rise to crosstalk from the digital to analog sections of the AD7545, particularly in circuits with high currents and fast rise and fall times. This type of crosstalk is minimized by using V_{DD} = +5 volts. However, great care should be taken to ensure that the +5V used to power the AD7545 is free from digitally induced noise.

Temperature Coefficients: The gain temperature coefficient of the AD7545 has a maximum value of 5ppm/°C and a typical value of 2ppm/°C. This corresponds to worst case gain shifts of 2LSBs and 0.8LSBs respectively over a 100°C temperature range. When trim resistors R1 and R2 are used to adjust full scale range, the temperature coefficient of R1 and R2 should also be taken into account. The reader is referred to Analog Devices Application Note "Gain Error and Gain Temperature Coefficient of CMOS Multiplying DACs", Publication Number E630−10−6/81.

SINGLE SUPPLY OPERATION

The ladder termination resistor of the AD7545 (Figure 1) is connected to AGND. This arrangement is particularly suitable for single supply operation because OUT 1 and AGND may be biased at any voltage between DGND and V_{DD}. OUT1 and AGND should never go more than 0.3 volts less than DGND or an internal diode will be turned on and a heavy current may flow which will damage the device. (The AD7545 is, however, protected from the SCR latch-up phenomenon prevalent in many CMOS devices.)

Figure 7 shows the AD7545 connected in a voltage switching mode. OUT1 is connected to the reference voltage and AGND is connected to DGND. The D/A converter output voltage is available at the V_{REF} pin and has a constant output impedance equal to R. R_{FB} is not used in this circuit.

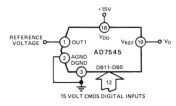

Figure 7. Single Supply Operation Using Voltage Switching Mode

The loading on the reference voltage source is code dependent and the response time of the circuit is often determined by the behavior of the reference voltage with changing load conditions. To maintain linearity, the voltages at OUT1 and AGND should remain within 2.5 volts of each other, for a V_{DD} of 15 volts. If V_{DD} is reduced from 15V or the differential voltage between OUT1 and AGND is increased to more than 2.5V the differential nonlinearity of the DAC will increase and the linearity of the DAC will be degraded. Figures 8 and 9 show typical curves illustrating this effect for various values of reference voltage and V_{DD}. If the output voltage is required to be offset from ground by some value, then OUT1 and AGND may be biased up. The effect on linearity and differential nonlinearity will be the same as reducing V_{DD} by the amount of the offset.

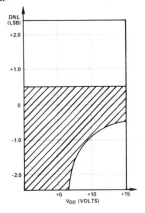

Figure 8. Differential Nonlinearity vs. V_{DD} for Figure 7 Circuit. Reference Voltage = 2.5 Volts. Shaded Area Shows Range of Values of Differential Nonlinearity that Typically Occur for L, C and U Grades.

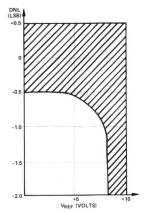

Figure 9. Differential Nonlinearity vs. Reference Voltage for Figure 7 Circuit. V_{DD} = 15 Volts. Shaded Area Shows Range of Values of Differential Nonlinearity that Typically Occur for L, C, and U Grades.

The circuits of Figures 4, 5 and 6 can all be converted to single supply operation by biasing AGND to some voltage between V_{DD} and DGND. Figure 10 shows the 2's Complement Bipolar circuit of Figure 5 modified to give a range from +2V to +8V about a "pseudo-analog ground" of 5V. This voltage range would allow operation from a single V_{DD} of +10V to +15V. The AD584 pin-programmable reference fixes AGND at +5V. V_{IN} is set at +2V by means of the series resistors R1 and R2. There is no need to buffer the V_{REF} input to the AD7545 with an amplifier because the input impedance of the D/A converter is constant. Note, however, that since the temperature coefficient of the D/A reference input resistance is typically ~300ppm/°C, applications which experience wide temperature variations may require a buffer amplifier to generate the +2.0V at the AD7545 V_{REF} pin. Other output voltage ranges can be obtained by changing R4 to shift the zero point and (R1 + R2) to change the slope, or gain of the D/A transfer function. V_{DD} must be kept at least 5V above OUT1 to ensure that linearity is preserved.

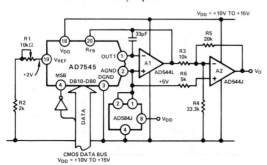

Figure 10. Single Supply "Bipolar" 2's Complement D/A Converter

MICROPROCESSOR INTERFACING OF THE AD7545
The AD7545 can interface directly to both 8- and 16-bit microprocessors via its 12-bit wide data latch using standard $\overline{CS}$ and $\overline{WR}$ control signals.

A typical interface circuit for an 8-bit processor is shown in Figure 11. This arrangement uses two memory addresses, one for the lower 8 bits of data to the DAC and one for the upper 4 bits of data into the DAC via the latch.

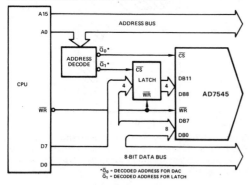

Figure 11. 8-Bit Processor to AD7545 Interface

Figure 12 shows an alternative approach for use with 8-bit processors which have a full 16-bit wide address bus such as 6800, 8080, Z80. This technique uses the 12 lower

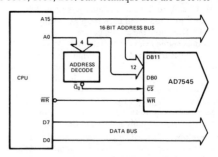

Figure 12. Connecting the AD7545 to 8-Bit Processors via the Address Bus

address lines of the processor address bus to supply data to the DAC, thus each AD7545 connected in this way uses 4k bytes of address locations. Data is written to the DAC using a single memory write instruction. The address field of the instruction is organized so that the lower 12 bits contain the data for the DAC and the upper 4 bits contain the address of the 4k block at which the DAC resides.

SUPPLEMENTAL APPLICATION MATERIAL
For further information on CMOS multiplying D/A converters the reader is referred to the following texts:

Application Guide to CMOS Multiplying D/A converters available from Analog Devices, Publication Number G479.

Gain Error and Gain Temperature Coefficient of CMOS Multiplying DACS — Application Note, Publication Number E630—10—6/81 available from Analog Devices.

Analog-Digital Conversion Notes — available from Analog Devices.

MECHANICAL INFORMATION

OUTLINE DIMENSIONS
Dimensions shown in inches and (mm).

20-PIN CERAMIC DIP (SUFFIX D)

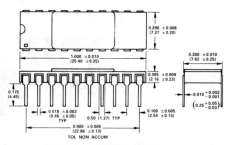

LEAD NUMBER 1 IDENTIFIED BY DOT OR NOTCH.
LEADS WILL BE EITHER GOLD OR TIN PLATED IN ACCORDANCE
WITH MIL-M-38510 REQUIREMENTS.

20-PIN PLASTIC DIP (SUFFIX N)   **20-PIN CERDIP (SUFFIX Q)**

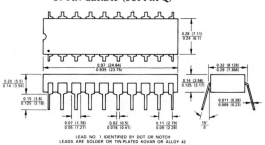

LEAD NO. 1 IDENTIFIED BY DOT OR NOTCH
LEADS ARE SOLDER OR TIN-PLATED KOVAR OR ALLOY 42

ANALOG DEVICES

Complete
12-Bit A/D Converter
AD574A*

FEATURES
**Complete 12-Bit A/D Converter with Reference
and Clock**
8- and 16-Bit Microprocessor Bus Interface
Guaranteed Linearity Over Temperature
  0 to +70°C – AD574AJ, K, L
  −55°C to +125°C – AD574AS, T, U
No Missing Codes Over Temperature
35μs Maximum Conversion Time
**Buried Zener Reference for Long-Term Stability
and Low Gain T.C. 10ppm/°C max AD574AL
                       12.5ppm/°C max AD574AU**
Ceramic DIP, Plastic DIP or PLCC Package

PRODUCT DESCRIPTION
The AD574A is a complete 12-bit successive-approximation
analog-to-digital converter with 3-state output buffer circuitry
for direct interface to an 8- or 16-bit microprocessor bus. A
high-precision voltage reference and clock are included on-chip,
and the circuit guarantees full-rated performance without external
circuitry or clock signals.

The AD574A design is implemented using Analog Devices'
Bipolar/I²L process, and integrates all analog and digital functions
on one chip. Offset, linearity and scaling errors are minimized
by active laser-trimming of thin-film resistors at the wafer stage.
The voltage reference uses an implanted buried zener for low
noise and low drift. On the digital side, I²L logic is used for the
successive-approximation register, control circuitry and 3-state
output buffers.

The AD574A is available in six different grades. The AD574AJ,
K, and L grades are specified for operation over the 0 to +70°C
temperature range. The AD574AS, T, and U are specified for
the −55°C to +125°C range. All grades are available in a 28-pin
hermetically-sealed ceramic DIP. The J, K, and L grades are
also available in a 28-pin plastic DIP and PLCC.

The S, T, and U grades are available with optional processing
to MIL-STD-883C Class B. The Analog Devices' Military Products
Databook should be consulted for details on /883B testing of the
AD574A.

PRODUCT HIGHLIGHTS
1. The AD574A interfaces to most 8- or 16-bit microprocessors.
   Multiple-mode three-state output buffers connect directly to
   the data bus while the read and convert commands are taken
   from the control bus. The 12 bits of output data can be read
   either as one 12-bit word or as two 8-bit bytes (one with 8
   data bits, the other with 4 data bits and 4 trailing zeros).

2. The precision, laser-trimmed scaling and bipolar offset resistors
   provide four calibrated ranges: 0 to +10 and 0 to +20 volts
   unipolar, −5 to +5 and −10 to +10 volts bipolar. Typical
   bipolar offset and full-scale calibration errors of ±0.1% can
   be trimmed to zero with one external component each.

3. The internal buried zener reference is trimmed to 10.00 volts
   with 0.2% maximum error and 15ppm/°C typical T.C. The
   reference is available externally and can drive up to 1.5mA
   beyond the requirements of the reference and bipolar offset
   resistors.

*Protected by U.S. Patent Nos. 3,803,590; 4,213,806; 4,511,413;
 RE 28,633.

One Technology Way; P. O. Box 9106; Norwood, MA 02062-9106 U.S.A.
Tel: 617/329-4700   Twx: 710/394-6577
Telex: 174059   Cables: ANALOG NORWOODMASS

SPECIFICATIONS

(@ = 25°C with V_{CC} = +15V or +12V, V_{LOGIC} = +5V, V_{EE} = −15V or −12V unless otherwise indicated)

Model	AD574AJ Min	Typ	Max	AD574AK Min	Typ	Max	AD574AL Min	Typ	Max	Units
RESOLUTION			12			12			12	Bits
LINEARITY ERROR @ +25°C			±1			±1/2			±1/2	LSB
T_{min} to T_{max}			±1			±1/2			±1/2	LSB
DIFFERENTIAL LINEARITY ERROR (Minimum resolution for which no missing codes are guaranteed)										
T_{min} to T_{max}	11			12			12			Bits
UNIPOLAR OFFSET (Adjustable to zero)			±2			±1			±1	LSB
BIPOLAR OFFSET (Adjustable to zero)			±4			±4			±2	LSB
FULL-SCALE CALIBRATION ERROR (with fixed 50Ω resistor from REF OUT to REF IN) (Adjustable to zero)			0.25			0.25			0.125	% of F.S.
TEMPERATURE RANGE	0		+70	0		+70	0		+70	°C
TEMPERATURE COEFFICIENTS (Using internal reference)										
T_{min} to T_{max}										
Unipolar Offset			±2(10)			±1(5)			±1(5)	LSB (ppm/°C)
Bipolar Offset			±2(10)			±1(5)			±1(5)	LSB (ppm/°C)
Full-Scale Calibration			±9(50)			±5(27)			±2(10)	LSB (ppm/°C)
POWER SUPPLY REJECTION										
Max change in Full Scale Calibration										
V_{CC} = 15V ±1.5V or 12V ±0.6V			±2			±1			±1	LSB
V_{LOGIC} = 5V ±0.5V			±1/2			±1/2			±1/2	LSB
V_{EE} = −15V ±1.5V or −12V ±0.6V			±2			±1			±1	LSB
ANALOG INPUT										
Input Ranges										
Bipolar	−5		+5	−5		+5	−5		+5	Volts
	−10		+10	−10		+10	−10		+10	Volts
Unipolar	0		+10	0		+10	0		+10	Volts
	0		+20	0		+20	0		+20	Volts
Input Impedance										
10 Volt Span	3	5	7	3	5	7	3	5	7	kΩ
20 Volt Span	6	10	14	6	10	14	6	10	14	kΩ
DIGITAL CHARACTERISTICS[1]										
Inputs[2] (CE, $\overline{CS}$, R/$\overline{C}$, A_0)										
Logic "1" Voltage	+2.0		+5.5	+2.0		+5.5	+2.0		+5.5	Volts
Logic "0" Voltage	−0.5		+0.8	−0.5		+0.8	−0.5		+0.8	Volts
Current	−20		+20	−20		+20	−20		+20	μA
Capacitance		5			5			5		pF
Outputs (DB11–DB0, STS)										
Logic "1" Voltage ($I_{SINK} \le 1.6mA$)	+2.4			+2.4			+2.4			Volts
Logic "0" Voltage ($I_{SOURCE} \le 500\mu A$)			+0.4			+0.4			+0.4	Volts
Leakage (DB11–DB0, High-Z State)	−20		+20	−20		+20	−20		+20	μA
Capacitance		5			5			5		pF
POWER SUPPLIES										
Operating Range										
V_{LOGIC}	+4.5		+5.5	+4.5		+5.5	+4.5		+5.5	Volts
V_{CC}	+11.4		+16.5	+11.4		+16.5	+11.4		+16.5	Volts
V_{EE}	−11.4		−16.5	−11.4		−16.5	−11.4		−16.5	Volts
Operating Current										
I_{LOGIC}		30	40		30	40		30	40	mA
I_{CC}		2	5		2	5		2	5	mA
I_{EE}		18	30		18	30		18	30	mA
POWER DISSIPATION		390	725		390	725		390	725	mW
INTERNAL REFERENCE VOLTAGE	9.98	10.0	10.02	9.98	10.0	10.02	9.99	10.0	10.01	Volts
Output current (available for external loads)[3] (External load should not change during conversion)			1.5			1.5			1.5	mA

NOTES

[1] Detailed Timing Specifications appear in the Timing Section.
[2] 12/8 Input is not TTL-compatible and must be hard wired to V_{LOGIC} or Digital Common.
[3] The reference should be buffered for operation on ±12V supplies.

Specifications subject to change without notice.

Specifications shown in boldface are tested on all production units at final electrical test. Results from those tests are used to calculate outgoing quality levels. All min and max specifications are guaranteed, although only those shown in boldface are tested on all production units.

Model	AD574AS Min	Typ	Max	AD574AT Min	Typ	Max	AD574AU Min	Typ	Max	Units
RESOLUTION			12			12			12	Bits
LINEARITY ERROR @ +25°C			±1			±1/2			±1/2	LSB
T_{min} to T_{max}			±1			±1			±1	LSB
DIFFERENTIAL LINEARITY ERROR (Minimum resolution for which no missing codes are guaranteed)										
T_{min} to T_{max}	11			12			12			Bits
UNIPOLAR OFFSET (Adjustable to zero)			±2			±1			±1	LSB
BIPOLAR OFFSET (Adjustable to zero)			±4			±4			±2	LSB
FULL-SCALE CALIBRATION ERROR (with fixed 50Ω resistor from REF OUT to REF IN) (Adjustable to zero)			0.25			0.25			0.125	% of F.S.
TEMPERATURE RANGE	−55		+125	−55		+125	−55		+125	°C
TEMPERATURE COEFFICIENTS (Using internal reference) T_{min} to T_{max}										
Unipolar Offset			±2(5)			±1(2.5)			±1(2.5)	LSB (ppm/°C)
Bipolar Offset			±4(10)			±2(5)			±1(2.5)	LSB (ppm/°C)
Full-Scale Calibration			±20(50)			±10(25)			±5(12.5)	LSB (ppm/°C)
POWER SUPPLY REJECTION Max change in Full Scale Calibration										
$V_{CC} = 15V \pm 1.5V$ or $12V \pm 0.6V$			±2			±1			±1	LSB
$V_{LOGIC} = 5V \pm 0.5V$			±1/2			±1/2			±1/2	LSB
$V_{EE} = -15V \pm 1.5V$ or $-12V \pm 0.6V$			±2			±1			±1	LSB
ANALOG INPUT										
Input Ranges										
Bipolar	−5		+5	−5		+5	−5		+5	Volts
	−10		+10	−10		+10	−10		+10	Volts
Unipolar	0		+10	0		+10	0		+10	Volts
	0		+20	0		+20	0		+20	Volts
Input Impedance										
10 Volt Span	3	5	7	3	5	7	3	5	7	kΩ
20 Volt Span	6	10	14	6	10	14	6	10	14	kΩ
DIGITAL CHARACTERISTICS[1]										
Inputs[2] (CE, $\overline{CS}$, R/$\overline{C}$, A_0)										
Logic "1" Voltage	+2.0		+5.5	+2.0		+5.5	+2.0		+5.5	Volts
Logic "0" Voltage	−0.5		+0.8	−0.5		+0.8	−0.5		+0.8	Volts
Current	−20		+20	−20		+20	−20		+20	μA
Capacitance		5			5			5		pF
Outputs (DB11–DB0, STS)										
Logic "1" Voltage ($I_{SINK} \leq 1.6mA$)	+2.4			+2.4			+2.4			Volts
Logic "0" Voltage ($I_{SOURCE} \leq 500\mu A$)			+0.4			+0.4			+0.4	Volts
Leakage (DB11–DB0, High-Z State)	−20		+20	−20		+20	−20		+20	μA
Capacitance		5			5			5		pF
POWER SUPPLIES										
Operating Range										
V_{LOGIC}	+4.5		+5.5	+4.5		+5.5	+4.5		+5.5	Volts
V_{CC}	+11.4		+16.5	+11.4		+16.5	+11.4		+16.5	Volts
V_{EE}	−11.4		−16.5	−11.4		−16.5	−11.4		−16.5	Volts
Operating Current										
I_{LOGIC}		30	40		30	40		30	40	mA
I_{CC}		2	5		2	5		2	5	mA
I_{EE}		18	30		18	30		18	30	mA
POWER DISSIPATION		390	725		390	725		390	725	mW
INTERNAL REFERENCE VOLTAGE	9.98	10.0	10.02	9.98	10.0	10.02	9.99	10.0	10.01	Volts
Output current (available for external loads)[3]			1.5			1.5			1.5	mA
(External load should not change during conversion)										

NOTES
[1] Detailed Timing Specifications appear in the Timing Section.
[2] 2/8 Input is not TTL-compatible and must be hard wired to V_{LOGIC} or Digital Common.
[3] The reference should be buffered for operation on ±12V supplies.
Specifications subject to change without notice.

Specifications shown in boldface are tested on all production units at final electrical test. Results from those tests are used to calculate outgoing quality levels. All min and max specifications are guaranteed, although only those shown in boldface are tested on all production units.

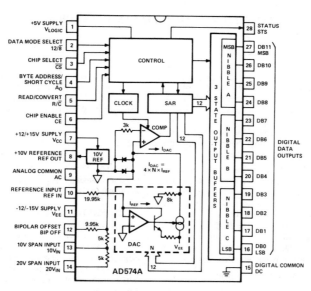

AD574A Block Diagram and Pin Configuration

ABSOLUTE MAXIMUM RATINGS*
(Specifications apply to all grades, except where noted)

V_{CC} to Digital Common . . . . 0 to +16.5V
V_{EE} to Digital Common . . . . 0 to −16.5V
V_{LOGIC} to Digital Common . . . . 0 to +7V
Analog Common to Digital Common . . . . ±1V
Control Inputs (CE, $\overline{CS}$, A_O, 12/$\overline{8}$, R/$\overline{C}$) to
     Digital Common . . −0.5V to V_{LOGIC} +0.5V
Analog Inputs (REF IN, BIP OFF, $10V_{IN}$) to
     Analog Common . . . . V_{EE} to V_{CC}
$20V_{IN}$ to Analog Common . . . . ±24V
REF OUT . . . . Indefinite short to common
     Momentary short to V_{CC}

Chip Temperature . . . . 175°C
Power Dissipation 825mW
Lead Temperature, Soldering . . . . + 300°C, 10 sec.
Storage Temperature (Ceramic) . . . . − 65°C to + 150°C
                (Plastic) . . . . . . − 25°C to + 100°C

*Stresses above those listed under "Absolute Maximum Ratings" may cause permanent damage to the device. This is a stress rating only and functional operation of the device at these or any other conditions above those indicated in the operational sections of this specification is not implied. Exposure to absolute maximum rating conditions for extended periods may affect device reliability.

AD574A ORDERING GUIDE

Model*	Temp. Range	Linearity Error Max (T_{min} to T_{max})	Resolution No Missing Codes (T_{min} to T_{max})	Max Full Scale T.C. (ppm/°C)
AD574AJ(X)	0 to +70°C	±1LSB	11 Bits	50.0
AD574AK(X)	0 to +70°C	±1/2LSB	12 Bits	27.0
AD574AL(X)	0 to +70°C	±1/2LSB	12 Bits	10.0
AD574AS(X)	−55°C to +125°C	±1LSB	11 Bits	50.0
AD574AT(X)	−55°C to +125°C	±1LSB	12 Bits	25.0
AD574AU(X)	−55°C to +125°C	±1LSB	12 Bits	12.5

NOTES
Package outlines illustrated at end of data sheet.

*X = Package designator. Available packages are:
  D (D28A) for all grades.
  E (E28A) for J, K, S, T, U grades.
  N (N28A) for J, K, and L grades.
  P for PLCC in J, K, L grades.
  Example: AD574AKN is K grade in plastic DIP.

THE AD574A OFFERS GUARANTEED MAXIMUM LINEARITY ERROR OVER THE FULL OPERATING TEMPERATURE RANGE

DEFINITIONS OF SPECIFICATIONS

LINEARITY ERROR

Linearity error refers to the deviation of each individual code from a line drawn from "zero" through "full scale". The point used as "zero" occurs 1/2LSB (1.22mV for 10 volt span) before the first code transition (all zeros to only the LSB "on"). "Full scale" is defined as a level 1 1/2LSB beyond the last code transition (to all ones). The deviation of a code from the true straight line is measured from the middle of each particular code.

The AD574AK, L, T, and U grades are guaranteed for maximum nonlinearity of ±1/2LSB. For these grades, this means that an analog value which falls exactly in the center of a given code width will result in the correct digital output code. Values nearer the upper or lower transition of the code width may produce the next upper or lower digital output code. The AD574AJ and S grades are guaranteed to ±1LSB max error. For these grades, an analog value which falls within a given code width will result in either the correct code for that region or either adjacent one.

Note that the linearity error is not user-adjustable.

DIFFERENTIAL LINEARITY ERROR (NO MISSING CODES)

A specification which guarantees no missing codes requires that every code combination appear in a monotonic increasing sequence as the analog input level is increased. Thus every code must have a finite width. For the AD574AK, L, T, and U grades, which guarantee no missing codes to 12-bit resolution, all 4096 codes must be present over the entire operating temperature ranges. The AD574AJ and S grades guarantee no missing codes to 11-bit resolution over temperature; this means that all code combinations of the upper 11 bits must be present; in practice very few of the 12-bit codes are missing.

UNIPOLAR OFFSET

The first transition should occur at a level 1/2LSB above analog common. Unipolar offset is defined as the deviation of the actual transition from that point. This offset can be adjusted as discussed on the following two pages. The unipolar offset temperature coefficient specifies the maximum change of the transition point over temperature, with or without external adjustment.

BIPOLAR OFFSET

In the bipolar mode the major carry transition (0111 1111 1111 to 1000 0000 0000) should occur for an analog value 1/2LSB below analog common. The bipolar offset error and temperature coefficient specify the initial deviation and maximum change in the error over temperature.

QUANTIZATION UNCERTAINTY

Analog-to-digital converters exhibit an inherent quantization uncertainty of ±1/2LSB. This uncertainty is a fundamental characteristic of the quantization process and cannot be reduced for a converter of given resolution.

LEFT-JUSTIFIED DATA

The data format used in the AD574A is left-justified. This means that the data represents the analog input as a fraction of full-scale, ranging from 0 to $\frac{4095}{4096}$. This implies a binary point to the left of the MSB.

FULL-SCALE CALIBRATION ERROR

The last transition (from 1111 1111 1110 to 1111 1111 1111) should occur for an analog value 1 1/2LSB below the nominal full scale (9.9963 volts for 10.000 volts full scale). The full-scale calibration error is the deviation of the actual level at the last transition from the ideal level. This error, which is typically 0.05 to 0.1% of full scale, can be trimmed out as shown in Figures 3 and 4.

TEMPERATURE COEFFICIENTS

The temperature coefficients for full-scale calibration, unipolar offset, and bipolar offset specify the maximum change from the initial (25°C) value to the value at T_{min} or T_{max}.

POWER SUPPLY REJECTION

The standard specifications for the AD574A assume use of +5.00 and ±15.00 or ±12.00V supplies. The only effect of power supply error on the performance of the device will be a small change in the full-scale calibration. This will result in a linear change in all lower-order codes. The specifications show the maximum full-scale change from the initial value with the supplies at the various limits.

CODE WIDTH

A fundamental quantity for A/D converter specifications is the code width. This is defined as the range of analog input values for which a given digital output code will occur. The nominal value of a code width is equivalent to 1 least significant bit (LSB) of the full-scale range or 2.44mV out of 10 volts for a 12-bit ADC.

CIRCUIT OPERATION

The AD574A is a complete 12-bit A/D converter which requires no external components to provide the complete successive-approximation analog-to-digital conversion function. A block diagram of the AD574A is shown in Figure 1.

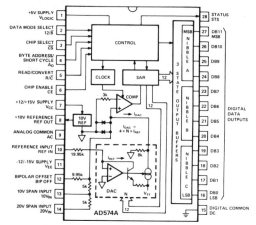

Figure 1. Block Diagram of AD574A 12-Bit A-to-D Converter

When the control section is commanded to initiate a conversion (as described later), it enables the clock and resets the successive-approximation register (SAR) to all zeros. Once a conversion cycle has begun, it cannot be stopped or re-started and data is not available from the output buffers. The SAR, timed by the clock, will sequence through the conversion cycle and return an end-of-convert flag to the control section. The control section will then disable the clock, bring the output status flag low, and enable control functions to allow data read functions by external command.

During the conversion cycle, the internal 12-bit current output DAC is sequenced by the SAR from the most significant bit (MSB) to least significant bit (LSB) to provide an output current which accurately balances the input signal current through the 5kΩ (or 10kΩ) input resistor. The comparator determines whether the addition of each successively-weighted bit current causes the DAC current sum to be greater or less than the input current; if the sum is less, the bit is left on; if more, the bit is turned off. After testing all the bits, the SAR contains a 12-bit binary code which accurately represents the input signal to within ± 1/2LSB.

The temperature-compensated buried zener reference provides the primary voltage reference to the DAC and guarantees excellent stability with both time and temperature. The reference is trimmed to 10.00 volts ± 0.2%; it can supply up to 1.5mA to an external load in addition to the requirements of the reference input resistor (0.5mA) and bipolar offset resistor (1mA) when the AD574A is powered from ± 15V supplies. If the AD574A is used with ± 12V supplies, or if external current must be supplied over the full temperature range, an external buffer amplifier is recommended. Any external load on the AD574A reference must remain constant during conversion. The thin-film application resistors are trimmed to match the full-scale output current of the DAC. There are two 5kΩ input scaling resistors to allow either a 10 volt or 20 volt span. The 10kΩ bipolar offset resistor is grounded for unipolar operation and connected to the 10 volt reference for bipolar operation.

DRIVING THE AD574 ANALOG INPUT

The internal circuitry of the AD574 dictates that its analog input be driven by a low source impedance. Voltage changes at the current summing node of the internal comparator result in abrupt modulations of the current at the analog input. For accurate 12-bit conversions the driving source must be capable of holding a constant output voltage under these dynamically changing load conditions.

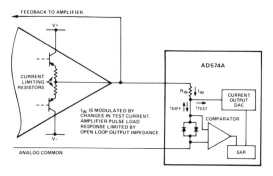

Figure 2. Op Amp – AD574A Interface

The output impedance of an op amp has an open-loop value which, in a closed loop, is divided by the loop gain available at the frequency of interest. The amplifier should have acceptable loop gain at 500kHz for use with the AD574A. To check whether the output properties of a signal source are suitable, monitor the AD574's input with an oscilloscope while a conversion is in progress. Each of the 12 disturbances should subside in 1μs or less.

For applications involving the use of a sample-and-hold amplifier, the AD585 is recommended. The AD711 or AD544 op amps are recommended for dc applications.

SAMPLE-AND-HOLD AMPLIFIERS

Although the conversion time of the AD574A is a maximum of 35μs, to achieve accurate 12-bit conversions of frequencies greater than a few Hz requires the use of a sample-and-hold amplifier (SHA). If the voltage of the analog input signal driving the AD574A changes by more than 1/2LSB over the time interval needed to make a conversion, then the input requires a SHA.

The AD585 is a high-linearity SHA capable of directly driving the analog input of the AD574A. The AD585's fast acquisition time, low aperture and low aperture jitter are ideally suited for high-speed data acquisition systems. Consider the AD574A converter with a 35μs conversion time and an input signal of 10V p-p: the maximum frequency which may be applied to achieve rated accuracy is 1.5Hz. However, with the addition of an AD585, as shown in Figure 3, the maximum frequency increases to 26kHz.

The AD585's low output impedance, fast-loop response, and low droop maintain 12-bits of accuracy under the changing load conditions that occur during a conversion, making it suitable for use in high-accuracy conversion systems. Many other SHAs cannot achieve 12-bits of accuracy and can thus compromise a system. The AD585 is recommended for AD574A applications requiring a sample and hold.

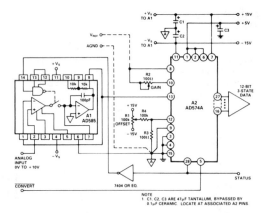

Figure 3. AD574A with AD585 Sample and Hold

SUPPLY DECOUPLING AND LAYOUT CONSIDERATIONS

It is critically important that the AD574A power supplies be filtered, well regulated, and free from high-frequency noise. Use of noisy supplies will cause unstable output codes. Switching power supplies are not recommended for circuits attempting to achieve 12-bit accuracy unless great care is used in filtering any switching spikes present in the output. Remember that a few millivolts of noise represents several counts of error in a 12-bit ADC.

Decoupling capacitors should be used on all power supply pins; the +5V supply decoupling capacitor should be connected directly from pin 1 to pin 15 (digital common) and the $+V_{CC}$ and $-V_{EE}$ pins should be decoupled directly to analog common (pin 9). A suitable decoupling capacitor is a $4.7\mu F$ tantalum type in parallel with a $0.1\mu F$ disc ceramic type.

Circuit layout should attempt to locate the AD574A, associated analog input circuitry, and interconnections as far as possible from logic circuitry. For this reason, the use of wire-wrap circuit construction is not recommended. Careful printed-circuit construction is preferred.

GROUNDING CONSIDERATIONS

The analog common at pin 9 is the ground reference point for the internal reference and is thus the "high quality" ground for the AD574A; it should be connected directly to the analog reference point of the system. In order to achieve all of the high-accuracy performance available from the AD574A in an environment of high digital noise content, the analog and digital commons should be connected together at the package. In some situations, the digital common at pin 15 can be connected to the most convenient ground reference point; analog power return is preferred.

UNIPOLAR RANGE CONNECTIONS FOR THE AD574A

The AD574A contains all the active components required to perform a complete 12-bit A/D conversion. Thus, for most situations, all that is necessary is connection of the power supplies ($+5$, $+12/+15$ and $-12/-15$ volts), the analog input, and the conversion initiation command, as discussed on the next page. Analog input connections and calibration are easily accomplished; the unipolar operating mode is shown in Figure 4.

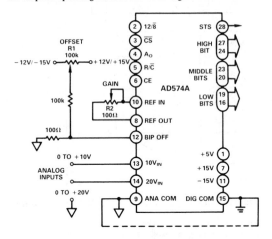

Figure 4. Unipolar Input Connections

All of the thin-film application resistors of the AD574A are trimmed for absolute calibration. Therefore, in many applications, no calibration trimming will be required. The absolute accuracy for each grade is given in the specification tables. For example, if no trims are used, the AD574AK guarantees $\pm 1LSB$ max zero offset error and $\pm 0.25\%$ (10LSB) max full-scale error. (Typical full-scale error is $\pm 2LSB$.) If the offset trim is not required, pin 12 can be connected directly to pin 9; the two resistors and trimmer for pin 12 are then not needed. If the full-scale trim is not needed, a $50\Omega \pm 1\%$ metal film resistor should be connected between pin 8 and pin 10.

The analog input is connected between pin 13 and pin 9 for a 0 to $+10V$ input range, between 14 and pin 9 for a 0 to $+20V$ input range. The AD574A easily accommodates an input signal beyond the supplies. For the 10 volt span input, the LSB has a nominal value of 2.44mV; for the 20 volt span, 4.88mV. If a 10.24V range is desired (nominal 2.5mV/bit), the gain trimmer (R2) should be replaced by a 50Ω resistor, and a 200Ω trimmer inserted in series with the analog input to pin 13 for a full-scale range of 20.48V (5mV/bit), use a 500Ω trimmer into pin 14. The gain trim described below is now done with these trimmers. The nominal input impedance into pin 13 is 5kΩ, and 10kΩ into pin 14.

UNIPOLAR CALIBRATION

The AD574A is intended to have a nominal 1/2LSB offset so that the exact analog input for a given code will be in the middle of that code (halfway between the transitions to the codes above and below it). Thus, the first transition (from 0000 0000 0000 to 0000 0000 0001) will occur for an input level of + 1/2LSB (1.22mV for 10V range).

If pin 12 is connected to pin 9, the unit will behave in this manner, within specifications. If the offset trim (R1) is used, it should be trimmed as above, although a different offset can be set for a particular system requirement. This circuit will give approximately ± 15mV of offset trim range.

The full-scale trim is done by applying a signal 1 1/2LSB below the nominal full scale (9.9963 for a 10V range). Trim R2 to give the last transition (1111 1111 1110 to 1111 1111 1111).

BIPOLAR OPERATION

The connections for bipolar ranges are shown in Figure 5. Again, as for the unipolar ranges, if the offset and gain specifications are sufficient, one or both of the trimmers shown can be replaced by a 50Ω ± 1% fixed resistor. Bipolar calibration is similar to unipolar calibration. First, a signal ½LSB above negative full scale (− 4.9988V for the ± 5V range) is applied and R1 is trimmed to give the first transition (0000 0000 0000 to 0000 0000 0001). Then a signal 1½LSB below positive full scale (+ 4.9963V for the ± 5V range) is applied and R2 trimmed to give the last transition (1111 1111 1110 to 1111 1111 1111).

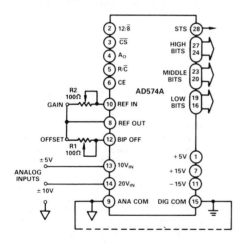

Figure 5. Bipolar Input Connections

CONTROL LOGIC

The AD574A contains on-chip logic to provide conversion initiation and data read operations from signals commonly available in microprocessor systems. Figure 6 shows the internal logic circuitry of the AD574A.

The control signals CE, $\overline{CS}$, and R/$\overline{C}$ control the operation of the converter. The state of R/$\overline{C}$ when CE and $\overline{CS}$ are both asserted determines whether a data read (R/$\overline{C}$ = 1) or a convert (R/$\overline{C}$ = 0) is in progress. The register control inputs A_O and 12/$\overline{8}$ control conversion length and data format. The A_O line is usually tied to the least significant bit of the address bus. If a conversion is started with A_O low, a full 12-bit conversion cycle is initiated. If

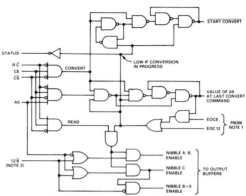

Figure 6. AD574A Control Logic

NOTE 1: WHEN START CONVERT GOES LOW, THE EOC (END OF CONVERSION) SIGNALS GO LOW. EOC8 RETURNS HIGH AFTER AN 8-BIT CONVERSION CYCLE IS COMPLETE, AND EOC12 RETURNS HIGH WHEN ALL 12 BITS HAVE BEEN CONVERTED. THE EOC SIGNALS PREVENT DATA FROM BEING READ DURING CONVERSIONS.

NOTE 2: 12/$\overline{8}$ IS NOT A TTL-COMPATIBLE INPUT AND SHOULD ALWAYS BE WIRED DIRECTLY TO V_{LOGIC} OR DIGITAL COMMON.

A_O is high during a convert start, a shorter 8-bit conversion cycle results. During data read operations, A_O determines whether the three-state buffers containing the 8 MSBs of the conversion result (A_O = 0) or the 4 LSBs (A_O = 1) are enabled. The 12/$\overline{8}$ pin determines whether the output data is to be organized as two 8-bit words (12/$\overline{8}$ tied to DIGITAL COMMON) or a single 12-bit word (12/$\overline{8}$ tied to V_{LOGIC}). The 12/$\overline{8}$ pin is not TTL-compatible and must be hard-wired to either V_{LOGIC} or DIGITAL COMMON. In the 8-bit mode, the byte addressed when A_O is high contains the 4 LSBs from the conversion followed by four trailing zeroes. This organization allows the data lines to be overlapped for direct interface to 8-bit buses without the need for external three-state buffers.

It is not recommended that A_O change state during a data read operation. Asymmetrical enable and disable times of the three-state buffers could cause internal bus contention resulting in potential damage to the AD574A.

An output signal, STS, indicates the status of the converter. STS goes high at the beginning of a conversion and returns low when the conversion cycle is complete.

CE	$\overline{CS}$	R/$\overline{C}$	12/$\overline{8}$	A_O	Operation
0	X	X	X	X	None
X	1	X	X	X	None
1	0	0	X	0	Initiate 12-Bit Conversion
1	0	0	X	1	Initiate 8-Bit Conversion
1	0	1	Pin 1	X	Enable 12-Bit Parallel Output
1	0	1	Pin 15	0	Enable 8 Most Significant Bits
1	0	1	Pin 15	1	Enable 4 LSBs + 4 Trailing Zeroes

Table I. AD574A Truth Table

TIMING

The AD574A is easily interfaced to a wide variety of microprocessors and other digital systems. The following discussion of the timing requirements of the AD574A control signals should provide the system designer with useful insight into the operation of the device.

CONVERT START TIMING – FULL CONTROL MODE

Symbol	Parameter	Min	Typ	Max	Units
t_{DSC}	STS Delay from CE			400	ns
t_{HEC}	CE Pulse Width	300			ns
t_{SSC}	$\overline{CS}$ to CE Setup	300			ns
t_{HSC}	$\overline{CS}$ Low During CE High	200			ns
t_{SRC}	R/$\overline{C}$ to CE Setup	250			ns
t_{HRC}	R/$\overline{C}$ Low During CE High	200			ns
t_{SAC}	A_O to CE Setup	0			ns
t_{HAC}	A_O Valid During CE High	300			ns
t_C	Conversion Time				
	8-Bit Cycle	10		24	μs
	12-Bit Cycle	15		35	μs

Figure 7 shows a complete timing diagram for the AD574A convert start operation. R/$\overline{C}$ should be low before both CE or $\overline{CS}$ are asserted; if R/$\overline{C}$ is high, a read operation will momentarily occur, possibly resulting in system bus contention. Either CE or $\overline{CS}$ may be used to initiate a conversion; however, use of CE is recommended since it includes one less propagation delay than $\overline{CS}$ and is the faster input. In Figure 7, CE is used to initiate the conversion.

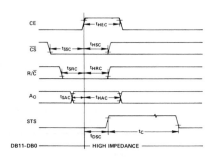

Figure 7. Convert Start Timing

Once a conversion is started and the STS line goes high, convert start commands will be ignored until the conversion cycle is complete. The output data buffers cannot be enabled during conversion.

Figure 8 shows the timing for data read operations. During data read operations, access time is measured from the point where CE and R/$\overline{C}$ both are high (assuming $\overline{CS}$ is already low). If $\overline{CS}$ is used to enable the device, access time is extended by 100ns.

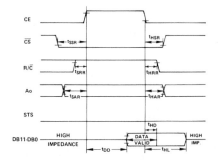

Figure 8. Read Cycle Timing

In the 8-bit bus interface mode (12/$\overline{8}$ input wired to DIGITAL COMMON), the address bit, A_O, must be stable at least 150ns prior to $\overline{CE}$ going high and must remain stable during the entire read cycle. If A_O is allowed to change, damage to the AD574A output buffers may result.

READ TIMING – FULL CONTROL MODE

Symbol	Parameter	Min	Typ	Max	Units
t_{DD}[1]	Access Time (from CE)			200	ns
t_{HD}	Data Valid after CE Low	25			ns
t_{HL}[2]	Output Float Delay			100	ns
t_{SSR}	$\overline{CS}$ to CE Setup	150			ns
t_{SRR}	R/$\overline{C}$ to CE Setup	0			ns
t_{SAR}	A_O to CE Setup	150			ns
t_{HSR}	$\overline{CS}$ Valid After CE Low	50			ns
t_{HRR}	R/$\overline{C}$ High After CE Low	0			ns
t_{HAR}	A_O Valid After CE low	50			ns

[1] t_{DD} is measured with the load circuit of Figure 8 and defined as the time required for an output to cross 0.4V or 2.4V.
[2] t_{HL} is defined as the time required for the data lines to change 0.5V when loaded with the circuit of Figure 9.

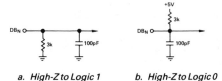

a. High-Z to Logic 1   b. High-Z to Logic 0
Figure 9. Load Circuit for Access Time Test

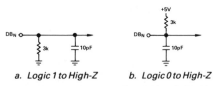

a. Logic 1 to High-Z   b. Logic 0 to High-Z
Figure 10. Load Circuit for Output Float Delay Test

"STAND-ALONE" OPERATION

The AD574A can be used in a "stand-alone" mode, which is useful in systems with dedicated input ports available and thus not requiring full bus interface capability.

In this mode, CE and 12/$\overline{8}$ are wired high, $\overline{CS}$ and A_O are wired low, and conversion is controlled by R/$\overline{C}$. The three-state buffers are enabled when R/$\overline{C}$ is high and a conversion starts when R/$\overline{C}$ goes low. This allows two possible control signals – a high pulse or a low pulse. Operation with a low pulse is shown in Figure 11. In this case, the outputs are forced into the high-impedance state in response to the falling edge of R/$\overline{C}$ and return

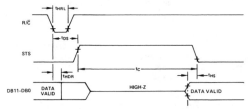

Figure 11. Low Pulse for R/$\overline{C}$ – Outputs Enabled After Conversion

AD574A 12-bit 25-μs A/D Converter

431

to valid logic levels after the conversion cycle is completed. The STS line goes high 600ns after R/C̄ goes low and returns low 300ns after data is valid.

If conversion is initiated by a high pulse as shown in Figure 12, the data lines are enabled during the time when R/C̄ is high. The falling edge of R/C̄ starts the next conversion, and the data lines return to three-state (and remain three-state) until the next high pulse of R/C̄.

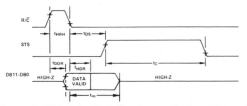

Figure 12. High Pulse for R/C̄ – Outputs Enabled While R/C̄ High, Otherwise High-Z

STAND-ALONE MODE TIMING

Symbol	Parameter	Min	Typ	Max	Units
t_{HRL}	Low R/C̄ Pulse Width	250			ns
t_{DS}	STS Delay from R/C̄			600	ns
t_{HDR}	Data Valid After R/C̄ Low	25			ns
t_{HL}	Output Float Delay			150	ns
t_{HS}	STS Delay After Data Valid	300		1000	ns
t_{HRH}	High R/C̄ Pulse Width	300			ns
t_{DDR}	Data Access Time			250	ns

Usually the low pulse for R/C̄ stand-alone mode will be used. Figure 13 illustrates a typical stand-alone confirguration for 8086 type processors. The addition of the 74F/S374 latches improves bus access/release times and helps minimize digital feedthrough to the analog portion of the converter.

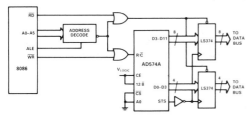

Figure 13. 8086 Stand-Alone Configuration

INTERFACING THE AD574A TO MICROPROCESSORS
The control logic of the AD574A makes direct connection to most microprocessor system buses possible. While it is impossible to describe the details of the interface connections for every microprocessor type, several representative examples will be described here.

GENERAL A/D CONVERTER INTERFACE CONSIDERATIONS
A typical A/D converter interface routine involves several operations. First, a write to the ADC address initiates a conversion. The processor must then wait for the conversion cycle to complete, since most ADCs take longer than one instruction cycle to complete a conversion. Valid data can, of course, only be read after the conversion is complete. The AD574A provides an output signal (STS) which indicates when a conversion is in progress. This signal can be polled by the processor by reading it through an

external three-state buffer (or other input port). The STS signal can also be used to generate an interrupt upon completion of conversion, if the system timing requirements are critical (bear in mind that the maximum conversion time of the AD574A is only 35 microseconds) and the processor has other tasks to perform during the ADC conversion cycle. Another possible time-out method is to assume that the ADC will take 35 microseconds to convert, and insert a sufficient number of "do-nothing" instructions to ensure that 35 microseconds of processor time is consumed.

Once it is established that the conversion is finished, the data can be read. In the case of an ADC of 8-bit resolution (or less), a single data read operation is sufficient. In the case of converters with more data bits than are available on the bus, a choice of data formats is required, and multiple read operations are needed. The AD574A includes internal logic to permit direct interface to 8-bit or 16-bit data buses, selected by connection of the 12/8̄ input. In 16-bit bus applications (12/8̄ high) the data lines (DB11 through DB0) may be connected to either the 12 most significant or 12 least significant bits of the data bus. The remaining four bits should be masked in software. The interface to an 8-bit data bus (12/8̄ low) is done in a left-justified format. The even address (A0 low) contains the 8MSBs (DB11 through DB4). The odd address (A0 high) contains the 4LSBs (DB3 through DB0) in the upper half of the byte, followed by four trailing zeroes, thus eliminating bit masking instructions.

It is not possible to rearrange the AD574A data lines for right-justified 8-bit bus interface.

	D7							D0
XXX0 (EVEN ADDR):	DB11 (MSB)	DB10	DB9	DB8	DB7	DB6	DB5	DB4
XXX1 (ODD ADDR):	DB3	DB2	DB1	DB0 (LSB)	0	0	0	0

Figure 14. AD574A Data Format for 8-Bit Bus

SPECIFIC PROCESSOR INTERFACE EXAMPLES
Z-80 System Interface
The AD574A may be interfaced to the Z-80 processor in an I/O or memory mapped configuration. Figure 15 illustrates an I/O mapped configuration. The Z-80 uses address lines A0-A7 to decode the I/O port address.

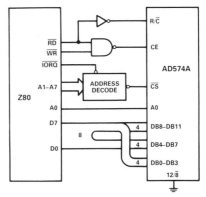

Figure 15. Z80 – AD574A Interface

An interesting feature of the Z-80 is that during I/O operations a single wait state is automatically inserted, allowing the AD574A to be used with Z-80 processors having clock speeds up to 4MHz. For applications faster than 4MHz use the wait state generator in Figure 16. In a memory mapped configuration the AD574A may be interfaced to Z-80 processors with clock speeds of up to 2.5MHz.

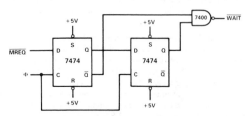

Figure 16. Wait State Generator

IBM PC Interface

The AD574A appears in Figure 17 interfaced to the 4MHz 8088 processor of an IBM PC. Since the device resides in I/O space, its address is decoded from only the lower ten address lines and must be gated with AEN (active low) to mask out internal DMA cycles which use the same I/O address space. This active low signal is applied to $\overline{CS}$. $\overline{IOR}$ and $\overline{IOW}$ are used to initiate conversion and read, and are gated together to drive the chip enable, CE. Because the data bus width is limited to 8 bits, the AD574A data resides in two adjacent addresses selected by A0.

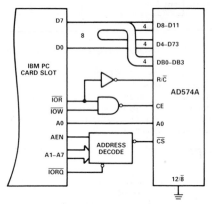

Figure 17. IBM PC – AD574A Interface

Note: Due to the large number of of options that may be installed in the PC, the I/O bus loading should be limited to one Schottky TTL load. Therefore, a buffer/driver should be used when interfacing more than two AD574As to the I/O bus.

8086 Interface

The data mode select pin $(12/\overline{8})$ of the AD574A should be connected to V_{LOGIC} to provide a 12-bit data output. To prevent possible bus contention, a demultiplexed and buffered address/data bus is recommended. In the cases where the 8-bit short conversion cycle is not used, A0 should be tied to digital common. Figure 18 shows a typical 8086 configuration.

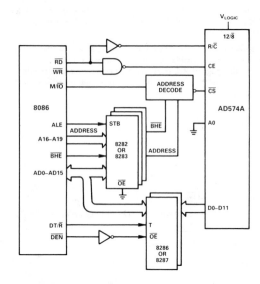

Figure 18. 8086 – AD574A with Buffered Bus Interface

For clock speeds greater than 4MHz wait state insertion similar to Figure 16 is recommended to ensure sufficient CE and R/$\overline{C}$ pulse duration.

The AD574A can also be interfaced in a stand-alone mode (see Figure 13). A low-going pulse derived from the 8086's $\overline{WR}$ signal logically ORed with a low address decode starts the conversion. At the end of the conversion, STS clocks the data into the three-state latches.

68000 Interface

The AD574, when configured in the stand-alone mode, will easily interface to the 4MHz version of the 68000 microprocessor. The 68000 R/$\overline{W}$ signal combined with a low address decode initiates conversion. The $\overline{UDS}$ or $\overline{LDS}$ signal, with the decoded address, generates the $\overline{DTACK}$ input to the processor, latching in the AD574A's data. Figure 19 illustrates this configuration.

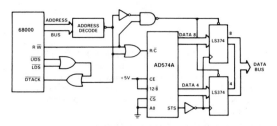

Figure 19. 68000 – AD574A Interface

OUTLINE DIMENSIONS
Dimensions shown in inches and (mm).

28-PIN CERAMIC DIP PACKAGE (D28A)

28-LEAD PLASTIC DIP PACKAGE (N28A)

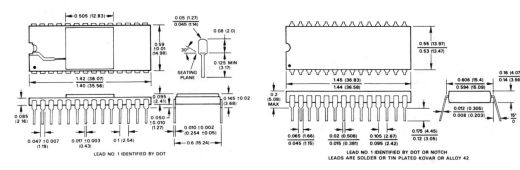

LEAD NO. 1 IDENTIFIED BY DOT

LEAD NO. 1 IDENTIFIED BY DOT OR NOTCH
LEADS ARE SOLDER OR TIN PLATED KOVAR OR ALLOY 42

28-TERMINAL PLCC PACKAGE

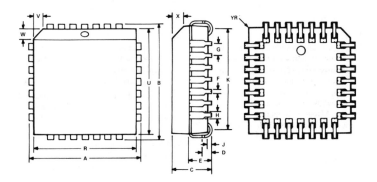

DIM	MILLIMETERS		INCHES	
	MIN	MAX	MIN	MAX
A	12.32	12.57	0.485	0.495
B	12.32	12.57	0.485	0.495
C	4.19	4.57	0.165	0.180
D	0.64	1.01	0.025	0.040
E	2.16	2.79	0.085	0.110
F	0.33	0.53	0.013	0.021
G	1.27 BSC		0.050 BSC	
H	0.66	0.81	0.026	0.032
J	0.38	0.63	0.015	0.025
K	9.91	10.92	0.390	0.430
R	11.43	11.58	0.450	0.456
U	11.43	11.58	0.450	0.456
V	1.07	1.21	0.042	0.048
W	1.07	1.21	0.042	0.048
X	1.07	1.42	0.042	0.056
Y	0.00	0.50	0.000	0.020

Low Cost Signal Conditioning 8-Bit ADC
AD670

FEATURES
Complete 8-Bit Signal Conditioning A/D Converter
Including Instrumentation Amp and Reference
Microprocessor Bus Interface
10µs Conversion Speed
Flexible Input Stage: Instrumentation Amp Front End
Provides Differential Inputs and High Common-Mode
Rejection
No User Trims Required
No Missing Codes Over Temperature
Single +5V Supply Operation
Convenient Input Ranges
20-Pin DIP or Surface-Mount Package
Low Cost Monolithic Construction

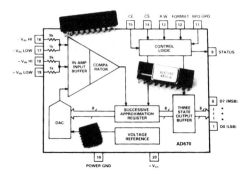

GENERAL DESCRIPTION
The AD670 is a complete 8-bit signal conditioning analog-to-digital
converter. It consists of an instrumentation amplifier front end
along with a DAC, comparator, successive approximation register
(SAR), precision voltage reference, and a three-state output
buffer on a single monolithic chip. No external components or
user trims are required to interface, with full accuracy, an analog
system to an 8-bit data bus. The AD670 will operate on the
+5V system supply. The input stage provides differential inputs
with excellent common-mode rejection and allows direct interface
to a variety of transducers.

The device is configured with input scaling resistors to permit
two input ranges: 0 to 255mV (1mV/LSB) and 0 to 2.55V
(10mV/LSB). The AD670 can be configured for both unipolar
and bipolar inputs over these ranges. The differential inputs and
common-mode rejection of this front end are useful in applications
such as conversion of transducer signals superimposed on common-
mode voltages.

The AD670 incorporates advanced circuit design and proven
processing technology. The successive approximation function is
implemented with I^2L (integrated injection logic). Thin-film
SiCr resistors provide the stability required to prevent missing
codes over the entire operating temperature range while laser
wafer trimming of the resistor ladder permits calibration of the
device to within ±1LSB. Thus, no user trims for gain or offset
are required. Conversion time of the device is 10µs.

The AD670 is available in four package types and five grades.
The J and K grades are specified over 0 to +70°C and come in
20-pin plastic DIP packages or 20-terminal PLCC packages.
The A and B grades (−40°C to +85°C) and the S grade (−55°C
to +125°C) come in 20-pin ceramic DIP packages.

The S grade is also available with optional processing to MIL-STD-
883 in 20-pin ceramic DIP or 20-terminal LCC packages. The
Analog Devices Military Products Databook should be consulted
for details on these configurations.

PRODUCT HIGHLIGHTS
1. The AD670 is a complete 8-bit A/D including three-state
   outputs and microprocessor control for direct connection to
   8-bit data buses. No external components are required to
   perform a conversion.
2. The flexible input stage features a differential instrumentation
   amp input with excellent common-mode rejection. This
   allows direct interface to a variety of transducers without
   preamplification.
3. No user trims are required for 8-bit accurate performance.
4. Operation from a single +5V supply allows the AD670 to
   run off of the microprocessor's supply.
5. Four convenient input ranges (two unipolar and two bipolar)
   are available through internal scaling resistors: 0 to 255mV
   (1mV/LSB) and 0 to 2.55V (10mV/LSB).
6. Software control of the output mode is provided. The user
   can easily select unipolar or bipolar inputs and binary or 2's
   complement output codes.

One Technology Way; P. O. Box 9106; Norwood, MA 02062-9106 U.S.A.
Tel: 617/329-4700   Twx: 710/394-6577
Telex: 174059   Cables: ANALOG NORWOODMASS

SPECIFICATIONS (@ V_CC = +5V and +25°C unless otherwise noted)

Model	Min	AD670J Typ	Max	Min	AD670K Typ	Max	Units
OPERATING TEMPERATURE RANGE	0		+70	0		+70	°C
RESOLUTION	8			8			Bit
CONVERSION TIME		10				10	μs
RELATIVE ACCURACY			±1/2			±1/4	LSB
T_min to T_max			±1/2			±1/2	LSB
DIFFERENTIAL LINEARITY ERROR							
T_min to T_max		GUARANTEED NO MISSING CODES ALL GRADES					
GAIN ACCURACY							
@ +25°C			±1.5			±0.75	LSB
T_min to T_max			±2.0			±1.0	LSB
UNIPOLAR ZERO ERROR							
@ +25°C			±1.5			±0.75	LSB
T_min to T_max			±2.0			±1.0	LSB
BIPOLAR ZERO ERROR							
@ +25°C			±1.5			±0.75	LSB
T_min to T_max			±2.0			±1.0	LSB
ANALOG INPUT RANGES							
DIFFERENTIAL (−V_IN to +V_IN)							
Low Range		0 to +255			0 to +255		mV
		−128 to +127			−128 to +127		mV
High Range		0 to +2.55			0 to +2.55		V
		−1.28 to +1.27			−1.28 to +1.27		V
ABSOLUTE (Inputs to Power Gnd)							
Low Range @ +25°C	−0.128		1.2	−0.128		1.2	V
Low Range T_min to T_max	−0.128		1.2	−0.128		1.2	V
High Range @ +25°C	−1.28		5	−1.28		5	V
High Range T_min to T_max	−1.28		5	−1.28		5	V
BIAS CURRENT (255mV RANGE)							
T_min to T_max		200	500		200	500	nA
OFFSET CURRENT (255mV RANGE)							
T_min to T_max		20	100		20	100	nA
2.55V RANGE INPUT RESISTANCE	8.0		12.0	8.0		12.0	kΩ
2.55V RANGE FULL SCALE MATCH + AND − INPUT		±1/2			±1/2		LSB
COMMON-MODE REJECTION RATIO (255mV RANGE)		1			1		LSB
COMMON-MODE REJECTION RATIO (2.55V RANGE)		1			1		LSB
POWER SUPPLY							
Operating Range	4.5		5.5	4.5		5.5	V
Current I_CC		30	45		30	45	mA
Rejection Ratio T_min to T_max			0.015			0.015	% of FS/%
DIGITAL OUTPUTS							
SINK CURRENT (V_OUT = 0.4V)							
T_min to T_max	1.6			1.6			mA
SOURCE CURRENT (V_OUT = 2.4V)							
T_min to T_max	0.5			0.5			mA
THREE-STATE LEAKAGE CURRENT			±40			±40	μA
OUTPUT CAPACITANCE		5			5		pF
DIGITAL INPUT VOLTAGE							
V_INL			0.8			0.8	V
V_INH	2.0			2.0			V
DIGITAL INPUT CURRENT							
(0 ≤ V_IN ≤ +5V)							
I_INL	−100			−100			μA
I_INH			+100			+100	μA
INPUT CAPACITANCE		10			10		pF

NOTES
Specifications subject to change without notice.
Specifications shown in boldface are tested on all production units at final
electrical test. Results from these tests are used to calculate outgoing quality
levels. All min and max specifications are guaranteed, although only those
shown in boldface are tested on all production units.

Model	AD670A Min	Typ	Max	AD670B Min	Typ	Max	AD670S Min	Typ	Max	Units
OPERATING TEMPERATURE RANGE	-40		+85	-40		+85	-55		+125	°C
RESOLUTION	8			8			8			Bit
CONVERSION TIME			10			10			10	µs
RELATIVE ACCURACY			±1/2			±1/4			±1/2	LSB
T_{min} to T_{max}			±1/2			±1/2			±1	LSB
DIFFERENTIAL LINEARITY ERROR T_{min} to T_{max}				GUARANTEED NO MISSING CODES ALL GRADES						
GAIN ACCURACY										
@ +25°C			±1.5			±0.75			±1.5	LSB
T_{min} to T_{max}			±2.5			±1.5			±2.5	LSB
UNIPOLAR ZERO ERROR										
@ +25°C			±1.0			±0.5			±1.0	LSB
T_{min} to T_{max}			±2.0			±1.0			±2.0	LSB
BIPOLAR ZERO ERROR										
@ +25°C			±1.0			±0.5			±1.0	LSB
T_{min} to T_{max}			±2.0			±1.0			±2.0	LSB
ANALOG INPUT RANGES										
DIFFERENTIAL ($-V_{IN}$ to $+V_{IN}$)										
Low Range		0 to +255			0 to +255			0 to +255		mV
		-128 to +127			-128 to +127			-128 to +127		mV
High Range		0 to +2.55			0 to +2.55			0 to +2.55		V
		-1.28 to +1.27			-1.28 to +1.27			-1.28 to +1.27		V
ABSOLUTE (Inputs to Power Gnd)										
Low Range @ +25°	-0.128		1.2	-0.128		1.2	-0.128		1.2	V
Low Range T_{min} to T_{max}	-0.08		1.2	-0.08		1.2	-0.005		1.2	V
High Range @ +25°C	-1.28		5	-1.28		5	-1.28		5	V
High Range T_{min} to T_{max}	-0.8		5	-0.8		5	-0.05		5	V
BIAS CURRENT (255mV RANGE) T_{min} to T_{max}		200	500		200	500		200	500	nA
OFFSET CURRENT (255mV RANGE) T_{min} to T_{max}		20	100		20	100		20	100	nA
2.55V RANGE INPUT RESISTANCE	8.0		12.0	8.0		12.0	8.0		12.0	kΩ
2.55V RANGE FULL SCALE MATCH + AND - INPUT		±1/2			±1/2			±1/2		LSB
COMMON-MODE REJECTION RATIO (255mV RANGE)		1			1			1		LSB
COMMON-MODE REJECTION RATIO (2.55V RANGE)		1			1			1		LSB
POWER SUPPLY										
Operating Range	4.5		5.5	4.5		5.5	4.75		5.5	V
Current I_{CC}		30	45		30	45		30	45	mA
Rejection Ratio T_{min} to T_{max}			0.015			0.015			0.015	% of FS/%
DIGITAL OUTPUTS										
SINK CURRENT (V_{OUT} = 0.4V) T_{min} to T_{max}	1.6			1.6			1.6			mA
SOURCE CURRENT (V_{OUT} = 2.4V) T_{min} to T_{max}	0.5			0.5			0.5			mA
THREE-STATE LEAKAGE CURRENT			±40			±40			±40	µA
OUTPUT CAPACITANCE		5			5			5		pF
DIGITAL INPUT VOLTAGE										
V_{INL}			0.8			0.8			0.7	V
V_{INH}	2.0			2.0			2.0			V
DIGITAL INPUT CURRENT ($0 \leq V_{IN} \leq +5V$)										
I_{INL}	-100			-100			-100			µA
I_{INH}			+100			+100			+100	µA
INPUT CAPACITANCE		10			10			10		pF

NOTES
Specifications shown in boldface are tested on all production units at final electrical test. Results from those tests are used to calculate outgoing quality levels. All min and max specifications are guaranteed, although only those shown in boldface are tested on all production units.

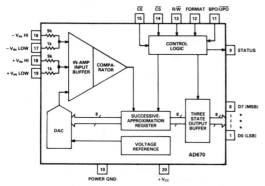

Figure 1. AD670 Block Diagram and Terminal Configuration
(All Packages)

ABSOLUTE MAXIMUM RATINGS*

V_{CC} to Ground . . . . 0V to +7.5V
Digital Inputs (Pins 11-15) . . . . −0.5V to V_{CC} +0.5V
Digital Outputs (Pins 1-9) . Momentary Short to V_{CC} or Ground
Analog Inputs (Pins 16-19) . . . . −30V to +30V
Power Dissipation 450mW
Storage Temperature Range . . . . −65°C to +150°C
Lead Temperature (Soldering, 10sec) . . . . +300°C

*Stresses above those listed under "Absolute Maximum Ratings" may cause permanent damage to the device. This is a stress rating only and functional operation of the device at these or any other conditions above those indicated in the operational sections of this specification is not implied. Exposure to absolute maximum rating conditions for extended periods may affect device reliability.

AD670 ORDERING GUIDE

Model	Temperature Range	Relative Accuracy @ 25°C	Gain Accuracy @ 25°C	Package*
AD670JN	0 to +70°C	± 1/2LSB	± 1.5LSB	Plastic DIP
AD670JP	0 to +70°C	± 1/2LSB	± 1.5LSB	PLCC
AD670KN	0 to +70°C	± 1/4LSB	± 0.75LSB	Plastic DIP
AD670KP	0 to +70°C	± 1/4LSB	± 0.75LSB	PLCC
AD670AD	−40°C to +85°C	± 1/2LSB	± 1.5LSB	Ceramic DIP
AD670BD	−40°C to +85°C	± 1/4LSB	± 0.75LSB	Ceramic DIP
AD670SD	−55°C to +125°C	± 1/2LSB	± 1.5LSB	Ceramic DIP

*Note: See last page for package outlines.

CIRCUIT OPERATION/FUNCTIONAL DESCRIPTION

The AD670 is a functionally complete 8-bit signal conditioning A/D converter with microprocessor compatibility. The input section uses an instrumentation amplifier to accomplish the voltage to current conversion. This front end provides a high impedance, low bias current differential amplifier. The common-mode range allows the user to directly interface the device to a variety of transducers.

The A/D conversions are controlled by R/W̄, CS̄, and CĒ. The R/W̄ line directs the converter to read or start a conversion. A minimum write/start pulse of 300ns is required on either CĒ or CS̄. The STATUS line goes high, indicating that a conversion is in process. The conversion thus begun, the internal 8-bit DAC is sequenced from MSB to LSB using a novel successive approximation technique. In conventional designs, the DAC is stepped through the bits by a clock. This can be thought of as a static design since the speed at which the DAC is sequenced is determined solely by the clock. No clock is used in the AD670. Instead, a "dynamic SAR" is created consisting of a string of

inverters with taps along the delay line. Sections of the delay line between taps act as one shots. The pulses are used to set and reset the DAC's bits and strobe the comparator. When strobed, the comparator then determines whether the addition of each successively weighted bit current causes the DAC current sum to be greater or less than the input current. If the sum is less, the bit is turned off. After all bits are tested, the SAR holds an 8-bit code representing the input signal to within 1/2LSB accuracy. Ease of implementation and reduced dependence on process related variables make this an attractive approach to a successive approximation design.

The SAR provides an end-of-conversion signal to the control logic which then brings the STATUS line low. Data outputs remain in a high impedance state until R/W̄ is brought high with CĒ and CS̄ low and allows the converter to be read. Bringing CĒ or CS̄ high during the valid data period ends the read cycle. The output buffers cannot be enabled during a conversion. Any convert start commands will be ignored until the conversion cycle is completed; once a conversion cycle has been started it cannot be stopped or restarted.

The AD670 provides the user with a great deal of flexibility by offering two input spans and formats and a choice of output codes. Input format and input range can each be selected. The BPO/$\overline{UPO}$ pin controls a switch which injects a bipolar offset current of a value equal to the MSB less 1/2LSB into the summing node of the comparator to offset the DAC output. Two precision 10 to 1 attenuators are included on board to provide input range selection of 0 to 2.55V or 0 to 255mV. Additional ranges of −1.28 to 1.27V and −128 to 127mV are possible if the BPO/$\overline{UPO}$ switch is high when the conversion is started. Finally, output coding can be chosen using the FORMAT pin when the conversion is started. In the bipolar mode and with a logic 1 on FORMAT, the output is in two's complement; with a logic 0, the output is offset binary.

CONNECTING THE AD670

The AD670 has been designed for ease of use. All active components required to perform a complete A/D conversion are on board and are connected internally. In addition, all calibration trims are performed at the factory, assuring specified accuracy without user trims. There are, however, a number of options and connections that should be considered to obtain maximum flexibility from the part.

INPUT CONNECTIONS

Standard connections are shown in the figures that follow. An input range of 0 to 2.55V may be configured as shown in Figure 2a. This will provide a one LSB change for each 10mV of input change. The input range of 0 to 255mV is configured as shown in Figure 2b. In this case, each LSB represents 1mV of input change. When unipolar input signals are used, Pin 11, BPO/$\overline{UPO}$, should be grounded. Pin 11 selects the input format for either unipolar or bipolar signals. Figures 3a and 3b show the input connections for bipolar signals. Pin 11 should be tied to +V_{CC} for bipolar inputs.

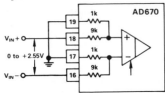

2a. 0 to 2.55V (10mV/LSB)

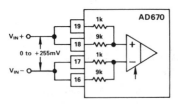

2b. 0 to 255mV (1mV/LSB)

NOTE: PIN 11, BPO/$\overline{UPO}$ SHOULD BE LOW WHEN CONVERSION IS STARTED.

Figure 2. Unipolar Input Connections

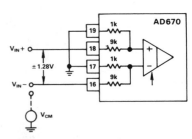

3a. ±1.28V Range

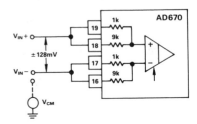

3b. ±128mV Range

NOTE: PIN 11, BPO/$\overline{UPO}$ SHOULD BE HIGH WHEN CONVERSION IS STARTED.

Figure 3. Bipolar Input Connections

Although the instrumentation amplifier has a differential input, there must be a return path to ground for the bias currents. If it is not provided, these currents will charge stray capacitances and cause internal circuit nodes to drift uncontrollably causing the digital output to change. Such a return path is provided in Figures 2a and 3a (larger input ranges) since the 1k resistor leg is tied to ground. This is not the case for Figures 2b and 3b (the lower input ranges). When connecting the AD670 inputs to floating sources, such as transformers and ac-coupled sources, there must still be a dc path from each input to common. This can be accomplished by connecting a 10kΩ resistor from each input to ground.

Common-Mode Performance

The AD670 is designed to reject DC and AC common-mode voltages. In order to ensure proper operation, the user should verify that the absolute range of input signals (referred to Power Ground) falls within the specified limits. Over the 0 to +70°C range, these limits allow full bipolar signals to be accommodated with a DC bias on either terminal that ranges down to 0V. At temperatures above +70°C, negative signals are more limited, but excursions below Power Ground can still be accommodated if the Absolute Input Range specifications are respected.

The excellent common-mode rejection of the AD670 is due to the differential nature of the instrumentation amplifier front end. The differential signal is maintained until it reaches the output of the comparator. In contrast to a standard operational amplifier, the instrumentation amplifier front end of the AD670 provides significantly improved CMRR over a wide frequency range (Figure 4a).

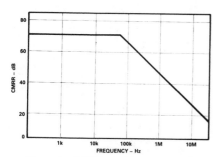

Figure 4a. CMRR over Frequency

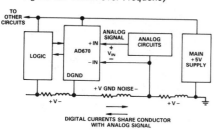

Figure 4b. AD670 Input Rejects Common-Mode Ground Noise

BPO/UPO	FORMAT	INPUT RANGE/OUTPUT FORMAT
0	0	Unipolar/Straight Binary
1	0	Bipolar/Offset Binary
0	1	Unipolar/2's Complement
1	1	Bipolar/2's Complement

Table I. AD670 Input Selection/Output Format Truth Table

$+V_{IN}$	$-V_{IN}$	DIFF V_{IN}	STRAIGHT BINARY (FORMAT = 0, BPO/UPO = 0)
0	0	0	0000 0000
128mV	0	128mV	1000 0000
255mV	0	255mV	1111 1111
255mV	255mV	0	0000 0000
128mV	127mV	1mV	0000 0001
128mV	−127mV	255mV	1111 1111

Figure 5a. Unipolar Output Codes (Low Range)

$+V_{IN}$	$-V_{IN}$	DIFF V_{IN}	OFFSET BINARY (FORMAT = 0, BPO/UPO = 1)	2's COMPLEMENT (FORMAT = 1, BPO/UPO = 1)
0	0	0	1000 0000	0000 0000
127mV	0	127mV	1111 1111	0111 1111
1.127V	1.000V	127mV	1111 1111	0111 1111
255mV	255mV	0	1000 0000	0000 0000
128mV	127mV	1mV	1000 0001	0000 0001
127mV	128mV	−1mV	0111 1111	1111 1111
127mV	255mV	−128mV	0000 0000	1000 0000
−128mV	0	−128mV	0000 0000	1000 0000

Figure 5b. Bipolar Output Codes (Low Range)

Good common-mode performance is useful in a number of situations. In bridge-type transducer applications, such performance facilitates the recovery of differential analog signals in the presence of a dc common-mode or a noisy electrical environment. High-frequency CMRR also becomes important when the analog signal is referred to a noisy, remote digital ground. In each case, the CMRR specification of the AD670 allows the integrity of the input signal to be preserved.

The AD670's common-mode voltage tolerance allows great flexibility in circuit layout. Most other A/D converters require the establishment of one point as the analog reference point. This is necessary in order to minimize the effects of parasitic voltages. The AD670, however, eliminates the need to make the analog ground reference point and A/D analog ground one and the same. Instead, a system such as that shown in Figure 4b is possible as a result of the AD670's common-mode performance. The resistors and inductors in the ground return represent unavoidable system parasitic impedances.

Input/Output Options

Data output coding (2's complement vs. straight binary) is selected using Pin 12, the FORMAT pin. The selection of input format (bipolar vs. unipolar) is controlled using Pin 11, BPO/UPO. Prior to a write/convert, the state of FORMAT and BPO/UPO should be available to the converter. These lines may be tied to the data bus and may be changed with each conversion if desired. The configurations are shown in Table I. Output coding for representative signals in each of these configurations is shown in Figure 5.

An output signal, STATUS, indicates the status of the conversion. STATUS goes high at the beginning of the conversion and returns low when the conversion cycle has been completed.

Calibration

Because of its precise factory calibration, the AD670 is intended to be operated without user trims for gain and offset; therefore, no provisions have been made for such user trims. Figures 6a, 6b, and 6c show the transfer curves at zero and full scale for the unipolar and bipolar modes. The code transitions are positioned so that the desired value is centered at that code. The first LSB transition for the unipolar mode occurs for an input of + 1/2LSB (5mV or 0.5mV). Similarly, the MSB transition for the bipolar mode is set at − 1/2LSB (−5mV or −0.5mV). The full scale transition is located at the full scale value −1 1/2LSB. These values are 2.545V and 254.5mV.

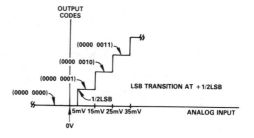

Figure 6a. Unipolar Transfer Curve

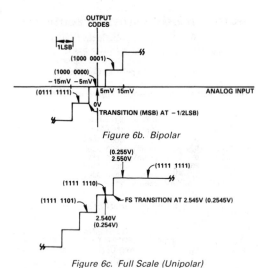

Figure 6b. Bipolar

Figure 6c. Full Scale (Unipolar)

Figure 6. Transfer Curves

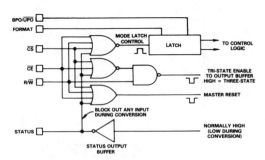

Figure 7. Control Logic Block Diagram

R/W̄	C̄S̄	C̄Ē	OPERATION
0	0	0	WRITE/CONVERT
1	0	0	READ
X	X	1	NONE
X	1	X	NONE

Table II. AD670 Control Signal Truth Table

CONTROL AND TIMING OF THE AD670
Control Logic
The AD670 contains on-chip logic to provide conversion and data read operations from signals commonly available in microprocessor systems. Figure 7 shows the internal logic circuitry of the AD670. The control signals, C̄Ē, C̄S̄, and R/W̄ control the operation of the converter. The read or write function is determined by R/W̄ when both C̄S̄ and C̄Ē are low as shown in Table II. If all three control inputs are held low longer than the conversion time, the device will continuously convert until one input, C̄Ē, C̄S̄, or R/W̄ is brought high. The relative timing of these signals is discussed later in this section.

Timing
The AD670 is easily interfaced to a variety of microprocessors and other digital systems. The following discussion of the timing requirements of the AD670 control signals will provide the designer with useful insight into the operation of the device.

Write/Convert Start Cycle
Figure 8 shows a complete timing diagram for the write/convert start cycle. C̄S̄ (chip select) and C̄Ē (chip enable) are active low and are interchangeable signals. Both C̄S̄ and C̄Ē must be low for the converter to read or start a conversion. The minimum pulse width, t_W, on either C̄S̄ or C̄Ē is 300ns to start a conversion.

Table III. AD670 TIMING SPECIFICATIONS
Boldface indicates parameters tested 100% unless otherwise noted. See Specifications page for explanation.

Symbol	Parameter	Min	Typ	Max	Units
WRITE/CONVERT START MODE			+25°C		
t_W	Write/Start Pulse Width	300			ns
t_{DS}	Input Data Setup Time	200			ns
t_{DH}	Input Data Hold	10			ns
t_{RWC}	Read/Write Setup Before Control	0			ns
t_{DC}	Delay to Convert Start			700	ns
t_C	**Conversion Time**			10	μs
READ MODE					
t_R	Read Time	250			ns
t_{SD}	Delay from Status Low to Data Read			250	ns
t_{TD}	**Bus Access Time**		200	250	ns
t_{DH}	Data Hold Time	25			ns
t_{DT}	**Output Float Delay**			150	ns
t_{RT}	R/W̄ before C̄Ē or C̄S̄ low	0			ns

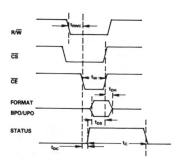

Figure 8. Write/Convert Start Timing

The R/$\overline{W}$ line is used to direct the converter to start a conversion (R/$\overline{W}$ low) or read data (R/$\overline{W}$ high). The relative sequencing of the three control signals (R/$\overline{W}$, $\overline{CE}$, $\overline{CS}$) is unimportant. However, when all three signals remain low for at least 300ns (t_W), STATUS will go high to signal that a conversion is taking place.

Once a conversion is started and the STATUS line goes high, convert start commands will be ignored until the conversion cycle is complete. The output data buffer cannot be enabled during a conversion.

Read Cycle

Figure 9 shows the timing for the data read operation. The data outputs are in a high impedance state until a read cycle is initiated. To begin the read cycle, R/$\overline{W}$ is brought high. During a read cycle, the minimum pulse length for $\overline{CE}$ and $\overline{CS}$ is a function of the length of time required for the output data to be valid. The data becomes valid and is available to the data bus in a maximum of 250ns. This delay between the high impedance state and valid data is the maximum bus access time or t_{TD}. Bringing $\overline{CE}$ or $\overline{CS}$ high during valid data ends the read cycle. The outputs remain valid for a minimum of 25ns (t_{DH}) and return to the high impedance state after a delay, t_{DT}, of 150ns maximum.

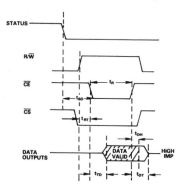

Figure 9. Read Cycle Timing

STAND-ALONE OPERATION

The AD670 can be used in a "stand-alone" mode, which is useful in systems with dedicated input ports available. Two typical conditions are described and illustrated by the timing diagrams which follow.

Single Conversion, Single Read

When the AD670 is used in a stand-alone mode, $\overline{CS}$ and $\overline{CE}$ should be tied together. Conversion will be initiated by bringing R/$\overline{W}$ low. Within 700ns, a conversion will begin. The R/$\overline{W}$ pulse should be brought high again once the conversion has started so that the data will be valid upon completion of the conversion. Data will remain valid until $\overline{CE}$ and $\overline{CS}$ are brought high to indicate the end of the read cycle or R/$\overline{W}$ goes low. The timing diagram is shown in Figure 10.

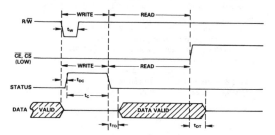

Figure 10. Stand-Alone Mode Single Conversion/ Single Read

Continuous Conversion, Single Read

A variety of applications may call for the A/D to be read after several conversions. In process control systems, this is often the case since a reading from a sensor may only need to be updated every few conversions. Figure 11 shows the timing relationships.

Once again, $\overline{CE}$ and $\overline{CS}$ should be tied together. Conversion will begin when the R/$\overline{W}$ signal is brought low. The device will convert repeatedly as indicated by the status line. A final conversion will take place once the R/$\overline{W}$ line has been brought high. The rising edge of R/$\overline{W}$ must occur while STATUS is high. R/$\overline{W}$ should not return high while STATUS is low since the circuit is in a reset state prior to the next conversion. Since the rising edge of R/$\overline{W}$ must occur while STATUS is high, R/$\overline{W}$'s length must be a minimum of 10.25μs (t_C + t_{TD}). Data becomes valid upon completion of the conversion and will remain so until the $\overline{CE}$ and $\overline{CS}$ lines are brought high indicating the end of the read cycle or R/$\overline{W}$ goes low initiating a new series of conversions.

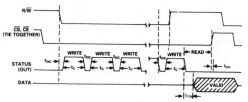

Figure 11. Stand-Alone Mode Continuous Conversion/ Single Read

APPLYING THE AD670

The AD670 has been designed for ease of use, system compatibility, and minimization of external components. Transducer interfaces generally require signal conditioning and preamplification before the signal can be converted. The AD670 will reduce and even eliminate this excess circuitry in many cases. To illustrate the flexibility and superior solution that the AD670 can bring to a transducer interface problem, the following discussions are offered.

Temperature Measurements

Temperature transducers are one of the most common sources of analog signals in data acquisition systems. These sensors require circuitry for excitation and preamplification/buffering. The instrumentation amplifier input of the AD670 eliminates the need for this signal conditioning. The output signals from temperature transducers are generally sufficiently slow that a sample/hold amplifier is not required. Figure 12 shows the AD590 IC temperature transducer interfaced to the AD670. The AD580 voltage reference is used to offset the input for 0°C calibration. The current output of the AD590 is converted into a voltage by R1. The high impedance unbuffered voltage is applied directly to the AD670 configured in the -128mV to 127mV bipolar range. The digital output will have a resolution of 1°C.

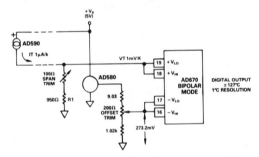

Figure 12. AD670 Temperature Transducer Interface

Platinum RTDs are also a popular, temperature transducer. Typical RTDs have a resistance of 100Ω at 0°C and change resistance 0.4Ω per °C. If a constant excitation current is caused to flow in the RTD, the change in voltage drop will be a measure of the change in temperature. Figure 13 shows such a method and the required connections to the AD670. The AD580 2.5V reference provides the accurate voltage for the excitation current and range offsetting for the RTD. The op-amp is configured to force a constant 2.5mA current through the RTD. The differential inputs of the AD670 measure the difference between a fixed offset voltage and the temperature dependent output of the op-amp which varies with the resistance of the RTD. The RTD change of approximately $0.4\Omega/°C$ results in a 1mV/°C voltage change. With the AD670 in the 1mV/LSB range, temperatures from 0 to 255°C can be measured.

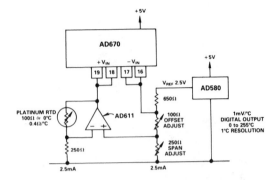

Figure 13. Low Cost RTD Interface

Differential temperature measurements can be made using an AD590 connected to each of the inputs as shown in Figure 14. This configuration will allow the user to measure the relative temperature difference between two points with a 1°C resolution. Although the internal 1k and 9k resistors on the inputs have $\pm20\%$ tolerance, trimming the AD590 is unnecessary as most differential temperature applications are concerned with the relative differences between the two. However, the user may see up to a 20% scale factor error in the differential temperature to digital output transfer curve.

This scale factor error can be eliminated through a software correction. Offset corrections can be made by adjusting for any difference that results when both sensors are held at the same temperature. A span adjustment can then be made by immersing one AD590 in an ice bath and one in boiling water and eliminating any deviation from 100°C. For a low cost version of this setup, the plastic AD592 can be substituted for the AD590.

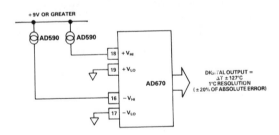

Figure 14. Differential Temperature Measurement Using the AD590

STRAIN GAUGE MEASUREMENTS

Many semiconductor-type strain gauges, pressure transducers, and load cells may also be connected directly to the AD670. These types of transducers typically produce 30 millivolts full-scale per volt of excitation. In the circuit shown in Figure 15, the AD670 is connected directly to a Data Instruments model JP-20 load cell. The AD584 programmable voltage reference is used along with an AD741 op-amp to provide the ±2.5V excitation for the load cell. The output of the transducer will be ±150mV for a force of ±20 pounds. The AD670 is configured for the ±128 millivolt range. The resolution is then approximately 2.1 ounces per LSB over a range of ±17 pounds. Scaling to exactly 2 ounces per LSB can be accomplished by trimming the reference voltage which excites the load cell.

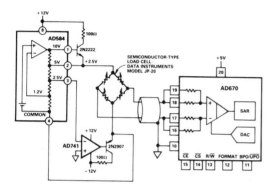

Figure 15. AD670 Load Cell Interface

MULTIPLEXED INPUTS

Most data acquisition systems require the measurement of several analog signals. Multiple A/D converters are often used to digitize these inputs, requiring additional preamplification and buffer stages per channel. Since these signals vary slowly, a differential MUX can multiplex inputs from several transducers into a single AD670. And since the AD670's signal-conditioning capability is preserved, the cost of several ADCs, differential amplifiers, and other support components can be reduced to that of a single AD670, a MUX, and a few digital logic gates.

An AD7502 dual 4-channel MUX appears in Figure 16 multiplexing four differential signals to the AD670. The AD7502's decoded address is gated with the microprocessor's write signal to provice a latching strobe at the flip-flops. A write cycle to the AD7502's address then latches the two LSBs of the data word thereby selecting the input channel for subsequent conversions.

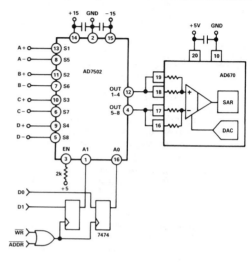

Figure 16. Multiplexed Analog Inputs to AD670

SAMPLED INPUTS

For those applications where the input signal is capable of slewing more than 1/2LSB during the AD670's 10μs conversion cycle, the input should be held constant for the cycle's duration. The circuit shown in Figure 17 uses a CMOS switch and two capacitors to sample/hold the input. The AD670's STATUS output, once inverted, supplies the sample/hold (S/H̄) signal.

A convert command applied on the C̄Ē, C̄S̄ OR R/W̄ lines will initiate the conversion. The AD670's STATUS output, once inverted, supplies the sample/hold signal to the CD4066. The CD4066 CMOS switch shown in Figure 17 was chosen for its fast transition times, low on-resistance and low cost. The control input's propagation delay for switch-closed to switch-open should remain less than 150ns to ensure that the sample-to-hold transition occurs before the first bit decision in the AD670.

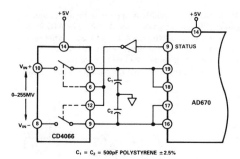

Figure 17. Low Cost Sample-and-Hold Circuit for AD670

Since settling to 1/2LSB at 8-bits of resolution requires 6.2 RC time constants, the 500pF hold capacitors and CD4066's 300Ω on-resistance yield an acquisition time of under 1μs, assuming a low impedance source.

This sample/hold approach makes use of the differential capabilities of the AD670. Because 500pF hold capacitors are used on both $V_{IN}+$ and $V_{IN}-$ inputs, the droop rate depends only on the offset current of the AD670, typically 20nA. With the matched 500pF capacitors, the droop rate is 40μV/μs. The input will then droop only 0.4mV (0.4LSB) during the AD670's 10μs conversion time. The differential approach also minimizes pedestal error since only the difference in charge injection between the two switches results in errors at the A/D.

The fast conversion time and differential and common-mode capabilities of the AD670 permit this simple sample-hold design to perform well with low sample-to-hold offset, droop rate of about 40μV/μs and acquisition time under 1μs. The effective aperture time of the AD670 is reduced by about 2 orders of magnitude with this circuit, allowing frequencies to be converted up to several kilohertz.

While no input anti-aliasing filter is shown, filtering will be necessary to prevent output errors if higher frequencies are present in the input signal. Many practical variations are possible with this circuit, including input MUX control, for digitizing a number of AC channels.

IBM PC INTERFACE

The AD670 appears in Figure 18 interfaced to the IBM PC. Since the device resides in I/O space, its address is decoded from only the lower ten address lines and must be gated with AEN (active low) to mask out internal (DMA) cycles which use the same I/O address space. This active low signal is applied to $\overline{CS}$. AO, meanwhile, is reserved for the R/$\overline{W}$ input. This places

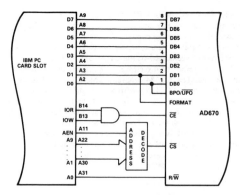

Figure 18. IBM PC Interface to AD670

the AD670 in two adjacent addresses; one for starting the conversion and the other for reading the result. The $\overline{IOR}$ and $\overline{IOW}$ signals are then gated and applied to $\overline{CE}$, while the lower two data lines are applied to FORMAT and BPO/$\overline{UPO}$ inputs to provide software programmable input formats and output coding.

In BASIC, a simple OUT ADDR, WORD command initiates a conversion. While the upper six bits of the data WORD are meaningless, the lower two bits define the analog input format and digital output coding according to Table IV. The data is available ten microseconds later (which is negligible in BASIC) and can be read using INP (ADDR + 1). The 3-line subroutine in Figure 19, used in conjunction with the interface of Figure 18, converts an analog input within a bipolar range to an offset binary coded digital word.

NOTE: Due to the large number of options that may be installed in the PC, the I/O bus loading should be limited to one Schottky TTL load. Therefore, a buffer/driver should be used when interfacing more than two AD670's to the I/O bus.

DATA	INPUT FORMAT	OUTPUT CODING
0	Unipolar	Straight Binary
1	Bipolar	Offset Binary
2	Unipolar	2's Complement
3	Bipolar	2's Complement

Table IV.

```
10   OUT &H310,1              'INITIATE CONVERSION
20   ANALOGIN = INP (&H311)   'READ ANALOG INPUT
30   RETURN
```

Figure 19. Conversion Subroutine

OUTLINE DIMENSIONS
Dimensions shown in inches and (mm).

20-PIN PLASTIC DIP (N)   **20-PIN CERAMIC DIP (D)**

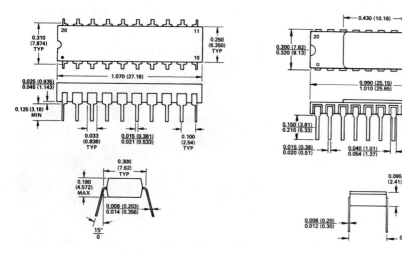

LEAD NO. 1 IDENTIFIED BY DOT OR NOTCH.

20-TERMINAL PLCC PACKAGE

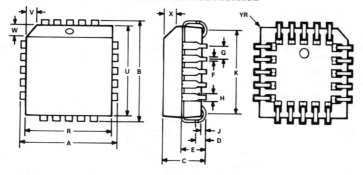

DIM	MILLIMETERS		INCHES	
	MIN	MAX	MIN	MAX
A	9.78	10.02	0.385	0.395
B	9.78	10.02	0.385	0.395
C	4.19	4.57	0.165	0.180
D	0.64	1.01	0.025	0.040
E	2.16	2.79	0.085	0.110
F	0.33	0.53	0.013	0.021
G	1.27 BSC		0.050 BSC	
H	0.66	0.81	0.026	0.032
J	0.38	0.63	0.015	0.025
K	7.37	8.38	0.290	0.330
R	8.89	9.04	0.350	0.356
U	8.89	9.04	0.350	0.356
V	1.07	1.21	0.042	0.048
W	1.07	1.21	0.042	0.048
X	1.07	1.42	0.042	0.056
Y	0.00	0.50	0.000	0.020

**ANALOG
DEVICES**

LC² MOS High Speed μP Compatible
8-Bit ADC with Track/Hold Function
AD7820

FEATURES
Fast Conversion Time: 1.36μs Max
Built-In Track-and-Hold Function
No Missed Codes
No User Trims Required
Single +5V Supply
Ratiometric Operation
No External Clock
0.3″ Wide, 20-Pin DIP

GENERAL DESCRIPTION
The AD7820 is a high speed, microprocessor compatible 8-bit analog-to-digital converter which uses a half-flash conversion technique to achieve a conversion time of 1.36μs. The converter has a 0V to +5V analog input voltage range with a single +5V supply.

The half-flash technique consists of 31 comparators, a most significant 4-bit ADC and a least significant 4-bit ADC. The input to the AD7820 is tracked and held by the input sampling circuitry, eliminating the need for an external sample-and-hold for signals with slew rates less than 100 mV/μs.

The part is designed for ease of microprocessor interface with the AD7820 appearing as a memory location or I/O port without the need for external interfacing logic. All digital outputs use latched, three-state output buffer circuitry to allow direct connection to a microprocessor data bus or system input port. A non-three state overflow output is also provided to allow cascading of devices to give higher resolution.

The AD7820 is fabricated in an advanced, all ion-implanted, high speed, Linear Compatible CMOS (LC²MOS) process and features a low maximum power dissipation of 75mW. It is packaged in a 0.3″wide, 20-pin DIP.

PRODUCT HIGHLIGHTS
1. Fast Conversion Time
   The half-flash conversion technique, coupled with fabrication on Analog Devices' LC²MOS process, enables very fast conversion times. The maximum conversion time for the WR-RD mode is 1.36μs, with 1.6μs the maximum for the RD mode.
2. Total Unadjusted Error
   The AD7820 features an excellent total unadjusted error figure of less than ½ LSB over the full operating temperature

range. The part is also guaranteed to have no missing codes over the entire temperature range.
3. Built-In Track-and-Hold
   The analog input circuitry uses sampled-data comparators, which by nature have a built-in track-and-hold function. As a result, input signals with slew rates up to 100mV/μs can be converted to 8-bits without external sample-and-hold. This corresponds to a 5V peak-to-peak, 7kHz sine wave signal.
4. Single Supply
   Operation from a single +5V supply with a positive voltage reference allows operation of the AD7820 in microprocessor systems without any additional power supplies.

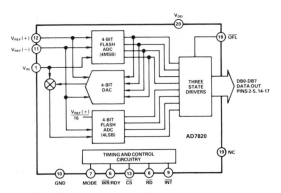

Functional Block Diagram

One Technology Way; P. O. Box 9106; Norwood, MA 02062-9106
Tel: 617/329-4700   TWX: 710/394-6577
West Coast   **Mid-West**   **Texas**
714/641-9391   312/350-9399   214/231-5094

SPECIFICATIONS

(V_{DD} = + 5V; V_{REF} (+) = + 5V; V_{REF} (−) = GND = 0V unless otherwise stated). All specifications T_{min} to T_{max} unless otherwise specified. Specifications apply for RD Mode (Pin 7 = 0V)

Parameter	AD7820KN[1]	AD7820LN	AD7820BQ AD7820TQ	AD7820CQ AD7820UQ	Units	Conditions/Comments
ACCURACY						
Resolution	8	8	8	8	Bits	
Total Unadjusted Error[2]	± 1	± 1/2	± 1	± 1/2	LSB	
Minimum Resolution for which						
No Missing Codes are guaranteed	8	8	8	8	Bits	
REFERENCE INPUT						
Input Resistance	1.0/4.0	1.0/4.0	1.0/4.0	1.0/4.0	kΩ min/kΩ max	
V_{REF} (+) Input Voltage Range	V_{REF}(−)/V_{DD}	V_{REF}(−)/V_{DD}	V_{REF}(−)/V_{DD}	V_{REF}(−)/V_{DD}	V min/V max	
V_{REF} (−) Input Voltage Range	GND/V_{REF}(+)	GND/V_{REF}(+)	GND/V_{REF}(+)	GND/V_{REF}(+)	V min/V max	
ANALOG INPUT						
Input Voltage Range	V_{REF}(−)/V_{REF}(+)	V_{REF}(−)/V_{REF}(+)	V_{REF}(−)/V_{REF}(+)	V_{REF}(−)/V_{REF}(+)	V min/V max	
Input Leakage Current	± 3	± 3	± 3	± 3	µA max	
Input Capacitance[3]	45	45	45	45	pF typ	
LOGIC INPUTS						
$\overline{CS}, \overline{WR}, \overline{RD}$						
V_{INH}	2.4	2.4	2.4	2.4	V min	
V_{INL}	0.8	0.8	0.8	0.8	V max	
I_{INH} ($\overline{CS}, \overline{RD}$)	1	1	1	1	µA max	
I_{INH} ($\overline{WR}$)	3	3	3	3	µA max	
I_{INL}	− 1	− 1	− 1	− 1	µA max	
Input Capacitance[3]	8	8	8	8	pF max	Typically 5pF
MODE						
V_{INH}	3.5	3.5	3.5	3.5	V min	
V_{INL}	1.5	1.5	1.5	1.5	V max	
I_{INH}	200	200	200	200	µA max	50 µA typ
I_{INL}	− 1	− 1	− 1	− 1	µA max	
Input Capacitance[3]	8	8	8	8	pF max	Typically 5pF
LOGIC OUTPUTS						
DB0–DB7, $\overline{OFL}$, $\overline{INT}$						
V_{OH}	4.0	4.0	4.0	4.0	V min	I_{SOURCE} = 360µA
V_{OL}	0.4	0.4	0.4	0.4	V max	I_{SINK} = 1.6mA
I_{OUT} (DB0–DB7)	± 3	± 3	± 3	± 3	µA max	Floating State Leakage
Output Capacitance[3]	8	8	8	8	pF max	Typically 5pF
RDY						
V_{OL}	0.4	0.4	0.4	0.4	V max	I_{SINK} = 2.6mA
I_{OUT}	± 3	± 3	± 3	± 3	µA max	Floating State Leakage
Output Capacitance[3]	8	8	8	8	pF max	Typically 5pF
SLEW RATE, TRACKING[3]	0.2	0.2	0.2	0.2	V/µs typ	
	0.1	0.1	0.1	0.1	V/µs max	
POWER SUPPLY						
V_{DD}	5	5	5	5	Volts	± 5% for Specified Performance
I_{DD}[4]	15	15	20	20	mA max	$\overline{CS}$ = $\overline{RD}$ = 0V
Power Dissipation	40	40	40	40	mW typ	
Power Supply Sensitivity	± 1/4	± 1/4	± 1/4	± 1/4	LSB max	± 1/16LSB typ V_{DD} = 5V ± 5%

NOTES
[1]Temperature Ranges are as follows:
AD7820 KN, LN   0 to + 70°C
AD7820 BQ, CQ   − 25°C to + 85°C
AD7820 TQ, UQ   − 55°C to + 125°C
[2]Total Unadjusted Error includes offset, full-scale and linearity errors.
[3]Sample tested at 25°C by Product Assurance to ensure compliance.
[4]See Typical Performance Characteristics.

Specifications subject to change without notice.

TIMING CHARACTERISTICS[1]   (V_{DD} = +5V; $V_{REF}(+)$ = +5V; $V_{REF}(-)$ = GND = 0V unless otherwise stated)

Parameter	Limit at 25°C (All grades)	Limit at T_{min}, T_{max} (K,L,B,C grades)	Limit at T_{min}, T_{max} (T,U grades)	Units	Conditions/Comments
t_{CSS}	0	0	0	ns min	$\overline{CS}$ TO $\overline{RD}/\overline{WR}$ Setup Time
t_{CSH}	0	0	0	ns min	$\overline{CS}$ TO $\overline{RD}/\overline{WR}$ Hold Time
t_{RDY}[2]	70	90	100	ns max	$\overline{CS}$ to Delay. Pull-Up Resistor 5kΩ.
t_{CRD}	1.6	2.0	2.5	μs max	Conversion Time (RD Mode)
t_{ACC0}[3]	t_{CRD} + 20	t_{CRD} + 35	t_{CRD} + 50	ns max	Data Access Time (RD Mode)
t_{INTH}[2]	125	–	–	ns typ	$\overline{RD}$ to $\overline{INT}$ Delay (RD Mode)
	175	225	225	ns max	
t_{DH}[4]	60	80	100	ns max	Data Hold Time
t_{P}	500	600	600	ns min	Delay Time between Conversions
t_{WR}	600	600	600	ns min	Write Pulse Width
	50	50	50	μs max	
t_{RD}	600	700	700	ns min	Delay Time between $\overline{WR}$ and $\overline{RD}$ Pulses
t_{ACC1}[3]	160	225	250	ns max	Data Access Time (WR–RD Mode, see Fig. 5b)
t_{R1}	140	200	225	ns max	$\overline{RD}$ to $\overline{INT}$ Delay
t_{INTL}[2]	700	–	–	ns typ	$\overline{WR}$ to $\overline{INT}$ Delay
	1000	1400	1700	ns max	
t_{ACC2}[3]	70	90	110	ns max	Data Access Time (WR–RD Mode, see Fig. 5a)
t_{IHWR}[2]	100	130	150	ns max	$\overline{WR}$ to $\overline{INT}$ Delay (Stand-Alone Operation)
t_{ID}	50	65	75	ns max	Data Access Time after $\overline{INT}$ (Stand-Alone Operation)

NOTES

[1]Sample tested at 25°C to ensure compliance. All input control signals are specified with tr = tf = 20ns (10% to 90% of +5V) and timed from a voltage level of 1.6V.

[2]C_L = 50pF.

[3]Measured with load circuits of Figure 1 and defined as the time required for an output to cross 0.8V or 2.4V.

[4]Defined as the time required for the data lines to change 0.5V when loaded with the circuits of Figure 2.

Specifications subject to change without notice.

Test Circuits

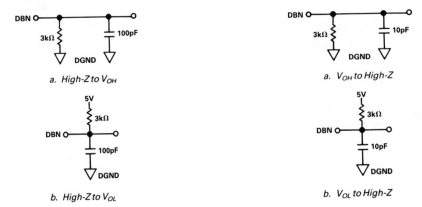

a. High-Z to V_{OH}

b. High-Z to V_{OL}

Figure 1. Load Circuits for Data Access Time Test

a. V_{OH} to High-Z

b. V_{OL} to High-Z

Figure 2. Load Circuits for Data Hold Time Test

ABSOLUTE MAXIMUM RATINGS*

V_{DD} to GND . . . . 0V, +7V
Digital Input Voltage to GND
Pins 6-8, 13) . . . . −0.3V, V_{DD} +0.3V
Digital Output Voltage to GND
(Pins 2-5, 9, 14-18) . . . . −0.3V, V_{DD} +0.3V
V_{REF} (+) to GND . . . . V_{REF} (−), V_{DD} +0.3V
V_{REF} (−) to GND . . . . 0V, V_{REF} (+)
V_{IN} to GND . . . . −0.3V, V_{DD} +0.3V
Operating Temperature Range
KN, LN . . . . 0 to +70°C

BQ, CQ . . . . −25°C to +85°C
TQ, UQ . . . . −55°C to +125°C
Storage Temperature Range . . . . −65°C to +150°C
Lead Temperature (Soldering, 10secs) . . . . +300°C
Power Dissipation (Any Package) to +75°C 450mW
Derates above +75°C by . . . . 6mW/°C

*Stresses above those listed under "Absolute Maximum Ratings" may cause permanent damage to the device. This is a stress rating only and functional operation of the device at these or any other conditions above those indicated in the operational sections of this specification is not implied. Exposure to absolute maximum rating conditions for extended periods may affect device reliability.

CAUTION:
ESD (Electro-Static-Discharge) sensitive device. The digital control inputs are zener protected; however, permanent damage may occur on unconnected devices subject to high energy electrostatic fields. Unused devices must be stored in conductive foam or shunts. The foam should be discharged to the destination socket before devices are removed.

PIN CONFIGURATION

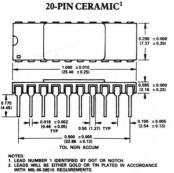

ORDERING INFORMATION

Total Unadjusted Error	Temperature Range and Package		
	Plastic 0 to +70°C	Cerdip[1] −25°C to +85°C	Cerdip[1] −55°C to +125°C
±1/2LSB	AD7820LN	AD7820CQ	AD7820UQ
±1LSB	AD7820KN	AD7820BQ	AD7820TQ

NOTE
[1]Analog Devices reserves the right to ship ceramic packages in lieu of cerdip packages.

PRICING (100's)

AD7820KN$ 9.95   AD7820CQ $20.95
AD7820LN $13.95   AD7820TQ $39.85
AD7820BQ $15.95   AD7820UQ $52.35

MECHANICAL INFORMATION
OUTLINE DIMENSIONS
Dimensions shown in inches and (mm).

20-PIN CERAMIC[1]

NOTES:
1. LEAD NUMBER 1 IDENTIFIED BY DOT OR NOTCH.
2. LEADS WILL BE EITHER GOLD OR TIN PLATED IN ACCORDANCE WITH MIL-M-38510 REQUIREMENTS.

20-PIN CERDIP (SUFFIX Q)

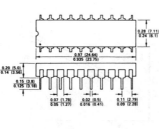

20-PIN PLASTIC DIP (SUFFIX N)

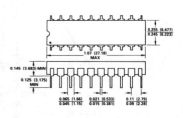

NOTE
[1]Analog Devices reserves the right to ship ceramic packages in lieu of cerdip packages.

Typical Performance Characteristics

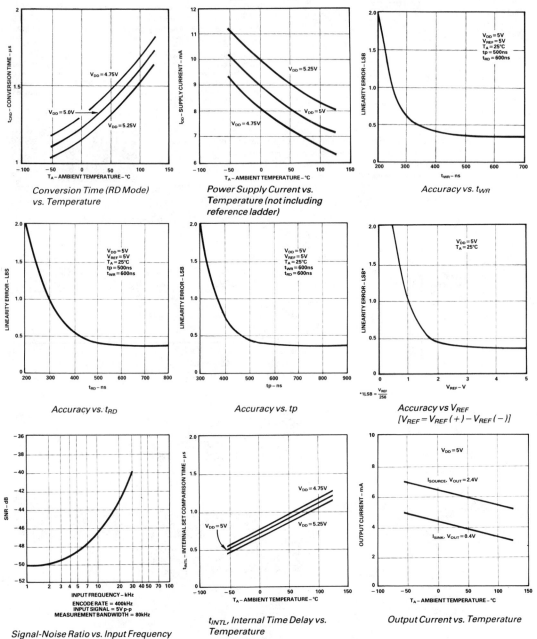

Conversion Time (RD Mode) vs. Temperature

Power Supply Current vs. Temperature (not including reference ladder)

Accuracy vs. t_{WR}

Accuracy vs. t_{RD}

Accuracy vs. tp

Accuracy vs V_{REF} [$V_{REF} = V_{REF}(+) - V_{REF}(-)$]

Signal-Noise Ratio vs. Input Frequency

t_{INTL}, Internal Time Delay vs. Temperature

Output Current vs. Temperature

PIN FUNCTION DESCRIPTION

PIN	MNEMONIC	DESCRIPTION
1	V_{IN}	Analog Input. Range: $V_{REF}(-)$ to $V_{REF}(+)$.
2	DB0	Data Output. Three State Output, bit 0 (LSB)
3	DB1	Data Output. Three State Output, bit 1
4	DB2	Data Output. Three State Output, bit 2
5	DB3	Data Output. Three State Output, bit 3
6	$\overline{WR}$/RDY	WRITE control input/READY status output. See Digital Interface section.
7	Mode	Mode Selection Input. It determines whether the device operates in the WR-RD or RD mode. It is internally tied to GND through a 50μA current source. See Digital Interface section.
8	$\overline{RD}$	READ Input. $\overline{RD}$ must be low to access data from the part. See Digital Interface section.
9	$\overline{INT}$	INTERRUPT Output. $\overline{INT}$ going low indicates that the conversion is complete. $\overline{INT}$ returns high on the rising edge of $\overline{RD}$ or $\overline{CS}$. See Digital Interface section.
10	GND	Ground
11	$V_{REF}(-)$	Lower limit of reference span. Range: $GND \leq V_{REF}(-) \leq V_{REF}(+)$
12	$V_{REF}(+)$	Upper limit of reference span. Range: $V_{REF}(-) \leq V_{REF}(+) \leq V_{DD}$
13	$\overline{CS}$	Chip Select Input. $\overline{CS}$, the decoded device address, must be low for $\overline{RD}$ or $\overline{WR}$ to be recognized by the converter.
14	DB4	Data Output. Three State Output, bit 4
15	DB5	Data Output. Three State Output, bit 5
16	DB6	Data Output. Three State Output, bit 6
17	DB7	Data Output. Three State Output, bit 7 (MSB)
18	$\overline{OFL}$	Overflow Output. If the analog input is higher than $(V_{REF}(+) - 1/2LSB)$, $\overline{OFL}$ will be low at the end of conversion. It is a non three state output which can be used to cascade 2 or more devices to increase resolution.
19	NC	No connection.
20	V_{DD}	Power supply voltage, +5V

CIRCUIT INFORMATION
BASIC DESCRIPTION

The AD7820 uses a half-flash conversion technique whereby two 4-bit flash A/D converters are used to achieve an 8-bit result. Each 4-bit flash ADC contains 15 comparators which compare the unknown input to a reference ladder to get a 4-bit result. For a full 8-bit reading to be realized, the upper 4-bit flash, the most significant (MS) flash, performs a conversion to provide the 4 most significant data bits. An internal DAC, driven by the 4 MSBs, then recreates an analog approximation of the input voltage. This analog result is subtracted from the input, and the difference is converted by the lower flash ADC, the least significant (LS) flash, to provide the 4 least significant bits of the output data. The MS flash ADC also has one additional comparator to detect input overrange.

OPERATING SEQUENCE

The operating sequence for the AD7820 in the WR-RD mode is shown in Figure 3. A set-up time of 500ns is required prior to the falling edge of $\overline{WR}$. (This 500ns is required between reading data from the AD7820 and starting another conversion). When $\overline{WR}$ is low the input comparators track the analog input signal, V_{IN}. On the rising edge of $\overline{WR}$, the input signal is sampled and the result for the four most significant bits is latched. $\overline{INT}$ goes low approximately 700ns after the rising edge of $\overline{WR}$. This indicates that conversion is complete and the data result is already in the output latch. $\overline{RD}$ going low then accesses the output data. If a faster conversion time is required, the $\overline{RD}$ line can be brought low 600ns after $\overline{WR}$ goes high. This latches the lower 4 bits of data and accesses the output data on DB0–DB7.

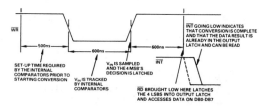

Figure 3. Operating Sequence (WR-RD Mode)

DIGITAL INTERFACE

The AD7820 has two basic interface modes which are determined by the status of the MODE pin. When this pin is low the converter is in the RD mode, with this pin high the AD7820 is set up for the WR-RD mode.

RD Mode

The timing diagram for the RD mode is shown in Figure 4. In the RD mode configuration, conversion is initiated by taking $\overline{RD}$ low. The $\overline{RD}$ line is then kept low until output data appears. It is very useful with microprocessors which can be forced into a WAIT state, with the microprocessor starting a conversion, waiting, and then reading data with a single READ instruction. In this mode, pin 6 of the AD7820 is configured as a status output, RDY. This RDY output can be used to drive the processor READY or WAIT input. It is an open drain output (no internal pull-up device) which goes low after the falling edge of $\overline{CS}$ and goes high impedance at the end of conversion. An $\overline{INT}$ line is also provided which goes low at the completion of conversion. $\overline{INT}$ returns high on the rising edge of $\overline{CS}$ or $\overline{RD}$.

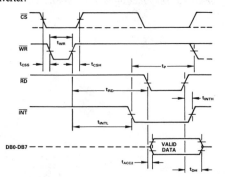

Figure 4. RD Mode

WR–RD Mode

In the WR–RD mode, pin 6 is configured as the WRITE input for the AD7820. With $\overline{CS}$ low, conversion is initiated on the falling edge of $\overline{WR}$. Two options exist for reading data from the converter.

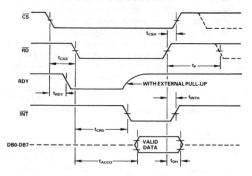

Figure 5a. WR-RD Mode ($t_{RD}>t_{INTL}$)

In the first of these options the processor waits for the $\overline{INT}$ status line to go low before reading the data (see Figure 5a). $\overline{INT}$ typically goes low 700ns after the rising edge of $\overline{WR}$. It indicates that conversion is complete and that the data result is in the output latch. With $\overline{CS}$ low, the data outputs (DB0-DB7) are activated when $\overline{RD}$ goes low. $\overline{INT}$ is reset by the rising edge of $\overline{RD}$ or $\overline{CS}$.

The alternative option can be used to shorten the conversion time. To achieve this, the status of the $\overline{INT}$ line is ignored and $\overline{RD}$ can be brought low 600ns after the rising edge of $\overline{WR}$. In this case $\overline{RD}$ going low transfers the data result into the output latch and activates the data outputs (DB0-DB7). $\overline{INT}$ also goes low on the falling edge of $\overline{RD}$ and is reset on the rising edge of $\overline{RD}$ or $\overline{CS}$. The timing for this interface is shown in Figure 5b.

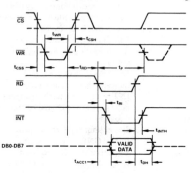

Figure 5b. WR-RD Mode ($t_{RD}<t_{INTL}$)

The AD7820 can also be used in stand-alone operation in the WR-RD mode. $\overline{CS}$ and $\overline{RD}$ are tied low and a conversion is initiated by bringing $\overline{WR}$ low. Output data is valid typically 700ns after the rising edge of $\overline{WR}$. The timing diagram for this mode is shown in Figure 6.

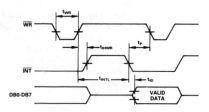

Figure 6. WR-RD Mode Stand-Alone Operation, $\overline{CS} = \overline{RD} = 0$

APPLYING THE AD7820
REFERENCE AND INPUT

The two reference inputs on the AD7820 are fully differential and define the zero to full-scale input range of the A/D converter. As a result, the span of the analog input can easily be varied since this range is equivalent to the voltage difference between $V_{IN}(+)$ and $V_{IN}(-)$. By reducing the reference span, $V_{REF}(+)-V_{REF}(-)$, to less than 5V the sensivity of the converter can be increased (i.e., if $V_{REF} = 2V$ then $1LSB = 7.8mV$). The input/reference arrangement also facilitates ratiometric operation.

This reference flexibility also allows the input span to be offset from zero. The voltage at $V_{REF}(-)$ sets the input level which produces a digital output of all zeroes. Therefore, although V_{IN} is not itself differential, it will have nearly differential-input capability in most measurement applications because of the reference design. Figure 7 shows some of the configurations that are possible.

INPUT CURRENT

Due to the novel conversion techniques employed by the AD7820, the analog input behaves somewhat differently than in conventional devices. The ADC's sampled-data comparators take varying amounts of input current depending on which cycle the conversion is in.

The equivalent input circuit of the AD7820 is shown in Figure 8a. When a conversion starts ($\overline{WR}$ low, WR-RD mode), all input switches close, and V_{IN} is connected to the most significant and least significant comparators. Therefore, V_{IN} is connected to thirty one 1pF input capacitors at the same time.

The input capacitors must charge to the input voltage through the on resistance of the analog switches (about $2k\Omega$ to $5k\Omega$). In addition, about 12pF of input stray capacitance must be charged. For large source resistances, the analog input can be modelled as an RC network as shown in Figure 8b. As R_S increases, it takes longer for the input capacitance to charge.

In the RD mode, the time for which the input comparators track the analog input is 600ns at the start of conversion. In the WR-RD mode the input comparators track V_{IN} for the duration of the $\overline{WR}$ pulse. Since other factors cause this time to be at least 600ns, input time constants of 100ns can be accommodated without special consideration. Typical total input capacitance values of 45pF allow R_S to be $1.5k\Omega$ without lengthening $\overline{WR}$ to give V_{IN} more time to settle.

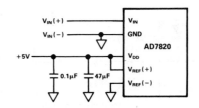

Figure 7a. Power Supply as Reference

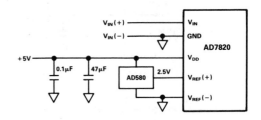

Figure 7b. External Reference 2.5V Full-Scale

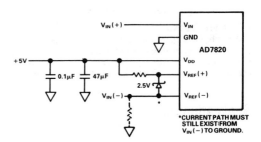

Figure 7c. Input Not Referenced to GND

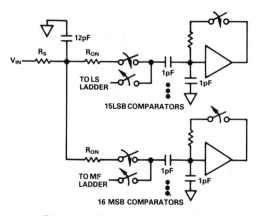

Figure 8a. AD7820 Equivalent Input Circuit

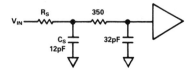

Figure 8b. RC Network Model

INPUT FILTERING

It should be made clear that transients on the analog input signal, caused by charging current flowing into V_{IN} will not normally degrade the ADC's performance. In effect, the AD7820 does not "look" at the input when these transients occur. The comparators' outputs are not latched while $\overline{WR}$ is low, so at least 600ns will be provided to charge the ADC's input capacitance. It is therefore not necessary to filter out these transients with an external capacitor at the V_{IN} terminal.

INHERENT SAMPLE-HOLD

A major benefit of the AD7820's input structure is its ability to measure a variety of high speed signals without the help of an external sample-and-hold. In a conventional SAR type converter, regardless of its speed, the input must remain stable to at least ½LSB throughout the conversion process if full accuracy is to be maintained. Consequently, for many high speed signals, this signal must be externally sampled and held stationary during the conversion The AD7820 input comparators, by nature of their input switching inherently accomplish this sample-and-hold function. Although the conversion time for the AD7820 is 1.36µs, the time through which V_{IN} must be ½LSB stable is much smaller. The AD7820 "samples" V_{IN} only when $\overline{WR}$ is low. The value of V_{IN} approximately 100ns (internal propogation delay) after the rising edge of $\overline{WR}$ is the measured value. This value is then used in the least significant flash to generate the lower 4-bits of data.

Input signals with slew rates typically below 200mV/µs can be converted without error. However, because of the input time constants, and charge injection through the opened comparator input switches, faster signals may cause errors. Still, the AD7820's loss in accuracy for a given increase in signal slope is far less than what would be witnessed in a conventional successive approximation device. A SAR type converter with a conversion time as fast as 1µs would still not be able to measure a 5V, 1kHz sine wave without the aid of an external sample-and-hold. The AD7820 with no such help, can typically measure 5V, 10kHz waveforms.

Applications

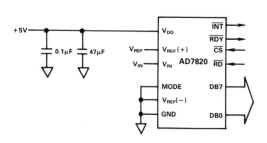

Figure 9a. 8-Bit Resolution

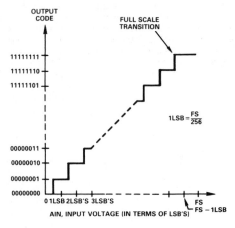

Figure 9b. Nominal Transfer Characteristic for 8-Bit Resolution Circuit

Applications

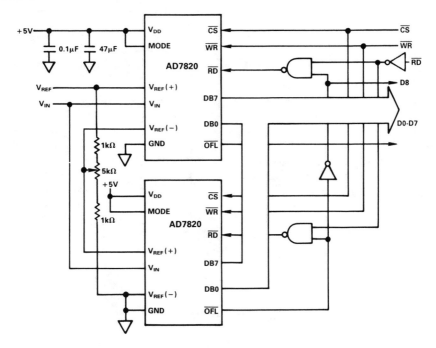

Figure 10. 9-Bit Resolution

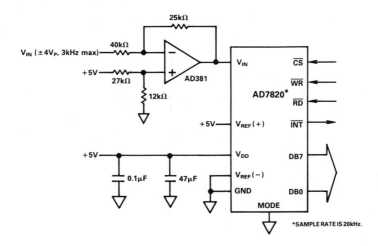

Figure 11. Telecom A/D Converter

Applications

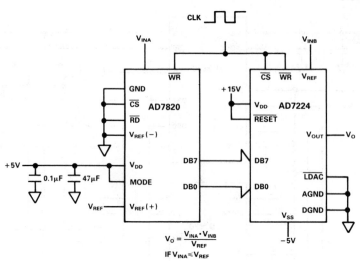

$$V_O = \frac{V_{INA} \cdot V_{INB}}{V_{REF}}$$

$$IF \; V_{INA} \le V_{REF}$$

Figure 12. 8-Bit Analog Multiplier

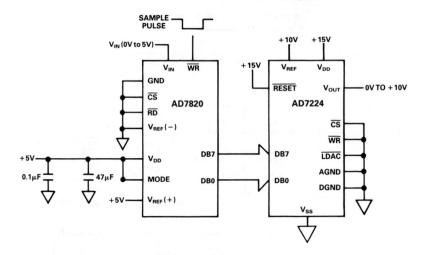

Figure 13. Fast Infinite Sample-and-Hold

Index